THE SPYGATE CONSPIRACY

BY
ROY D. DAVIS

THE SPYGATE CONSPIRACY

BY ROY D. DAVIS

©2025, all rights reserved

ISBN 978-1-942790-29-7

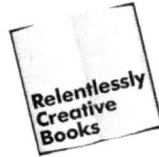

Published by Relentlessly Creative Books LLC
https://relentlesslycreativebooks.com/
books@relentlesslycreative.com

Dallas, Texas, USA

THIS BOOK IS DEDICATED TO
LIEUTENANT GENERAL MICHAEL FLYNN

"We have an army. As a soldier and a retired general, we have an army of digital soldiers. That's what we call them, what I call them, because this was an insurgency folks, this was run like an insurgency. This was irregular warfare at its finest in politics and that story will continue to be told. But we have what we call citizen journalists because the journalists that we have in our media did a disservice to themselves actually—more than they did to this country. They did a disservice to themselves because they displayed an arrogance that is unprecedented. And so, the American people decided to take over the idea of information. They took over the idea of information, and they did it through social media."

—General Flynn

Table of Contents

An Introduction:

'The SpyGate Conspiracy' is an encyclopedic DOSSIER of the people, events, and crimes related to the political conspiracy nicknamed SpyGate. This book will be an unfolding playbook of the primary characters involved in these many illegal criminal conspiracies as the truth is finally publicly revealed.

Since late 2015 several interconnected intelligence operations were planned and conducted against then candidate Donald Trump. Incredibly the attacks against now re-elected President Donald Trump continue to this very day. Operation Trump officially started in early 2016 beginning with the complete exhortation of Hillary Clinton/Aides (ObamaGate). Next came the creation/distribution of the knowingly false Trump-Russia Dossier by British spy Christopher Steele (RussiaGate). Third was the use of the fake Steele Dossier to obtain FISA Court approved FISA Title-1 surveillance warrants and FISA 702 searches for communication chain HOPS against Trump Campaign staffers (SpyGate). Last came what FBI Agent Peter Strzok termed the 'Insurance Policy' which was the criminal prosecution of President Trump first via the DOJ then later by Special Counsel Robert Mueller.

The book you are about to embark on is the result of three years of research and writing by one of our country's most persistent and insightful citizen journalists: Roy D. Davis (aka CaptainRoyD). Author Captain Roy has been chronicling the people and events surrounding "SpyGate" (sometimes known as ObamaGate) and publishing the results of his work on Redditt and other platforms.

Roy is one of the co-authors, collectively known as WWG1WGA, of the bestselling book *QAnon: An Invitation to the Great Awakening*. And like so many of the citizen journalists who have written on topics related to the election and first term of Donald J. Trump as POTUS—and the posts of QAnon—his work has been vilified and censored multiple times.

We are sure that Captain Roy would agree: Writing about current events in the Trump era makes the work of WaterGate-era journalists, those who spilled the beans on Nixon and the break-in at the WaterGate Hotel, perhaps the biggest political scandal prior to now, look like child's play. As QAnon—the anonymous 8Chan contributor frequently quoted in this book—reminds followers: THIS IS NOT A GAME.

Roy and others who research, write and broadcast about the topics contained in this book have bravely persevered despite abusive attacks by the mainstream media and censorship by social media and search-engine platforms and sometimes by the people they love the most. They have the scars to show for it. Despite all, this book is a complete encyclopedia of information about SpyGate.

Ironically, many of the "Anons" (anonymous followers of QAnon's posts) have spent months discussing and worrying about, "How are we going to let the others know what's going on?" They are endlessly concerned about friends and family, neighbors and co-workers.

For many, the driving motivation for their work as researchers, writers, broadcasters and publishers, is to "red pill" (alert, awaken or otherwise share what they have learned) with those they care about. Others feel that it is their civic duty as patriotic Americans to let their fellow citizens know what's really going on. In other words, most are motivated by love and caring for others—and not power or wealth. Seriously, many of us pray about how to talk about SpyGate, etc.

Why all the concern you may wonder? It's because we know what happens when people are red pilled because most of us have been there. Learning the truth about what's happening can be mentally challenging, even painful, because:

- It is difficult to face unwanted realities. (Think of learning about the death of a dear one or discovering that your spouse has been cheating.)
- It is made worse when that reality has been hidden from you for many years.
- It is extremely difficult to keep an open mind when some of your most cherished views are being challenged.
- It is hard to know who to trust in a world full of thieves and liars.
- Many of the worst liars are the people we trusted the most.
- Some of the crimes we've learned about involve innocent children.

If you want a sterling example of the kind of deception that is difficult to face, think of how the mainstream media news promoted the notion that Donald Trump was a Russian asset or was somehow involved with colluding with Russians. For nearly three years we were subjected to a daily tirade of accusations: Russia! Russia! Russia!

The release of the Mueller report, and Robert Mueller's appearance before Congress made clear that the endless barrage of accusations was baseless. Many people were shocked by the fact that the news sources that they trusted to provide complete and accurate reporting had not just been wrong, but to many it appeared that they were lying to viewers for nearly three years! The ratings for most mainstream media news programs have dropped as people are catching on.

But it may even be worse than that. Consider that the Russia collusion story might have been concocted by those seeking to overthrow a duly elected President illegally as an act of treason. And consider that it might have also served as a distraction to keep you from learning about other important events including other illegal acts. That's why this book is important.

This book will fill you in on some of the stories you may have missed because they weren't covered by the daily news. The truth is far more complicated than Russia! Russia! Russia! SpyGate involves many people in top government posts and some of them are not household names. There are so many that it is nearly impossible to hold all the people involved in SpyGate, their names and histories, in your head. It is tempting to just give up.

Please don't give up. The unfolding events that surround us now represent some of the most horrifying and simultaneously many of the most amazing that will happen in our lifetimes. As crimes are being revealed and criminals are tried and sentenced, the doors will open upon new vistas of opportunity and prosperity. The implications of the takedown of the Deep State will be felt worldwide. This is your guidebook to the players involved, a literal Who's Who of Spygate. It can be a companion to keep handy as you hear the news or start doing your own research.

QAnon reminds us that the Patriots, those of us who love God, family and country, are in charge now. Given that the grip the Deep State has held us in is sure to loosen, we can sit back and enjoy the show. But it is hard to enjoy what you don't understand. This book will help.

A few reader tips:

Most of the QAnon quotes in this book are just snippets of longer posts. We strongly encourage you to read the posts in their entirety. http://www.QAGG.news is a good place to start.

If you want to learn more about QAnon, Relentlessly Creative Books' bestselling title *QAnon: An Invitation to the Great Awakening* is a great compilation by a dozen author/contributors. It has over 3000 5-star reviews but is no longer available on Amazon.com due to censorship.

Since print books cannot contain active links that you merely click on as you can with ebooks, in most cases you can simply search for the text shown in the link. You can use Duck Duck Go, Google or any browser you prefer.

All of the links shown as resources in this book were working at the time of publication, but the Internet, being an environment of rapid change, may thwart our best efforts. Please send us email about bad links and we will fix them in future editions: books@relentlesslycreative.com

Many people prefer printed books, but an advantage of ebooks is that hyperlinks are active in many ebook readers. So, you might want to consider getting the ebook version, too, and have the best of both worlds.

Enjoy the show!

SpyGate Update: 3 Spies/2 LURES/4 Coded Ops

This is more than Spy vs Spy or even White Hat vs Black Hat, it is basically a global war between Good vs Evil. 'Q' has helped to foster General Flynn's Army of Digital Soldiers. SpyGate is a combination of several different planned illegal operations against both then candidate and elected President Trump. BHO would use HRC's phony 2016 Russia Dossier as the keystone to launch his illegal surveillance campaign against President Trump with RussiaGate and Crossfire Hurricane.

Post Q# 3898
> The key that opens all doors.
> The 'Start.'

One part of SpyGate involved an operation code named Crossfire Hurricane. The scorecard can chalk up 3 confirmed official spies and 2 foreign "LURES" or intelligence assets involved in this portion of the coup plot. All of these paid individuals were inserted or planted into Trump World during the 2016 Presidential campaign cycle and transition period. President Trump would begin to seek legal recourse with his 2022 Federal lawsuit against HRC/DNC/Perkins Coie/others related to the unfolding SpyGate political scandal. It was revealed in 2024 that the US Intel Community requested from its FIVE EYES partners to illegally spy upon selected Team Donald Trump aides in 2016.

Post Q# 1939
> "This is the case with Halper, who is now proven to be a spy."

These actions unbelievably began prior to the official start now claimed by the FBI of the summer of 2016. The FBI's Counterintelligence Division investigation of candidate Trump by agent Peter Strzok has the official beginning launch date of 7/31/16 and not when they occurred earlier that year. The DOJ in essence was using the element of time travel to help retroactively justify this illegal surveillance operation.

Post Q# 4011
> CROSSFIRE HURRICANE

The four main components of the political coup attempt nicknamed **Operation Trump**:
- Exoneration of HRC/Aides (ObamaGate)
- False Trump-Russia Dossier creation/distribution (RussiaGate)
- FISA Title-1 Warrants/Section 702 (SpyGate)
- The 'Insurance Policy' (Crossfire Hurricane)

Post Q# 1938
> BO - UK - AUS.
> AUS -UK -BO.
> BO - Alexander Downer (FVEY) (EX1).

DOJ/FBI came up with a special classic code named (hat top to reporter John Solomon) programs generally under 'Operation Trump' or the specific internal FBI nickname of 'Arctic Frost' as early as December 2015. Several operational plans were colorfully code-named Crossfire Hurricane/Operation FISA Dragon/Crossfire Typhoon/and Crossfire Razor to name a few. The Deep State and the HRC campaign needed to associate Donald Trump with Russians. In the intelligence community, the art of 'bumping' or dirtying-up by contact is an age-old tradecraft method of setting up targeted individuals.

Post Q# 1589

ABUSE OF EXEC POWERS.
ILLEGAL SPYING.
INSERT ASSETS.

Incredibly back in February 2014 the first known public meeting between Halper, Donald Trump, and General Flynn occurred in England. The event was an annual gathering of past and current intelligence community folks at famed Cambridge University/London. In hindsight this may have been the early approach by the White Hats to enlist the billionaire New York developer into the plan to save the world.

Post Q# 3061

Another piece to the puzzle.
AUTISTS SAVING THE WORLD.

Operative Stefan Halper dutifully sent a report back to CIA Director John Brennan about Flynn seemingly being really cozy with a Russian (FSB) woman. Also, the chance meeting between Donald Trump and General Mike Flynn was of note in Halper's follow up surveillance report. The connection to head clown Brennan is key as he would be the quarterback of SpyGate.

Post Q# 1164

Not Public: Five Eyes/UK/AUS POTUS targeting using pushed RUS decoy meetings/campaign insertions.

I make a distinction between the spies and the LURES within SpyGate. Spies like Halper/Mifsud/ and Nader arranged the various 'sting' meetings involving various Trump aides. We would find out from 'Q' as to many other deliberate plants inserted into the Trump circle like Carter Page and Paul Manafort.

Post Q# 3125

The attempted 'COUP' [TREASON] opens the public's door to more serious.......

Downer and Millian acted more like international OCONUS (outside continental U.S.) LURES, shown to their intended targets as dangling the preverbal forbidden fruit. Several internal Peter Strzok text messages to lover FBI lawyer Lisa Page in December 2015 acknowledged foreign intelligence assets (LURES) were now being deployed against candidate Trump. The Strzok/Page texts will also reveal physical threats against President Trump by this criminal cabal.

Post Q# 2128

USE OF BACKCHANNEL SURV/SPY INSERTION [BODY 1, 2, and 5).

These paid assets were the primary co-enablers in this coordinated SpyGate plot against Candidate/President-Elect Trump:

Campaign SPY: Stefan Halper is an American scholar who teaches courses at Cambridge. Halper has had a long working history with both the CIA and MI6 in informational gathering assignments.

Halper has been involved with 3 prior Republican Presidential Administrations. This was his entry card to be hovering around various 2016 RNC/Trump campaign officials. He is noted in history as the 'banker' of President Bush's Iran-Contra scandal.

George Papadopoulos already prepped by Mifsud by accepting a $3k contract, was tasked to go to London in May to do a seminar and write a paper for Halper. This led to the 'chance' encounter with Alexander Downer in a pub and overhearing talk of obtaining some HRC 'dirt' by PapaD.

Professor Halper additionally set-up meetings with both Carter Page in July and Sam Clovis in August 2016, designed to entrapped them. Department of Defense's Office of Net Assessment (ONA) has awarded Halper contracts totaling over $1M over the last several years.

Post Q# 4422
Change We Can Believe In.

Transition SPY: George Nader is a shadowy international figure that has been regularly connected to the UAE Crown Prince Mohammed bin Zayed. Nader arranged two very suspicious meetings with Trump World people during the 2016/17 transition period.

In December 2016 Nader/Crown Prince meet at Trump Tower with Kushner and Bannon to discuss future options in the Middle East. No commitments were finalized but it was an olive branch extension by the UAE Crown Prince.

In January 2017 Nader arranged for Erik Prince to meet in the Seychelles (Indian Ocean) with notorious Russian Kirill Dmitriev and the Crown Prince bin Zayed. This meeting was to talk about future 'Back-Channels' between Trump and Russia with Erik being the conduit.

Team Mueller tried to tie in a Kushner friend Richard Gerson with this Erik Prince meeting, primarily because Gerson was vacationing in the Seychelles at the same time of this Nader meeting. Also note Q-dropped the iconic hot tub photo w/Slick Willy and Nader, this was just days before the Erik Prince meeting.

Post Q# 4011
CROSSFIRE HURRICANE
CROSSFIRE TYPHOON

Foreign SPY: Joseph Mifsud is the mysterious 'Maltese Professor' with direct ties to the Kremlin. Joseph inserted himself into the 2016 Presidential Campaign when he met George Papadopoulos in Italy in March 2016. Mifsud dangled the HRC 'dirt' as bait to 'LURE' in PapaD and to further assist Halper with his continuing role.

Then again on April 26, 2016 Mifsud meet PapaD in London, this time bringing along the infamous so-called "niece" of Putin. This second follow-up meeting was to set the hook and trap the young PapaD.

Ties to Brennan/CIA are also part of Mifsud's intelligence working background. Mifsud had been missing for a while but has reappeared in photos in the company of several nude ladies.

Post Q# 1972
BIGGER THAN WATERGATE.
BIGGEST SCANDAL IN US HISTORY.

Foreign LURE Asset # 1: Alexander Downer was an Australian diplomat and former High Commissioner to the UK. Downer has been the center of attention trying to justify a prior $25 million donation to the Clinton Foundation from Australia.

Downer meet Papadopoulos and Halper on 5/10/16 at London's Kensington Wine Room for cocktails. Downer overhearing PapaD claiming access to the deleted HRC emails, and this is the historic starting point of Trump-Russia. SC John Durham's final report submitted in 2023 outlines Downer's testimony that PapaD never mentions 'HRC Dirt,' which was the false prediction to launch Crossfire Hurricane.

It is the pivotal pub event that supposedly launches the entire DOJ/FBI Counterintelligence Probe (Crossfire Hurricane) into then candidate Trump. SpyGate and the Insurance Policy will go down in infamy.

Foreign LURE Asset # 2: Sergei Millian is a Belarusian-American businessman. Sergei Millian contacted George Papadopulos (PapaD) in the Summer of 2016 with various business opportunities and would physically meet on July 23, 2016. Millian had been the President of the Russian American Chamber of Commerce and was considered to be a solid source of intelligence.

PapaD was offered a lucrative $30,000 per month job as long as he was involved with the Trump Campaign. The cover story was they would form an energy related business, that would be financed by mysterious Russian oligarch billionaires. Millian would be Steele's source conduit via Igor Denchenko a researcher for Orbis. This however turned out to be a frame job against Millian as records proved he never communicated with Danchenko about the fake Russia dossier.

Post Q# 3990
FBI CHAIN OF COMMAND FISA-RUSSIA-POTUS-FLYNN-STONE-PAPADOP-MANAF?

Sergei Millian (a claimed sub source) would pass along to Chris Steele the fake 'pee per' story he heard from Oleg Deripaska. Millian now denies ever talking to the arrested Denchenko. Oleg Deripaska laughed with Putin saying even the stupid Americans will never fall for this phony tall hotel room tale. HRC first floated the Alfa Bank server hoax and followed that up with several phony dossiers concerning the fake Russian collusion narrative against Donald Trump.

Post Q# 1238
Not "official" product-5 Eyes.

IG Michael Horowitz/SP John Huber/Special Counsel (SC) John Durham have been looking into the "SpyGate" along with the FISA abuses. SC Durham's indictment of Perkins Coie/Clinton campaign lawyer Michael Sussmann connects HRC, DNC, Fusion GPS, CrowdStrike, Google, plus many other coup plotters. Judgement Day is coming and the truth about SpyGate will be revealed. SC John Durham submitted his final report in 2023 and will be the foundation for future judicial accountability.

Post Q# 2043
DECONSTRUCT INCLUDES D2_SPY INSERT.

It has been uncovered in Strzok/Page text messages that several 'spy' operations were being conducted alongside Crossfire Hurricane (Razor/Typhoon/Dragon). There are unknown additional paid intelligence assets known as sleepers and coded operations yet to be uncovered in this coup plot. With the re-election of President Trump in 2024, let's pray that all the SpyGate secret details will finally be publicly revealed.

Post Q# 3858
THIS REPRESENTS A CLEAR AND PRESENT DANGER TO THE CONSTITUTIONAL REPUBLIC IN THE UNITED STATES.

Links
Epoch Times-SpyGate: The Inside Story

FOX News-Patel found Thousands of Sensitive Trump Russia Probe Docs

The Federalist-Unsealed Crossfire Hurricane Docs prove RussiaGate a Hoax

Just the News-Declassified Russia Collusion Documents

Real Clear Politics-What the ObamaGate Scandals Mean

Markets Work-SpyGate: The Inside Story

America First Legal-The Shellenberger/Taibbi Files

The Hill-Willful Blindness by Media over BHO Administration Spying

John Seaman-Durhan Investigation: Answering the 5 W's

Real Clear Investigations-How the FBI Copied Parts of the Steele Dossier

Real Clear Politics-To Spy on a Trump Aide: The FBI Pursued a Dossier Rumor

The Federalist-SpyGate 101: A Primer on the Russia Collusion Hoax

Tablet Magazine-Here Comes the Limited Hangout

Patel Patriot-Devolution: Part 11 CrowdStrike/SpyGate

Red State-Lisa Page Text to Peter Strzok: 'You get our OCONUS Lures Approved?'

The Last Refuge-SpyGate: The Big Picture

Undercover Huber-Downer/Mifsud/PapaD

Elizabeth Lea Vos-All RussiaGate Roads lead to London

The War Economy-Fusion GPS

Front Page Mag-BHO used HRC's Dossier to Spy on Trump

Clinton Foundation Timeline-March 14, 2016: Flashpoint of SpyGate/RussiaGate

Markets Work-SpyGate: The True Story of Collusion

The Last Refuge-Mifsud, PapaD and Downer

Markets Work-List of Participants

Red State-Remembering Strzok/Page 'Insurance Policy Exchange'

Markets Work-Ties that Bind: Halper/Mifsud/Downer/and Papadopoulos

Real Clear Investigations -The Maltese Phantom of RussiaGate

Millennium Report-SpyGate: The Reign of the Psychopaths is Over

Capital Research Center-Cast of the Trump Russia Collusion Hoax

Markets Work-Time Magazine details 'Shadow Campaign' against Trump

American Thought Leader-Inside Story of How SpyGate was Uncovered

Senate Judiciary Committee: 2021 Crossfire Hurricane DECLAS

Justice.gov-Crossfire Hurricane Timeline

OIG.Justice.gov-DOJ OIG FISA Report

Crossfire Hurricane Docs-Joseph Mifsud Interview

Crossfire Hurricane Docs-Halper Files

Clinton Foundation Timeline-2025 Crossfire Hurricane Docs

Justice.gov-SC John Durham 2023 Report

'Jumping Jack Flash' and Operation Crossfire Hurricane

'Jumping Jack Flash' is a hit Rolling Stones tune which features the term 'Crossfire Hurricane.' As most of us know by now President Trump always includes a song or two from the Rolling Stones at all his jam-packed rallies. This Crossfire Hurricane theme will become the critical illegal operation in 2016 against then candidate Donald Trump. In 2022, President Trump would file a federal RICO lawsuit against HRC/DNC/Perkins Coie/others related to the unfolding SpyGate scandal.

Post Q# 3505
Nunes to receive a special package from BARR?

Perverted by criminal elements from within the Department of Justice, Crossfire Hurricane was a coded intelligence operation designed at stopping Candidate/President Elect Donald J. Trump. The top leadership of the DOJ formed a 'Secret Society' to craft an elaborate plot to help achieve their political goals. HRC's created 2016 Russia Dossier was the setup BHO needed to launch the next phase against Donald Trump with FisaGate and Crossfire Hurricane.

Post Q# 2478
Let the unsealing begin.
Let the DECLAS begin
Let the WORLD witness the TRUTH.

Sadly, we are discovering that this planned sting entrapment coup plot has continued throughout President Trump's first term in office. History will not be kind to all of those that assisted and enabled this failed coup plot. As the illegal Biden administration is in the process destroying of nation, the Digital Soldiers of 'Q' continue to push out the truth while awaiting the future lawful return of President Trump.

Post Q# 4230
This is only the start.

AG William Barr signaled the release of all documents as were lawfully ordered by President Trump in late 2020 but sadly that did not transpire. The old 'temp cleanup' strategy had certainly worked perfectly over at the DOJ as well as troubled swampy areas like CIA and the State Department. Of a historical side note is the theory naming the operation against candidate Trump as Crossfire Hurricane was due to the playing of Rolling Stone songs at his rallies. Termed generally as 'Operation Trump' or the internal FBI nickname of 'Arctic Frost/Haze' was the many operations to discredit or outright remove President Trump from power.

Four main coup plot components of **Operation Trump:**
- Exonerate HRC/Aides (ObamaGate)
- Dossier development/distribution (RussiaGate)
- FISA Title-1 Surveillance Warrants/Section 702 (SpyGate)
- The 'Insurance Policy' (Crossfire Hurricane)

Post Q# 3993
If [AS] was privy to GANG OF EIGHT classified material would he not know the same FACTS (TRUTH) as NUNES?
Think NUNES memo v SCHIFF.

IG Michael Horowitz had already laid out criminal findings in his prior reports on the HRC emails and FISA abuse. The ball is now in Special Counsel (SC) John Durham's court from Horowitz and he has begun to drop criminal indictments related to the illegal surveillance operations of SpyGate. It would be revealed in 2024 that John Brennan/CIA asked FIVE EYE intel alliance partners to illegally spy on US citizens as just another example of the lawlessness in Washington DC.

Post Q# 1816
FISA. [20].

Phase Two of the OIG's inquiries focused on both the FISA Court abuses and the SpyGate/Crossfire Hurricane elements. Then Rep. Devin Nunes from the House side along with Senators Grassley and Johnson headed the Senate Congressional inquiring committees. BHO held a pivotal Oval Office meeting on 1/5/17 with planned Trump carryovers James Comey/Sally Yates along with VP Biden, Susan Rice, and Valerie Jarrett to finalize the coup plot. The illegal FISA surveillance operations of 2016 also included Crossfire Razor which was against General Flynn and Crossfire Typhoon which was against candidate Ted Cruz.

Post Q# 2462
Who briefed NUNES on classified intel re: HUSSEIN spy campaign v. POTUS?

The country has already witnessed in a small part, the wholesale cleansing out of both the FBI/DOJ/and Intelligence communities. President Trump has said of Nunes "This guy will go down into dungeons/basements, he'll find a document, no matter what." President Trump had ordered the declassification of many Crossfire Hurricane documents just prior to leaving office. President Trump's own copy of Crossfire Hurricane documents was the focus of the 2022 Mar-A-Lago raid by the DOJ/FBI. The entire set illegal operations against Donald Trump blended from ObamaGate to RussiaGate to SpyGate often employing the same corrupt government officials in these various operations.

Post Q# 4133
Why did [Schiff] illegally surveil [phone] members of WH legal team, media, and Congress?

Rumor had it that Devin Nunes had originally planned back in 2018 to read the critical previously totally redacted page number twenty [20] of the Carter Page FISA warrant live from the Congressional House floor. Representative Devin Nunes announced he will leave Congress in 2022 to run Trump's TruthSocial media company. SC John Durham completed his report in 2023 to show the public the scope of the various treasonous coup plots in President Trump. With the re-election of President Trump in 2024, many pray past political secrets will finally be publicly revealed.

Post Q# 4011
CROSSFIRE HURRICANE
CROSSFIRE TYPHOON

You didn't think the statement by POTUS re: 'CALM BEFORE THE STORM' was just random did you?

Links
Washington Times-John Durham going Deep into RussiaGate

FOX News-Patel found Thousands of Sensitive Trump Russia Probe Docs

Just the News-FBI Opens Grand Conspiracy Probe

The Federalist-FBI Revelations Show the Mueller Special Counsel was a Cover-Up

Markets Work-SpyGate: The Inside Story

Town Hall-Why the FBI Ransacked Mar-A-Lago

NY Post-CIA and Foreign Intel Agencies Illegally Targeted 26 Trump Aides

Lee Smith-BHO's January 5th Conspiracy

Washington Times-Retribution for Crossfire Hurricane

Shipwrecked Crew-How Crossfire Hurricane Came to Be

John Seaman-FBI Coverup of the Crime of the Century

Real Clear Politics-Ratcliffe: Brennan Briefed Obama and Biden about HRC's Plan

The Hill-FBI Docs Confirm Trump Campaign Investigated without Justification

Clinton Foundation Timeline-Crossfire Hurricane

Buster Hyde-Crossfire Hurricane (Operation Dung Castle)

FOX News-Rolling Stones Song inspired 'Crossfire Hurricane' Codename

The Federalist-Code Name "Crossfire Hurricane"

Grays Economy-Nunes to Read Crossfire Hurricane

The Last Refuge-FISA 702 Searches

Susan Whitney-Get to know Michael Ellis and Ezra Cohen-Watnick

The American Spectator-Crossfire Hurricane: Category 5

Patel Patriot-Devolution: Part 11 CrowdStrike/SpyGate

PJ Media-ObamaGate is Real and It's Spectacular

Rolling Stones-Crossfire Hurricane (trailer)

Front Page Mag-BHO used HRC's Dossier to Spy on Trump

Taibbi/Shellenberger-US Government is Hiding Documents

American Thought Leader-The Inside Story of How SpyGate was Uncovered

OIG.Justice.gov-DOJ OIG FISA Report

Senate.gov-Crossfire Hurricane: Timeline of Key Events

Crossfire Hurricane Docs-Christopher Steele Binder

Justice.gov-2023 SC John Durham Report

Inquiring Minds want to Know about 'The Insurance File'

NYPD prosecuted a highly publicized underage child pornography case with national political news coverage involving former New York Congressman Anthony Weiner. One shared laptop computer with Anthony Weiner's wife and several other electronic devices were seized in this raid by the New York police authorities. 'Q' pointed out in the beginning of the drops as to the importance of Huma and the Muslim Brotherhood (MB).

Post Q# 1371

Did they view the Insurance file?
This is not a game.

Criminal charges were later filed against husband Weiner and he was ultimately released early from jail after an usually light sentence. Anthony Weiner is a serial repeat sex offender and fortunately is getting court mandatory mental treatment. Weiner's then underage sexting partner would later become a famous OnlyFans online internet sensation. Already a failed U.S. House Congress member, Anthony Weiner filed in late 2024 to run for a seat in NYC Council. Anthony Weiner's primary underage 'sext' victim was Sydney Leathers.

Post Q# 1981

Huma - Muslim Brotherhood.
Matters of NAT SEC.

IG Michael Horowitz's several reports have highlighted bizarre and yet to be explained official actions involving classified emails found on Weiner's laptop. One example from Horowitz 1.0 report is on page 281, where former FBI Director James Comey [JC] describes himself as having a "reasonably good memory" while physically demonstrating to the contrary.

Post Q# 2697

Coleman Authored.
Hillary Clinton and Foundation.
Crime Against Children.

Incredibly during the same IG interview session, Comey states "I didn't know that I knew Weiner was married to Huma was married to Weiner." [JC] the only person in the world not aware of this high-profile Washington DC power marriage and tries to dismiss the obvious national security concerns.

Post Q# 3920

Define 'Traitor.'
Data exchange(s) can be very dangerous.

OIG Horowitz's 1.0 report highlights on page 294 a troubling reference "Crime Against Children." This information was found on the Weiner/Huma's seized computer laptop under a special section labeled the 'Insurance File' (Arkancide prevention).

Post Q# 45

What did HRC instruct Huma to do re: Classified markings?

FBI Counterintelligence Director Randy Coleman gave FBI Director Comey a briefing on 10/4/16 about the shared Anthony Weiner/Huma Abedin laptop. Randy Coleman made notes that the forensic review found in the digital data that reflects 'crime against children.' Knowing all about the Clinton Body Count', Huma Abedin created her 'Insurance File' for safety/security reasons.

Post Q# 4845
> Roger that, Madam Secretary.
> [C] = classified [State]
> Nothing is ever truly deleted.

On 9/27/16 the assigned Assistant US Attorney/SDNY had official correspondences with the local NY FBI. An email was exchanged between the FBI/SAC and DOJ/AUSA about search terms to be used while reviewing Werner's laptop. These restrictions were to prevent exposure of the truth contained within this insurance file. Years later the public as well as leading political figures are still calling for the release of the data obtained from the Weiner/Abedin laptop.

Post Q# 1235
> Don't forget about Huma.

The Abedin/Weiner 'Insurance File' had evidence of crimes related to the sexual exploitation of children, enticement, blackmail, and obscenity. The sexual emails were stored alongside classified top-secret emails between then Secretary HRC and longtime trusted aide Huma Adebin. Many have hinted that trips onboard Jeff Epstein's jet to the infamous 'Island' involving HRC videos are in this insurance file. In addition to the thousands of HRC emails contained on the seized laptop, the mysterious 'insurance fie' is of much interest to the public.

Post Q# 1552
> IG email investigation (weakest of set).
> Opens door to:
> Weiner HRC / Others - crimes against children.
> Noose.

The FBI discovered on Weiner's laptop approximately 675,000 emails, with 49,000 being HRC's related to government duties per FBI Bill Priestap. Huma Abedin from a young age has been HRC's closest advisor and constant companion/partner for over 20 years. Many have long suspected that Huma Abedin is in fact a planted 'sleeper agent' for the Muslim Brotherhood. Abedin would face in 2015 Congressional hearings over the deadly 2012 Benghazi attacks as she was a top State Department aide to then Secretary HRC.

Post Q# 8
> Huma.
> Husband in jail.
> HRC, Muslim Brotherhood, or child?

FBI laptop forensic review discovered many of these stored HRC emails were very highly classified. The Special Access Programs (SAP) emails could not be read by most FBI investigators assigned to this case and special security clearances were needed to access this laptop data. As demonstrated in the past by the coverup FBI in regards to the seized laptops from HRC aides Cheryl Mills and Heather Samuelson, the FBI only reveals publicly less damaging computer data.

Post Q# 1287
> How do you introduce evidence into an investigation (legally)?
> Insert Rudy.

"Lordy" many of these emails had SAP designations, meaning big legal trouble for those caught in possession of this top-secret material. Incredibly the FBI itself was restricted from reviewing this compartmentalized secret SAP material and required from various issuing government agencies written permits to view.

Post Q# 4484
Importance of SDNY control?
Jurisdiction:
Weiner evidence collection
Clinton Foundation

FBI Counterintelligence Division partnered with the DOJ National Security Division, as quarterbacking the entire Crossfire Hurricane coup plotters. FBI Director Randy Coleman wrote "Crime Against Children" and "HRC and Foundation" immortalizing event.

Post Q# 15
11.6 - Huma indicted.

Comey/McCabe/and Strzok knowingly sat on these Weiner emails for over a one month. The FBI then started back up the Midyear Exam (MYE) , which was the HRC email probe in late October 2016 just days before the election.

Post Q# 1828
[SPY OP]
[[HRC] [BC] [HA] [CM]......] [FAKE NEWS]

The threat to go public by the NYPD forced the reopening on the MYE email 'matter.' AG Loretta Lynch [LL] got involved in stopping future leaks or inquiries by threatening direct retaliation against the NYPD force. Lynch used corrosion tactics to put a lid of silence concerning the laptop data. Seized laptops would stay in the MSM news cycle due primarily to Hunter Biden's Laptop from Hell.' President Trump and others continually make to correct comparisons to the incriminating data discovered on both the Biden as well as Weiner/Abedin devices.

Post Q# 484
Who are the Muslim Brotherhood?
Who is Huma?

[LL] was using old leverage from the Eric Garner case, thus keeping NYPD in-sync with demands from main Justice. Pressure applied from headquarters central, always seems to get the required judicial/political results. Blackwater founder Erik Prince did a Breitbart interview explaining the horrific data discovered on the Weiner/Abedin electronic devices.

Post Q# 1345
Define bribe.
Define kickback.
Special Interest Groups (SIG).

Huma Abedin has been connected in terms of her involvement with the Muslim Brotherhood (MB). Huma Abedin's family has long been involved with the most radical elements of the MB operating in the Middle East. Rep. Michele Bachmann in 2012 attempted to start investigations into both Huma Abedin and the Muslim Brotherhood. Post illegal Biden administration's capitulation of Afghanistan, Huma Abedin honored the Muslim women at a fancy gala event.

Post Q# 2365
[Pg 294].
Crime Against Children +++.

The DOJ's secret society members all had private emails (non .GOV) accounts. Private accounts are perfect for avoiding lawful FOIA requests and to hide illegal communication activities like Gmail 'ghost draft' messages. Special Counsel (SC) John Durham was tasked to explore the numerous criminal referrals from IG Horowitz related to the SpyGate scandals. Of an odd relationship, in 2024 Huma Abedin and Alex Soros, son of globalist George Soros, would secretly get engaged in 2024 and marry in 2025 -truly a match made in hell by the Devil himself.

Post Q# 2
>Where is Huma?
>Follow Huma.

Much public speculation has swirled around the confiscated shared laptop of Huma Abedin. Huma and HRC had a reunion in the Hamptons and their decades long relationship seems intact. Inquiring minds want to know all of the secrets contained within the 'insurance file' on the Weiner/Huma laptop. SC Durham has dropped criminal indictments and submitted his final report in 2023. With the re-election of President Trump in 2024, many mysteries like the Weiner/Abedin laptop will finally be publicly revealed.

Post Q# 1236
>Q posted Anon comment:
>OHHH!! This is one of my reasons why POTUS keeps bringing up witch hunt!

Links

NY Post-Huma Abedin Remains a Mystery

The Hill-Huma Abedin's Ties to the Muslim Brotherhood

FOX News-Huma Abedin and Alex Soros Marry in Swank Hamptons

Last Refuge-Tens of Thousands of Emails Belonging to Abedin on Weiner's Laptop

People Magazine-Huma Abedin Facts

Breitbart-Erik Prince: NYPD Ready to Make Arrests

FOX News-Disgraced Weiner Receives Campaign Donation from Unexpected Source

NY Post-Classified Docs Found on Abedin/Weiner's Laptop

The Hill-Anthony Weiner's Political Comeback Fails

NY Post-The Moment FBI Agents found HRC Emails on Weiner's Laptop

FOX News-State Department releases Huma Abedin Emails

Clinton Foundation Timeline-2025 Crossfire Hurricane Docs

Justice.gov-SC John Durham Report

Admiral Mike Rogers: A Quiet Hero's Two 'Infamous' Deeds

Admiral Michael S. Rogers (Adm R) has retired from proud years of service as the Director National Security Agency (NSA). After years of dedication to this country unwavering service to President Trump, Admiral Mike Rogers has turned over the keys to NSA/U.S. Cyber Command to General Paul Nakasone. Cyber Command would start a new unit in 2022 designated Cyber Military Intelligence Group (CMIG) that will utilize public open-source data to support cyber operations.

Post Q# 2637
> Rogers departure. Intel.
> Notice a pattern?

History books will correctly show Admiral Mike Rodgers to be the true Patriot that he really was when this saga is fully publicly revealed. There are two critical dates that NSA Rogers performed heroic actions that will long be remembered by all Patriots. Admiral Rogers bucked the powers to be when in 2016 he shutdown NSA FISA 702 general search inquiries and additional links informed then President Elect Donald Trump of ongoing illegal surveillance operations being conducted in his New York City Trump Tower.

Post Q# 8
> POTUS installed his people within each top spot at each 3-letter agency except 1 (good reason).
> Adm R kick started this and scrubbed all POTUS nominations to verify oath.

On April 18, 2016, Admiral Rogers shutdown the previous unrestricted flow of NSA's FISA 702 search inquiries gathering raw data to outsider private contractors (Fusion GPS/CrowdStrike). Early in 2016 an internal review alerted NSA Mike Rogers to the suspicious use of 702 'About Queries', which are general searches by outside entities that did not have authority to access. These NSA data searches were primarily 'fishing' expeditions into unsuspecting selected targets.

Post Q# 2937
> Define 'game theory.'
> Define 'plausible deniability.'

General search or FISA 702 'Queries' allow for the collection of all emails, text, voice, and other electronic data on a specific targeted individual. Normally highly restricted 702 searches can travel both upstream as well as downstream informational captures. Admiral Mike Rogers saw this top-secret raw intel data was going to outside contractors and immediately put a stop to this illegal process.

Post Q# 1380
> When did Adm R step down?
> Reconcile.

Outside shady contractors like Fusion GPS and CrowdStrike were the recipients of these questionable NSA's 702 database inquiries and obviously known to Adm R. This raw intelligence helped the coup plotters construct the discredited Christopher Steele Trump-Russia fake dossier. Blackmail material was also gathered to keep all coup plotters dutifully onboard.

Post Q# 4646
> Nothing [digital] is ever really lost.

The shut-down action by Admiral Mike Rogers now forced the Deep State to switch over to using human intelligence assets (HUMIT) like planted spies. Now comes the entrance of international Five Eyes/Halper/Hakluyt/Downer and co-conspiracy friends into the 'sting-like/entrapment' operation.

Post Q# 151
> Why is Adm R. so important?
> Nothing is as it appears.

The classic nickname that Sundance/CTH (Hat Tip) gave to this phase of Admiral Rogers' plan was "Operation Condor." Reference being that Mike Rogers plays the actor Robert Redford's character (watch out for the mailman) in this hit Hollywood film. Spies and covert surveillance of one's enemies is as old as human history itself.

Post Q# 4310
> NSA Mike Rogers _TT [SCIF secure] [date]?

In that popular Hollywood movie Redford/Rogers exposes and ultimately brings down the corrupt CIA Clowns. Our hero Admiral Rogers performed in real life way better than any Hollywood actor could ever pretend to portray. 'Q' has stressed that in fact we are all watching a scripted movie and many movie similarities have been made in past 'Q' drops.

Post Q# 270
> Adm r No Such Agency (W and W) + POTUS/USMIL = Apply the Keystone.

On November 17, 2016, Mike Rogers goes outside his chain of command boss DNI Clapper and visits President Elect Trump at Trump Tower. No one knows exactly was said in the newly constructed Sensitive Compartmented Information Facility (SCIF) between POTUS and NSA Rogers that day, but everything changed on that fateful day. Many Anons feel that was the beginning of The Storm and President Trump's plan for payback.

Post Q# 3389
> Why did Rogers retire?
> Why did POTUS move his transition command center (base of ops) from TT the VERY NEXT DAY?

We do however know what Team Trump's immediate reaction to this confidential news from Admiral Rogers was. President Trump is well known for being a person of immediate action when needed and Team Trump packed up for immediate departure to a new base of operations in NJ. Trump's golf club in Bedminster/NJ would remain a trusted location especially in 2021.

Post Q# 144
> What council do the Wizards and Warlocks control?

Then President Elect Trump along with his top staffers were swiftly evacuated over to Trump National Golf Club in Bedminster/NJ the very next morning after NSA's visit. I'm looking into rumors of additional physical "bugs" being planted within the Trump Tower during this Presidential transition period.

Post Q# 1981
> Who knew?
> Adm Rogers?
> Matters of NAT SEC.

It is obvious to most folks that Admiral Rodgers told President Elect Donald Trump about the ongoing FISA surveillance (SpyGate) operation. I still feel that a physical threat against President Trump was another option being considered by the inner circle of the SpyGate coup plotters.

Post Q# 144
> +++Adm R+++
> What agency is at war w/Clowns In America?

Assassination was the final option under their 'Insurance Policy' part of Crossfire Hurricane/Operation Dragon/Crossfire FISA operations. The sad legacy with all these ObamaGate/SpyGate criminals, will be the utter failure of this sophisticated coup plot. History would ultimately vindicate Admiral Rogers as being a lone voice among top government officials in denouncing the RussiaGate/Steele Dossier scandalous claims against then Presidential candidate Donald Trump.

Post Q# 279
> Why is the USSS protecting key members of No Such Agency?

Of interesting timing (remember dates are important) is what happened on April 18, 2016. This was one day after FISA raw intel was shut down by NSA Rogers and the DNC claims a major computer system data breach. Perhaps this April breach was the initial downloads performed by murdered DNC IT staffer Seth Rich.

Four main components in the coup plot nicknamed **Operation Trump:**
- Exonerate HRC/Aides (ObamaGate)
- Fake Trump-Russia Dossier creation/distribution (RussiaGate)
- FISA Title-1 Surveillance Warrants/Section 702 (SpyGate)
- The 'Insurance Policy' (Crossfire Hurricane)

Post Q# 120
> Why is the NSA limited re: ability to capture and unmask US persons?

This was the Guccifer 2.0 intrusion claim that led to the CrowdStrike forensic review with their Cozy and Fancy Bear Russian hacking claims. This event marks the start of public claims of Russian election interference in the 2016 Presidential election. Special Counsel (SC) John Durham was tasked to explore the various criminal activities involved with the SpyGate scandal stemming out of IG Horowitz's prior reports. Since Admiral Rogers retired in 2018, records indicated he has been cooperating with the John Durham investigation.

Post Q# 3319
> Michael S. Rogers.

Please note that the DNC/DWS refused both the FBI and DHS access to their breached computer servers. Never in the recorded FBI's files were such bizarre actions performed in an effort to exonerate HRC of her obvious crimes. SC John Durham has dropped criminal indictments and submitted his final report in 2023. Admiral Mike Rogers would join the Board of Directors of Quantum Xchange in late 2022 and we all wish him well in his private life.

Post Q# 585
> TRUST Adm R.
> He played the game to remain in control.

Thank you, Admiral Rogers, for both your years of devotion to our country as well as your two points of historic national intervention. You will be remembered by Patriot for your valiant actions.

General Paul Nakasone will keep up the outstanding tradition you established in Cyber Command as well as the entire NSA. With the re-election of President Trump in 2024, many feel past hidden government secrets will finally be publicly revealed.

Post Q# 3212
> Think Rogers T-Tower meeting (right after SCIF set up in Tower).
> Think POTUS campaign leaving T-Tower (base of operations) THE VERY NEXT DAY.
> 1 + 1 = 2

Links

Intercept-Former NSA Director (Rogers) Cooperating Trump-Russia Investigation

Just the News-Steele Dossier Cited in 2016 ICA Claim about Putin

The Last Refuge-Original BHO and HRC 2008 Agreement

Clinton Foundation Timeline-Admiral Rogers on Russian Collusion

The Federalist-Unsealed Crossfire Hurricane Docs prove RussiaGate a Hoax

CVFC-Admiral Mike Rogers saved USA

FedScoop-New Army Unit will combine Military Intelligence with Open Source Data

Tapa Talk-Operation Condor: How Admiral Mike Rogers saved America

The Last Refuge-Admiral Rogers

NPR-NSA Head meet with Trump but didn't give Heads Up to BHO

The Last Refuge-FISA 702 Searches

Markets Work-The Uncovering: Rogers' Investigation, Section 702 Abuse and FBI

Epoch Times-NSA Admiral Rogers Disclosed FISA Abuse

Red State-Expanding Scope of Inquiry include "To/From" Queries in NSA Database

Shift Frequency-The Great Unmasker

Markets Work-The Uncovering: Admiral Rogers Investigation

Wired-The Man who Spoke Softly and Commands a Cyber Army

Markets Work-A Quiet Hero Admiral Rogers Retires

Daily Beast (pre Q)-Inside the "Q Group" Hunting Snowden

C-SPAN-Admiral Rogers: Cybersecurity Threats

The Last Refuge-Admiral Rogers/FISA 702

Quantum XChange-Michael S. Rogers

NSA.gov-Central Security Services (CSS)

ODNI.gov-DNI Clapper Email to Admiral Rogers: 2017 ICA

Crossfire Hurricane Docs-Admiral Mike Rogers Interview

Justice.gov-2023 SC John Durham Report

A Stroll Down Memory Lane—The Early 'Q' Days

"A CROSSROADS IN THE HISTORY OF OUR CIVILIZATION"

Q Clearance Patriot or 'Q' (termed QAnon by the media) was a group of less than 10 individuals, started posting drops at the POL board on 4chan in late October 2017. Team-Q due to security issues switched over to 8chan by late 2020. Throughout 2020 'Q' was dropping exclusively on 8KUN (DoD servers) which replaced 8chan due to a Deep State shutdown. The drops paused in early December 2020 but have begun again after a two-year break. Drops began on the same day as the Supreme Court's Roe decision and past drops reference 11.3 (part of Roe). There also seems to be a special 'Q' account at President Trump's Truth Social new media platform that appears to be related to the 'team.'

Post Q# 4955

It had to be done this way.

'Q' ultimately got a private dedicated board site called the Calm before the Storm (CBTS) on 8chan, which mirrored the Reddit subs CBTS followed by Great Awakening subreddits. Posts had regularly appeared for over three years and few that have followed from the jump have no doubt of the accuracy of 'Q.' 'Q' proofs would help to confirm the closeness of the Q-Team to President Trump. JoeM outlined what we know as 'The Plan' and Patel Patriot outlined his Devolution theory with the Continuity of Government (COG) program that seem to possibly be in play.

Post Q# 2450

A beautiful brave new world lies ahead.
We take this journey together.
One step at a time.
WWG1WGA!

The 'Q' informational drops are exclusively posted at the individual Q-Research and Patriots Fight boards on 8chan/8KUN. Dedicated Anons and Bakers have been decoding this valuable information and interacting on a cyber basis with the Q-Team for over three year and almost 5,000 posts. Then magically after a two-year break, the 'Q' team returned on the day Roe (6/24/22) was overturned to start new drops. Reporters John Solomon and Sara Carter in a FOX News interview recounted two mysterious intelligence officials approached them to release information to the public.

Post Q# 3683

We are all equal in this fight.
No person is above another.
United We Stand.

President Trump and the Patriots have long voiced concerns over the extreme danger posed by the Deep State. The real enemy of the American people is the Fake News or controlled corporate Mockingbird news media, which has acted as gatekeepers for the NWO Globalist Marxist bent on the complete destruction of the United States of America. In 2018 Time Magazine would include 'Q' (QAnon) in their list of the world top 25 internet influencers of which President Trump was also included.

Post Q# 1777

WE ARE Q

Let's all take a minute to look back at the beginning of this epic historic Second American Revolution. Patriots are now witnessing the start of the 'Storm' phase as all part of the 'Great Awakening' process of public enlightenment. The entire country awaits the coming 'Judgement Day' and the return of equal justice under the law in the United States. A popular 'Q' term that will obviously become more relevant with time is "Future proves Past."

Post Q# 4881
> There is 'Q.' 1
> There are 'Anons.' 2
> There is no 'QAnon.' 3

I'm sure many of us even if Red Pilled already, first learned of 'Q' at one of the early Patriot YouTube broadcasts. The 'Q' was a back-channel informational program designed for a worldwide growing number of truth seekers. President Trump's back channel of information (Q-drops) would last from the Fall of 2017 through the 2020 election cycle otherwise known as the steal of the century. The House of Representatives would pass an official resolution in 2020 condemning QAnon and the so-called conspiracy theorists surrounding the international 'Q' movement.

Post Q# 96
> Your President needs your help.
> Everything stated is for a reason.

At the end of 2019 Jesse Watters/FOX News had 'Q' at 10% accepted by the entire USA population and by March 2020, Pew Research had 15% were alright with 'Q.' The start of 2021 had 'Q' at a 16% favorable opinion and 40% recognition factor. Independent polls had 'Q' at close to 18% acceptance factor in 2022. A December 2024 poll would show that 'Q' is at 19% accepting rate within the USA. We all have come a long way from late 2017 and indications are more Patriots are coming onboard every day to this 'Great Awakening' worldwide process.

Post Q# 225
> You are here to help guide.
> Future proves past.
> You are the calm before and during the storm.

Included below are a few of the videos that 'Q' has recommended for us all to watch in past board drops. The drops are intended to help guide General Flynn's Army of Digital Soldiers and to be a backchannel of information bypassing the narrative control of the Mockingbird MSM. As the 'Q' drops get confirmed using our phase of 'future proves past', the destruction of the fake news based upon their false SpyGate statements will be evident for the world to witness.

Post Q# 38
> Note false flags.
> Prepare messages of reassurance based on what was dropped here to spread on different platforms.

Special Counsel (SC) John Durham's criminal indictment of Perkins Coie/Clinton campaign lawyer Michael Sussmann and Steele Dossier source Igor Danchenko confirms some of the prior 'Q' drops concerning SpyGate. SC Durham would publicly term his discoveries as a vast 'Joint Venture Conspiracy'. Many feel the 'Q Operation' began in 2004 and was first made public in 2014 (NSA Q Group) then full blown to the public (Anons) in late 2017.

Post Q# 4407
ONLY AT THE PRECIPICE [moment of destruction] WIIL PEOPLE FIND THE WILL TO CHANGE.

The older Patriots have been focused since JFK and younger folks have become enlightened since 9/11. Please note that Judgement Day is forthcoming and SC Durham has submitted his final report in 2023. With President Trump's re-election in 2024, many pray that justice will finally prevail and past secrets will be publicly revealed.

Post Q# 62
This will be considered the biggest 'inside' 'approved' dump in American history.

Links

The Atlantic-Reddit QAnon Ban Evasion Policy

Clinton Foundation Timeline-2025 Crossfire Hurricane Docs

Awaken Greatly-Ask the 'Q'

Wired-Kash Patel: The Hero QAnon has been Waiting For

NBC News-Reddit bans QAnon/Great Awakening Subs

NPR-Why QAnon hasn't Gone Away

Rolling Stone-QAnon Conspiracy: Trump Timeline

AMG-Q: Greatest Military Intelligence Operation

Raw Story-Steve Bannon: QAnon was Right

Martin Geddes-Information Architecture of the Q

Business Insider-FBI couldn't Find QAnon

CNN-Q Group: Manhunt Under Way for NSA Leaker

Axios-Trump praises QAnon Supporters

General Flynn-Army of Digital Soldiers

The War Economy-John Solomon meets Q Team

Markets Work-Time Magazine details the 'Shadow Campaign' against Trump

The Atlantic-The Prophecies of Q

NBC News-Amazon under Fire: QAnon Book Climbs Best-Seller List

Burning Bright-We Are Q

American Thinker-An Introduction to Q

Time Magazine-2018 Top 25 Internet Influencers

Britannica-QAnon Conspiracy Theory

NBC News-Trump on QAnon Conspiracy Theory

VICE News-Over 30 Million People believe in QAnon

AMG-JFK: The Beginning and Origin of 'Q'

VICE TV-QAnon Influencers

Congress.gov-2020 HR 1154: Condemning QAnon

Crossfire Hurricane Docs-Christopher Steele Binder

QAnon: The 2nd most Attacked Entity—All for a LARP

WE ARE Q

Post Q# 4881
> There is 'Q.' 1
> There are 'Anons.' 2
> There is no 'QAnon.' 3

The war on QAnon or 'Q', is the war on President Trump and the America First movement. 'Q' has told us what is obvious to observe, these continued waves of attacks are from all sides of the corrupt DC Swamp. 'QAnon' is a straw man persona created by the Mockingbird news media to be able to attach their false narrative propaganda. Every day for over seven years there has been at least one if not many, MSM news hit piece concerning 'Q.' President Trump's army of digital soldiers welcome the future as our previous investigative research will help to show the public outlines of the 'plan' and possible devolution programs under the Continuity of Government (COG) operations.

Protest if you wish Q, Anons existed before Q showed up on 4chan. "Anon" applied to anyone who was not posting using their own name. It simply meant they were anonymous.

Post Q# 2491
> #2 attacked entity by FAKE NEWS [+ Swamp [R + D]].

It is incredible to read that 'Q' is both unpopular and that the same time the most attacked entity in the world behind only President Trump. One must question all the serious media's (both MSM and Alternative) attention paid merely to a pretender or make-believe online 'LARP.' In a 2021 CNN townhall, even Sleepy Joe bemoaned 'QAnon' saying that we all need to 'get beyond this conspiracy.' The 2022 Russian special military operation into Ukraine would bring 'Q' into the news concerning both the bioweapons' labs and Nazi's.

Post Q# 3167
> #2 re: attacked.
> PANIC.

Free thinking individuals may wonder why the Mockingbird Fake News media continues to expend valuable resources to fight a phony baloney like 'Q.' The gatekeepers of the 'Old Guard' news media want exclusive control of the flow of information to the public and jointly go after those that threaten this exclusive narrative stranglehold. The citizen journalist of the 'Q' digital army and the counter argument represented by the Anons, has the Mockingbird press media going insane. In 2022 Biden would order the Pentagon to review US psyops on social media (investigate 'Q').

Post Q# 2936
> At what stage in the game do you play the TRUMP card?

These coordinated attacks upon 'Q' are well financed and come in the form of scheduled informational waves because they are not organic in nature. Professional shills/trolls combine with previously inserted FAKE MAGA 'Trojan Horses' and their blue check marked famous assistants to push out false narratives designed to hurt the 'Q' movement. Coordination and representation of the given media narrative is one of the keystones to control the mass population.

Post Q# 4333

> HRC direct attack re: Q?
> 2,200+ [attack] MSDNC articles written/pushed in past 2 years?

The age-old infamous strategy of the divide and conquer method has been employed against 'Q' from the jump. Deliberately hanging out for a while in the movement, is followed by a swift public departure by the shills. Amazon removed both of our #1 bestselling QBooks on 1/12/21 in an act of modern-day book burning and in desperation to stop the spread of our message. In a criminal act of corporate collusion, on the same day Amazon stopped printing my 'NEW' books, eBay removed all of our 'USED' books. To this day if you were lucky enough to buy one of my books before Amazon's ban, you can't purchase these books on eBay. Congress released in 2024 the 'Amazon Files' which shows the U.S. Government pressured Amazon to censor selected books in a direct violation of our precious First Amendment.

Post Q# 3597

> Do you think we are targeted attacked by the largest media co's in the world because we're a LARP?

You attack those that are always the biggest threat and thus those you fear the most. Being the funnel that controls the information narrative, seems the narcissistic goal of most broadcasters on the mainstream and alternative media. 'Q' was an instant threat to both the corporate media as well as the reverse of that coin being the controlled alternative media. Recall the distinct pattern of the Mockingbird MSM news by either a full frontal coordinated attack campaign against 'Q' or a complete ignoring/blackout of anything related to 'Q' in media lockstep coordination.

Post Q# 4612

> #2 attacked topic [POTUS #1].
> ALL FOR A 'CONSPIRACY.'
> INFORMATION WARFARE.

The continued hateful public assaults on 'Q' has been non-stop from the Fake News/MSM. Rounds of [Attack] [Ignore] [Infiltrate] [Gaslighting] have become a predictable pattern from most media outlets. Often the lazy media outlets will change only one or two words from the 'talking point' making it even more obvious to the watchful observer.

Post Q# 3896

> Occam's razor simply states that of any given set of explanations for an event occurring, the simplest one is most likely the correct one.

The Mockingbird news media has no problem hooking up with the Progressive Communist Socialist Leftists and Never-Trump loyalists to remove President Trump. Attempts to silence, fragment, and censor the worldwide 'Q' movement have not succeeded to date. Thousands of hit pieces have been written and aired against the messages from Team-Q since the end of 2017.

Post Q# 3310

> Other than POTUS, can you name a group more attacked than 'Q' by the FAKE NEWS media.

The sad fact is we expect this type of treatment from the Leftists, but the Republican RINO side has been just as vicious to 'Q.' Jesus Christ talked of the 'Sin of Pride' and it is very evident in the actions by all that thought HRC "would never lose" and that the 2020 election is a 'Big Lie.' HBO aired in 2021 a six-part documentary titled Q-Into the Storm and HBO was caught hiding negative tweets about the customer reviews.

Post Q# 2030
> QAnon yesterday (poll).
> POTUS today (poll).
> Notice any similarities?

Beginning in late February 2018 the first round of Fake MAGA 'plants' activated over the controversy of the Internet Bill of Rights (IBOR) issue. Several Q-YouTubers claimed "trip codes" were compromised as the false basis for their highly publicized instant departures from the young 'Q' movement.

Post Q# 4814
> Why are we being censored?
> Why are we being attacked daily?
> Why are we being condemned by Congress?

It is not a coincidence that these Fake MAGA YouTubers claimed in unison that 'Q' is a LARP. Despite huge losses in subscribers and YouTube view counts, they all stayed magically fully funded to continue broadcasting their anti-Q propaganda.

Post Q# 22
> Biggest drop to ever be provided on Pol.

The Jerome Coris/Alex Jones (AJ) stunts in late April 2018 also included more Q-YouTubers coincidentally leaving the movement at the same time. The fake censorship of AJ was really the total banning/de-platforming/and full censorship of 'Q.'

Post Q# 148
> NYT/Clowns in America article released today re: Q-Group is a DIRECT attack/warning
> re: what is being dropped here.

The Deep State ordered Reddit totally ban 'Q' to occur at this exact same time as the InfoWars fake censorship hype. There are no coincidences, and it is obvious many cheered on the silencing of 'Q.' The 2020 election cycle had caused big tech/social media firms like Twitter/Facebook/Alphabet/and Amazon to follow Reddit with total bans upon all 'Q' associated accounts and products.

Post Q# 1865
> We target NBC.
> NBC targets Q.

Throughout these unrelenting attacks one theme has remained apparent, 'Q' will not go away. Encouraging critical thinking individuals to seek the truth out for themselves is our motto and way of life for Anons enlisted in General Flynn's Army of Digital Soldiers. General McInerny has classified this current conflict as 'Hybrid Warfare' involving a different breed of warrior.

Post Q# 4622
> Ask yourself a very simple question-
> Why is everything re: 'Q' being censored, banned, and attacked?

'Q' is one of the unique 'cults' where the leadership is totally anonymous to all of the members. Most feel that this is not a bad foundational pillar on which to build a world changing international following. Critical thinking and independent investigation is a proven method at trying to arrive at the truth.

Post Q# 4954
    Shall we play a game once more?

President Trump has bypassed the Fake News and has enlisted a new breed of citizen journalist reporters to distill the flow of public information. Anons are the new media and traditional/alternative broadcasters are losing their minds over this change of power. President Trump has continued to troll his many enemies via reposting 'QAnon' related memes on his TruthSocial platform.

Post Q# 3112
    So much effort to 'KILL' a LARP.
    Nothing to see here.

What the MSM/Alternative Media fear the most is loss of their monopoly control of the distillation of public information. MSM want to remain the funnel through which all pre-selected/pre-approved narrative information flows. Special Counsel (SC) John Durham was tasked with working on criminal referrals from IG Horowitz, which in large part vindicates the 'Q' drops surrounding SpyGate. SC Durham submitted his final report in 2023 and will be the foundation for future judicial accountability.

Post Q# 2788
    PROOF'S NEGATE FALSEHOODS/CONSPIRACY ATTACKS.

'Q' has stressed that all information should 'Be Free.' This doesn't play well in the minds of greedy broadcasters and their Mockingbird affiliated networks. Censorship and total bans have been employed against 'Q' accounts by Reddit/Facebook/Twitter/YouTube and Amazon. Beyond cancel culture censorship is the formation in 2021/22 of LawFare groups of attorneys targeting 'Q' influencers. President Trump would begin to hold legally accountable those who promoted during the 2016 election a false Russian collusion narrative with his filing in 2022 of a federal RICO lawsuit.

Post Q# 3857
    Highly sophisticated 'State-level' attacks [v 8kun] followed by FAKE NEWS attacks [v Q] the next day?
    Ask yourself a simple question — why?
    It's time to wake up.

The nonstop Mockingbird news media attacks continue and have grown since President Trump temporarily left office. The drops have begun after a two-year break oddly on the day the Supreme Court announced their Roe decision (11.3 as a marker). It was revealed last in 2024 that USAID has plotted with the US Gov't to censor selective narrative dissent like 'Q.' With the re-election of President Trump in 2024, many hope past political secrets will finally be publicly revealed.

Post Q# 900
    Why are we providing this much sensitive detail in a public [known] forum?

Links

HBO-QAnon: Into the Storm

Awaken Greatly-Ask the 'Q'

MSNBC-Durbin questions Pam Bondi about QAnon

Just the News-FED Disinfo Team Coalesced around Russia/QAnon to Dismiss Hunter Laptop

Raw Story-Steve Bannon on QAnon

The Black Vault-FBI releases Files on QAnon

Burning Bright-We Are Q

Axios-QAnon Grows before 2020 Election

The Hill-When the FBI Attacks Critics as 'Conspiracy Theorists'

The Verge-The Pentagon has Ordered a Review of US Psyops on Social Media

Gizmodo-Twitter Censored Tweets on HBO QAnon Show 'Q: Into the Storm'

CBC News-QAnon Conspiracy about Ukraine Bioweapons became Mainstream Disinformation

Policy Forum-What Governments can do about QAnon Believers

Patriots Soapbox-General Paul Vallely Confirms Existence of "Q"

Epoch Times-Amazon Removing QAnon Products from Marketplace

Time-The Secret History of the Shadow Campaign (2020 Election)

NBC News-Amazon Bans QAnon Merchandise from its Marketplace

The Hill-Lawmakers introduce House Bill condemning QAnon Conspiracy Theory

Forbes-South Park set to Tackle QAnon

Revolver-General McChrystal: Deploying Military Grade Information Warfare Tools

The Hill-Witch joins QAnon to Find Children on SNL

VICE News-Tucker Carlson can't Find QAnon's Website

General Mike Flynn- "Army of Digital Soldiers"

VICE TV-Fanatics: The Deep End/QAnon (trailer)

NY Times-Shadow Brokers: Security Breach Shaken the NSA

CNN-Q Group: Manhunt Under Way for NSA Leaker

Medium-QAnon Derangement Syndrome

Hot Air-The Amazon Files

Foundation for Freedom-USAID Documents Reveal Gov't Plot to Promote Censorship

Congress.gov-US House Intel Committee 10/15/20 Transcript

Congress.gov-US HR 1154 Resolution Condemning QAnom

Crossfire Hurricane Docs-Halper Files

Justice.gov-2023 SC John Durham Report

Saul's "Rules for Radicals": Time for a New Playbook

The poster boy for the hard-core Progressive Leftists Communist movement is Saul David Alinsky (1909-1972). Chicago born and educated, Alinsky was known best for his "Rules for Radicals" 1971 publication, which oddly came out shortly before he died. Both sides employ Alinsky methods, and the illegal Biden administration is using the old street organizer's playbook. The country would witness in 2020 the CCP Virus, election steal, the summer of love and many more of the tactics outlined by Saul Alinsky.

Post Q# 4650
> Past playbook used today?
> Knowledge is power.

Alinsky was a famous community organizer as well as a political activist, humanitarian and a writer. BHO was only 11 years old when Saul died but he had a huge impact on both his and HRC political philosophies. The evil socialism and Marxism being displayed by the woke left should finally help to wake up the sleeping masses.

Post Q# 2349
> Playbook [FAIL].

A young HRC was introduced to Alinsky by Rev. Don Jones. HRC would write her senior college thesis on Saul Alinsky and described him as a great seducer of young minds. HRC would evidentially send several personal letters to Alinsky, and she was a firm supporter of his radical playbook.

Post Q# 2207
> NEW PLAYBOOK NEEDED?

Alinsky preached a mix of cultural communism/Marxist propaganda as the method to overthrow the ruling elite class. Saul Alinsky would start his organizing campaigns always in the poor/ghetto sections of U.S. major cities. Saul Alinsky would be dancing in his grave over Biden's DHS forming in 2022 a new 'Ministry of Truth' department to combat all narratives that counter the DC Swamp.

Post Q# 4806
> [D] party con.
> [D] party playbook.
> THE WORLD IS WAKING UP.

Diana West's "Red Thread" series highlights the current infiltration into the government by these communists' radical elements. Alinsky has pushed these same radical progressive ideas to extreme applications all across the United States. The planned infiltration of the USA by the Muslim Brotherhood has been decades in the making.

Post Q# 3903
> [infiltration instead of invasion]

Sad to witness adept pupils like Cass Sunstein (Sam Power's husband and HRC's USSC likely pick) and other liberals continue these communist Alinsky principles. Socialism and communism are on the rise within the new Leftists. It is suggested that the illegal Biden administration can take a few lessons from the Alinsky playbook to help rescue their regime.

Post Q# 4626
> FIFTH COLUMN.

A section in Saul's infamous book goes "The first radical known to man who rebelled against the establishment and did it so effectively, that he at least won his own kingdom." The upcoming Great Awakening will open the eyes of many as to these infiltration plans.

Post Q# 3596
> What advantages might exist when you know the other sides playbook?
> Enjoy the show!

A man of many quotations, this is yet another bizarre Alinsky quote "Hell would be heaven for me." These classic sayings give you a glimpse into the soul and Alinsky's real character. Saul Alinsky's top fans like BHO and HRC are emblematic of this philosophy being pushed upon an unsuspecting general public.

Post Q# 4362
> Keyword: Insurgency

President Trump and 'Q' have suggested that it is time for the Deep State to come up with a new 'Playbook.' When your entire game plan comes to the 'Insurance Policy', it's game/set/match. Special Counsel John Durham has dropped criminal indictments related to SpyGate and submitted his final report in 2023. With the re-election of President Trump in 2024, the coming of Judgement Day quickly approaches.

Post Q# 626
> OP Mockingbird FAILURE.

Links

Famous People-Saul Alinsky Bio

FOX News-Democrats pulled Greatest Con Job Ever

Ada Nestor-They All Knew it was a Lie

Town Hall-So Much for The Rule of Law

Red State-Biden's Ministry of Truth Director Turns out to Be a Raving Lunatic

Front Page-Three Foreign Billionaires financed Dark Money in 2020 Election

American Thinker- 'Let's Go Brandon' is Alinsky Method

Breitbart-Virgil-Saul Alinsky on 'Rules for Radicals' and 2020 Election

WND-Biden's Actions explained by Cloward Piven Strategy

Washington Times-Coronavirus and the Smell of Saul Alinsky

Center for Security Policy-U.S. Muslim Brotherhood and Saul Alinsky

Town Hall-Russian Collusion by Saul Alinsky

American Spectator-HRC/Alinsky/Lucifer Connection

The Federalist-Who is Saul Alinsky?

The Blaze: Cloward-Piven Strategy Alive and Well at Border

New Yorker-Cass Sunstein

Archive.org- "Rules for Radicals"

NY Post-Celebrating the Collapse of HRC's Big Lie

FBI.gov (vault)-COINTELPRO

State.gov-U.S. Government Counterinsurgency Guide (2009)

Clinton Foundation Timeline-2025 Crossfire Hurricane Docs

Justice.gov-2023 SC John Durham Report

Lest We Forget: That Lingering Question of Eligibility

The 'Birtherism' issue was first brought up by Sid 'Vicious' Blumenthal in the 2008 Presidential election cycle. Blumenthal's work was in an effort to help HRC defeat BHO in their highly contested Democrat party primaries. In later years the leftist would attempt to pin the origins of the birth certificate issue at the feet of President Donald Trump. President Trump filed in 2022 a federal RICO lawsuit against many of the BHO officials connected to the promotion of the false Russian collusion narrative during the 2016 election cycle.

Post Q# 1508
Why are Hussein records sealed?

For almost a decade Sheriff Joe Arpaio and the Cold Case Posse have been searching for BHO's original birth certificate. Under Sheriff Joe the Maricopa County/Arizona commissioned several investigators to assist with his search. Odd that Maricopa County would become the epicenter of the 2020 election voter fraud forensic examinations.

Post Q# 3837
BIGGER THAN YOU CAN IMAGINE
Crimes against Humanity.
The Silent War Continues.....

Helping out Sheriff Joe was well known NSA/CIA Whistleblower Dennis Montgomery. Also helping Sheriff Joe was the Cold Case Posse (CCP) under Mike Zullo's expert leadership. BHO has given contradictory claims of both who are who true bloodline parents as well as his actual birthing hospital.

Post Q# 894
When we're done he'll claim Kenyan citizenship as a way to escape.

John 'Clown' Brennan has been assisting BHO since before the 2008 campaign. The Deep State has a lot of resources in keeping secret the truth and silencing any eligibility issues involving BHO. Many historians question especially who the real father of BHO is and where he actually spent the early years of his deliberately obscure childhood.

Post Q# 3601
Many who 'represent' us, do not love us.

Thankfully POTUS gave Patriot Joe a full pardon from his targeted conviction under BHO's reign of terror. Dinesh D'Souza/The Bundy's pardons give us hope for equal justice in the future. In 2021 former Sheriff Joe Arpaio has stated he is going to run for Mayor of Fountain Hills Arizona and all Patriots look forward to his return to public service.

Post Q# 3518
How did someone die from this type of accident?
Severity of impact?

The Zullo/CCP have proven scientifically using top independent labs the '9-Points of forgery' with BHO's long-form Birth Certificate. 'Q' has hinted at BHO's eligibility issues for the highest office. The 'Manchurian Candidate' theme has corrected swirled around BHO from his sponsored Harvard education onward. In the hit movie 'The Matrix', there is the ability on the future to build 'constructs' that mimic reality perfectly.

Post Q# 111
    Why would this former President be funded pre-political days?

The heat remains on this long-time smoldering subject of BHO's eligibility. Worldwide searches continue looking for BHO's authentic undiscovered original and his true birthplace. This tired narrative of being unable to produce your original birth certificate is becoming more unbelievable by the year. Historians will reflect that this major deception marked a major societal downfall within the USA.

Post Q# 4158
    SHADOW PRESIDENCY.
    SHADOW GOVERNMENT.
    INSURGENCY.

The hunt for BHO's birth certificate includes the bizarre death of Loretta Fuddy, who was the Director of the Hawaii Department of Health. Fuddy drowned and was the lone death as a small commercial plane crash landed off of Molokai in Hawaiian waters on December 11, 2013. It was revealed in 2023 that at least 6 BHO officials (including BHO) used fake non-governmental email accounts in efforts to avoid FOIA requests and shielding their shady activities.

Post Q# 4588
    Do not give up the citizen investigation.

The bizarre story goes BHO when pressed on the subject couldn't even remember the correct name of his birth hospital. Who else on this planet doesn't know where there were born or even the name of their birth hospital? Odd that BHO would make an unannounced White House appearance in 2024 at State Dinner for Kenyan President. Special Counsel John Durham has submitted his final report in 2023 related to the ObamaGate/SpyGate scandals. With the re-election of President Trump in 2024, many past secrets will finally be publicly revealed.

Post Q# 3514
    One or both of his parents fluent in Russian?
    Is Russian a common language to learn?
    Farms develop necessary (unique) skill sets in order to produce results.

Links

Newsweek-Sheriff Joe Resurrects "Birtherism"

The Federalist-BHO used NPR to Launder Lies

Clinton Foundation Timeline-2025 Crossfire Hurricane Docs

CBS News-Arpaio: BHO Birth Certificate definitely Forged

Revolver News-BHO: A Shadowy Cryptic Figure

Just the News-Sheriff Joe Arpaio about the U.S. Border

BBC News-The Birth of the BHO 'Birther' Conspiracy

American Spectator-The Scandal Obama still won't Acknowledge

Thread Reader-Remember Loretta Fuddy?

NPR-Sheriff Arpaio Releases Findings on BHO's Birth Certificate

The Savage Citizen-BHO/Birth Certificate

AZ Central-Sheriff Joe still a "Birther"

Tablet Magazine-How RussiaGate began with BHO's Iran Deal

The Matrix (1991)-The 'Construct' Scene

FOX News-Clinton Campaign/Blumenthal Fight back against 'Birth Rumor'

Video-Carl Gallup interview w/Mike Zullo (2018)

ABC15 News-Mike Zullo Update on BHO's Birth Certificate

Tru News-BHO removes Link to Birth Certificate

Newsie-Sheriff Joe Arpaio and the Birth Certificate

AZ Central-Man behind Vote Fraud Theory pushed Debunked Info with Arpaio

Tablet Magazine-The BHO Factor

Conservative Twins-Software to Show BHO's Birth Certificate is Fake

Crossfire Hurricane Docs-DJT and Flynn Defensive Briefing

Justice.gov-2023 SC John Durham Report

Julian Assange—Soon to be [ACTIVATED]

Not so long ago, some thought that the 'Q' Elf on the Shelf reference maybe for a sidelined player like Julian Assange (JA). Assange had been arrested in London and British courts have previously ruled no to the legal decision over extradition to the USA. The USA had won the appeal over Assange's extradition and after months of exhausting appeals with the British courts, JA just may be coming across the pond facing 175 years for war crimes. Beginning in late April 2022 and continuing through 2024, UK authorities were working with their USA counter parts to arrange Julian Assange's physical transfer.

Post Q# 1286
> Why no contact w/WL / JA?
> What is being investigated?

Progress would continue in 2023 with the U.S. Ambassador Caroline Kennedy to Australia is hopeful a deal can be reached for immunity and transportation finally for Julian Assange. British courts will hear the final extradition appeal in February 2024. Julian Assange has been a player on the sidelines, but the world is dying to hear his side of this intriguing DNC email tale. JA can clear up once and for all the true identity of the infamous 2016 DNC/Podesta email source to WikiLeaks. Assange and his infamous WikiLeaks have been in the forefront of accurate whistleblower information for decades. In a late plea deal with the U.S. DOJ, Assange has agree to violating the Espionage Act and is free from prison in June 2024 with time served.

Post Q# 3312
> We have the source.

'Q' has stressed we are way past playing checkers and onto 4-D chess. Life can be viewed as a chess board that demonstrates a strategy of moves vs countermoves, were two sides battle toward ultimate victory-checkmate thank you for playing. We have been told that 'actors' are involved with plan to defeat the NWO in playing out elaborate scripted roles in various 'movies'.

Post Q# 459
> CONF_WHITE_WHITE.

The Australian government announced it had issued a passport to JA. Assange was one step closer to freedom prior to arrest/removal from Ecuadorian embassy when he had stayed for yes. Now inquiring minds want the full scoop on the role played by murdered DNC staffer Seth Rich.

Post Q# 4963
> Whistleblowers.
> Time to show the world.

Rumors have been swirling about federal charges stemming from the Chelsea Bradley Manning theft saga and not related to the DNC. Assange and WikiLeaks (WL) had a 10-year perfect track records in releasing authentic material that they have obtained.

Post Q# 1844
> Could a new Telecommunications Act be on the way?

The 2016 computer intrusion of the DNC's servers has been ground zero in the false Trump-Russia collusion narrative. NSA expert Bill Binney has forensically proven this was a leak not a hack based upon the DNC data download time was at very high transmission speed rates. Assigned Special Counsel (SC) John Durham had revealed via 2022 court filings that SpyGate researchers could have relied on 'spoofed' data related to the 2016 DNC server breach and the subsequent investigation by Perkins Coie hired CrowdStrike.

Post Q# 1773
> Track last.
> JA offline cause.

Patriot Bill Binney concluded that the DNC intrusion was a leak contrary to claims by hired CrowdStrike. POTUS advised then CIA Director Pompeo (KANSAS) to meet with Binney and to review his scientific findings from the intrusion. It has later been revealed that the CIA has plans drawn up to either kidnap or assassinate Assange. SC John Durham had previously announced through a court filing that his office is investigating the 2016 DNC computer intrusion.

Post Q# 1707
CrowdStrike?
Servers.
SR.
JA.

Self-admissions by former British Ambassador Craig Murray, has a DNC insider passing him the 'stolen' email data via a thumb drive in Washington/DC. Additionally, a batch of Skippy Podesta's emails were included with the 'leaked' DNC emails that were ultimately handed over to WikiLeaks in 2016.

Post Q# 2595
Think 'Elf on the Shelf.'

JA/WL displayed their classic 'drip' strategy in the systematic releasing these DNC/Podesta emails prior to the 2016 Presidential election. A crescendo of non-disputed emails from the least to most impactful, were timely released almost daily by WikiLeaks.

Post Q# 531
Anon post: JA's post concerning a famous chessboard (D5) move
Q reply: Impressive Anon!

Many have pointed to murdered DNC staffer Seth Rich (SR) as the insider that physically performed these data downloads. Sadly, we all recall the brutal killing of "Panda" by his DC apartment, occurred shortly after discovery of the DNC computer intrusion email leak.

Post Q# 1462
What recent news came out re: SR/JA/WL lawsuit?

Information is still being collected regarding the possible use by SR of SecureDrop. SecureDrop was a whistleblower submissions site operated by the Freedom of the Press Foundation (FOTP) John Perry Barlow and Company. 'Q' has emphasized the Mockingbird MSM news media get daily 4am 'talking points' from their CIA overlords.

Post Q# 1198
SR connect to DNC.
MS_13.
JA.

It appears that the Deep State's intelligence assets intercepted SR's initial correspondence to JA/WL via SecureDrop. Recall the rash of untimely deaths surrounding FOTP founders like John Perry Barlow/Aaron Schwartz/and James Dolan during this timeframe. Odd through the several years of the Mueller Russia collusion probe, Assange was never interviewed about WikiLeaks role.

Post Q# 2499
[House Of Cards] re: Maggie NYT re: WL.

JA had helped with the escape route and advanced coordination for C_A operative Edward Snowden. Oddly both JA and Snowden, along with reporters Glenn Greenwald/Laura Poitras/Daniel Ellsberg and actor John Cuzak, were all founding core members of the FOTP.

Post Q# 1626
Server or JA = truth exposed (SR).

Debbie Wasserman-Schultz and Perkins Coie lawyer Michael Sussmann hired CrowdStrike to review the DNC computers. Often overlooked was the existing personal relationship between Sussmann and Shawn Henry (President of CrowdStrike) in this scheme involving the DNC computer forensic review. SC John Durham's criminal indictments of Perkins Coie lawyer Michael Sussmann connects to HRC/DWS/the DNC and many more treasonous coup plotters.

Post Q# 4709
Julian Assange

CrowdStrike concluded the Russian/Ukraine hacker groups Fuzzy and Cozy Bear were solely responsible for the DNC 'hack.' Compliments of JA/WL the CIA Vault 7 release showed the ability to plant false intrusion fingerprint trails within most outside computer hacking operations. Rolling Stone news has claimed the then CIA Director Mike (KANSAS) Pompeo considered the assassination of Julian Assange over the classified Vault 7 leak.

Post Q# 3764
How does one provide content to WL?
comp-to-computer
person-to-person [1]

The Deep State then produces Guccifer 2.0 to help muddy the political hacking waters. Smoke, mirrors, and deception is the trademark of the DNC fake computer intrusion fiasco and false Russian collusion narrative cover story. History will show a web of false narratives combined with extensive intelligence operations combined to form the unfolding scandal termed SpyGate.

Post Q# 874
JA-have you learned and eliminated L-6?

Assange had been holed up in London's Ecuadoran Embassy for almost 7 years prior to his recent incarnation. Team 'Q' has alerted us that JA will be returning, and the courts have confirmed his extradition to the USA. Assange has stood for decades as a symbol of independent journalism acting as a watchdog against corruption. Assange's health has deteriorated exponentially since his stay at the Embassy and subsequent harsh prison confinement. Assange has suffered a stroke under the strain of his extradition process and unfortunately this stoke has affected his memory. In a positive development, the British court granted Assange's marriage to long-term partner Stella Morris on 3/23/22.

Post Q# 2322
[Pg. 20 - Assange Arrest].
By: Marty Torrey [Mad Hatter].

U.S. House Representative Dana Rohrabacher did meet with Assange in 2017. Dana through Senator Rand Paul, claim they got JA's vital information passed along to the proper people. No guarantees of pardons had been made by Rep. Rohrabacher or by the Trump administration to JA. Special Counsel John Durham has dropped criminal indictments related to SpyGate and past illegal activities by BHO/HRC/and Biden, as well as submitting his final report in 2023. With the re-election of President Trump in 2024, many are hopeful of the long overdue Presidential pardon for Julian Assange.

Post Q# 1591
JA in the news?
Think JC.
Server unlocks SR.

Already declared a citizen of Ecuador and a worldwide journalist hero, JA is ready to be finally heard. 'Q' told us JA was not stateside a while ago and now we all wait the extradition hearing outcome. Ecuador would eventually cave to Globalists pressure in 2021 and revoke Assange's passport while he rots in British custody. Oddly Mexico has stepped up to offer sanctuary for Julian Assange, but his current confinement is under judicial review. Sad to announce that in June 2023 Assange lost yet another appeal against extradition to the USA from England and in 2024 the drama continues to drag out in international courtrooms until a late deal in June 2024.

Post Q# 4153

> internal DL [terminal 1] speed?
> WL publish v SR 187?

Many people have been waiting to see how the Assange 'card' gets played out in the future. JA has married his longtime partner Stella Morris while still in prison. The UK court has previously ordered psychological testing for Julian Assange as a prerequisite before granting permission to marry his partner while in prison. Julian Assange in 2024 plead guilty to violating the Espionage Act and is a free man for time served in deal from the U.S. DOJ. We all hope for a classic winning checkmate (D5) move with the freedom and the subsequent activation of hero Julian Assange.

Post Q# 3341

> Under protection.
> Key to DNC 'source' 'hack' '187.'

Links

AP News-Julian Assange Wins Appeal over US Extradition

American Thinker-Was the Death of Seth Rich a Hit?

The Federalist-Unsealed Crossfire Hurricane Docs prove RussiaGate a Hoax

BBC News-Who is WikiLeaks/Julian Assange?

Just the News-Julian Assange makes Public Appearance following Prison

Revolver News-Worst Snakes still Hate Assange

Daily Mail-Julian Assange Plea Deal with the DOJ

Reuters-WikiLeaks' Assange gets Married in UK High-Security Jail

Justice.gov-WikiLeaks Founder charged in Superseding Indictment

Markets Work-Is Julian Assange our Guy?

The Nation-Free Julian Assange!

LA Times-Assange Tried to warn W/H about Classified Doc Leak

Breitbart-Julian Assange Receives Australian Passport

Boing Boing-Assange and John Perry Barlow Joint Interview

Nieuwsuur-Julian Assange on Seth Rich

Neon Revolt-At the Highest Levels (part 1)

FBI.gov/Vault-Seth Rich (part 1 of 2)

Gadgets-NSA's Tailored Access Operations intercepts Computer Data

Crossfire Hurricane Docs-Christopher Steele Binder

Justice.gov-2023 SC John Durham Report

Bombardier to Pilot Sharyl Attikisson "We're Over the Target"

Sharyl Attkisson is a premier reporter and DOJ whistleblower who has been the target of unauthorized surveillance. Ms. Attkisson has long been the champion for truth, transparency and exposure of corrupt governmental/elected officials. Sharyl Attkisson would be asked by Congress in May 2022 to testify about the past illegal surveillance conducted on her by the U.S. government.

Post Q# 1728
Unauthorized missile fired.
POTUS AF1.
Biggest threat to the American people.

Ms. Attkisson's has a pending lawsuit case against the DOJ/FBI that has finally reached the USSC. Oral arguments began on 1/29/19 for the unlawful computer intrusion by our government on Ms. Attkisson's personal equipment. As of mid 2022, various court filings are still going on, but Ms. Attkisson has been winning at each legal level to date.

Post Q# 2578
Sometimes 'intrusions' have a way of safeguarding people and evidence.

Sharyl Attkisson has published an outstanding article about the timeline of the "Collusion Against Trump." This superb article demonstrates just how far back in time all the pieces were put in place to help ensnare our POTUS. Ms. Attkisson would continue be a champion for the truth and justice through all of the unfolding political scandals.

Post Q# 214
What is the FBI?
Spying tool?
Nothing is what it seems.

Sharyl Attkisson has been credited for her 2012 groundbreaking journalistic investigations into tragic Fast and Furious as well as the Benghazi scandals. Sharyl had several unexplainable computer issues while covering these BHO-era political scandals. History will show that prior to the unlaw surveillance of candidate Doanld Trump in 2016, Ms. Attkisson was spied upon around 2014.

Post Q# 2581
Name IDEN Public and FBI 'intrusion' and Lawsuit and Response to lawsuit and Public Reveal (otherwise sealed?).

Attkisson's superb reporting drew her to attention of the Deep State enemy and ultimately into their crosshairs. This legal battle has been ongoing for years and we wish Sharyl success in uncovering the truth and her due reparations from civil court. It has appeared the legal worm has turned, and justice will prevail.

Post Q# 113
Controlling stake in CBS?

Ms. Attkisson's employer at the time of her first computer intrusion was CBS News. CBS's team of computer experts established through neutral forensic analysis, that a Governmental agency(s) had penetrated her personal computer. The government could never refute these independent analysis findings concerning penetration of Ms. Attkisson's personal electronics. Sharyl Attkisson would later publicly state that some of the implanted false data files included child porn images.

Post Q# 4961
Endless surveillance.
Who will put an end to the endless?

IP addresses were linked in this review directly to the government and was the means of initial electronic intrusion. All roads point to the NSA/CIA and recent FISC/FISA abuses bear that out. Rep. Devin Nunes has demonstrated the use of 'HOPS' which are jumps in lines of individuals communications allowing for legal mass surveillance.

Post Q# 4620

Intel community [NAT SEC_WH] essential to control [infiltration] to prevent DECLAS_public exposure of true events [illegal surv [R] candidates 1+2, House members 1-x, Senate members 1-x, Journalists 1-x, Amb 1-x] + CLAS 1-99 events.

This critical 'intrusion' discovery led to the current $32 million dollar lawsuit by Sharyl Attkisson against the U.S. Government. Attkisson's legal filings got a boost when it also has recently been discovered that one of her hard drives had been totally replaced by the FBI/DOJ without her knowledge.

Post Q# 1943

Could FISA warrants be issued/active for numerous in-the-news now/future U.S. targets.

The swapping out of Attkisson's hard drive occurred while it was in the sole possession/custody of the Department of Justice. Watch for the fireworks as Sharyl has just also sued Rod Rosenstein personally for spying on her computers. Ms. Attkisson is currently helping to expose the Covid-19 origins, fake news media, as well as the 2020 election fraud. The MSM coverup of Hunter Biden's 'Laptop from Hell' is yet another example of how corrupt DC Swamp politicians can use the news media to create false narratives.

Post Q# 2959

Hussein gave the order to start the spy campaign.
The More You Know.

Then departing AG Bill Barr upgraded SP John Durham to a full Special Counsel in order to protect him from illegal Biden while looking into this vast 'Joint Venture Conspiracy' criminal behavior. All SpyGate roads lead back to BHO, and Special Counsel John Durham has dropped criminal indictments and submitted his final report in 2023. With the historic re-election of President Trump in 2024, the 'Judgement Day' is coming and equal justice under the law will be restored to our Republic.

Post Q# 2005

The 'Marathon Media' is working hard.
The Flood Is Coming-BOOM!

Links

PJM-Attkisson Accuses DOJ of Swapping Hard Drive

Sharyl Attikisson-New Details about Spying on Me and My CBS Computers

Headline USA-Reporter Tells Congress the Hard Truth

Sharyl Attkisson-BHO Era Surveillance Timeline

Sharyl Attkisson-Journalist Sharyl Attkisson Testifies about Surveillance Abuse

The Federalist-How Media Covered the Russia Hoax vs. Hunter Biden's Laptop

Sharyl Attkisson-Investigates Covid-19 Origins

Gregg Jarrett-Former CBS Reporter: "A Target of Illegal Spying under BHO

Epoch Times-Journalist sues Rod Rosenstein for Spying on Her Computers

Sharyl Attkisson-Lt. Gen. Flynn Personally Fired by DNI Clapper in 2014

Sharyl Attkisson-Countdown to USSC Oral Arguments

Real Clear Politics-Attkisson: How did the Media get Trump-Russia so Wrong

Sharyl Attkisson-Timeline of 'Sabotage' of Trump in 2016

Sharyl Attkisson-Cybersecurity and The Awan Brothers

Breitbart-Attkisson: CIA Under Brennan Spied on Whistleblowers

Full Measure-Sharyl Attkisson interviews President Trump

Open Democracy-Attkisson: "Fake News" didn't Start with Trump

Sharyl Attkisson's website-great articles

Clinton Foundation Timeline-2025 Crossfire Hurricane Docs

Justice.gov-2023 SC John Durham Report

Imran Awan: Bigger Than You Can Imagine

Imran Awan's 'Judgement Day' was on July 3, 2018, for his Federal court appearance date. Imran signed a cooperating plea deal at that time and ultimately received a light sentence (so far). The mystery of this alleged Pakistani intelligence operative continues to this very day. In 2023 Federal Judge Tanya Chutkan who oversaw Awan's case, would be assigned President Trump's criminal case related to January 6th.

Post Q# 2385
Mathematically impossible or every detail planned?
WWG1WGA!

It was expected to bring fireworks in terms of the U.S. House's espionage allegations but ultimately ended in a strange plea deal. Awan got a slap in the wrist for minor bank fraud charges, temporarily holding off the espionage related charges that will hopefully flow in the future. Remember there are no statute of limitations concerning treasonous actions against our nation.

Post Q# 1978
AWAN - Pakistan Intelligence?

Imran Awan lost all Capitol computer access on 2/2/17 and an official USCP (Capitol Police) investigation dutifully began. Federal authorities were brought in when off-site servers and possible classified informational breaches were discovered at Awan owned properties. Imran Awan would recruit several families' members and friends into his IT work for the U.S. House of Representatives.

Post Q# 1626
AWAN is bigger than you can imagine.

Imran Awan was first hired by Xavier Becerra in 2004 as a Congressional IT staffer. The USCP were also investigating Xavier Becerra for turning over a fake copy of his House server when he left Congress in response to Awan's questionable computer activities. Becerra now has returned to government now as Biden's Secretary of HHS.

Post Q# 4933
Watergate x 1000.

Awan got several family members hired at the maximum allowed pay for Congressional IT staffers into what ultimately were 'Ghost Jobs.' The combined Awan Cabal took in $7 million over their several years of government employment. Imran Awan additionally operated side grift schemes involving stolen computer and Blackberry phones among other Congress staff.

Post Q# 1983
Think Server Access [granted].
Money talks.

House members routinely waved the lawful required background security checks for the Awan's. The deliberate waving of background checks is critical in incriminating Congressional co-conspirators. Rumors on the Hill constantly swirled of highly discounted hot stolen equipment being offered by the Awan's.

Post Q# 1328
THERE WILL COME A TIME THEY WILL NOT BE SAFE WALKING DOWN THE STREET.

Look way beyond the unauthorized data access, selling stolen computer equipment, and shady bank loan fraud issues to get to the real Awan mission. 'Q' said that in fact real investigations were ongoing into espionage by the entire Awan cabal.

Post Q# 1250
When did AWANs mission op go green?

Imran Awan additionally ran side used car companies and these are directly connected to the Hezbollah /Project Cassandra narcoterrorism. Car dealerships are notorious fronts for money laundering operations worldwide. In the works of espionage, cars are often needed in operations involving foreign nationals within the USA.

Post Q# 674
AWAN/DWS/Paki intel/MB.
decode: MB = Muslim Brotherhood

There needs to be a serious look as to any Pakistan Intelligence/MB ties with the Awan's. Stories involve Imran's real Father being observed turning over thumb drives to Pakistan Intelligence agents. It would come as no surprise to learn that Imran Awan is treated like royalty every time he returns to his native Pakistan.

Post Q# 949
Trust the plan.
Full control.

President Trump's first major military action was in Yalka/Yemen in January 2017. Tragically due to an advance informational leak, Navy Seal Ryan Owen died. Intel on this mission was absolutely compromised, and the Awan's are the prime suspects. We will never forget Ryan nor his wife's tearful acknowledgment of President Trump's words at that memorable State of the Union speech.

Post Q# 4245
HOW DO YOU CREATE A DIVERSION?
HOW DO YOU SHIFT THE NARRATIVE?

President Trump as well as all us want to know the specific details about DWS's Pakistan 'Mystery Man.' 'Q' has advised in multiple drops that Imran Awan has already fully cooperated with authorities, and much more will be forthcoming. Special Counsel (SC) John Durham has been tasked to prosecute the many criminal referrals from IG Horowitz centering around the political SpyGate scandal.

Post Q# 3532
DNC server(s) hold many answers.
[AWAN]
You didn't think the plea deal was the end did you?

To quote [DWS] protests with the U.S. Capital Police returning in regard to her previously lost personal laptop, "There will be consequences." Not to worry Noodles Judgement Day is coming and is part of the Great Awakening to counter the NWO's global Great Reset. SC John Durham has dropped criminal indictments and submitted his final report in 2023. With the re-election of President Trump in 2024, past hidden political secrets will finally be revealed.

Post Q# 3634

[D]'s (internal) infiltration issue(s) w/protecting NAT SEC?
Deliberate?
Awan IT scandal

Links

FOX News-Imran Awan avoids Jail Time

Clinton Foundation Timeline-2025 Crossfire Hurricane Docs

Medium-Imran Awan Timetable

Observer-DWS: Corruption Scandals are Piling Up

The Federalist-Special Counsel's Office is Investigating DNC Server Hack

Western Journal-Remember Imran Awan? DOJ Confirms part of Sealed Criminal Matter

Red State-The Awan Story Disappeared but One Judge is Still asking Questions

Markets Work-IT Intrigue: Imran Awan and Debbie Wasserman Schultz

Judicial Watch-Luke Rosiak/Daily Caller Interview: Imran Awan

NY Times-Congress pays $850,00 to Muslim IT Aides in Inquiry

Daily Caller-Awan's Money Laundering Car Dealerships

Breitbart-Fast Facts about Imran Awan

Daily Caller-DWS's Hard Drive Central to Awan Case

Unz Review-The Tale of the Brothers Awan

Daily Caller-44 House DEMs waived Awan's Background Checks

Epoch Times-Luke Rosiak: Epstein and Imran Awan

Crossfire Hurricane Docs-Christopher Steele Binder

Justice.gov-2023 SC John Durham Report

Who is James Baker?
How is Baker Connected to ObamaGate ?

Former FBI General Counsel James Baker [JB] personally prepared, approved, and signed-off on all the Title-1 FISA Surveillance warrants. Baker was the FBI's gatekeeper of the required Woods Procedure paperwork needed prior to presentation in front of the FISA Court. To be able to obtain such intrusive governmental surveillance, the FBI is held to a very high threshold of incriminating evidence in advance. President Trump would file in 2022 a federal RICO lawsuit against those officials involved with the promotion of the false Russian collusion narrative back during the 2016 election cycle. The Republican controlled House plans to call James Baker to testify in regards to his employment at Twitter following his release from the FBI.

Post Q# 2157
Panic in DC.
James Baker testifying against Comey?

It has finally been confirmed that FBI's James Baker had been under investigation for leaking to the news media and discussions with Perkins Coie lawyer Michael Sussmann over Alfa Bank acquisitions. James Baker is just another in a long line of lying leaking corrupt DOJ officials and is now cooperating with the John Durham's criminal probe. Baker had long standing contacts with DNC lawyer Michael Sussmann over the Alfa Bank information concerning Donald Trump that would later prove to be totally false. Sussmann would be found not guilty, but Baker did testify at that trial helping to setup Durham's vast 'Joint Venture Conspiracy'.

Post Q# 2135
"Review of the new documents raises grave concerns regarding an apparent systematic culture of media leaking by high-ranking officials at the FBI and DOJ related to ongoing investigations".

John Solomon reported several FBI/DOJ email chains indicated that the Carter Page FISA warrants may have been illegally altered or doctored. This might allow some of the FISA signers off the hook in technical legal terms but will lead to more criminality via the conspiracy laws. History will let us know if James Baker was completely duped by the cooked-up phony Alfa Bank and Trump tale or if more sinister motives are involved.

Post Q# 2229
Panic in DC re: Baker confirm?

FBI's head lawyer James Baker was the final legal authority by which our country's top government lawyers all turned for advice. Baker was FBI Director James Comey's right-hand person and was neck-deep involved with the evil coup plot against President Trump. History will show a vast amount of both DOJ and FBI officials were deeply involved with this treasonous activity against candidate Donald Trump back in 2016.

Post Q# 3815
They will not be able to walk down the street.
THE GREAT AWAKENING.

These high-level clicks of officials formed the 'Small Group' within the Department of Justice and nicknamed themselves as the 'Secret Society.' Surprisingly James Baker claims now there always was enough evidence to charge HRC/Aides in the server/email 'matter.'

Post Q# 2071

FBI and DOJ CORRUPTION.
FEDERAL BUREAU OF 'INVESTIGATION.'
James Baker, General Counsel-FIRED.

Appointed from Special Prosecutor to a Special Counsel (SC) John Durham have been tasked to look into FISA Court abuses by the DOJ/FBI. Additionally, the elements of SpyGate/Crossfire Hurricane related scandals have been added to the ongoing criminal probes by Durham. Baker along with FBI colleagues Bill Priestap/Peter Strzok/Joe Pientka/and Lisa Page were said by 'Q' to be early cooperating witnesses.

Post Q# 2323

James Baker closed door testimony + previous to IG/GJ statements sealed.

Baker will soon come back into the media spotlight because of his prior key position of preparing all FISA applications. President Trump had authorized declassification of every Carter Page FISA warrant prior to leaving office but this pending DECLAS did not occur in 2020. SC Durham would paint a vast coordinated criminal conspiracy involving both government officials as well as private outside actors.

Post Q# 3595

F2F 1-4 US person(s) initiated scope memo.

In past testimony before Congress, James Baker revealed that [RR] did not 'joke' about wearing a wire (25th Amendment) to try to entrap POTUS. Baker admitted he meet with Perkins Coie attorney Michael Sussmann to receive Trump-Russian collusion intelligence concerning Alfa Bank. SC Durham has indicated Sussmann for lying to the Baker in 2016 over Alfa Bank but all feel Baker knew he was working for the Clinton campaign.

Post Q# 1316

James Baker/FIRED [reported today-resigned [false]]/removed Jan/Fired 4.21.

Walk down memory lane with a few of Baker's contributions to SpyGate/ObamaGate:

- 4/26/16 Baker attends back-to-back meetings at the White House with DOJ attorneys and Obama officials over FISA.
- 5/5/16 Baker and protégé' Lisa Page go to W/H to brief BHO on FISA status.
- May-June 2016 Baker is part of inner-circle loop on all changes/revisions to Comey's HRC exoneration memo.
- 10/31/16 Baker leaks classified material on the Trump Dossier to David Corn of Mother Jones media.
- Late December 2016 Director Wray effectively fires Baker with severe demotion and removal as FBI General Counsel.
- 2017 Baker joins fellow cooperating DOJ/FBI staffer Priestap/Page/Ohr/and Strzok. All the folks still working now for the US Government and testifying. Baker was demoted/reassigned later in 2017.
- 2018 Baker seems to have changed course and is now fully cooperating. He resigned prior to Chris Wray's confirmation as new FBI Director.
- 2020 Baker is involved with the coverup of Hunter Biden's Laptop from Hell' and other crimes.
- 2021 SC John Durham's indictment of Baker's pal Michael Sussmann for lying to the FBI over Alfa Bank.

- 2022 Baker is coopering with Durham to testify against Sussmann (found not guilty) and Elon Musk exposes Twitter/Baker's involvement in past censorship of free speech. Musk would fire Baker in December 2022 upon release of the Twitter Files and would be called to testify to the U.S. House.

Post #Q 953
How bad is the corruption?
FBI (past/present). + 29 (16).
decode: 29 have already quit or been fired and 16 still are employed.

James Baker and James Comey worked together first at Justice as Federal Prosecutors. Later they had a very profitable stint together at Bridgewater Associates. The revolving golden door of DC political nepotism is obvious when watching longtime politicians go into cushy high paying private gigs then return to government as the political winds shift again. The DC Swamp/Deep State have perfected this significant 'reward' program for their aligned political allies.

Post Q# 4153
[FBI Floor 7] James Baker - Perkins Coie [shell 2]

Mueller/Comey cleared famed Sandy "Burglar" Berger from classified document theft and destruction of official U.S. records. Berger was caught with classified documents stuffed down his pants/socks while leaving the U.S. National Archives Building. History will show high ranking government officials covered up many previous political scandals for several Presidential administrations. Incredibly it would be revealed that James Baker had a hand in the coverup of Hunter Biden's 'Laptop from Hell' and Rosemont Seneca Partners relationship with then VP Joe Biden.

Post Q# 1910
Who signed the CP FISA?

Like on any merry go round these crooked cops always circle back to crimes. Baker along with McCabe and Rybicki backed-up Comey's false version of the private talk with a President Trump over General Mike Flynn. SC Durham has publicly announced James Baker will testify against Clinton campaign lawyer Michael Sussmann confirms his status as a cooperating witness. Durham would produce during Sussmann's discovery period several text messages from Sussmann to Baker confirming his outright lies and fabrication of the Alfa Bank false connection to candidate Donald Trump.

Post Q# 2331
"Former general counsel James Baker met during the 2016 season with at least one attorney from Perkins Coie, the Democratic National Committee's private law firm."

FBI James Baker testified previously to grand juries that Perkins Coie cyber lawyer Michael Sussmann gave the FBI Alfa Bank false allegations about Trump Tower. Baker was a conduit with Perkins Coie/Fusion GPS/DOJ and to the BHO's White House. SC John Durham's indictment of Michael Sussmann was due to lying to the FBI lawyer James Baker in 2016 regarding Alfa Bank claims involving Trump Tower. NSA Jake Sullivan and operative Dan Jones have also been implicated in the false Alfa Bank collusion narrative promoted by HRC/DNC.

Post Q# 3173
The calm before the storm?
FIRE AT WILL COMMANDER.

James Baker's replacement at the suggestion of Director Chris Wray as the top FBI lawyer was Dana Boente. Boente would be subsequently forced out by AG Bill Barr and departed the FBI in June 2020. Twitter had hired Baker to be their Deputy General Counsel, but Elon Musk would fire Baker in early December 2022 upon release of the Twitter Files. James Baker would land in 2024 at the far left-wing Protect Democracy Project. President Trump won the 'keys' in 2016 to unlock past secrets, and Elon Musk now can look behind Twitter's 'curtain' to see what exactly James Baker has done to prevent free speech in the USA. SC John Durham submitted his final report in 2023. With the re-election of President Trump in 2024, many hope past hidden political secrets will finally be revealed.

Post Q# 4359
Update the list.

Links

NY Post-Twitter Hires former FBI Chief Counsel as Deputy Lawyer

Just the News-HRC's Plan tying Trump and Russia

The Federalist-Senate Expands Probe into FBI's Ability to Hide Documents

Clinton Foundation Timeline-FBI Revelations Show the Mueller Special Counsel was a Cover-Up

American Report-The Ghost: Who is James Baker?

FOX News-James Baker Twitter Lawyer fired by Elon Musk played Key Role in Russia Collusion

The Federalist-Baker behind RussiaGate/Biden Laptop now Part of Election Network

John Seaman-FBI: Coverup of the Crime of the Century

Daily Mail-Elon Fires Twitter's General Counsel James Baker

The Federalist-SpyGate 101: A Primer on the Russia Collusion Hoax

National Review-Former FBI General Counsel: Page FISA Unacceptable

Business and Politics-Grenell: FBI wasn't Duped by Lying Attorney

Washington Examiner-John Durham grills Former FBI Lawyer James Baker

Markets Work-Baker's Testimony Reveals Concerns about FBI Probe

Clinton Foundation Timeline-diGenova: FBI's Baker is Cooperating with Durham

Red State-JoeD: Former FBI General Counsel has Flipped

Epoch Times-Baker testifies Perkins' Sussmann gave FBI Alfa Bank Allegations

Judicial Watch-Durham uncovers New Clinton/FBI Connections

Markets Work-Resignations and Complicity at the FBI

Crossfire Hurricane Docs-Christopher Steele Binder

Justice.gov-2023 SC John Durham Report

(Answer is:) Huma's CF Contact
(Question:) Who is Doug Band?

The public has been made aware of an official ongoing DOJ criminal investigation of the Clinton Foundation (CF). Headquartered at the DOJ's Little Rock office, this special task force has impaneled a real live grand jury and has been at this investigation for several years. President Trump filed in 2022 a federal RICO lawsuit against those involved with the promotion of the false Russian collusion narrative during the 2016 election cycle.

Post Q# 3674
DOJ plane(s).
CF.

The several criminal investigations ongoing into the CF is a MOAB type of a big BOOM that's just waiting to be detonated. A grand jury has been impaneled and a full fledge official DOJ investigation of the CF is finally underway. Special Counsel (SC) John Durham indicated Perkins Coie/Clinton campaign lawyer Michael Sussmann and his law firm connects to directly to HRC/CF/and the DNC.

Post Q# 3875
[Epstein]
The story goes much deeper [darker].

Douglas Band was both Deputy Assistant and Legal Counsel to then President Bill Clinton. Band founded Teneo, which was an advisory and investment firm with several top Fortune 500 clients within their client portfolio.

Post Q# 1220
Clinton Foundation conflicts of interest.

Band co-mingled his clients financially as well as personally into the spiderweb known as the Clinton Global Initiative (CGI)/CF/and Bill Clinton Inc. This was done in exchange for valued access to Slick Willy and big-league political favors in classic political quid pro quo.

Post Q# 4820
THE CLINTON FOUNDATION.
WHITE HOUSE FOR SALE.

Band's designated contact over at HRC's State Department was via longtime aide Huma Abedin. Band and Huma Abedin handled the dirty details concerning the 'pay to play' scheme with the CF and their financial contributors.

Post Q# 48
Who would have to goods on U1?

Band is credited with the creation and management of the CGI. A public squabble developed between Band and Chelsea Clinton primarily over his handling of operations/accounting of the CF/CGI.

Post Q# 1345
U1 [donations to CF].

Chelsea Clinton's CYA actions involved bringing in her friend Eric Braverman as the new CEO of the CF. Ultimately Band won out and Eric Braverman was let go, creating a negative public appearance for the CF/CGI.

Post Q# 10
> Why did FBI have an investigation into CF and was dropped?

Of interesting note was the relationship between the CF and lobbying firm APCO. APCO made large donations to the CF, while being paid by Tenex/Rostom to push the Uranium One deal through final CIFUS approval.

Post Q# 479
> How much did AUS donate to CF?
> How much did SA donate to CF?

Band worked primarily through Huma Abedin to coordinate so called client 'In-Kind Services.' Huma Abedin was the funnel at the U.S. State Department from which all access and thus special political favors flowed. Huma was a gatekeeper for HRC while Doug Band was a similar gatekeeper for Bill Clinton.

Post Q# 2872
> Hillary Clinton and Foundation.
> Crime Against Children.

Huma/Anthony Weiner may have included Band in their famed 'Insurance File.' The NYPD seized a shared laptop from Weiner's sexting case and hopefully soon these emails will reveal unbelievable secrets. It has been revealed Band flew several times with Bill Clinton on Jeff Epstein's special plane to St. John's Island and Europe. Epstein Island would be the focus of an international group of globalists sexually frolicking with underage children.

Post Q# 1431
> Those who are the loudest....
> Suicide weekend?
> Pain.

In return for given political favors, large cash donations to the CF were accepted and highly encouraged. Band's dual hat roles (business/government) made him the number one person in the world, for those wanting 'Clinton Access.' SC John Durham has dropped criminal indictments and submitted his final report in 2023. Durham's report will be the foundation future judicial accountability. With the historic re-election of President Trump in 2024, many past hidden political secrets will finally be revealed.

Post Q# 4241
> Think Chess.
> QUEEN protects KING?

Links

Forbes-Doug Band: Chief of Staff William J. Clinton Foundation

FOX News-House Panel Subpoenas Clintons/Others in Epstein Probe

CBS News-Clinton Foundation Pressed Donors to Steer Business to Bill Clinton

Clinton Foundation Timeline-2025 Crossfire Hurricane Docs

Daily Mail-Top Bill Clinton Aide Doug Band links to Epstein

Breitbart-Elites Rush to Embrace Clinton Global Initiative

Vanity Fair-Confessions of a ClintonWorld Exile

Ivan Pentchoukov-Huma Abedin to Doug Band

We Love Trump-Doug Band is Reportedly a Whistleblower

Daily Mail-Chelsea Pushed out of CF Bill's 'Surrogate Son'

The Last Refuge-Abedin/Weiner Laptop

New Republic-Scandal at Clinton Inc.

The Federalist-Emails show Huma did Favors

The Atlantic-Doug Band: Center of Bill Clinton Inc.

TPM-5 Ways Aides Funneled Money into Clinton Foundation

New Yorker-Trouble with Doug Band

Corey's Digs-Rudy, RICO, and Clinton Inc.: Racketeering

NY Post-Doug Band is Shocked to Discover Clintons are Slimy

Judicial Watch-Teneo and The Clinton Machine

Observer-6 Clinton Foundation Scandals You need to Know

Crossfire Hurricane Docs-State Department Steele Binder

Justice.gov-2023 SC John Durham Report

The 'Grateful' Bard of the Internet—meet John Perry Barlow

Post Q# 2262

MUSIC IS ABOUT TO STOP.

John Perry Barlow (1947-2018) died on 2/7/2018 of an apparent 'heart attack' at the age of 70. Nicknamed the 'Bard of the Internet' and incredibly was an original Grateful Dead band member, all would concur that Barlow was a unique individual. John Perry Barlow (JPB) would accurately be described as an early pioneer in the worldwide Internet, human rights activist, security from surveillance consultant, classic song writer and as a leader in the acid rock music movement.

Post Q# 952

The link.
(John Perry Barlow).

John Perry Barlow meet up at the age of 15 with Bobby Weir and along with Jerry Garcia, this trio would form the core of the historic Grateful Dead Band. Classic songs like Mexicali Blues, Looks Like Rain, and Estimated Prophet are JPB written classic originals. The 'Dead' would be in the forefront of a worldwide acid rock movement and performed live weekend long concerts for decades.

Post Q# 3025

John Perry Barlow POST January 27, 2018
John Perry Barlow DEAD February 8, 2018.
This is not a game.

JPB has been in addition to a founding member of the famous Grateful Dead, a rancher, cowboy, political activist, cyber libertarian, and Internet guru. Barlow is credited in giving many inspirational speeches that motivated early Internet pioneers like Julian Assange (WikiLeaks) and Aaron Swartz (Reddit). Assigned Special Counsel (SC) John Durham had revealed in 2022 court filings of an existing relationship involving Julian Assange's WikiLeaks company and criminal activity related to the unfolding RussiaGate/SpyGate scandal.

Post Q# 730

Coincidence "Truth to Power "?
Coincidence Barlow?

The Electronic Frontier Foundation (EFF) was started by JPB in 1990. This was the forerunner to his 2012 Freedom of the Press Foundation (FOTP) organization which helped to establish anti-censorship core foundations. This unique group acted as a center self-monitoring body of Internet professionals striving for internet freedoms. The EFF would file an Amicus brief (neutral basis) in 2023 with the U.S. 5th Circuit Court in the critical free speech case (Big Tech censorship) of Biden vs Missouri.

Post Q# 722

Think BDT NYC 'attempt' and Barlow.

JPB joined Assange, Edward Snowden, and Aaron Swartz as founding Board of Directors for FOTP. Barlow took over Swartz's website 'SecureDrop' after the sudden mysterious deaths of Aaron Swartz and his co-founder James Dolan. Suspicion would be an understatement surrounding this rash of bad luck among the original SecureDrop founders. JPB published in 1996 his fortitude thesis 'A Declaration of the Independence of Cyberspace,' which predicted mass censorship as well as the advent of BitCoin.

Post Q# 790
> JOHN PERRY BARLOW.
> DEFINE THE END?

FOTP core founders were John Perry Barlow/Edward Snowden/Aaron Swartz/Glenn Greenwald/ Laura Poitras/Daniel Ellsberg/and John Cusak. The 'star power' of this group instilled a trust factor with SecureDrop, that would be later exploited by the C_A/Clowns. Control of the narrative is the number one assigned to the cooperative Mockingbird news media and their corrupt governmental officials. Edward Snowden would reveal in 2013 that NSA's PRISM computer program is a data collection tool originally designed to target foreign intelligence but was deliberately turned inward domestically against all opposition groups.

Post Q# 628
> Freedom of the Press.
> John Perry Barlow.
> SecureDrop [Whistleblowers]?
> SecureDrop - Clowns In America.
> NOBODY IS SAFE.

'Q' has pointed out that SecureDrop had been taken over by the C_A/Clowns. Edward Snowden's stolen NSA source codes has enabled the 4am MSM 'talking points' to be transmitted via SecureDrop (aka ShadowNet) for the entire Mockingbird network of news reporters. Heroic reporter Julian Assange would lose his final legal appeal from extradition to the USA from England in 2023 but ultimately gain freedom in 2024. Of an interesting note was a personal relationship between JPB and JKF,Jr.

Post Q# 677
> Heart attacks can be deadly.

To say the John Perry Barlow was just a worldwide web/Internet pioneer would be a gross understatement. JPB hung out with Timothy O'Leary (LSD Experience), regularly attended the Burning Man Festival, leading outspoken advocate for the Marijuana Policy Project, and much more. To help restore equal justice and revenge for the murder of JPB. SC John Durham had been tasked to act on criminal referrals from IG Michael Horowitz. The future would see that Nerds/ Censorship/and the Internet will play keys roles in the salvation of freedom vs tyranny.

Post Q# 770
> John Perry Barlow-187 post name [DROP].

'Q' has directed our attention to JPB on several occasions and JPB figures into this puzzle in a major fashion. Barlow was a whistleblower himself and help to defend all whistleblowers via SecureDrop. It came as no shock to Anons that some of the whistleblowers as well as the SecureDrop developers ended up dead. The Great Awakening will usher a new Republic and SC Durham has dropped criminal indictments related to SpyGate and submitted his final report in 2023. With the re-election of President Trump in 2024, hopefully some of these mysteries will finally be publicly revealed.

Post Q# 760

Thank you for showing the world how Clowns pass the narrative to journalists 4AM
Reread crumbs re: SecureDrop.
John Perry Barlow.

Links

EFF-John Perry Barlow: Internet Pioneer (1947-2018)

Wired-Mourning the 'Bard' of the Internet

PBS-Julian Assange is Now Free

NY Times-John Perry Barlow: Internet Champion of Unfettered Internet

Dead.net-John Perry Barlow

Reason-The Insanely Eventful Life of John Perry Barlow

EFF-John Perry Barlow Library

BitCoin News-Pioneer John Perry Barlow who Influenced Assange is Dead

Variety-Internet Pioneer dead at 70

NBC News-Internet Champion and Grateful Dead Member Dies at 70

Rolling Stone-Grateful Dead Lyricist Dies at 70

WROR-10 Grateful Dead Songs w/Lyrics by JPB

Grateful Dead video-"Looks Like Rain" lyrics by JPB/Weir

BitCoin News-John Perry Barlow's Declaration of the Independence of Cyberspace

CNET-What is the NSA's PRISM Program?

EFF-2023 Amicus Brief: Missouri vs Biden

Eko-Override

Clinton Foundation Timeline-2025 Crossfire Hurricane Docs

Justice.gov-2023 SC John Durham Report

AG Barr's Departing Gesture: Special Counsel Durham

Public optics do not matter when employing the cleaver 'Scaramucci Model.' As professionally demonstrated by Anthony Scaramucci in removing some longtime RINO's and anti-Trump staffers. Former Attorney General (AG) Bill Barr had been known for employing various forms of professional deception in performing his duties. It does not shock any Anon to see the seemingly negative interactions play out in the media between President Trump and Bill Barr (actors will act).

Post Q# 2681
-Barr install.
-Barr (w/Whitaker) pull DECLAS review assignment from OIG.
-Barr executes order to DECLAS.

Former White House staffers Priebus and Spicer found out the hard way about temporary President Trump hires being very dangerous. Acting AG Whitaker had the broom in-hand after Jeff Sessions and swept out the leftover garbage from the DOJ/FBI headquarters before returning AG Bill Barr took over. President Trump relied upon his different top law enforcement officers to help complete his plan to save America.

Post Q# 2654
Scaramucci model?
Public opinion (optics) do not matter.
Temps can be very dangerous to those who are targeted.

The U.S. Senate confirmed William Barr as the new U.S. Attorney General for the second time in his public service career. Bill Barr served without major blemish as AG for President Bush 41 from 1991-93 (Boomerang). Due to Barr's past experience with Bush, the Republican RINOS as well as the Leftists accepted this nomination to become President Trump's new AG. Historians will either view AG Barr as the most disloyal backstabbing appointee or one of the best villain actors playing a role and really was a Trump White Hat all along.

Post Q# 3932
The House will push for Barr removal.
The Silent War Continues....

AG William Barr brings to the table both prior outstanding work experience as well as big league credibility. Barr headed the DOJ's Office of Legal Counsel (the lawyers' lawyer) for many years. Both sides of the political isle respect Bill Barr and President Trump has shown full confidence with this key judicial appointment. As the final acts in the Storm play out under the illegal Biden administration, true behind the scenes heroes will be revealed.

Post Q# 3806
Boomerang.
"And the rockets red glare, the bombs bursting in air, gave proof through the night that our flag was still there."

The U.S. Senate began hearings on Barr's nomination on 1/15/19 and he sailed through without a major hitch. AG Barr has been 'read-in' quickly on all pending ObamaGate/SpyGate investigations and is coordinating with SP Durham and SP Huber for the many ongoing criminal investigations.

Post Q# 2776
> Mueller to Barr: "With regards to the President we have found no links or ties to any foreign entity etc."

Two little blips on the radar map had appeared in William Barr's history. One question mark surrounds the Iran Contra fiasco and the other incredibly involves his past working relationships within the CIA. Having a history with the CIA Clowns is a resume point that needs to be examined in depth.

Post Q# 3036
> Did POTUS just install a rouge AG who allows for the indictment of his children based on false pretenses?
> Do UNICORNS exist?

"Compromised: Clinton, Bush, and the CIA" by former CIA officer Terry Reed, highlights Barr's possible CIA connections. Due to extensive scrubbing of Barr's CIA background, exact facts are still largely unconfirmed other than Barr was employed from 1973-77. Having public records scrubbed is always a red-light warning that shenanigans are afoot.

Post Q# 3595
> AUS, IT, UK co-opt DOJ (Barr, Durham, CLAS 1-4).

Connections have definitely placed AG Barr way back with Bush 41 when he was the CIA Director. Barr's claimed undercover name was Robert Johnson. Barr/Johnson worked with Col. Oliver North and Barry Seal with the infamous Iran Contra guns-drugs operations.

Post Q# 3668
> Planned/coordinated attacks on BARR coming [smear campaign].
> Information warfare.

The high-powered law firm of Kirkland and Ellis has employed Barr between his government gigs. Other notable Kirkland alumni include John Bolton and Ken Starr. AG Barr had added another Special Prosecutor US Attorney John Bash from Texas to looking the massive 2016 unmasking requests. Special Prosecutor (SP) John Huber and Special Counsel (SC) John Durham have been handing the criminal referrals from DOJ's OIG Michael Horowitz. A retired AG Bill Barr would explain in 2022 that HRC's actions surrounding the scandal known as RussiaGate would be considered 'seditious.'

Post Q# 4486
> Was Barr a member of the board?
> What advantages might exist to incoming AG Barr re: member of external advisory board (CIA)?

President Trump said in a 2019 news conference that "By appointing acting Cabinet heads, it gives me much more flexibility." Anons already knew that thanks to the Scaramucci Model and the looming stealth bombers devastating releases. Former AG Bill Barr has emphasized that the DOJ needs to look into the Hunter Biden laptop and the implications of the data contained. It was demonstrated to the public in late 2020 (just prior to the Presidential election) of an effort to hide the validity Hunter's 'Laptop from Hell' in a coordinated fashion by the CIA/Media/and Big Tech.

Post Q# 3410
> Stealth Bomber.
> B(2).

Bill Barr would publicly state in 2022 the need for the SCOTUS to have a special counsel selected to investigate the leak of the internal secret draft on the upcoming Roe vs Wade debate. Additionally, Barr would state publicly that he will vote the Republican ticket in 2024. One of AG Barr's final tasks was to upgrade US Attorney John Durham to full Special Counsel (SC) status to head criminal investigations steaming from past IG Horowitz's reports related to SpyGate. Judgement Day is coming as SC John Durham has outlined a vast 'Joint Venture Conspiracy' and has dropped criminal indictments. SC Durham submitted his final report in 2023. With the re-election of President Trump in 2024, exact roles of all players will finally be revealed.

Post Q# 3671
> When does the B2 drop the FIRST BOMB?
> Bill Barr fit into [8] spaces?

Links

USA Today-SpyGate: William Barr

The Federalist-DOJ Officials didn't know Database Allowed FBI to Bury RussiaGate Docs

Just the News-HRC's Plan tying Trump and Russia

The Federalist-Unsealed Crossfire Hurricane Docs prove RussiaGate a Hoax

FOX News-Jesse Watters: Durham Report tells Us what We Knew

The Hill-Bill Barr will Vote Republican Ticket in 2024

Just the News-Barr: DOJ went too Far in Prosecuting J6 Capitol Riot

Blaze Media-Bill Barr Rips RussiaGate as 'Seditious': Origins of Durham Probe

FOX News-Barr: Durham Appears to have 'Dug Deep' on Russia Probe

The Federalist-6 New Revelations in the John Durham SpyGate Probe

Aaron Mate-RussiaGate has No Bottom

Real Clear Politics-No Durham Report likely before Elections

Just the News-Government hints at Undisclosed Flynn Case Information

FOX News-Durham Assumed parts of John Huber's Clinton Foundation Review

Vanity Fair-Tale of a Young Bill Barr

Red State-AG Barr Continues to Question Media's Role in Russia Collusion Caper

Markets Work-Where Bill Barr Failed the President

New Yorker-Trump's Sword and Shield

OIG.DOJ.gov-Report on 2020 Election Fraud

Crossfire Hurricane Docs-Christopher Steele Binder

Justice.gov-2023 SC John Durham Report

Benghazi Debacle Revisited: Pre Heroic "13 Hours"

R.I.P. -Chris Stevens / Sean Smith / Tyrone Woods / Glen Doherty

Judicial Watch (thanks to Tom Fitton) had obtained videos a FOIA requests informative documents from the Defense and State Departments about the 9/11 2012 attack in Benghazi. Records reflect the BHO Administration knew that al Qaeda would attack the U.S. Consulate facility a full 10-days in advance. Many today feel that BHO/HRC permitted this assault on our diplomatic Libyan compound and U.S. Embassy to coverup several ongoing illegal Benghazi based operations. The public would still witness in both the Afghanistan and Ukraine deliberate Biden endorsed military decisions that are not in the best interest of the USA.

Post Q# 2180
Define 'Traitor.'
2. a person who commits treason by betraying his or her country.
Synonym = Renegade.

The U.S. Consulate complex located in Benghazi/Libya was assaulted on 9/11/12 by ongoing waves of crazed Islamic militants. The historical site significance of September 11th goes without question, and this date was targeted for the attacks in Benghazi. Tragically this unprovoked attack resulted in the deaths of 4 brave Americans based in the compound complex. History has recorded the heroism displayed by everyone caught in this attack. Then Chief of Staff Denis McDonough gave a White House Oval Office briefing on 9/11/12 to BHO about the status of the attacks in Benghazi.

Post Q# 1884
LIBYA [ACCESS] PENDING [MAIN PORT CLOSED] [LIMITED].

Conditions were in flux in terms of authority and civil rebellion ruled the entire Benghazi region. It is unconscionable that our brave personnel were left exposed with no backup rescue forces. President Trump had shown in Iraq how we will defend U.S. interests worldwide as well as payback to Iranian terrorist Soleimani for his past murders of Americans. Unfortunately, the illegal Biden administration has displayed total weakness to our enemies with the debacle in Afghanistan and the military has testified their strategic combat advice was totally ignored. The global war against the democratic West is ongoing and witnessing new strategic alliances taking place.

Post Q# 2149
We Will Never FORGET!
We Will Never FORGIVE!

Visiting U.S. Ambassador Chris Stevens (to Libya) had a small Foreign Service protection detail at his residence on 9/11/12 and the nearby CIA Annex had a somewhat larger security force that would combine in the Alamo-like last defensive stand. Ambassador Chris Stevens knew of the BHO/HRC/C_A Clown mission of shipping illegal arms from Libya over to Syria. Ambassador Stevens and his laptops were a liability to BHO/HRC that had to be cleaned up. BHO, then VP Joe Biden and HRC were running out of the nearby CIA Annex in Benghazi a secret weapons program codenamed "Zero Footprint'.

Post Q# 3683
" Put on the full armor of God, so that you can take your stand against the devil's schemes."

These two sets of assigned protection contractors fought for hours with an Alamo-like defense of both compounds in this historic epic stand. This last stand has been immortalized in the Hollywood movie "13 Hours: The Secret Soldiers of Benghazi." As fate would have it, this movie was a huge box office hit and helped in part to spread some of the truth behind Benghazi. Blackwater founder Erik Prince would lay some blame on private citizen Sid Blumenthal for advising HRC on foreign policy (Libya/Benghazi) affairs. It would later be revealed that HRC and BHO knew in advance that the Benghazi attacks would definitely occur, and their fateful conduct will be forever remembered.

Post Q# 4845
(Hussein dir, Benghazi, MB, CIA assets, crimes against humanity....)

Special Counsel (SC) John Durham has dropped criminal indictments related to illegal surveillance operations and has submitted his final report in 2023. HRC's Benghazi helper Jake Sullivan, now Biden's NSA, has been connected to the indicted Michael Sussmann indictment as 'Foreign Policy Advisor.' Many pray that with the re-election of President Trump in 2024, the many still unanswered questions surrounding the Benghazi incident will finally be made public.

Post Q# 2147
ATTENTION ON DECK.
BATTLE STATIONS.

Several key reasons laid the foundation for the general chaos in Benghazi. The ultimate responsibly of this tragedy falls right into the laps of both BHO and HRC:

- Toppling of Qaddafi/Arab Spring/and Muslim Brotherhood to destabilize area.
- Secret CIA compound/Annex and NSA listening post which ran operation 'Zero Footprint" an international gun running program.
- Gun-Running scheme: Libya to Turkey to Syria that Stevens ran covert operation with Marc Turi.
- 7 Red Crescent workers kidnapped prior to raid and released just after deadly attack due to Iran's demands.
- Theory that Iran was behind raid to kill U.S. Ambassador over arming ISIS (Soleimani hit).
- 7 Davey Crockett nuclear mortars.
- 400 Surface-to-Air Stinger missiles lost/stolen.
- HRC's extra server with Special Access Programs for the bin Laden Family and others.
- Cover-up of real motive (video caused attack) due to BHO's re-election campaign.

Post Q# 56
Libyan militia leader Abdelhakim Belhadj, a known al Qaeda associate, and saluted him as "my hero" during a visit to Benghazi.
decode: Talking about No Name's visit to the region one year before the deadly attack on the US Consulate and Annex in Benghazi.

Post Q# 4255
Where. We. Go. One. We. Go. All.

Arming both al Qaeda and ISIS was the fuel that ignited and then destabilized the entire Middle East. President Trump previously firing missiles into Syria and had properly defended the Iraq Green Zone. President Trump had temporarily enhanced our international public image due to the past damage caused by Secretary of State HRC and BHO. With the disasters of both Afghanistan and Ukraine, the illegal Biden/Harris administration has reversed all previous international goodwill gains the United States had made. With the historic re-election of President Trump in 2024, many pray to the return of political sanity in the White House.

Post Q# 2640

What was the 16-year plan to destroy America?

Links

Breitbart-New Documents Blow Lid off Benghazi

Just the News-Book Manuscript supports Kash Patel's Benghazi Narrative

Real Clear Politics-Hillary Clinton's Greatest Masterpiece

Judicial Watch-Susan Rice/HRC/and Benghazi

AMG News-Phone Transcript of HRC Admitting She knew in Advance of Benghazi Attack

The American Report-Former US Military Personnel Exposes Truth of Benghazi

Thread Reader-Benghazi Notes

Judicial Watch-BHO Administration knew 10-Days in Advance of Benghazi

Daily Caller-Benghazi led Directly to Crossfire Hurricane

True Pundit-Classified Memo proves HRC Supplied Weapons from Benghazi to ISIS

Business Insider-Intrigue Surrounds Secret CIA Operation in Benghazi

Breitbart-Benghazi Gun Running Scheme armed Islamic State

Free Beacon-FEDs knew Benghazi Attack Planned in Advance

Red State-Tom Fitton vs HRC: Chapter 19

Breitbart-Rep. Jordan same Song different Dance: Kabul/Benghazi

Michelle-Benghazi Won't Go Away

The Last Refuge-Denis McDonough 9/11/12

Rated Red-The Real Story of Benghazi

Breitbart-Erik Prince: HRC should be Unemployable

CCNS-Benghazi Timeline

US Congressional Hearing-HRC Benghazi Testimony

13 Hours: Official 2016 Movie Trailer

Crossfire Hurricane Docs-Christopher Steele Binder

Justice.gov-2023 SC John Durham Report

Mueller/Comey cleared Sandy 'What's in Your Pants' Berger

Imagine this scene in your mind, a middle-aged man stumbling in a disheveled appearance from the National Archive Building in 2004. Incredibly obvious to all observers of this scene, are various official government documents stuffed down this odd person's pants/pockets/and even his socks. The National Archives and Records Administration (NARA) would stay in the news under BHO's Presidential Library as well as with President Trump's records requested by various witch-hunting Congressional committees.

Post Q# 4310
HOW DO YOU ADD LAYERS OF PROTECTION?
INSTALL A SPECIAL COUNSEL TO LOCK [FREEZE] EVERYTHING RE: RUSSIA?

Meet Bill Clinton's infamous NSA Director Samuel Richard 'Sandy' Berger (1945-2015) aka Sandy "The Burglar." This stalwart of modern society was at one point in time the National Security Adviser to President Slick Willy and held unlimited high security clearances. Biden's current NSA is Jake Sullivan and is a similar buffoonish political hack like Sandy Berger. History will show the total rot and political corruption from within the FBI/DOJ began during this period.

Post Q# 18
Why did Mueller meet POTUS 1-day prior to FBI announcement of Muller COULD NOT be offered director due to prev term limits rule?

Sandy Berger still had the security clearance to look but certainly not to steal (then later destroy) reams of highly classified material. This was the lawless attitude that many surrounding the Clinton criminal cabal freely demonstrated time and time again. The nickname of the Clinton Crime Cabal was truly earned during this turbulent period.

Post Q# 4620
Mueller installed [Comey termination loss of power] [POTUS inside a box] [prevent counterattack].

This national treasure theft of historical Osama bin Laden (UBL) intel documents occurred back in 2003. Berger claimed he solely was on and informational scouting mission for Bill Clinton prior to the upcoming 9/11 Commission review proceedings. The nation would witness in 2024 scary parallels with the witch-hunt by Special Counsel (SC) Jack Smith in the NARA documents case against President Trump compared to the double standard treatment of Sandy Berger.

Post Q# 3473
[MUELLER] [Epstein bury and cover-up].
2019 - YEAR OF THE BOOMERANG.

Congress was looking for information on any signal's intelligence received by the White House before the terrorists' attacks on 9/11 in NYC and Pentagon on that fateful September day. Talk at that time was UBL was previously well known and on the radar of American intelligence agencies. Many feel the unfolding events of today are directly related to 9/11 and the Great Reset plan.

Post Q# 3790
If FISA warrants deemed to be illegal [ALL SURV LEAPFROG HOPS] what happens to MUELLER's case(s)?

Berger promptly scrubbed all damaging information from the National Archives regarding UBL known intelligence data during the President Bill Clinton-era. To this day no one knows exactly what was removed and ultimately destroyed by Sandy "The Burglar" Berger. This would be similar to the wanton destruction of our Nation's founding documents and the National Archives official duty to jealousy guards our historical records.

Post Q# 1008

Why is Mueller going after inside plants?

In 2005 the ever-generous Deputy AG James Comey and FBI Director Bob Mueller gave Berger a sweetheart plea deal. For admitting to removing and destroying classified records, Sandy was ultimately allowed to skate free. Sandy Berger was the 'Scientology' liaison and additionally regularly gave John Travolta personal briefings.

Post Q# 2512

Mueller will face charges re: U1.
He's working to save himself.

Sandy Berger got a minor slap on the wrist with some easy community service and paying a small $50k fine. The National Archive entire staff is to this day are still very ashamed of losing this historic classified material on Osama bin Laden. Unpublished safeguards have been put into place in a direct response to this theft. President Trump would go on the offensive in 2022 by filing a federal RICO lawsuit against Comey/HRC/DNC/and others involved with promoting the false Russian collusion narrative around the 2016 election.

Post Q# 1289

Do you believe in coincidences?
Think recent Mueller drops.
Think private comes.

Mueller and Comey have been safeguarding and protecting the criminal Clinton Cabal for decades. This 'Pretorian Guard' is why no Clinton or known associates ever has gotten indicted or criminally prosecuted to date. 'Q' has advised us that this prior protection is no longer in place. Judgement Day will soon be here in the form of future judicial accountability stemming from the final report by SC John Durham submitted in 2023. 'Q' also poised the obvious question about why Mueller meet with President Trump at the White House under the guise of applying to be the FBI Director again.

Post Q# 3

Open your eyes.
It finally came out that Rod/Bob were key players in the Uranium scandal.
Why did POTUS meet Bob under the cover of FBI DIR interview?

Several of the SpyGate coup plotters, like did Bill/Hillary Clinton, traveled over to Epstein/Pedo Island and engaged in the well-known sexual debauchery. An evil alliance between BHO and HRC occurred when they teamed up jointly to remove President Trump. Everyone would witness the hypocrisy of Sandy Burger and the treatment of President Trump's Mar-A-Laga documents raid and subsequent prosecution. With the re-election of President Trump in 2024, he would instantly fire the head National Archivist Colleen Shogan. The return to the rule of law is a foundational pillar of MAGA/Great Awakening is forthcoming.

Post Q# 2118
    If Mueller is dirty, [RR] must also be dirty.

Links

Politico-Former NSA Sandy Berger Dies

Western Journal-Subpoenaed Robert Muller said to be in Memory Care Facility

Clinton Foundation Timeline-2025 Crossfire Hurricane Docs

Epoch Times-Trump Promises to Replace Head of US Archives

The Federalist-FBI Revelations Show the Mueller Special Counsel was a Cover-Up

American Thinker-Mueller, Comey, and Rescue of Sandy Berger

Huff Post-No Robert Mueller/James Comey aren't Heroes

Buster Hyde-Clinton Cabal/Comey/Berger

Real Clear Politics-Sandy Berger: What did He Take and Why?

Lew Rockwell-BHO's Role in Scandals: SpyGate and EmailGate

The Atlantic-Sandy Berger's Washington

The War Economy-SpyFall

American Thinker-Mueller/Comey have Massive Clinton Foundation Problems

US News-Berger's Theft still Weight on Archive Agents

Washington Times-Sandy Berger's Crime

FOX News-Former Clinton Aide Pleads Guilty

WAPO-HRC's Sandy Berger Problem

Matt Taibbi-RussiaGate is this Generation's WMD

The Hill-Trump Fires National Archivist

Just the News-Biden White House Collaborated on Trump Documents Probe

Archive.gov-Notable Thefts from the National Archives

Crossfire Hurricane Docs-State Department Steele Binder

Justice.gov-2023 SC John Durham Report

NSA Whistleblower Bill Binney:
"Leak NOT Hack"

William Binney is "A Good American," who served this country for over 35 years as a Senior U.S. Military Intelligence Officer. Bill became an early NSA Whistleblower (pre-Edward Snowden) and revealed ongoing illegal mass surveillance programs by the NSA. The role of false whistleblowers became apparent in one of the failed impeachment attempts against President Trump as well as good whistleblowers within the IRS concerning Hunter Biden.

Post Q# 394
We have the USSS, NSA, and DHS, also protecting this message.

Bill Binney was involved with not only helping to build these surveillance computer programs but in ultimately exposing their purposes. NSA would later name Bill Binney's creations Stellar Wind/Thin Thread/and Trailblazer.

Post Q# 2332
How the [SPY OP] re: Russia hacking + POTUS-Russia False Narrative + Installation of Mueller was CONSTRUCTED.

These new computer filters were able to selectively capture all historical data by using key identifying words. Ultra-google-like search/capture software programs were incorporated within the fastest known super computers.

Post Q# 386
PATRIOT of the highest caliber.

These special types of innovative secret computer programs ended up being misused by the NSA. Bill Binney felt compelled to make these secret surveillance collection projects known to the American public.

Post Q# 151
Who do you trust to keep secrets?

These NSA programs were involved with the total capturing of all USA phone/data collection (the whole enchilada Snow White) against US law. Producer Oliver Stone asked Bill to assist and technically advise with his Hollywood hit movie called "Snowden". Snowden would be revealed by Team-Q as a traitor who stole from the NSA on instructions by the C_A.

Post Q# 384
Bill Binney.

Bill Binney claimed that the NSA had been using spying mechanisms and computer programs successfully by past Presidential administrations. Mass surveillance programs have operated ever since the travesty that was 9/11 (Patriot Act). Cyber security firm CrowdStrike would be brought in by the law firm Perkins Coie and would become central in the false Russian hacking forensic results.

Post Q# 1661
What role can MI INTEL play?
What role can NSA play?
BANG!

Bill Binney worked alongside several other NSA Whistleblowers like Thomas Drake and Kirk Wiebe to form a forensic team called Veteran Intelligence Professionals for Sanity (VIPS). This group of VIPS whistleblowers examined and ultimately scientifically disprove the "hack theory" due to high download speed rate (22.7 megabytes) of the so-called DNC breached computer server.

Post Q# 3841
RUSSIA DID NOT 'HACK' [penetrate] THE DNC SERVER.
internal DL / release.
crowdstrike manipulation of source.

Binney has made several comments directly related to the ongoing political ObamaGate/SpyGate scandals. Binney has backed up claims by President Trump that in fact POTUS was wiretapped by the U.S. Intelligence Community/Department of Justice.

Post Q# 166
Expand your thinking.
Jason Bourne (Deep Dream).

At the request of President Trump, the then CIA Director Captain Mike Pompeo (KANSAS) and Binney had a sit-down over the DNC data intrusion. Bill Binney's scientific studies of the port/download transmission rates of the infamous DNC computer breach proved beyond question that it was a leak.

Post Q# 4016
Was the DNC (was) hacked by Russia?
Seth Rich internal DL hand-to-hand pass USA?

Binney's forensic team has shown that the DNC intrusion was a leak/physical download (Thumb Drive) as opposed to a hack/Internet outside download. A physical download proves it was a LEAK not HACK by all standard observations. Perkins Coie/DNC retained cyber security firm CrowdStrike muddied the waters with the false Russian hack via Cozy/Fancy Bear and Guccifer.

Post Q# 1002
The BITE that has no CURE-NSA.

The difference in 'speed' is the pivotal factor in what started this entire ObamaGate/SpyGate ordeal. This throws out the false Russian narrative and brings right into play both the murder of Patriot Seth Rich and the release by WikiLeaks. Special Counsel John Durham has dropped criminal indictments regarding the many tentacles of the SpyGate treasonous coup plot and submitted his final report in 2023. With the historic re-election of President Trump in 2024, many feel past hidden political secrets will finally be revealed.

Post Q# 4153
comp-to-comp [transfer] speed [hack]?
internal DL [terminal 1] speed?
hand-to-hand transfer?

Links

NBC News-NSA Bill Binney says Trump pushed for CIA Meeting

The Federalist-HRC and the FBI Set Up Trump

Real Clear Investigations-Hidden over Two Years DEM Sworn Testimony of No Hack

Consortium News-Secrecy and HRC

Real Clear Politics-RussiaGate: HRC/Perkins Coie/Fusion GPS/CrowdStrike

The Guardian-NSA Utah Data Facility

Peter Collins-Interview: Former NSA Technical Director Bill Binney

The American Spectator-Durham and Amazing Disappearing DNC Hack

Breitbart-NSA Whistleblower Binney: Page FISA Gateway into Trump Spy Campaign

The Intercept-CIA Director meets with NSA Whistleblower Binney

Documentary-William Binney: A Good American

Breitbart-Binney: "Absolutely Tapping Trump's Calls"

Bill Binney-How the NSA Tracks You

Daily Mail-Cybersecurity Experts Abandon some Russia Hack Claims

Markets Work-The Uncovering: Mike Rogers//FISA/and FBI

Bill Binney: The Future of Freedom

The American Report-Woolsey/Brennan/Clapper/and Comey Framed Trump

PBS-William Binney: NSA before 9/11

The Last Refuge-SpyGate: The Big Picture

The American Report-Biden used Hammer/Scorecard just like BHO

Gadgets-NSA's Tailored Access Operations intercepts Computer Data

Whistleblower.org-BIO: Bill Binney and Kirk Wiebe

Clinton Foundation Timeline-2025 Crossfire Hurricane Docs

Justice.gov-2023 SC John Durham Report

Who is Sid Blumenthal?
How is He Connected to ObamaGate?

Sid "Vicious" Blumenthal has been a close confidant of both Clintons going back for several decades. Blumenthal served Slick Willy as White House Senior Advisor and was the primary funnel to the Mockingbird media from both Bill Clinton and HRC. President Trump would file in 2022 a federal RICO lawsuit against HRC/DNC/and others who promoted the false Russian collusion narrative during the 2016 Presidential election.

Post Q# 2872
> Hillary Clinton and Foundation.
> Crime Against Children.

Known as the 'Fixer' of all Clinton related scandals, Blumenthal dutifully earned this cleaver nickname of "Sid Vicious." Sid Vicious has been a Clinton enforcer and has been as a known trickster in the DC political arena forever. Each side sadly has its own dirty tricks department and shady characters like Blumenthal are always in demand by the DC Swamp.

Post Q# 3858
> THIS REPRESENTS A CLEAR AND PRESENT DANGER TO THE
> CONSTITUTIONAL REPUBLIC OF THE UNITED STATES OF AMERICA.

Blumenthal's devious fingerprints are all over several major historic Clinton related scandals. Ultimately the Christopher Steele Russia Dossier will bring Blumenthal to the attention of assigned Special Prosecutor John Huber and now Special Counsel (SC) John Durham. SC Durham's indicated of Perkins Coie/Clinton campaign lawyer Michael Sussmann will bring the entire Clinton crime family once again into the legal spotlight.

Post Q# 571
> NOBODY PLAYING THE GAME GETS A FREE PASS.
> NOBODY.

Sid Vicious and loyal sidekick Cody Shearer worked through Victoria Nuland/Jonathan Winer of the BHO's U.S. State Department. This criminal team helped funnel additional opposition research into Christopher Steele's final Trump-Russia Dossier. SC Durham's indictment of Sussmann connects HRC, DNC, Fusion GPS, CrowdStrike, Google, and Blumenthal. Blackwater founder Erik Prince would give testimony in the Benghazi Congressional hearings that Sid Blumenthal as a private citizen had no right to advise HRC in foreign policy affairs.

Post Q# 2876
> CLINTON PANIC.
> CLINTON FEAR.
> JUDGEMENT DAY COMING.

- 2008: Sid Blumenthal is credited with starting the "Birtherism" topic while a Senior Advisor to HRC 2008 Presidential Campaign.
- 2011: Sid teams up with Jake Sullivan/State Department and Marc Turi in Operation Zero Footprint. BHO/HRC's goal to help arm ISIS with gun running scheme in Libya (Benghazi) onto rebels in Syria.
- 2013: A Romanian hacker known as Guccifer breaks into Blumenthal's email account to gain HRC messages. The discovery and revelations lead to the uncovering of the HRC private email server during the Benghazi Hearings.

- 2016: Blumenthal teams up with long-time sidekick Cody Shearer to author the 2nd Steele Trump-Russia Dossier. The pair work with Winer and Nuland at the U.S. State Department to funnel made-up opposition researcher to Chris Steele and the FBI.
- 2019: Blumenthal tried unsuccessfully with Center Street/Hatchet Book Group to block the publication of Lee Smith's' new book about RussiaGate.
- 2020: Senators Johnson and Grassley subpoena Blumenthal to testify at Congressional hearing over RussiaGate.
- 2021: SC John Durham indictments of Perkins Coie/Clinton campaign lawyer Michael Sussmann.

Post Q# 357
>Trip code on 4 working.
>FLYSIDFLY

Blumenthal is an author by trade but has been employed for many years at the Clinton Foundation. BHO had forbidden Sid Blumenthal from any work within the government due to that pesky 'Birth Certificate' issue Sid Vicious first started in 2008. As could be expected from Team Clinton, the BHO birth certificate hunt would be blamed upon private citizen Donald Trump.

Post Q# 4227
>[Russia] narrative ALL FAKE?

Blumenthal is partially credited with starting the entire Trump-Russia 'Collusion Delusion.' Judgement day is coming soon for Sid Vicious and all the failed coup plotters. SC Durham submitted his final report in 2023. With the historic re-election of President Trump in 2024, beware of all the SpyGate/RussiaGate coup plotters.

Post Q# 3125
>The PUBLIC must be prepared for what is about to come.
>"THE CLINTON FOUNDATION"

Links

Washington Times-Sidney Blumenthal Emerges in Russia Dossier Case

Just the News-HRC Plan tying Trump and Russia

Clinton Foundation Timeline-2025 Crossfire Hurricane Docs

Washington Examiner-Meet the Men behind HRC's Private Spy Network

Real Clear Politics-HRC's Greatest Masterpiece

National Review-Sidney Blumenthal: HRC's Enabled in Chief

Vanity Fair-HRC's oldest Confidant

Political Willie-Steele/Winer/Blumenthal/and Shearer

Red State-Pay-to-Play at HRC's State Department

Daily Caller-Johnson Subpoenas Blumenthal/Shearer: HRC's Second Dossier

The Guardian-HRC's Second Russia Dossier Authored by Cody Shearer

Real Clear Investigations-Unpacking the Other HRC Russia Dossier

Washington Examiner-Trey Gowdy: Blumenthal used to Collaborate Steele Dossier

Breitbart-Winer: I Feed Oppo Research from Sid Blumenthal to Chris Steele

Washington Examiner-Russian Collision Hoax meets Unbelievable End

The Federalist-4 Times Sid was More than HRC's Friend

Judicial Watch-Russian Dossier: Enter Sid

Epoch Times-SpyGate: The Inside Story

Michelle-Benghazi Won't Go Away

The Federalist-35 Key People Involved in Russia Hoax need Investigated

Breitbart-Erik Prince: HRC should be Unemployable

Crossfire Hurricane Docs-State Department Steele Binder

Justice.gov-2023 SC John Durham Report

Migrant Caravan Hordes Invading—POTUS to the Rescue

POTUS: "WITHOUT A WALL, YOU DON'T HAVE A COUNTRY."

President Trump had ordered our Southern border closed back in 2019 and sent in Military/National Guard to secure the nation. Armed troops were to protect against incoming hordes of South/Central American migrants coming in various waves and potentially carrying harmful viruses. These waves of illegal aliens are not organic in nature but part of a larger scheme to destabilize the USA via a broken border inherited from BHO. History will show that under the illegal regime of Biden/Harris , over 20 million invaders from 117 different countries would easily cross over our open Southern border.

Post Q# 2502

Border Security = National Security.

Back in 2017 President Trump had acquired the wall funds and completed over 500 miles upon the end of his first term and fixed the open border crisis. History will show the wall was near completion when the illegal Biden administration stopped all construction as one of his first acts. Caravan waves originally from Mexico and Central American countries have been followed by now millions of illegal immigrants worldwide. Biden/Harris implemented a replacement voter/worker policy of unlimited immigration that now poises a real national security threat. Miraculously after President Trump's 2024 reelection, marching migrant caravans turned around from our current porous border.

Post Q# 2049

WHO ARE THE WHITE RABBITS?

President Trump had cut-off all U.S. foreign aid to 3 Central American countries as well their NAFTA involvement to pressure cooperation. A total shutdown of the entire Southern border was then threatened by our great President Trump and they all instantly capitulated. Under the illegal Biden/Harris regime, the now open Southern border has become an item of national security concern with flights of thousands of unvetted Afghanistan refugees bringing terrorism onto our shores.

Post Q# 2454

Border under attack.
Do you understand why?

President Trump had successfully negotiated with the leaders of Central/South America a policy to accept the return of caught illegals. Additional new waves of migrant caravans have been forming and steadily marching northward in attempting to overrun our border. The influx of COVID-19 contagious aliens is overwhelming our already taxed hospitals and worn thin Border Patrol officers. Odd that American citizens were forced to take experimental vaccines while the millions of entering illegal immigrants had no such medical requirements.

Post Q# 2395

See the 'gun' tucked in the pants of the 'money man'?

This article was first posted mid-2018 with the original first major funded/coordinated caravan assault on our southern border. Now well into 2024, a much larger wave of thousands ate forming in Central America for the long-organized migrant trek northward. Estimates show over 20 million illegals have crossed into the USA since Biden/Harris reversed President Trump's successful border policies. Stephen Miller has pointed out both the pending border crisis as well as the folly of the 'Catch and Release' policy.

Post Q# 988
> Immigration Bill.
> Border.
> Wall.

The Deep State had an on-going political coup against President Trump and has thus allied with many Anti-Trump factions. To help achieve their goal of total domination. a wide variety of internal and external resistance groups have now merged. The reach of the globalist power can be measured in their release of the COVID-19 and vaccine operations. Biden inherited the best Southern border ever and within months our nation is being overrun by hordes of illegal immigrants. Estimated at over 20+ million illegal immigrates crossings since 2021 and the waves of organized caravans continue to roll northward. President Trump has vowed in his second term, that on day one he will use our U.S. military to forcibly deport them all.

Post Q# 3407
> Re: Border Fight.
> Worth remembering.

You would normally think that your average Progressive Leftists would be sickened by extreme Muslim practices. No problem joining hands and overlooking the vial treatment of minority's rights if you are against Trump/MAGA and the USA. Decades of internal infiltration has been going on by the sworn enemies of America primarily the Muslim Brotherhood. The NWO globalist goal is a replacement population for the USA of illegal immigrants as a new voter base going forward.

Post Q# 4481
> Difficult truths.
> THREE ALLIANCE GROUPS:
> RED-Progressive Communist/CCP
> GREEN-Radical Muslim Brotherhood
> BROWN-Central/SA Migrant Caravans

Incredibly these disparate groups have aligned themselves for communal advancement against the freedom demonstrated by the USA. Beware a war is raging for on a global basis for ultimate control of mankind. Some say the culmination of this epic struggle will be of biblical proportions. The NWO globalist have decided to have China/CCP takes over from the USA as the superpower on the planet. Special Counsel John Durham has dropped criminal indictments related to past illegal surveillance activities and submitted his final report in 2023.

Post Q# 3750
> What is the 'real' total number of illegal immigrants currently in the US?
> By flooding costal States controlled by [D]s does this 'pull' votes out of the Heartland?
> THE GREAT REST AGENDA:
> NWO/UN/EU/World Control • Elimination of America/Western Society
> No Borders/Unlimited Immigration
> Two-Tier Lawless Justice System
> Global Climate Accords/Carbon Tax
> Eroding Constitution/Amendments
> Deep State Worldwide Control
> The 16-Year Plan to Destroy America

Post Q# 2656

   Anons knew? (Border Security)

These are but a few of the main goals of these various factionalized groups. They do form the pillar of Anti-USA philosophy that lies at the core of this worldwide NWO ruling elite cabal's schemes. An open border and subsequent destruction of the United States is a shared globalist goal with the illegal Biden/Harris regime. The Haitian surge of the Fall of 2021 will be the straw that broke the camel's back with our Southern border crisis. The courts would rule in 2023 that the BHO era policy of protecting the young DACA/Dreamer immigrants as being unconstitutional. A central campaign promise by winning 2024 candidate President Trump is that he will finish the southern border wall and depot all those (estimated around 20 million) who illegally entered the United States under Biden/Harris.

Post Q# 100

   Why are migrants important?
   Why are migrants so important?

Resistance was led by BHO/HRC along with their domestic RINO partners. The Never-Trump/Anti-Q/Fake MAGA individuals are more than happy to hitch their wagon with these globalist rulers. International funding for this invasion is compliments of the Muslim Brotherhood and Communist along with partnered foreign intelligence agencies. Besides the replacement population aspect, the migrants are bringing unique diseases like Dengue Fever. The illegal Biden/Harris administration would reverse the gains made by President Trump and in 2023 the Border Patrol would cut Texan laid razor wire to let in migrants. The systemic planned invasion of all Western countries by hordes from Third world 'hell holes' by the ruling elite Globalist is a key element of a New World Order.

Post Q# 1009

   Troops to Border.
   Clown Black Ops.
   Private funds.
   Raised how?

Please look at Diana West's series "The Red Thread," as she highlights the Red-Green merger. The Red-Green alliance began in Europe but has spread to the USA via the Communist (CCP) and the Muslim Brotherhood (Iran). Our southern border is now wide open under the illegal Biden/Harris administration, and the flow of illegal aliens is nonstop. Texas Governor Abbot is attempting to close his border with an unprecedented line of vehicles and National Guard as 95,000 migrants march from Mexico. With the re-election of President Trump in 2024, time to finish the Southern border and as per one of his first Executive Orders, send in the military and let the mass deportation begin.

Post Q# 4813

   How close did we come to losing it?
   What if our borders remained open?

Links

FOX News-Migrants from 117 Countries accept Biden's Open US Border Policy

Revolver News-Calls to Ban all Third World Immigration

FOX News-Trump's Border Miracle

Just the News-FBI has Arrested more than 10,000 Illegal Immigrants

Daily Wire-Trump Dead Serious about Border

Sara Carter-Trump sends 10,000 Troops to the Border

Washington Examiner-From 9/11 to Today

Breitbart-Guatemala Minister: Migrant Caravans "Planned not Spontaneous"

Daily Wire-FEDs Cut Razor Wire Placed by Texans to let in Illegals

Newsweek-Understanding the Red/Green Alliance

Conservative Daily News-Migrant Caravan brings Dengue Fever and Disease

Daily Wire-Thousands of Migrants March toward US Border from Mexico

Just the News-Orchestrated Crisis: Tens of Thousands Pour across Southern Border

Center for Security Policy-The Red Green Axis

Lew Rockwell-Reduction and the Collapse of the West

Millennium Report-The Trojan Horse Rolled into America

The Blaze: Cloward-Piven Strategy Alive and Well at Border

American Thinker-CAIR: Islamic Trojan Horse

Radio Free Europe-Islamic World combining with China against the Uyghurs

Crossfire Hurricane Docs-State Department Steele Binder

Justice.gov-2023 SC John Durham Report

The Braverman 'BRIDGE':
Clinton Foundation to Schmidt Charities

Timing is everything when changing corporate jobs, especially at the CEO level of major institutions. You may wonder then why a young individual would virtually disappear from the face of the earth after being fired and supposedly seeking new employment. Eric Schmidt/Charities would continue to be a major player in the war against President Donald Trump and MAGA through the midterms of 2022.

Post Q# 2581 on 12/11/18:
> Why is the 'CLINTON FOUNDATION' back in the news?

Most young top executives would normally want to be quickly exposed as being available in the open job market. That is unless you have just been let go by the Clinton Foundation (CF) and you fear a case of 'Arkancide' may yet occur.

Post Q# 2872 on 2/22/19:
> Hillary Clinton and Foundation.
> Crime Against Children.

So strange was this sudden invisibility act, that several major conspiracy theories developed via the internet. Many people had believed Eric Braverman either dead, MIA, or hiding out in a foreign country for personal protection.

Post Q# 4516 on 6/24/20:
> GOOG threat analysis group _entry catalogue.
> Deep dreaming, young dragonfly.

Bear in mind as you go through this article, Mr. Eric Braverman (emphasize on the BRAVE) fortunately escaped CF employment with his life. So many people that have crossed the Clinton's have meet with bizarre untimely demises (aka Arkancide).

Post Q# 10 on 10/29/17:
> What countries donated big money to CF and why?

Eric Braverman was hired in 2013 by the Clinton Foundation (CF) based upon Chelsea's stern insistence. Chelsea was disturbed by an audit that showed financial irregularities and disapproved of Doug Band's current leadership.

Post Q# 3798 on 1/28/20:
> Play a game of 'Where Are They Now?'
> Think CEOs.
> THE BEST IS YET TO COME.

Big surprise when an outside independent financial audit found many accounting problem areas. Chelsea brought in her friend Braverman to serve as the CF's new CEO to help clean things up. Nepotism and inbreeding seem to be a required characteristic of the DC Swamp.

Post Q# 71 on 11/4/17:
> How much money was provided to the CF by SA during 15/16?

This of course started a turf war with Doug Band, who is Slick Willy's right-hand dude. Chelsea's new initiative was geared to improving the CF's tarnished public image, but this went against the 'pay-to-play' model.

Post Q# 4484 on 6/20/20:
> Importance of SDNY control.
> Jurisdiction:
> Clinton Foundation.

Braverman was accused by CF staff of leaking company records to the Mockingbird media. Braverman denied these charges but resigned anyway after serving only two years. In later Wikileaks email disclosures, records seem to prove that Eric was indeed the media leaker.

Post Q# 3674 on 12/14/19:
> DOJ plane(s).
> CF.

Wild rumors swirled around the Internet of Erik's possible murder, going into the Witness Protection Program, changed his identity via plastic surgery, or was hiding out in a foreign country. After the 2016 Presidential election, Eric Schmidt fired the Podesta Brothers and hired Braverman to spearhead his charities.

Post Q# 4105 on 5/4/20:
> DARPA / FB / TWITTER / GOOG [D] coord and dev of [AI] tool in attempt to counter (your) reach [now public - see prev drop]

Braverman was put in charge of the Philanthropic Division of the Eric/Wendy Schmidt Group (Alphabet/YouTube/GMail/Google). Headquarters is in beautiful Menlo Park/Silicon Valley and the Schmidt Group controls millions in different charitable foundations.

Post Q# 1935 on 8/27/18:
> Define DARK MONEY.

Eric Braverman is currently Chief Executive of Schmidt Futures (SF), which he helped to create with Eric Schmidt. SF's stated mission is applying technology to make society work better, while solving the world's toughest problems. It was revealed in 2024 that Google had interfered in past U.S. elections over 41 documented instances.

Post Q# 53 on 11/2/17:
> List of all who have foundations.
> How can donations be used personally?

Why you might ask is someone still breathing that has so publicly betrayed the Clinton's. I think it is exclusively due to Chelsea's intercession and assistance in sparing he longtime buddy Braverman.

Post Q# 89 on 11/5/17:
> FBI/MI currently have open investigation into the CF.

Chelsea originally hired Braverman to go after Doug Band, so she must have been involved with the negative media leaks on some level. Braverman got extremely lucky to be able to walk away and continue breathing. President Trump would file in 2022 a federal RICO lawsuit against HRC/DNC/and other related to the promotion of the false Russian collusion narrative during the 2016 Presidential election.

Post Q# 3125 on 3/20/19:
> The PUBLIC must be prepared for what is about to come.
> "THE CLINTON FOUNDATION"

The U.S. Attorney's Office based out of Little Rock Arkansas is currently investigating the CF. Please note that the Weiner/Abedin laptop is included with the ongoing official DOJ CF investigation originally headed by SP John Huber and turned over to Special Counsel (SC) John Durham. Durham's indictment of Perkins Coie/Clinton campaign lawyer Michael Sussmann had brought Eric Schmidt and Alphabet directly into this fake Russian collusion scheme.

Post Q# 1220 on 4/21/18:
Clinton Foundation conflicts of interest.

The DOJ has had a prosecution team looking into HRC's State Department pay to play schemes by the CF before President Trump. It is rumored Braverman may have been involved on some level with the Podesta/WikiLeaks emails. SC Durham submitted his final report in 2023. With the historic re-election of President Trump in 2024, many feel past hidden political secrets will finally be publicly revealed.

Post Q# 4072 on 5/2/20:
Treason doesn't pay well in the end.

Links

Stream.org-Mysterious Disappearance of C/F CEO

Clinton Foundation Timeline-2025 Crossfire Hurricane Docs

NY Post-Google Interfered in US Elections 41 Times

Tores Says-Ukraine/BHO/Biden: Mafia Global Election Interference

FOX news-Former Google CEO Emerges as Key Democratic Power Player

Breitbart-Eric Schmidt Pushes Deeper Ties between Big Tech and Defense Industry

Revolver News-Worst Snakes still Hate Assange

NY Post-Durham Report proves HRC was Putin's Puppet not Trump

CNET-Eric Schmidt (Google) has Left Company

WSJ-Justice Department hits Google with Antitrust Lawsuit

The Goldwater-Eric Braverman CF Former CFO in FBI Protective Custody

SVBJ-Former CEO of the Clinton Foundation to head Schmidt Charities

Epoch Times-SpyGate the Inside Story

Schmidt Futures-Chief Executive Eric Braverman

PolitiFact-Former CF CEO Eric Braverman is Not Missing

Urban Dictionary-Meaning of 'Arkancide'

WikiLeaks-Eric Braverman Emails

Crossfire Hurricane Docs-State Department Steele Binder

Justice.gov-2023 SC John Durham Report

Let's Peel Back Some Layers on DNC Stalwart Donna Brazile

Often is the case when digging into the background character of these Deep State political hacks, you will find an intriguing resume. Donna Brazile has been a long time top Democratic strategist and Washington DC power broker. President Trump would file in 2022 a federal RICO lawsuit against HRC/DNC/and others related to the promotion of the false Russian collusion narrative. Even Brazile would recognize and openly state in 2023 that Donald Trump's 'movement' is to be respected.

Post Q 4227
> [Russia] narrative ALL FAKE?

Brazile broke the barrier to become the first African American woman to direct a national political (Democrat) campaign. Donna Brazile has in fact twice headed this party; in 2011 and 2016 she was the acting Chairperson of the DNC. Brazile's role as head of the DNC in 2016 will be under intense scrutiny when the full details of President Trump's lawsuit become publicly available.

Post Q# 1493
> SR 187 DISCOVERY.

Some of Donna Brazile's many other resume accomplishments include national media network analyst, successful author, college lecturer, and political consultant. Brazile has run the past political election campaigns for Al Gore, Jessie Jackson, and Bill Clinton. 2022 would be the beginning of the public unveiling of the illegal surveillance against then candidate Donald Trump.

Post Q# 1591
> Server unlocks SR.

Prior to the 2016 national DNC Convention, Debbie Wasserman-Schultz [DWS] was fired and Brazile stepped in to take over. Brazile inherited the infamous DNC computer leak/hack and worked closely with the hired forensic team from CrowdStrike.

Post Q# 3532
> DNC server(s) hold many answers.
> [DWS]
> House of Cards.

Brazile as she has done in the past, stepped up to take over the DNC chair role from DWS. Ultimately, Donna Brazile will be entangled in the Seth Rich murder, the Perkins Coie and CrowdStrike's criminal coverup elements.

Post Q# 4016
> Was the DNC (was) hacked by the Russians?
> HOW FAR BACK DID IT GO?

As 'Q' has advised several times, that the DNC computer intrusion was an inside leak and not an outside hack. Bill Binney/Thomas Drake documented that the file transfer rate on the download could only be done physically in-person and not from an outside internet hack.

Post Q# 1008
> SETH RICH?
> MS_13 187 [2] -24- Distance?

CrowdStrike was retained under [DWS] but Brazile did the final sign off of their false intrusion report. CrowdStrike maintained the outside hack theory was via mysterious Russian's Fancy/Cozy Bear groups.

Post Q# 3764
> Interning for the DNC can be deadly.
> The hole is DEEP.

Brazile was working for CNN during the 2016 campaign season and was involved with her own informational "leak". Donna gave to HRC the debate questions to be asked, well in advance of a Bernie Sanders debate. The FEC would fine in 2022 the DNC and HRC's campaign for over $1M for payments made to Fusion GPS in preparing the false Steel Dossier during the 2016 election cycle.

Post Q# 45
> Why is Donna running for cover?
> Was a deal granted in exchange for something?
> Who made the deal?

Do we care about Donna or those who instructed her to violate the law?

This was just one of many helping efforts done to assist HRC against both Sanders and then ultimately candidate Trump. The Awan's did dirty computer tricks/robot calls against the Sanders campaign as well as their Congressional computer server espionage program.

Post Q# 1462
> What recent news came out re: SR/JA/WL lawsuit?

CNN fired Brazile after the leaked Sanders debate questions became public. It would be over one year later that Donna would be pinned down and finally have to confess to this improper action. FOX New hired Brazile only to fire her due to meltdowns and now she is with ABC News as a contributor.

Post Q# 3815
> They will not be able to walk down the street.
> THE GREAT AWAKENING.

Donna would go on to pen a popular book titled "Hacks" in 2017. Brazile's book dedication surprised many, as it was to murdered DNC staffer Seth Rich. This of course was an effort to steer the narrative back toward the Russians.

Post Q# 3994
> How does Soros comm [secure] w/DNC leaders?

His name was Seth Rich (Panda) and he was brutally murdered after WikiLeaks started to publish the Podesta/DNC leaked emails. Recent inquiries have shown that magically Brazile and the DC mayor were at the hospital the night Seth was brought in and tragically passed away.

Post Q# 4620
> 6. Delay [D] convention _strategic take-over of nominee post conf.

Brazile mentions in her book that the Seth Rich murder "Was anything but a robbery gone wrong". The other theme running through "Hacks" was the fact of HRC's complete takeover of the DNC operations from the top down.

Post Q# 1515

These reporters and networks have been named in the WikiLeaks to have colluded with the DNC or Hillary campaign during the 2016 election cycle.

Inquiring minds demand to know the true events surrounding the tragic death of Patriot SR. 'Q' has told of MS 13's involvement and other particulars which should assist in the continued murder investigation of Seth Rich. Special Counsel (SC) John Durham's indictment of Perkins Coie/Clinton campaign lawyer Michael Sussmann connects to HRC and the DNC. SC Durham submitted his final report in 2023. With the re-election of President Trump in 2024, many pray past hidden political secrets will finally be revealed.

Post Q# 2885

They NEVER thought Crooked Hillary would lose.

Links

Variety-Donna Brazile joins ABC News as Contributor

The Federalist-The FBI Set Up Trump and We Watched it Happen

Just the News-HRC Plan tying Trump and Russia

Clinton Foundation Timeline-2025 Crossfire Hurricane Docs

Washington Examiner-Clinton Campaign, Elias, DNC, and Fusion GPS battle Durham

Techno Fog-John Durham, Michael Sussmann, and the Broader Clinton Conspiracy

Real Clear Politics-RussiaGate: HRC/Perkins Coie/Fusion GPS/CrowdStrike

Washington Examiner-Brazile Finally Admits to giving HRC Debate Questions

Clinton Foundation Timeline-Brazile's: CrowdStrike was Asked to Wait One Month

Daily Dot-Donna Brazile denies Report She was at Hospital

The Atlantic-Brazile's Book Troubling for All the Wrong Reasons

FOX News-DNC/HRC Campaign Pay FEC fines over Fusion GPS/Trump Dossier

Victor Davis Hanson-How to Commit Democratic Party Suicide

Crossfire Hurricane Docs-State Department Steele Binder

Justice.gov-2023 SC John Durham Report

The Traitorous Art of Projection: John "Clown" Brennan

"Clowns to the left of me, Jokers to the right....."

Ex-CIA Director John Brennan had publicly accused President Trump of "treason" at the Summit in Helsinki. This is a textbook example of what psychiatrists' call 'projection.' Brennan will be viewed by historians as the quarterback of SpyGate and the treasonous coup plot against then sitting President Trump. Brennan would join former DNI James Clapper and others former intel officials totaling 51 that penned a letter claiming Hunter Biden's laptop was Russian disinformation and would later admit under Congressional testimony in 2024 that letter was purely political. A newly re-elected President Trump would pull the security clearances of all of the 51 Intel officials.

Post Q# 3836
> $2 + 2 = 6$?
> Define projection.

Psych expert Sigmund Freud says one 'projects' one's own motivations, thoughts, desires and feelings upon others. Projection is the Progressive Leftists classic form of a psychological defensive mechanism and the narrative changing tactic. Narrative control is the main objective of the ruling class and the need for informational intelligence against the opposition is a top priority. Late in 2022 Elon Musk began to reveal via his Twitter Files series the exact collusion between Big Tech and the U.S. government in the suppression of free speech.

Post Q# 1161
> SC-Supreme Court.
> RBG.
> AS 187 / Clown Black (Brennan).

Converted to Islam, fluent in Arabic, voted for the Communist Party in a Presidential election, and once head of the world's premier spy outfit, are true characteristics of the former CIA Director John Brennan [JB]. Brennan is a colorful character that may go down as a principal conductor in ObamaGate/SpyGate. It would be revealed in 2024 that in 2016 then CIA Director Brennan had the FIVE EYES intel partnership illegally spy on 26 Trump aides and set off RussiaGate.

Post Q# 1017
> The Analysis Corporation (TAC).
> Happy Hunting!

Brennan took his oath of office as BHO's Director of the CIA using an original copy of the U.S. Constitution, minus the Bill of Rights. [JB] used this stunt as opposed to the Bible, which has normally been the customary long-standing practice for incoming public servants. The Muslim Brotherhood has long attempted to infiltrate the U.S.A. and the globalist seem intent on pushing Islam onto the rest of the world.

Post Q# 3762
> Brennan CLAS SEC DIV - spy_T?
> Meeting(s) w/Durham?

John Brennan goes back to the early BHO days with his 2008 election campaign and was part of the BHO transition team. [JB] earned his wings when his team altered/scrubbed the U.S. Passport Records Office of BHO's past travel history files. Brennan additionally played a part in the creation of the controversial BHO long-form birth certificate. Fast forward to 2023 and John Brennan would be at the center of a new organization ordered by Biden under the Department of Homeland Security (DHS) labeled the 'Homeland Intelligence Experts Group.'

Post Q# 875
Who performs in a circus?

JOHN BRENNAN NOTABLE ACTIONS:
- Changing BHO Passport Files
- I.C.A. Report-17 Different Agencies
- Benghazi/Libya Coverup
- CIA Agent Peter Strzok's Handler
- Edward Snowden NSA Operation
- Shuttered Project Cassandra/DEA
- Interfered in Israel's Election
- Crossfire Hurricane/SpyGate
- Steele Dossier(s) and Alfa Bank (server)
- Lead 51 Former IC Officials in Hunter Laptop Narrative
- Dossier/FISA Title-1 Surveillance
- Khobar/SA -USAF Base Bombing

Post Q# 4712
Guccifer 2.0

Please take the time to look at Diana West's "Red Thread" series. Ms. West outlines the Communists/Marxist of yesterday, are the same as the radical Progressive Leftists of today. The illegal Biden administration is showing everyone examples of living under a totalitarian ruling communist society. Head clown Brennan would be the quarterback on many of the BHO-era illegal operations and the entire intelligence community has been in an all-out against President Trump from the very jump.

Post Q# 3120
John Brennan picture=Placeholder

People are once again calling into question the validity of the 2016 Intelligence Community Assessment (ICA). Brennan/Clapper recruited FBI agent Peter Strzok and clown Eric Ciaramella to be the main ICA report authors. CIA official then and now with Biden's DoD, was involved with the Alfa Bank false information from indicted Perkins Coie lawyer Michael Sussmann. Records released in 2022 show that John Brennan and the CIA were getting the illegally obtained data on candidate Donald Trump as early as April 2016.

Post Q# 4331
Intelligence was manipulated by [Brennan].
Watch the news.

The ICA relied heavily upon the now disproven Christopher Steele Trump-Russia Dossier (aka the 'Crown Material') as the primary supportive evidence. IG Michael Horowitz's declassified footnotes revealed a deliberate use of Russian disinformation by both Steele and FBI. The ICA was then used to justify the launch of the Special Counsel (SC) Robert Mueller's notorious witch-hunt. It was revealed in 2023 that John Brennan and James Clapper headed a secret DHS Intel Group focusing on the censorship of Americans.

Post Q# 3881
> Backgrounds are important.
> Muslim Brotherhood.

Of odd history was Peter Strzok's role as a CIA agent in Iran under handler [JB.]. The wizard hidden behind the SpyGate curtain is proclaimed converted Muslim John Brennan. Brennan was just denied access to classified material as he researches for an upcoming book and preps for his upcoming SC John Durham testimony. Durham's indictment of Perkins Coie lawyer Michael Sussmann connects Brennan/CIA to the false Alfa Bank scheme.

Post Q# 4016
> Was the DNC (was) hacked by Russia?
> CIA [BRENNAN] FORCE?

[JB] has been the puppet master behind this planned Coup d'état. Recall Edward Snowden's operation began same time Brennan took over CIA. 'Q' says "Up is Down and Left is Right" in the realm of international espionage and traitorous circus clowns. SC Durham has dropped criminal indictments related to SpyGate and submitted his final report in 2023. With the re-election of President Trump in 2024, many past hidden political scandals will finally be revealed.

Post Q# 2933
> No punishment [Brennan] by HUSSEIN ADMIN re: SURV of Senate etc.

Links

Revolver News-This Guy is Still Running Key Parts of the CIA

NY Post-BHO's Russia Collusion Report was Corrupt from the Start

The Hill-The Rise and Fall of John Brennan

FOX News-DOJ Receives Gabbard's Criminal Referral

Real Clear Investigations-BHO Administration turned Unverified Report into RussiaGate

FOX News-Trump pulls Security Clearance of 51 National Security Officials

Markets Work-How Much did Brennan/BHO/Comey Know before Investigation Opened

Epoch Times-John Brennan used Unofficial Intel to Create Russia Hoax

NY Post-CIA and Foreign Intelligence Agencies Illegally Targeted 26 Trump Aides

Sharyl Attkisson-BHO Era Surveillance Timeline

The Federalist-SpyGate 101: A Primer on the Russia Collusion Hoax

American Report-HAMMERING Out their Cover Story 2 Days before Inauguration

Markets Work-Brennan and Clapper: Complicity, Lies, and Bill Priestap

Undercover Huber-John Brennan/Steele Dossier

Markets Work-SpyGate: The True Story of Collusion

The American Spectator-Who ran Crossfire Hurricane?

American Report-John Brennan's "Fusion Center" Fable

The War Economy-SpyFall

Real Clear Investigations-The Brennan Dossier: Prime Mover of RussiaGate

Lew Rockwell-Unfolding Facts of John Brennan's Career of Treachery

American Spectator-The Three Stooges of SpyGate

Senate Intelligence.gov-CIA's use of Journalists/Clergy in Intel Ops

Clinton Foundation Timeline-CIA and Sussmann

DHS.gov-Mayorka Establishes the Intelligence Experts Group

Crossfire Hurricane Docs-Christopher Steele Binder

Justice.gov-2023 SC John Durham Report

Devin Nunes has Targeted CIA's John "Bullseye" Brennan

Then Representative Devin Nunes/House Intelligence Committee had completed in 2018 their Phase Three of government corruption investigations. This third phase had emphasis on the Chris Steele Dossier and the interactions between members of BHO's Intelligence Community. Former CIA Director John Brennan [JB] would join 50 former intel officials in penning a letter just prior to the 2020 Presidential election claiming that the now infamous Hunter Biden 'Laptop form Hell', is Russian disinformation and in fact not reality (nothing to see here-move along). The truth about the Intelligence Community's letter was proven to be of a 'political' nature and newly re-elected President Trump would pull the security clearances of them all.

Post Q# 2933
No punishment [Brennan] by HUSSEIN ADMIN re: SURV of Senate etc.

Phase One was primarily focused on the misconduct in the DOJ/FBI and the illegal surveillance/unmasking during the BHO regime. Phase Two looked at the 2nd Clinton Dossier (Sid Blumenthal/Cody Shearer) that was run through the U.S. State Department via Jonathan Winer and Victoria Nuland. Nunes had staff helpers like Ezra Cohen-Watnick, Michael Ellis and Kash Patel getting many of these coup plotters under official testimony that is proving helpful to Special Counsel (SC) John Durham.

Post Q# 717
Public: FBI/DOJ/O-WH/SD.
Private: Clowns Clowns Clowns.
Expand your thinking.

Ex-CIA Director [JB] has been the key person or quarterback of the SpyGate plot against President Trump. Brennan is the central figure in getting Senator Harry Reid in August 2016 to contact FBI Director Comey over the Steele Dossier. HRC and the DNC contracted with law firm Perkins Coie to hire Fusion GPS and CrowdStrike to assist with the SpyGate plans. Records later would show that John Brennan and the CIA was provided with data illegally collected on candidate Donald Trump as early as April 2016.

Post Q# 4110
[Brennan] and [Comey] assessment [Clapper assist] [hard-push]?

James Comey was advised by Senator Reid to launch an official counterintelligence probe into candidate Trump. The evidence that Brennan passed along was the fake Christopher Steele Trump-Russia Dossier. Senator Harry Reid and No Name worked together in this bi-partisan coup plot against then candidate Trump.

The four main components of OPERATION TRUMP:
- Exoneration of HRC/Aides (ObamaGate)
- False Trump-Russia Dossier creation/distribution (RussiaGate)
- FISA Title-1 Warrants/HOPS (SpyGate)
- The 'Insurance Policy' (Crossfire Hurricane)

Post Q# 1589
LL IS KEY to CONNECTING TO WH / HRC/BC/JB/JC/SP/EH......

Clown director Brennan goes back to doing White House intel briefings for then President Bill Clinton. [JB] worked for many years at the CIA and was station chief in Saudi Arabia (FBI agent

Peter Strzok was briefly stationed there) and converted to a Muslim religion. Brennan's defense of the Muslim Brotherhood (MB) would be more apparent under the BHO reign.

Post Q# 1887

What is JB's background?

Brennan left government work temporarily back in 2005 to delve into the private sector of shady intelligence work. JB] would become the CEO of The Analysis Corporation (TAC) and this firm would become involved with some very sinister deals. Like today's Fusion GPS or its British cousin Hakluyt, spies for hire has always been fashionable.

Post Q# 4711

John Brennan

Brennan's TAC was found out and later admitted to being involved with unauthorized access to the U.S. Passport Office. Lt. Quarles Harris was an employee of TAC and has admitted to performing this computer intrusion prior to his unexplained 2008 murder. Clown Brennan would be the quarterback on many of the BHO era shady operations and the intelligence community has engaged in all-out total war against President Trump from the jump.

Post Q# 1892

NEVER FORGET.
BLACK OPS AGAINST THE USA.
TOTAL TAKEOVER OF OUR COUNTRY .
WHAT NO-AGENCY LEAKED THE DATA?
TRAITORS ALL.

United States Passport files that were change or altered by Lt. Harris stealth computer intrusion were BHO/HRC/and No Name. BHO had JB consulting his 2008 Presidential Campaign and later appointed him as the CIA Director or head of the Clowns. The corrupt intelligence community would continue to attack President Trump through his first term and into the illegal Biden administration. Brennan and his sidekick James Clapper would use the ultrasecret supercomputer nicknamed 'The Hammer' to conduct surveillance upon their political enemies like Donald Trump.

Post Q# 559

Who used private email addresses?
JB.

I feel [JB] will be singled out as one of the main criminal ring leaders in SpyGate. John Brennan can be spotted these days on any number of MSM cable news shows crying about the pulling of his security credentials or orange man bad. As more information is publicly revealed concerning the SpyGate scandal, all roads lead to Brennan being the quarterback of these treasonous operations. It would be revealed in 2023 that the FBI/DOJ spied upon then Rep. Nunes and his staff (Kash Patel and Ezra Cohen Watnick) by subpoenaing their personal phone/email records while investigating Crossfire Hurricane/John Brennan. It would be revealed in 2024 that then CIA Director John Brennan targeted 26 Trump aides to be illegally spied upon by the FIVE EYES intel partnership.

Post Q# 4310

[Brennan] [Clapper] [Carter] push to TERM _NSA Mike Rogers [date]?

Brennan helped produce the fake Benghazi video, the very suspicious BHO birth certificate and is mentioned in several key Strzok/Page texts. [JB] played a central role in quarterbacking all operational facets for this coup plot on behalf of ringleader BHO. SC John Durham has made criminal indictments and finished his report in 2023 related to RussiaGate and they connect to Brennan/CIA via the false Alfa Bank collusion scheme. Sussmann met with both FBI James Baker and CIA Director John Brennan in 2016 representing the false Alfa Bank story. America First Legal revealed in 2024 that the Brennan/Clapper led DHS Committee recommended that folks turn in their neighbors into the FEDS for any suspicious activities.

Post Q# 1017

> The Analysis Corporation (TAC).
> Happy Hunting!

The BHO ordered Intelligence Community Assessment (I.C.A.) that Brennan lead and rushed the report out in early January 2017 to setup President Elect Trump. The I.C.A. had disgraced FBI agent Peter Strzok push the phony Steele Dossier as a central supporting evidentiary basis. This phony I.C.A. would be used as the foundational claim upon which to unleash Special Counsel (SC) Robert Mueller. Late in 2022 Elon Musk would begin to reveal in his Twitter Files series the exact collusion between Big Tech and the U.S. government in the suppression of free speech.

Post Q# 3881

> Backgrounds are important.
> Muslim Brotherhood.

Daily new evidence all points toward coordination with the DOJ's 'Secret Society' in the implementation of Crossfire Hurricane/Crossfire Razor/Dragon FISA/and others. SC Durham is beginning to lay out via court filings a vast 'Joint Venture Conspiracy' that involves many from both inside/outside the U.S. government. Brennan and the CIA were involved with the Alfa Bank, DNC computer intrusion, Crossfire Hurricane, and most aspects of SpyGate. With the re-election of President Trump in 2024, factual information and the truth will be finally revealed to help usher in judicial accountability in the upcoming Judgement Day.

Post Q# 3762

> Brennan CLAS SEC DIV - spy?
> Meeting(s) w/Durham?

Links

Breitbart-Third Phase of Nunes' Probe to focus on CIA Director Brennan

FOX News-Brennan directed Implausible Reports claiming Putin Preferred Trump

Just the News-FBI Opens Grand Conspiracy Probe

FOX News-John Brennan/James Comey under Criminal Investigation

YouTube-Devin Nunes Exposes BHO Administration's Illegal Spying Targeting Trump

The Last Refuge-Original BHO and HRC 2008 Agreement

The Federalist-Unsealed Crossfire Hurricane Docs prove RussiaGate a Hoax

Real Clear Politics-What the ObamaGate Scandals Mean

FOX News-Trump pulls Security Clearance of 51 National Security Officials

Revolver News-The CIA Interfered in the 2020 Election

Markets Work-How Much did Brennan/BHO/Comey Know before Investigation Opened

NY Post-CIA and Foreign Intelligence Agencies Illegally Targeted 26 Trump Aides

Lee Smith-BHO's January 5th Conspiracy

American Report-HAMMERING Out their Cover Story 2 Days before Inauguration

Buster Hyde-The Dung Castle: Operation Crossfire Hurricane

Michael Schellenberger-CIA and Crossfire Hurricane

Markets Work-SpyGate: The True Story of Collusion

American Spectator -Who Ran Crossfire Hurricane?

BBC-Democrat Hack: Who is Guccifer 2.0?

Millennium Report-The Hammer Ultra Secret Supercomputer

Undercover Huber-Brennan/Steele Dossier

The Federalist-Brennan Lied about not Including Steele Dossier in I.C.A.

Real Clear Investigations-The Brennan Dossier: Prime Mover of RussiaGate

The American Report-John Brennan's "Fusion Center" Fable

DNI.gov-FISA Memo 2017

Crossfire Hurricane Docs-Christopher Steele Binder

Justice.gov-2023 SC John Durham Report

U1 FBI Confidential Informant: Meet William Campbell

Vlad Putin had the idea to corner the world supply of uranium in an effort to give Mother Russia the monopoly over a critical global natural resource. For six years Patriot William 'Doug' Campbell worked as an Under Cover Confidential Informant (UCCI) for the FBI. Campbell poised as an average American businessman in the Nuclear Energy Industry as his base cover. The global events related to Russia's 2022 special military operation into Ukraine will resurface the past events connected directly to the Uranium One (U1) deal.

Post Q# 726
> Over the TARGET.

Of odd historical note is Russia sold its entire financial stake in Uranium One shortly before their military operation into Ukraine in 2022. Mr. Campbell pretended to represent Putin's illegal attempts to gain worldwide control of various uranium deposits via bribery. Then Rep. Mark Meadows had Mr. Campbell in for official Congressional testimony on 12/13/18.

Post Q# 1306
> Where did the U1 material end up?

The Russians gained leverage in the uranium market by using old fashion bribes, kickbacks, extortion and complex money laundering schemes. These criminal actions were aimed at gaining influence in the ultimate purchase of Uranium One.

Post Q# 2657
Post public release of CLAS NSA PRO and U1?
> What country was involved with U1?

William Campbell documented many violations of the U.S. Foreign Practices Act to the FBI while working deep undercover. This whistleblowing effort was intended to block the U1 sale, which represented the sale of over 20% of the total U.S. uranium ore reserves.

Post Q# 3893
Backchannels are important when the 'news' itself is untrustworthy [controlled].
> WWG1WGA!!!

Putin's atomic energy giant Rosatom needed lots of uranium and Russia wanted total global market domination. Frank Giustra's Canadian firm UrAsia was absorbed in 2007 by U1 to assist with this multi-nation complex scheme.

Post Q# 3035
> [MUELLER] connection to U1 and Russia?

Frank Giustra was a long-time Clinton ally who directed various groups to contribute millions into the Clinton Foundation (CF) coffers. It is estimated that over $145 million in new donations flowed into the CF directly due to the U1 transactional purchase.

Post Q# 1345
> U1 [donations to CF].

Putin's Rosatom gains majorly ownership control over U1 in June 2010. Coincidentally it was on 6/29/10 that Bill Clinton gave and was paid $500,000 for an infamous very short Moscow speech. Rosatom would receive special exemption status in 2022 in regard to the various economic sanctions imposed by the USA/EU over the Russia military operation into Ukraine.

Post Q# 689

Re_read recent drops re: U1/informant.

To most people the fact of selling our uranium reserves to Russia is a horrible idea on its face. U1 produced 'Yellow Cake' which is highly enriched uranium and can be used by the military for lethal applications.

Post Q# 3837

BIGGER THAN YOU CAN IMAGINE.
More than selling of Uranium.

The processed Yellow Cake went out via illegal shipping routes through Canada to multiple international locations. All uranium was to stay in the USA per approval guidelines by CIFUS and not out to our known enemies.

Post Q# 2512

Mueller will face charges re: U1.
He's working to save himself.

Mr. Campbell has testified in multiple closed-door interviews to Congress and SP Huber/SC Durham. Mr. Campbell has as his able lawyer Victoria Toensing (White Hat) and she has outlined much of these details on various network TV news programs.

Post Q# 520

The MAP is the KEY.
PLANNED for [3] years.

Both the premature release of Mr. Campbell's identity and the shameful comments made by Democrats over his memory issues (suffering from a serious brain tumor), were professionally unconscionable acts. Ms. Toensing has been considering additional legal repercussions due to this unethical treatment of her brace client.

Post Q# 1069

Systematic weakening of the US.
U1.
Cash flow funnel.

Our prayers go out for Mr. Campbell's personal struggles with his ongoing ill health. Our nation will be forever thankful for heroic whistleblowers like Mr. William Campbell.

Post Q# 674

Public interest [keep high].
U1 FBI informant.

Peter Schweizer's book "Clinton Cash" details the extensive payments into the Clinton Foundation. These millions were paid to purchase political favor in textbook classic pay to play corruption schemes. All sides saw the economic windfalls and strategic benefit of the trading such a scare and powerful natural resource such as uranium.

Post Q# 2217

U1 Funnel and Canada and X.

This was one reason for the use of a private email server by HRC, so as to hide the 'Pay to Play' between the State Department and the CF. The coordinators were Huma Abedin at the State Department and Doug Band over at the CF. History will show that BHO/HRC/and Biden tried to bribe and manipulate Russia all while President Trump had a good personal relationship with Putin.

Post Q# 964

U1 CAN EU RUSSIA IRAN NK SYRIA PAK

The larger crime was the FBI/Mueller keeping Campbell's evidence from the 2010 CFIUS panel. Ultimately BHO's CFIUS group unanimously approved the Uranium One sale and the loss of 20% reserves of this precious element. The 2020-21 government data shows that the USA imports annually nearly 1/3 of our needed supply of uranium from Russia.

Post Q# 3

It finally came out that Rod/Bob were key players in the Uranium scandal.

The critical testimony given by Mr. Campbell will assist the efforts by the DOJ. Headquartered out of the Little Rock US Attorney's office is a probe. Finally, a real grand jury has been empaneled for this criminal ongoing investigation into the CF. Special Counsel John Durham has dropped criminal indictments related to HRC/BHO/as well as their treasonous co-conspirators and submitted his final report in 2023. With the historic re-election of President Trump in 2024, Val Putin will play a key role in stabilizing both Uranium as well as Ukraine.

Post Q# 3836

Think U1 [sale of US uranium to Russia]
Sold out US to benefit Russia for personal financial gain?

Links

NY Times-Cash Flowed into the Clinton Foundation

The Federalist-Senate Expands Probe into FBI's Ability to Hide Docs

Badlands Media-The Biggest Cover Up in American History

Breitbart-Uranium One: 7 Facts

Just the News-The BHO/Biden/HRC Nuclear Giveaway to Russia

Radio Free Europe-The Rosatom Exemption: Russia's Nuclear Giant has Escaped Sanctions

The Hill-FBI's 37 Secret Page Memo about HRC and U1

Larry Beech-Uranium One and CrowdStrike

Defcon News-Russia Sold its Stake in Uranium One before Invading Ukraine

Victor Davis Hanson-Russia Russia Forever Obsession

New Yorker-5 Questions about the Clintons and Uranium One

WGBH-News-Crooked Hillary Redux: Making Sense of Uranium One

House.gov-BHO Era Russian Uranium One Deal

Markets Work-Russian Collusion: Bribes, Coverup, Clinton, and U1

Daily Mail-Russia Paid Millions to Influence HRC with U1

The Hill-U1 Informant makes Clinton Allegations to Congress

Buster Hyde-HRC/CF: Blurred Lines

The Hill-FBI knew of Russian Plot Prior to CFIUS

NPR-The Alternative 'Russia Scandal'

Millennium Report-The Last Clinton Scandal

Breitbart-Timeline: Bill Clinton's Uranium Windfalls for the Foundation

Web Archive.org-Uranium One Timeline

Justice.gov-President of Transportation Company found Guiltily

Crossfire Hurricane Docs-State Department Steele Binder

Justice.gov-2023 SC John Durham Report

John Carlin: DOJ NSD Chief
Who Approved Altered FISA Spy Warrants

John Carlin [JC] was the former Assistant Attorney General for the National Security Division of the Justice Department (DOJ). Carlin resigned from DOJ on 10/15/16, which oddly is the day after he signed off on the department's 2016 FISA annual review report. History will show that Carlin's FISA filings began the crossover from RussiaGate to SpyGate.

Post Q# 2645
> WE WILL NOT GO SILENT INTO THE NIGHT.
> EO ACTIVE.

Oddly October 2016 is the time period when the first Carter Page FISA surveillance warrant application was approved by the FISA Court (FISC). It is widely believed that Carlin had his fingerprints on the very first Carter Page FISA that was denied in the Summer of 2016. Carlin definitely was involved with the second Carter Page FISA application which gained FISC approval.

Post Q# 2129
> THE US GOVERNMENT UNDER HUSSEIN, KNOWINGLY, PRESENTED FALSE
> EVIDENCE TO FISC IN AN EFFORT TO OBTAIN 'LEGAL' US INTELLIGENCE
> 'UMBRELLA' SURV OF POTUS [IDEN TARGET] FOR THE SOLE PURPOSE OF
> INFLUENCING THE 2016 ELECTION OF THE PRESIDENCY.

Per trusted reporter John Solomon, FBI/DOJ email chains indicate that the Carter Page FISA warrant(s) were in fact intentionally altered/doctored by the FBI. This would ease the future liability of some FISA original signers but leads to more criminality within the lower ranks of the DOJ/FBI. FBI lawyer Kevin Clinesmith has been criminally referred to SP John Durham for knowingly altering FISA information.

Post Q# 2248
> RATS RUNNING?
> THE WORLD WILL KNOW.
> ANONS KNEW.

Inquiring minds now want to know if John Carlin approved any of the 'doctor' or altered Carter Page FISA surveillance warrants. These highly illegal actions normally need directions given from a senior level authority from main Justice due to normal oversight by the department Inspector General.

Post Q# 3921
> FISA INDICTMENTS = START

We are waiting for confirmation on who within the DOJ/FBI signed off on the Carter Page October 2016 FISA application. Carlin had the authority within the to give final rubber stamp approval for the altered Carter Page FISA Title-1 warrant(s).

Post Q# 1316
> John Carlin, Asst. AG-Head of DOJ's National Security Division-FIRED/FORCE.
> THE SWAMP IS BEING DRAINED.

ObamaGate/SpyGate plans were coordinated through the National Security departments of both the DOJ and FBI. Deliberately organized in this fashion due to DOJ Assistant AG Sally Yates not allowing normal OIG oversight by Michael Horowitz, who was in charge of the DOJ.

Post Q# 1828
[DOJ [LL] [SY] [BO-CS] (UK) [DL] [PS] [DNI] [JC] [MM] [RB]] - [BC].

John Carlin was responsible for examining, writing recommendations and pre-approving most FISA applications. Carlin also oversaw prosecutions of espionage cases, domestic terror cases, oversight of NSA surveillance, and representing the U.S. Government in front of the FISA Court.

Post Q# 1147
SC/LL deal drop.
Tarmac.

Thanks to Admiral Mike Rogers forced review of prior NSA access abuses by outside contractors (Fusion GPS/CrowdStrike/Orbis), hard questions were now being directed toward the DOJ and FISC. It is accepted that Carlin along with DNI James Clapper, lobbied BHO to fire Admiral Rogers over his November 2016 Trump Tower unauthorized visit to President Elect Trump.

Post Q# 3673
It was over before it began.

One of John Carlin's duties was the approval of raw data NSA stored data only accessible via FISA/FISC orders. These FISA 702 'About Queries' within the NSA database, featured inclusive searches of all upstream mega captures of select targeted subject's personal data records. Special Counsel John Durham has started to drop criminal indictments related to past illegal surveillance operations termed SpyGate.

Post Q# 4352
Thank you for playing.
Have a Nice Day.

Carlin has also been connected to the entire Lynch/Clinton 'Tarmac' episode and apparent coverup efforts by both the DOJ/FBI. Carlin helped with the [Lynch] talking points and worked with FBI's James Rybicki with the official released joint media statements concerning the "Tarmac' meeting.

Post Q# 1720
When does a bird sing?

Lisa Page's closed-door testimony confirms that John Carlin was kept in the Trump-Russia loop aka the 'Secret Society'. Carlin was regularly updated personally by FBI leaders Andy McCabe and Randy Coleman. Carlin additionally failed to advise the FISA Court that Carter Page had previously worked with both the FBI and CIA (Kevin Clinesmith).

Post Q# 3595
F2F 1-4 US person(s) initiate scope memo.

According to our guy Joe D, "Nobody in a Senior Department post resigns 3 weeks before an election, when you think HRC is going to win". Inquiring minds also want to look back upon the very first FISA against Carter Page that was miraculous turned down by the FISC. SpyGate assigns Special Counsel John Durham submitted his final report in 2023. With the historic re-election of President Trump in 2024, many past hidden political secrets will finally be revealed.

Post Q# 3667
Did you learn (4) FISAs last week re: POTUS?
Non_public prior?

Links

The Federalist-DOJ Officials didn't know Database Allowed FBI to Bury RussiaGate Docs

Clinton Foundation Timeline-2025 Crossfire Hurricane Docs

Real Clear Investigations-Deception by Redaction

The Federalist-SpyGate 101: A Primer on the Russia Collusion Hoax

Markets Work-Biden Officials had Roles in Surveillance of Trump

Breitbart-Acting DAG Carlin: DOJ Investigating Jan. 6th

Real Clear Politics-DOJ Official John Carlin on Russia Controversy

Markets Work-Uncovering: Mike Rogers' Investigation Section 702 FISA Abuse/FBI

Just the News-Durham File: Documentary on the FBI against Trump

Clinton Foundation Timeline-Lisa Page on John Carlin's Role

Markets Work-John Carlin: Enabled FBI's Carter Page FISA Warrant

Epoch Times-Testimony by FBI Lawyer Trisha Anderson Reveals Extensive Role

Bloomberg-The FBI's Investigation into Trump/Russia looks Worse Now

Markets Work-Bypassing the IG: Sally Yates/DOJ's National Security Letter Carve-Out

DNI.gov-FISC Top Secret Report on FISA (2017)

Justice.gov-IG Horowitz: Review of 4 FISA Applications

Senate Judiciary Committee-2021 Crossfire Hurricane DECLAS

Justice.gov-2023 SC John Durham Report

Deep State's Point Man: James 'The Hammer' Clapper

History books will show that former Director of National Intelligence (DNI) James Clapper was a key central figure in ObamaGate/SpyGate. DNI Clapper was the Deep State's point person that coordinated surveillance against all of BHO's political enemies. All of the 17 different intelligence agencies report under the DNI and thus Clapper is the ultimate gatekeeper of all top secret classified information.

Post Q# 1828
[SPY OP].
[DNI] [JC].

James Clapper [JC] previously held the same job as did General Mike Flynn being the Director of the Defense Intelligence Agency (DIA) and was a Lt. General in the U.S. Air Force. BHO made Clapper the fourth DNI in 2010 and held that lead intelligence position through the end of BHO's second term. James Clapper and then CIA Director John Brennan would join to form a total of 51 retired intelligence officials in penning a letter claiming Hunter Biden's 'Laptop from Hell' was not real and only a product of Russian disinformation, thus effecting the 2020 Presidential vote of over 17% of the population. A newly re-elected President Trump would instantly pull the security clearances of all 51 Intel officials. It was also revealed in 2024 that the US Intel community requested from its FIVE EYES (FVEY) international partners to illegally spy upon targeted Team Donald Trump aides back in 2016.

Post Q# 1164
HUSSEIN HRC LL BRENNAN CLAPPER NAT SEC WH SIT RM OP UK AUS
assist/set up.

Eon Musk would release late in 2022 his Twitter Files which confirm U.S. governmental influence in the suppression of free speech just before the 2020 Presidential election. The DNI oversees all 17 intelligence agencies within the U.S. government. BHO ordered DNI Clapper to prepare an Intelligence Community Assessment (ICA) over suspected Russian 2016 Presidential campaign interference. Clapper farmed out most of the ICA to CIA Director John Brennan, who in turn had FBI agent Peter Strzok do most of the final paper. This later discredited ICA report in January 2017 set the stage for the ensuing Trump-Russia Dossier operation.

Post Q# 1708
Co-sponsor insurance policy re: POTUS election.
Clapper.

James Clapper's tenure was marred dramatically by Edward Snowden's 2013 theft of NSA top secret files. In March 2013 ironically just a few months prior to Snowden, Clapper gave his infamous 'Big Lie' to Congress over mass surveillance of the American public. Note that NSA's internal investigation force called the 'Q Team' began the international hunt for traitor Edward Snowden.

Post Q# 2129
DIR BRENNAN DIR CLAPPER W/PDB REGULAR UPDATES + LIVE
STREAMING.

Clapper testified to Senator Ron Wyden about the 'Prism' surveillance data collection programs created by NSA whistleblower Bill Binney. James Clapper in responding to unlawful surveillance against millions of Americans replying, "No sir, not wittingly." This was the 'Big Lie' that James Clapper escaped any accountability for willfully lying to Congress. Also recall it was behind the back of his boss (Clapper) that Admiral Mike Rogers went to visit then President Elect Trump over in Trump Tower to warn of the ongoing surveillance.

The four main components of the elaborate coup plot nicknamed Operation Trump:
- Exonerate HRC/Aides (ObamaGate)
- Fake Trump-Russia Dossier creation/distribution (RussiaGate)
- FISA Title-1 Surveillance Warrants/Section 702/HOPS (SpyGate)
- The 'Insurance Policy' (Crossfire Hurricane)

Post Q# 4310
[Brennan] [Clapper] [Carter] push to TERM _NSA Mike Rogers [date]?

DNI Clapper was noted for the vast expansion of the SCIF network, as he knew all about 'The Hammer' and other mass surveillance programs. The Hammer supercomputer system was publicly highlighted by whistleblower Dennis Montgomery, and it involved the capturing all fiber data by the CIA/NSA. The Hammer was a signals intelligence network program that was housed within governmental super computers.

Post Q# 2662
"The treachery revealed by Comey, Clapper and Brennan requires accountability."

Nicknamed HAMR or The Hammer is a top-secret supercomputer surveillance program used by the CIA/NSA. The HAMR was used illegally against 17 different Trump businesses as well as many judges/news media/business leaders/ and Congressional members. FBI J. Edgar Hoover was noted for using illegally obtained material as leverage against everyone in DC. DNI Clapper and CIA Director (head clown) Brennan would lead many of BHO's illegal 2016 schemes against then candidate Donald Trump.

Post Q# 4802
Spy campaign failed.
Russia Russia Russia failed.
BIGGER THAN YOU CAN IMAGINE.

Bear in mind this mass surveillance happened a few years before Donald Trump even declared his Presidential 2016 candidacy. James Rosen/FOX TV News and Sharyl Attkisson/CBS TV News were two media news reporters that were directly spied upon by BHO using the notorious HAMR surveillance system. President Trump would file in 2022 a federal RICO lawsuit against many of the main SpyGate characters who promoted the false Russian collusion narrative in 2016. Scarily in 2023 Biden announced the formation of a new unit under DHS titled the 'Homeland Intelligence Experts Group' of which notorious villains John Brennan and James Clapper would head. This censorship team would recommend (per America First Legal in 2024) that any suspicious neighbors be reported to the FEDS.

Post Q# 3595
2010 - 2017 [Clapper] [bulk]

WikiLeaks confirmed Montgomery's claims in their 2017 'Vault 7' dump about CIA hacking tools and The Hammer. Other CIA hacking tools like 'false fingerprints' on computer intrusions come into play with the ObamaGate/SpyGate scandals being revealed. Special Counsel (SC) John Durham was tasked to explore referrals by IG Horowitz made related to the illegal surveillance surrounding the political scandal known as SpyGate. SC Durham's indictment of Perkins Coie/Clinton campaign lawyer Michael Sussman launched the beginning of the judicial accountability phase and his final report submitted in 2023 will be the foundation for future cases.

Post Q# 1764
WH visitor logs: NO NAME/BRENNAN/CLAPPER/RICE.

Clapper commented on Edward Snowden "He saw deceiving the American people as what he does as his job, as something completely ordinary." That appears to be a textbook example of projection 101 or old guard saying of the pot calling the kettle black. History will show the arrogance and utter contempt these failed coup plotters had against President Trump and all of his MAGA supporters. Late in 2022 Elon Musk began to expose the exact collusion between Big Tech and the U.S. government in the suppression of free speech. SpyGate villains like Clapper, Strzok, and McCabe would be rewarded with cushy TV gigs and lucrative book deals.

Post Q# 4110
[Brennan] and [Comey] assessment [Clapper assist] [hard-push]?

Historians will reflect upon the misleading letter regarding Hunter's laptop being Russian disinformation as one of James Clapper's (and intel friends) as being one of the worst violations of the public trust. James Clapper's new book titled "Facts and Fears: Hard Truths from a Life in Intelligence" might turn out to be clairvoyant. Clapper left out the important part, where he calls news reporter Michael Isikoff to "Take the kill-shot on Flynn". Judgement Day is coming as evidence by SC Durham has dropped criminal indictments and submitted his final report in 2023. With the historic re-election of President Trump in 2024, many pray that past political secrets will be revealed and lead to judicial accountability.

Post Q# 3116
James Clapper picture - Placeholder

Links

American Report-BHO Surveillance HAMMER on Trump Worse than Watergate

FOX News-Clapper pushed to Comprise Normal Steps

The Federalist-BHO's ODNI Scuttled Intelligence Briefing

NY Post-BHO's Russia Collusion Report was Corrupt from the Start

Clinton Foundation Timeline-2025 Crossfire Hurricane Docs

FOX News-Trump pulls Security Clearance of 51 National Security Officials

America First Legal-Brennan/Clapper led DHS Committee: Report Neighbors to FEDS

Sharyl Attkisson-BHO Era Surveillance Timeline

The Federalist-SpyGate 101: A Primer on the Russia Collusion Hoax

American Report-HAMMERING Out their Cover Story 2 Days before Inauguration

Tablet Magazine-RussiaGate began with BHO's Domestic Spying

Markets Work-Brennan and Clapper: Complicity, Lies, and Bill Priestap

The Last Refuge-SpyGate: The Big Picture

The American Spectator-The Three Stooges of SpyGate

Millennium Report-'The Hammer' Ultra Secret Computer/Surveillance System

American Thinker-James Clapper: Deep State Point Man

The Guardian-Video of Clapper's 2013 'Big Lie' to Congress

American Report-The Hammer is the Key to the Coup

DHS.gov-Mayorkas Establishes the Intelligence Experts Group

Judiciary.House.gov-The Hunter Biden Statement

ODNI.gov-DNI Clapper Email to Admiral Rogers: 2017 ICA

Crossfire Hurricane Docs-Christopher Steele Binder

Justice.gov-2023 SC John Durham Report

Rarer than Unicorns—Clinton Foundation Whistleblowers

For the last several decades no one has dared to testify against the Clinton Foundation (CF). Finally, as their grip on power diminishes a few brave whistleblowers have begun to emerge. History will show that a small group of accountants acting as financial bounty hunters would be the first the crack the Clinton Foundation empire. The FEC in 2022 would fine both the DNC and HRC over $1M for the false Fusion GPS opposition research used in the 2016 Presidential election cycle.

Post Q# 2560

Why is "The Clinton Foundation" back in the news?

Rep. Mark Meadows held a Congressional hearing on 12/13/18 in regard to oversight of non-profit organizations. This sub committee's titled event is called "A Case Study on the Clinton Foundation". These initial public hearings would be the first glimpse at actions behind the scenes which may finally produce judicial results.

Post Q# 48

> What is Q Clearance?
> Who would have the goods on U1.

Andrew Kessel joined the CF in 2004 as the Chief Financial Officer (CFO). Kessel previously worked at Kidder Peabody and Barclays. Andrew is also a graduate of the Wharton School of Business just like our great POTUS.

Post Q# 89

> FBI/MI currently have open investigation into the CF.

Price Waterhouse Coopers is the accounting firm of record for the CF. They along with Kessel signed all of the annual federal tax statements for the global charity. The financial bounty hunters Larry Doyle and John Moynihan filed paperwork with the IRS to claim any future percentage of collected funds from their whistleblowing campaign.

Post Q# 3881

> THIS IS NOT SIMPLY ANOTHER 4-YEAR ELECTION.
> [assumptions correct - package well rec [known]]

Federal charity law often carries harsher civil and criminal penalties than does normal U.S. corporate regulations. The final untangling of the den of corruption will be a massive endeavor.

Post Q# 2578

> [post OIG WB status + docs handover protocols].

The CF had additionally hired outside independent experts to do periodic reviews for compliance purposes. Highlighted in supplemental reports was systemic co-mingling of funds and non-disclosure of foreign donors to the foundation.

Post Q# 1876

> Coord w/AID ORGS for [illegal] plans.

The MDA Analytics company filled comprehensive whistleblower reports in 2017 with both the FBI and IRS. Performed at their own expense, MDA hopes to collect a commission 'bounty' on any past IRS tax funds reclaimed.

Post Q# 3605
>PAY-FOR-PLAY only works when you hold a position of POWER.

MDA only selects only large charities as they are paid based upon their whistleblower's success. In the forensic accounting industry, they are known commonly as "Financial Bounty Hunters". Even though the DC Swamp has thrown roadblocks in front of Doyle and Moynihan, they both have persisted in uncovering the truth about the corrupt Clinton foundation.

Post Q# 2562
>Why 'all of a sudden' are people talking about the CLINTON FOUNDATION (including whistleblowers and hidden company established to investigate covertly (ex_ABCs)).

CFO Kessel is one of the several CF whistleblowers working with MDA. This organization has already turned over 6,000 pages of evidence and IG Michael Horowitz have access to these records.

Post Q# 2578
>The moment your name went 'live' there was no other choice
>Keep the faith, Patriot.

In a public sideshow the FBI raided the home of another CF whistleblower to siege evidence. Nathan Cain had already given testimony and turned over his CF/U1 information to both Rep. Devin Nunes/HPSCI and AG Barr/IG Horowitz.

Post Q# 4278
>[2016 campaign [+CF] contributions [HRC] by media]
>Control of narrative.

MDA is a collection of former Federal prosecutors, investigators, and accounting experts working on behalf of these brave CF whistleblowers. Patriot Charles Ortell has been working hard to expose the charity fraud at the CF via forensic accounting methods.

Post Q# 1345
>U1 [donations to CF].

The 'Pay to Play' element is the core backbone of the criminal charity known as the CF. Foundation Directors incredibly included Cheryl Mills, serving while she was HRC's Chief of Staff at the U.S. State Department. We have hope in Special Counsel (SC) John Durham as he has begun criminal indictments related to SpyGate.

Post Q# 1868
>Do not link to CF.
>[CF] docs kept in NYC and Utah.

The stench of sinister guaranteed "quid-pro-quo" deals abounded at the CF. Recall that the Clinton Global Initiative (CGI) was shut down due to lack of funds just prior to President Trump taking office in 2017. The international grifting schemes of Clinton Inc. never recovered from HRC's stunning upset in 2016.

Post Q# 4820
>THE CLINTON FOUNDATION.
>WHITE HOUSE FOR SALE.

Since the 2016 election outcome, the contributions flowing into the CF have stopped due to the lack of political influence. With loosing political power, came the end of Pay to Play, the big-league money and the fear of 'Arkancide' to any possible whistleblowers. Financial bounty hunters Doyal and Moynihan continue in 2022 to press the courts on resolution to their various pending claims.

Post Q# 259
Funds raised vs distributed?
7/10 plane crashes are targeted kills.

Frank Giustra and the Uranium One deal is the poster child that exemplifies this personal enrichment scheme by the Clintons. Giustra coordinated with Cheryl Mills/Huma Abedin from State and with Doug Band at the CF directing over $145 million into the Clinton Foundation. The Deep State of tens uses foundations and non-governmental organizations to shelter their financial activities.

Post Q# 3036
Do UNICORNS exist?

Claims of uncontrollable personal expenses by both BC/HRC are combined with the cost of Chelsea's wedding as examples of criminality. Co-mingling of funds and use of charity donations for personal expenses are major crimes. SC Durham's criminal indictment of Perkins Coie/Clinton campaign lawyer Michael Sussmann connects HRC, DNC, and many others to this failed coup plot.

Post Q# 4963
Whistleblowers.
Time to show the world.

BC told reporters recently that all of the accounting woes of the CF can be blamed on the accountant. Every too quickly shift the blame, BC said "The guy that filled out the forms made an error". The era of accountability and equal justice is returning again via Judgement Day. Of hope is the fact that SP John Huber turned over all of his investigations into the Clinton Foundation to SC John Durham in 2020. SC Durham submitted his final report about SpyGate in 2023. With the historic re-election of President Trump in 2024, many past hidden political secrets will finally be revealed.

Post Q# 3598
"Whistle Blower Trap"

Links

CNN-What is The Clinton Foundation?

The Federalist-HRC and the FBI Set Up Trump

Clinton Foundation Timeline-2025 Crossfire Hurricane Docs

Just the News-Durham Report breathes New Life into CF Whistleblower Case

Washington Examiner-FEC fines DNC and Clinton for Trump Dossier Hoax

Warfoo-John Moynihan and Larry Doyle on Clinton Foundation

Clinton Foundation Timeline-CF Whistleblowers: Moynihan/Doyle/and Durham

Vigilant News-Clintons Reopen their Pay-to-Play Global Initiative

FOX News-Durham Assumed Parts of John Huber's Clinton- Foundation Review-

Just the News-Judge orders IRS Reveal Documents on Clinton Whistleblowers

Just the News-Federal Tax Judge allows Whistleblower Case against CF to Proceed

Washington Examiner-Judge Orders IRS to Check the Clinton Foundation

Red State-CF "Pay to Play" Allegations 6,000 Pages from Whistleblowers

We Love Trump-Doug Band is a Clinton Whistleblower

PJ Media-Clinton Appointed Judge Refuses to Unseal CF Whistleblower's Documents

Clinton Foundation-2020 Timeline for Whistleblowers

The Hill-FEDs received Whistleblower Evidence in 2017

Daily Mail-CF Whistleblowers claim Quid-Pro-Quo

PJ Media-Another Suspicious Body Drops around Hillary Clinton

FOX News-John Solomon on CF Whistleblowers (12/6/18)

LW Doyle-Financial Bounty Hunters

US House Oversight-A Case Study on the Clinton Foundation

Crossfire Hurricane Docs-Christopher Steele Binder

Justice-gov-2023 SC John Durham Report

'Clinton Mob': Teams of Enforcers / Spies / and Lawyers

To run any successful enterprise, one needs an integrated staff of professionals that operates seamlessly together. If you are dealing with a major criminal business enterprise, then caution and coordination becomes absolutely paramount. Rewarding the loyal is a keystone of a continued successful operation and kickbacks up to the boss is mandatory in the world of DC Swamp politics. President Trump would begin to extract revenge in 2022/2023 with his filing of a federal RICO lawsuit against HRC and many others who promoted the false Russian collusion narrative during the 2016 election cycle.

Post Q# 570
THEY NEVER THOUGHT SHE WOULD LOSE.

'Clinton 3-STEP' relies on the following defensive actions:
- Use friendly MSM for Intimidation
- Defame and Attack the Attacker's
- Oh That's "Old News" Trick

Post Q# 4782 on 9/28/20:
CLINTON FOUNDATION AT THE CENTER.

BC/HRC have both long relied on these '3-step' critical maneuvers along with selective memory issues to escape being legally trapped. BC didn't get but rather earned his iconic appropriate nickname of 'Slick Willy.' The magician's sleight of hand has been employed by the Clinton gang to fool the public while always doing something completely different behind closed doors. Least we never forget the past treasonous acts of Slick Willy giving the Chinese miniature Nuke tech and HRC gave Russia hypersonic missile tech. Odd that the events surrounding the Russian special military operation into Ukraine would bring the attention to several past political scandals involving the Clinton Mob.

Post Q# 3856
Define Evergreen [HRC USSS code name]
Non-standard definition.
Think depopulation.

For decades the public has witnessed the illegal activities of the Clinton Crime Cabal firsthand. Beginning back with Whitewater through the HRC email scandal, contributions flowed into their cash laundry machine-aka The Clinton Foundation (CF). The CF was caught in Haiti assisting Laura Silsby in trafficking children and now HRC is involved with charter flights involving Afghanistan refugees. Bestselling author Peter Schweizer gets credit for terming the Clintons as being masters of 'Disaster Capitalism' with their various grifting schemes.

Post Q# 2723
Chatter - Bill and Hillary's 'public' health will begin to rapidly deteriorate.

Misdirection and transference were the standard operating procedure with both HRC/BC. The CF was a setup front and operated as a global criminal 'pay to play' enterprise. A cooperative MSM has been the supportive foundation allowing the Clintons free reign for their political corruption schemes. Shuttered due to lack of donations in 2017, the CF/CGI started backup in 2022 under the guise of assisting Ukraine.

Post Q# 1959

CrowdStrike managed the infiltration program based on payments to CF.

Also don't forget the looting of the White House furniture due to the Clintons being flat broke. Clinton aide Eric Hothem spearheaded the theft of the people's property upon the Clinton's White House departure in 1999. Grifting of the populace had been refined to the professional ranks during the Clinton era of control.

Post Q# 4386

Expect us.

CLINTON ENABLERS/CRONIES:

- Larry Nichols: Self-confessed 'Hit Man' for the Clintons-admitted to several murders and recently died himself.
- Harold Ickes: Lawyer/Mob Union ties and W/H Counsel to Bill. Also, he started the Shadow Party w/Soros.
- Sid Blumenthal: Political Consultant and W/H Advisor to Bill. Sid Vicious is co-author of the 2nd Trump/Russia Dossier.
- •ack Palladino: Private Eye admits HRC paid him to harass Kathleen Willey and did work for Harvey Weinstein in recent years.

Post Q# 4333

HRC direct attack re: Q?

- James Carville: Lead strategist for Bill's presidential campaigns as well as in 2008 for HRC's campaign.
- Cody Shearer: Brother In-Law to Strobe Talbott and constant sidekick of Blumenthal. Co-author of the 2nd Dossier run through the State Dept.
- Anthony Pellicano: Private Eye hired exclusively to silence Bill's mistresses.
- Cheryl Mills: HRC's Chief of Staff and personal lawyer-a long list of coverups.
- Doug Band: W/H Advisor to Bill, owned Tenno, started Clinton Global Initiative and worked at the CF as the CEO.
- Marc Elias: Lawyer at Perkins Coie and served as General Counsel to both HRC and the DNC for several elections' cycles. Pushed the Fusion GPS phony Russian dossier(s) against Trump.
- Michael Sussmann: Lawyer at Perkins Coie who specializes in technology and cyber. Indicated by SC John Durham and was personal pal with CrowdStrike's Sean Henry as well as peddling the false Alfa Bank/Russian collusion server story.
- David Kendall: The main personal lawyer for Bill and Hillary since 1993. Personally, oversaw the sorting and deletions of HRC's emails.

Post Q# 3396

Re: BC/RC Epstein Plane Pic.
What age is RC in picture?
[15]

BC/HRC figured out early in the game, that to have a successful criminal organization you need crooked aides. Demonstrated in the creation of a permanent "War Room" regardless of being in or out of elected public office. This same combative mentality has followed the Clinton Crime gang from the jump.

Post Q# 3423

[Wheels Up] flight logs [CLAS 1-99] under investigation by FBI/DOJ?

The Clinton's have shown the ability to have any and all opposition silenced quickly (Arkancide). Very few if any whistleblowers have ever come out publicly against the Clinton Mob. We must not overlook the shady connections with Jeff Epstein and the infamous Lolita Express for international escapades and subsequent honey pot blackmail evidence. HRC would in 2023 publicly call for the Soviet-style 'de-programming' of Trump MAGA supporters. History will sadly show that both Bill and Hillary Clinton accepted foreign money from regimes like China/Russia/Iran/Saudi Arabia and others to sellout America.

Post Q# 3875
[Epstein]
The story goes much deeper [darker].

Rarer than unicorns flying, CF whistleblowers appeared on December 13, 2018, to testify before Congress. The House Subcommittee on Government Operations was focused on the "Oversight of Nonprofit Organizations" a case study on the CF. Perkins Coie/Clinton campaign lawyer Michael Sussmann lied to FBI James Baker about false Alfa Bank claims while being paid by HRC's 2016 campaign. Incredibly in 2023 the NWO 'elites' still rush to support and attend Clinton Global Initiative gala events.

Post Q# 4743
CRIMES AGAINST HUMANITY.

The U.S. Attorney in Little Rock began the investigation of the CF under BHO and was continued through the first Trump term. President Trump has cut off the international funding and the CF has been hemorrhaging donations ever since the 2016 election cycle. The Presidential election of 2020 demonstrated that the political clout of the Clintons has faded. Under the illegal Biden administration, many of the Clintons associates are back into governmental power.

Post Q# 3035
The Clinton Connection.
PAY-FOR-PLAY SPIDER WEB.

Recent CF financial statements reflect a $50m operating loss since the 2016. The legal glue that will bind all of these criminals will be RICO-RACKETEER INFLUENCED and CORRUPT ORGANIZATIONS ACT. SC John Durham's first criminal indictment of Perkins Coie/Clinton campaign lawyer Michael Sussmann connects HRC, DNC, and Google with the failed Russian collusion scheme. SC Durham submitted his final report in 2023 laying the basis for judicial accountability. With the re-election of President Trump in 2024, predictably Bill Clinton signals for a preemptive pardon for HRC by outgoing Biden.

Post Q# 4820
THE CLINTON FOUNDATION.
WHITE HOUSE FOR SALE.

Links

The Atlantic-Clinton Primer: From Whitewater to Benghazi

Just the News-HRC Plan tying Trump and Russia

FOX News-House Panel Subpoenas Clintons/Others in Epstein Probe

The Federalist-Unsealed Crossfire Hurricane Docs prove RussiaGate a Hoax

Clinton Foundation Timeline-2025: Trump Posts Video of Mysterious Deaths and Suicides

NY Post-Inside the Clinton Dossier

Pepe Lives Matter-Clinton Plundered Haiti through Guise of 'AID'

WSJ-The Totalitarian Heart of HRC

Just the News-HRC Factor: Evidence shows Russia Collusion Story Began/Ended with HRC

WSJ-The Clinton Foundation, State and Kremlin Connections

News Punch-Bill Clinton invited Epstein 17 Times to White House

Real Clear Politics-RussiaGate: HRC/Perkins Coie/Fusion GPS/CrowdStrike

NY Times-Clinton approves Technology Transfer to China

Corey's Digs-Rudy, RICO, and Clinton Inc: Racketeering

National Review: The Clintons: New York's Sixth Crime Family

The Sun-Clinton Tarmac Reporter Chris Sign is Dead

American Spectator-ChinaGate and the Clintons

Markets Work-CGI's closing Confirmations

The Millennium Report-The Clinton Crime Family

The Hill-Chelsea Clinton Reaps $9M from Corporate Board Position

WikiLeaks-CF and Pay to Play: HRC/Skippy Email Chains

C Reason-The Clinton Cabal

Breitbart-Journalist who Unveiled HRC's Spy Network

Video-Clinton Cash (Directors Cut)

Shad Budge-Clinton Body Count-Railroad Teen Murders

Observer-6 Clinton Foundation Scandals You need to Know

Video-The Clinton Chronicles

Crossfire Hurricane Docs-David Kendall Defensive Interview

Justice.gov-2023 SC John Durham Report

'Q' said "Important to Remember"— Ezra Cohen-Watnick

The one key governmental body that is not corrupt is our faithful U.S. Military/Military Intelligence (MI). President Trump gained entry with his own MI conduit (spy) directly into the Department of Justice. President Trump had sent Ezra Cohen-Watnick (ECW) back over to the Pentagon/DOD as Deputy Assistant Secretary (Counter Narcotics). Patel Patriot's excellent series on Devolution points out the key role that ECW would continue to play post President Trump's first term.

Post Q# 2462
> Who was assigned directly to SESSIONS by POTU?
> Mandate charged to Ezra Cohen-Watnick [Defense Intelligence]?
> NAT SEC ADVISOR TO SESSIONS [Counterintelligence and Counterterriosm]?

ECW is currently the chair (appointed by President Trump in 2020) of the Public Interest Declassification Board (PIDB) and has vowed to release very soon previously classified records related to events like JFK and 911. Ezra Cohen-Watnick has been under President Trump the National Security Adviser to the U.S. Attorney General. Cohen-Watnick had reported to AG Bill Barr after first assisting AG Jeff Sessions and then acting AG Matt Whitaker. ECW would ultimately finish President Trump's first term back over to the Pentagon where he had originally started.

Post Q# 1539
> Important to remember.
> decode: Q link to NY Mag article ECW

One of ECW's first primary tasks was to stop the unprecedented amount of MSM news reporters receiving top secret classified material leaks. Cohen-Watnick's unique high security clearance level allows unrestricted probing into every governmental computer system. President Trump had his own 'sniffer' trying to plug the almost daily White House leaks.

Post Q# 11
> Key:
> Military Intelligence v FBI/CIA/NSA.

ECW began at the Defense Intelligence Agency (DIA) as an analyst under General Mike Flynn. ECW was a rising star and became General Flynn's trusted protégée while serving under BHO at DIA. General Flynn would have a professional clash with BHO over the handling of ISIS as well as the Middle Eastern conflicts.

Post Q# 3702
> This is not another 4-year election.
> Game theory.

ECW was part of General Flynn's inner-circle known in intelligence circles as the 'FlynnStones.' This original core of Patriots is still performing heroic deeds on behalf of our country under the illegal Biden administration. True President Trump continues to lead all Patriots in the ongoing struggle to reclaim our Republic.

Post Q# 4620
> McMaster removal of 'loyalist' intel community _NAT SEC

Cohen-Watnick had received and still holds the highest level of top-secret security clearance ('Q' Level). ECW has often been termed as being way too young and at times brash and very ambitious. ECW just barrels ahead performing flawlessly for each task he has been assigned from Defense to the Justice Departments and back again.

Post Q# 144
Who has clearance to full picture?
What council do the Wizards and Warlocks control?

Appointed originally under BHO, ECW was assigned to General Mike Flynn in the Deference Intelligence Agency. ECW was one of the very few high-level carryovers into President Trump's new administration. Cohen-Watnick would show both a natural leadership ability as well as serious intelligence analysis.

Post Q# 2462
Who briefed Goodlatte and Gowdy on classified intel re: DOJ and FBI?
" _ _ "
Hint: (Ezra Cohen-Watnick)

ECW personally did many of the daily intelligence briefings during President Elect Trump's transition period. ECW has the full support from both POTUS and of course General Flynn/FlynnStone crew. These Intel briefs were key due to BHO deliberately withholding information to the Trump transition team in the fall of 2016.

Post Q# 1661
Think stages.
What role can MI play?
BANG!

Under NSA Director General Flynn, ECW was made part of President Trump's new National Security Council. ECW along with several other NSC members were later dismissed by the new NSA General McMaster. McMaster would personally hunt down for removal all of the loyal FlynnStones. The Deep State intentionally first targeted for instant removal General Flynn and his FlynnStones above all of the new Trump Administration.

Post Q# 3211
Bake your noodle.

ECW gets a White Hat Award for tipping off Devin Nunes on 3/21/17 to the past mass surveillance/unmasking. ECW and White House lawyer Michael Ellis brought Devin Nunes along with aide Kash Patel into the specifics of past surveillance crimes during the BHO reign. Ellis would again assist President Trump in preserving in a secure White House computer server the original transcript from the Ukrainian Presidential phone call from being altered.

Post Q# 2057
Ezra Cohen-Watnick.
BRIDGE connecting people.

On March 22, 2017, the infamous Rep. Devin Nunes presser was held on Capitol Hill and was the start of public discourse. Rep. Nunes had looked at BHO's Presidential Daily Brief (PDB) with Ezra/Ellis down in the White House Sensitive Compartmented Information Facility (SCIF). President Trump has said of Nunes, "This guy goes down into dungeons/basements, he'll find a document, no matter what."

Post Q# 4202
It's like having all the pieces of the puzzle but only after [news unlocks] can the puzzle [full picture] be put together.

'Q' has said ECW would later brief both Representatives Gowdy and Goodlatte on the discovered surveillance intelligence. Operation Latitude was the BHO designed dissemination of unmasking intel and fake Russia Dossier material via the widely distributed Presidential Daily Brief (PDB). Public exposure of this operation was thanks to Dr. Evelyn Farkas spilling the beans on MSNBC.

Post Q# 3463
Ezra Cohen-Warnick.

Rep. Devin Nunes found items like unmasked names, oppo research from Steele, FISA Title-1 warrants, illegally gained NSA FISA 702 Queries, and improperly obtained raw intelligence in umbrella HOPS coverage. BHO had led a massive illegal domestic spying operation against his perceived enemies using the weaponized police/intelligence agencies.

Post Q# 1126
Ezra re-emerges at Justice Dept.
decode: 'Q' linked NYT article about Ezra

President Trump had ordered ECW initially to be located at Attorney General's right hand at Justice before returning to the Pentagon. ECW had made a civilian stop at big tech giant Oracle in between his vital government gigs. Many in the Mockingbird media are asking if ECW is 'Q' and of course you already know his response.

Post Q# 4800
RED OCTOBER.

ECW has some 'FARM' CIA background training at Camp Perry and was sent by Flynn over to train in Afghanistan. ECW had returned to the place he first started back at the Pentagon/Department of Defense a the end of the first President Trump's first term. Cohen-Watnick was the Acting Under Secretary of Defense serving Secretary Chris Miller. With the historic re-election of President Trump in 2024, ECW will continue to offer sound advice to our new POTUS.

Post Q# 2462
Mandate charged to Ezra Cohen-Watnick [Defense Intelligence]?

'Q' has repeatedly pointed toward Ezra Cohen-Watnick as playing important roles in the future. ECW was put in charge by President Trump of the civilian Declassification Board in late 2020. ECW was pressuring the illegal Biden administration to release the final batch of JFK assassination files, but the files were punted yet again down the road of history. Special Counsel John Durham has dropped criminal indictments and submitted his final report in 2023. Reports from IG Horowitz and SC Durham will be the foundation for the coming justice phase and coming Judgement Day.

Post Q# 131
POTUS NAT SEC E briefing 3:02am

Links

Forward-3 Things About Ezra Cohen-Watnick

Know your Meme-RussiaGate: Ezra Cohen Watnick

Clinton Foundation Timeline-2025 Crossfire Hurricane Docs

PIDB-Public Interest Declassification Board: Members

Ezra Cohen Twitter/X-New US Army 4th PSYOP Video

Huffington Post -2 Officials that helped Devin Nunes get Intelligence Reports

Dauntless Dialogue-DEVOLVED: A New Cold War

Daily Beast-Infamous MAGA Figures Rush into Purged Pentagon

Bloomberg-Former Trump Aide who Left in Controversy Rejoins Pentagon

Daily Caller-Inside Ezra Cohen-Watnick's Future DOJ Role

Daily Mail-Ezra to Stop Cascade of DOJ Leaks

Breitbart-Ezra Cohen-Watnick Joins the DOJ under Sessions

Susan Whitney-Lets Get to Know Michael Ellis and Ezra Cohen-Watnick

NY Mag-Fired White House Official Hired by DOJ at Trump's Insistence

NY Times-Aide Ousted from White House Emerges at Justice

Washington Examiner-National Security Aide to join Justice

Haaretz-Meet 30-Year Old Ezra Cohen-Watnick

NBC-Meet the "FlynnStones"

NY Times-2 White House Officials give Nunes Intel Reports

Forward-Meet Ezra Cohen-Watnick: The Secret Source

Just Security-Ousted NSC Official takes Job at Oracle

Daily Beast (pre Q)-Inside the 'Q Group' Hunting Snowden

WAPO-NSC: Trump Loyalists at War with Career Aides (FlynnStones)

Clinton Foundation Timeline-SpyGate: Lead Investigator Kash Patel tells All

How Stuff Works-The SCIF

Crossfire Hurricane Docs-FISA Notes

Justice.gov-2023 SC John Durham Report

Earned his own 'Q' Drop: Meet Google's Jared Cohen

Jared Cohen went from HRC's U.S. State Department Policy and Planning staff, directly over to Eric Schmidt's Google in 2010. This poaching of high-level Clinton staffers would be repeated again by Schmidt with the hiring to run his vast charities of Eric Braverman back in 2016. Under the illegal Biden regime, Schmidt would pay for science staffers and continue to lobby on behalf of Big Tech. Jared Cohen would be hired in the summer of 2022 by Goldman Sachs, primarily to influence the political landscape on behalf of the firm and its clients.

Post Q# 2375
> Court order to preserve ALL data sent to GOOG?
> Think GOOG+ / Gmail / etc.
> Comms cleanup?
> The More You Know.

Cohen additionally serves as an Adjunct Senior Fellow at the Council of Foreign Relations. Jared Cohen has co-authored a book with Eric Schmidt using the snappy title, "The New Digital Age: Reshaping the Future of People, Nations and Businesses". This book did relatively well but the underlying theme is alarming to many observers.

Post Q# 839
> Do you trust Google?

When Cohen arrived at Google, he was put in charge of the new Google Ideas division. Google Ideas primary focus was on emerging technologies that will make the future a better place for all mankind. Alphabet like many of its Big Tech cohorts made a corporate decision to go 'Woke.' Alphabet operates Google/YouTube/GMail/and other businesses that teamed up to coordinate censorship/woke narratives.

Post Q# 964
> GOOG coming soon.
> TIDAL WAVE INCOMING.

Progressive Communist Leftist agendas have combined with modern technology, seemingly to improve the entire planet. Lock step Socialist's theory following upon the original community organizer Saul Alinsky's grand utopian vision. The illegal merger of government with partnered Big Tech/MSM, the birth of cancel culture and out of control censorship was the obvious outcome. It was revealed in 2024 that Google itself had interfered in past U.S. elections over 41 documented instances.

Post Q# 3798
> Play a game of 'Where Are They Now?'
> Think CEOs.
> THE BEST IS YET TO COME.

In late 2015 Eric Schmidt created a new Google company called Groundwork. Groundwork heavily assisted the 2016 HRC campaign in digital databases and targeting large social media platforms. Recall that Alphabet made a $100M financial investments into CrowdStrike background in 2015. Google along with their Big Tech partners would attempt to silence all opposition by coordinating complete censorship of all dissenting voices from the UniParty plans.

Post Q# 4105
> DARPA / FB / TWITTER / GOOG [D] coord and dev of [AI] tool in attempt to counter (your) reach [now public - see prev drop]

Julian Assange highlighted in published Wikileaks emails, that Google's Schmidt and Jared Cohen were assisting HRC's 2016 election campaign efforts. This was not startling news to anyone that had observed the actions by Google and could see the quid pro quo a President HRC offered to Schmidt/Cohen. What was successful overseas in changing 'minds' through propaganda, Google turned their money and algorithms into influencing American elections. Google unsuccessfully tried to elect HRC in 2016 but did influence over 6 million votes to Joe Biden in the 2020 Presidential election.

Post Q# 428
> Clown contribution in exchange for access code?
> Google home?

Cohen turned Google Ideas into a new company called Jigsaw. Jigsaw focused on developing interesting software applications to be used by various intelligence agencies around the globe. Enhanced AI programs can be used to effect public opinions or sway general elections. Working with the Defense Advanced Research Projects Agency (DARPA) and individuals such as General Stanley McCrystal, these terrorists targeting computer tools would be turned on the American public.

Post Q# 4516
> GOOG threat analysis group _entry catalogue.
> Deep dreaming, young dragonfly.

One huge Jigsaw design was a mapping/removal of content tool used to track dissidents and defectors in civil war conflicts was termed Altitude. This computer program could easily be switched from military to civilian use. Jared Cohen himself was on the ground in Egypt evaluating the effects with the Arab Spring. Scarily these military-grade algorithms developed by Alphabet/Jigsaw and deployed by Google/YouTube, were turned domestically to track and target perceived enemies of the DC 'Administrative' Deep State.

Post Q# 2587
> What if GOOG already gave access to China?

Chilling tracking concept when possibly applied to an entire general civilian population. Google has been working with North Korea and China in developing advanced internet civilian tracking censorship programs. Through these actions Jared Cohen earned the nickname of Google's 'Censorship Architect.' Assigned Special Counsel (SC) John Durham was tasked to investigating all elements of the SpyGate political scandal as well as the 2016 DNC computer intrusion. Google and Eric Schmidt would play key financing roles to the Democrats in the 2016/2020/and 2024 Presidential elections trying to thwart Donald Trump.

Post Q# 1947
> DEFEND GOOG AT ALL COSTS.
> GOOGLE TO BE REGULATED.

The Jigsaw program was put to work against Syrian President Bashar al-Assad in an effort to overthrow him. The Google Home is even a more evasive domestic consumer home voice-activated speaker using the Google Assistant platform. Big Tech is activity colluding with governmental intelligence agencies in eroding even more civil liberties via mass selective censorship. Records later revealed that both Jared Cohen and Eric Schmidt worked with HRC back in 2011 in planning the proposed 2014 political coup in Ukraine.

Post Q# 1024

> Coming to a theater near you.
> Jared Cohen.

When you look at the number of people associated with both Google/Clinton Foundation it is alarming. Through past connections you get 60 total people involved in some fashion with both organizations. SC John Durham indictment of Perkins Coie/Clinton campaign lawyer cyber expert Michael Sussmann set the stage. SC Durham submitted his final report in 2023. directly connects HRC, DNC, and Eric Schmidt from Alphabet/Google.

Post Q# 2587

> GOOG (upcoming) financial statements should receive extra scrutiny [10-Q].
> Follow the money.

Ironically in 2023 Alphabet/Google cut the staff at Jigsaw to a 'skeleton crew' to focus on more profitable companies. The 'Spider Web' is messy and tangled to be sure. The Justice Department has hit Google with a huge antitrust lawsuit. President Trump has filed a major class action lawsuit against Alphabet/Google. With the re-election of President Trump in 2024, the 'White Hats' will start to drain the Swamp and usher in the Great Awakening.

Post Q# 3584

> GOOG whistleblower
> Project Deep Dream?

Links

Guardian-Google's Jared Cohen Interview

FOX News-Trump 1.0 Alums Share Chilling Google Message

Revolver News-Worst Snakes still Hate Assange

Forbes-Google Cuts Jigsaw to a 'Skeleton Crew'

VICE News-Google's Jigsaw became a Toxic Mess

Transcend-US Gov't Perpetuated 2014 Coup in Ukraine

NY Post-Google Interfered in US Elections 41 Times

FOX News-Former Google CEO Emerges as Key Democratic Power Player

Breitbart-Goldman Sachs Teams Up with Google's 'Director of Regime Change'

Wired-Altitude: Terrorism Content Removal Tool

Daily Mail-Google Billionaire Eric Schmidt has PAID the Salaries of Biden's Science Office

PJ Media-Analysis Shows Google Steered 6 Million Voters to Biden in 2020

FOX News-DEMs Deploying DARPA Information Warfare Tool

Breitbart-Eric Schmidt Pushes Deeper Ties between Big Tech and Defense Industry

NBC News-Eric Schmidt and Jared Cohen meet Pope Francis

Fast Company-Can Alphabet's Jigsaw solve Google's Vexing Problems?

CNET-Eric Schmidt (lead Google) has Left the Company

Breitbart-Assange says Google Engaged the HRC Campaign

Revolver-Meet General Deploying Military Grade Information Warfare Tools

Breitbart-4 Times Google was directly Linked to HRC

Daily Mail-Does Google Basically Work for the White House

The Independent-Google helped Syrian Rebels bring down Assad

Time-100 Most Influential People 2013: Jared Cohen

CFR-Adjunct Senior Fellow: Jared Cohen

Tuffs Fletcher School-Schmidt and Cohen: "The New Digital Age"

Crossfire Hurricane Docs-State Department Steele Binder

Justice.gov-2023 SC John Durham Report

President Trump's Influential Mentor: Meet Roy Cohn

Starting back in antiquity with the ancient Greeks, the mentoring of the young was encouraged civilization wide. Lucky were those individuals that were educated and mentored by the tribal elders. No question that lawyer Roy Cohn (1927-1986) had skeletons in his closet, but a young Donald Trump obviously took the good advice from this mentor. Many would theorize that the infamous 2023 Georgia 'mug shot' of President Trump reflects a little of the Roy Cohn New York 'Mob Gangster-Style' influence.

> **Post Q# 1145**
> Trust POTUS.

Donald Trump was extremely fortunate to have a mentor relationship with lawyer Roy Cohn beginning back in 1973. Cohn was an established New York power broker as well as a successful famed MOB lawyer.

> **Post Q# 14**
> What must occur to allow for civilian trials?

Roy Cohn has famously been involved with both the Rosenberg's trial/execution and with the infamous McCarthy hearings of the 1950's. Cohn was Chief Counsel to Senator Joe McCarthy during the communism scare and was at McCarthy's side during the public hearings.

> **Post Q# 1831**
> Does POTUS make statements that are false?

President Trump admits that Roy Cohn planted the seeds of public office back in 1984 and that was the first time he considered entering into presidential politics. Don't forget at the time Donald Trump sued the NFL over the new USFL and eventually won a ceremonial $1.00 court victory judgement.

> **Post Q# 151**
> How do you capture a dangerous animal?
> Nothing is as it appears.

Roy Cohn helped young Donald Trump as his personal lawyer with many successful large real estate development ventures. Cohn helped to guide our beloved POTUS through the treacherous corporate construction world. Roy Cohn is credited with helping Donald Trump in securing union contracts and political approvals in his various New York City skyscrapers building projects including famed Trump Tower.

> **Post Q# 4076**
> This is about regaining POWER.
> Every asset deployed.
> WIN OR DIE.

Cohn cemented his three pillars of success into Trump's inner being. The pillars begin to always attack, then counterattack, and never ever apologize. Roy Cohn's death from HIV/Aids has always been in question by his close friends. 'The Apprentice' would be a 2024 movie (Jermy Strong as Cohn) featuring the life of President Trump and highlighted subsequent relationship lawyer Roy Cohn with a young Donald Trump.

> **Post Q# 2333**
> Nothing to See Here.....

Characteristics like hitting your attacker back ten times harder and to win at all costs were core values instilled by Roy Cohn into the young Trump. You can observer characteristics of "The Art of War" laced into the philosophy of our President Trump. The Great Awakening is integral to the plan to save our Republic and citizen Donald Trump accepted the challenge. The MSM's coverup of Hunter Biden's 'Laptop from Hell' is a classic example of the manipulation of the news media to creative false narratives.

Post Q# 4543
Loyalists _critical.
Remember your oath.
Defend and protect at all costs.

Roy Cohn's careful legal mentoring has had a big-league influence on Donald Trump. It can be said with the luxury of hindsight that Cohn was indeed a modern day 'king maker', reflected in his protege's rise to the U.S. Presidency. Judgement Day is coming and Special Counsel John Durham submitted his final report in 2023. With the historic re-election of President Trump in 2024, many feel past hidden political secrets will finally be revealed.

Post Q# 14
How is POTUS always 5-steps ahead?

Links

Politico- "He will Brutalize for You"

BBC-Roy Cohn: Mysterious Lawyer who Helped Donald Trump Rise to Power

The Federalist-How Media Covered the Russia Hoax vs. Hunter Biden's Laptop

New Yorker-Eavesdropping on Trump and Roy Cohn

Rolling Stone-Real Life Mob Families of 'The Irishman': Donald Trump Knew Them

Vanity Fair-How Trump/Cohn Symbiosis Changed the World

CNBC-FBI releases Files on President Trump's late Lawyer

Daily Caller-What Roy Cohn taught Donald Trump

People's World-Donald Trump's Mentor was Roy Cohn

NY Mag-The Original Donald Trump

Deadline-Roy Cohn: Right Hand of McCarthy and Trump's Lawyer

Esquire-Donald Trump Interview: Where's my Roy Cohn?

Daily Mail-All the Lawyers Counseling President Trump

NPR-President Trump Calls for Roy Cohn

The Guardian-Man Who Taught Trump Power of Publicity

History-1951 The Rosenberg Trial Begins

Quod Verum-Endgame: POTUS Trump's Vindication Nears

Time-Donald Trump's Mug Shot

Crossfire Hurricane Docs-Christopher Steele Binder

FBI Scribe and Office Matchmaker: Meet Randy Coleman

Randy Coleman was the FBI's Director of Counterintelligence (CI) and was a notable scribe when it came to taking notes. Coleman recommended agent Peter Strzok to run the HRC probe and to have lawyer Lisa Page be Strzok's liaison with FBI Deputy Director Andy McCabe (matchmaking 101). President Trump would file in 2022 a federal RICO lawsuit against McCabe/Strzok/Page/and others related to the promotion of the false Russian collusion narrative during the 2016 election cycle.

Post Q# 3990
THE FEDERAL BUREAU OF "INVESTIGATION"
Randy Coleman - Assistant Director Counterintelligence Div-REMOVED.

Coleman was Peter Strzok's immediate boss prior to Bill Priestap taking over in December 2016. Randy Coleman conveniently setup Lisa Page to work closely with Peter as they performed their intelligence tradecraft make believe love affair.

Post Q# 2365
[Pg 294].

[Meeting between Comey and Coleman on October 4].

Hillary Clinton and Foundation.
Crime Against Children.

IG Horowitz's 1.0 report outlined on page 294, some of Coleman's notes from a 10/4/16 meeting in Director James Comey's office. Randy Coleman made a comprehensive presentation briefing for Comey on the discovered forensic date from Anthony Weiner's laptop.

Post Q# 1180
'Insurance File.'

According to Coleman's documented notes, Weiner's laptop contained not only hundreds of thousands of emails but disturbing illegal sexual material. Randy Coleman would record evidence that exists in Weiner's recorded data for "Crime Against Children."

Post Q# 1978
How might this OPEN THE DOOR to [Weiner] / [Huma] / [HRC].

Of odd note was the apparent speed at which the FBI reviewed over 600,000 emails of these Weiner/Abedin records. James Comey would later comment this extraordinary pace was "Thanks to the wizardry of our technology,"

Post Q# 4343
2 + 2 = 5?

Most of the emails were between Weiner's wife Huma Abedin and HRC involving official government work. Besides the numerous classified/top secret emails, recovered were sensitive Special Access Programs (SAP). Coleman and Strzok handled the July 2016 FBI deposition of HRC.

Post Q# 1807
Randy Coleman?
GREATEST COVER UP IN US HISTORY.

No agent on the investigation team or their immediate FBI supervisors, had required top secret clearances to even touch any of the discovered SAP. The originator agencies have the final say and to this day many still have refused permission on several SAP emails.

Post Q# 1371
>   Did they view the Insurance file?

Remember that James Comey and Andy McCabe would 'sit on' this information for almost one full month. It would not be until days before the 2016 Presidential election that Comey would reopen the HRC email probe. Much of the 7th floor headquarters of the FBI/DOJ's top management is connected in some fashion to the false Russia narrative of the 2016 Presidential election cycle.

Post Q# 1978
WHY WAS THE INFORMATION ON WEINER'S LAPTOP IN THE FIRST PLACE?

Convicted sex offender Anthony Weiner and estranged wife Huma Abedin had a computer folder marked 'Insurance File.' Blackwater's Erik Prince has said publicly that sickening sexual material was discovered by NYPD/FBI in that particular computer program file. Assigned Special Counsel (SC) John Durham has slowly been developing a vast 'Joint Venture Conspiracy' involving the 2016 surveillance of Team Trump and the criminal political scandal becoming known as SpyGate.

Post Q# 4598
>   [note the pen]
>   You have more than you know.

Coleman is currently the Chief Security Officer at industrial giant Caterpillar. Some Anons have questioned a SEC probe of Caterpillar and the link back to Priestap's wife Melissa Hodgman. Randy Coleman was friends and worked at the FBI with Shawn Henry the COO of CrowdStrike. SC John Durham's indictment of Perkins Coie/Clinton campaign lawyer Michael Sussmann connects directly to CrowdStrike and many others.

Post Q# 2692
>   Re-read drops re: 'Midyear.'
>   OIG........and review graphics.

Coleman left just prior to POTUS taking office and is a part of the cleaned out corrupt 7th Floor at the Department of Justice. SC Durham has dropped criminal indictments and submit his final report in 2023, signaling the oncoming Judgement Day. With the historic re-election of President Trump in 2024, we all expect the return to the rule of law and the Great Awakening!

Post Q# 3921
>   FISA INDICTMENTS = START

Links

Brass Balls-Caterpillar Hired Strzok's Boss to Stop SEC Probe

Just the News-FBI Timeline Exposes Political Corruption

FOX News-Patel found Thousands of Sensitive Trump Russia Probe Docs

Clinton Foundation Timeline-FBI Revelations Show the Mueller Special Counsel was a Cover-Up

The Federalist-Unsealed Crossfire Hurricane Docs prove RussiaGate a Hoax

The Last Refuge-Key Brennan Email to Comey and Strzok

The American Spectator-John Durham and the Steele Dossier

Brother Street Joy-Randy Coleman/Weiner Laptop

Gray's Economy-Weiner's 'Insurance File'

The Last Refuge-SpyGate: The Big Picture

Markets Work-A Listening of Participants

Clinton Foundation Timeline-Randy Coleman

Washington Examiner-Officials Upset at BHO's Comments About HRC's Emails

Senate Judicial Committee: 2021 Crossfire Hurricane DECLAS

Crossfire Hurricane Docs-Christopher Steele Binder

Justice.gov-2023 DC John Durham Report

Paul Combetta: Infamous BleachBit and Reddit Promoter

Both Reddit and BleachBit can be thankful to Platte River Network's (PRN) IT Tech Paul Combetta. Combetta gave big-league huge national media exposure during his Congressional testimony. The Clinton crime family always has relied upon the technical assistance of dubious computer experts. Special Counsel (SC) John Durham dropped criminal indictments and submitted his final report in 2023. The entire Deep State is an ongoing coordinated effort by many governmental officials to prevent past accountability (coverups) while continuing the unrelenting attacks against President Trump.

Post Q# 4078
> Locked on target [painted].
> Planned and immediate.

Combetta made several requests to the Anons via Reddit for technical computer program information. Paul (aka 'Stonetear') Combetta requested programs dealing with both email stripping tools as well as total data deletion computer software. PRN worked with data storage firm Datto, Inc. in off-site backup of the Clinton server.

Post Q# 2076
> Pages 33 and 34.
> The More You Know......

Paul Combetta gets credit for making BleachBit a common household name. Combetta indirectly has coined both terms of "Oh Shit Guy" and "A Very VIP." Not often does one person claim credit in starting several catchy and ultimately trending national phrases. HRC's computer server and associated emails are the central focus point of the start of the initial crime that has led to the many coverup related operations with the political scandal known as SpyGate.

Post Q# 4616
> NOTHING CAN STOP WHAT IS COMING.
> NOTHING.

This of course led to a lot of folks discovering what the heck exactly was BleachBit. Additionally, it brought Reddit back into the MSM notoriety like that of FBIAnon and the Silk Road days. The 'Q' informational drops would bring Reddit back into the worldwide spotlight. SC John Durham announced in March 2022 that his probe includes the DNC computer intrusion during the 2016 election cycle.

Post Q# 3634
> [D]'s (internal) infiltration issue(s) w/protecting NAT SEC?
> Deliberate?
> Clinton server - China relay

Paul Combetta got into legal hot water when he deliberately deleted all of HRC's emails and electronic data. Combetta oversaw the host server that Platte River Networks operates for HRC's backups. After HRC left government service she needed a new private computer company to handle the Clinton server.

Post Q# 1223
> Think private email addresses.
> They think they are cleaver.

This deletion came while PRN had received from Congress both subpoenas for all data and an extra preservation order for all technical records and history of all system backups. The possibility of China hacking HRC's server, was already known to the FBI via prior briefings.

Post Q# 559
    Nothing is ever truly erased/deleted.

Fortuitously indeed that Paul Combetta received from FBI Director James Comey an Immunity deal for his apparent crimes. Director Comey and the loyal FBI always to the rescue, historically bailing out HRC and her staffers. Datto storage had done full back up operations to the Clinton sever and FBI's Peter Strzok would psychically remove this server from Datto and keep for his coverup scheme.

Post Q# 453
    (including her 33,000 illegally deleted emails)

decode: HRC emails were under a Congressional subpoena and all data was included in a preservation order not to be deleted or erased.

Post Q# 1818
    Did they ask Combetta for advice?

IG Horowitz's 2.0 report focused in on the FISA abuses by underlings of BHO/HRC. Watch for Paul Combetta/Cheryl Mills/Heather Samuelson/John Bentel/and Brian Pagliano to seek future cooperation deals as the truth gets exposed . With the re-election of President Trump in 2024, Judgement Day is coming soon as the Great Awakening continues.

Post Q# 438
    HRC SAPs (private server).
    EVIL.

Links

Daily Caller-US House seeks Charges against Paul Combetta

PJ Media-Bombshell Report Reveals about HRC Email Scandal

The Federalist-Unsealed Crossfire Hurricane Docs prove RussiaGate a Hoax

Real Clear Investigations-The Apparent Trump-Hillary Double Standard: For Her

Clinton Foundation Timeline -Platte River Networks Employee Deletes all Clinton Emails

Daily Mail-Security Farce at Datto Inc that held Hillary Clinton's Emails

Town Hall-HRC's IT Guy Created an Encrypted Gmail Account

Ivan Pentchoukov-Paul 'BleachBit' Combetta

AP News-Witnesses refuse to Testify in Hearing (HRC's Emails)

PJ Media-Platte Rivers Network Employee expressed Concern over HRC Emails

Judicial Watch-Fitton Victory: Court Orders HRC Deposition on Emails/Benghazi

Washington Examiner-Gohmert: Unclear if HRC IT Aide is Lying

Epoch Times-HRC's Emails sent to Address of a China Company

Breitbart-Gowdy: Tantamount to Letting Trigger Man go Free

FOX News-DOJ grants Immunity to Combetta

Daily Caller-The Immunized Five

US News-Combetta May have asked for Reddit Help

Clinton Foundation Timeline-Paul Combetta Immunity Deal

Epoch Times-SpyGate the Inside Story

Poynter Institute-Bleach and Hammers

Platte Rivers Network-Employee Spotlight: Paul Combetta

Grassley.Senate.gov-Security Incidents Related to HRC Emails

Crossfire Hurricane Docs-HRC Lawyer Defensive Briefing

Justice.gov-2023 SC John Durham Report

Goodies Found in 'Leakin Lying' James Comey's FBI Office Safe

IG Michael Horowitz issued a report on a separate investigation into 'Leakin' FBI Director James Comey [JC] back in 2018. James Comey's leaking of his infamous classified personal 'memos' and lying to Congress is not going to be prosecuted (this crowd is always escaping justice) at this time. Special Counsel (SC) John Durham was tasked to explore IG Horowitz's several criminal referrals and indictments have been dropped. President Trump named Comey along with HRC/DNC/Perkins Coie/and others in his 2022 federal RICO lawsuit stemming from the illegal activities surrounding the SpyGate political scandal.

Post Q# 1828
[SPY OP].
[DNI] [JC].

'Leakin' James Comey is a tall, strange dude that has displayed in the past very questionable memory issues while giving sworn Congressional testimony. IG Horowitz/SC Durham will see what other assorted criminal baggage resides in James Comey's dark closet. Like all longtime DC Swamp creatures Director Comey has done many political favors in his decades at the DOJ. It would be revealed in 2024 by a whistleblower that [JC] placed 'Honeypot' agents into President Trump's 2016 campaign, thus solidifying the online information of nefarious operations by the Deep State via 'Q' drops.

Post Q# 4110
[Brennan] and [Comey] assessment [Clapper assist] [hard-push]?

Since being fired without advance notice some interesting items were discovered in Director Comey's FBI office safe. Found in Comey's safe that is of huge interest was a special white binder simply labeled 'Clinton Emails.' It strains credulity to accept Comey's many public claims as to not seeing any criminality when you are holding the evidence in your FBI office safe. It would later be learned that James Comey had secret rooms within the FBI headquarters building that incriminating evidence was hidden in 'burn bags.'

Post Q# 2805
Drop put you on notice?
Traitor's Justice.

We are now discovering that the Deep State coup plotters were planning on the Comey Memos being an 'obstruction trap.' They all knew conspiracy was a non-starter, so they went with Plan B with the old reliable entrapment scheme against then President Trump. Drafting a fictional account of a top-secret Presidential meeting afterwards is typical of back covering corrupt bureaucrats.

Post Q# 3865
Bigger [slam-dunk] charges coming?

Fired FBI Director [JC] has admitted to sitting on critical evidence during several ongoing criminal probes. Exemplified by the one-month delay in reviewing the thousands of classified emails found on Weiner/Abedin's laptop. Comey and his FBI co-conspirators underlings like Peter Strzok assisted in the cover up of the Weiner/Abedin laptop. History would show that Comey's personal friend, Columbia professor Daniel Richman, regularly leaked classified information to the media to shape RussiaGate collusion false narratives on behalf of FBI Director Comey.

Post Q# 1912
> Will you stand tall or cower?
> Smile for the camera.
> Patriots in control.

James Comey attended the infamous Oval Office meeting on 1/5/2017 where Obama/Biden instructed Sally Yates and Comey to sabotage the incoming Trump administration. History will show that during this time period the total rot at the highest levels of the FBI/DOJ took root. As FBI Director Chris Wray cleans out the remnants of the 7th Floor, let's look back at some infamous James Comey's historical FBI lowlights:

- HRC Exhortation-Mid Year Exam.
- Comey had a private non-Gov email.
- Signed Many/Approved all FISA warrants.
- Weiner/Abedin Laptop-held 1 month.
- HRC Foreign (China) Server Intrusion.
- Told Rep. Stefanik he didn't notify Congress about Trump Investigation.
- Admitted under oath to 'Leaking.'
- Placed 2 FBI 'Honeypot' agents into 2015/16 Trump Campaign.
- Ignored NSA Berger's Archives Theft.
- Removal/Distribution of the Classified Comey-Trump Presidential Memos.
- Killed the Assange Immunity Deal.
- Montgomery Whistleblower Case.

Post Q# 4310

What was really discussed during [Jan 5] meeting?

Dennis Montgomery was an intelligence contractor with CIA and NSA. Montgomery was tasked with developing new surveillance programs like the infamous 'Hammer' (HAMR) mass collection supercomputer and the 'Scorecard' software program that can alter election computations.

Post Q# 2164

How do you inflict MAX PAIN / DAMAGE?

> drop/release MOAB?

Dennis Montgomery copied over 600 million classified files onto 47 hard drives in 2015. Montgomery went the internal government 'Whistleblower' route in an effort to expose NSA/CIA wrongdoing. At one period in time, governmental whistleblowers were held in high esteem by the news media as well as law enforcement.

Post Q# 2323

Did James Baker just testify behind closed doors [RR] and [JC] coordinate to appoint Mueller?

Montgomery made the mistake (unlike Snowden) of going to the FBI with this evidence of illegal domestic data collection. When it appeared that the FBI might turn on him, Dennis Montgomery made the difficult choice of going public with this classified information. [JC] as well as much of the FBI leadership has developed an earned mistrust by a majority of the American public.

Post Q# 3599
> A Higher Loyalty [Y].

Dennis Montgomery sought immunity from the DOJ under the Federal Whistleblower status. Montgomery was later granted immunity by AUSA Deborah Curtis for testimony and gave up the stolen hard drives. James Comey routinely had his name deliberately misspelled to read 'Corney' in a preemptive maneuver to avoid future FOIA requests. Bizarrely James Comey also insert two female FBI Agents into the 2015/16 Trump Campaign hoping to entrap 'Team Trump' staff via 'honeypot' operatives.

Post Q# 2943
Anons IDEN the 'error' made re: Corney v Comey?

Comey/Mueller exonerated NSA Sandy Berger after he stole National Archive document. Older tales but still demonstrate Comey's sorted history and pressure tactics often employed. It was revealed in 2024 the U.S. Intel community requested its FIVE EYES (FVEY) foreign intelligence partners to illegally spy (bump) targeted Team Donald Trump aides back in 2015 helping the FBI to start the phony Trump-Russia investigation.

Post Q# 10
Why did Comey drop CF?
decode: CF = Clinton Foundation.

One classic drop was about JC's use through Twitter of secret code words.

Post Q# 645
JC Tweet Translation.

Issues exist with Strzok ignoring foreign intrusion (China) evidence within HRC's computer server and stored metadata. FBI Director Comey sat on the Weiner/Abedin laptop classified emails until just days before the 2016 general election. Obviously trying to play both sides is a classic political DC 'Swamp Creature' move by Comey not knowing HRC would absolutely win this late in the campaign. Elon Musk's Twitter Files would expose the extend the FBI went to censor free speech. SpyGate villains like Comey, McCabe and Strzok have been rewarded with cushy TV gigs and lucrative book deals.

Post Q# 2365
[Pg 294]
[Meeting between Comey and Coleman on October 4].

IG Horowitz's 1.0 report reignited the Weiner/Abedin 'Insurance File' emails/sex crimes against children issues. Additionally, the Clinton Foundation's 'pay to play' schemes are under current ongoing grand jury federal investigations. James Comey had predictable 'memory loss' during his public testimony at several Congressional hearings. Many of the various political scandals that [JC] had an active role, will come to light via the criminal probes out of the Special Counsel's office.

Post Q# 3121
James Comey picture - Placeholder

Horowitz 2.0 report highlighted many illegal activities involved with the Carter Page FISA warrants. The grand finale everyone is waiting for are the continued SC John Durham has dropped indictments and submitted his final report in 2023. The highly coordinated coup conspiracy of 2016 will bring the Director Comey and the entire 7th floor of the FBI back to center public stage. With the re-election of President Trump in 2024, nothing can stop what is coming, nothing!

Post Q# 2156

Panic in DC.

Comey in communication w/McCabe re: 'testimony' 'story.'

Links

WAPO-Timeline: James Comey Decision Making on HRC Probe

PJ Media-James Comey's Blackmail Treachery against Trump

Just the News-Comey Media Mole told FBI He Shaped Russia Narrative

FOX News-Patel found Thousands of Sensitive Trump Russia Probe Docs

NY Post-FBI Launches Criminal Investigations of James Comey/John Brennan

Just the News-Jim Jordan Timeline: Comey Spying on Trump's 2016 Campaign

Washington Times-FBI James Comey had 'Honeypot' Operatives Infiltrate Trump Campaign

Lee Smith-BHO's January 5th Conspiracy

Markets Work-How Much did Brennan/BHO/Comey Know before Investigation Opened

Tablet Magazine-How the FBI Hacked Twitter

Real Clear Investigations-FBI Comey Misled Congress's 'Gang of 8' over RussiaGate

Millennium Report-The Hammer Ultra Secret Supercomputer

Brass Balls-James Comey Named to HSBC Board

Buster Hyde-James Comey and Clinton Cabal

Markets Work-Highlights: IG's Report on James Comey

The Last Refuge-Mid Year Review/Exam

The American Report-Woolsey/Brennan/Clapper/and Comey framed Trump

Video-Rep. Elise Stefanik Grills James Comey

The Federalist-Obama/Biden Oval Office Meeting on 1/5/2017

Lew Rockwell-Twin Pillars of RussiaGate Crumble

Google Docs-SpyGate Deep State's Timeline

The American Report-John Brennan's "Fusion Center" Fable

CBS News-Trey Gowdy grills James Comey over HRC Emails

FBI.Vault.Gov-FISA Surveillance Court Applications

Scribe-FBI Declaration about James Comey's Memos

Crossfire Hurricane Docs-James Comey Text Messages

Justice.gov-2023 SC John Durham Report

Trump's CFIUS Said NO
Under BHO and Biden 'NO Problem'

President Trump had vowed to tighten up all future Committee on Foreign Investment (CFIUS) requests. This certainly had not been the case for CFIUS under the past traitorous reign of BHO and now Biden. Time will tell how the CFIUS board members will handle the interests of our country under the new Biden administration. The 2022 Russian special military operation into Ukraine would back into the spotlight past international sketchy deals like Uranium One and Skolkovo. History will show that under both BHO and Biden administrations, international deals were made with the mortal enemies of the United States.

Post Q# 1306
SUM OF ALL FEARS.

The CFIUS BOARD is tasked to safeguard critical resources like:
- Manufacturing
- Finance and Information
- Mining and Utilities
- Wholesaler and Retail Trade

Post Q# 1220
Clinton Foundation conflicts of interest.

HRC under BHO would start the Russian Reset agenda back in 2009 with the Skolkovo technology project where in fact our hypersonic missile information would be transferred to Russia. Peter Schweizer's "Clinton Cash" first raised the alarm over the Clinton Foundation's (CF) large donations related to the Uranium One (U1) sale. Under BHO/HRC, the CFIUS Board gave approval for the sale of U1 to the Russian government owned Rosatom in 2013.

Post Q# 4820
THE CLINTON FOUNDATION.
WHITE HOUSE FOR SALE.

Of odd timing was the fact Bill Clinton was paid $500k for a speech by Renaissance Capital in Moscow during this same period. This pricey speech was just a few months prior to the CFIUS final U1 committee vote. Of similar strange note was that Russia sold its entire financial stake in Uranium One shortly before their 2022 special military operation into Ukraine.

Post Q# 2643
TRUTH AND TRANSPARENCY IS THE ONLY WAY FORWARD.

Renaissance Capital has direct ties to Putin/Russian FSB Intelligence sources. Russians paid Slick Willy 3 times his normal appearance/speech fee for this very short Moscow talk. Overpaying for personal speaking appearances is a classic method of influence peddling to political figures.

Post Q# 3605
PAY-FOR-PLAY only works when you hold a position of POWER.

The information from William Campbell, the FBI UC confidential informant, was directly told to FBI Director Mueller. The FBI was advised of the illegal bribery and kickbacks occurring directly around the pending U1 deal.

Post Q# 953
> TRUMP ADMIN v2?
> PUBLIC AWAKENING.

Mueller/DOJ deliberately withheld these whistleblowers reported crimes surrounding the U1 deal from the CFIUS panel. William Campbell went several years' operating undercover and reporting the U1 shenanigans to the FBI. Campbell's Russian handlers were the same running the ten spies under the FBI's Operation Ghost Stories, which was made famous in the hit TV series called the 'Americans'.

Post Q# 2576
> Those who 'knowingly' broke the law in a coordinated effort [treason] are the most vocal.

CFIUS has a lot of power and can sway approvals by flexing it's given muscle on select deals. Conversely panel members can deliberately ignore glaring warning signs and green light those special proposals. We must examine the underlining political reasons for the approvals of these questionable foreign deals confirmed by the CFIUS panel.

Post Q# 3168
> Nobody walks away from this.

Only the current POTUS can approve a sale, while CFIUS directs a recommendation to POTUS one way or the other. HRC and Mueller made sure of the final vote by the manipulation of the U1 evidence.

Post Q# 4360
> Insurrection Act of 1807.

BHO's CFIUS BOARD MEMBERS:
> • Hillary Clinton (State)
> • Eric Holder (DOJ)
> • Janet Napolitano (DHS)
> • Tim Geithner (Treasury)
> • Bob Gates (Defense)
> • Penny Pritzker (Commerce)
> • Steven Chu (Energy)
> • John Holdren (Science/Technology)

Post Q# 4158
> INSURGENCY.

BHO had his finger on the scales with the U1 sale, as it helped both his and HRC's 2009 Russian Reset efforts and global NWO plans. U1 greased the path for BHO's signature Iranian Nuclear Deal. History will show that both BHO and Biden attempted to either attack or befriend Putin/Russia, all while the real true relationship was with President Trump.

Post Q# 3837
> BIGGER THAN YOU CAN IMAGINE.
> More than selling of Uranium.

March 6, 2009 in Geneva HRC gave to Russian Minister Lavrov a red plastic button that was to read 'Reset' to symbolize a new era of peace. This phony 'Russian Reset' story gave the Mockingbird MSM ammunition to sway the unwashed public in false narratives. Citizens were convinced that giving Russia 20% of our uranium reserves was a very good thing indeed after all.

Post Q# 194

U1-CA-EU-ASIA-IRAN/NK.

We can't forget Robert Mueller's direct involvement in famed FBI "Ghost Stories". Bob Mueller caught ten Russian spies in an operation that would become a hit TV series. FX's "The Americans" is based on real life family sets of Russian spies from this event.

Post Q# 46

Why is the information re: BO important re: U1 and export approval to Canada to EU?

One of these Russian spies got very close to HRC before the entire family spy ring was captured. Quickly and quietly the 10 spies ultimately were exchanged for 4 captured US/UK intelligence assets.

Post Q# 4620

[infiltration]
Traitors everywhere.
Welcome to the Revolution.

HRC wanted everything to go away fast and with little to coverage from the MSM. Mueller acted as a transport 'mule' for BHO/HRC, when he personally flew several uranium ore test samples over to Europe for inspection.

Post Q# 2087

Those who are the loudest.....
Have the most to FEAR [hide]?

By sending FBI Director Mueller with the sample to inspect for strength prior to the sale, it signaled to Vlad that the deal was cool indeed. Top level criminals need reassurance when involved in major financial transactions.

Post Q# 3181

BLIND JUSTICE UNDER THE LAW WILL RETURN TO OUR REPUBLIC.
There is a reason why a sword is held.

'Q' has mentioned Uranium One deal many times for extra emphasis. The $145 million-dollar total kickback to the Clinton Foundation is record breaking even among thieves. Special Counsel (SC) John Durham was tasked with reviewing criminal referrals from IG Horowitz related to HRC/CF/DNC/and many others.

Post Q# 1345

U1.
Risk the welfare of the world.
U1 [donation to CF].

HRC was BHO's quarterback and was allowed to skim the kickbacks via the Clinton Foundation. Frank Giustra (U1) was already well known and was welcomed into the 'Pay to Play' deal by that administration. Let's see how the illegal Biden administration handles future CFIUS national security inquiries. SC Durham has dropped criminal indictments and submitted his final report in 2023 as Judgement Day quickly approaches. With the re-election of President Trump in 2024, Putin will be a key partner in stabilizing Uranium as well as Ukraine.

Post Q# 3673

It was over before it began.

Links

FOX News-BHO Era Uranium One Deal

Badlands Media-The Biggest Cover Up in American History

Just the News-The BHO/Biden/HRC Nuclear Giveaway to Russia

The Hill-FBI Uncovered Russian Bribery Plot before CIFUS Approval

Defcon News-Russia Sold its Stake in Uranium One before Invading Ukraine

Just the News-Uranium: How Russia got stronger as Bidens/Clintons got Richer

The Hill-U1 Informant makes Clinton Allegations

Clinton Foundation Timeline-2025 Crossfire Hurricane Docs

Victor Davis Hanson-Russia Russia Forever

WSJ-The Clinton Foundation, State and Kremlin Connections

Breitbart-Uranium One: 7 Facts

National Law Review-Trump and CFIUS

Holland and Knight-New CFIUS Regulations take Effect

Jonathan Turley-Brennan briefed BHO: "A Means of Distracting the Public"

Markets Work-Russian Collusion: Corruption, HRC, and BHO

Breitbart-Clinton Cash in Uranium One Deal

Larry Beech-Uranium One and CrowdStrike

National Review-Russian Collusion Clinton Style

FOX News-U1 Informant: Moscow paid Millions

Breitbart-U1 Deal Approved by CIFUS Panel

The Federalist-Russia/Clinton Uranium One is Crazy

Observer-6 Clinton Foundation Scandals You need to Know

DOJ.gov-Former President of Transportation Company found Guilty

Covington Burling Law-CFIUS in the Biden Administration

US Treasury-CFIUS Board Composition

Justice.gov-Lisa Monaco: Chatham House Remarks on CFIUS

Crossfire Hurricane Docs-Christopher Steele Binder

Justice.gov-2023 SC John Durham Report

COINTELPRO / Controlled Opposition / and Fake-MAGA

Post Q# 2499
> CORSI [attempt infiltrate] Q.
> FAKE MAGA.
> TRANSPARENCY IS THE ONLY WAY.

The popular sub-Reddit called CBTS was deleted in March 2018 and the sub-Reddit called Great Awakening was removed in September 2018 by main Reddit to mark the start of censorship against 'Q'. 2018 marked the onset of a coordinated campaign on behalf of the federal government with the big tech censorship of the new 'Q' back channel informational movement. The FBI started in the late 1990's a code-named project Patriot Conspiracy (PATCON) with the goal of infiltration of right-wing groups by undercover FED 'Glow Boys' exemplified by the Whitmer kidnapping plot as well as January 6th Capitol event. PATCON was in high gear post 9/11 tracking terrorists both first foreign threats and later domestic.

Post Q# 2746
> Why are we attacked by pro MAGA?

No Anon is pro-censorship in the least and in 2022 Biden's DHS had formed a 'Ministry of Truth' section to go against their sworn political enemies. Our various social media platforms have been under nonstop attacks by big tech due to our America First (MAGA) stance and reporting on the whistleblower called 'Q'. Government sponsored COINTELPRO (CIP) from the 1960/70's as anti-Vietnam war communist infiltration, acting as controlled opposition programs have been a similar constant companion to the 'Q' movement. Amazon even resorted to unconstitutional political book burning when they removed both of my 2019 #1 bestselling QBooks in January 2021, marking a steep increase in the level of mass censorship.

Post Q# 4850
> What happens when too many people don't buy what they are selling?

> What happens when they lose control of the digital battlefield?

The glaring issue had been the attempted odd return in 2018, after public disavowing of 'Q', by disinformation Fake MAGA like Jerome Corsi and others paid controlled opposition agents under the InfoWars banner. These Fake MAGA decry 'Q' then leave and attempt to re-infiltrate again later on with their divide and conquer clown strategy. Today the Deep State plants false narratives or cognitive false information operations like Flat Earth/JFK Jr. into current organizations. The CIA began Operation Mockingbird in the 1950's which was the placement of intelligence assets into the U.S. new media and ran through the Church Committee exposure in the 1970's.

Post Q# 678
> The ART of illusion.

Many 'Q' followers have already been banned or de-platformed by big tech as well as wiped out by main Reddit (CBTS/Great Awakening) in the past. No Anon endorses bans/censorship of any person or platform regardless of affiliation but we are mindful of controlled opposition infiltration. Basically, the alternative news media is the mirror opposite of the Mockingbird media (nicknamed from the old CIA operation) and the Deep State needed to have total control of the press. Many older Alternative Media outlets looked upon the new 'Q' movement as direct competition to their audience base and tried to co-opt through inserting paid agents.

Post Q# 4957
> 50 years of propaganda.
> 50 years of lies.

Alex Jones is only mentioned here in terms of his years long continued public bashing of 'Q' and his coining the repulsive term of 'Q-Tards'. Alex Jones' attempted the insertion of his own paid Zack as the new 'Q' and tried unsuccessfully to co-opt this worldwide Patriot movement by inserting paid InfoWars operatives like Jerry Corsi. Professional psychology operations (psych ops) have been run by our intelligence community for years against our international adversaries and these tools have been turned domestically against Patriots.

Post Q# 2142
> Shills only shill.
> Patriots WIN.

The upcoming Great Awakening welcomes all followers of Alex Jones and other alternative media influencers to come back over to rejoin the Digital Soldiers of 'Q.' Many were fooled early on by these professional COINTELPRO (CIP) agents as well as their partnered news media political tricksters. CIP is yet another covert project by the FBI aimed at surveillance and infiltration of domestic political groups. The US Army put out a special video in 2022 titled 'Ghosts in the Machine-Psywar' (link below) and it is a must watch for a look in the real world of military phycological operations.

Post Q# 529
> 4-6% LOST FOREVER.

Jerome Corsi sprung into the 'Q' community while being a paid Washington DC news correspondent for Alex Jones/InfoWars. Corsi all along pitched his new book within the movement but his book purposely left out any mention of 'Q.' As an author myself and knowing publisher's abilities, surely Corsi could've added in a 'Q' section if he wanted due to the publication date. One operation many will remember was Jack Posobiec/OAN did a failed hit piece on 'Q' interviewing MicoChip about falsified 'ChatLogs.'

Post Q# 1343
They attempted to infiltrate, repackage and rebrand as their own.

> Profit-vehicle.
> Destroy through [misinformation].
> Re-route traffic to other platforms.

Things went sideways in late April 2018, not long after the first big 'Q' public march and a simple planned InfoWars Press Club event. Corsi and team Alex Jones began an on-air discrediting campaign of 'Q' and all worldwide supporters, that has continued to this day. Post January 6th, the entire staff at InfoWars tried to deflect DC Capitol events onto others like the Patriots following 'Q'.

Post Q# 3310
> Threat to Controlled Narrative.
> DIVIDERS will FAIL.

Not only did Corsi/Jones attempt to spin a false narrative about compromised 'trip codes' but they pushed their own 'Q' replacement figure named Zack. AJ said Zack was no LARP like was 'Q' but in fact a real high-level intelligence source that knew everything much better than did 'Q.' Yet another co-opting tactic employed by AJ in his ongoing attempts to commandeer and take control of this new worldwide Patriot movement.

Post Q# 2102
Who is testifying before Mueller tomorrow?

What happens if Mueller 'proves' 'Free Speech Systems LLC' aka 'InfoWars' is linked to a Foreign Intel Agency or other Non_Domestic entity?

Disinformation and division are classic Saul Alinsky tactics employed in the past and now Cass Sunstein infiltration tactical methods are being used widely. Please remember we are dealing with trained professionals familiar with psychological warfare and public mass brain washing techniques. The CIA/FBI enjoys developing false flag operations like the January 6th Capitol event to then blame on their targeted groups.

Post Q# 3597
Do you think we are targeted and attacked by the largest media co's in the world because we're a LARP?

The Jones/InfoWars/Corsi betrayal stunt will tried being explained away as just a horrible corporate business decision gone south. Controlled opposition sponsored by the 'Clowns' constantly churn out disinformation, it's the primary role of the alternative media's limited hangout routine. President Trump has long emphasized that the MSM is the "Enemy of the People".

Post Q# 1343
"Be careful who you follow."
"Some are profiting off this movement."
Those guilty immediately reacted (predictably).

Shockingly many YouTubers split-off from 'Q' at this exact timeframe of the public Corsi stunt. These Q-Tubers were once devoted followers, but they jumped ship simultaneously to sow divisions and sway away 'Q' followers. The continued attacks by Team InfoWars during the entire Q informational program demonstrates the degree of resources that media institutions will commit to destroy promoting a counter-narrative.

Post Q# 1008
Why is Mueller going after 'inside plants'?

Incredibly many disinformation promoters outing themselves for just being called out by team 'Q' for their profiteering motivation. 'Trojan Horse' infiltration tactics were employed under managed controlled opposition of the entire alternative media complex. Post January 6th Capitol event, a coordinated campaign was launched through the Alternative Media to associate 'Q' with the 1920's Russian 'Operation Trust'. Recycling Psychological Warfare Operations or PsyWars due to the old guard mentality has been a trade mark of the CIA/Clowns of changing populations thoughts via Fifth Generation Warfare methods for a very long time.

Post Q# 4962
Why are they manipulating you?
PUT AN END TO THE ENDLESS.

Try to catch Praying Medic's or SerialBrain2's excellent post on the meaning of implanted 'Sleeper Cells.' All past videos have been deleted by big tech but print copies still remain. These implanted Judas figures are being exposed by 'Q' throughout this Great Awakening process and will be held accountable for their slanderous statements. President Trump filed in 2022 a federal RICO lawsuit against those government/media officials that crafted the false Russian collusion narrative.

Post Q# 3655

> Deconstruction of foreign controlled [intel].
> US media [+ alt] critical.

We were dealt a huge favor by 'Q' calling out these false voices and their greedy underlying control of the narrative. FAKE MAGA motives are not based upon normal economics, as they lost followers but act per orders from their Deep State handlers who provide the income lost by their ordered departure. The coverup of Hunter Biden's 'Laptop from Hell' by the MSM and former intelligence officials just prior to the 2016 election, it a case study in crafting a false public narrative. Elon Musk would begin to reveal the exact scope of the suppression of free speech by our government with his Twitter Files series. In late 2023 a whistleblower revealed the existence of Cyber Threat Intelligence League (CTIL) which bridged public and private censorship of American citizens.

Post Q# 2104

> "Jerome Corsi who I outed as a Mossad asset/agent in a 1997 sting operation in London."

All you have to do is look at the average views of these Fake MAGA videos from before they trashed 'Q', compared to their new broadcast of today. Economically they must have suffered unless they have mysterious supplemental income still flowing into their accounts from their NWO Globalists overlords. Dr. Robert Malone (MNRA developer) has explained that the population has been under a planned Mass Formation Psychosis or general brainwashing. The MSM's coverup of the Hunter Biden 'Laptop from Hell' scandal is a classic example of the coordination of the media with the corrupt political DC Swamp.

Post Q# 225

> You are the voice.
> We are here to help guide.

You are the calm before and during the storm.

When will the Progressive Left/Mockingbird Media/Never Trump/Anti-'Q'/Fake-MAGA ever just admit the truth? An old fashion dose of Humble Pie would be in order and a first step toward repairing this fractured Republic. The leftist will soon start attacking themselves as the LawFare boomerang of legal justice is coming. President Trump won in 2016 and was the victim of a stolen election in 2020. The Mockingbird media and Big Tech teamed up with the corrupt elements of the DC UniParty Swamp to attack non-stop both President Trump and the 'Q' Digital Patriots.

Post Q# 4824

> Combat tactics, Mr. Ryan.

The Sin of Pride can fog normal rational actions and cause vanity to keep pushing out a false narrative. Controlled opposition agents like AJ/Corsi's relevancy days are long over and history will not be kind to the entire lot of alternative media news influencers that has constantly attacked 'Q.' The extreme censorship of 'Q' (QAnon) from the very beginning gave credence to the tireless efforts of all Anons. Special Counsel John Durham has dropped criminal indictments related to past illegal surveillance operations and submitted his final report in 2023. With the monumental re-election of President Trump in 2024, the never Trumpers and Anti-MAGA are more irrelevant than ever -"The Best is Yet to Come."

Post Q# 873
>Re: IBOR.
>Loss of control.
>Must be regulated to prevent censorship and narrative push.

Links

US Army SOF-GHOSTS IN THE MACHINE

Daily Dot-Alex Jones Claims He urged Mike Flynn to Come Out as 'Q'

General Flynn-CIA Propagandizing Americans

Clinton Foundation Timeline-2025 Crossfire Hurricane Docs

Keihatsu-False Narratives Drive the World

Revolver News-FBI Sinister PATCON: Internet Best kept Secret

Tablet Mag-Hoax of the Century: Thirteen Ways Looking at Disinformation

CTIL Files-US/UK Military Subcontractors

The New American-Propaganda and the US Government

Code Monkey-Framing Techniques for Mass Persuasion

Starfire Codes-Operation Mockingbird

Axios-QAnon Grows before 2020 Election

The Federalist-How Trump Derangement gave Birth to the Censorship Industrial Complex

Burning Bright-Overton Goalpost

American Greatness-Conspiracy Theories as Reality/Reality as Conspiracy Theories

Radix Verum-The Whitmer Case and the FBI's PATCON Legacy

NY Post-FBI, Big Tech, Big Media: Partners in Collusion

Epoch Times-PATCON: Records Provide Glimpse of FBI Infiltration Ops

Real Clear Politics-Dr. Robert Malone: Mass Formation Psychosis

Breitbart-Time Magazine: Secret/Well Funded Cabal worked to Protect 2020 Election

Jordan Sather-COINTELPRO: The Anatomy of a Psych-Op

American Thinker-Darryl Cooper/Martyr Made's Mega Thread

The Intercept-How Covert Agents Infiltrate to Manipulate the Internet

Revolver News-Trump uses Cleaver Trick to Break Deep State

Newsweek-Alex Jones: QAnon Rant Watched over 2 million Times

The Guardian-To Trap a Spy (Operation Trust)

JSTOR-PATCON

Medium-Operation Mockingbird: The CIA's Secret Control of the Media

FBI.gov (vault)-COINTELPRO

Crossfire Hurricane Docs-Christopher Steele Binder

Meet the Original 'Q'-Patriot William Cooper

Milton William Cooper (1943-2001) was a leading conspiracy theorist and much sought-after public speaker. Bill Cooper held in the mid-1970's, a very special Top Secret Military Security of 'Q' level clearance. For good reason 'Q' has specifically pointed on several occasions to both Bill Cooper and his iconic 1991 bestselling book 'Behold a Pale Horse.' The Great Awakening and MAGA movements have brought back a new appreciation for many different revelations that Bill Cooper presented in the past.

Post Q# 48
What is Q Clearance?

Future proves past once again when it comes to many of Bill Cooper's bold futuristic predictions. Cooper was a maverick and helped to 'Red Pill' the general public during his many educational speaking seminars. To this day, many Patriots still listen to the historical recorded broadcasts by Mr. Cooper. Cooper had an 8-hour live broadcast on that fateful September 11th day.

Post Q# 4407
ONLY AT THE PRECIPICE [moment of destruction] WILL PEOPLE FIND THE WILL TO CHANGE.

Cooper's 'Majesty Twelve' revelation was about the planned formation of a world totalitarian socialist ruling government. Cooper exposed the globalists plans for a New World Order (NWO) before most even understood the reality of events. To say that Bill Cooper was ahead of his time in the discussion of many 'difficult truths', would be a huge understatement.

Post Q# 3774
Moves and countermoves.
The 'silent' war continues.

Cooper was in the forefront of JFK/NWO/MK Ultra/UFO-Aliens/Illuminati /Masonic Secret Societies/Osama bin Laden /9/11/etc. Many believe that Cooper's very public views on the run up and aftermath of 9/11, ultimately led to his violent gunfight death. It is hard to pick a favorite subject that Cooper highlighted but most would find something of interest from his vast collection.

Post Q# 2563
At some point, the Q will be asked.

Many of Cooper's original lectures have now been uploaded to popular YouTube videos. Please take the time to watch Cooper and listen to his both these video recordings and his famous hourlong radio shows. Just as many of us see the wisdom in the Q drops, Bill Cooper was dropping big league crumbs long before it was fashionable. Mr. Cooper pioneered in the 1990's shortwave and later satellite broadcasting of his famed The Hour of the Time radio show.

Post Q# 157
Who unlocked the door of all doors?
Why are non MSM platforms cast as conspiracy and/or non-credible?

Cooper produced a popular video series called Mystery Babylon with NWO theories explained. Bill also did a long-running radio show called the Hour of the Time (links below). Cooper's iconic book 'Behold the Pale Horse' remains today on many top 100 sellers lists long after the initial publication date. 'Pale Horse' is a must read for all Patriots and was also suggested from Team-Q.

Post Q# 166

Expand your thinking.

Jason Bourne (Deep Dream).

Bill Cooper has long been held as a historical leader in the 'truther movement.' Cooper sets the standard that many follow today as a true American 'White Hat Patriot." The current worldwide widespread movement of individuals seeking the truth, can be traced in part back to folks like Mr. Cooper. Bill Cooper had a weekly radio broadcast titled 'The Hour of the Time' and produced several hundred interesting programs.

Post Q# 3670

Scope and size far greater than you can imagine.

Bill Cooper was a 'pathfinder' to older Patriots and current modern day Patriots that follow in Cooper's footsteps are Patriotic notable figures such as Rogers/Huber/Binney/Kellogg/Pompeo/Durham/Flynn/Horowitz/Cohen-Watnick/Patel/Nunes/Team 'Q'/etc. One of 'Q' favorite sayings fits Bill Cooper like a glove, "Future proves Past".

Post Q# 4964

We are not prophets.

Focus on the mission.

The 8chan board on 2/16/18 had a picture and short article from Cooper's 1991 book 'Behold the Pale Horse.' In a classic direct 'Q' response to this Anon's inquiry about Cooper, the reply post from the Q-Team just simply stated "BIG". Also bear in mind that the CIA/Intel Community has a long history of planting false UFO stories to distract the public from other issues.

Post Q# 782

BIG!

Cooper was on the run from the U.S. Marshalls Service who were attempting to deliver a bogus warrant on trumped up tax charges. Bill Cooper had kept one-step ahead other governmental agencies for several years until he was ultimately cornered in Arizona. Going against the given public narrative is a risk-taking endeavor and one must be prepared for the personal flak that surely will follow.

Post Q# 34

Q Clearance Patriot.

A deadly confrontation occurred on 11/5/2001 with local sheriff's deputies in Apache County/AZ. Police were attempting to arrest Bill Cooper and he was shot dead in a gunfight. History will long remember your early contributions fellow Patriot Milton William Cooper. Special Counsel John Durham has dropped criminal indictments related to SpyGate and submitted his final report in 2023. With the re-election of President Trump in 2024, this definitely signals the oncoming Great Awakening/Judgement Day.

Post Q# 3585

Project Looking Glass?

Links

Behold a Pale Horse Comparisons

My Takes Video-To the Shills and The Sheeple (Bill Cooper)

Hour of the Time-Bill Cooper Radio Show collection (Series 1-5)

AZ Central-Bill Cooper and QAnon

Felix Matamoros-The Legacy of William Cooper HOTT

Rolling Stone-Grandfather of Conspiracy Theories

Revolver News-CIA has History of Planting False UFO Stories

Publisher Weekly-Who was William Cooper?

End of Innocence-The Coming Alien Hoax

Bill Cooper's Mystery Babylon Series

Esquire Magazine-Behold a Pale Horse Book Review

MK Ultra Productions-Bill Cooper: History of Egyptian Magic

Bill Cooper's Mystery Babylon Series (Audio Edition)

Archive.org-William Cooper's Mystery Babylon Series (Full Text Version)

Wikipedia-U.S. Security Clearance Chart

Archive.org-William Cooper's Behold a Pale Horse book

Wikipedia-Q Clearance

Clinton Foundation Timeline-2025 Crossfire Hurricane Docs

Justice.gov-2023 SC John Durham Report

(Answer is:) Justin Cooper
(Question:) Clinton Tech with No Security Clearance?

Justin 'Hammering' Cooper was an adviser and employee of the Clinton Foundation (CF). Cooper was in charge initially of setting up the Clinton personal home email/server with Eric Hothem. The Clinton criminal cabal has relied heavily upon shady IT and technical enablers to assist with the global corrupt grifting schemes.

Post Q# 3815
> They will not be able to walk down the street.
> THE GREAT AWAKENING.

Odd coincidence is that Special Counsel (SC) Robert Mueller's right-hand investigator Aaron Zebley represented Justin Cooper in the past. Zebley defended Cooper as he testified in front of several Senate committees about the HRC email server scandals. Special Counsel (SC) John Durham has dropped criminal charges related to referrals from IG Michael Horowitz and submitted his final report in 2023.

Post Q# 3045
> HOW DID HRC OBTAIN SAP (SPECIAL ACCESS PROGRAMS) ON HER
> PERSONAL SERVER(S)?
> TREASON.

Justice is coming to Justin Cooper as he was forced testify in a Judicial Watch lawsuit and get his lies on the record. Judge Lambert will hear answers about Benghazi and the secret HRC server from most of HRC's aides, but she and Cheryl Mills got a pass from the judge not having to go under judicial oath.

Post Q# 4125
> WIN BY ANY MEANS NECESSARY.
> Everything is at stake.

Justin Cooper gets his clever and appropriate nickname from our President Trump at several 2016 campaign stump speeches. Always at his best in rally settings President Trump gave a glimpse into Justin's real past duties working for HRC.

Post Q# 1551
> Weiner HRC/Others-crimes against children.

The minds-eye iconic image that comes from the 2016 campaign trail is one of Justin Cooper enthusiastically hammering away at HRC's phones. Cooper destroyed several of HRC's BlackBerry phones so well demonstrated by then candidate Trump wildly swinging his arms in demonstration on stage the destruction of these implicating phones.

Post Q# 1223
> Think private email addresses.
> Hussein.
> HRC.

Eric Hothem (also Hoteham) was the original domain owner of clintonemail.com and along with Cooper, put the secret server/email system together. This 'home brew' system was fired up on the swearing in day of HRC as BHO's new U.S. Secretary of State. Hoteham worked closely with Cooper as well as Bryan Pagliano in the upkeep of the Clinton computer systems.

Post Q# 1972
>BIGGER THAN WATERGATE.
>BIGGEST SCANDAL IN US HISTORY.

Cooper never received training on any level or formal instructions of U.S. governmental security clearances. Cooper was additionally lacking any advanced knowledge about computer intrusion prevention and complex encryption programs. Typical of the criminal thugs known to circle around the Clintons orbit.

Post Q# 3634
>Clinton server - China relay
>It's only a matter of time.

Justin Cooper combined with Bryan Pagliano to oversee the day-to-day management of the Clinton email server. When HRC left State, Cooper worked with Platte River Networks (PRN) tech Paul Combetta to let PRN manage the Clinton computer server. Certainly, history will show that the incompetence level went down when PRN entered into the Clinton email server saga.

Post Q# 4820
>THE CLINTON FOUNDATION.
>WHITE HOUSE FOR SALE.

Tech Combetta leads directly to the infamous Reddit/BleachBit/email address 'Scrubbing' fiasco. Story goes that Combetta had to remove BHO's (VIP) emails from HRC's history records using specialized software striping programs. Unobtainable to the public were the required computer tools, Combetta turned to BleachBit to completely erase everything.

Post Q# 2876
>CLINTON PANIC.
>CLINTON FEAR.
>JUDGEMENT DAY COMING.

Cooper was questioned for his role involving the HRC email server by famed FBI agent Peter Strzok. The spider web seems to be all encompassing with this criminal Cabal and past Deep State working relationships. SC John Durham submitted his final report in 2023 and will be the foundation for future judicial accountability.

Post Q# 809
>HRC open source server?
>[Missing emails].

Generously the Clinton's are now paying for all of the legal fees encountered by Justin Cooper. Not sure if Cooper's no-shows are billed at the same level as his Congressional subpoenaed private closed-door appearances. 'Q' has pointed out that this all is a perfectly scripted movie, and that justice will prevail.

Post Q# 3674
>DOJ plane(s).
>CF.

Legal fees of $250,000 have been spent to date on Cooper's defense. History shows that when dealing with the Clinton Crime Family, some get rewarded, while some get 'Arkancided.' There has been for decades a palpable fear of death for anyone that would ever dare to cross the Clinton crime family. Like with many Clinton aides, Justin Cooper worked simultaneously with Doug Band's Teneo firm receiving a salary and benefits.

Post Q# 2514
> Future will prove past.
> History books.

Recently crack reporter John Solomon revealed that a group of financial bounty hunters is making headway as CF whistleblowers. Inquiring minds believe that it is either Hammering Justin or CEO Eric Braverman will join the already squealing past CF CFO Andrew Kessel. With the historic re-election of President Trump in 2024, Judgement Day is coming for all of these treasonous coup plotters.

Post Q# 1551
> CF investigation ongoing.

Links

Clinton Foundation Timeline-Justin Cooper was Administrator of Clinton's Server

Breitbart-Clinton Aide with No Security Clearances

Real Clear Investigations-The Apparent Trump-Hillary Double Standard: For Her

CBS News-Clinton Foundation Pressed Donors to Steer Business to Bill Clinton

Real Clear Politics-Hillary Clinton's Greatest Masterpiece

Western Journal-Investigation of 2016 DNC Hack Resurfaces

AP News-Witnesses refuse to Testify in Hearing

Free Beacon-Cooper Destroyed Devices with a Hammer

Business Insider-HRC Aide Broke Phones with a Hammer

GOP.com-Memo: Who is Justin Cooper

Judicial Watch-JW Releases Testimony of HRC Email Administrator

Daily Caller-Clinton's Paying Cooper's Legal Bills

Red State-Pay-to-Play at HRC's State Department

Politico-12 of the Juiciest Bits from HRC's FBI Report

Town Hall-HRC's IT Guy Created Encrypted Gmail Account

Poynter Institute-Bleach and Hammers

Grassley.Senate.gov-Security Incidents Related to HRC Emails

State Dept.gov-FOIA: HRC Recovered Emails

Clinton Foundation Timeline-2025 Crossfire Hurricane Docs

Justice.gov-2023 SC John Durham Report

Deep State's 2016 July 4th Weekend "Will Go Down in Infamy"

At this point in time, there is little doubt of an orchestrated past Deep State coup plot against then President Donald Trump by various U.S. governmental forces. Discovery of the exact origins of these treasonous plans and all of the different co-conspirators, are being slowly rolled out with details of SpyGate/ObamaGate scandals. President Trump would file in 2022 a federal RICO lawsuit against HRC/DNC/and other related to the promotion of false Russian collusion narratives during the 2016 election cycle.

Post Q# 3858
> THIS REPRESENTS A CLEAR AND PRESENT DANGER TO THE CONSTITUTIONAL REPUBLIC OF THE UNITED STATES OF AMERICA.

Special Counsel (SC) John Durham would be tasked to investigate the false Russia collusion narrative and would slowly rollout through court filings in 2022 the elements of a coordinate criminal conspiracy against candidate Donald Trump. We can all look for a central focal point where all of these various elements seem to convergence. One such time period came over the 2016 July 4th Holiday weekend. Many can compare these historic events to past evil plans against our country invoking that this time period "Will go down in infamy."

Post Q# 3683
> "Put on the full armor of God, so that you can take your stand against the devil's schemes."
> Below is a recap of that very special weekend and significant activity that occurred:

07/01/16:
- Loretta Lynch publicity announces her "partial recusal" from the HRC investigation due to Tarmac meeting and defers prosecutorial decision making over to James Comey/FBI.
- FBI agent Mike Gaeta meets Christopher Steele in London and receives first installment of the 'Dossier' memos. Gaeta's trip was authorized by US State Department official Victoria Nuland.
- FBI Strzok/Page texts sarcastically referenced about Lynch, "A real profile in courage, since she knows no charges will be brought".
- BHO began holding secret W/H basement meetings concerning Crossfire Hurricane. NSA Susan Rice ordered recording equipment to be turned off for these official meetings.
- Islamic militants (ISIS) storm cafe in Dhaka/Bangladesh in country's worst terror attack.
07/02/16:
- HRC's 3.5 hour-long FBI interview with agents Coleman and Strzok. Allowed to attend (targets themselves) as HRC attorneys were Cheryl Mills and Heather Samuelson.
- Stefan Halper contacts Carter Page about scheduled upcoming (7/11/16) London trip for the 'Spy' symposium at University of Cambridge/UK. Campaign aide Stephen Miller was also invited by Halper to attend Cambridge but fortunately he declined.
- FBIAnon first appearance on 4Chan offering insider information about HRC email and Clinton Foundation probes.

Post Q# 4502
> The doubters will soon be believers.
> **07/03/16:**
- HRC does several Sunday morning MSM talk shows claiming she was "Eager to talk to the FBI about her emails."

- False Flag/narrative shift w/ISIS claims responsibility for major bombing in Baghdad hundreds killed in the Karida Market District.
  07/04/16:
  Surprising Day-Off (HRC polls begin dropping)

Post Q# 96
> Your President needs your help.
> **07/05/16:**

- FISC denied first Carter Page FISA warrant for Trump World surveillance.
- FBI officially closes its investigation of HRC.
- James Comey holds infamous presser exonerating HRC and Aides for emails.
- Chris Steele gives to an old contact from the FBI in Rome his first memo (start of the Dossier) against then Republican candidate Donald Trump.
- Guccifer now 2.0 version falsely claims to have hacked the DNC system-a second real download breach (22.7 megabytes p/second transfer rate) did however occur.
- Bill Binney/VIPS forensically determine that DNC intrusion was an internal leak via a USB/Thumb Drive as opposed to an external server hack.
- AU Alexander Downer shares his London/UK Papadopoulos contact w/Five Eyes.

Post Q# 4645
> A CRITICAL MOMENT IN TIME.
> **07/06/16**

- Loretta Lynch announces the official end of the DOJ's HRC email investigation.
- State and foreign governments are investing heavily into the Clinton Foundation/Campaign.
- Victoria Nuland/Jonathan Winer hand off the 2nd Dossier memos (Sid and Cody) to the FBI.
  07/10/16

- Seth Rich murdered (RIP)
- DOJ Bruce Ohr meets with Chris Steele

Post Q# 3771
> Do you believe in coincidences?
> The TRUTH will be told.

The four main components of the political coup operation nicknamed Operation Trump:
> Exoneration of HRC/Aides (ObamaGate)
> False Trump-Russia Dossier creation/distribution (RussiaGate)
> FISA Title-1 Warrants/Section 702 (SpyGate)
> The 'Insurance Policy' (Crossfire Hurricane)

Post Q# 4011
> CROSSFIRE HURRICANE

'Q' has mentioned all of the above mentioned events from the suspicious Tarmac meeting to the FBI lovers text messages. On a sad note, is the death of hero ABC news reporter Chris Sign, who originally broke the Tarmac meeting story. One of President Trump's last official action on 1/19/21 was to order the total declassification of the FBI's Crossfire Hurricane material. Hopefully 2025 will be the year of justice with the coming 'Storm/Judgement Day' and the Great Awakening!

Post Q# 4289
> It's a marathon not a sprint.

This special Holiday Weekend saw both the complete legal exoneration of HRC and the launch of the false Trump-Russia 'collusion delusion' narrative. The trust factor by the American public has been shattered with these two illegal actions by the Department of Justice. President Trump would file in 2022 a federal RICO lawsuit against those who promoted the false Russian collusion narrative during the 2016 election cycle. It was revealed in 2024 that the US Intel Community did request from its FIVE EYES partners to illegally spy on Trump related aides.

Post Q# 2164
> How do you inflict MAX PAIN / DAMAGE?
> drop/release MOAB?

Now comes the pain and justice phase, as our President Trump is known to always hit back 10-times harder. Special Counsel John Durham has dropped criminal indictments concerning SpyGate and submitted his final report in 2023. With the re-election of President Trump in 2024, to quote 'Q', "Nothing can stop what is coming-nothing."

Post Q# 3680
> OP activity pre_July 2016?

Links

Epoch Times-SpyGate Timeline (info-graph)

FOX News-Patel found Thousands of Sensitive Trump Russia Probe Docs

Just the News-FBI Opens Grand Conspiracy Probe

The Federalist-Unsealed Crossfire Hurricane Docs prove RussiaGate a Hoax

Markets Work-SpyGate: The Inside Story

Washington Times-How the BHO Administration's SpyGate 'trumps' WaterGate

Sharyl Attkisson-Collusion against Trump Timeline

America First Legal-Matt Taibbi/Shellenberger Files

Rolling Stone-How did RussiaGate Start?

Tablet Magazine-How the FBI Hacked Twitter

Western Journal-Investigation of 2016 DNC Hack Resurfaces

Clinton Foundation Timeline-July 2016 Archives

The Federalist-Strzok Texts show FBI Investigating Trump before Crossfire Hurricane

WSJ-When Carter Page met Stefan Halper

Markets Work-Details of Victoria Nuland's Role in SpyGate

The Last Refuge-SpyGate: The Big Picture

Undercover Huber-Bruce Ohr meet Steele 3 Times in July 2016

Patel Patriot-Truth is a Force of Nature

Markets Work-FBI Contractors, FISA Abuses and the Steele Dossier

National Review-IG Horowitz did Not Endorse the FBI's Predication

Capital Research Center-Cast of the Trump Russia Collusion Hoax

NSA.gov-Central Security Services (CSS)

Ann Phelm Scoop-ObamaGate Movie

HSGAC.Senate.gov-Crossfire Hurricane Timeline

Crossfire Hurricane Docs-FISA Notes

Crossfire Hurricane Docs-Christopher Steele Binder

Judtice.gov-2023 SC John Durham Report

Operation Trump vs Operation Condor:
Classic Coup vs Countercoup

There is little doubt in many minds of a 'coup plot' against Donald Trump dating to at least late 2015. A 'countercoup' has since been launched by President Trump beginning in 2016 against traitorous dark forces within our own government. This epic struggle between good and evil continues to play out under the illegal Biden administration. Outside private contractors would be established as a source of classified leaks that undermine privacy rights of Americans. This real-life political drama would come to have colorful nicknames like Operation Trump/Arctic Frost and Operation Condor.

Post Q# 533
> WE THE PEOPLE ARE TAKING BACK OUR COUNTRY (and WORLD) FROM THE EVIL LOSERS WHO WOULD DO US HARM.
> 4, 10, 20.

Fired FBI agents Strzok/Page had exchanged personal text messages indicating that a codenamed 'Operation Trump' also called internally at the FBI as 'Arctic Frost', began early in December 2015. The associated National Security Divisions of DOJ/FBI/and White House along with Brennan/CIA and Clapper/DNI, all combined to form the treasonous secret society (aka the Small Group) coup cabal. This secret society relied upon its co-conspiracy partners in the MSM news to assist with this coup plot.

Post Q# 3125
> The attempted 'COUP' [TREASON] opens the 'public' door to more serious......

Without oversight from Inspector General (IG) Michael Horowitz, and thanks to a DAG Sally Yates directive, this 'Small Group' conducted their coup plans without fear of outside exposure from watchdog departments like the IG. The given overall code name was Operation Trump and consisted of several highly coordinated cooperative intelligence components. Cleaver sub-ops had coded names as Crossfire Hurricane/Typhoon/Razor/and many to be yet discovered.

Post Q# 26
> The only way is the military.

OPERATION TRUMP FOUR-PART COUP PLOT:
- Exonerate HRC and involved Aides (ObamaGate)
- Russia Dossier creation and distribution (RussiaGate)
- FISA Title-1 Surveillance Warrants and Section 702 Intel (SpyGate)
- The 'Insurance Policy' (Crossfire Hurricane)

Post Q# 144
> What council do the Wizards and Warlocks control?

These all were well organized collapsing plans, each needed upon the failure of the prior one. This Globalist NWO crowd is not used to their first plan failing, let alone be on the emergency option of the last final plan (always a Plan Z). Having multiple mutual beneficial outcomes is very much a key part of these complex narrative schemes. The entire RussiaGate/SpyGate coup plot exemplified the insidious relationship between government officials and outside private contractors working alongside a compliant news media.

Post Q# 3212
> Think Rogers T-Tower meeting (right after SCIF set up in Tower).
> Think POTUS campaign leaving T-Tower (base of operations) THE VERY NEXT DAY.
> 1 + 1 = 2

SpyGate was a multipronged surveillance tool used within this conspiracy that relied on foreign (FVEY) intelligence assets or 'Spies/Lures' as well as domestic agents. These Five Eyes assisted foreign assets were used as bait to entrap several Trump World associates. Christopher Steele's infamous Trump-Russia dossier was nicknamed 'Crown Material' and was additionally included in Brennan's phony early 2017 I.C.A. History would ultimately vindicate Admiral Rogers as a lone voice among top government officials in denouncing the RussiaGate/Steele Dossier claims against Presidential candidate Donald Trump.

Post Q# 4646
> Nothing [digital] is ever really lost.

Beginning in the Winter of 2016, NSA Director Mike Rogers (Adm R) uncovered widespread abuses of the FISA 702's mass database. General "About Queries" can be made with the NSA system to cull all upstream/downstream digital data on the selected FISA/FICA approved surveillance target(s). The uncovering of purposefully redacted names of American citizens follows the NSA query process. Future oversight reports would demonstrate to the public that the DOJ/FBI has been conducting vat illegal searches of American citizens without proper FISA warrants.

Post Q# 270
> Adm R./No Such Agency (W and W) + POTUS/USMIL=Apply the Keystone.
> Paint the picture.

Admiral Mike Rogers put an end to this illegal practice of unauthorized 702's on 4/18/15. Outside contractors like Fusion GPS and CrowdStrike lost their inside source of raw intel via the 'about queries' ultimate searches. Special Counsel (SC) John Durham's indictment of Perkins Coie/Clinton campaign lawyer Michael Sussmann directly connects back to CrowdStrike and his pal Sean Henry.

Post Q# 3841
> RUSSIA DID NOT 'HACK' [penetrate] THE DNC SERVER.
> RUSSIA DID NOT INTERFERE WITH US ELECTION OF 2016.

The NSA's nickname for this internal uncovering program was 'Operation Condor' after the famous movie starring Robert Redford. Admiral Mike Rogers crippled the Deep State's ability to freely access comprising raw intelligence on their opposition targets. The use of human intelligence operatives began the instant Admiral Mike Rogers shutdown this back door avenue. Timeline confirms that SpyGate's Crossfire Hurricane operation spun up with planted 'LURES' and intelligence operatives as early as late 2015.

Post Q# 3934
> [Placeholder - Acts of Treason + support Articles]
> [Placeholder - FISA _pub]

Admiral Rogers came to our countries rescue once again on 11/17/16 in a meeting at Trump Tower. NSA Mike Rogers waited until the new Sensitive Compartmented Information Facility (SCIF) was completed in New Jersey and told President Elect Trump about the ongoing illegal surveillance currently in place at his New York Trump Tower and at the White House/Executive Offices complex.

Post Q# 585
> TRUST Adm R.
> He played the game to remain in control.

Remember that then President Elect Trump evacuated his top staff the very next morning to his golf club at Bedminster/NJ. This brave deed by Admiral Rogers will go down in the American history books and will be long remembered. SC John Durham would slowly unveil in 2022 to the public a vast coordinated conspiracy beginning in 2016 against candidate Donald Trump by both government officials and outside private contractors. Admiral Mike Rogers would join Quantum Xchange as a member of their Board of Directors in late 2022.

Post Q# 1981
> Who knew?
> Adm Rogers?
> Matters of NAT SEC.

The counter coup is ongoing and the original failed coup plotters better beware. Hold the line Patriots as multiple movies such as Panic in DC, Guardians of the Pedophiles, and FisaGate as simultaneously playing now. It will be an epic historic struggle of Good vs Evil, as this all plays out in the coming Judgement Day. SC John Durham has dropped criminal indictments and submitted his final report in 2023. With President Trump's re-election in 2024, future judicial accountability will be based on the reports from IG Horowitz and SC Durham, bringing everyone into the Great Awakening!

Post Q# 3319
> Michael S. Rogers.

Links

Red State-Expanding Scope of 'To/From' NSA Database Queries

FOX News-Clapper Pushed to Compromise Normal Steps

NY Post-HRC's Plan to Smear Trump with Russia Collusion

The Last Refuge-Orignal BHO and HRC 2008 Agreement

Clinton Foundation Timeline-Admiral Rogers on Russian Collusion

Just the News-Trump NSA Director Shot Down WAPO Story

CVFC-Admiral Mike Rogers saved USA

Security Boulevard-Mike Rogers: The Rise of Machine Identities

The Last Refuge-FISA 702

CBS News-Face the Nation: Admiral Mike Rogers (2020)

Business Wire-Admiral Mike Rogers Joins Quantum Xchange

NPR-NSA Head meet with Trump but didn't give Heads Up to BHO

The Federalist-SpyGate 101: A Primer on the Russia Collusion Hoax

Tapa Talk-Operation Condor: How Mike Rogers saved America

The Last Refuge-Admiral Rogers/FISA 702

Epoch Times-SpyGate: The Inside Story

Markets Work-The Uncovering: Mike Rogers' Investigation, Section 702 Abuse

Buster Hyde-The Dung Castle: Operation Crossfire Hurricane

American Report-Woolsey/Brennan/Clapper/and Comey Framed Trump and Flynn

Red State-Unsung Hero: Admiral Mike Rogers

Markets Work-Three Subpoenas: Unmasking the Unmaskers

Daily Beast (pre Q)-Inside the "Q Group" Hunting Snowden

The Last Refuge-The Insurance Policy

NSA Archive.GWU.edu-NSA Tracking of U.S. Citizens

Senate Judiciary.gov-Declassified Docs Undercut Steele Dossier/Page FISA Warrants

Crossfire Hurricane Docs-Admiral Mike Rogers Interview

Justice.gov-2023 SC John Durham Report

Memo to CrowdStrike: We Have the Server

The spider web of connections is overflowing when it comes to the DNC's infamous 2016 computer intrusion. All of the regular suspects appear from ObamaGate/SpyGate unfolding scandals when it comes to the origin of the Russian collusion hoax. The DNC email leak and subsequent investigation by CrowdStrike is the epicenter of this coup plot. Many believe CrowdStrike will ultimately appear in a Special Counsel (SC) John Durham's final report related to the unfolding SpyGate political scandal.

Post Q# 2692
BIGGEST COVER UP IN US HISTORY [ATTEMPTED].

CrowdStrike's (CS) co-founder Dmitri Alperovitch is a Senior Fellow at the Atlantic Council with all of its globalist New World Order tendency's. The President of CS is Sean Henry, who had an extensive FBI cyber official in past years. CrowdStrike magically received millions in startup funding from George Soros in a major investment effort that now, in hindsight makes logically sense.

Post Q# 1959
China hacked HRC server?
Access was granted.

The Deep State's favorite law firm has been for years the shady lawyers from Perkins Coie. Perkins retained both Fusion GPS and cyber security firm CrowdStrike on behalf of both HRC/DNC during the 2016 campaign cycle. Perkins Coie has personally assisted BHO, HRC, DNC, and many other top politicians in the past.

Post Q# 4016
Was the DNC (was) hacked by Russia?
CrowdStrike code insert?

Fusion GPS and CrowdStrike were outsider private contractors that were allowed access to the sensitive NSA database. This unlawful use of FISA 702 queries by outside contracting firms was unfortunately common practice prior to Admiral Rogers shutting it all down in 2016. Citizens personal data was used by these contractors in the construction of dossiers and leaked attack news media hit pieces.

Post Q# 3764
Possible to layer/insert code [CrowdStrike] to designate intruder [intended target]?
The hole is DEEP.

What makes a good movie besides great actors, is a very plausible thrilling plot. Then DNI Dan Coats declassified the 98-page FISA Court review in May 2018 and specifically mentioned the two outside contractors involved with unauthorized access to FISA 702 quires. Logically thinking this information points squarely at private firms like Fusion GPS and CrowdStrike. SC Durham would roll out in 2022 the general outline of his 'conspiracy' involving all of the different SpyGate players.

Post Q# 1666
We have the server.

HRC/DWS/and the DNC panicked on 4/30/16, when a computer server breach was officially reported. DNC Chair Debbie Wassermann-Schultz retained Perkins Coie as point investigative firm and subsequently employed CrowdStrike to review the DNC mainframe computer system and the data downloads. President Trump would bring up CrowdStrike and their servers being located in Ukraine with the then new Ukrainian President Zelensky in their infamous July 2019 phone call.

Post Q# 809
> [Missing emails]
> [CrowdStrike]

Privately what CS and their in-house cyber expert Captain Johnston found, was a leak not a hack download by a DNC IT staffer named Seth Rich. Later in 2016 Julian Assange of WikiLeaks would publicly put the spotlight on the murder of Seth Rich in Washington DC. While publicly CrowdStrike proclaimed Russian hackers Cozy Bear and Fancy Bear were to blame for the DNC computer intrusion. This public claim was in direct opposition to the discovered DNC computer intrusion and the forced testimonies of CS executives having to fess up in court.

Post Q# 4153
> CrowdStrike testimony re: DNC and Russia [hack]?
> manipulation of source?

Both Directors James Comey/FBI and Jeh Johnson/DHS were denied their requested physical access to the breached DNC computer equipment. Eric Schmidt/Google infused $100M into CS in 2015 and another $100M in 2017 to become the biggest investor in CrowdStrike. SC John Durham is making a connection with the indictment of Perkins Coie lawyer Michael Sussmann and various private tech contractors to help setup candidate Donald Trump.

Post Q# 1008
> No investigation on WL receipt of information?

Eric Schmidt had been the self-appointed HRC's 2016 campaign computer advising guru. Along with Jared Cohen's from Jigsaw (Google Ideas), they combined to offer HRC an unbeatable virtually complimentary tech playbook for 2016. Many Big Tech companies will prove to have played roles in the many treasonous coup plots.

Post Q# 1960
> CrowdStrike managed the infiltration program based on payments to CF.

Co-founder of CS is Dmitri Alperovitch, who is a Russian expat with ties to both HRC and George Soros, is a major international heavyweight. Having shady owners and partners is a perfect environment for criminals to have legal operational cover. It was temporarily thought 'Tech Exec #1' from Sussmann's indictment is Alperovitch since he was slated to be HRC's Cyber Czar, but Durham showed it was Rodney Joffe.

Post Q# 3990
> FBI CHAIN OF COMMAND DNC HACK? [CIA BRIDGE - UKRAINE - CROWDSTRIKE_BRENNAN]?

Adding to this mix of corrupt tech contractors, is the President of CrowdStrike Services Shawn Henry. Henry and Perkins Coie's Michael Sussmann are longtime personal friends and coordinated media leaks. Obvious to political observers is Sussmann's indictment and the direct ties back to all of these connected players. SC Durham has issued new grand jury subpoenas focusing on private outside tech firms and executives that assisted the DNC/HRC in these various schemes.

Post Q# 3841
> RUSSIA DID NOT INTERFERE WITH US ELECTION OF 2016.
> Crowdstrike manipulation of source.

Thomas Drake and Bill Binney started Veteran Intelligence Professionals for Sanity (VIPS) to scientifically review computer data. VIPS forensic teams found proof that the DNC intrusion was a "Leak not a Hack" due to transmission download speeds. Binney on President Trump's direct orders gave then CIA Director Pompano (KANSAS) a full briefing on these documented results. Hard to argue with scientifically proven data like download time involved with a computer intrusion.

Post Q# 436
> GOOG.
> CROWDSTRIKE.
> DNC.

'High Profile' cases involving national security normally are not handled by a third-party private company. One of many abnormalities that have surrounded ObamaGate/SpyGate are the obvious irrational explanations proffered by the coup plotters and media co-conspirators. Recall President Trump specifically asked the Ukraine President about CrowdStrike in that infamous phone call. Many believe that the physical CrowdStrike computer server containing the fake records used to implant the Russian 'breadcrumbs' as part of the DNC computer intrusion investigation.

Post Q# 1462
> The 'server' brings down the house.

Conveniently the Russian hacking narrative helps to cover the DNC's own internal mistakes. Patriot Seth Rich's mysterious death surrounds the Trump-Russia collusion, while Seth was trying to expose the rigging against Bernie Sanders. SC John Durham has dropped an indictment on Sean Henry pal Perkins Coie's cyber lawyer Michael Sussmann and has plead not guilty awaiting a May 2022 federal criminal trial.

Post Q# 3603
> FISA goes both ways.
> Information warfare.

Inquiring minds want to know the real 'skinny' on CrowdStrike and its involvement with SpyGate. This will ultimately expose the true facts surrounding the murder of Seth Rich and the real intrusion of the DNC computer system. SC Durham submitted his final report in 2023. In early 2024 Microsoft and CrowdStrike would be headline news over a global IT computer outage that effected many institutions from airlines to government services. With the re-election of President Trump in late 2024, many feel that the 'Great Awakening' will usher in a new American era.

Post Q# 3815
> They will not be able to walk down the street.
> THE GREAT AWAKENING.

Links

CrowdStrike-How CrowdStrike stops Recent Cozy Bear Phishing Attack

The Federalist-The FBI Set Up Trump and We Watched it Happen

Just the News-HRC Plan tying Trump and Russia

Clinton Foundation Timeline-CrowdStrike is Confused on Eleven Key Details

BBC-Microsoft and CrowdStrike

Vigilant News-CrowdStrike: House of Cards

Real Clear Investigations-What Durham Skipped: CrowdStrike

Clinton Foundation Timeline-Perkins Coie Contracts with CrowdStrike and Fusion GPS

Larry Beech-CrowdStrike and Uranium One

Real Clear Politics-RussiaGate: HRC Campaign/Perkins Coie/Fusion GPS/CrowdStrike

Aaron Mate-Clinton Lawyer hired CrowdStrike

Patel Patriot-Devolution: Part 11 CrowdStrike

The American Spectator-Durham and Amazing Disappearing DNC Hack

Breitbart-HRC's Law Firm Paid for Dossier/Recruited CrowdStrike

Lew Rockwell -Twin Pillars of RussiaGate Crumble

Medium-Former NSA Official questions Intel Community's Assessment

BBC-Democrat Hack: Who is Guccifer 2.0?

Markets Work-Listing of Participants

Breitbart-Common Funding Link Whistleblower and CrowdStrike

The Last Refuge-Admiral Rogers and CrowdStrike

Real Clear Investigations-Hidden over Two Years DEM Testimony of No Hack

Senate Judiciary Committee-2021 Crossfire Hurricane DECLAS

Crossfire Hurricane Docs-Christopher Steele Binder

Justice.gov-2023 SC John Durham Report

Steele's "Pee Pee" Dossier Author:
Meet Oligarch Oleg Deripaska

Regardless of your feelings about ObamaGate/SpyGate, this coup plot has produced many colorful characters. One of the most mysterious actors exposed so far has been Oleg Deripaska and he had a direct hand in the creation of Steele's Dossier. 'Q' stresses that future proves the past, so the recent FBI raid of Deripaska's DC/NYC homes should come as no surprise. Deripaska would shockingly find his London mansion being occupied by squatters due to the Russian invasion of Ukraine in 2022.

Post Q# 678
The ART of illusion.

Oleg Deripaska is considered a close friend of Vlad Putin and earned his Russian oligarch status in the aluminum metal industry. Considered to be one of the wealthiest individuals in Russia in 2008. Deripaska was also very much connected and involved with notorious international organized crime rings. Oleg Deripaska and his businesses had sanctioned imposed by the U.S. Treasury Office in 2018 and by the United Kingdom in 2022 related to the Ukraine special military operation.

Post Q# 3316
If the dossier was known to be unverified and fake, how then was an investigation started to begin with?

History will show that the 'Pee Pee' story was the keystone section of Steele's infamous Trump-Russia Dossier. Oleg playing the role as original creator of this 'Pee Pee' affair as had heard this tall tale one night in a Moscow bar and the essence was passed along to both Igor Danchenko and Sergei Millian, then back to Steele for the dossier. Normally bar gossip is hearsay at best, but this was an outright fabricated story made up out of whole cloth. The world knows about President Trumps' 'germaphobia' and on the surface this entire tall tale makes no common sense at all.

Post Q# 2776
"Was FISC made aware of all details surrounding the dossier?"

This sick story (pee pee/golden showers) was an off shoot of a 2013 Miss Universe pageant that was held in Russia. The Miss Universe owner Donald Trump, professional Russian ladies and a Ritz-Carlton Moscow hotel room were pivotal elements to this false tale. Oleg Deripaska joked with Vlad Putin that the even the stupid Americans would never fall for such a bogus phony "golden showers" story as well as Trump being an asset of Russia.

Post Q# 1745
FISA IMPLICATES SENIOR MEMBERS OF UK, MI5/6, US INTEL, WH, FVEY, R PARTY (CONGRESS/SENATE) OF KNOWN CORRUPTION IN EFFORT TO RETAIN POWER AND RIG ELECTION.

Deripaska has long been restricted entry into the USA and has been attempting to change that travel status. Contacted in 2009 by the FBI (including Andy McCabe), Oleg Deripaska was officially asked to assist in the release of former FBI/DEA agent Robert Levinson from Iranian held captivity.

Post Q# 436
BRIT INTEL. HRC CAMP PAY. DNC PAY. STEELE.

Deripaska would spend $25 million personally and it looked very much like the release of Levinson would actually occur. Oleg Deripaska had financial and metal interests ongoing in Iran, as well as high ranking politicians in his preverbal oligarch pocket. Deripaska had developed around Russian spy master Vlad Putin and knew exactly how to play the 'stupid Americans.'

Post Q# 3815

> They will not be able to walk down the street.
> THE GREAT AWAKENING

Then the entire Levinson hostage deal was scrubbed unexplainable by HRC in 2010. Sadly, reports out of Iran stated that Levinson had passed away in March 2020 while still in captivity. Deripaska has been Paul Manafort's partner in some businesses and claimed Manafort cheated him out of $10 million. The DOJ would fine Paul Manafort in 2022 over $3M for bank fraud/tax evasion directly related various shady international dealings with Russian Oligarch Oleg Deripaska.

Post Q# 1935

> Define 'Projection.'
> Define DARK MONEY.

Oleg Deripaska has retained in the past high profile DC lawyer Adam Waldman at a sweet $40,000 monthly lobbying fee. Deripaska has swirled around the DC Swamp and has made many inside the beltway political connections. Waldman had ties with DC powerbroker Daniel Jones who also knew Oligarch Deripaska and this whole crew played side roles in SpyGate operations. Daniel Jones assisted Fusion GPS with both the Trump-Russia dossier and the false Alfa Bank plots.

Post Q# 1164

> Avoid US data collection laws.
> Public: Dossier FISA.

In the Fall of 2016, the FBI again contacted Oleg Deripaska once again for mutual assistance help. This time Deripaska was questioned about possible Trump-Russia ties and about the Moscow hotel 'pee pee' portion of Christopher Steele's laughable dossier research. Understand that Vald Putin and Deripaska are longtime pals and trolling the FBI is a fun sport for them both. The FBI and IRS in turn would file complaints against Deripaska for U.S. asset forfeitures like luxury properties and even the sale of his California music studio.

Post Q# 4933

> Watergate x 1000.

Oleg Deripaska laughed uncontrollably back to the FBI (Andy McCabe was present) about their unbelievable Putin/Trump Russian collusion narrative tale. Go to the real-life mobsters if you really want to know what in fact is going on out in the world. The FBI unbelievably seem to disbelieve that the Russian hookers in a Moscow hotel was sheer fooling around fantasy. An odd fact is that Deripaska's DC mansion was next door to Donald Trump critic George Conway.

Post Q# 1626

> Putin/U1 will come out post summit.

Oleg Deripaska offered to testify to Congress in 2017 but for some reason that idea was rejected outright by the DOJ. Deripaska and lobbyist lawyer Adam Waldman got involved with Sen. Mark Warner in his efforts to meet personally with Christopher Steele in March 2017. Once again it would seem the Russian prankster was stringing along the corrupt Warner as this meeting never materialized. Deripaska would return to the media headlines during the 2022 Russian special military operation in the Ukraine and the sanctions imposed upon many Russian Oligarchs. In early 2023 the ongoing U.S. sanctions against Oleg Deripaska would be the legal basis in the arrest of former FBI agent Charles McGonigal. Disgraced FBI agent McGonigal plead guilty in August 2023 and received four years in prison for collaborating/working with Oleg Deripaska, and their ties back to the false RussiaGate hoax would resurface.

Post Q# 4738
THE DISEASE CALLED CORRUPTION.

Odds are that in fact the 'Our Guy' is Deripaska that is refereed in the released email exchanges between DOJ official Bruce Ohr and Christopher Steele. Unearthed Hunter Biden emails show a scheme involving aluminum reports to Alcoa concerning Deripaska. Inquiring minds want to know if Oleg Deripaska will be indicted by Special Counsel (SC) John Durham for his role in ObamaGate/SpyGate. SC Durham submitted his final report in 2023. With the re-election of President Trump in 2024, many look forward to hidden political secrets to be publicly revealed.

Post Q# 3331
You are witnessing the systematic destruction of the OLD GUARD.

Links

The Hill-5 Things About Oleg Deripaska

The Blaze-The Case against Clinton/Brennan/and Comey is Stronger than Ever

The Federalist-The Russia Collusion Hoax is Worse than You Think

Just the News-Steele Dossier Cited in 2016 ICA Claim about Putin

Clinton Foundation Timeline-2025 Crossfire Hurricane Docs

Just the News-Fallen FBI CI Agent had Role in Trump Russia Hoax

Daily Mail-Putin Henchman Turned Tables on FBI

Forbes-Oleg Deripaska

The Daily Beast-Putin's Shady Billionaire Buddy Who could Hold the Keys

The Last Refugee-Oleg Deripaska/Peeing Story

NY Magazine-Fusion GPS: The Pee Pee Tape

The Last Refuge-Oleg Deripaska

The Hill-Mueller May have a Conflict: A Russian Oligarch

Buster Hyde-Oleg Deripaska and Resistance

The Last Refuge-SpyGate: The Big Picture

Daily Mail-FBI asked Oligarch to Spend $25M to Help Rescue Hostage

Markets Work-Deripaska and Waldman's Role in Assange Negotiations

Forbes-Russian Billionaire Oleg Deripaska describes US Money Laundering

Clinton Foundation Timeline-Oleg Deripaska

FOX News-Sen. Warner texted Russian Oligarch to meet with Steele

Washington Examiner-Emails show Links: Steele/Ohr/Simpson and Deripaska

PBS.org-"It's all a Lie": Russian Billionaire Deripaska

Classic Video-Vlad Putin takes Oleg Deripaska to Task

Senate.Judiciary.gov-Declassified Docs Undercut Steele Dossier/Page FISA Warrants

Crossfire Hurricane Docs-Christopher Steele Binder

Justice.gov-2023 SC John Durham Report

Trend Setting NSA Whistleblower: Thomas Drake's 'Q' Pins

Ten years before Edward Snowden there was a 'White Hat' named Thomas Drake. Drake worked with the likes of Bill Binney and Kirk Wiebe at the National Security Agency (NSA) developing mass surveillance programs. The NSA would be the gatekeepers of all collected data and assigned the filtering process to obtain relevant information. Drake/Wiebe/and Binney would form the core of the Thinthread Whistleblowers group.

Post Q# 2581
> NORMALLY, A WHISTLEBLOWER IS PROTECTED AND SHIELDED FROM ALL NON ESSENTIAL (CLAS).

History will show that all 3 became famous government whistleblowers. Drake let the cat out of the bag by reporting on the illegal use of these sophisticated computer programs against the general public. Stringent privacy laws were put in place to protect the general public against unauthorized surveillance.

Post Q# 1661
> What role can NSA play?

Drake specialized in various NSA computer programs related to mass collection of electronic data. The primary NSA's big surveillance programs were nicknamed Thin Thread/Trailblazer/and Stellar Wind. Credit must be given to Drake and his whistleblower colleagues in the creation of these specialized data collection software programs.

Post Q# 4153
> internal DL [terminal 1] speed [hack]?

The 'Trailblazer' project was the most abused program and the one Drake turned into the OIG of the Defense Department. Even though Binney/Weibe were also joint whistleblowers, only Drake was the only one of this group ultimately prosecuted. Later supercomputer and software enhancements lead to the development of the HAMR or Hammer program abused by DNI James Clapper and CIA Director John Brennan.

Post Q# 2042
> UK ASSIST + FISA SURV INCLUDED ALL UPSTREAM COLLECTION +TANGENT CONTACTS (UMBRELLA SURV).

Thomas Drake tried to do things correctly by working through the 1989 Whistleblower Protection Act. By notifying both the Inspector General of the DOD and Congress, you would think the proper channels would both listen and over proper protection. The protection of the Fourth Amendment had been paramount throughout the history of the United States.

Post Q# 394
> We have the USSS, NSA, and DHS, also protecting this message.

Thomas Drake got his life destroyed by reporting his observed NSA surveillance violations. Drake's whistleblowing on NSA's 'dark' projects highlighted illegal warrantless domestic mass spying on U.S. citizens later admitted under oath at Congressional hearing by DNI Clapper.

Post Q# 3181
> BLIND JUSTICE UNDER THE LAW WILL RETURN TO OUR REPUBLIC.
> There is a reason why a sword is held.

This sounds like a familiar tactic used today by the Deep State (Future proves Past). The groundwork laid by Drake helps us comprehend the FISA abuses being exposed in ObamaGate/SpyGate. Special Counsel John Durham has begun to drop criminal indictments related to the illegal surveillance operations of SpyGate.

Post Q# 1876
Why was No Such Agency created?

One of Drake's classic quotes is "I will not live in Silence". Non-action by both internal governmental watchdog and Congressional groups caused Drake to go public. Hopefully whistleblower laws and protections will prevent this type of unfair treatment.

Post Q# 2514
History books.
Justice.

Drakes attempted disclosures were discovered and lead to Federal Espionage charges. Thomas Drake ultimately agreed to a plea deal of 1-year probation and some local community service. Thankfully the government backed off and some leniency was given to Drake.

Post Q# 3990
FBI CHAIN OF COMMAND DNC HACK? [CIA BRIDGE - UKRAINE - CROWDSTRIKE_BRENNAN]?

Drake's revelations were the biggest since the Daniel Ellsberg/Pentagon Papers. Bear in mind that Drake's disclosures were all released in the pre-Edward Snowden 2013 time period. If more brave Patriots stood up like Thomas Drake, our country would not be in the communist takeover we are experiencing in 2021 under Biden.

Post Q# 3670
Scope and size far greater than you can imagine.

Thomas has to be viewed as an early Patriot much like colleague Bill Binney and older Bill Cooper. Drake teamed up with Bill Binney and Kurt Weiner to form Veteran Intelligence Professionals for Sanity (VIPS). VIPS in part was which an informational gathering consortium that specialized in scientific computer reviews. VIPS would run forensic testing on the 2016 DNC email data to scientifically prove "Leak not Hack".

Post Q# 14
How is POTUS always 5-steps ahead?

Please check out Thomas Drake's own Twitter account (where he addresses the 'Q-Pin' controversy. Drake was way ahead of his time with displaying and promoting 'Q' in public realm. The unique designs inspired by the 'Q' movement would be displayed in shirts, hats, signs and flags following Drake's early lead.

Post Q# 1678
Trolling is fun!

Thomas Drake swears by constantly wearing his special Q-Pin that it doesn't mean that he is part of Team-Q. Wordsmith and evasive tactics are drilled into all young government intelligence candidates. However, Drake does acknowledge our worldwide internet movement in his various public speeches today. With the re-election of President Trumps in 2024, hopefully past whistleblowers will be vindicated.

Post Q# 3903
    [infiltration instead of invasion]

Links

Smithsonian-Thomas Drake Story: Leaks and the Law

Just the News-HRC's Plan tying Trump and Russia

VICE News-Sitting down with Whistleblower Thomas Drake

Techno Fog-U.S. Intelligence Operations against Americans

The Atlantic-BHO's War on Whistleblowers

Jonathan Turley-Six Degrees from Brookings: Think Tank in Russian Collusion

CBS News-Thomas Drake: The Dark Side of Data and the NSA

Daily Dot-Who is Q: Internet's most Mysterious Poster

New Yorker-The Secret Sharer: Thomas Drake

NPR-Whistleblowers before Snowden who Lifted the Veil

The Guardian-How Pentagon Punished Whistleblowers

Sic Sempre Tyrannis-Binney/Johnson: Why the DNC was not Hacked by Russians

PBS-Drake Compares 9/10 to 9/11

Sam Adams Award-Thomas Drake Receives the Sam Adams Award

Thomas Drake-Disavows any Relationship: Report For The President

Whistleblower.org-Whistleblower Profiles: Thinthread Whistleblowers

Thomas Drake/Twitter-'Q' Pins

Crossfire Hurricane Docs-FISA Notes

Justice.gov-2023 SC John Durham Report

Bauer and Dunn: Yet Another ObamaGate 'Dirty Couple'

What do you get when you hitch a partner of Perkins Coie + BHO's White House Communications Director? Oddly when combining this match, you get yet another ObamaGate/SpyGate 'Dirty Couple.' The law firm of Perkins Coie has played pivotal roles in many of the unfolding scandals of today. In his filed 2022 federal RICO lawsuit, President Trump would specially name Perkins Coie along with HRC/DNC/Fusion GPS/and others for damages surrounding the promotion of the false Russia collusion narrative in 2016 then leading to the SpyGate political scandal.

Post Q# 2700
Establish 'financial checks/reviews' of those reviews senior (critical) positions (audits) + direct family (close proximity).

Special Counsel (SC) John Durham would be in charge of unwinding this elaborate criminal conspiracy that involved lawyers, government officials, and outside private contractors. Marriage vows draw attention toward this White House husband/wife combo of the Bauer's. It is becoming more apparent this couple was involved neck deep in ObamaGate/SpyGate as were several other married partner teams. History will show this modern-day Bonnie and Clyde criminal pairings like Bruce/Nellie Ohr.

Post Q# 4077
The World is waking up.

Robert Bauer was the original forming partner of the Political Law Division at Perkins Coie. Prior to organizing this high-profile political group, Bob Bauer was BHO's White House Counsel and primary personal attorney. Many of these in the political lawyers group later would become entangled in the same scandals they were hired to sweep under the proverbial DC rug. Bauer was the office boss of both infamous lawyers Marc Elias and Michael Sussmann.

Post Q# 2331
[Part re: Fusion GPS, Perkins Coie now being revealed?]

Robert Bauer also was General Counsel for 2008/2012 elections for BHO and represented the DNC in that capacity as well. Marc Elias also from Perkins Coie served the same dual roles for HRC/DNC in the 2016 election cycle. This internal coordination among Perkins lawyers was beneficial to shady DC Swamp clientele like HRC and the DNC.

Post Q# 4896
HOW IS THE GAME PLAYED?

Bauer brought several other Obama-era staffers over to join his political division at Perkins Coie. Perkins retained in 2016 Fusion GPS to create the infamous Trump-Russian Christopher Steele Dossier. Coordination by Perkins lawyer Michael Sussmann was with DOJ Bruce Ohr and wife Nellie Ohr under contract with Fusion GPS. SC John Durham indicated Sussmann for lying to FBI General Counsel James Baker in 2016 over Alfa Bank.

Post Q# 809
HRC open source server?
[Missing emails]
[CrowdStrike]

Additionally, Perkins Coie hired CrowdStrike to look at DNC computer breach in 2016, bizarrely over the FBI. Perkins hired Fusion GPS to get dirt against No Name in 2012 and 2008 for BHO, concerning the Birther issue and U.S. Passport office records coverups using John Brennan's TAC firm. Bob Bauer combined with fellow Perkins lawyers Michael Sussmann and Marc Elias in the RussiaGate/SpyGate political scandals and coverups. Bob Bauer would be tapped by Biden in 2023 to help defend against the numerous classified (SCI level) documents discovered at various locations.

Post Q# 2121
Knowledge is POWER!

Loving wife of Bauer is Anita Dunn, who also worked at the BHO White House. Dunn was BHO's White House Communications Director and media strategy/speechwriting coordinator. It was not uncommon for BHO to poach staffers like Dunn and Jake Sullivan from both HRC as well as Biden's staff. Sullivan would reappear in the illegal Biden administration as the National Security Adviser. Many consider Anita Dunn one of the architects of the 2020 Biden campaign and she has continued to assist this illegal administration. Early in 2023 Anita Dunn would make Biden's short list for the new Chief of Staff position being vacated by Ron Klein. Revolver News would aptly nickname Anita Dunn the 'Brawler-In-Chief' and she is a controlling force along with wife Jill. In typical DC revolving door fashion, Anita Dunn departed the White House soon after Joe Biden dropped out of the 2024 race for a position with a Kamala Harris Super PAC.

Post Q# 1828
[SPY OP]
[PERKINS COIE] (Shell2)

Anita Dunn had helped Harvey Weinstein strategize before media exposure and subsequent arrest. Bauer and Dunn have given testimony to Congressional committees about their knowledge and roles in the SpyGate scandal. SC John Durham will clean up this corrupt couples past involvement and began with Perkins Coie lawyer Michael Sussmann. Anita Dunn has been a principal partner in a DC powerful political strategy firm called SKDK (Anita is the 'D'). All of America First can thank Anita Dunn for coming up with the term 'Ultra MAGA', which everyone now wears as another badge of honor in the Information War. History will show both Bauer and Dunn were part of the inner White House circle that managed (autopen) the USA policy due to mental cognitive decline of Biden.

Post Q# 964
BIDEN/CHINA VERY IMPORTANT MARKER.

Bob and Anita join fellow 'Dirty Couples'-M/M McCabe and M/M Strzok and M/M Ohr and M/M Pientka and Murray-King and Power-Sunstein, to name a few involved in SpyGate/ObamaGate. Similar to Bauer's sudden departure fellow Perkins Coie lawyer Marc Elias has resigned ahead SC John Durham's indictment/trial of lawyer Michael Sussmann. late in 2022 Elon Musk would call out Perkins Coie/Sussmann for an "Attempt to corrupt a Presidential election". SC Durham submitted his final report in 2023. With the historic re-election of President Trump in 2024, many past hidden political secrets will finally be revealed.

Post Q# 3702
This is not another 4-year election.
Game theory.

Links

Political Vel Craft-Anita Dunn's Husband and Council for BHO

FOX News-Biden Insider Anita Dunn Confronted after Grilling from GOP

Just the News-Evidence Suggests FBI Conspired with HRC to Legitimize RussiaGate

Clinton Foundation Timeline-Perkins Coie Contracts with CrowdStrike and Fusion GPS

NY Post-Biden Campaign Aides under Fire over Debate Debacle

NY Times-Anita Dunn and Bob Bauer: Couple at Center of Biden's Inner Circle

Revolver News-The Big Gun running Biden Behind the Scenes

FOX News-Who is Bob Bauer?

Breitbart-Elon Musk Calls out Sussmann/Perkins Coie for 'Attempt to Corrupt an Election'

WAPO-Anita Dunn and SKDK: Power and Profit in Biden's Washington

Real Clear Politics-RussiaGate: HRC Campaign/Perkins Coie/Fusion GPS/CrowdStrike

Dawson Field-Perkins Coie and HRC Campaign

CNBC-Joe Biden Shakes up Campaign: Elevating Strategist Anita Dunn

WSJ-Bob Bauer/Anita Dunn: In and Out at the White House

National Review-When Scandals Collide

Daily Beast-BHO Aides "Pissed Off" about Anita Dunn

Markets Work-Devin Nunes List of 42 Named Referrals

American Thinker-How Husband/Wives Figure in Latest Scandal Revelations

NBC News-Power Couple at Center of Biden's Political Universe

Influence Watch-Perkins Coie

Grassley.Senate.gov-Crossfire Hurricane Timeline

House.gov-Anita Dunn Request to Testify (AutoPen)

Crossfire Hurricane Docs-FISA Notes

Justice.gov-2023 SC John Durham Report

Elevated to Special Counsel: Meet John 'Bull' Durham

John H. 'Bull' Durham was the longstanding US Attorney (USA) for District of Connecticut until his retirement this year. 'Bull' Durham has had a history of cleaning up political corruption in the New England region. Now elevated to a Special Counsel (SC) status within the DOJ, Durham is playing a historical role in the upcoming SpyGate/ObamaGate criminal political indictments. One of the final posts by 'Q' just said "Durham" as this will be key in the general public's awakening process. SC Durham concluded his extensive investigation in 2023 and his final report was a vindication of our own research.

Post Q# 2603
> What if there's another prosecutor (outside of DC) assigned by SESSIONS w/the same mandate/authority?

John 'Bull' Durham had served Connecticut for over 35 years and was the Deputy USA before being appointed the head in 2/22/18. John Durham was serving as the interim USA for CT on October 28, 2017 (note: same day as first 'Q' drops and tasked by AG Sessions to prosecute the Storm). Most agree that SC Durham is a straight-shooting prosecutor that cannot be dissuaded from his judicial duty. Durham would roll out in his 2002 court filings a vast coordinated criminal conspiracy against candidate Donald Trump by both government officials as well as outside private contractors.

Post Q# 3718
> Durham discoveries can lead to early retirement(?)

Durham was assigned from 2008-2012 as Acting USA for the Eastern District of Virginia. John Durham was tasked to investigate the CIA's torture of terrorist detainees and the destruction of video tape evidence. Durham's political independence was solidified by his own prior judicial actions in handling several high-profile criminal corruption cases. All sides seem to universally agree as to John Durham's airtight image of serious independence.

Post Q# 3784
> DECLAS CoC
> POTUS - Barr
> Barr - Durham

John Durham is also credited in 1999 with cleaning up the notorious Boston criminal mobs. Inspiring the Oscar-winning film 'The Departed', Durham brought down the infamous James 'Whitey' Bulger crime syndicate. Bulger's nephew would become a partner with Hunter Biden/Chris Heinz/and Devon Archer in the infamous Rosemont Seneca (Bohai) Partners international investment fund. The illegal Biden administration has floundered in trying to address issues concerning Hunter and his colorful partner's hard to explain business deals.

Post Q# 3389
> Durham and Rogers meeting(s)?

Under questioning from Congressional committees, former FBI lawyer James Baker admitted to being under criminal investigation by SC John Durham for leaks to the news media. James Baker's attorney pointed out to Rep. Jim Jordan that Durham is overseeing a criminal probe involving their client. Durham has indicated Perkins Coie lawyer Michael Sussmann over lying to the James Baker in 2016 concerning Alfa Bank and Fusion GPS opposition research (Steele

Dossier) rumors. SC Durham would slowly role out in 2022 through various court filings a vast 'Joint Venture Conspiracy' involving HRC/DNC/Perkins Coie/and many others.

Post Q# 3800
> Think Durham start.
> Think 'Q' start.
> You have more than you know.

I had previously written that Acting AG Matt Whitaker was one of 'Q''s Stealth Bombers and now please add SC Durham to the top of that list. Former AG Barr had previously clarified that SP John Huber was investigating the CF/U1 and SC Durham is specifically handling FISA abuses and 'spying.' 44 Republican Senators are demanding AG Garland made SC Durham's report made public. SC Durham would assume much of John Huber's investigations into the Clinton Foundation in 2020.

Post Q# 4489
> Lock down(s) + C: Halt travel of called witnesses re: pending investigation [Durham (known)] _legal out deployed by witness "I do not feel comfortable and/or safe traveling due to COVID-19 health concerns."

'Q' had pointed out the possibility of a second Special Prosecutor (SP) in addition to John Huber way back in 2018. AG Barr has also assigned at that time SP John Durham to review the Trump-Russia probe and the legal predication of the inception of this treasonous plot against President Elect Trump. One of the last official moves by AG Barr was to elevated John Durham to Special Counsel prior to the end of the first Trump Presidential term. SC Durham would continue to expose the layers of criminal plans involved with the 2016 false Russia collusion narrative against candidate Donald Trump, including Alfa Bank/Steele Dossier/Trump Tower and more.

Post Q# 4952
> Durham.

It is logical to assume that Durham has been prosecuting the many media leak investigations and working plea agreements with cooperating witnesses. President Trump's first actions ordered Stealth AG Jeff Sessions to open 27 different federal leak probes (Reality Winner/James Wolfe). Now POTUS jokingly asks if John Durham actually exists, Anons know this as being answer-moves and countermoves. Durham's criminal probes continue and fresh grand jury subpoenas flow from the Special Counsel's office.

Post Q# 3595
> AUS, IT, UK co-opt DOJ (Barr, Durham, CLAS 1-4).

Former FBI lawyer James Baker had been fingered by FBI lawyer Lisa Page as leaking classified information to reporter David Korn from Mother Jones News. AG Jeff Sessions had made illegal leaks his first mission and DOJ's biggest priority. SC Durham's lead investigator William Aldenberg has been briefed by Sundance/CTH as to what is known by the public (Digital Soldiers) about SpyGate. Former DNI Ratcliffe had given SC Durham over 1,000 intelligence documents that will ultimately usher in many criminal indictments and per court filings, Durham had released over 60,000 newly declassified documents in discovery proceedings.

Post Q# 3932
> The House will open investigations into Barr-Durham [lack of confidence].
> The Silent War Continues....

With the re-election of President Trump in 2024, hopefully we will witness real justice and poised for the final act in this historic movie. SC Durham dutifully and as common practice submitted his resignation as an U.S. Attorney in the beginning of the under the illegal Biden administration. Kevin Clinesmith was the first to be indicted, with Perkins Coie/Clinton campaign lawyer Michael Sussmann the second criminal indictment and Chris Steele's dossier researcher Igor Danchenko being the third in SC John Durham's record. The reports from IG Horowitz and SC Durham will be the foundation for future judicial accountability. With the re-election of President Trump in 2024, we hope to get the full details behind these past political scandals. President Trump would instantly appoint Mr. Durham's son John J. Durham the U.S. Attorney for the Eastern District of NY (BOOM).

Post Q# 3581
Month/Day 'Q' public campaign initiated?
Month/Day 'Durham' initiated?

Links

Epoch Times-Infographic: Timeline of Durham Investigation

FOX News-Patel found Thousands of Sensitive Trump Russia Probe Docs

The Federalist-DOJ Officials didn't know Database Allowed FBI to Bury RussiaGate Docs

Just the News-FBI Opens Grand Conspiracy Probe

The Federalist-Unsealed Crossfire Hurricane Docs prove RussiaGate a Hoax

Newsweek-Donald Trump: RussiaGate Hoax

The Federalist-FBI Revelations Show the Mueller Special Counsel was a Cover-Up

Washington Examiner-Durham Report: 5 Key Takeaways

Breitbart-Durham Report Exonerates Trump Vindicating Russian Hoax

CBS News-SC John Durham Testifies to Sobering Findings

Justice.gov-SC John Durham 2023 Report

FOX News-Durham Assumed Parts of John Huber's Clinton Foundation

Techno Fog-Investigating-the Investigators

Washington Examiner-RussiaGate claim exposes FBI and DOJ's Misinformation Campaign

PJ Media-SC John Durham Investigation of ObamaGate Expansion

NY Magazine-The Trials of John Durham

The American Spectator-John Durham and the Steele Dossier

Markets Work-Durham Investigating whether CIA withheld Information

National Review-Last trusted Prosecutor in Washington

Time-CIA Abuse Investigator: John Durham

Bloomberg Law-Special Counsel's Probe Explained

DEA.gov-DEA/FBI Dismantle Drug Trafficking in NY/CT

Justice.gov-John J. Durham appointed US Attorney for Eastern District of NY

Justice.gov-Statement of U.S. Attorney John H. Durham

Crossfire Hurricane Docs-Christopher Steele Binder

Justice.gov-SC Office: Michael Sussmann Indictment

Sayonara Five Eyes (FVEY): Let's Welcome Three Eyes

The new developing global intelligence alliance might possibly be called Three (not Five) Eyes. Five Eyes (FVEY) was the old Western intelligence sharing group formed out of necessity between the Allies in 1941 during the onset of global war. The obvious need for sharing of critical wartime information carried over into peacetime for the victorious allied partners. 'Q' has pointed us to the possibility of a secret alliance between President Trump with Russia/Saudi Arabia/China/and others.

Post Q# 2657
> Was FVEY established and designed by the INTEL COMM as a backchannel SURV apparatus to avoid domestic laws, triggers, and Congressional/Senate oversight?

Current FVEY member nations consist of the U.S./U.K./Canada/Australia/and New Zealand. Unlimited intelligence flows to/from each nation but SpyGate demonstrates that FVEY has been used illegally from time to time. Membership automatically insures full cooperation on both intelligence as well as diplomatic levels. It was theorized that Deep State actors would travel to foreign based Sensitive Compartmented Information Facilities (SCIF) nicknamed 'tanks', to nefariously removed top secrets with no real paper trail.

Post Q# 140
> Why did POTUS receive a sword dance when visiting SA?

What if China, Russia, and others are coordinating w/POTUS to eliminate the NWO?

The three U.S. agencies involved with the FVEY partnership are the NSA/FBI/and National Geospatial Intelligence Agency. Exclusive clubs tend to hide behind closed doors as do the identities of their active secret memberships. The heavy hitters operating the FVEY intelligence operations are the CIA (clowns). Keep in mind often it is Spy vs Spy with various psychological operations and driven narratives that surround any international intelligence sharing agreements.

Post Q# 4153
> FVEY [unofficial].
> FVEY UK-AUS reverify AUTH_WH [unusual req special instructions]

Recent years has offered an expansion into both the Nine Eyes (Denmark/France/Netherlands/Norway) and the Fourteen Eyes (Germany/Spain/Sweden/Spain/Belgium) sharing partnerships. Signals intelligence (SIGINT) captures all electronic communications transmitted on a global basis. Sadly it was revealed in 2024 that former CIA Director John Brennan had FIVE EYES illegally target 26 Team Trump aides back in 2016, which set off the Russia Russia Russia false narrative giving cover to FBI/HRC's operations.

Post Q# 1603
> If you are smart (stupid) you know what just occurred at the meeting in Russia.
> [Objective] to keep POTUS away from PUTIN failed.
> EVIL has no place here.
> GOD WINS.

This century has witnessed abuses by countries 'farming-out' surveillance to each other to avoid their own domestic s spying laws. If for some reason the U.S. couldn't spy on candidate/President Donald Trump, they would hand off the surveillance job to a fellow FVEY co-conspirator partner.

There is much significance behind the Saudi Sword Dance as was in the gift of a Russian World Cup soccer ball by Putin to Trump in Helsinki. 'Q' hinted that a computer chip may have been secreted inside by Putin to give to President Trump as part of their NWO takedown plan.

Post Q# 4299
> 702 collection [minimization procedures] v CIA v FVEY

Originally named the Atlantic Charter, this intelligence alliance was later called ECHELON during the Cold War period. Public exposure in the late 1990's combined with the tragedy of 9/11 forced the existence of Five Eyes into a shocked mass public. The 2022 Ukraine invasion by Russia is possibly demonstrating pre-agreed upon plans to takedown the Deep State/NWO Cabal.

Post Q# 72
> SA is the primary, US is secondary (Asia/EU).....
> Alice and Wonderland.

The new Three Eyes intelligence alliance might possibly be the U.S./Saudi Arabia/and Russia. President Trump even rubbed the mysterious glowing orb and did the rare 'Sword Dance', which in essence was the start of a Storm. Our old partners have all turned coup plot traitors and new trustworthy allies need to be found. History will show that to much of the amazement of the world, China reaffirmed their commitment to Russia despite the Ukraine war of 2022.

Post Q# 2681
> UK/AUS narrative shift re: in country spy campaign v POTUS (hops 1 to 2, 2 to 3, 3 to 4, 4 to target).

Jared Kushner and Ezra Cohen-Watnick had been the liaisons on the ground in Saudi Arabia and developing this critical new partnership that led to the Abraham Peach Accord. Main goals are for a lasting Middle East peace plan and solidifying a new possible Three Eyes intelligence alliance partnership. The illegal Biden administration is beginning to sink FVEY as partner New Zealand is fuming over a sneaky nuclear sub deal with Australia. Biden's NSA Jake Sullivan would in 2022 piss off the Saudi Crown Prince Mohammed bin Salman over the death of Jamel Khashoggi and damage the relationship with the USA developed under President Trump.

Post Q# 2938
> If not tasked and targeted under FVEY-what legal authority existed to engage the targeting?
> Think Nunes statement "not through normal collection, gathering, and reporting/oversight re: (FVEY).
> What US Ally completed the collection of false data?

Picture in your mind the infamous Helsinki soccer ball toss between President Trump and Vladimir. There are new alliances forming in the wake of discovered abuses made by FVEY partners against President Trump. The rarely discussed 2-EYES (US and Israel) may also become a thing of the past as well. We may be witnessing a new alliance of super-powers with USA joining with Russia/Saudia Arabia/China/and others in defeating the globalist attempted New World Order. The formation by a group of nations of the BRICS gold backed currency and President Xi disavowing the G20 shows the background of President Trump's plan. Many now feel the FBI raid upon President Trump's Mar-A-Lago home was to obtain the RussiaGate/Crossfire Hurricane classified folder.

Post Q# 190
> Necessary to form WW alliances to defeat.

The 'New Alliance' are the current contingency of modern-day White Hat Patriots. The 'Storm' was 23 core Generals/Admirals plus MI/NSA/Team-Q all forming "The Plan" to enlist President Trump. Judgement Day is coming to this criminal cabal and Special Counsel (SC) John Durham has dropped criminal indictments related to past illegal surveillance operations and submitted his final report in 2023. The reports from IG Horowitz and SC Durham will be the foundation for future judicial accountability. Vald Putin would praise the courage bravery shown by President Trump after the failed Butler assassination attempt as well as early congratulations on his 2024 re-election victory.

Post Q# 4647

44, Brennan-lead + [F] assist.
Matters of NAT SEC.

Links

Burning Bright-Righteous Russia: Enemy of my Enemies

Journal of World Affairs-All Eyes on Five Eyes

The Last Refuge-The Big Picture

Clandestine-Game of Thrones

Jonathan Turley-The EYES have It

NY Post-CIA and Foreign Intelligence Agencies Illegally Targeted 26 Trump Aides

NZ Herald-New Zealand Hosts Five Eyes Network Gathering

The New American-Propaganda and the US Government

The Intercept-Saudi/Russia Collusion is Driving up Gas Prices/Ukraine Crisis

The Hill-Putin's Soccer Ball Gift to POTUS Contains Transmitter Chip

Restore Privacy-Five Eyes, Nine Eyes, 14 Eyes Explained

US Treasury.gov-US and Saudi Open New Terror Center

Reuters News-Five Eyes Alliance Builds Coalition to Counter China

Providence Mag-What to Know about Five Eyes (FVEY)

UK Defense-Five Eyes: The Intelligence of the Anglosphere

Daily Mail-Saudi Crown Prince and Kushner Share Intelligence

The Atlantic-Is the 'Five Eyes Alliance' Conspiring to Spy on You?

The Guardian-U.S./U.K. Struck deal to Unmask Personal Data

Jerusalem Post-Saudi Arabia/Egypt/Qatar/UAE welcome Trump Peace Plan

Privacy End-Five Eyes, Nine Eyes, Fourteen Eyes Alliance

Clinton Foundation Timeline-Key Foreign Intelligence SpyGate Players

The Guardian-One Orb Slightly Used: MBS Reveals Fate of Mysterious Saudi Sphere

Epoch Times: Renewal of US-Saudi Alliance Under Trump: Game Changer

US Army 4th PSYOP Group-Ghost in the Machine 2

Crossfire Hurricane Docs-Christopher Steele Binder

Justice.gov-2023 SC John Durham Report

Nunes Advises "Follow the HOPS"—Not the White Rabbit

In the shadowy world of intelligence gathering, the term 'HOPS' refers to the ability to jump or 'leapfrog' communications chains between individuals (no White Rabbit). FISA Title-1 allows a total of 2 contacts or 2-degrees of separation to be captured. 2022 would mark the beginning of the public unveiling of the vast coordinated conspiracy against then candidate Donald Trump and those aides in his political orbit.

Post Q# 2043
FOREIGN TARGET DESIGNATOR(S) CREATE LEAPFROG (HOPS) TO ISOLATE 'REAL' TARGET(S).

In lay terms you call up Ken and then he calls Barbie, now all 3 people are under this total net of surveillance. It is a series of HOPS or 'leapfrogging' method to ensnare suspects especially the target. These 'warrant less' surveillance techniques were allowed under FISA 702 queries into the chains of conversations between targets.

Post Q# 1826
[Past 24hrs - Nunes Attack].

Crossfire Hurricane was a classic example of reverse engineering of Title-1 surveillance warrants. Candidate/President Trump was the real intended objective and target, not volunteer campaign advisor Carter Page.

Post Q# 2681
UK/AUS narrative shift re: in-country spy campaign v POTUS (hops 1 to 2, 2 to 3, 3 to 4, 4 to target).
decode: UK/AUS employs 3-HOPS whereas US lowered to 2-HOPS.

FISA warrants allow these HOPS to collect all communications records like phone calls, texts, data, FAXES, social media, DM, HAM communications, Xbox chat logs, Gmail ghost drafts, blogs, etc. "The whole Enchilada Snow White" as was told to Edward Snowden in "Citizen Four" movie.

Post Q# 4647
The illegal spy campaign by 44 [upstream collection] went far beyond that of 45s transition team.

The total number of 'friends of friends' is over 4,000 people after the 2nd Degree HOP is applied. This method is termed 'umbrella surveillance' due to the large radius of total coverage. The 3-HOPS rule captures +1 million 'friends' (UK/AUS employed).

Post Q# 1498
[[RR]] approved/signed FISA-warrant application(s) to extend surveillance on POTUS/others.

To obtain a FISA Title-1 surveillance warrant law enforcement must demonstrate to the secret court/FISC that the 'target' is an agent of a Foreign Power. This is a very high threshold and the required documentary evidence needs to be iron clad.

Post Q# 3608
WASHINGTON CIVIL WAR [CONTROL THE NARRATIVE].
[SELF PRESERVATION]

Naturally a very high bar to reach except during the illegal surveillance reign of BHO. We are discovering extras FISA's were granted besides the notable Carter Page warrant (Trump/Flynn/PapaD/Cruz/etc). It was revealed in 2024 that the CIA/Director Brennan asked Five Eye (FVEY) intelligence sharing partners to spy upon U.S. citizens and employing the extra 'HOP' level.

Post Q# 2489
[Placeholder - OIG Report-Umbrella SPY and Targeting].

In this case Carter Page is a foreign agent who appears regularly on FOX News with no lawyer. Not the normal routine for a high level covert secret foreign Russian intelligence asset (spy).

Post Q# 151
How do you capture a very dangerous animal?

Carter Page attended a London symposium at the request of Stefan Halper. The carrot that was dangled to Carter Page was some juicy HRC opposition research.

Post Q# 3212
Think Rogers T-Tower meeting (right after SCIF set up in Tower).

This interchange was one of the genesis events from which sprang the entire Trump-Russia collusion fraud. George Papadopoulos had his own 'dirty-up' London pub entrapment operation as part of Crossfire Hurricane.

Post Q# 3595
[1-3 jumps primary target], T WH spy insertion NATSEC C.

Recall the famed Devin Nunes presser in front of the White House in 2017. Ezra Cohen-Watnick and Michael Ellis showed Nunes the BHO Presidential Daily Briefings (PDB) and illegal unmasking of Trump campaign staffers that had occurred.

Post Q# 2462
Who briefed NUNES on classified intel re: HUSSEIN spy campaign v. POTUS?

This meeting was held in the White House Sensitive Compartmented Information Facility (SCIF). BHO's had his PDB spread out via a mass dissemination method called "Operation Latitude" (Dr. Evelyn Farkas). Leave no doubt that all of the various coup operations against Donald Trump began and were approved by BHO.

Four main components of the coup plot nicknamed Operation Trump:
- Exonerate HRC/Aides (ObamaGate)
- False Trump-Russia Dossier creation/distribution (RussiaGate)
- FISA Title-1 Surveillance Warrants/Section 702 (SpyGate)
- The 'Insurance Policy' (Crossfire Hurricane)

Post Q# 4489
Can you see and understand their attempts to slow-stop accountability?

Patriot Devin Nunes saw unmasked names, opposition research from Steele, illegal NSA Section 702 queries, and more in BHO's PDBs. As a Gang of 8 member, Nunes has the absolute highest level security clearance to see all of this evidence of illegal surveillance operations. Admiral Mike Rogers exposed in 2016 the abuses by the FBI of the warrantless Section 702 wiretaps and HOPS communication chains.

Post Q# 3788

Correction will be needed: ALL SURV re: POTUS [hops] will be concluded that there was "insufficient predication to establish probable cause."

It takes near 'Q-level' clearance even be allowed to access this very high-level top-secret material. Ezra Cohen-Watnick is an original "FlynnStone" member alumni and is held in the highest regard by President Trump and Devin Nunes. President Trump spoke of Nunes "This guy down into dungeons/basements, he'll find a document, no matter what."

Post Q# 436

[FISA 2]
decode: Minimum 2 FISA Title-1 Surveillance warrants have been approved-Carter Page (Flynn/Manafort/Papadopoulos/Ted Cruz/etc.).

Devin Nunes has said publicly that the DOJ used unverified 'opposition research' in the original Rod Rosenstein Scope Memo, This establishes the origins of the Trump-Russia witch hunt was launched using the known fake Christopher Steele Dossier.

Post Q# 4196

Why did [Schiff] illegally surveil [phone] members of WH legal team, media, and Congress?

Staffer to Nunes was Kash Patel and he played a critical role in helping uncover the Russian Hoax. Patel went over from the NSC to help then acting ODNI Richard Grenell to straighten out the corrupt intelligence committees. Representative Nunes announced he is retiring from Congress at end of 2021 to become CEO of Trump's new media company.

Post Q# 2043

P talks to X.
X talks to Y.
Y talks to Z.
P, X, Y, Z = BULK DATA COLLECTION.
[UMBRELLA].

IG Horowitz/SP Huber/SC Durham have all taken on the investigation of alleged abuses by the DOJ/FBI with past FISC-FISA applications. Horowitz's 2.0 report demonstrated the Carter Page FISA four applications were illegally obtained through falsehoods to the FISC. SC John Durham is on the final stages of these ongoing criminal probes.

Post Q# 3993

If [AS] was privy to GANG OF EIGHT classified material would he not know the same FACTS (TRUTH) as NUNES?
Think NUNES memo v SCHIFF.

The ACLU/Civil Libertarians should be shouting and howling at the sky about governmental surveillance abuses. Unfortunately, from this concerned crowd all we are hearing is nothing but crickets. SC John Durham's final report was submitted in 2023 and will be the basis for future judicial accountability. With the historic re-election of President Trump in 2024, many past hidden political secrets will finally be revealed.

Post Q# 570

Sessions/Nunes Russian OPS.

Links

The Atlantic-NSA Admits it Analyzes more People's Data than Revealed

Just the News-Steele Dossier Cited in 2016 ICA Claim about Putin

The Federalist-Unsealed Crossfire Hurricane Docs prove RussiaGate a Hoax

Wired-FBI Officials urge Agents to use Warrantless Section 702 Queries

Tablet Magazine-FISA's License to HOP

CSIS.org-Reforming Section 702 FISA

Conservative Brief-Nunes: I've sent 14 Criminal Referrals to John Durham

The Last Refuge-FISA 702

Markets Work-The Uncovering: Mike Rogers/FISA/and FBI

War Economy-Four FISA/Crossfire Hurricane

YouTube-Devin Nunes Exposes the BHO Administration's Illegal Spying Targeting Trump

Tablet Magazine-FISA Title 1 Surveillance

Epoch Times-IG Horowitz and FISA Abuses

The Last Refuge-SpyGate: The Big Picture

Dawson Field-2 HOP Surveillance

Markets Work-FBI's Contractors, FISA Abuse, and Steele Timeline

WTPO-NSA Surveillance "HOPS"

The Guardian-3 Degrees of Separation: HOPS

Red State-Expanding Scope of Inquiry to include "To/From" Queries in NSA Database

NPR-3 HOPS gives NSA Millions of Phone Records

The Guardian-U.S. and U.K. Struck Secret Spying Arrangement

Forward-Nunes gets Secret Intel from Ezra

US House.gov-FISA Title-1 Summary

The American Report-Biden used Hammer/Scorecard just like BHO

Susan Whitney-Michael Ellis and Ezra Cohen-Watnick

Markets Work-FISA Surveillance: Title 1/3 and Section 702

Judiciary.Senate.gov-Crossfire Hurricane Interviews

Crossfire Hurricane Docs-Christopher Steele Binder

Justice.gov-2023 SC John Durham Report

Flynn Targeted Vendetta by McCabe over EEOC Case

FBI Whistleblower Supervisory Special Agent Robyn Gritz was fired in 2015. Robyn had been a highly decorated counter-terrorism expert. General Flynn has written a letter of commendation for Robyn back in 2014, in support of agent Gritz's job performance. President Trump would assist General Flynn in seeking revenge against McCabe and others in his 2022 federal RICO lawsuit against the main SpyGate characters promoting the false Russian collusion narrative.

Post Q# 97
Game theory.
What is Flynn's background?
Was he involved with intel ops?

General Flynn even tried to testify at Ms. Gritz's hearings but was deliberately denied this opportunity. Robyn Gritz filed an Equal Opportunity Employment Commission (EEOC) complaint against both the FBI and Deputy Director Andrew McCabe. General Flynn would file in 2022 a $50 million claim against the DOJ/FBI in part over the Robyn Gritz past EEOC case as well as the entire SpyGate/Russia probe of 2016.

Post Q# 3388
There is a big [direct] reason why Flynn's new attorney is seeking security clearance.

Robyn Gritz was the FBI agent who supervised the Robert Levinson case in 2009. This brings in Mueller/McCabe/and John Pistole along with Robyn working with Russian Oligarch Oleg Deripaska, in trying to free Levinson from Iranian captivity.

Post Q# 4620
Flynn 1st strike designed to 1. cripple 2. prevent exposure of illegal acts [Hussein WH CoC] through NAT SEC [intel] discovery

History shows that Oleg spent $25 million of his own funds, in this joint effort to get Levinson out of Iran. The deal was all set for Levinson's release, only to be terminated at the last minute by HRC/US State Department.

Post Q# 1282
Who interviewed Flynn?

The crux of this EEOC case began with a sexual discrimination charge over a promotion and was later upgraded to include workplace retaliation. Once McCabe had learned of the pending EEOC complaint, he engaged in what was later proven to be harsh workplace penalties directed at Ms. Gritz.

Post Q# 3693
Same evidence to FREE FLYNN currently being used to INDICT others [GJ]?
[6] counts.
FBI agent [1] [P] - FLYNN interview......

This was inflicted by Andrew McCabe as payback for her pending EEOC discrimination complaint. The vindictive nature of McCabe has been shown to Robyn Gritz, General Flynn, the MAGA movement and President Trump.

Post Q# 4607
Are you ready to serve once again?
decode: Q-Team asking General Flynn

Past releases from the FBI's Office of Professional Responsibly showed McCabe leaked information to the MSM media about General Mike Flynn in February 2017. This is an ongoing pattern of unauthorized media leaks by the top echelon of the Justice Department/FBI.

Post Q# 1265
> We all have a part to play.
> We knew FLYNN would be challenged.
> Part of the plan?

Future proves past as it now appears there was a coordinated attack to remove then NSA Mike Flynn. Involved with this plan to setup and force the removal of Flynn, were senior officials of both the FBI and DOJ (Flynn/Yates/Strzok/etc).

Post Q# 2164
> SESSIONS and FLYNN [targeted] for [immediate] removal/recusal?

Flynn's FBI 'sting' operation featured an intercepted phone call from Russian Ambassador Sergey Kislyak. Later the nature of this call was the basis of NSA Flynn's removal for so-called misleading of VP Mike Pence of this routine phone conversation.

Post Q# 2043
> FISA warrant issued / approved - FLYNN.

Then NSA Director Flynn was questioned by two FBI agents in an impromptu informal interview in the White House on 1/24/17. Comey/McCabe sent agents Peter Strzok and Joe Pientka to question Flynn with no legal counsel being present.

Post Q# 4506
> The People's General.
> Soon.

Code named Crossfire Razor, this entrapment operation against Flynn was one of several sub-plans within Crossfire Hurricane. In addition to the FISA warrants, BHO issued National Security Letters (NSL) to illegally surveil General Flynn in Operation Crossfire Razor. Crossfire Typhoon was the use of the Foreign Agents Registration Act (FARA) by Team Mueller against Flynn/Manafort/Gates/and PapaD.

Post Q# 1280
> Define 'on record.'
> Who knows where the bodies are buried?

Sally Yates soon advised President Trump of this 'compromising' phone call by NSA Flynn. Potential future compromising blackmail by the Russians was the excused by Yates for her suggested General Flynn's removal as the NSA. The confusion with VP Pence sealed the deal for General Flynn and we pray for his total exoneration.

Post Q# 4025
> CLEARED OF ALL CHARGES.
> TRUMP ADMIN v2?

Unfortunately, a tragic and strange death occurred to a very close friend of Robyn's. Investigative journalist Jen Moore was found dead in a DC hotel room under very suspicious circumstances. During both the Clinton and Obama eras, many investigative journalists were found dead under beyond mysterious circumstances. The term 'Arkancide' became a popular public label for many of these very suspicious deaths.

Post Q# 3330
> FBI 302's.
> FISA (spy) - Flynn.

Will newly discovered evidence (AG Barr-SDNY) FREE FLYNN?

Jen Moore had just told Robyn Gritz she had discovered documents that tie both of the Clintons into a pedophile ring and that now she feared for her life. Robyn Gritz had been telling of unethical and coercive tactics previously employed by the DOJ/FBI. Patriots would witness General Mike Flynn continue to support President Trump throughout the turmoil of the stolen 2020 election period.

Post Q# 4140
> LET FREEDOM RING!

Inquiring minds want to know how far this political corrupt will go to achieve Deep State goals. Fortunately, the DOJ has dropped all charges against General Flynn, and we await his return to governmental duty very soon. Special Counsel John Durham has dropped criminal indictments related to the illegal surveillance of SpyGate and submitted his final report in 2023. With the re-election of President Trump in 2024, hopefully all these hidden political secrets will finally be publicly revealed.

Post Q# 131
> POTUS NAT SEC E briefing 3:02am

Links

The Intercept-The Digital General

Kings Intel-New Evidence Unveils McCabe's Deception

Clinton Foundation Timeline-May 2014: McCabe Accused of Sexual Discrimination

Real Clear Investigations-Flynn backed FBI Agent charging Sex Bias

The Federalist-FBI closes Flynn Case Dubbed Crossfire Razor

NPR-Former FBI Agent Speaks Out

Tablet Magazine-RussiaGate began with BHO's Domestic Spying

Western Journal-Gen. Flynn: Deep State Pushing U.S. toward Final Military Conflict

The Federalist-BHO/Biden Oval Office Meeting on January 5th was Key

Tampa Bay Times-FBI Agent Fred Humphries calls McCabe Firing Justified

Epoch Times-Was Strzok's Interview really about McCabe's SpyGate Role?

Lamar-ObamaGate

The Federalist-Susan Rice Email Confirms Michael Flynn was Targeted

The Last Refuge-FISA 702 Searches

American Thinker-Flynn Entrapment was McCabe's Revenge

American Spectator-Gritz Found out McCabe is No Gentleman

Quo Verum-The Great Sacrifice: General Flynn

The Federalist-8 Times U.S. Intelligence Set People Up to Fabricate the Russia Story

SOTT-Collateral Damage (Flynn): SpyGate Figure Stefan Halper

Vabelle2010-Robyn Gritz/EEOC

Western Journal-General Flynn: New Type of Warfare

Lift the Veil-Robyn Gritz and George Webb: The Jen Moore Investigation

Justice.gov-Crossfire Hurricane Timeline

Crossfire Hurricane Docs-Andrew McCabe Memos

Justice.gov-2023 SC John Durham Report

Deep State's Early Targets:
The General and His 'FlynnStones'

Special Counsel (SC) Robert Mueller's recommendation for no jail time for General Michael Flynn, ultimately was honored by the DOJ in dropping all pending federal charges. General Flynn's attorney Sidney Powell has done heroic work highlighting the government's past "Bad Faith" actions and obvious prosecutorial misconduct. The American public would start to see in 2022 the full extent of past illegal surveillence operations conducted against candidate Donald Trump and those in his inner circle.

Post Q# 144
> Who has clearance to full picture?
> What council do the Wizards and Warlocks control?

Judge Emmet Sullivan was the corrupt Federal judge overseeing General Flynn's case, was ordered by the Appeals Court to go along with the DOJ's decision to drop all charges. The gross misconduct of the DOJ as well as Flynn's prior counsel, was in front of several different courts and General Flynn rightfully was exonerated after much legal jockeying. General Flynn would file a $50 million claim against the DOJ/FBI for the 2016 Russian probe and this eventually will lead to a full lawsuit.

Post Q# 1283
> If the FBI found NO evidence of lying why was Flynn charged?

More exculpatory evidence (Brady Material) kept unfolding as the sentencing phase in the Flynn case dragged out for several years. The December 2016 Russia event that Mike Flynn attended, was used as leverage by the DOJ but the DIA as per intelligence protocol, had been fully informed in advance of this international meeting. It was discovered BHO used National Security Letters (NSL) as well as FISA warrants in Operation Razor to illegally surveil General Michael Flynn.

Post Q# 2462
> Mandate charged to Ezra Cohen-Watnick [Defense Intelligence Agency]?

The Deep State's first targeted victim from the new Trump Administration was Lt. General Mike Flynn. The operation against Flynn was code named Crossfire Razor. A routine phone call to Russian Ambassador Kislyak was used as the basis for unmasking of many of Flynn's contacts and well as bogus Logan Act charges and FARA violations.

Post Q# 4620
> Flynn 1st strike designed to 1. cripple 2. prevent exposure of illegal acts [Hussein WH
> CoC] through NAT SEC [intel] discovery

President Trump's new NSA General McMaster, then routed out and fired all of Mike Flynn's remaining National Security Council (NSC) staff known affectionately in intelligence circles as the "FlynnStones". I believe the idea of Flynn's "Army of Digital Soldiers" is built from around this core base of loyal Patriots.

Post Q# 4025
> Who knows where the bodies are buried?
> CLEARED OF ALL CHARGES.
> TRUMP ADMIN v2?

At a security seminar held in Cambridge/London in February 2014, the first known meeting occurred between General Flynn and Stefan Halper. Like a Super Bowl for spies, these London seminars always attract the world's leaders in the shadowy intelligence field.

Post Q# 4196
Why did [McMaster] target and remove loyal intel operatives inside WH?

Stephan Halper dutifully reported back to CIA Director John Brennan about Flynn talking to a female Russian FSB agent (Svetlana Lokhova). The basis for 'Crossfire Hurricane' was being laid abroad by contract intelligence assets such as Stefan Halper.

Post Q# 4506
The People's General.
Soon.

The deliberate purging of loyal top intelligence officials from the NSC by new NSA McMaster, was designed intentionally to hobble President Trump. This is censorship in the worse possible manor to a new incoming President, it virtually blinds any leader by the removal of top trusted aides.

Post Q# 4224
Subject: Flynn.
Topic: Rule of Law @ Risk.
Can you prosecute without prosecutors?

BHO tried to restrict intelligence given to President Elect Trump by altering his own PDB's shared with the transition team. This is when POTUS stopped getting the BHO PDB and relied on General Flynn and Ezra Cohen-Watnick's own personal daily intelligence briefings instead of what was being offered. Any information obtained via the FISA or NSL concerning General Flynn could then be included in BHO's PDB.

Post Q# 36
Military Intelligence.
Focus on Flynn.
Background and potential role.

General Mike Flynn put together a very loyal band of Patriots beginning from his time under BHO at the D.I.A. Those chosen to go over to the NSC in Trump's mew administration were termed by many in the intelligence community as the 'FlynnStones.' It was always said about General Flynn and thus the Deep State feared this correct phrase, "Flynn knows where the bodies are buried ".

Post Q# 2043
FISA warrant issued/approved - FLYNN.

Proud 'FlynnStone' members included K.T. McFarland, Gen. Keith Kellogg, Michael Anton, Derek Harvey, Rich Higgins and Flynn's loyal protégé' Ezra Cohen-Watnick. Some of these heroes are still assisting President Trump and will be remembered kindly by historians.

Post Q# 4762
Not long now.

The old guard intelligence community was always skeptical of this inner circle of General Flynn. After President Trump's appointment of Flynn as the new NSA, he filled his National Security Council team from this special core of intelligence individuals mainly from his old Department of Defense/Army crew.

Post Q# 1282
> Why did Flynn take the bullet?
> Rubber bullet?

Ezra Cohen-Watnick (ECW) was NSA's Senior Director for Intelligence Programs under NSA Director Flynn. Cohen-Watnick's position gave him the authority to inspect the files all of 17 US Intelligence agencies for past wrongdoing and corruption activities.

Post Q# 2218
> In the end, all will be right.
> Patriots protect Patriots

ECW held a powerful post that's designed to coordinate/liaise between all of the various Intelligence Community entities and the White House. Ezra Cohen-Watnick gained the trust of POTUS as he regularly gave the daily intel briefings during the transition period.

Post Q# 4956
> Are you ready to serve your country again?
> Remember your oath.

decode: Q-Team asking General Flynn and he immediately changed his social media banner in positive response and Q in # 4608 said "Acknowledged".

Ezra Cohen-Watnick is credited with first alerting Devin Nunes to unmasking and illegal surveillance abuses. ECW along with W/H lawyer Michael Ellis took Nunes to the W//H SCIF to view the incriminate evidence.

Post Q# 3693
> [302]_mod [1] count.
> FBI agent [1] [P] - FLYNN interview.......

By order of the POTUS, Ezra had once again returned back to government service. This time assisting Attorney General/DOJ as National Security Adviser responsible for both counterintelligence and counterterrorism.

Post Q# 3626
> Targeted and silenced (gag) for a reason?
> Pain coming.

Ezra Cohen-Watnick had faithfully served Stealth Jeff/Matt Whitaker and AG Bill Barr before joe going back to the Pentagon. Cohen-Watnick will be the Deputy Assistant Secretary in charge of counter narcotics at the Defense Department.

Post Q# 26
> Think about it logically.
> The only way is the military.

President Trump had formed a legal dream team with AG William Barr along with SP Huber/SC Durham/IG Horowitz/and IG Storch to do criminal probes. The pending DECLAS followed by unsealing of criminal indictments, will usher in the Great Awakening. SC John Durham would ultimately submit his final 'report' in 2023.

Post Q# 1370
> Does Flynn know?
> Define "on the record."

Everyone will always remember Nunes' media news presser in front of the White House in 2017. Devin Nunes was signaling alarm bells and ECW along with Michael Ellis helped make that all possible. The main illegal (FISA) surveillance operations of 2016 were Crossfire Hurricane against candidate Trump, Crossfire Razor against General Flynn, and Crossfire Typhoon against candidate Ted Cruz.

Post Q# 3330

FISA (spy) - Flynn.
Will newly discovered evidence (AG Barr-SDNY) FREE FLYNN?

Having Military Intelligence (think 'Q' level clearance) in the DOJ is an important chess piece for President Trump. Several times Team 'Q' has emphasized young ECW as being a key player. SC John Durham was tasked to explore several criminal referrals from IG Horowitz and did drop a few indictments related to the illegal surveillance operations under SpyGate.

Post Q# 1008

Flynn is safe.

Former law enforcement officer Roscoe Davis has tied the Clinton Foundation to Benghazi. Roscoe additionally claims DIA Mike Flynn was targeted because he knows exactly where all the bodies are buried (sounding like 'Q').

Post Q# 4140

LET FREEDOM RING!

Patriots are hoping for the gallant return into Government service of their favorite General as miraculously President Trump won re-election in late 2024. We need General Flynn to help 'Drain the Swamp' and reconstitute his famous band of Patriots called 'FlynnStones.' The illegal Biden administration and Congress has subpoenaed General Flynn over in regard to their January 6th witch-hunt committee's probes.

Post Q# 3388

There is a big [direct] reason why FLYNN'S new attorney is seeking security clearance.

Links

Epoch Times-Flynn Case: 85 Lies, Contradictions, and Oddities

Just the News-Whistleblower told FBI Schiff approved Leaking Classified Intel

The Federalist-BHO/Biden Oval Office Meeting on January 5th was Key

Lee Smith-BHO's January 5th Conspiracy

Sharyl Attkisson-BHO Era Surveillance Timeline

PJ Media-Biden/BHO Officials Sought to Torpedo incoming Trump Adm

Tablet Magazine-RussiaGate began with BHO's Domestic Spying

The Last Refuge-Why Flynn Lied

The Federalist-FBI closes Flynn Case Dubbed Crossfire Razor

Epoch Times-Year of Vindication: Lt General Michael Flynn

War Economy-McCabe: "Fuck Flynn, then We Fuck Trump"

Markets Work-Were the Events Surrounding Flynn's Moscow visit Misframed?

Lamar-ObamaGate

SOTT-Collateral Damage (Flynn): SpyGate figure Stefan Halper

NBC News-Meet the "FlynnStones"

Forward-Meet Ezra Cohen-Watnick

Susan Whitney-Let's Get to know Michael Ellis and Ezra Cohen-Watnick

Quad Verum/Rex-The Great Sacrifice: General Flynn

WAPO-NSC: Trump Loyalists at War with Career Aides (FlynnStones)

Markets Work-Time Magazine details 'Shadow Campaign' against Trump

Justice.gov-Crossfire Hurricane Timeline

Crossfire Hurricane Docs-Flynn Interview

Justice.gov-2023 SC John Durham Report

Devin's Dungeoneers:
Basement Dwellers Ezra and Ellis

All great tales have certain recognizable focal points that draw historical attention. The Great Awakening and America 2.0 will become a reality in President Trump's second term, as we are witnessing the major acts in this unfolding real-life drama. Former official Kash Patel has said Special Counsel (SC) John Durham's indictment of Clinton campaign lawyer Michael Sussmann, even though eventually found not guilty, will ultimately lead to the exposure of a major coordinated operation termed a 'Joint Venture Conspiracy' against then candidate Donald Trump during the 2016 Presidential election cycle.

Post Q# 2462
Who was assigned directly to SESSIONS by POTUS?
Mandate charged to Ezra Cohen-Watnick (Defense Intelligence Agency)?
NAT SEC ADVISOR TO SESSIONS.

President Trump gave remarks at the White House after his exoneration of the first false impeachment charges. President Trump pointed out many Patriots that have been assisting this effort and placed particular emphasis on the role of Representative Devin Nunes. Representative Nunes announced his retirement from the U.S. Congress at end of 2021 to become CEO of Trump's new TruthSocial media company. One of President Trump's last official actions on 1/19/21 was to order the total declassification of the FBI's Crossfire Hurricane material.

Post Q# 2959
Hussein gave the order to start the spy campaign.

Author Lee Smith's popular new book 'Plot against the President' explains how Devin Nunes helped to uncover the biggest political scandal in U.S. history. Nunes jumped into an Uber late in the night of March 22, 2017 and raced to the White House for a rendezvous with destiny. As 'Q' has pointed out on many occasions in prior drops, there are no coincidence. Kash Patel was lead investigator for Nunes and was instrumental in helping with the White House secret discoveries.

Post Q# 1125
What was just released to Nunes?
IT'S HAPPENING.

The two whistleblowing White Hat Patriots that were waiting at the White House to meet Rep. Nunes along with aide Kash Patel, were NSC official Ezra Cohen-Watnick (ECW) and lawyer Michael Ellis. These two notorious 'basement dwellers' would escort Nunes/Patel down into the basement White House Sensitive Compartmented Information Facility (SCIF) to review a few dozen top secret documents concerning past illegal surveillance. ECW was a protege of General Flynn and Ellis was a White House lawyer (nicknamed Midnight Run).

Post Q# 4429
Have faith in God.
The Great Awakening.

Representative Nunes held a press conference the very next day on March 23rd and announced to the disbelieving Mockingbird MSM, about illegal surveillance and unmasking activities conducted by the BHO administration. This would be the beginning of the public rollout of the Deep State's

SpyGate coup plot including nicknamed operations like Crossfire Hurricane, Crossfire Razor, and FISA Dragon.

Post Q# 11
> Key:
> Military Intelligence v FBI CIA NSA.

ECW was the young prodigy of Trump appointed NSA General Flynn and part of a group originally at the Defense Intelligence Agency and later to the National Security Council. The infamous 'FlynnStones' included besides ECW, K.T. McFarland, General Keith Kellogg, Mike Anton, Rich Higgins, and Victoria Coates as key figures within this loyal core. This group followed General Flynn over from the Department of Defense to the Trump White House.

Post Q# 144
> Who has clearance to full picture?
> Who are the Wizards and Warloc[k]s?

The FlynnStones and ECW were specifically targeted by General McMaster after the Deep State successfully removed General Flynn as NSA. President Trump ordered the rehiring of ECW (after a quick Oracle private job stint) and placed him at the DOJ as NSA to AG Sessions/Whitaker/and then Barr. ECW was tasked in sniffing out' the many remaining leakers and anti-Trump traitors still part of the stay-behind resistance effort. ECW is currently the chair (appointed by President Trump in 2020) of the Public Interest Declassification Board (PIDB) and has vowed to release previously classified files on events like JFK and 911.

Post Q# 2057
> Ezra Cohen-Watnick.

Michael Ellis had been a long serving White House lawyer and advisor to the President. In addition to his heroic 'dungeon duty' in 2017, Ellis has again saved the day for our republic. Ellis along with colleague John Eisenberg, placed the official Ukrainian Presidential phone call transcript in a secure White House server where no one (Col. Alexander Videman) could alter this critical conversation. It would be revealed in 2023 that the DOJ subpoenaed the phone/email records of Congressional staffers connected to probing then the Crossfire Hurricane scandal. The infamous 'Red Folder' (sought after in Mar-a-Lago raid) was written by Nunes/Kash/and Ezra outlining the origins of RussiaGate/SpyGate.

Post Q# 1481
> Kashyap Patel - name to remember.

Both Ellis and Eisenberg were eventually cleared by an independent review panel of the false charges brought by the Democrats. These two brilliant White House lawyers also assisted in the successful defense of President Trump against the recent House of Representatives impeachment counts. Ellis was involved with the clearance of John Bolton's new book and pointed out subsequent NDA violations in that publication. It was revealed in 2023 that the DOJ/FBI spied on Kash Patel and other Congressional staffers that were probing the Crossfire Hurricane plot.

Post Q# 1661
> Think stages.
> What role MIL INTEL play?
> BANG!

Ellis was installed as acting top NSA lawyer but resigned due to an extended confirmation delay. Cohen-Watnick went from the DOJ back over to the Pentagon to assist Acting Secretary of Defense Chris Miller. Devin Nunes announced he was leaving Congress in 2022 to run President Trump's new social media platform called TruthSocial. We seem to be entering into the 'Storm' portion of 'The Plan', as 'Judgement Day' is coming with the re-election of President Trump in 2024. Devin Nunes will serve as chairman of President Trump's Intelligence Advisory Board.

Post Q# 4196

Why did [McMaster] target and remove loyal intel operatives inside the WH?

Links

Federalist-Nunes says Trump's most Important Accomplishment is Outing Hostile Media

FOX News-Patel found Thousands of Sensitive Trump Russia Probe Docs

Know your Meme-RussiaGate: Ezra Cohen Watnick

The Federalist-DOJ Officials didn't know Database Allowed FBI to Bury RussiaGate Docs

Clinton Foundation Timeline-2025 Crossfire Hurricane Docs

Washington Times-Nunes: Trump wants to End Politicalizing Intel Agencies

Just the News-Probe Opened into FBI Targeting US House Intel Staffers

PIDB-Public Interest Declassification Board: Members

Rolling Stone-How did RussiaGate Start?

Huffington Post-2 Officials that gave Devin Nunes Intelligence Reports

Just Security-The Gravity of Michael Ellis' Promotion to Senior Director for Intelligence

Conservative Brief-Nunes: I've sent 14 Crimes Referrals to be Reviewed

The Hill-Former GOP Operative Installed as NSA Top Lawyer Resigns

Epoch Times-Years of Vindication Part 4: Devin Nunes

Susan Whitney-Michael Ellis and Ezra Cohen-Watnick

Politico-'Are You QAnon?': One Trump Official's Brush with an Internet Cult

Breitbart-Fusion GPS Leader bragged Planting False Evidence against Devin Nunes

NBC News-Meet the FlynnStones

AP News-Impeachment Inquiry Focuses on 2 White House Lawyers

Bloomberg-Former Trump Aide who Left in Controversy Rejoins Pentagon

NY Magazine-Fired White House Official Hired by DOJ

The Atlantic-The Man McMaster Couldn't Fire

Business Insider-Trump Ordered DOJ to hire Controversial Aide

Forward-Controversial Aide Ezra Cohen-Watnick joining DOJ

YouTube-Devin Nunes Exposes the BHO Administration's Illegal Spying Targeting Trump

The Atlantic-Ever Deepening Mystery of Devin Nunes

CNBC-Devin Nunes Defends his Visits to the White House

WAPO-NSC: Trump Loyalists at War with Career Aides (FlynnStones)

Clinton Foundation Timeline-Spygate: Lead Investigator Kash Patel tells All

How Stuff Works-The SCIF

American Thought Leader-Inside Story of How SpyGate was Uncovered

Justice.gov-Crossfire Hurricane Timeline

Crossfire Hurricane Docs-FISA Notes

Justice.gov-2023 SC John Durham Report

FBI's Purposely Forgotten HRC Related Laptops

The new modus operandi of our FBI is to destroy and suppress evidence on a selective basis. This past decade has witnessed the political 'weaponization' of the Department of Justice (DOJ) and other government agencies. The majority of the American population has lost confidence in the independence of both the DOJ as well as the courts.

> **Post Q# 1279**
> We have it all.

Two more mysterious laptop computers must be added to the current existing ObamaGate/SpyGate list. Seized laptops and servers will ultimately reveal the totality of the treasonous coup plot against President Trump. A second failed impeachment came on the heels of the 2020 Presidential election steal bringing the importance to removing Trump/MAGA.

> **Post Q# 3045**
> Did a Foreign State gain access to the SAP/SCI material on the server?
> TREASON.

KEY SEIZED SPYGATE LAPTOPS:
- Weiner/Abedin laptop=NY PD/FBI
- Seth Rich laptop=Metro PD
- Imran Awan/DWS laptop=Capitol PD
- Mills/Samuelson/Hunter Biden laptops=FBI

Please notice the complete 'Cone of Silence' by the co-conspirators MSM media that conveniently surrounds all of these seized personal laptop computers. This is not by accident but of deliberately planned coordinated actions to control their crafted public narrative. By coordinating the DOJ and a compliant news media, covering the truth is a relatively easy task. Strange that laptops like Hunter Biden's 'Laptop from Hell' would continue to play important roles in the unfolding SpyGate political scandal.

> **Post Q# 559**
> Nothing is ever truly erases/deleted.

Cheryl Mills was the former Chief of Staff to then Secretary HRC and was also her personal attorney. Lawyer Heather Samuelson started out as a low-level campaign staffer and later joined Secretary of State HRC as an office assistant. Mills and Samuelson would later be teamed to delete all of HRC's emails from their time at the State Department.

> **Post Q# 158**
> What is immunity?

The hierarchy was that Samuelson worked under Cheryl Mills and they both were overseen by lead attorney David Kendall. According to Lisa Page's testimony, the FBI struggled with disagreements for months about the handling of these two incriminating laptops. It was obvious to all that data existed on these two laptops that would cause extreme difficulty to HRC and other top BHO officials.

> **Post Q# 1815**
> We have the server[S].

Both Heather Samuelson and Cheryl Mills would receive from Lynch/Comey, sweetheart get out of jail immunity deals. Both admitted in this plea deal to the deliberate destruction of subpoenaed emails as did Paul Combetta the computer server technician from Platte River Networks. Unbelievable that top level lawyers admitted deliberating committing criminal acts but ultimately received immunity from the government.

Post Q# 2872
> Hillary Clinton and Foundation.
> Crime Against Children.

Beyond being very gracious Mills and Samuelson got special immunity agreements that let them skate totally free. These extraordinary arrangements including several incredible bonus "side-bar" deals that the DOJ tried hard to keep secret. Normally to get a special deal, relevant testimony must be provided but no person was held accountable.

Post Q# 1978
> What if access to the server(s) was deliberate?

Senator Chuck Grassley smelled a rat and had pushed hard for the public exposure of the famed Wilkerson letters. These Wilkerson letters inappropriately restrict the FBI's scope of data review as well as permitted the previously unheard of destroying the Mills/Samuelson's laptops after giving immunity. History will record this very special sweetheart deal as a criminal act in itself.

Post Q# 2876
> CLINTON PANIC.
> CLINTON FEAR.
> JUDGEMENT DAY COMING.

In addition to general get-outa-jail-free cards, separate side deals were agreed upon to limit the scope of the exact data search on their devices. Specific time ranges were imposed to restrict finding uncomfortable data. Deal included the destruction of these laptops by the FBI after their restrictive review process.

Post Q# 3966
> Average people must be able to digest and accept [factual] events.
> FISA lead-in [stage 1 act 1].

The Justice Department agreed not to look at any information/data on either laptop after 1/31/15. This in essence guaranteed that no evidence of obstruction of justice involving HRC's emails would be ever found. It is as if HRC herself was directing the exact scope of the investigation process. It was revealed in 2023 that at least 6 top BHO officials used fake non-governmental email accounts with HRC known to have used 3 aliases.

Post Q# 1978
> How might this discredit the FBI's investigation into HRC's emails?

Then by having the FBI destroy the Mills/Samuelson laptops, this guaranteed no future review could alter their warped findings. It was standard operating procedures by the previous corrupt Justice Department to clean up any potential bad loose ends to would alter their narrative.

Post Q# 4230
> This is only the start.

TIMELINE OF EVENTS:
- 10/15/2014: HRC Team instructs Datto/Platte River Networks to delete emails from back-up storage servers.
- 3/3/2015: HRC Teams asks PRN to confirm Clinton email scrub.

- 3/31/2015: Paul Combetta/PRN realizes he forgot and uses BleachBit.
- 6/24/2015: Classified emails found on HRC email/server turned over to FBI.
- 10/3/2015: FBI seizes PRN and Brian Pagliano's (Clinton's NY home) servers.
- 9/16/21: SC John Durham indicates Perkins/Clinton campaign lawyer Michael Sussmann and submits his final report in 2023.

Post Q# 3815
They will not be able to walk down the street.
THE GREAT AWAKENING.

In defiance of clear leadership orders, a few brave Patriots from inside the FBI did not destroy these 2 critical laptops. Additional rumors state known copies of all the data from of these laptops have been downloaded. Former FBI agent Lisa Page would admit under oath to DNI John Ratcliffe in 2019 that BHO ordered the DOJ to 'stand down' in regards to HRC's email/documents scandal.

Post Q# 247
Think HRC email, Weiner laptop, etc.

To come up with a believable HRC/Aide's exoneration theory, the FBI/DOJ had to contort like circus acrobats. These 'uniquely crafted' immunity deals will be long remembered by legal historians. Judgement Day is coming, and SC John Durham has begun drop criminal indictments connected to HRC/DNC/Big Tech and more.

Post Q# 2365
Initial analysis of laptop-thousands of emails.
Hillary Clinton and Foundation.

All of these seized laptops plus the related servers, will form foundational evidence of future criminal proceedings. Special Counsel John Durham indictment of Perkins Coie/Clinton campaign lawyer Michael Sussmann was the beginning, and his final report was submitted in 2023. With the historic re-election of President Trump in 2024, the coming justice phase of the 'Storm' will be upon all of these Deep State criminals shortly.

Post Q# 3125
The PUBLIC must be prepared for what is about to come.
"THE CLINTON FOUNDATION"

Links

WND/HRC Aide's Laptops not Destroyed

FOX News-Patel found Thousands of Sensitive Trump Russia Probe Docs

PJ Media-Bombshell Report Reveals Details about HRC's Email Scandal

The Federalist-Senate Expands Probe into FBI's Ability to Hide Docs

Clinton Foundation Timeline-FBI Revelations Show the Mueller Special Counsel was a Cover-Up

Law and Crime-Judge orders Investigation of Clinton Lawyers

NY Post-How the FBI Wound Up Destroying Evidence

Breibart-6 BHO Officials used Alias Emails

Real Clear Investigations-The Apparent Trump-Hillary Double Standard: For Her

Washington Examiner-Federal Judge Shocked Cheryl Mills was Granted Immunity by DOJ

Daily Beast-3 HRC given Immunity by FBI

PJ Media-FBI Agreed to Destroy Laptops of HRC's Top Aides

The Last Refuge-Mid Year Team: Weiner Laptop/HRC Emails

Washington Examiner-Gohmert: Unclear if HRC IT Aide is Lying

Breitbart-IG Report: FBI hasn't Destroyed Laptops

The Hill-FBI Destroying/Suppressing Evidence

Red State-DOJ 'Does Not Want' FBI to Examine Laptops

American Thinker-diGenova: FBI Agents Refused to Destroy Laptop

Judicial Watch-Weiner Timeline: FBI have HRC Covered during Election

Sen. Grassley.gov-Wilkerson Letters: Mills/Samuelson Laptops

Crossfire Hurricane Docs-Halper Files

Justice.gov-2023 SC John Durham Report

Perkins Coie hired Fusion GPS and CrowdStrike

The Deep State's favorite 'go to' law firm is Perkins Coie. Perkins retained both Fusion GPS and cyber security firm CrowdStrike (CS) on behalf of HRC and the DNC. Of recent odd note have been the 2020 resignation of Robert Bauer, Durham's indictment of Michael Sussmann, and the sudden departure of Mark Elias from Perkins Coie. President Trump would include Perkins Coie/Fusion GPS/HRC/DNC and others in his 2022 federal RICO lawsuit related to damages surrounding the SpyGate political scandal. The RICO conspiracy charge concerns all those who promoted the false Russian collusion narrative against candidate Donald Trump during the 2016 election cycle.

> ### Post Q# 3764
> Possible to layer/insert code [CrowdStrike] to designate intruder [intended target]?
> The hole is DEEP.

The FEC would fine both the DNC and HRC over $1M for the Fusion GPS opposition research used in the 2016 Presidential election cycle. What makes a good movie besides great actors, it is a very plausible plot. Watch the Black Hats continue to push the false narrative of Russia-Russia-Russia and POTUS begins the counter coup. Several key lawyers at Perkins Coie including Michael Sussmann and Marc Elias, played key roles in the treasonous SpyGate coup plot. Michael Sussmann got not guilty from the bias DC jury at his trial, but it was confirmed that HRC personally directed the RussiaGate coup plot. Special Counsel (SC) John Durham is slowly unveiled a vast coordinated 'Joint Venture Conspiracy' of a false Russia collusion narrative against candidate Donald Trump during the 2016 Presidential election cycle.

> ### Post Q# 1008
> No 'direct' investigation into CS?
> FBI/SC/DOJ/FED G simply TRUST CS's report on data breach?

Incredibly it was learned via a 2022 whistleblower of a designated secured office workspace and computer portal for the FBI at the DC office of Perkins Coie law firm. HRC/DWS/and the entire DNC all soiled themselves on 4/30/16, when a campaign IT aide reported a computer server breach within the DNC framework. Rep. Wassermann-Schultz (DWS) retained Perkins Coie to subcontract CrowdStrike to review the DNC mainframe computer system. DWS had IT relationships with both Seth Rich and Imran Awan.

> ### Post Q# 809
> [Missing emails]
> [CrowdStrike]

Privately what CS (lead investor was Captain Johnston) found was a leak by DNC staffer Seth Rich. While publicly CS proclaimed that Russian hackers Cozy Bear and Fancy Bear were the sole culprits of this computer intrusion. These are glaring contrary claims that will be the pivotal starting point to much of the false Russian narrative. BHO used HRC's false 2016 Russia Dossier as the excuse to launch the next phase against Donald Trump with FisaGate and Crossfire Hurricane.

Post Q# 4016
> CIA [BRENNAN] FORCE?
> Crowdstrike code insert?
> HOW FAR BACK DID IT GO?

Both Comey/FBI and Johnson/DHS were denied access to the breached DNC computer data but accepted completely the outside results from CS. Eric Schmidt/Alphabet magically infused $100 million into CS earlier in 2016. Several Big Tech companies made the decision to back the HRC campaign and were committed to defeat Donald Trump at any cost.

Post Q# 2331
> [Part re: Fusion GPS, Perkins Coie now being revealed?].

Eric Schmidt had been HRC's Campaign computer guru and provided critical 2016 voter data information. Schmidt's sidekick Jared Cohen assisted HRC with Google's Jigsaw and Groundwork tech services divisions. 'Q' has directly pointed to Cohen and Google in prior drops. SC John Durham would discover in his criminal investigations that Perkins Coie retained other private contractors like Rodney Joffe to assist in this various coup plot schemes,

Post Q# 1960
> CrowdStrike managed the infiltration program based on payments to CF.

Co-founder of CS is Dmitri Alperovich (Atlantic Council fame), a Russian expat with ties to both HRC and Soros. Having questionable owners/partners provides the perfect environment for criminals to have legal cover to maintain on-going operations. It is assumed that 'Tech Exec #1' mentioned in a SC Durham indictment is Rodney Joffe, as he was slated to be HRC's Cyber Czar.

Post Q# 1866
> Why did POTUS move his entire operation out of TT the DAY AFTER the ADM
> ROGERS [SCIF] MEETING?

Perkins Coie lawyer Michael Sussmann has a personal relationship with CrowdStrike's co-founder Shawn Henry. James Baker has testified Sussmann gave the FBI false allegations about Alfa Bank at Trump Towers. SC John Durham's criminal probe is focusing upon the relationship between Alfa Bank, Perkins Coie, FBI, and HRC aides. SC Durham is additionally focused upon the other firm contracted by Perkins Coie and the role of Fusion GPS in the creation of the Steele Dossier.

Post Q# 3990
> FBI CHAIN OF COMMAND DNC HACK? [CIA BRIDGE - UKRAINE
> CROWDSTRIKE_BRENNAN]?

Thomas Drake and Bill Binney formed Veteran Intelligence Professionals for Sanity (VIPS) to scientifically exam computer data. The VIPS forensic team found proof that the 2016 DNC computer intrusion was 'Leak not a Hack.' Documented evidence confirmed data transfer had to be internal not external, due to fast transmission download speeds. SC John Durham had requested previously held 'privileged' documents and issued a new round of subpoenas directly related to tech firms that assisted Fusion GPS/Perkins Coie/HRN/and the DNC in the SpyGate criminal conspiracy.

Post Q# 2330
> "Former FBI general counsel James Baker met during the 2016 season with at least one
> attorney from Perkins Coie, the Democratic National Committee's private law firm."

On direct orders from President Trump, Bill Binney gave CIA Director Pompeo (KANSAS) a full briefing on these computer test results. Proving that an insider (SR) used a thumb drive memory stick, as opposed to international outside hacking group(s). History will show that Seth Rich became the epicenter of the treasonous RussiaGate/SpyGate coup plot against President Trump and Julian Assange/WikiLeaks assisted with the initial public exposure.

Post Q# 436
GOOG.
CROWDSTRIKE.
DNC.

Who believes that in any other related high-profile case that the FBI/DHS would accept results from an outside third-party? It is unheard of for the FBI to 'farm-out' investigative operations to private contractors. This third-party review would represent just one of many strange anomalies surrounding the handling of the DNC server breach probes. Oddly in 2024 CrowdStrike would be at the center of a global IT outage that shutdown computers worldwide in Airlines/Banks/Government institutions.

Post Q# 1828
[SPY OP].
[FUSION GPS] (Shell2) and (CS) and [NO NAME] and [PERKINS COIE] (Shell2).

Conveniently the Russian hacking narrative helps to cover the DNC's own internal mistakes. It was the conclusion from CS that helped initially to launch the Trump-Russia collusion delusion narrative. With the help of a cooperative fake news media, this treasonous theme against President Trump and the Russians took hold over a portion of the population. SC Durham's probe has led to the discovery of a tech guru named Rodney Joffe that was also paid by Perkins Coie to spy on Trump World. Durham additionally is looking into the 2016 DNC claimed computer 'hack' of the email system and the exposure by WikiLeaks before the Presidential election. SC Durham submitted his final report in 2023 and will be the foundation for future judicial accountability.

Post Q# 1051
Anon: BackPage website shutdown.
QAnon: That didn't take long.

Perkins Coie has had almost $3M seized by the government for BackPage connections. Sex and human trafficking were the core sleazy business of BackPage. Emblematic of the 'DC Swamp' that is in the process of being drained and replaced. Crack reporter Diana West is now linking Perkins Coie as having a copy of murdered DNC staffer Seth Rich's laptop. In 2022 Elon Musk would call out Perkins Coie/Michael Sussmann for an "Attempt to corrupt a Presidential election". With the historic re-election of President Trump in 2024, all security clearances were pulled from Perkins Coie and many past hidden political secrets will finally be publicly revealed.

Post Q# 4153
[FBI Floor 7] [UK assist] Steele - B_Ohr - N_Ohr - Fusion GPS [shell 2]

Links
Shift Washington-Seattle Law Firm connected to Clinton 'Pay for Play' Scandal

The Federalist-The FBI Set Up Trump and We Watched it Happen

Just the News-HRC Plan tying Trump and Russia

The Last Refuge-Original BHO and HRC 2008 Agreement

NY Post-Nellie Ohr Perjured Herself in Trump Russia Probe Testimony

Clinton Foundation Timeline-CrowdStrike is Confused on Eleven Key Details

Real Clear Investigations-What Durham Skipped: CrowdStrike

NY Magazine-Fusion GPS and the Steele Dossier

Biz Pac Review-Gaetz: FBI Maintains Workspace in Office of Perkins Coie

The Federalist-SpyGate 101: A Primer on the Russia Collusion Hoax

Aaron Mate-Clinton Lawyer hired CrowdStrike

Real Clear Politics-RussiaGate: HRC/Perkins Coie/Fusion GPS/CrowdStrike

Dawson Field-Perkins Coie and HRC Campaign

Front Page Mag-BHO used HRC's Dossier to Spy on Trump

The American Spectator-Durham and Amazing Disappearing DNC Hack

Markets Work-Ongoing Fusion GPS Revelations

Breitbart-HRC's Law Firm that Paid for Dossier also Recruited CrowdStrike

Real Clear Investigations-DOJ Official and Wife had Big Roles in Dossier

The War Economy-Alfa Bank/Fusion GPS/and Perkins Coie

Markets Work-FBI Outside Contractors, DNC Servers and CrowdStrike

Clinton Foundation Timeline-Perkins Coie hires Fusion GPS and CrowdStrike

Markets Work-Listing of Participants

Influence Watch-Perkins Coie

Senate Judiciary Committee-2021 Crossfire Hurricane

White House.gov-Addressing Risks from Perkins Coie

Crossfire Hurricane Docs-Steele Dossier through Simpson and McCain

Crossfire Hurricane Docs-Nellie Ohr Interview

Justice.gov-2023 SC John Durham Report

Steele's FIFA Dossier Connects to Trump Dossier via FBI Gaeta

FBI agent Michael Gaeta headed the Eurasian Crime Division and had a working relationship with Christopher Steele. Gaeta's FBI team gets credit for uncovering a massive bribery in the bidding process of FIFA's (Federation Int'l Football Association) future World Cup soccer matches. Gaeta would be promoted by Biden to become Deputy Assistant Attorney General reporting under BHO's Lisa Monaco. President Trump would file in 2022 a federal RICO lawsuit against those who promoted the false Russian Dossier narrative during the 2016 election cycle.

> **Post Q# 2160**
> Panic in DC.
> Steele req non_extradition to U.S.?
> US-UK extradition treaty 2003.

The economic benefits to the winning host country of a World Cup event, is the financial equivalent to hosting a Super Bowl. Gaeta's investigations lead to the resignation of several top FIFA staff including top dog Sepp Blatter. Christopher Steele would remain a pivotal figure in the unraveling of the political SpyGate/RussiaGate scandal.

> **Post Q# 4153**
> [FBI Floor 7] [UK assist] Steele - B_Ohr -.N_Ohr - Fusion GPS [shell 2]

Sepp Blatter was the head of the FIFA from 1998-2015 and presided during the host bid rigging scandal. Christopher Steele worked for a 'spies for hire' firm called Orbis during this same time period. Later some of the Qatar officials involved with FIFA Cup bribery scheme would be implicated in a political scandal nicknamed QatarGate with Israel.

> **Post Q 2630**
> How many senior FBI and DOJ officials have been removed?

In 2010 Orbis/Steele got a contact from the U.K. government to help land the 2018 World Cup bid. Russia magically got the 2018 event combined with Qatar garnishing the 2022 matches, causing other bidding countries to go ballistic over these apparent corrupt bids. It was revealed in 2024 that the US Intel community requested from its FIVE EYES (FVEY) partners to illegally spy/bump upon targeted Team Trump campaign aides back in 20216.

> **Post Q# 4072**
> Treason doesn't pay well in the end.

Chris Steele produced a FIFA Dossier and shared it with FBI agent Mike Gaeta, who was an acquaintance from an Oxford England seminar. Michael Gaeta's takedown of FIFA leadership, lead to Chris Steele providing ongoing intelligence information to BHO's State Department through official Victoria Nuland. Many feel that Gaeta's conveyance upon returning from Rome of the first copy of the Christopher Steele Dossier to Victoria Nuland in early July 2015, was the true beginning of SpyGate.

> **Post Q# 1708**
> Creation of fake intel dossier using ex spy.

State official Victoria Nuland would receive various Steele's memos concerning Russia/Ukraine activities from 2014-16. This laid the foundation for Steele being a past credible source for both the FBI and State Department. Appointed Special Counsel (SC) John Durham was tasked to explore the many criminal aspects related to the SpyGate political scandal.

Post Q# 1974

> If the FAKE Steele Dossier constitutes the 'bulk' of the 'facts submitted' to FISC to obtain FISA warrant(s) against POTUS.....

In the Spring of 2016, coup plot leaders decided to incorporate Christopher Steele into their Crossfire Hurricane/SpyGate plans. Victoria Nuland green-lighted the 7/5/16 London/England meeting with Steele and FBI's Pete Strzok/Gaeta/and Andy McCabe. The FEC would fine in 2022 the DNC and HRC's campaign over $1M for payments made to Fusion GPS for their preparation of the false Steele Dossier during the 2016 election cycle. Michael Gaeta's role in RussiaGate and the 'Dossier' would involve direct contact with Christopher Steele as well as with DOJ's Bruce Ohr.

Post Q# 43

> [DNC BREACH / DOSSIER]
> STEELE

The official FBI's Counterintelligence Division probe of candidate Donald Trump would not begin officially until 7/31/16. This was the launch point of the Russian 'collusion delusion' narrative by the Deep State and was not the beginning of the illegal surveillance programs. Now at DOJ, Mike Gaeta assures the public that all of SC Durham's probes will be disseminated. It was learned during the Igor Danchenko trial that the FBI offered Chris Steele $1M to verify his own fake Trump dossier in the Fall of 2016.

Post Q# 718

> 71 [187]
> [1] targeted.
> Dossier.
> U1.

FBI lawyer Lisa Page has given prior testimony, which reveals Mike Gaeta personally received the Trump-Russia Dossier directly from Chris Steele. Lisa Page described Gaeta as both Stefan Halper and Chris Steele's official 'handler' for the FBI. SC John Durham has been tasked to follow up on the numerous criminal referrals from IG Horowitz relating to the illegal surveillance operations of SpyGate.

Post Q# 2253

> FISA DECLAS WILL BRING THE HOUSE DOWN.

Certainly not a shocker as former FIFA President Seth Blatter is indicted for fraud in late 2021. The interconnecting spiderweb elements of ObamaGate/SpyGate reach out on an international basis. SC Durham has dropped criminal indictments and submitted his final report in 2023. With the re-election of President Trump in 2024, many of past political scandals like SpyGate will finally be publicly revealed.

Post Q# 4362

> Keyword: Insurgency

Links

ESPN.com-The FBI vs FIFA

The Blaze-The Case against Clinton/Brennan/and Comey is Stronger than Ever

The Federalist-HRC and the FBI Set Up Trump

Just the News-Steele Dossier Cited in 2016 ICA Claim about Putin

Real Clear Investigations-FBI Man in Europe undercuts Ohr's Claims in RussiaGate Role

Markets Work-SpyGate: The True Story of Collusion

FOX News-FBI offered Christopher Steele $1M to Corroborate Trump Dossier

AP News-Qatar paid former CIA Official to Spy on FIFA for Bid

The Guardian-How Russia Won the World Cup

Daily Caller-Steele's FBI Handler called Him 'Completely Untrustworthy'

Undercover Huber-Gaeta meets Steele in London

Real Clear Investigations-How Rome FBI Team gave Steele Guarded Secrets

Clinton Foundation Timeline-July 5, 2016: Michael Gaeta Travels to London

Judicial Watch-State Department Handler for Steele used Personal Email

Newsweek-Bruce Ohr and Chris Steele tried to Turn an Oligarch into Informant

The Last Refuge-FISA 702 Searches

Washington Times-BHO Aide Nuland started Steele/FBI Alliance

The Guardian-Qatar World Cup Stadium Dream

FIFA-World Cup Qatar 2022

FBI.Vault.gov-FISA Surveillance Court Applications

OIG.Justice.gov-DOJ OIG FISA Report

Crossfire Hurricane Docs-State Department Steele Binder

Justice.gov-2023 SC John Durham Report

'Farm Kid' Devin Nunes:
Gang of Eight's Lone White Hat

Various committees are formed for Congressional oversight of the many U.S. intelligence agencies. One special group tasked for being the main intelligence watchdog is called the Gang of Eight. This special select group of elected officials coordinate the most secret aspects of our government. President Trump would vindicate then committee chair Devin Nunes past SpyGate investigation efforts with his 2022 federal RICO lawsuit against HRC/DNC/Perkins Coie/Fusion GPS/and others.

Post Q# 2643
What happens when a member of the House Intel Comm purposely leaks FAKE and FALSE data to 'friendly' news sources in order to maintain and portray a FALSE NARRATIVE to the public?

This select group of Congressional leaders are regularly briefed in secret by members of the Executive Branch. Representative Devin Nunes alone broke ranks to help President Trump with draining the corrupt DC Swamp. Nunes has announced he will leave Congress in 2022 to run Trump's new media company.

Post Q# 4310
HOW DO YOU ADD LAYERS OF PROTECTION?
INSTRUCT CONGRESS TO FILE ARTICLES OF IMPEACHMENT?

Nunes has stood tall in the face of sabotage, MSM attacks and violent mobs of protesters. Let's set the stage and take Devin out of this picture and imagine "Hear no evil, speak no evil, see no evil".

Post Q# 2294
"House Speaker Paul Ryan (R-Wis)- a member of Congress's "Gang of Eight" that was briefed more than anyone else about the inadequacies of the Russia evidence - believes you should declassify."

The other 7 members may well be called to account for their deliberate inactions. History will not be kind on governmental leaders that joined in this coup plot or ultimately helped with the diabolical cover-up.

Post Q# 3679
If [AS] was privy to GANG OF 8 classified material would he not know the same FACTS (TRUTH) as NUNES/others?
'Knowingly.'

The permanent membership resides in select Congressional elected positions. The Gang of Eight members is divided evenly with 4 DEM/4 REP for an equal political balance. The even split does not factor in the UniParty influence and the dire consequences our country has faced with this DC Swamp mindset.

Post Q# 3173
The calm before the storm?
FIRE AT WILL COMMANDER.

This is the makeup and membership of the 2017 U.S. National Intelligence Gang of Eight (Warner replaced Feinstein):

- Speaker of the House (Ryan)
- Minority House Leader (Pelosi)
- Senate Majority Leader (McConnell)
- Senate Minority Leader (Schumer)
- House Intelligence/Ranking (Nunes)
- House Intelligence/Minority (Schiff)
- Senate Intelligence/Ranking (Burr)
- Senate Int'l Comm. Minority (Warner)

Post Q# 2462

Who briefed NUNES on classified intel re: HUSSEIN spy campaign v. POTUS?

This special group has access (almost Q-Level) to our country's highest top secret classified information. This type of information is stored at Sensitive Compartmented Information Facility (SCIF) in various locations in the USA.

Post Q# 1126

What was just released to Nunes?
"A clean [H]ouse is very important.

Understandability the White House would want all of their secrets housed within the White House's SCIF. The same private sand box theory applies with all of the other 3-letter agencies in terms of keeping their top-secret information held tightly internally.

Post Q# 1481

Kashyap Patel - name to remember.

Devin Nunes held a infamous presser on March 22, 2017 in front of the White House. Devin Nunes accompanied by aide Kash Patel, had earlier meet with whistleblowers Ezra Cohen-Watnick (an original FlynnStone member) and lawyer Michael Ellis at the White House Sensitive Compartmented Information Facility (SCIF) to review past massive illegal surveillance.

Post Q# 3241

[Knowingly] disseminating FALSE information is illegal.
GANG OF 8 (INTEL)

Ezra/Ellis showed Nunes/Patel a peek as to what really had been going on under BHO. Specifically the improper mass surveillance and illegal unmasking of many Trump Campaign staffers. The unfolding events surrounding the entire SpyGate scandal are vindicating both President Trump as well as Representative Nunes.

Post Q# 4824

Combat tactics, Mr. Ryan.

The DOJ/FBI National Security units launched their official investigation of Trump-Russia on July 31, 2016. Evidence is coming forth refuting this official narrative behind the real origins of this coup plot against President Trump.

Post Q# 3690

GANG OF 8 DECLAS = [[[AS]]]
"Knowingly."

Now it looks like December 2015 was the start date of this 'Russian Witch Hunt' entrapment operation. Certainly, everyone would agree that the FBI claimed launch date of 7/31/16 is false. It was revealed in 2023 that the FBI/DOJ spied on Congressional staffer's personal phone/email records that were probing Crossfire Hurricane.

Post Q# 3505

Nunes to receive a special package from BARR?

'Leakin' James Comey failed to mention the FBI's ongoing Trump Russian probe to Congress. In a public hearing Comey was blindsided by Rep. Elise Stefanik asking about the lack of required notification.

Post Q# 3993

If [AS] was privy to GANG OF EIGHT classified material would he not know the same FACTS (TRUTH) as NUNES?
Think NUNES memo v SCHIFF.

On 3/20/17 Rep. Stefanik nails James Comey about his failure to report the Trump investigation as he is required to give notice to the Congress. This public interview began the finger pointing and division within the 'Secret Society.' Representative Nunes announced his retirement from Congress in 2021 to become CEO of Trump's new media company called TruthSocial.

Post Q# 2657

C_A 'illegal' SURV - SEN INTEL COMM?

Congressional notice of any FBI counterintelligence investigations is required not optional. This is where FBI Director James Comey blames this lack of proper timely notice directly onto FBI Counterintelligence Director William Priestap. Special Counsel (SC) John Durham indictment of Perkins Coie/Clinton campaign lawyer Michael Sussmann will help to unravel the SpyGate scandal. IG Michael Horowitz revealed in his 2024 report about illegal surveillance on Rep. Devin Nunes and his close RussiaGate investigative staffers.

Post Q# 643

REAL TIME: [7] Congressional members + [3] Senators + [2] former O-senior officials + [4] OUTSIDE CONTRACTORS.
[NO C/TOP/SENS-LEVEL CLEARANCES] @ SCIF.
[DC-CAP].

Devin Nunes alone broke away from the Gang of Eight who would have kept the illegal activities of the BHO Administration secret. Our country will be forever in the debt of White Hat Patriots like Devin Nunes and Ezra Cohen-Watnick/Michael Ellis. Mr. Nunes would become CEO of President Trump's social media platform TruthSocial. SC Durham submitted his final report in 2023 and know that Judgement Day is coming very soon. With the re-election of President Trump in 2024 and Devin Nunes appointed as chairman of the Intelligence Advisory Board, many secrets from Crossfire Hurricane will finally be publicly revealed.

Post Q# 3063

ADAM SCHIFF IS PART OF THE 'GANG OF EIGHT' (INTEL).
IT WILL BECOME CRITICAL ONCE 'GANG OF EIGHT' MATERIAL IS DECLASSIFIED.

Links

Washington Monthly-Devin Nunes was Trump's Mole Inside the Gang of Eight

FOX News-Patel found Thousands of Sensitive Trump Russia Probe Docs

Just the News-Steele Dossier Cited in 2016 ICA Claim about Putin

The Federalist-DOJ Officials didn't know Database Allowed FBI to Bury RussiaGate Docs

Just the News-DOJ Spied on Congressional Staff Probing Crossfire Hurricane

The Last Refuge-Current vs Prior Gang of 8

Real Clear Investigations-FBI Comey Misled Congress's 'Gang of 8' over RussiaGate

Breitbart-Nuned Refers 10 BHO Officials to DOJ

The Last Refuge-Oleg Deripaska/Bruce Ohr/and Gang of 8

Conservative Brief-Nunes: I've sent 14 Criminal Referrals to Durham

The Last Refuge-Gang of 8/Carter Page FISA

Town Hall-Devin Nunes Devastates Schiff with Fiery Opening Statement

Independent UK-Devin Nunes allowed Access to Classified Docs

Undercover Huber-Brennan/Steele Dossier

Business Insider-"What the Hell is Nunes doing at the White House?"

Susan Whitney-Let's Get to know Michael Ellis/Ezra Cohen Watnick

NY Times-Inquiry by CIA affirms it Spied on Senate Panel

Markets Work-Devin Nunes, Classified Intel, and Schiff's Pretense

DNI.gov-DNI FISA Memo 2017

Senate.gov-SSCI Report on Trump 2016 Russia Contacts

Scribd-Sen. Mark Warner text with Russian Oligarch's Lobbyist

Crossfire Hurricane Docs-James Wolfe Interview

Justice.gov-2023 SC John Durham Report

The Gingerbread Express Elevator and Hidden Mickeys

Shall we play a game once more?

The Trump Hotel in Chicago got into the 2018 Christmas season by creating a unique functional holiday display. Team Trump designed the Gingerbread Express Elevator, fully functional and made out of real delicious edible ingredients. This outstanding corporate media stunt paid dividends as international press coverage highlighted this unique holiday-themed elevator. In 2022 on the new media platform TrusthSocial, President Trump is resending out memes with 'Q' clearly represented.

> **Post Q# 2595**
> What are the odds of a 'Q' stocking?
> Think 'Elf on the Shelf.'

A group of skilled professional chefs (Bakers) employed by the Trump Hotels, baked hundreds of edible gingerbread blocks and added masterful designs to this fully operational passenger elevator. Anons found several hidden clues throughout this masterpiece, with 'Q' references and shout outs from our beloved President Trump. Since the election steal of 2020 and the installation of the illegal Biden administration, our nation is falling apart while we patiently await the rightful return of President Trump.

> **Post Q# 2857**
> We thank you for your service, Bakers.

Walt Disney World has committed a team of professional "Imagination Artists" to run the Hidden Mickey program. Hidden Mickeys (HM) are a partial or complete image of the famed Mickey Mouse, that is imprinted upon a part of the Walt Disney worldwide empire. Anons will easily see the comparison between HM and that of the many different depictions of hidden Pepe the Frog memes.

> **Post Q# 4938**
> PLEASE FIX THE BREAD AND TIDDY UP THE SHIP.

These dedicated Walt Disney artists create these iconic 'Mickeys' and deliberately place them in various semi-hidden locations throughout all of the properties. Discovery of these HM are a joy to those searching. Incredibly thousands search year-round, high and low over all of the many Disney worldwide facilities and several cruise ships.

> **Post Q# 2419**
> What # does the passcode add up to?
> For Anons.....

The HM are not just to be found at the various worldwide customer theme parks but all Disney locations. HM can be spotted at Walt Disney hotels, theme parks, restaurants, shopping complexes, transportation vehicles, movie studios, the town of Celebration/Florida, and even aboard their luxury cruise ships.

> **Post Q# 3876**
> Thank you, Baker(s)!
> THE BEST IS YET TO COME!

The insertion of the HM has been decades long by Disney and several books have been written about this phenomenon. Similar to the strategic insertion of the number 17 and the letter Q by

POTUS, the imagination of the hidden concept is extraordinary. As part of the Gingerbread Express Elevator and another hat tip to the Anons, there was a picture of Santa Claus holding a 'hammer' as signed QA.

Post Q# 1296
Personal thank you to BO, Bakers, and Autists/Anons who continually dedicate their time and energy to the GREAT AWAKENING.

The '17/Q' has always been recognized as one of the biggest shout outs to the entire Anon community. No question the Gingerbread Express is a direct nod to the hard-working Anons/Bakers by our great Commander in Chief. Special Counsel (SC) John Durham has dropped criminal indictments related to SpyGate and submitted his final report in 2023. SC Durham's report in part validates prior 'Q' drops on the illegal surveillance operations of Crossfire Hurricane and SpyGate. With the re-election of President Trump in 2024, expect the Great Awakening to swing into high gear.

Post Q# 4438
Not all posts are meant for Anons.

The number 17/letter Q has been regularly used in sly verbal and hand waving references, as well as in Time Delta proofs and written into Presidential tweets. 'Q' would start posting after a two-year break oddly on the day Roe is overturned by the Supreme Court. Trolling of the Fake News media with insertion of hidden 'Q' codes within The Gingerbread Expresses is absolutely priceless, unique and will long be remembered by all Anons/Bakers-WWG1WGA.

Post Q# 2598
Confirmed.
'QA' - 'QAnon' - Hammer.

Links

NWI Times-Trump Hotel Gingerbread Express Elevator

Elevator.com-Trump Hotel Chicago Decorates Elevator for Christmas

WTTW-Trump Hotel Chicago Transforms Elevator into Gingerbread Express

The Federalist-Corrupt Media didn't Fall for Russia Hoax: They were Part of It

President Trump-Gingerbread Express Elevator

Huffington Post-Trump Tower in Chicago: Elevator Made out of Gingerbread

ABC News-Hidden Mickey Photos

WDW Info-The Hidden Mickeys

Mashable-Trump's Words (17) Fuel the QAnon Fire

Commercial Elevator-Trump Hotel Chicago decorates Elevator

Wikipedia-Hidden Mickey

Florida Tix-Top 10 Hidden Mickeys at Disney World

Deadline-Elon Musk Tweets about Pepe the Frog

FOX 13 News-Judge Bans Elf on a Shelf during Holiday Season

Windy City Elevators-The Gingerbread Express Elevator

The Trump Organization-Tour the Gingerbread Express Elevator

Watching over the Purse Strings—TRUST GRASSLEY

Senator Chuck Grassley (R-Iowa) moved over from being the chair of the prestigious Judiciary Committee to the Finance Committee, while remaining a member of Judicial. Senator Grassley has initiated several critical investigations into the Clinton Foundation/Biden Family/Uranium One/and other political scandals. Both Senators Grassley and Ron Johnson continue to lead the probes into Hunter Biden's 'Laptop from Hell' and the possible national security implications from the incriminating data information. Both Senators Grassley and Ron Johnson would be blocked by the DOJ in 2022 in seeking answers on the Hunter Biden laptop criminal investigation.

Post Q# 4457
SENATE WAS THE TARGET.

Chuck Grassley combined with U.S. House Representative James Comer in 2023 to focus on the Biden Family corruption by issuing Congressional subpoenas. Senator Grassley through the Senate Judiciary was critical in getting President Trump's three USSC and Federal Judges appointed. The keys to all governmental tax and spending flow from the Senate Finance Committee. Currently Senator Grassley is continuing to hold the many corrupt political figures accountable with both committee investigations and media appearances.

Post Q# 1553
Sessions informed Congress in his letter that all the matters recommended for investigation by Goodlatte, Gowdy, and Grassley are "fully within the scope of [Huber's] existing mandate."

Also remember Grassley valiantly held the line with BHO's Merrick Garland USSS nomination attempt in March 2016. Few expected that a President Trump would fill that empty seat (AS) as the media repeatedly proclaimed HRC would be victorious.

Post Q# 4310
What was really discussed during [Jan 5] meeting?
[Hussein] order preventing sharing of intel re: Russia?

Sen. Grassley is taking over from retiring Orin Hatch and has twice before served on this important Senate committee. Chuck vows to return to bipartisan common-sense solutions to tax relief and universal tax fairness policies.

Post Q# 49
Follow Sen Grassley.

Why does Grassley (one example) have a higher than normal amount of security detail?

Additionally, Senator Grassley will become the President Pro Tempore (2nd highest) of the U.S. Senate. Grassley will be remembered by the number of Federal Judges he heled shepherd through these past two years as well as his fiscal conservative eye.

Post Q# 2657
C_A 'illegal' SURV and SENATE INTEL COMM?

Two important probes that Grassley is interested in getting resolved are with Susan Rice [SR] and FBI agent Joe Pientka. Pientka was Peter Strzok's partner that interviewed General Flynn at the White House. Sen. Grassley will help ensure both are followed through properly in the powerful Senate Judiciary committee before Special Counsel John Durham finishes the judicial job.

Post Q# 2444
> Shift to Senate Judiciary.

Susan Rice wrote an unusual, classified memo and sent it to herself on January 20, 2017 (Inauguration Day). Rice was immortalizing an Oval Office meeting from 1/5/17 that she attended. This would be last face-to-face meeting of the coup plot leadership and given final marching orders by BHO. The main topic of discussion per John Brennan's notes (not Rice's memo) concerned covering HRC's email deletions with the Trump/Russia hoax.

Post Q# 1496
> Nunes/Grassley/Freedom C push for docs.

In attendance besides BHO and SR were Biden/Comey/and Sally Yates. Rice's C.Y.A. bizarre memo to herself after she was no longer employed, emphasized BHO stressing "by the book". In fact, BHO was updated on the fake Trump-Russia narrative and pushed to use the Logan Act against General Flynn.

Post Q# 49
> Why is Grassley and others held in a secure location?

Senator Grassley has a longstanding interest in receiving the documents from General Flynn's FBI interview in early 2017. FBI agents Peter Strzok and Joe Pientka interviewed General Flynn without his lawyer being present and felt no lying occurred.

Post Q# 659
> Those who stood chanting "USA" were FREED.
> The shot heard around the world.
> FREEDOM DAY.

Sen. Grassley has been demanding the records of these FBI's 302 forms for months. Mueller's court filings have backed up Grassley's hunch in suspecting shenanigans were at play. The walls are finally closing in on this entire cabal. Luckily Chuck Grassley has announced he will seek another term in the Senate representing Iowa and has received President Trump's complete endorsement.

Post Q# 2445
> TRUST GRASSLEY.
> Senate Judiciary Chairman.
> [House of Cards].

Patriot Chuck Grassley is truly beloved by Iowa and all of fly-over country. Senator Grassley has always promoted youth internships and mentoring programs. SC Durham's indictment of Perking Coie/Clinton campaign lawyer Michael Sussmann exonerates Senator Grassley's past efforts in the SpyGate inquiries. Grassley would reveal in 2023 that the FBI had credible reports of criminal activity for years from 40 'Confidential Sources' against the Biden Crime Family, while obliviously the DOJ protected them.

Post Q# 4603
> How many Senate members were illegally surv?

White Hat Patriots within the U.S. Senate are rare as purple unicorns. SC Durham has dropped criminal indictments and submitted his final report in 2023. Senator Grassley is pursuing Hunter Biden's laptop from hell. Senator Grassley revealed in June 2023 of the existence of 17 audio recordings of Biden taking Ukraine bribes. In 2024 Sen. Grassley would press the USSS/DHS as to details into the attempted assassination of President Trump just prior to his re-election. When 'Q' states that we should "TRUST GRASSLEY," that is good enough in my book fellow Patriots. With the historic re-election of President Trump in 2024, many hidden political secrets will finally be revealed.

Post Q# 1553

"Matters recommended for investigation by Goodlatte, Gowdy, and Grassley are 'fully within the scope' of [Huber's] existing mandate."

Links

NBC News-Sen. Grassley opts to Cede Judiciary Committee

Just the News-Chuck Grassley Condemns FBI Handling of HRC Email Investigation

FOX News-Senators Grassley/Johnson demand Answers about Undercover J6 Sources

Grassley.Senate.Gov-Grassley Obtains FBI Records alleging VP Biden Bribery Scheme

The Federalist-Grassley's Bombshells show House Investigators where to Aim Subpoenas

Just the News-FBI had 40 Sources providing Intel against the Biden Family

FOX News-Grassley: Burisma Executive who Paid Biden has Audio Tapes

Daily Wire-Chuck Grassley on Clinton Campaign: Spied on Trump

Sen.Grassley.gov-Democratic Coverup of Hunter Biden Laptop Investigation

Markets Work-Grassley's Letter to Susan Rice

WSJ-FBI's Dubious Briefing for Senators Grassley and Johnson

Real Clear Investigations-Susan Rice's Testimony doesn't Add Up

The Federalist-BHO/Biden White House Meeting on January 5th was KEY

The Hill-Rice's Odd Memo: Did BHO withhold Intel from Trump?

The Last Refuge-Chuck Grassley and Christopher Steele

Sen.Grassley.gov-Wilkerson Letters: Mills/Samuelson Laptops

FOX News-Susan Rice's Memo (Top Secret/Unclassified)

Senate Judiciary Committee: 2021 Crossfire Hurricane DECLAS

Crossfire Hurricane Docs-Steele Dossier through Simpson and McCain

Grassley.Senate.gov-Declassified Document Proves Fusion GPS Contractor Nellie Ohr Lied

Justice.gov-2023 SC John Durham Report

Hakluyt: Fusion GPS's British Cousin

Hakluyt and Company is a British strategic intelligence and advisory firm. The obvious comparison is now being made between Fusion GPS and it's "shagadelic" British espionage cousin Hakluyt. The importance of accurate intelligence becomes all the more critical in the age of a pending global Great Reset. President Trump would go on the offensive in 2022 with his filing of a federal RICO lawsuit against Chris Steele/HRC/DNC/and others related to the SpyGate scandal.

Post Q# 4647
44, Brennan-lead + [F] assist.
Matters of NAT SEC.

Hakluyt has offices and clients around the globe. Originally opened in 1995 by several former top ranking MI6 agents that including prior heads of GCHQ Sir Richard Dearlove and Robert Hannigan. The British Secret Intelligence Service (SIS) is commonly called MI6 and known for the world's top agents. The RussiaGate/SpyGate coup plot in 2016 against candidate Donald Trump highlights the insidious relationship than can exist between corrupt governmental officials from different countries.

Post Q# 1929
TREASONOUS ACTS [MOVIES 1-3 FULL LIST].

Hakluyt was renamed to Holdingham Group Limited in 2011. The primary core services offered by Hakluyt are corporate espionage and opposition intelligence research. Spying is used just as much in the private corporate arena as against each other's foreign intelligence services. Just like the USA will outsource shady activities to intelligence firms like Fusion GPS, the British similarly would use private companies like Hakluyt for international/domestic spying operations.

Post Q# 4620
[infiltration]
Traitors everywhere.
Welcome to the Revolution.

This shadowy security firm sells competitive intelligence to corporate clients through the use of placed operatives as does Project Veritas. 'Spooks for Hire' should be engraved on Hakluyt's own front door as this is the moniker duly earned over the years. Americans got to witness the illegal surveillance performed by outside contractors like Fusion GPS.

Post Q# 4
Focus on Military Intelligence/State Secrets why might that be used vs any three letter agency.

Hakluyt is a cross between companies like Fusion GPS and Texas based Stratfor. Stratfor is the Austin/TX based (Alex Jones) intelligence firm connected to Mossad and the CIA 'Clowns.' It should come as no surprise that many of the employees of these intelligence firms are former government spooks.

Post Q# 3850
How do you 'awaken' the 'induced coma public [FAKE NEWS control] from their long sleep?
Sometimes you allow your enemies to [openly] attack... ...

The work product of British national Christopher Steele's Trump-Russia Dossier is one example of services that Hakluyt provides to international clients. Chris Steele worked for competitor London based Orbis, which is like Hakluyt in selling out intelligence products.

Post Q# 1286
> The Brits-raw intel/dossier/5 Eyes.

Hakluyt's own internal Advisory Board has been populated by several notorious chaps in recent years. The Australian diplomat Alexander Downer, Joseph Mifsud, and U.S. Ambassador Louis Susman are high-profile individuals connected to Hakluyt. All of these intelligence related individuals would play a role in the Crossfire Hurricane coup plot against President Trump.

Post Q# 1238
> Not 'official' product-5 Eyes.

Ambassador Downer helped organize a $25 million payment to the Clinton Foundation. Downer was directly involved with the Stefan Halper/George Papadopoulos London pub crawl affair. That evening would be the origins of the RussiaGate/Crossfire Hurricane plot both rouge Americans and their Five-Eyes international co-conspirators.

Post Q# 3786
> Globalism dead?

Ambassador Downer gained international notoriety in 2004 when he was caught spying on one country while serving as a UN Peace Envoy from yet another country. ObamaGate/SpyGate seems to have reunited this band of old school global spies. Sir Dearlove would continue beating the 'Never Trump' drum in 2024 by predicting a national security risk to the U.K. and potentially the end of Western Democracy if President Trump is re-elected.

Post Q# 1746
> FISA = START.
> FISA=IMPLICATES SENIOR MEMBERS OF UK MI5/6/SIS, US INTEL, WH, FVEY, R PARTY (CONGRESS/SENATE), OF KNOWN CORRUPTION IN EFFORT TO RETAIN POWER AND RIG ELECTION.

Stephan Halper was Bush's banker in Iran-Contra and advised Bush 43 as well. Many of the colorful British spies that assisted Bush also helped the BHO regime in secret surveillance activities. The former U.S. Ambassador to the U.K. was Louis Susman. Louis Susman has dutifully earned his nickname of the 'Vacuum Cleaner.'

Post Q# 1972
> BIGGER THAN WATERGATE.
> BIGGEST SCANDAL IN US HISTORY.

Susman is famous for sucking out money from one source and funneling it out to another. It should not be a shocker that Louis Susman has been a huge fundraiser for BHO/JK/and HRC. Large campaign bundlers are important in funneling 'dark money' into selected political races. Special Counsel (SC) John Durham was tasked to criminal referrals from IG Horowitz centering around the Clinton Foundation and the SpyGate scandal.

Post Q# 972
> Intelligence A's across the globe in partnership to spy on citizens.

FBI agent Peter Strzok went over to London on 8/3/16 to meet with Ambassador Downer. The coordination of these foreign intelligence components was synced at the top of the DOJ with final approval always by BHO. It was important to gain the help of Five-Eye allies with the illegal plot against sitting President Trump. SC Durham has dropped criminal indictments related to the illegal surveillance operations both domestic and international involving SpyGate. SC Durham submitted his final report in 2023. With the re-election of President Trump in 2024, we pray these past political hidden secrets will finally be publicly revealed.

Post Q# 4153
    [DOSSIER DISCREDIT PRIOR-TO [KNOWN]]

Links

Real Clear Investigations-RussiaGate's Architects Suppressed Doubts to Peddle False Claims

FOX News-Patel found Thousands of Sensitive Trump Russia Probe Docs

Racket News-The Spies who Hijacked America

Mediaite-Former Head of MI6 warns Trump's Re-election is a National Security Risk

WSJ-The Clinton Foundation, State and Kremlin Connections

The Guardian-Former Head GCHQ now Advising Hakluyt Intelligence Firm

The War Economic-SpyFall

Powerbase-Hakluyt and Company

Markets Work-Dearlove Connections: Hakluyt, Downer, Halper and PapaD

The Guardian-British Spies First to Spot Trump Team Links to Russia

Mark Steyn-Tinker, Tailor, Clapper, Downer, Carter, Halper Spy

The Federalist-Steele Testifies HRC and Susan Rice knew about Dossier

Elizabeth Lea Vos-All RussiaGate Roads lead to London

News Comm-UK Worried over Hakluyt Ties to AU

Markets Work-Sir Richard Dearlove and UK Intelligence

Epoch Times-SpyGate: The Inside Story

The Guardian-GCHQ Chief Robert Hannigan Quits

Clinton Foundation Timeline-Key Foreign Intelligence SpyGate Players

Crossfire Hurricane Docs-State Department Steele Binder

Justice.gov-2023 SC John Durham Report

Planted 2016 Trump Campaign Spy—Meet Stefan Halper

Hat tip to Dan Bongino (ex-US Secret Service and now FBI AD) for first advancing the 'Dirty Up' theory with Trump-Russia. What has become obvious is certain lower-level Trump campaign advisors, were specifically targeted to have meetings with paid intelligence assets which would make them 'dirty.' President Trump would file in 2022 a federal RICO lawsuit against those officials involved with the promotion of the false Russian collusion narrative back in 2016.

Post Q# 2489
>[Placeholder - OIG Report-Umbrella SPY and Targeting].

These entrapment/sting operations get togethers, could later be tied into the Russian 'collusion delusion' narrative. Elaborate plans and professionally execution was the hallmark of the SpyGate/ObamaGate operations. The designated domestic spies or foreign LURES would 'touch' or dirty-up the targeted individual in an entrapment operation.

Post Q# 1164
>Not Public: Five Eyes/UK/AUS POTUS targeting using pushed RUS decoy meetings/campaign insertions.

It was revealed in 2024 that the US Intel community requested from its FIVE EYES (FVEY) partners to illegally spy upon Team Donald Trump aides back in 2016. Stefan Halper is a syndicated columnist, college professor, defense contractor, past White House Adviser, and has close ties to both CIA/MI6. Halper goes back to Iran-Contra (he was the banker) and is no stranger to international covert black operations.

Post Q# 1589
>ILLEGAL SPYING.
>FRAME.
>INSERT ASSETS.

Stefan Halper arranged several very suspicious meetings with Trump officials during the 2016 Presidential campaign. Joseph Mifsud worked for MI6 and was a colleague of Halper who assisted with these various sting operations (Crossfire Hurricane).

Post Q# 2601
>NOBODY IS ABOVE THE LAW.
>THE WORLD IS WATCHING.

In July 2016 Stefan Halper set-up a meeting in London with Carter Page just days after Page's Russia trip that became part of the Steele Dossier. Halper contracted Page to attend a symposium at Cambridge. Globalist featured speakers like Madeleine Albright spoke of Global Politics and the upcoming U.S. election.

In August 2016 Stefan Halper reached out to then co-Chair of the Trump campaign Sam Clovis. According to Victoria Toensing (Clovis attorney) Halper meet with Clovis in Virginia to offer his expertise in foreign relations. Additionally offered to assist in the election of candidate Donald Trump with any information that may be of value that Halper might later discover about HRC.

NOTE: On 8/2/16 a gala party was held at the Australian Embassy in London. FBI Peter Strzok flew over to attend this event and specifically meet with Downer/Halper at the AU embassy.

In September 2016 Halper contacts George Papadopoulos and they agree to have a meeting. Stefan bragged to George repeatedly that his Russian contacts had the missing HRC emails. He offered his personal help and to turn over the emails to the Trump campaign. Halper's assistant Azra Turk (her alias and known CIA asset) was setup to accompany George Papadopoulos on trip to England as his sexual partner (honeypot).

Originally back in May 2016 Papadopoulos was introduced by an Israeli Diplomat to Alexander Downer. George PapaD was in London to speak at a lecture and write a paper, under a $3,000 plus expenses contract job. It makes more sense that the low level Trump Officials would be targets as opposed to source information for the FIVE EYES (FVEY) intelligence network.

Post Q# 3181
BLIND JUSTICE UNDER THE LAW WILL RETURN TO OUR REPUBLIC.
There is a reason why a sword is held.

While out pub crawling at the Kensington Gardens, George PapaD was overheard bragging by Australian diplomat Alexander Downer, talking about Russian 'dirt' on HRC. This casual off-hand comment would be the 'predication' upon the granting of the Carter Page FISA warrant(s).

Post Q# 3966
FISA lead-in [stage 1 act 1]

This famous off-hand bar talk led to onset of the Russian collusion narrative. The DOJ points to this 'Intel' as the sole reason used to first launch the FBI's counterintelligence probe into Trump-Russia on July 31, 2016. Stefan Halper also invited Trump Campaign Adviser Stephen Miller to attend the July 2016 University of Cambridge event that was where SpyGate was born.

Post Q# 4958
How do you insert a plant?

Records indicate that Stefan Halper has received almost $1.2 million from the Department of Defense's Office of Net Assessment (ONA) over the last several decades. Halper was paid to prepare four separate research contracted projects and transmit his findings in prepared reports. Many of the characters of the SpyGate political scandal were motivated by either financial or personal power gains.

Post Q# 1935
Focus Here "raise troubling questions about Halper, who was believed to have worked with the CIA and part of the matrix of players in the bureaus 'Crossfire Hurricane.'

Stefan Halper has past ties various intelligence agencies due to his roles with the Nixon/Ford/and Reagan administrations. Halper has been paid to act as an intelligence asset for the CIA in the past. Folks are still searching for the identity of Halper's FBI handler with signs pointing towards the elusive Joe Pientka.

Post Q# 3595
C_A HUMINT domestic placement - T campaign.

Stefan Halper will be confirmed as one of several paid FBI moles planted within the Trump campaign. This destroys the previously given timeline and the actual start date of the real origins of the FBI Counterintelligence on candidate Donald Trump probe. History will record that a group of corrupt government officials joined with private outside contractors in a treasonous coup plot.

Post Q# 972
    Intelligence A's across the globe in partnership to spy on citizens.

IG Horowitz's past reports publicly showed abuses of the FISC/FISA process by the DOJ/FBI. SC John Durham will look for the real basis on which the Carter Page Title-1 FISA warrant(s) were originally granted. Halper was taped in a conversation stating that Trump's new NSA (Flynn) would be gone soon in an astonishing clairvoyant prediction of future events.

Post Q# 4153
    [FBI Floor 7] [CIA] spy_insert 1-3 [AUS assist] POTUS_campaign.

The FBI claims July 31, 2016, as the official counterintelligence launch date. Unbelievably this flawed timeline is based upon select Papadopoulos's public drunken bar tales and not their actual SpyGate/Crossfire Hurricane operations. Special Counsel (SC) John Durham is looking into all of the part illegal surveillance and criminal activity surrounding SpyGate and is building a vast 'Joint Venture Conspiracy (RICO) case.

Post Q# 2043
    UK ASSIST + FISA SURV INCLUDED ALL UPSTREAM COLLECTION +
    TANGENT CONTACTS (UMBRELLA SURV).

Figuring out the real FBI start date will help expose the roots of this traitorous plot. Understanding and connecting the various components of Crossfire Hurricane/Dragon FISA/and Crossfire FISA programs will reveal the truth. 2021 will usher in the biblical justice long overdue as well as the public Great Awakening as SC Durham has submitted his final report in 2023. With the re-election of President Trump in 2024, many Hope long hidden political secrets will finally be revealed.

Post Q# 678
    The ART of illusion.

Links

The Federalist-Stefan Halper likely Lied to FBI on Purpose

Clinton Foundation Timeline-Stefan Halper

Sara Cater-Russia Collusion Informant Stefan Halper received $1.2 Million

Just the News-FBI kept Defending Crossfire Hurricane's Stefan Halper

Racket News-The Spies who Hijacked America

The Intercept-Stefan Halper: FBI Informant who Monitored Trump Campaign

FOX News-Who is Hiding RussiaGate's Stefan Halper?

The Federalist-Did SpyGate source Stefan Halper work for the HRC Campaign?

Real Clear Politics-Stefan Halper, Longtime 'Zelig' of U.S. Scandals

Washington Examiner-Stefan Halper: FBI Crossfire Hurricane Operative

Daily Caller-Stefan Haper's Honeypot Azra Turk

Markets Work-Stefan Halper's Role in Crossfire Hurricane more Significant

Daily Caller-SpyGate Professor told FBI Salacious Rumor about Flynn

Jeff Carlson-The Art of War

The Federalist-8 Times U.S. Intelligence Set People Up to Fabricate the Russia Story

The Last Refuge-Downer/Mifsud

Undercover Huber-Alexander Downer and PapaD

American Spectator-The Three Stooges of SpyGate

Markets Work-Ties that Bind: Halper/Downer/Mifsud/and PapaD

Washington Examiner-Stefan Halper: Cambridge 'Don' FBI sent to Spy on Trump

The Last Refuge-Origins of Russia Probe

Clinton Foundation Timeline-Key Foreign Intelligence SpyGate Players

Crossfire Hurricane Docs-Stefan Halper Files

Justice.gov-2023 SC John Durham Report

BHO's own 'Body Count' List:
TAC Employee Lt. Quarles Harris

Lt. Quarles Harris Jr. (1982-2008) was found mysteriously murdered in his parked car on April 18, 2008. Lt. Harris was shot in the head and his vehicle was parked in front of a Washington DC church. The untimely and bizarre nature of many deaths of those surrounding both the Clintons as well as BHO, is now of legendary vengeance. In the creation of a 'Manchurian Candidate' an extensive false legend (personal history) is required.

Post Q# 3973
> Who trained/supplied ISIS?
> Knowledge is power.

Quarles Harris had worked at The Analysis Corporation (TAC) as an intelligence operative. TAC was headed by John Brennan and his company was implicated in the breach of the U.S. Passport Records. It is rumored then acting DNI Grenell had turned over to AG Barr declassified documents showing a history of spying/leaking from Brennan's TAC.

Post Q# 1887
> What is JB's background?
> Muslim by faith?

Passport data on citizen travel records is permanently contained within the U.S. State Department. U.S. State Department launched an investigation into this affair in April 2008. Computer files showed a breach where BHO's history was accessed and forensically altered by an outside entity. BHO and Brennan would oversee the first half of the 16-Year Plan and act as the Shadow President once again under illegal Joe Biden. Department of Justice AG's Holder and Lynch assisted in these many nefarious operations.

Post Q# 1017
> The Analysis Corporation (TAC).
> Happy Hunting!

At the time of Quarles's tragic murder, he was an active key cooperating federal witness for the FBI. Lt. Harris was to meet with several FBI agents on the evening of his untimely murder. TAC and Brennan has ties to China that are also being revealed as the SpyGate/ObamaGate scandals begin to publicly unravels. Special Counsel (SC) John Durham has dropped criminal indictments related to SpyGate and submitted his final report in 2023.

Post Q# 4711
> John Brennan

Quarles Harris had already told authorities of his and another co-conspirator's (Rodney Quarles-oddly similar) involvement with changing BHO's records on behalf of TAC. With a confession in hand by the authorities the inquiry should have had some momentum to move full speed forward. The political corruption of the DC Swamp extends from politicians to the justice and intelligence agencies of government. BHO and John Brennan would work together on many more illegal/shady operations in the years to come.

Post Q# 2657
> What was BRENNAN's background re: SAUDI ARABIA?

The 'cleaning up' operations into BHO's true background was ordered by Perkins Coie attorney Bob Bauer. In an attempt to mask the obvious changing of only BHO's travel history, TAC was tasked for more covert work to muddy the trail. Quarles Harris went back in days later to altered both HRC and No Name's passport files to muddy the waters of any future probes. All recall the many varying accounts given by BHO as to both who are his true bloodline parents as well as the actual hospital of his own birth.

Post Q# 4331
> Intelligence was manipulated by [Brennan].
> Watch the news.

BHO later admitted to a previously undisclosed personal trip to Pakistan during his wayward college days in 1981. One heck of a field trip to take and to keep it under wraps until pressed on the subject-vintage obfuscation by BHO. Joan Rivers fans will recall her public comments days prior to her untimely death about BHO being gay and Michelle a trannie. The steal of the century of the 2020 election and installation of the illegal Biden administration was engineered by the Shadow President himself (BHO).

Post Q# 1380
> No Such Agency vs Clowns In America.

Of very odd note was the bizarre death of Rolling Stone reporter Michael Hastings. Hastings was looking into the murder of Quarles Harris when he died in a very suspicious auto accident. Additionally award winning journalists Andrew Breitbart/Bre Payton/and Joe Rago all died relatively young under mysterious circumstances. 'Q' often reminds us that there are no coincidences. President Trump would file in 2022 a federal RICO lawsuit against all those that promoted the false Russian collusion narrative. BHO/Brennan/and Clapper were briefed about HRC's planned 'RussiaGate' operation against candidate Trump before the FBI opened their probe.

Post Q# 2933
> No punishment [Brennan] by HUSSEIN ADMIN re: SURV of Senate etc.

In the documentary 'ShadowGate', CIA Director Brennan uses contractor Edward Snowden to build computer bridges. Snowden gave a direct full data link from the NSA mainframe computers to outside TAC. This was the basis of the 'Hammer' surveillance system of the public by BHO's intelligence agencies and utilized in the 2020 election steal. With the re-election of President Trump in 2024, 'Judgement Day' is coming and the full hidden truth will be revealed.

Post Q# 4620
> [infiltration]
> Traitors everywhere.
> Welcome to the Revolution.

Links

Epoch Times-Brennan's Role during the 2016 Elections

Revolver News-BHO's 2016 NPR Interview comes back to Haunt

FOX News-DOJ Receives Gabbard's Criminal Referral

Just the News-Ratcliffe's Review finds John Brennan pushed Steele Dossier

Revolver News-BHO: A Shadowy Cryptic Figure

Broken Anthem-BHO: Total Control

American Spectator-The Scandal Obama still won't Acknowledge

The Last Refuge-The Analysis Corporation

Tore Says-John Brennan and Michael Hastings

True Pundit-Intel Operative who Altered BHO's Passport Records is Murdered

Washington Times-BHO Passport Files Violated: 2 Workers Fired/1 Rebuked

The War Economy-SpyFall

PJ Media-Brennan: BHO's Assassination Czar

Rense-Key Witness in BHO Passport Fraud Case Murdered

Washington Times-Passports Probe Focuses on Worker

American Thinker-BHO Passport Breach: Unanswered Questions and Murder

An Informed Populace-Quarles Harris Jr.

Washington Examiner-State Department Employee pleads Guilty to Identity Theft

CNBC-What did the Analysis Corporation do?

Tony Heller-Joan Rivers: BHO is gay and Michelle Transgender

Tablet Magazine-The BHO Factor

Crossfire Hurricane Docs-DJT and Flynn Defensive Briefing

Justice.gov-2023 SC John Durham Report

Rich Higgins' NSC Memo: Red Flare Warning

In late May 2017 Rich Higgins (1974-2022) formerly of the National Security Council (NSC), wrote a 7-page memo outlining a 'Deep State Coup' against President Trump. This fortuitously predictive memo got Higgins fired on 7/21/17 by the new director of the NSA/NSC General H. R. McMaster. Foreign operations to 'capture' via compromise plans has been employed against US officials forever. Sad to report the passing early in 2022 of Patriot Rich Higgins due to heart failure and be assured that history will always remember his heroic NSC memo.

Post Q# 4543
Remember your mission.
Infiltration not invasion.

Higgins did however have many correction assumptions and accurate predictions of the ultimate coup. Operation Crossfire Hurricane would be one component of an elaborate coup coined ObamaGate/SpyGate. These unfolding political scandals will prove to be much larger than Watergate and bring accountability to all of these traitors.

Post Q# 2729
Bigger than the 25th amendment attempt to remove.
Depth of this is very serious.

Higgins came from the Pentagon over to the NSC and became part of the famed group nicknamed the 'FlynnStones.' This crew of close inner-circle staffers of DIA/NSA General Mike Flynn (K.T./Ezra/Kellogg/Anton/etc.) were all extremely loyal and dedicated Patriots.

Post Q# 144
What council do the Wizards and Warlocks control?

Higgins worked as the Director of the Strategic Planning Office of the NSC. Rich Higgins was an early hire by NSA General Flynn and along with Ezra Cohen-Watnick were part of the famed FlynnStones who all were targeted for removal by General McMaster.

Post Q# 2640
What was the 16-year plan to destroy America?

Rich Higgins' main memo theme was that President Trump is facing a coup plot comparable to a Mao type insurrection from the Deep State. Higgins could not have been more correct and omnipotent in his warning President Trump of this pending danger. The Chinese CCP has long has a detailed plan known as the '3 Warfare's' doctrine of infiltration. The combination of the MB along with the Chinese CCP brings two enemies against the USA.

Post Q# 2572
Drops 'layered' to provide 'advance knowledge.'

Higgins also points out the combination of the Progressive Hard Left/Cultural Marxist with the Radical Islamic Movement (Muslim Brotherhood). A sinister Red/Green Axis was formed to fundamentally transform America, in what we know as the '16-Year Plan to Destroy America.' In 2021 we see the continuing of the plan with the wide-open borders and the humiliation of the fall of Afghanistan. The world would witness in 2024 the merger of Red/Green with the numerous pro Hamas/anti-Israel protests.

Post Q# 131
POTUS NAT SEC E briefing 3:02am

Higgins' coup plot elements involve the weaponized DOJ and Leftists 'resistance' in coordinated attacks. BHO's Organizing for Action (OFA) were the foot soldiers of BLM/Antifa and had been the main quarterback directing the attacks on President Trump to this day. Many alumni from the BHO era are now back with the illegal Biden Administration. The Ukraine conflict of 2022 would give Saudi Crown Prince Mohammed bin Salman (MBS) the opportunity to make beneficial arrangements with both Russia and China.

Post Q# 1661

What role can NSA play?

Higgins outlines the much larger conspiracy is at play termed the '16-Year Plan.' The goal has always been to bring down President Donald Trump at all costs so as regain control and insure they never lost power again. The election steal of 2020 would exemplify the desperation of the guilty Deep State DC Swamp. US Admiral James Lyons echoed in 2015 similar concerns to Higgins surrounding the serious national security threat posed by the Muslim Brotherhood.

Post Q# 4196

Why did [McMaster] target and remove loyal intel operatives inside the WH?

Look how many failed coup plotters will face huge criminal charges. ObamaGate/SpyGate include incredibly many married couples: Ohr's/Strzok's/McCabe's/Dunn-Bauer/Murray-King. Many BHO alumni have returned in the Biden administration and are completing the third term via a Shadow Presidency. Biden constantly telling reporters he is 'not allowed' to answer certain questions per his handlers confirms Biden's puppet position. Hunter Biden's infamous 'Laptop from Hell' was confirmed to the public in 2022 and the incriminating trove of emails will show corruption at the highest levels.

Post Q# 570

[The 16 Year Plan to Destroy America].

Thanks to President Trump's direct order, we had the return of Ezra Cohen-Watnick (ECW) over to the DOJ and then over to work with acting Secretary of Defense Chris Miller. DOD made changes to special forces being out of the loop for CIA and directly under the President. Patel Patriot has outlined a possible Continuance of Government (COG) operation that President Trump may have instituted at the end of his first term.

Post Q# 2219

None are protected.
None are safe.

Sadly, we are now witnessing the second half of the 16-year plan under Biden. IG Horowitz's 2.0 exposed many illegal violations with FISA/Dossier/and SpyGate activities under review by Special Counsel (SC) John Durham. Rep. Devin Nunes had sent 14 criminal referrals for SC John Durham and finally there is a chance at governmental accountable for past crimes. It would later be learned that the corrupt USAID would indirectly fund many Islamic organizations/charities that passed money onto terrorists, which highlights the brave accomplishments of Rich Higgins.

Post Q# 4360

Insurrection Act of 1807.
Call the ball.

Recall that Rep. Michele Bachmann in 2012 attempted to start investigations into both Huma Abedin and the Muslim Brotherhood. The world would focus in 2024 upon the continued global struggle between Islam/Muslim Brotherhood and the West with the war between Israel and Hamas. General Michael Flynn is President Trump's secret ace in the hole, and all will be finally revealed in 2025 being the year of Justice. Judgement Day is coming, and SC Durham has dropped criminal indictments related to ObamaGate/SpyGate and submitted his final report in 2023. With the re-election of President Trump in 2024, many past political secrets will finally be publicly revealed.

Post Q# 154
> Who financed 9-11?
> Who was Bin Laden's handler?
> Fantasy land.

Links

Daily Caller-Rich Higgins "Interview and Article"

Emerald TV-The Most Famous Memo of the Trump Era

Real Clear Politics-Eulogy for a Bureaucrat with a Conscience

Unconstrained Analytics-POTUS and Political Warfare (aka Higgins Memo)

American Thinker-Islamic Infiltration and Death of Richard Higgins

Epoch Times-Infiltrating the West

Breitbart-'Blood Money': The Secret Chinese Warfare Manifesto

WSJ-The Red Green Alliance: Pro Hamas Protests

Lori Anderson-2015 Admiral James Lyons on Muslim Brotherhood Threats

Real Clear Politics-Mark Levin: The Muslim Brotherhood has Infiltrated our Government

Independent Sentinel-George Soros: Plan to Destroy America

Foreign Policy-Here's the Memo that Blew Up the NSC

National Review-How BHO Sided with the Muslim Brotherhood

Free Beacon-Taxpayer USAID Group funded Terrorism tied to Islamic Charity

WSJ-Rich Higgins: The White House fired Me over Loyalty

Breitbart-McMaster "Detonated" over Higgins NSC Memo

The Atlantic-NSC Staffer Forced out over Memo

The Last Refuge-Jake Sullivan and the Muslim Brotherhood

Free Beacon-Fired NSC Aide reveals Political Warfare against Trump

Rush Limbaugh-The Barack Obama Shadow Government Coup against Trump

Politico-Secret Backstory of how BHO let Hezbollah Off the Hook

American Thinker-Darryl Cooper: Martyr Made's Mega Thread

House.Oversight.gov-The Muslim Brotherhood's Global Threat

Crossfire Hurricane Docs-State Department Steele Binder

Justice.gov-2023 SC John Durham Report

(Answer is:) Mrs. Peter Strzok
(Question:) Who is Melissa Hodgman ?

Melissa Hodgman has been promoted from the Associate Director (Enforcement Division), to acting Director of the Securities Exchange Commission. Melissa Hodgman's first big promotion was on 10/14/16, correlating to her husband's (Peter Strzok) special work assignment at the FBI. Biden recently promoted Hodgman to the acting Director, continuing the transparent reward scheme. President Trump would file in 2022 a federal RICO lawsuit against husband Peter Strzok/HRC/DNC and others who promoted the false Russian collusion narrative during the 2016 Presidential election.

Post Q# 1742
Follow the family.
Think texts between PS/MH.

As Dan Bongino (ex-USSS) often says "dates are important" and we also know by now that there are no coincidences, this huge Fall 2016 promotion smells of an inside governmental payoff scheme. Anons have uncovered a rash of husband/wife teams involved with this coup plot against President Trump. Hodgman's suspiciously timed big promotion and her ongoing role as head of the SEC investigations into the Clinton Foundation pegs her into the SpyGate scandal.

Post Q# 1621
You have more than you know.
Fireworks.

Melissa Hodgman has been with the SEC since 2008. She is married to infamous and subsequently fired FBI Counterintelligence agent Peter Strzok. It was Hodgman who first alerted the FBI about this affair, after discovering emails in her husband's phone and not through FBI discovery.

Post Q# 1278
National crisis.
Reveal Gmail draft comms.

The Strzok's met while attending college at Georgetown University. They are incredibly still married after Peter's firing from the FBI and the highly publicized 'love affair' with his co-worker FBI lawyer Lisa Page.

Post Q# 2211
THE CORRUPT SWAMP

Melissa Hodgman graduated from the School of Foreign Service from Georgetown University. There have been rumors swirling for years about Georgetown being a primary recruiting ground for various intelligence agencies and covert governmental services.

Post Q# 247
Who is Melissa Hodgman?
Date of promotion of wife?
Follow the wives.

Let's recall in October 2016 that Melissa gets a huge promotion at the SEC while overseeing investigations into the Clinton Foundation (CF) as well as Pete's work at the FBI. The CF investigations for the last several years were primarily under Hodgman's direct security enforcement division.

Post Q# 1278
> Reveal Gmail draft comms.

Hodgman's special promotion occurred while her husband Peter was neck-deep in the FBI's operation Crossfire Hurricane. Strzok and FBI 'lover' Lisa Page were planning an 'Insurance Policy' against then candidate and later President Donald Trump.

Post Q# 2158
> Panic in DC
> Lisa Page testifying against Peter Strzok.

Fired FBI Deputy Director Andy McCabe's office was where these diabolical plans were first hatched. This Justice Department crew of coup plotters nicknamed themselves the 'small group' or the mysterious 'Secret Society.'

Post Q# 4089
> Sometimes you can't TELL the public the truth.
> YOU MUST SHOW THEM.

COUP PLOT (Crossfire Hurricane):
- Completely exonerate HRC/Aides (ObamaGate)
- Fabricate Russia Dossier to damage Trump (RussiaGate)
- FISA Title-1 Surveillance on Trump World (SpyGate)
- Final stage 'Insurance Policy' would be the removal of the POTUS by any means (Crossfire Hurricane)

Post Q# 4362
> Keyword: Insurgency

Of public interest are the text messages exchanged between Strzok and Lisa Page. Apparently, they were having an affair and exchanged 50,000 personal messages during this critical time period of late 2016 and early 2017.

Post Q# 586
> Discussed the assassination (possibility) of the POTUS.
> AS THE WORLD TURNS.

Only a small portion of Strzok/Page texts have been declassified and made public. Inquiring minds want to know do any messages reveal plans of physical harm or assassination plot discussions against POTUS/Family members?

Post Q# 250
> Date Peter/Comey cleared Weiner emails?
> Date wife was promoted?
> Do you believe in coincidences?

Remember Peter Strzok lead both the Hillary Clinton and Donald Trump official FBI criminal investigations. Additionally, Strzok interviewed HRC/Mills/Abedin/Flynn and later was placed on the Robert Mueller's Team. Peter Strzok and Lisa Page would win their lawsuits in 2024 against the DOJ for private claims and government job dismissal due to SpyGate related activities..

Post Q# 4124
> Why do they always include their spouse, son, daughter, etc.?
> Follow the money.

In this entire corruption scandal commonly known as ObamaGate/SpyGate there are a surprising amount of married 'dirty' couples. The law preventing testimony against each other may have been a selection factor. Melissa Hodgman would become involved with the 2022 SEC investigation of President Trump's social media firm Truth Social and would drag out for SEC approval through 2023.

Post Q# 1271
Note 187.

In addition to the Strzok's others are McCabe's / Ohr's / Dunn and Bauer / Murray and King / Abedin and Weiner. Married 'dirty couples' would be a hallmark of this sad government operation against a Presidential candidate. Hodgman is credited to first alerting the FBI about hubby Pete's love affair, not discovery via an internal FBI search. Special Counsel (SC) John Durham has many criminal referrals from IG Horowitz related to illegal surveillance operations under BHO/HRC.

Post Q# 2700
Establish 'financial checks/reviews' of those in senior (critical) positions (audits) + direct family (close proximity).

Hodgman's SEC division have recently been investigating Patrick Byrne and OverStock.com. Hodgman is credited with the insider stock deal and subsequent prosecution for lying of Martha Stewart. SC Durham has dropped criminal indictments related the ObamaGate/SpyGate treasonous coup plotters and submitted his final report in 2023. With the historic re-election of President Trump in 2024, many hope past hidden political secrets will be revealed.

Post Q# 3481
Important to remember correlation between FISA abuse [treason remove DA_POTUS] and midyear investigation?

Links

FOX News-Democrats pulled Greatest Con Job Ever

Clinton Foundation Timeline-2025 Crossfire Hurricane Docs

Just the News-SEC Chair draws Republican Scrutiny over Trump's Social Media Merger

Politico-FEDs Settle Page/Strzok Privacy Claims

Washington Examiner-Strzok pushed Falsehood on Trump-Russia Inquiry Origin in 2017

The Federalist-Senate Expands Probe into FBI's Ability to Hide Documents

SEC.gov-Melissa Hodgman named Acting Director of Enforcement

Washington Examiner-Peter Strzok's Wife discovered Lisa Page Affair on his Phone

American Report-Exposing What is in Plain Site (Melissa Hodgman)

Justice.gov-Cyber Division Recovers Strzok/Page text Messages

FOX News-Nunes: Russian Hoaxer Strzok's Wife SEC Appointment

Breitbart-"7th Floor FBI Top Brass Involved": Strzok keeping Flynn Case Open

Epoch Times-SpyGate: The True Story of Collusion

American Thinker-How Husband/Wives Figure in Latest Scandal Revelations

Brass Balls-Peter Strzok's Insurance Policy: Wife Melissa Hodgman

Eric "Take the 5ᵗʰ" Holder—No Free Passes

Eric Holder [EH] was the first African American to serve as U.S. Attorney General. Eric Holder was appointed AG in 2009 and demonstrated his unwavering loyalty to BHO time after time until his forced resignation in 2015. Holder was often described as BHO's wingman due to his constantly having to bail out the corrupt elected official.

Post Q# 36
> How does Soros, Obama, Clinton, Holder, Lynch, etc all net many millions of dollars (normally within a single tax year).

Many political scandals occurred under Holder's watch at the Department of Justice, while none ever touched BHO. The protection of BHO is the central axis point of the political corruption known as ObamaGate/SpyGate. In typical DC hypocrisy, Holder would publicly state in 2022 that President Trump "has to be held accountable' for January 6th Capitol riot.

Post Q# 1431
> Those who are the loudest....
> Suicide weekend?
> Pain.

Eric Holder also holds the dubious title of the first Attorney General to be held in contempt of Congress. [EH] would ultimately be forced to resign as AG in total disgrace back in 2015. History would show that it would be Biden's AG Merrick Garland that was discussed by Congress to be held in contempt. Additionally Holder and BHO would be involved with Qualcomm and an illegal microchip transfer to China terribly adversely impacting our national security.

Post Q# 1601
> NOBODY IS ABOVE THE LAW.
> THE WORLD IS WATCHING.

Holder outright refused to answer scandal related questions ("I take the 5th") about Fast and Furious to Congressional oversight committees. Not many high office holders have ever thumbed their nose at Congress and outright refused to answer basic questions under while oath as a public servant.

Post Q# 436
> HOLDER RELAY SPEC RUSSIA

Holder's successor for Attorney General was Tarmac Queen Loretta Lynch (aka Elizabeth Carlisle). We wonder today if things went from bad to worse with this change at the top of the Justice Department with the change of leadership. It would be revealed in 2023 that at least 6 BHO administration officials had fake non-governmental emails and Eric Holder had 3 known alias accounts.

Post Q# 1589
> LL IS KEY to CONNECTING to WH / HRC / BC / JB / JC / SP / EH.....

Holder has his fingerprints on a wide range of political scandals. Here are just a few of the all-time BHO-era favorites:
- IRS Targeting of Conservatives
- Fast and Furious Scandal
- Refused to Prosecute Voter Fraud

- ATF Agent Brian Terry's Murder
- Ferguson/Missouri Riots
- Iran Nuclear Deal/Hostage Payoff
- Qualcomm Microchip to China
- Punishing select Journalists
- Private non-GOV email accounts
- Withholding FOIA Documents
- Contempt of Congress charge

Post Q# 895
> Don't drop the soap.

As we know from 'Q' an evil plan was concocted involving a planned Supreme Court USSC (AS) vacancy. A President HRC would fill the empty seat (Cass Sunstein) from (AS) and make Loretta Lynch wait for RBG to later step down. In 2022 the Mexican government finally charges 7 nationals with Fast and Furious weapons trafficking indictments.

Post Q# 1149
> LL remains AG HRC.
> HRC appoints new AS replacement.
> RBG steps down.
> LL steps up.
> New AG
> 'The Plan'

I feel that we will be hearing from Eric Holder again in the months to come. Everyone has hopes that Special Counsel (SC) John Durham is going to claw-back past crimes that the DOJ previously gave out free passes. It a twist of political irony and hypocrisy, Congressional leaders are holding Trump aides in contempt while they had claimed the opposite with BHO's AG Eric Holder.

Post Q# 155
> How do you capture a very dangerous animal?

ObamaGate/SpyGate prosecutions will keep folks busy for years to come. There are many unjust prosecutions that need to be reviewed with possible reversals and pardons granted. SC Durham has dropped criminal indictments related to the illegal activities surrounding SpyGate and submitted his final report in 2023. Rep. Jim Jordan sent a letter to ATF in late 2022 demanding that they retain all records concerning the Fast and Furious scandal.

Post Q# 1071
> EH CA.
> Relevant soon.

Remember what 'Q' has said about the top-tier ObamaGate/SpyGate failed coup criminals- "Nobody gets a free pass". I firmly believe that once all has been exposed these treasonous coup plotters will not be able to walk down the street. With the re-election of President Trump in 2024, we enter the final Storm and approaching Judgement Day in conjunction with the worldwide Great Awakening.

Post Q# 3870
> THEY WILL BE HELD ACCOUNTABLE.
> NOBODY WALKS AWAY FROM THIS.

Links

Rolling Stone-Eric Holder: Wall Street Double Agent

Just the News-BHO Endorses Bogus CIA Claims about Trump and Putin

FOX News-House Panel Subpoenas Clintons/Others in Epstein Probe

Revolver News-Did BHO and Eric Holder get Paid to Rig Court Cases

The Last Refuge-AG Eric Holder

Breibart-6 BHO Officials used Alias Emails

Forbes-BHO's War on the Fast and Furious Whistleblowers

Sharyl Attkisson-BHO Era Surveillance Timeline

The Atlantic-Eric Holder: Contempt of Congress/Fast and Furious

Legal Insurrection-Mexican Government charges 7 with Fast and Furious related Crimes

Sheryl Attkisson-Fast and Furious Story Links

Politico-BHO Relents in Fight over Fast and Furious Docs

Town Hall-BHO's Bloodiest Scandal Reemerges as Mexico Demands an Apology

Real Clear Politics-Past Attorney General went Unpunished for Contempt

True Pundit-Mother of Murdered Border Agent: Son Feared for His Life

Ammo.com-Operation Fast and Furious: Forgotten History of ATF's Gun Scandal

CSM-BHO 'Stooge' Eric Holder

Washington Times-Not so Fast BHO: Your Biggest Scandal is Unfolding

The Guardian-Eric Holder held in Contempt of Congress

CBN-Scandals call Holders Legacy into Question

Real Clear Politics-Real Reasons behind Eric Holder's Resignation

Western Journal-Eric Holder Snaps "Shut the Hell Up" to Paul Sperry

NY Times Archive-The Eric Holder Letter

Crossfire Hurricane Docs-FISA Notes

Justice.gov-2023 SC John Durham Report

Think Huber / Trust Huber / Meet Big John Huber

Then AG 'Stealth' Jeff Sessions announced with little fanfare that the U.S. Attorney for Utah John Huber has been appointed to be a Special Prosecutor (SP). SP Huber has silently been working alongside OIG Michael Horowitz and then SP John Durham since November 13, 2017. I believe history will show John Huber to have been a key player in holding past political corruption to full account.

Post Q# 2506
> To all those that doubted SESSIONS and HUBER you ALL WILL PAY THE PRICE VERY SOON.

The DOJ cancelled SP Huber's expected testimony to the U.S. House on December 13, 2018. Then AG Barr had announced that John Huber was wrapping up his HRC investigations (Clinton Foundation and Uranium One/U1) and criminal indictments should be forthcoming.

Post Q# 1517
> IG started long before Huber setting stage.
> IG = FBI.
> Huber = DOJ (no DC).

SP's Huber/Durham and IG Horowitz have been conducting extensive internal reviews of the DOJ/FBI. In this unique setup, Horowitz acts like the FBI for the investigations and Huber/Durham act as the DOJ for the prosecutions.

Post Q# 2554
> WHITAKER, HOROWITZ, HUBER, and WRAY.
> Long meeting held within a SCIF [unusual].

Horowitz/Huber/Durham first were focused on the misconduct by the DOJ/FBI over the HRC email investigation. Horowitz/Huber/Durham's scope has now expanded to include elements of FISA/Dossier/SpyGate/CF and U1 probes of criminal misconduct.

Post Q# 1682
> Who does Huber report to [directly]?

OIG Horowitz's 1.0 500-page report on the HRC investigation showed a bias and a deliberate effort to exonerate HRC. Horowitz's 2.0 report on FISA abuses (17 major errors) has been referred to SP John Durham for criminal investigations.

Post Q# 2462
> Who is HUBER?
> Mandate charged to HUBER?
> Resources provided to HUBER?

Horowitz's 2.0 report demonstrated concerns FISA/FISC abuses and the activities of Stefan Halper in SpyGate. The entire Crossfire Hurricane/Razor illegally surveillance plots will be the focus for the criminal probes.

Post Q# 1644
> Timing is everything.
> Think Huber.

SP Huber has been referred affectionately as a "Jock with the soul of a Geek." Big John Huber was a very smart former college football player and that helps with the overall projected personal 'smart jock' image.

Post Q# 4486
It's what you don't see.
Durham is not the only game in town.

Huber has been serving in various positions in the Utah District U.S. Attorney's Office since April 2002. Huber took over after the helm in 2015 as the U.S. Attorney. Always considered a straight shooter, Huber has always left politics at the door and performed admirably in his differing justice roles.

Post Q# 3674
Huber.
DOJ plane(s).
CF.

Professor Jonathan Turley said the combination of Huber's prosecutor abilities along with that of the investigational tools of IG Horowitz's large staff, should do the job in place of a second appointed Special Counsel. 'Q' has reposted Turley's spot-on comment many times on the board concerning this entire group of professional prosecutors.

Post Q# 2524
HUBER FISA(S) [2-way street]

Sen. Orion Hatch has praised John Huber's independence and his outside of the DC Swamp perspective on many critical issues. Huber has many supporters and professional admirers from both sides of the DC political aisle.

Post Q# 1660
Ask yourself: does Huber have the ability to file across all 50 states?

Horowitz/Huber/Durham have been hunting government criminals for a few years now. Their specialty is exposing foreign LURES, domestic spies, and corrupt political traitors.

Post Q# 2676
ZERO leaks re: HUBER?
ZERO.
Do not mistake 'public' silence for inaction.

Please note that Utah still carries the death penalty and has access to impartial non-swamp juries. 'Q' has hinted about future MOAB BOOMS, which coincidentally is a Utah city. John Huber would leave his post at the DOJ in January 2021 after many years of dedication. Mr. Huber is a shareholder of the prestigious Salt Lake City law firm of Greenberg Traurig.

Post Q# 1122
TRUST HOROWITZ.
TRUST HUBER.

Captain Jeff (TRUST SESSIONS) had kept the John Huber/John Durham appointments secret for a long time. AG Barr/Huber/Horowitz/Storch/Durham/Bash and others assisting POTUS with this cleanup justice phase. The DOJ discovered a letter sent from then Chief of Staff Matthew Whitaker from AG Jeff Sessions on 11/22/17 advising John Huber to revisit the Clinton Foundation and Uranium One probes.

Post Q# 2562

> When was HUBER activated by SESSIONS?
> Who was/is assigned to HUBER?

Another reason for Huber's selection is that Utah has large uranium (U1) mining operations. Utah may very well become the base of future prosecutions for the Uranium One case.

Post Q# 2397

> OIG works w/HUBER [important to remember].

Coincidentally NSA maintains a supercomputer data facility that's very handy to Huber's location. Wizards and Warlocks are actively at play in forming half of the 'Keystone.' Special Counsel John Durham has dropped criminal charges related to the SpyGate scandal and the areas SP Huber had initially reviewed. John Huber turned over all his Clinton Foundation investigations to SC Durham in 2020.

Post Q# 2662

> 'That can only happen through a federal grand jury investigation headed by John W.
> Huber, the U.S. Attorney in Utah who has been appointed to investigate FISA criminality
> by the Obama FBI and DOJ.'

Jurisdiction will come into play due to the location of these many uranium mines. Also untainted grand juries' pools can be empaneled for the indictment phase stemming from SP John Huber's CF/U1 review. POTUS has recently tweeted about SP Huber and that normally signals the 'chess board' is active.

Post Q# 1552

> Weiner HRC / Others-crimes against children.
> Noose.
> Ref to Huber?

SP Huber has spoken up previously on behalf of both "Kate's Law" and "No Sanctuaries Act." SC John Durham will finish the justice phase of SpyGate and submitted his final report in 2023. As is normal with new administrations, John Huber resigned per Joe Biden's request in February 2021. It was mentioned several times in the drops as to Huber + 470 and only time will reveal the exact details of this reference. With the re-election of President Trump in 2024, many expect hidden political secrets to finally be revealed.

Post Q# 2681

> Barr meeting with Huber and OIG.
> Barr/Whitaker re: DECLAS, SC report, Huber, etc....

Links

Washington Times-U.S. Attorney John Huber

Real Clear Investigations-RussiaGate's Architects Suppressed Doubts to Peddle False Claims

Justice.gov-John Huber leaves his DOJ Post

The Federalist-FBI Revelations Show the Mueller Special Counsel was a Cover-Up

FOX News-Durham Assumed Parts of John Huber's Clinton Foundation Review

Breitbart-Inspector General will Declare FBI/DOJ Broke the Law

Daily Beast-DOJ finds Letter Ordering Scrutiny of Uranium One and Clinton Foundation

ABC News-U.S. Attorney for Utah Resigns

The Last Refuge-SpyGate: The Big Picture

Epoch Times-Mr. Huber goes to Washington

Salt Lake Trib-Utah's own John Huber

Justice Department-US Attorney John Huber

Markets Work-Why Sessions chose Huber

Lee Rockwell-Trust Sessions/Huber/and Horowitz

Greenberg Traurig Law-John Huber (Shareholder)

US Attorney Utah-SP Huber meets David Schwendiman

US Attorney John Huber Twitter-Funereal Services for K-9 "Hondo"

Crossfire Hurricane Docs-Steele Dossier through Simpson and McCain

Justice.gov-2023 SC John Durham Report

Operation Crossfire Hurricane and the 'Insurance Policy'

The four main components of the political coup plot nicknamed OPERATION TRUMP:

- Exonerate HRC/Aides (ObamaGate)
- Trump-Russia Dossier creation/distribution (RussiaGate)
- FISA Title-1 Surveillance Warrants/Section 702 (SpyGate)
- The 'Insurance Policy' (Crossfire Hurricane)

Just like coming to the final song at a concert or the final act in a play, DOJ's Small Group/Secret Society is out of options. The fourth and final phase of Operation Trump was the very threateningly sounding 'Insurance Policy' last option. Top level bureaucrats do have a knack for producing voluminous white papers and advanced strategy policies memorandum. President Trump would file in 2022 a federal RICO lawsuit against HRC/DNC/and others related to the promotion of the false Russian collusion narrative during the 2016 election cycle.

Post Q# 2731
[2] accounted for?
IDEN remaining incoming.

Claimed to be officially started on 7/31/16 was the FBI's Russia Counterintelligence probe nicknamed Crossfire Hurricane. Additional parallel plans like Crossfire FISA and Operation Dragon were also conducted by the DOJ/FBI during this treasonous coup plot. Critical to the plan to remove Donald Trump if he happened to win was the false Russian association with Team Trump which was confirmed in 2024 via the FIVE EYES (FVEY) revelation.

Post Q# 1728
Unauthorized missile fired.
POTUS AF1.
POTUS re-routes
Biggest threat to the American people.

The Deep State Cabal is currently watching in combined disbelief their professional pre-laid plans crumbled one by one with the Great Awakening process. Dire panic has truly now set in and is being displayed in desperate attempts to change the current narrative of a global Great Reset operation. In what would turn out to be the most watch show of all time, Tucker Carlson interviewed President Trump in 2023 and warned specifically of a potential assassination attempt before the 2024 Fall election, predicting the shots fired in Butler/PA in mid July.

Post Q# 2856
Are 'new' investigations designed to be an 'insurance' extension?
Retain the 'insurance' policy?

This criminal group from within our own government, even met off-campus on more than one occasion. Cabal members tried to refine their coup plot against our great President Trump with these surveillance avoidance ultra-secret meetups. The Deep State in DC consists of both Democrats and RINO Republicans combining to form the 'UniParty.'

Post Q# 154
Perhaps someday people will understand 'they' had a plan to conduct 'another' mass extinction event.

I firmly believe that some of the Strzok/Page text messages will reveal a diabolical scheme against President Trump and his family. Devin Nunes had pushed hard for all of the DOJ/FBI documents concerning SpyGate and Crossfire Hurricane operations to be released to the public. One of President Trump's last official actions on 1/19/21 was to order the total declassification of the FBI's Crossfire Hurricane material.

Post Q# 3734
Also think 'White Squall' (Q-typo) re: Cuban M Crisis/JFK.
Bigger than you can imagine.
Expand your thinking.

Please check out the below reporter Kevin Jackson's interview on FOX News where he broaches the 'Assassination' topic. Kevin Jackson shocked the FOX TV network hosts and got the assassination talk instantly quashed via a silenced microphone. SC Durham would slowly unveil in multiple 2022 court filings, a vast coordinated conspiracy involving both government officials as well as outside private actors.

Post Q# 4235
What 'Insurance' did they have?
Infiltration of US GOV?
That fact alone should scare every American.

Devin Nunes has said that if there was a "Spy or Two" inserted into the Trump campaign that is a 'Red Line' no American will accept. If there are documented assassination discussions against POTUS/FAMILY, that is another line that will not be tolerated, nor should it ever be allowed. Questions of an assassination attempt would arise in the 2024 FBI raid on President Trump's Mar-a-Lago home over classified documents and the issue by the FBI to use 'deadly force.'

Post Q# 586
What would happen if texts originating from an FBI agent to several [internals] discussed the assassination of the POTUS or member of his family?

OIG Horowitz/SP Huber/SC Durham/IG Storch had focused on the "SpyGate" element to their various criminal probes. Fingers crossed and popcorn ready for the much-anticipated flood of indictments by Special Counsel John 'Bull' Durham. SC Durham's indictment of Perkins Coie/Clinton campaign lawyer Michael Sussmann is the first major domino to fall. USSS whistleblowers would warn officials of additional assassination efforts after the failed 2024 Butler/PA Trump Rally and Trump International Golf Club/FL attempts.

Post Q# 3125
The attempted 'COUP' [TREASON] opens the door to more serious......

The Small Group Cabal always was big on nicknames like the phrase "Mid-Year Exam" (MYE), in reference to the HRC Email/Server "matter". History may show both the Trump-Russia Witch-hunt and Congressional Impeachment spectacle, were preludes to more desperate attempts at removal. It would be learned in 2023 that President Trump deliberately took many of the SpyGate (President had declassified) documents to his home at Mar-A-Lago/Florida for safe keeping.

Post Q# 1559
LP "Viva Le Resistance."
Viv[a] vs Viv[e]
Why classified by intel comm @ highest level?

Of sad ironic note is the use by the Black Hats of this nickname in terms of an American tragedy. Recently deceased famed JFK investigator Jim Marrs, purposely named his classic book "Crossfire: The Plot That Killed Kennedy." History would show that President Trump was under intense threats after his first term and thankfully our brave USSS kept watch. It would be revealed in 2024 that John Brennan/CIA asked FIVE EYES intel alliance partners to illegally spy in 2016 on US citizens. Incredibly the FBI would foil a plot by Iranian Republican Guard to stalk/assassinate President Trump in 2024.

Post Q# 4829
>Do you remember when they told you this was a helicopter
>decode: Unauthorized missile fired at AF1

There is a church outside of DC aka the Secret Society's Clubhouse, that was at that time being monitored and recorded by the NSA White Hats. Newscaster Keith Opbermann as well as other MSM journalists would post on X/Twitter in 2024 of "Hopes for Trump's assassination." Scarily in July 2024 at a campaign rally in Butler/PA President Trump was shoot in the right ear in an assassination attempt. Judgement Day is coming, and SC Durham has submitted his final report in 2023 related to the various SpyGate scandals. President Trump won re-election in 2024, and a new era of American excellence began.

Post Q# 30
>Would you believe a device was placed somewhere in the WH that could actually cause harm to anyone else in the room and would in essence be undetected?
>Fantasy, right?

Links

Revolver News-J13 Quietly Disappears

The Last Refuge-Weiner/Abedin Laptop

FOX News-White House: Condemns James Comey for Attempt to Put a 'Hit' on President

Revolver News-New Theory about Trump's would-be Assassin

NY Post-Iranian Agent Instructed to Stalk/Assassinate Trump

Newsweek-What we Know: How many Trump Assassination Attempts?

Just the News-FBI's Arctic Haze

Revolver News-President Trump: "The Bullets are Flying"

The Federalist-USSS Whistleblower Warns of more Assassination Attempts

Washington Times-Tucker Carlson warns Donald Trump about Assassination

NY Post-CIA and Foreign Intel Agencies Illegally Targeted 26 Trump Aides

Conserative Brief-Dan Bongino: President Trump remains Under Threat

Clinton Foundation Timeline-Crossfire Hurricane

(Answer is:) BHO's Iranian Consigliere
(Question:) Who is [VJ]

Valerie Jarrett [VJ] was born in Shiraz/Iran and served BHO as his most Senior Adviser. The Italian Mob call a Capo's top counselor the Consigliere and is undoubtedly the most fitting title for Jarrett. In 2008 BHO talked Jarrett out of the Illinois Senate race for a White House gig. BHO would use HRC's 2106 false Russia Dossier to spy on candidate Donald Trump.

Post Q# 1510
Why are Hussein records sealed?

Valerie Jarrett was the sole gatekeeper of the Oval Office and was the 'fixer' to the many of the BHO-era scandals. [VJ] was the hand that gave or slapped back political favors from the White House's Oval Office. Jarrett was tangential involved with the Blagojevich political bribery scandal with her 2008 Senate consideration. President Trump would file in 2022 a federal RICO lawsuit against all those officials involved with the creation and promotion of the phony dossier during the 2016 election cycle.

Post Q# 1887
What is VJ's background?
Muslim by faith?

Roseanne Barr refocused public attention back upon Valerie Jarrett via "Planet of The Apes" meme. Roseanne Barr would go on to publicly state that Jarrett was "a product of the Muslim Brotherhood combined with the Planet of the Apes." After her statement and funny meme went viral, bad news followed due to the negativity generated and almost instantly the network cancelled Barr's current hit TV series. This would demonstrate an evil new trend that later would be coined 'cancel culture' and show the extent of censorship to be applied to all those with counter narratives.

Post Q# 3881
THE SWAMP RUNS DEEP.
Backgrounds are important.
Muslim Brotherhood.

It is without dispute that all major decisions coming from the BHO White House were run by and given final approved from Jarrett. [VJ] relished her powerful Oval Office Consigliere position and BHO often used her as a 'sniffer' of loyalty. Jarrett's control would run through the first term of President Trump and into the illegally installed Biden Administration.

Post Q# 1948
Who is Valerie Jarrett?
Where was she born?

Jarrett continues in her predominant position when she has moved into BHO's swank post President new DC mansion. This is the new command headquarters for the Progressive Leftists 'resistance' movement, and all conveniently funded by George Soros and other NWO Globalists. This was in effect a Shadow Government during President Trump and acting as such controlling Biden today.

Post Q# 1235

Don't forget about Huma.
AWAN.
VJ.

VJ's fingerprints and stench are on these infamous BHO scandals:
- Fast and Furious (AG Holder lying)
- Libya/Benghazi Stand-Down Order
- SpyGate/Operation Crossfire Hurricane
- Journalists Files/Computers Seized
- Secret Service-Prostitution Deal
- Edward Snowden NSA Leaks
- Imran Awan's Pakistani Spy Cabal
- BHO's "Sniffer" Routing Military
- Excessive Drone Strikes/Kills
- HRC Email/Server Handling
- •armac Meeting Coverup

Post Q# 3634

[VJ] direct relay - Iran pre/post Iran deal [future marker].

In recent times [VJ] has taken to the MSM to pronounce BHO had no real scandals during his two terms. As the ObamaGate/SpyGate scandals continue to unfold, [VJ] may need to revisit some of these prior public statements. History will show a vast RICO-like conspiracy involving many high-level governmental officials coordinating with private outside contractors.

Post Q# 1828

[SPY OP].
[WH] [Hussein] [VJ] [DM] [JB] [RE].

Valerie Jarrett comes from a family of hard leftist communist sympathizers. Father In-Law Vernon Jordan was a noted author and Chicago community activist of some notoriety in his own right. Jarrett has pushing as of late the role of Black Women in leading business positions.

Post Q# 50

Where is BO today?
Where is VJ?
Alice and Wonderland.

It will become clear in future DECLAS events that many BHO governmental officials had secret email accounts. Gmail 'ghost drafts' emails, Xbox Live Chats, and HAM radio communications were all utilized with the blessing of BHO. These extracurricular accounts are primarily to avoid both future FOIA requests as well as communications exposure to surveillance programs.

Post Q# 4832

SHADOW PRESIDENT.
SHADOW GOVERNMENT.

Jarrett is credited with spearheading the Muslim/Communist infiltration within the USA. [VJ] will be back in the news with the 2023 release of the Special Counsel (SC) John Durham's final report. Odd that former Governor Cuomo reached out to Jarrett when the NY AG was beginning criminal investigations into the nursing home murders.

Post Q# 1098

Why did HUSSEIN PROTECT ISIS?

Valerie Jarrett will be shown as playing a central role in ObamaGate/SpyGate. Bad enough when we had to battle one Jarrett, but this crowd is steeped in nepotism with Jarrett's daughter being implanted over at CNN. Remember that 'Q' has repeatedly mentioned to 'watch the families. IG Horowitz has made many criminal referrals related to the unfolding scandal nicknamed SpyGate. After government service, Valerie Jarrett would become the CEO of the BHO Foundation.

Post Q# 4373
INFILTRATION V INVASION
INSURGENCY.
IRREGULAR WARFARE.

Laura Jarrett (no real journalistic background) was the Justice Department reporter and general news correspondent for CNN. Laura Jarrett worked at the time the network was helping to setup candidate Trump with the fake Steele Dossier and Russian collusion narrative. History will be very harsh on the traitorous Mockingbird news media when the truth is revealed.

Post Q# 669
VJ phone call w/AS.
[2 listeners - no IDEN].
Article 3.
Section 3.

Make no mistake Valerie Jarrett is still BHO's tip of the 'Resistance Spear.' [VJ] has the final say as Consigliere stating "It will never happen" about Michelle Obama ever running for elected office. A Shadow Presidency can work both ways as the BHO/Biden criminal cabal is learning the hard way. Judgement Day is coming as SC Durham's 2023 report is the foundation for future judicial accountability. With the re-election of President Trump in 2024, many hope hidden political secrets will finally be revealed.

Post Q# 3954
Missing [29] connections - National.
Missing [98] connections - Local.

Links

LifeZette-Jarrett must Explain Her Clinton Foundation Coverups

Clinton Foundation Timeline-2025 Crossfire Hurricane Docs

The Federalist-SpyGate 101: A Primer on the Russia Collusion Hoax

Real Clear Politics-Ratcliffe: Brennan Briefed Obama and Biden about HRC's Plan

Tablet Magazine-How RussiaGate began with BHO's Iran Deal

Ronan Farrow-Valerie Jarrett and Preet Bharara

American Thinker-Jarrett and BHO are behind SpyGate

Front Page Mag-BHO used HRC's Dossier to Spy on Trump

Washington Examiner-Jarrett: I Still haven't Accepted Trump is President

Breitbart-VJ, Chicago, and Iran Deal

The Last Refuge-SpyGate: The Big Picture

Washington Times/BHO Scandals Overlooked by VJ

FOX News-Jarrett's rumored Role in Iran Deal

Epoch Times-SpyGate: The True Story of Collusion

Judicial Watch-FBI Files on Communist Jarrett Family

American Thinker-VJ's CNN Daughter useful Tool

RD RLL-Laura Jarrett

Talking Points Memo-Valerie Jarrett Dropped out of Senate Race for WH

US News-10 Things You didn't Know about Valerie Jarrett

Jeff Carlson-Strzok's Notes

New Republic-Valerie Jarrett: BHO Whisperer

Chicago Magazine-Valerie Jarrett

Crossfire Hurricane Docs-Christopher Steele Binder

Justice.gov-2023 SC John Durham Report

Thankfully Senator Johnson is Picking at Those FBI Scabs

Senator Ron Johnson is a leader on the powerful Senate Homeland Security and Governmental Affairs committee. Senator Johnson keeps probing and needling the FBI/DOJ for relevant documents concerning the ObamaGate/SpyGate scandals. Johnson's official attention has turned to the Hunter Biden laptop, COVID/VAX issues and 1/6/21 U.S. Capitol events. The New York Times admitted in March 2022 as to the authenticity of the infamous Hunter Biden 'Laptop from Hell' and now both Senators Johnson and Chuck Grassley want testimony from the complicit news media and Big Tech.

Post Q# 1698
> You owe it to your country.
> We stand with you.
> The time is now.

Senator Johnson knows that the Department of Justice/FBI has many 'scabs' that may turn into open wounds if he just keeps picking at them all. A model more Republicans should employ to assist in the needed cleanup of the corrupt DC Swamp. President Trump had shown all Republicans how to be aggressive in combating the entrenched political corruption head on.

Post Q# 4227
> [Russia] narrative ALL FAKE?

Senator Johnson keeps requesting from FBI Director Wray select documents that will unveil the truth about past corrupt activity. President Trump has pushed AG Barr for the full public DECLAS to help with Senate probes, but time unfortunately ran out. Senators Johnson and Chuck Grassley have carried on with pressure from their respective committees for answers. Johnson and Grassley are also leading the probes into the disgusting Hunter Biden laptop and the very possible national security concerns.

Post Q# 4816
> Think drop today re: Sen Johnson re: redaction(s) [GSA vs FBI].
> "Let's see what happens."

Documents requested by Johnson's HSGAC committee from Wray had been previously directed at 16 current/former FBI/DOJ officials. Coordination with SC John Durham's investigations should bring 'light to dark' with this entire ObamaGate/SpyGate treasonous coup plot. Senator Johnson is also 'picking' at both Hunter's laptop and the truth with the 1/6 U.S. Capitol event. Both Senators Johnson and Chuck Grassley would be blocked by the DOJ in 2022 with answers on the Hunter Biden investigation.

Post Q# 659
> Those who stood chanting "USA" were FREED.
> Shot heard around the world.
> FREEDOM DAY.

Sen. Johnson had requested all documents from 1/15/15 to the end of 2020 from the following FBI key Crossfire Hurricane players: Comey / McCabe / Strzok / Page / Rybicki / Bowdich / Giacalone / Baker / Turgal / Moffa / Anderson / Priestap / Toscas / Coleman / Brooks / Kortan

Post Q# 4603
> How many Senate members were illegally surv?

Senator Johnson has been probing the FBI hard in recent time and promises future Senate hearings. Ron Johnson has raised several critical questions concerning past actions and conduct by the upper levels of the Justice Department/FBI/and intelligence agencies. Ron Johnson has pledged a self-imposed two-term limit and would run again only if a Republican replacement is not found.

Post Q# 1887
Operation Cyclone - Mujahideen/Afghanistan.

Senator Johnson additionally has pressured the DOJ in terms of the mystery Hunter Biden laptop, the 1/6 Capitol Riot, Afghanistan and demanding the public release of the John Durham report. Almost all alone Johnson has stood up to the illegal Biden/Harris administration reign. Senator Johnson would instantly call for all USSS records regarding the failed Butler/PA rally assassination attempt on President Trump in July 2024.

Ron Johnson has a stellar list of accomplishments, and a few are highlighted in the below section.

SEN. JOHNSON'S AREAS OF INQUIRY:
- Text messages between Page/Strzok
- One month delay with Weiner's Laptop
- USSS/Rally Assassination attempt
- Documents from 16 Top FBI Agents
- Members of the 'Secret Society'
- Details about FBI's 'Insurance Policy'
- Excessive Unmasking
- Hunter Biden's 'Laptop from Hell'
- U.S. Capitol event on 1/6
- SpyGate/ObamaGate Hearings
- Afghanistan Investigations
- 2022 COVID Panels/Helping VAX Injured

Post Q# 111 on 11/5/17:
They never thought she would lose.
POTUS is our savior.
We are at war.

The only way to get the truth behind all these troubling questions, is via documents and sworn testimony. Then the unsealing of indictments will be the 'Hammer' to drives home the nail in the Deep State's coffin. The ultimate loyal team player, Sen. Johnson has said he will not run for re-election if another Republican has a better chance to hold this seat due to unrelenting media attacks, but it appears Senator Johnson will serve once again.

Post Q# 3603
FISA goes both ways.
Information warfare.

Senator Johnson certainly seems to be wearing a "White Hat" as he keeps picking at the FBI/DOJ obvious scabs. Special Counsel John Durham's final report submitted in 2023 vindicates Senator Ron Johnson/Grassley and the Anons. Recently Ron Johnson has opened an inquiry into credible reports that Americans were turned away at the Kabul International Airport. The tragedy in Afghanistan and Biden's accountability is yet another item on the plate of all loyal Patriots like Senator Johnson. Ron Johnson would continue to press for the truth surrounding both Joe and

Hunter Biden, especially the sweetheart plea deal concerning taxes/gun charges. With the re-election of President Trump in 2024, Sen. Ron Johnson calls on USSS/FDA/HHS/CDC and others to persevere their records for future hearings.

Post Q# 2682
Prosecution and Transparency is the only way to save our way of life.

Links

ABC News-Johnson on Getting Shots: "What do You Care"

Western Journal-GOP Senator says Duped or Complicit Reporters return RussiaGate Awards

Just the News-Ron Johnson calls for Accountability Amid FBI Grand Conspiracy Probe

Clinton Foundation Timeline-2025 Crossfire Hurricane Docs

RonJohnson.Senate.gov-Federal Failed Response to COVID

Just the News-Sen. Ron Johnson: FBI Disinterested in Investigating

Daily Mail-Republican Senator: Much larger Story behind Elon Musk's 'Twitter Files'

The Guardian-'Mosquito in a Nudist Colony': Ron Johnson targets Fauci/Hunter

Real Clear Politics-Sen. Johnson Hearing: A Second Opinion COVID-19

The Guardian-Ron Johnson is Blend of QAnon and the Tea Party

The Federalist-FBI's Failed Setup of Ron Johnson: A Case Study of Corruption

The Last Refuge-SpyGate: The Big Picture

Breitbart-Senator Johnson: Highest Level of Corruption in Investigation of Trump

Daily Caller-Sen. Johnson Subpoenas Blumenthal/Shearer: HRC's Second Dossier

FOX News-McCabe/Page Texts reveal High Level Intel Meeting: Post 2016 Election

HDGAC gov-Interim Report: FBI Texts and Emails

Epoch Times-Senate Intel Committee: No Collusion

Clinton Foundation Timeline-Ron Johnson

OIG.Justice.gov-Cyber Division Recovers Strzok/Page Text Messages

FOX News-Susan Rice's Memo (Top Secret/Unclassified)

Crossfire Hurricane Docs-Steele Dossier through Simpson and McCain

Justice.gov-2023 SC John Durham Report

Dan Jones: A Common Name That May Become "Household"

When will the 'Progressive Leftists' finally give up and accept the reality that former President Donald Trump won originally back in 2016? Daniel Jones is a former Senate Intelligence Committee staffer of Senator Diane Feinstein and also a past senior FBI agent. Jones had a past relationship with Special Counsel (SC) John Durham over the CIA torture programs. SC John Durham would paint a vast conspiracy surrounding the false Russia collusion narrative during the 2016 election involving both government officials as well as outside private actors.

Post Q# 4465
> Biblical Times.

Then Rep. Devin Nunes had sent 42 names of current and former government officials to testify to a Congressional Task Force under Senate control. Then acting DNI Rick Grenell had recently released several dozens of these declassified Congressional testimonies. SC John Durham had interviewed Daniel Jones and indicated Perkins Coie/Clinton campaign lawyer Michael Sussmann for lying to the FBI about Alfa Bank.

Post Q# 2657
> C_A 'illegal' SURV and SEN INTEL COMM.

Daniel Jones is part of this select lot and will have to explain his continued post-election "Trump Dossier" quest. Some folks just don't realize when the have been totally defeated and refuse to accept the reality of current events. Incredibly a second near identical false second Trump-Russia dossier was explored.

Post Q# 1345
> THEY NEVER THOUGHT SHE WOULD LOSE.

Jones now runs the Penn Quarter Group (PQG), which deals in informational 'oppo' research projects. PQG operates in much the same fashion as does Fusion GPS/CrowdStrike/and Hakluyt International as international information contractors. Jones was involved with the false tip to the FBI about Alfa Bank having Russian computer servers involving Mr. Trump's personal companies. President Trump would file in 2022 a federal RICO lawsuit against those involved with the promotion of the false Russian collusion narrative during the 2016 election cycle.

Post Q# 4158
> SHADOW GOVERNMENT.
> INSURGENCY.

Daniel Jones has prior connections to the George Soros backed PR firm called The Democracy Integrity Project (TDIP). TDIP's goal was to pump out daily 'opposition research' enforcing the fake Trump-Russia collusion narrative. Jones seems to have a hand in several Deep State operations in the past and is a go to guy for the DC Swamp powerbrokers.

Post Q# 1963
> Mortified?
> What is the purpose of a BRIDGE?

Jones /PQG received over $50 million in March 2017 to continue the same Russian opposition research on Trump as had HRC/DNC. This extremely large payment was from 7-10 different

NY/CA based (Soros/OSF linked) major Democratic leftist donors. The influence from globalist to influence our elected officials and to sway elections is part of the Great Reset plan.

Post Q# 4962
Why are they manipulating you?
PUT AN END TO THE ENDLESS.

Incredibly Jones rehired both Fusion GPS and Christopher Steele to continue the same failed Russian "oppo research". Trying to recycle the already discredited fake Trump-Russia Dossier into a version 2.0, is unbelievably irrational to say the very least. The attempted second impeachment and continued Russian collusion witch-hunts continue today under the illegal Biden administration against President Trump.

Post Q# 1238
Not 'official' product-5 Eyes.

It is mind bending to watch the continued Anti-Trump bias and sheer hatred of our twice duly elected POTUS. Dan Jones' ongoing efforts to fund Fusion GPS/Steele is a prime example of this extreme hatred and of classic Trump Derangement Syndrome (TDS). The impeachment efforts along with the illegal surveillance operations of SpyGate demonstrates that the opposition to President Trump and our movement will never stop.

Post Q# 11
Military Intelligence vs FBI CIA NSA.

Jones/Fusion GPS were trying to retroactively validate the debunked original Christopher Steele Trump-Russia Dossier. This continued work was done under the false guise as to look for new "Russian Dirt" that was yet to be discovered. The injection of false memos by private outside contractors like Fusion GPS and CrowdStrike bolstered the ongoing efforts by Dan Jones. Skippy Podesta along with Jones re-engaged Fusion GPS to continue the Russian dossier project.

Post Q# 4021
Public truths of some events force wars.
WWIII prevent.
Hello, Feinstein.

Daniel Jones wrote a top-secret report in 2012 on alleged torture by the CIA during past conflicts in the Middle East. Daniel Jones' Senate Intelligence Committee report would later be turned into a movie titled 'The Report.' Then a DOJ investigator John Durham along with then CIA Director Gina Haspel dealt directly with the torture reports coming from Dan Jones. Many Congressional White Hats were glad to see Dan Jones finally leave government service in 2016. The Alfa Bank false Russia/Trump narrative is centered around data that was 'user created' and many feel Dan Jones had a hand in this operation as well as the Fusion GPS second dossier project.

Post Q# 1840
[Fish]ing is fun.
These people are stupid.

Daniel Jones was involved with trying to help Senator Mark Werner personally meet with Christopher Steele. Arrangements were centered around a mutual buddy Adam Waldman. Waldman is also the lawyer for Russian oligarch Oleg Deripaska and is also a known acquaintance of Daniel Jones. Deripaska bagged to FBI McCabe in a 2017 interview that he was originator of the made-up Pee Pee memo included in the Steele Dossier.

Post Q# 2345
See EVIL in the face of FEINSTEIN?

Senator Chuck Grassley says it looks like Glenn Simpson/Fusion GPS have lied under oath to Congress about Christopher Steele's Dossier. Daniel Jones' own records and statements are at direct odds with that given by Fusion GPS head Glenn Simpson's prior testimony. Much of the primary funding for all of these operations against President Trump comes from George Soros related organizations.

Post Q# 2444
Thank you, Patriots.
The Senate means everything.

Oddly one of Jones' personal buddies is James Wolfe, the infamous arrested/jailed leaker from the U.S. Senate Intelligence Committee. Jones is suspected of also being a leaker via Wolfe's media lover/squeeze, MSM news reporter Ali Watkins. The DC Swamp is appropriately termed due to the incessant coordination between the MSM news and the politicians they are assigned to cover. With financial support from Reid Hoffman (Linkin), Daniel Jones began Project Birmingham which was really just Trump-Russia 2.0 Dossier.

Post Q# 2281
[FEINSTEIN] THREAT TO MURKOWSKI?
EVIL BE GONE.

Daniel Jones also has recently been mentioned by Michael Caputo when he screamed "God Damn you to hell Jones." A 2019 movie titled "The Report" features a character based directly upon the real-life Daniel Jones (actor Adam Driver). Before the dossiers Jones was involved with the Alfa Bank and Russian servers at Trump Tower hoax narrative. No Name would assist Jones with Alfa Bank as well as the first Steele Dossier. Jones coordinated his fake Trump Tower/Alpha Bank computer 'pinging' narrative with Glenn Simpson from Fusion GPS and ultimately out to the Mockingbird news media.

Post Q# 280
Watch the news.
Leakers exposed.
These people are stupid.

Michael Caputo was directing his verbal anger generally at the Senate Intel Committee and at Daniel Jones in particular. The Senate Intelligence Committee is the most corrupt group within the entire swamp called Congress. Since Jones was involved partially with the Alfa Bank false server narrative back in 2016, the indictment of Sussmann ties Jones, HRC, DNC, Fusion GPS, CrowdStrike, Google/Alphabet, and many others into the mix.

Post Q# 1286
Fusion GPS.
The Brits-raw Intel/dossier/5 eyes.

Per crack reporter John Solomon, the DOJ/FBI used false information to initially entrap General Flynn. Some of this fake "intel" used by the DOJ/FBI, may have been developed/fabricated by Dan Jones and Fusion GPS. SC John Durham submitted his final report in 2023 and will be the foundation for future judicial accountability. With the re-election of President Trump in 2024, many past political secrets will finally be publicly revealed.

Post Q# 4832
INFORMATION WARFARE.
IRREGULAR WARFARE.
INSURGENCY.

Links

News Blaze-FBI asks Dan Jones how $50M Relates to Trump-Russia

NY Post-HRC's Plan to Smear Trump with Russia Collusion

Clinton Foundation Timeline-2025 Crossfire Hurricane Docs

Markets Work-Former Feinstein Staffer involved with Fusion GPS During 2016 Elections

Time-The True Story behind the Movie 'The Report'

The Federalist-Soros funded 'Disinformation' Group paid $1M to Steele Dossier

Clinton Foundation Timeline-Dan Jones Archive

The War Economy-Daniel Jones/Alfa Bank

New Yorker-The Contested Afterlife of Trump Alfa Bank Story

Real Clear Investigations-Trump Russia 2.0 Dossier

The Last Refuge-August 16, 2016: FBI denied FISA

Red State-Durham Investigation has taken Interest in Daniel Jones

Meaning in History-Why the Daniel Jones Story is Significant

Clinton Timeline-Durham Subpoenas Dan Jones/Alfa Bank

The Federalist-Former Feinstein Staffer hires Fusion GPS and Steele

Esquire-The Report: Real Story Dan Jones vs Adam Driver

Breitbart-Jones Hired Fusion to keep "Exposing Russian Meddling"

The Federalist-Daniel Jones: Running a Post-Election "Steele Dossier Operation"

The Last Refuge-Insurance Policy/Deripaska/Steele/and Daniel Jones

Influence Watch-Daniel Jones

Scribd-Sen. Mark Warner Text with Russian Oligarch's Lobbyist

Crossfire Hurricane Docs-Christopher Steele Binder

Justice.gov-2023 SC John Durham Report

Clinton Coverup Lawyer: Meet David Kendall

David Kendall Esq. has been a partner with the law firm of Williams and Connelly LLP since 1981. Kendall has been the Clinton's primary personal lawyer for many decades and the keeper of all the secrets. Kendall is considered one of the top DC political lawyers and is with one of the leading legal firms. President Trump would file in 2022 a federal RICO lawsuit against HRC/DNC/and others related to the promotion of false Russian collusion narratives during the 2016 election cycle.

Post Q# 2692
> Baker's heads up on the Kendall call was sent to:

It is of no shock that David Kendall is again representing the Clinton Criminal Cabal in President Trump's RCIO lawsuit. Kendall's term of legal service ranges for all of the Bill and Hillary Clinton infamous scandals. David Kendall began back in the Whitewater days through the secret "email server" issue and with RussiaGate of today, remembering that sexy Monica Lewinsky is sandwiched in between. Every criminal organization needs expert legal advice and rescue from the law on a routine basis.

Post Q# 576
> The flood is coming.
> Emails, videos, audio, pics, etc.

The investigation specifically into the HRC's personal server/emails by IG Horowitz/SP Huber/and now Special Counsel (SC) John Durham, will ultimately reveal the true extent of Kendall's personal involvement. The Clinton crime machine requires constant expert legal assistance to avoid any tricky future entanglements. The indictment of Perkins Coie/Clinton campaign lawyer Michael Sussmann will connect back to Kendall.

Post Q# 1504
> Re-read drops re: private emails re: convicting HRC convicting themselves.

Kendall oversaw both Cheryl Mills and Heather Samuelson (lawyers themselves) with the sorting and deletion of HRC's emails. This bulk email sorting process was to comply with lawful FOIA requests as well as several Congressional document production subpoenas and not intended for deletions.

Post Q# 4788
> Those that scream the loudest...

David Kendall and Cheryl Mills later were involved in several joint server/email mass deletion discussions with computer backup firm Platte River Networks (PRN). PRN became the new hosting/backup computer service for the Clinton server and email system. When Kendall requested a system scrub of the Clinton servers, it was known about prior data protection orders by Congress.

Post Q# 2848
> Being a Clinton donor really pays off!

Paul Combetta from PRN had incredibly forgotten to erase all the email data as ordered previously by Mills. This is where Reddit (strip out all VIP addresses) and "BleachBit" became famous in the dark underworld of the internet due to Paul Combetta's computer generated acid-washed HRC email deletions.

Post Q# 1978
> What if access to the server(s) was deliberate?

Bear in mind everyone knew that HRC's estimated 33,000 email records were under current U.S. Congressional preservation orders. Nevertheless, all these co-conspirators destroyed all traces permanently (BleachBit) of HRC's email history. The FBI seized the laptops of both Cheryl Mills and Heather Samuelson in 2016 were of paramount concern to David Kendall, who ensued noting would be gleamed from officials searches. The term 'BleachBit' would become a household name after the infamous computer erasure incident.

Post Q# 4216
> They have officially retained lawyers.

Judicial Watch has received documents via FOIA showing that FBI James Baker sent a copy of James Comey's letter to Congress (HRC/Weiner's laptop) to Kendal. David Kendal commented after this heads-up letter was "tantalizingly ambiguous and highly ominous." A group of HRC's lawyers, headed by David Kendal, meet with the FBI to give a 'defensive' briefing trying to exonerate HRC from any involvement with the Russian collusion narrative.

Post Q# 2691
> You are witnessing the greatest 'DISINFORMATION' campaign to ever be pushed by a political party.

Kendall may rue the day he didn't get one of the ultra-special Comey/Lynch 'Immunity' deal agreements. Mill/Samuelson/and Combetta all we're granted various forms of immunity from future DOJ prosecution. SC John Durham has dropped criminal indictments and has submitted his final report in 2023.

Post Q# 2878
> CROOKED [[[HILLARY]]].

Mills and Samuelson were advised that their laptops would be destroyed after a very limited search by the FBI. Lucky for us a few patriotic FBI agents did not destroy these two laptops as they had been so ordered. With the historic re-election of President Trump in 2024, Judgement Day is coming for all of these many past political scandals.

Post Q# 2885
> Enemy of the People.
> Facts matter.

Links

NY Times-From Whitewater to Emails: Clinton's Dogged Lawyer

The Federalist-HRC and the FBI Set Up Trump

Town Hall-Comey's FBI Deliberately Sandbagged Clinton Email Investigation

Clinton Foundation Timeline-2025 Crossfire Hurricane Docs

Law and Crime-Judge orders Investigation of Clinton Lawyers

PJ Media-Why did HRC's Lawyers meet with the FBI?

Just the News-Evidence show Russia Collusion Story Began/Ended with HRC

Bloomberg-How David Kendall Fights for the Clintons

FOX News-DOJ and Clinton Lawyers limit FBI Access to Clinton Foundation Emails

2xWide-David Kendall

Judicial Watch-FBI Baker and Clinton Lawyer Kendal Spoke About Weiner's Laptop

The Last Refuge-HRC Emails on Abedin/Weiner Laptop

Founders Code-Who is David Kendall?

National Review-Why HRC's Lawyers are Problematic

Daily Caller-Meet HRC's email Lawyers

Power Line-Kendall's Whitewater Op-Ed

FOX News-Emails show FBI Scrambling to Respond to Clinton Lawyer

The Atlantic-Whitewater to Benghazi: Clinton Scandal Primer

Front Page-New Evidence unveils Disturbing Facts about HRC's Email Scandal

State Dept.gov-FOIA: HRC Recovered Emails

Crossfire Hurricane Docs-David Kendall Defensive Interview

Justice. gov-2023 SC John Durham Report

Secret Society's Clinesmith Altered Carter Page's Renewal FISA Docs

FISA INDICTMENTS = START

"I have initiated the destruction of the Republic" brags "low level" FBI lawyer Kevin Clinesmith, who is now heavily embroiled in SpyGate. IG Horowitz's FISA documented Clinesmith's altering of the three Cater Page renewal FISA applications. Special Counsel (SC) John Durham will indicate Clinesmith first and Perkins Coie lawyer Michael Sussmann will be the second indicted in this criminal probes. President Trump would include Clinesmith in his 2022 federal RICO lawsuit based upon damages surround the SpyGate political scandal.

> **Post Q# 1559**
> LP "Viva Le Resistance."
> Viv[a] vs Viv[e]

Kevin Clinesmith was not a low-level lawyer but in fact worked as Peter Strzok's right-hand helper at the FBI Counterintelligence Division. Clinesmith primarily was assigned under the FBI National Security and Cyber Branch. Clinesmith along with Strzok and agent Joe Pientka gave candidate Trump his first Intel briefing in 2016.

> **Post Q# 2365**
> [Pg 294]
> [Meeting between Comey and Coleman on October 4]
> Crime Against Children +++

Clinesmith was tasked in early 2015 to the HRC email probe nicknamed the Mid-Year Exam (MYE), the FBI Trump-Russia C/I probe in 2016, and finally the Mueller Team in 2017. This 'Small Group' core would guide all these investigations in the direction ordered by their Deep State 'Puppet Masters.'

> **Post Q# 2381**
> [Batter's Box]
> Kevin Clinesmith

Robert Mueller had to remove Clinesmith early in his Trump-Russia "Witch-hunt" due to the discovery of prior bias email/text messages. We come to find out now that young Kevin was the author of the infamous post-election FBI internal email chain, first sent to Lisa Page, known as 'Viva Le Resistance."

> **Post Q# 26**
> The only way is the military. Fully controlled. Save and spread (once 11.3 verifies as 1st marker).

Clinesmith was part of the original 'Secret Society' or 'Small Group' within the upper ranks of the DOJ/FBI. This 7th Floor Cabal first set on exonerating HRC of her unapproved illegal home-brew computer server and subsequent destruction of subpoenaed evidence. History will should that a group of corrupt government officials coordinated with private outside contractors in a treasonous coup plot against then candidate Donald Trump.

Post Q# 3570
> [C] before [D].
> possible decode: Clinesmith (not Coats) before DECLAS.

Clinesmith is referred to as FBI Agent #2 in IG Horowitz's first report (page 455) concerning the HRC email probe. Indications are that Clinesmith was involved with the Weiner/Abedin laptop coverup affair. History will show that this entire group of government officials knowingly engaged in their treasonous coup plots against President Trump.

Post Q# 2697
> Where are they now?
> Kevin Clinesmith - track and follow.

HRC's email matter (not an investigation per (LL) was coined the MYR and was quarterbacked by FBI Deputy Director of Counterintelligence Peter Strzok, with legal advice from FBI lawyers Lisa Page (Pete's paramour) and Clinesmith. Operation Crossfire Hurricane and other spy insertions were overseen by this 'Secret Society.' Clinesmith magically was also assigned to the Weiner laptop email/data review team.

Post Q# 1828
> [SPY OP]
> [FBI] [JC] [AM] [JR] [MS] [BP] [PS] [LP] [JB] [MK] [JC] [SM] [TG] [KC]
> decode: [KC] = Kevin Clinesmith

Next up for this traitorous band was the counterintelligence investigation (Crossfire Hurricane) of Candidate/President Trump by the FBI. In 2017 Robert Mueller picked up this ongoing FBI 'witch-hunt' as well as Clinesmith and his Deep State treasonous DOJ/FBI cohorts.

Post Q# 4130
> Advocating overthrow of Government?

The IG Horowitz 2.0 report on FISA Abuse had named Clinesmith as illegally altering (adding false information) the three Carter Page FISA renewal applications. Incredibly Clinesmith was having a romantic affair with fellow FBI agent Sally Moyer (Office of General Counsel), who was involved with applying the critical Woods Procedure.

Post Q# 1807
> FBI Chain of Command for the: Midyear Investigation.
> Kevin Clinesmith?
> BIGGEST COVERUP IN US HISTORY.
> [ATTEMPTED]

Moyer's FBI duties included signing off on the required Woods Procedure on all FISA requests. This imports step was to help ensure all material, especially exculpatory facts, would fairly be presented to the FISA Court (FISC). Of odd note is both Clinesmith/Moyer worked previously with ICIG Michael Atkinson.

Post Q# 3481
> Important to remember.
> Correlation between FISA abuse [treason remove DE_POTUS] and midyear investigation?

DNI Radcliffe declassified FBI documents reflecting Clinesmith attended defensive briefings given to candidate Trump in August 2016. FBI agents Peter Strzok/Joe Pientka lead these briefings that were being used to lay the foundation for the 'Insurance Policy' component of Crossfire

Hurricane. It would later be revealed that the judge who oversaw Kevin Clinesmith's criminal case also played a key role in the 2016 RussiaGate FISA scandal.

Post Q# 4621
[Placeholder - Indictments Tracking— Non_Civ]
1. Kevin Clinesmith [KC] [11.3]

Clinesmith is a known marathon runner, and his plea deal will allow him to continue his freedoms. Within days of Clinesmith interviewing with IG Horowitz, he quit governmental service. SC Durham accepted the guilt of Clinesmith for altering FBI documents. Incredibly the DC Bar Association has reinstated Clinesmith's law license in late 2021. SC Durham submitted his final report in 2023. With the re-election of President Trump in 2024, many hope past hidden political secrets will finally be revealed.

Post Q# 3045
IF THE TOP FBI CHAIN OF COMMAND FOR THE MIDYEAR INVESTIGATION WERE 'ALL' FIRED DOES ONE CONCLUDE THE INVESTIGATION WAS NOT CONDUCTED PROPERLY?

Links

Law and Crime-SC John Durham asks Judge to Send Message to Clinesmith

Clinton Foundation Timeline-FBI Revelations Show the Mueller Special Counsel was a Cover-Up

The Federalist-Unsealed Crossfire Hurricane Docs prove RussiaGate a Hoax

Just the News-Judge Blocking Trump Deportations Played Key Role in FISA Scandal

John Seaman-Durham Investigation: Answering the 5 W's

The Federalist-Notes Show FBI Agents Mislead DOJ on Trump-Russia Investigation

Real Clear Investigations-To Spy on a Trump Aide: FBI Pursued a Dossier Rumor

Just the News-Trump suing HRC/DNC over Russia Collusion Narrative

Washington Examiner-Durham Report: 5 Key Takeaways

Daily Caller-Kevin Clinesmith receives Probation

The Last Refuge-Clinesmith and PapaD

Politico-FBI Lawyer Spared Prison Time for Altering Records

Markets Work-FBI Lawyer Referred for Criminal Prosecution

The Last Refuge-SpyGate: The Big Picture

WSJ-The FBI's Dossier Deceit

Breitbart-FBI Lawyer Doctored Email to Coverup Errors in FISA

Clinton Foundation-Timeline: Kevin Clinesmith

Markets Work-FISA Surveillance: Title 1/3 and Section 702

OIG.Justice.gov-DOJ OIG FISA Report

Senate Intelligence Committee: 2021 DECLAS

Justice.gov-FBI Attorney admits Altering Email used in FISA Application

Crossfire Hurricane Docs-FISA Notes

Who is Mike Kortan? How is He Connected to SpyGate?

Michael Kortan [MK] was the Head of Public Affairs at the FBI and ultimately left under cloud of disgrace. Kortan was the final authority on all media statements making his position very key within the SpyGate scandal. [MK] retired suddenly after 33 years of service over his involvement with taking unauthorized gifts from the media as well as his direct involvement with ObamaGate/SpyGate. It has later come out Kortan was in fact fired for accepting free Washington Nationals baseball club box tickets on multiple occasions in 2016.

Post Q# 2692
Michael Kortan, FBI assistant director for public affairs, now retired.

Kortan was connected in July 2016 via Peter Strzok text messages as "Mike" within the 'Small Group.' One overt tactic employed by Deputy Director Andy McCabe, was sending out a memo stating that HRC will get a FBI 'Headquarters Special' Kortan helped to author many of these types of sketchy FBI memos in attempts to cover the DOJ Secret Society's coup plot tracks.

Post Q# 1316
Mike Kortan, FBI Assistant Director for Public Affairs-FIRED [cooperating under 'resigned' title].

Mike Kortan gave his stamp of approval to the final James Comey HRC 2016 exoneration memo. It appears that Mike Kortan and Peter Strzok helped with critical word 'editing' of James Comey's infamous July 2016 news media presser. Judicial Watch won a FOIA request in 2022 for the release of all of the government officials on the 2016 Peter Strzok memo to start FBI's operation codenamed 'Crossfire Hurricane', the spy campaign against candidate Donald Trump.

Post Q# 1986
Mike Kortan -cooperating under 'resigned' title-TO BE CALLED?

Kortan was part of the DOJ/FBI's inner circle's or "Secret Society" and vital part of ObamaGate/SpyGate planning. This small group from with the Justice Department ran Crossfire Hurricane and various surveillance programs against the Trump administration. BHO and his key White House aides were the quarterbacks of these various spying operations.

Post Q# 4352
Thank you for playing.
Have a Nice Day.

Prior publicly released Strzok/Page text messages implicit "Mike" being directly in the coup plot loop. Kortan was caught talking/leaking on the phone with FBI Lawyer Lisa Page and WSJ news reporter Devlin Barrett. [MK] was one of the central contacts for the complicit Mockingbird news media in the distribution of the given FBI narrative of the day.

Post Q# 1829
FBI [JC] [AM] [JR] [MS] [BP] [PS] [LP][JB] [MK] [JC] [SM] [TG] [KC].

FBI lawyer Lisa Page leaked statements as per Asst. Director Andy McCabe's instructions, was one pivotal reason for Kortan's firing. This leaked false media story concerned Andy's wife Dr. Jill McCabe's questionable VA State Senate campaign donations. Dr. McCabe's failed campaign would total in excess of $1 million received in a state where losers can keep their unspent donations.

Post Q# 3815

They will not be able to walk down the street.

THE GREAT AWAKENING.

Dr. Jill McCabe had received big league contributions from questionable insider Democratic/Clinton donor sources. Then VA Governor Terry McAuliffe was credited for directing over $700,000.00 to Dr. McCabe's campaign. 'Q' has posted [MK] within a select FBI group of 29 past officials on a list of FBI criminals.

Post Q# 953

How bad is the corruption?
FBI (past/present) + 29 (16).

The entire cabal of treasonous coup plotters will be exposed in the coming Judgement Day. Special Counsel John Durham has dropped criminal indictments related to SpyGate and submitted his final report in 2023. With the re-election of President Trump in 2024, have the popcorn ready Patriots, as panic breaks out and the rats in the DC Swamp are running as the Storm progresses.

Post Q# 2692

BIGGEST COVER UP IN US HISTORY [ATTEMPTED].

Links

FOX News-Another Longtime Comey Aide leaving FBI

The Federalist-Senate Expands Probe into FBI's Ability to Hide Docs

Clinton Foundation Timeline-FBI Revelations Show the Mueller Special Counsel was a Cover-Up

Just the News-Kash Patel sends Declassified Crossfire Hurricane Docs to Congress

Judicial Watch-Court Orders FBI to Provide Details on Officials Listed in Strzok Memo

The Federalist-SpyGate 101: A Primer on the Russia Collusion Hoax

Minuteman Militia-Mike is Out

The Federalist- Alfa Bank Hoax is Looking a Lot like Crossfire Hurricane

Washington Examiner-Senior FBI Official Resigned after Lying about Baseball Tickets

Daily Caller-OIG Report finds FBI Official accepted Unauthorized Gifts from Media

Buster Hyde-The Dung Castle: Operation Crossfire Hurricane

The Last Refuge-SpyGate: The Big Picture

Epoch Times-Lisa Page's Testimony Fingers Mike Kortan as a Leaker

Markets Work-SpyGate: The Inside Story

FOX News-BHO's FBI Brass Hollowed Out after Last Resignation

The Last Refuge-Kortan/Strzok/and Page

Power Line Blog-The FBI's Anti-Trump "Leak Strategy"

American Thinker-FBI Departures Indicate "Jig Is Up"

Red State-FBI Official who took Illegal Gifts Retires with Full Benefits

Judicial Watch-FOIA Records: Kortan/Strzok/Rybicki/Page

Markets Work-FISA Title One Surveillance Warrants

Grassley.Senate.gov-Crossfire Hurricane Timeline

Scribd-DOJ/OIG Report on Mike Kortan

OIG.DOJ.gov-Investigation of Unauthorized Contacts by FBI with the Media

Crossfire Hurricane Docs-Christopher Steele Binder

Justice.gov-2023 SC John Durham Report

Meet 'Secret Society' Member David [DL] Laufman

David [DL] Laufman formerly was the DOJ's Deputy Assistant AG in the National Security Division (NSD). Laufman oversaw counterintelligence, export control, FARA applications, counterespionage, and cyber security for the DOJ. Laufman would return to the news headlines in 2022 by commenting on the possible mishandling of classified documents by President Trump in the secure storage facility at his Mar-A-Largo compound.

Post Q# 2070
David Laufman, Chief of the Justice Department's Counterintelligence and Export Control Section [NAT SEC-HRC email invest]-FIRED/FORCE.

Laufman was a former C_A officer and federal prosecutor who worked directly under Assistant AG John Carlin. Coincidently and incredibly odd, they both resigned around the same time. [DL] was a proud member of the DOJ's small group or 'Secret Society' of coup plotters against President Trump.

Post Q# 100
Secret Society.

Per crack reporter Sara Carter, General Flynn's lead attorney Sidney Powell had requested government security clearance, so as to fully exam all of the case evidence. It appears DOJ Laufman had pressured General Flynn to sign incorrect FARA forms and is partially to blame for the confusion surrounding this case.

Post Q# 1828
[SPY OP]
[DOJ] [LL] [SY] [BO-CS (UK)] [DL] [PS] [DL] [JC] [MM] [RB].

This criminal small group from within the DOJ/FBI was deliberately kept from OIG Horowitz's oversight by Deputy AG Sally Yates. SpyGate/Crossfire Hurricane coup plot was hatched and implemented by this rouge 'Secret Society' knowing was above official review by the OIG.

Post Q# 2107
Who signed?
'Knowingly' used FALSE intelligence.

Laufman assumed his NSD leadership role in 2014 and was one of the key players in both the HRC email server and Russia DNC hack investigations. David Laufman was involved with prepping the July 2016 FBI interviewing agents Peter Strzok and his superior Randy Coleman in advance of HRC's sit down session.

Post Q# 4011
CROSSFIRE TYPHOON.

[DL] also had a hand in launching the probes under the Foreign Agents Registration Act (FARA) against Paul Manafort, Rick Gates and General Flynn. David Laufman ends up recently representing Monica McLean (Dr. Blasey Ford's pal) in the bizarre Judge Kavanaugh hearings.

Post Q# 1978
What if this is 'known' within the FBI and DOJ?
decode: HRC's Server hacked by China

DOJ official Laufman had a close working relationship with Secret Society member and the DOJ's #4 Bruce Ohr. The entire rouge Secret Society was racing against Admiral Rogers investigations and in their getting the Carter Page FISA Title-1 approved in October 2016. The various illegal surveillance operations under SpyGate like Crossfire Hurricane would all become unraveled by IG Michael Horowitz.

Post Q# 3815

They will not be able to walk down the street.
THE GREAT AWAKENING.

Admiral Rogers had shut down all outside contractors (Fusion GPS/CrowdStrike) from accessing NSA FISA 702 'about queries. Admiral Rogers had also launched a review of FISA past abuses and presented his findings to the FISA Court (FISC). Head FISC Judge Rosemary Collier issued a scathing report outlining the past abuses by the FBI and totally vindicating Admiral Rogers.

Post Q# 1979

Evidence of an ongoing investigation.

The original Carter Page FISA request was turned down once (Summer 2016) by the FISC and everyone was pushing hard in the Fall of 2016 for this important approval. Operation Trump has gone from clearing HRC to going after Presidential candidate Trump now via code name Crossfire Hurricane.

Post Q# 1975

What are the odds that the FBI and DOJ are right on top of this?

The Secret Society needed the Carter Page surveillance warrant to be able to 'HOP' communication chains from targeted aides to ultimately reach candidate Donald Trump. The intended individual is reverse targeted using this legal ability to 'leap-frog' several degrees of communications for one individual to the next, to form an umbrella surveillance net of thousands to be captured electronically. After learning the DOJ, David Laufman was made a partner at Wiggin and Dana making the news again in 2024 helping to represent Joe Biden in interviews during classified document case with Robert Hur.

Post Q# 2494

Nothing can stop what's coming.
Nothing.

A crossroads in the history of our civilization.

The Deep State used Laufman to push phony violations of the Foreign Agents Registration Act (FARA) in Crossfire Typhoon to entrap Trump Campaign staff. Crossfire Typhoon targets by the FBI included Flynn/Manafort/Gates/and PapaD. Governmental officials colluded with private contractors in a treasonous coup plot against candidate Donald Trump.

Post Q# 1402

Think DOJ and FBI.
Think cleaning.

Time is growing near fellow Patriots that the prior hidden truths and diabolical coup plots are all going to be publicly exposed. Special Counsel John Durham has dropped criminal indictments related SpyGate and submitted his final report in 2023. With the historic re-election of President Trump in 2024, the long-awaited justice phase is finally here.

Post Q# 4933
 Watergate x 1000.

Links

WAPO-DOJ Official who Oversaw Clinton Probe Steps Down

The Federalist-DOJ Officials didn't know Database Allowed FBI to Bury RussiaGate Docs

Real Clear Investigations-Why is RussiaGate Origin Story still Redacted?

The Federalist-Unsealed Crossfire Hurricane Docs prove RussiaGate a Hoax

Conservative Brief-Trump Hillary Double Standard

NPR-Justice Department is Reviewing how Classified Material Wound up at Mar-a-Lago

The Federalist-SpyGate 101: A Primer on the Russia Collusion Hoax

Epoch Times-IG Audit finds 'Widespread' Problems with FBI's FISA Applications

Daily Caller-Senators seek Igor Danchenko and David Laufman Records

The Last Refuge-SpyGate: The Big Picture

Real Clear Investigations-No Need for Real Evidence for Collusion Probe

Daily Wire-Senate to Subpoena BHO Officials over Crossfire Hurricane Scandal

Red State-Senior Justice Department Official David Laufman suddenly Resigns

Markets Work-Resignations, Demotions, and Complicit

Just the News-Durham File: Documentary into the FBI against Trump

Daily Caller-David Laufman representing Monica McLean from Dr. Ford Case

NPR-David Laufman: Consequences if Trump Releases Secret Doc's

Paul Sperry-Why is Adam Schiff Withholding Transcript of ICIG Atkinson's Testimony

Markets Work-Listing of Participants

Epoch Times-SpyGate: The Inside Story

OIG.Justice.gov -Investigative Summary February 2019

DNI-FISC Top Secret Report on FISA (2017)

Senate.Judicial.gov-Sen. Graham: Subpoena Power related to Crossfire Hurricane

Crossfire Hurricane Docs-FISA Notes

Justice.gov-2023 SC John Durham Report

Dr. Jill and Andy McCabe:
Another ObamaGate "Couple"

Give BHO's Consigliere Valerie Jarrett credit for setting up this 'Mafia Style' crew of corrupt individuals. The BHO Administration was littered with many 'dirty' married couples. Incredible to believe this practice of married couples engaging in criminal activities has continued under the illegal Biden administration. So many BHO alumni have recycled back into power that we need to continue to follow the wives and families as 'Q' had pointed out in the drops. President Trump would file in 2022 a federal RICO lawsuit against Andrew McCabe/HRC/DNC/and others related to the promotion of the false Russian collusion narrative during the 2016 election cycle.

Post Q# 4777
Follow the family.
Think McCabe's wife.
The money never flows directly.

Corrupt married couples that were willing to go along with every bizarre plot and scheme are normally hard to find. Political goals to advance the Progressive Leftists Alinsky agenda comes first before anything else in the minds of this crowd. The NWO globalist are pushing the Great Reset and America has been under attack both internationally and domestically. A hybrid of Alinsky and the Cloward-Piven strategy is at play the Deep State against the free world.

Post Q# 4124
Why do they always include their spouse, son, daughter, etc.?
Follow the money.

History will record these infamous married couples to include McCabe's/Ohr's/Strzok's/Power-Sunstein/Pientka's/Priestap's/Dunn-Bauer/Murray-King /Simpson-Jacoby/Abedin-Weiner and sadly several more. Bonnie and Clyde's gangster image can be witnessed today with these real-life corrupt married teams. More and more complicated threads of relationships and political scandals are being unraveled as time goes on.

Post Q# 3122
Andrew McCabe picture=Placeholder

We also had the unmarried FBI team of Strzok/Page just pretending to be 'lovers' as their roles in Crossfire Hurricane. Counterintelligence or the spy tradecraft at its best was on display with this elaborate coup plot scheme. Special Counsel (SC) John Durham is working on criminal referrals from IG Horowitz in connection with the illegal surveillance operations stemming around SpyGate.

Post Q# 2265
[McCabe] leaked memos to NYT re: [RR].

'Q' has correctly pointed out that we should "Follow the Wives" and trace "How were they paid?" These references go to the insidious parts played by various married teams that were integral to ObamaGate/SpyGate coup plans. Andy and Jill McCabe are as devious of a political couple as you can find within the DC Swamp. Future proves past in 2024 as Andy McCabe finally publicly admits many mistakes were made by the FBI in the Trump FISA scandal.

Post Q# 1744

> #2 in FBI?
> Wife connection?
> Follow the wives.

Least we don't forget about the real puppet masters pulling the strings of these crooked married couples. The devil's own evil kingpins of the BHO/HRC and their obvious shame marriages. Stories of strange marital boundaries as well as skepticism over the exact sexual preferences of both of those couples.

The four main components of the coup plot nicknamed Operation Trump:
- Exonerate HRC/Aides (ObamaGate)
- Fake Trump-Russia Dossier creation/distribution (RussiaGate)
- FISA Title-1 Surveillance Warrants/Section 702 (SpyGate)
- The 'Insurance Policy' (Crossfire Hurricane)

Post Q# 2324

> 'McCabe Memos' = SOURCE DOCS for NYT article re: [RR] 'wear a wire' - 25th amendment?
> Enjoy the show.

Dr. Jill McCabe ran unsuccessfully campaign for the Virginia State Senate in 2015. Terry McAuliffe's PAC gave almost $1 million to Jill's campaign and the McCabe's were permitted legally to pocket the mostly unspent campaign funds. McAuliffe is a longtime Clinton crony and known for illegal campaign schemes. McAuliffe is currently running for VA Governor but is behind in his primary campaign.

Post Q# 543

> How can FBI Deputy Director Andrew McCabe, the man in charge, along with leakin' James Comey, of the phony HRC investigation (including her 33,000 illegally deleted emails) be given $700,000 for wife's campaign by Clinton Puppets during investigation.

On 10/15/15 Andy McCabe told FBI investigators that HRC will get a 'HQ Special.' Meaning lenient treatment to the point of total clearance and legal exoneration of all charges against HRC/Aides. McCabe along with FBI Director James Comey would make sure the wheels of justice moved slow and encountered many internal roadblocks. It was revealed in 2024 that the US Intel community requested its FIVE EYES (FVEY) foreign partners to illegally spy upon targeted Team Donald Trump aides back in 2016 helping the FBI to begin the false Trump-Russia investigation.

Post Q# 645

> I wish Andy [187] well. I also wish continued strength for the rest of the FBI [GENERAL THREAT TO OTHERS].

The FBI's nickname for the HRC email probe was the "Midyear Review" and these investigators went out of their way to clear HRC. Andy McCabe had begun to spill the beans about the shenanigans performed in this coup plot in an effort to get himself a get out of jail free card. Moves and countermoves would mark the entire SpyGate scandal and the various married couples that actively played a role. SpyGate's villains like Andy McCabe and Peter Strzok would receive cushy TV gigs and lucrative book deals.

Post Q# 2732
> Dark to Light.
> The orders came from the highest office in the land.

McCabe now publicly acknowledges in 2021 that the DOJ attempted a coup against candidate and President Donald Trump. Elon Musk's 2022/23 Twitter Files public release would expose the exact extend the FBI went to censor free speech. SC John Durham has begun to drop criminal indictments surrounding the SpyGate coup plotters (couples are included). Hopefully SC Durham's final report submitted in 2023 will unravel the treasonous surveillance activities deployed during SpyGate. Andy McCabe revealed in early 2024 that the entire Intel Community is scared of a President Trump 2.0 with Kash Patel as the new FBI Director. With God's assistance in Butler/PA, President Trump won re-election in 2024 and hopefully is going to jail all those connected to the RussiaGate/SpyGate political scandal.

Post Q# 447
> SEARCH crumbs [#2].
> Who is #2?
> No deals.

Links

Daily Mail-Trump Blasts McCabe as "Major Sleaze-Bag"

Kings Intel-New Evidence Unveils McCabe's Deception

Judiciary.Senate.gov—Report shows FBI Cut Corners in HRC Email Investigation

Clinton Foundation Timeline-FBI Revelations Show the Mueller Special Counsel was a Cover-Up

Just the News-McCabe Memos show FBI Leader kept Russia Collision Hoax Alive

FOX News-Trump Orders FBI Declassify Docs from Crossfire Hurricane

Daily Wire-FBI McCabe Concedes many Mistakes in Trump FISA

FOX News-Figures Exposed in Durham Report Rewarded Cushy TV Gigs/Lucrative Book Deals

American Report-HAMMERING Out their Cover Story 2 Days before Inauguration

The Last Refuge-Andrew McCabe gets a Pass

Red State-Remembering Strzok/Page 'Insurance Policy' Exchange

Judicial Watch-FBI Releases McCabe's Texts

The Last Refuge-Crossfire Hurricane

New Yorker-Pete/Lisa and Andy/Jill

NY Magazine-Terry McAuliffe Aided Wife of FBI Official

Markets Work-McCabe says He was 'Unfairly Branded a Liar'

The Last Refuge-McCabe/Insurance Policy

Senate Judiciary Committee: 2021 Crossfire Hurricane DECLAS

OIG.Justice.gov-2018 Investigation Related to Andrew McCabe

Justice.gov-Crossfire Hurricane Timeline

Crossfire Hurricane Docs-Andrew McCabe Memos

The Keating Five Scandal-No Name's Early Shame

"EVERY DOG HAS ITS DAY"

Hey 'No Name' (aka John McCain), what happened to all of the old local community Savings and Loan banks? To quote No Name about his involvement in the Keating Five scandal, "It was the worst mistake of my life". Bear in mind this characterization of magnitude of shame is from one of the most corrupt politicians of all time. Senator John McCain (1936-2018) earned the appropriate nickname of 'No Name' because some military Patriots do not like to say his name.

Post Q# 1707
No Name in the redacted portion of FISA application?

When did No Name last travel to the UK one may ask? Long ago No Name teamed up with several of his corrupt Senatorial buddies to become what infamously is known as the Keating Five, part of the collapse of the nationwide Savings and Loan banking system.

Post Q# 1764
Think FISA.
Think NO NAME.

As time normally does tell, No Name has turned out to be one of the most corrupt U.S. Senators of all time. No Name's trail of deception began back in Vietnam (Songbird was his nickname) and was ongoing through to the Trump-Russia coup plot scandal. No Name almost sunk in 1967 aircraft carrier USS Forestal with a 'wet-start' jet plane start-up stunt. It is unique that Vietnam erected a memorial to No Name on the spot of his capture and celebrating his plane being shot down in 1967.

Post Q# 2633
US SEN NO NAME
NEWS SHOP
BUZZF

This special group of corrupt U.S. Senators at the urging of Charles Keating Jr., changed some critical core U.S. banking laws and regulations. This loosing of key banking rules, ultimately lead to the collapse of the Savings and Loan community banking system in the 1980's/early 90's.

Post Q# 1649
Think SC vote to confirm (coming).
No Name action.
Every dog has its day.

The Keating Five's lineup of corrupt U.S. Senators included No Name/Glenn/DeConcini/Cranston/ and Riegle. Charles Keating along No Name were the kingpins and had a long-standing personal relationship prior to the Savings and Loan Banks financial shenanigans.

Post Q# 261
Since POTUS elected what changed w/Mc_I?

No Name even took his family down to vacation at the Keating's secluded compound located on the privately held Bahamian Island of Cat Cay. Cat Cay Bahamas was an international haven for the jet setter NWO crowd back in 1970's/80's/and 90's. Other notable Cat Cay members included

Al Rockwell (Rockwell Int'l), James Ryder (Ryder Trucks), Wayne Huizenga (Marlins and Blockbuster), and Bebe Rebozo (Richard Nixon pal).

Post Q# 1092
We love phones!
No name should know better.
note: Title pic is from this drop

Time has shown that No Name was the pivotal Congressional link to banking mogul Charles Keating. Keating was the initiator and his bought off crooked politicians which caused the demise of this once very popular rural area banking system. Corrupt career American politicians combined with global banking interests against independent banking systems is a recipe for loss of sovereignty.

Post Q# 1326
No Name prev meeting(s)?
Discussions of death/funeral?
Medical or escape?

The Senate Ethics Committee after a long hearing process, formally cleared No Name of any ethical charges. The Senate committee did however issue a reprimand to No Name and John Glenn. The other 3 Senators didn't seek re-election, thus getting their preverbal free passes out of this public disaster. Widow No Name is back on the public dole/family grift accepting Ambassador to the UN Food Program.

Post Q# 373
MAVERICK.
JUSTICE_FED_J[1-4]_remove + appellate

Global banking (NWO) interests rejoiced at the destruction of the popular USA local community banking system. Charles Keating turned out to be a discredited financier and the ugly public face of the Savings and Loan banking crisis. Many of the same financial shenanigans are being played out again today between elected government officials and state acting private corporations.

Post Q# 1706
No name returning to headlines...

Keating and his oldest son Charles III went to Federal Prison over criminal related charges stemming from this banking fraud. No Name has been trying to dodge this scandal for the past 25 years as well as numerous other improprieties. Navy Seal son Charles 4th was killed fighting ISIS in 2016.

Post Q# 5
What if John M never had surgery and that was a cover for a future out if needed against prosecution?

No Name was connected to the Christopher Steele Dossier through his aide David Kramer. Court documents later would show Kramer gave the Christopher Steele Dossier to Buzzfeed News, US Congressional members, and other Mockingbird news outlets back in November 2016. Additionally, No Name worked with political operative Dan Jones in pushing the false Alfa Bank server narrative. Now from the grave, a comment by No Name concerning current Secretary of State Blinken as "dangerous to America has gone viral on social media.

Post Q# 25
John M (some of us refuse to say his last name for a reason).

Additionally, No Name's busy aides have been tied to the past IRS targeting of the Tea Party. FeistyCat (I agree) connected a 'Q' term 'Iron Eagle' as possibly being Senator Lindsey Graham and him being a witness to treason charges issued against No Name. No Name is credited with the formation and funding of ISIS and other middle eastern terror organizations. Ironically the Arizona forensic audits of the stolen 2020 Presidential election is highlighting the extensive corruption from No Name territory.

Post Q# 1935
[He did not depart on his own terms].
Exactly [30].

Anons knew No Name would be 'Actioned in 30' and held fully responsible. Apparently, the well-known General Erwin Rommel 'option' (by Hitler) was offered and accepted by No Name/Family. The infamous Rommel option was a hero state funeral after self-suicide (No Name's cancer claim/facial scar), in lieu of a trail as a traitor and public execution. Q' has stated that false medical claims will not be any excuse to avoid or escape judgement day (Biden's dementia or HRC's illnesses). Special Counsel (SC) John Durham was tasked to explore the criminal referrals from IG Horowitz related to all aspects of the unfolding SpyGate scandals. 'Q' would foreshadow the death of No Name by exactly 30 days in advance with the 'returning to headlines' classic post.

Post Q# 4153
[NO MAME ASSIST [SENATOR STAMP _credible]_FBI FLOOR 7_DNI_POTUS PDB]

SC John Durham has dropped criminal indictments and submitted his final report in 2023. The Great Awakening is happening now largely due to the re-election of President Trump in 2024 and those still alive will be held fully accountable for their past criminal conduct under the law. History may show that No Name was the first of many to be held accountable for past crimes as Judgement Day is coming to all of the treasonous coup plotters.

Post Q# 4830
How much was McCain [McCain Institute] paid to peddle the Steele dossier?

Links

AZ Central-No Name Pictured with ISIS Leaders

Clinton Foundation Timeline-No Name sends Kramer to meet with Chris Steele

Markets Work-Deposition Reveals Late No Name's Role in SpyGate

Lew Rockwell-John McCain is NOT a Hero

LA Times-Charles Keating: Fraud Figure was Emblem of 1980's

FOX News-Court Files: No Name and Associate spread Anti Trump Dossier

Financial Dictionary-The Keating Five

CBS News-Keating Scandal still Haunts No Name

Business Insider-No Name: Describes Receiving the Steele Dossier

Time-History of the Keating Five

Politico-BHO Hit No Name on Keating 5

Jeff Carlson-David Kramer (No Name Associate)

AZ Central-No Name in a "Hell if a Mess"

Phoenix News-No Name most Reprehensible of Keating 5

FOX News-No Name brags "I would do it Again"

Video-1989 No Name's Keating 5 Explanation

The Last Refuge-No Name

Video-No Name's Vietnam Confession

Markets Work-No Name Associate provided Steele Dossier to BuzzFeed

USNI News-Update: Officials describe Fight that Killed Navy Seal

History Channel-General Rommel (aka The Desert Fox) Dies by Suicide

USNI-Dissecting Carrier Disaster

Crossfire Hurricane Docs-Steele Dossier through Simpson and McCain

Justice.gov-2023 SC John Durham Report

BHO's McDonough Linked to Dossier: Welcome to the "Show"

IG Michael Horowitz's several oversight reports have led to many ongoing criminal investigations now headed by Special Counsel (SC) John Durham. Horowitz was tasked with looking into DOJ abuses involving FISA Title-1 Surveillance/Steele Dossier/FISC/SpyGate and making criminal referrals. It has been confirmed that BHO's DOJ illegally spied on Carter Page per the FISA Court, and the many criminal investigations would start to become public in 2022.

Post Q# 4310
What was really discussed during [Jan 5] meeting?

Lest we forget about the existing DOJ ongoing investigations like Uranium One/Clinton Foundation/MSM Leaks/etc. Many carpet bombs are going to drop with several major MOABs with be produced indictments from SC John Durham's coming Judgement Day. BHO used HRC's 2016 false Russia Dossier as the evidence to spy on candidate Donald Trump. President Trump would file in 2022 a federal RICO lawsuit against all those who promoted the false Russian collusion narrative during the 2016 campaign cycle.

Post Q# 382
SATAN has left the WH.
Day of days.

Some old familiar names will be resurfacing along with a few individuals not so prominent now with the illegal Biden administration. One such person to lookout for is BHO's final Chief of Staff and highly trusted White House aide Denis McDonough. McDonough in now a very familiar move by many former BHO alumni, is now returning to government service as Biden's new Secretary of Veterans Affairs. President Trump would publicly call for BHO to release all emails from his McDonough concerning the 2016 election cycle.

Post Q# 1223
Think private email addresses.
They think they are cleaver.

Bear in mind that Denis McDonough's role was the equivalent to that of Trump's Chief of Staff Mark Meadows. Denis McDonough began with the start of BHO's second Presidential term and lasted until the bitter end as his 'Chief.' McDonough will ultimately be involved with the notorious January 5, 2017, Oval Office meeting. Of historical note, McDonough would be the main White House official to brief BHO on 9/11/12 over the tragic events in Benghazi and the status of the secret operation codenamed 'Zero Footprint' (CIA Annex weapon deals).

Post Q# 2943
Group-Think.
NATIONAL CRISIS.

McDonough has once again teamed up with his old BHO-era cronies within the Biden administration. Denis McDonough along with the likes of Ben Rhodes/Susan Rice/Samantha Power/Jake Sullivan, had formed a new PAC called National Security Action (NSA). Many of these figures are once again back at the White House.

Post Q# 2129

> [LIVE STREAMING] WH HUSSEIN NON-OVAL [SITUATION ROOM] COORDINATION.

This BHO hit group is focused on the continued attack of President Trump on all fronts. NSA is considered the resistance headquarters for the anti-Trump movement and the tip of the spear.

Post Q# 151

> How do you capture a very dangerous animal?

Recently released documents show that Denis McDonough meet with CIA John Brennan [JB] in mid-August of 2016 about Trump/Russia. John Brennan showed the Christopher Steele Dossier first to BHO on 8/10/16 and later to the inner circle or Secret Society of coup plotters.

Post Q# 1504

> They all had them.
> Why did the entire Hussein admin use private emails.

[JB] then meet Sen. Harry Reid on 8/25/16 to go over the dirty details in the Trump-Russia Dossier. Not the normal flow or chain of command for delivering classified intelligence information but a classic Deep State work around. Senators Reid and the traitor 'No Name' were instrumental in the early stages of their false Russian narrative campaign against candidate Trump.

Post Q# 4216

> They have officially retained lawyers.

Senator Harry Reid on 8/27/16 sent FBI Director James Comey a letter to officially investigate these Russian collusion accusations. This action would mark the official beginning of the Trump-Russia probe and the continuance of operations Crossfire Hurricane/Razor/Typhoon.

Post Q# 571

> NOBODY PLAYING THE GAME GETS A FREE PASS.
> NOBODY.

In some of the classical FBI 'Lovers' text messages between Strzok/Page, McDonough's name appears several times. MSM leaks were the first area AG Sessions publicity announced he was going to investigate, eliminate, and prosecute fully.

Post Q# 976

> Wonder who leaked this.
> Fire in the hole.

Denis McDonough had also tried to shift the blame of election Russian collusion over to Senator Mitch McConnell. McDonough made claims against Mitch for watering down early reports of Russia's attempts to interfere with the 2016 Presidential election cycle. Special Counsel (SC) John Durham is working on criminal referrals from IG Horowitz related to illegal surveillance during the BHO reign.

Post Q# 4686

> WATERGATE x1000

Governmental agencies like the DOJ and CIA are supposed to be independent and neutral in all domestic politics. Any coordination done with the White House and ongoing investigations would be highly inappropriate and borderline on treasonous conduct. SC John Durham has dropped criminal indictments concerning SpyGate and submitted his final report in 2023. Reports filed by Horowitz and Durham will be the foundation for future judicial accountability.

Post Q# 4301
Who was the quarterback?

Denis McDonough was acting as the main White House conduit between Brennan/Reid/Comey in regard to the circulation of the Steele Dossier. McDonough is part of a large contingency of BHO alumni that Biden has recycled back into the DC Swamp. With the re-election of President Trump in 2024, the continuing 'Great Awakening' will hopefully open everyone's eyes to the longstanding political corruption.

Post Q# 603
TODAY Former President Barack HUSSEIN Obama formerly retained counsel (9/WW).

Links

Politico-McDonough is BHO's Obama

Just the News-BHO Endorsed Bogus CIA Claims about Trump and Putin

PJ Media-Biden/BHO Officials Sought to Torpedo incoming Trump Adm

NY Post-Sen. Blackburn launches Probe into VA's Denis McDonough

Washington Times- Steele Dossier: FBI Nurtured biggest Hoax in American History

The Federalist-SpyGate 101: A Primer on the Russia Collusion Hoax

American Spectator-The Scandal BHO still won't Acknowledge

The Last Refuge-Denis McDonough Actions on 9/11/12

Jonathan Turley-Brennan briefed BHO: "A Means of Distracting the Public "

Buster Hyde-Chief of Staff Denis McDonough

Front Page Mag-BHO used HRC's Dossier to Spy on Trump

BuzzFeed-The Mystery of Denis McDonough

The Last Refuge-BHO/Biden/and McDonough

FOX News-List of BHO Officials Unmaking Flynn: Among them BHO's Chief of Staff

The Atlantic-Who is Denis McDonough?

The Federalist- Alfa Bank Hoax ss Looking a Lot like Crossfire Hurricane

True Pundit-FBI Memo: BHO State Department in Communication 'Pee' Dossier

The Federalist-BHO's Chief of Staff Admits they want Tyranny

Kyle Cheney-Denis McDonough and James Wolfe

Epoch Times-The Origins of SpyGate: 10 Questions

Crossfire Hurricane Docs-Christopher Steele Binder

Justice.gov-2023 SC John Durham Report

Judgement Day Brings Military Tribunals

Post Q# 4955
> It had to be done this way.

'Q' often asked besides great actors, "What makes a movie GOOD?" The answer is a perfect ending to a well scripted and exceptionally choreographed movie but of course. The anticipated ending starts with assigned Special Counsel (SC) John Durham's final report submitted in 2023, thus triggering Judgement Day, followed by the justice phase including Military Tribunals. In classic Deep State projection, many of the SpyGate coup plotters are calling for Nuremberg-style tribunals for Putin over his Ukraine special military operation of 2022.

Post Q# 740
> Max cap
> [1] other prison being prepped.
> note: Anon Question-How full is GITMO going to be?

As the 'Storm' descends upon the entrenched DC Swamp Shadow Government, the final scene is about to start in the Great Awakening. Movies [1], [2] and [3] are upon us all now and the scope of the past traitorous criminal conduct is slowly being publicly revealed. What began as a coverup of past crimes by attempting to remove President Trump, led directly to a biological weapon being released and military biological labs discovered in the Ukraine.

Post Q# 589
> What would happen if texts originating from a FBI agent to several [internals] discussed the assassination of the POTUS or member of his family?

'Q' has repeatedly mentioned the possibility of Military Tribunals for the top-tier ObamaGate/SpyGate criminals. At every rally for candidate/President Trump, and now former POTUS, a reoccurring chant of "Lock Her Up" has been a certainty among MAGA loyalists. There is a distinct feeling of accountability and equal justice being applied. President Trump filed a federal RICO lawsuit in 2022 against many of the SpyGate characters listed below.

Post Q# 3600
> For those who decide to save the taxpayers some money.
> There is no escaping God.

'Q' has stressed there will be "No Deals" and there has been a slight quickening feel to unfolding events. The return to the rule of law under one fair justice system is now demanded by all MAGA American Patriots and the majority of citizens. The failed impeachments, the election steal of 2020, and the virus/VAX operations are all interconnected via a cabal of evil globalists. Rusia's 2022 special military operation into Ukraine highlighted bioweapons labs/Neo-Nazis/Computer Server Farms/and a center of operations for the New World Order (NWO).

Post Q# 669
> VJ phone call w/ AS.
> [2 listeners - no IDEN].
> Article 3.
> Section 3.

At the end of the European portion of World War 2, an International Military Tribunal (IMT) was formed to render justice for crimes against humanity. The IMT selected a total of 24 (two dozen) of the important people from the German military, political, judicial, and business leadership to face legal judgement. Judges from all of the victorious allied countries were represented on the IMT panel. It was revealed in 2024 that the US Intel community requested its FIVE EYES (FVEY) partners to illegally spy upon select Team Donald Trump aides back in 2016.

Post Q# 520
Prison.
Death.
[CLAS_GITMO_J z9-A [89].

When it comes to certain lists, everyone has their own and these outlined below seem the worthiest related to SpyGate/RussiaGate. Please note this post was originally made in late 2018 prior to impeachment(s), virus pandemic (crimes against humanity will have their own list), and the 2020 Presidential election steal:

- Hussein • HRC • Biden • Lynch
- Comey • Jarrett • Brennan • Rice
- Clapper • Yates • McCabe • BC
- Nuland • Ohr • Monaco • Holder
- Power • Rhodes • Sullivan • Schiff
- Simpson • Steele • Halper • Kerry

Post Q# 2876
JUDGEMENT DAY COMING.

Please note that the early 'Songbirds' like Priestap/Strzok/Page/Baker/Pientka/Kortan and Bruce Ohr (fighting to save wife Nellie) all have been cooperating witnesses. Due to their early singing, they sheltered themselves against the worst of the possible legal GITMO outcome. CBS reporter Katherine Herridge outlines the massive expansion projects ongoing at GITMO in spite of Biden wanting to close. President Trump on 12/21/27 signed the historic Executive Order blocking property of persons involved with human rights abuse or corruption.

Post Q# 4414
RED5: NAT MIL COM CEN
RED6: SEC OF DEF _instruct1 USSS
CASTLE_ROCK

President Trump tried hard during his first four years to drain the DC Swamp, now the White Hats will turn the tables on the Deep State. Patriots must remain united and steadfast against this entrenched evil enemy facing our Republic. NWO Globalists want us divided and the continued control of the public narrative. In an Orwellian action back in 2021 post J6, the FBI declares it's targeting Trump supporters legit due to them being domestic terrorists and combines with various in-house DHS teams to pressure Big Tech to censor many MAGA followers, and later HRC publicly called for 're-education camps' for over half of the country.

Post Q# 4908
Crimes against children unite all humanity [cross party lines]?
Difficult truths.

The puppet masters of the Deep State Shadow Government have failed in their coup attempt to eliminate President Trump. The 2020 election was stolen in the 'Big Lie' and state forensic audits will confirm this fraud. SC John Durham was tasked to look into the criminal referrals by IG

Michael Horowitz. SC Durham did get Kevin Clinesmith/Michael Sussmann/Igor Danchenko criminal indictments connected to SpyGate. The final reports from IG Horowitz and SC Durham will be the foundation for future judicial accountability. History will show that President Trump vanquished his political enemies like Clinton/Biden/and Obama into permanent irrelevance.

Post Q# 2980

Death Blossom.

The price for failed ringleaders from any failed coup attempts in the past has always been the same throughout recorded history. Traitors from ObamaGate/SpyGate through the global pandemic, should all receive the same ultimate justice for their criminal acts against the world. The world is craving an IMT 2.0 to bring these evil doers to global justice. President Trump has led the resistance to the illegal Biden/Harris administration, and all Patriots await his 2025 return for the revitalization of America. Many from the news media and government employees fear the return of President Trump and justice for their prior crimes, known by the Anons as 'Panic in DC.' President Donald Trump has often stressed the need for "Quick Trials and Swift Justice".

Post Q# 802

Traitor
1. a person who betrays another, a cause, or any trust.
2. a person who commits treason by betraying his or her own country.

With the historic re-election of President Trump in 2024, the table is set for judicial accountability for all the Deep State criminals. Popcorn at the ready for the grand finale of this historic 'movie' fellow Patriots. Bring on the required pain and the justice phase of the Great Awakening. Judgement Day is coming, and it will involve a full legal accounting for all of these failed coup plotters. International tribunals have occurred in the past at Nuremberg and oddly enough history has a way of repeating.

Post Q# 1098

Bring back the gallows!

Links

National WW2 Museum-Military Tribunals: Justice at Nuremberg

FOX News-Who could be Indicted in Russia Collusion Hoax?

The Federalist-The FBI Set Up Trump and We Watched it Happen

General Flynn-Many Empires have Fallen

Lew Rockwell-2025 Deagel Forecast: War and Population Reduction

CNN-Trump Amplifies Posts calling for Military Tribunals

Taibbi/Shellenberger-Origins of SpyGate

American Media Group-Military Tribunals

Washington Times-Retribution for Crossfire Hurricane

History-WW2: The Nuremberg Trials

CBS News-Katherine Herridge: GITMO 2021 Expansion

Video-KGB Defector Yuri Bezmenov: Manipulation of US Public

The Guardian-Final Moments of Nazis Executed at Nuremberg

Shawn Ryan-Mike Benz: They are Media Mercenaries

Time Magazine-Secret History of Shadow Campaign that Saved 2020 Election

Buster Hyde-The Dung Castle: Operation Crossfire Hurricane

US Holocaust Museum.org-The Nuremberg Code

Epoch Times-SpyGate: The Inside Story

BBC News-What is a War Crime?

Georgetown.edu-Military Tribunals and Case Law

White House.gov-EO blocking Property of Persons Involved with Corruption

Crossfire Hurricane Docs-Christopher Steele Binder

Justice.gov-2023 SC John Durham Report

Tormenting Progressive Liberals:
Master Troll Stephen Miller

Stephen Miller was Senior Advisor to President Trump during his first term and will return as Deputy Chief of Staff in the Trump 2.0 administration. Sill in his early 30's while advising our President Trump, Stephen Miller has already made a big-league name for himself. After the first Trump term, Stephen Miller started America First Legal (AFL) group, which is designed to legally help Patriots and combat the Biden/Harris administration. Stephen Miller would find himself subpoenaed and compelled to testify in 2022 to the January 6th U.S. House panel about some of his 2021 privileged Presidential conservations.

Post Q# 648
Did you miss the most important line in the entire speech?

Miller's AFL would take the lead in 2022 by accusing Walt Disney of violating civil rights and religious freedom laws. Stephen Miller has been a staunch supporter of free speech and Biden's DHS formation in 2022 of a new "Ministry of Truth' department to counter all opposition to the approved political narrative. Miller joined the Trump Campaign in January 2016 as the Senior Policy Advisor. Stephen Miller was generous given over to the growing Donald Trump 2016 Presidential campaign by then Sen. Jeff Sessions.

Post Q# 2691
FAKE NEWS DESIGNED TO KEEP THE FAKE NARRATIVE IN PLAY [COVER].

Miller had previously served Stealth Jeff Sessions as his Communications Director/Press Secretary. Candidate Trump knew what he was getting with Stephen Miller and Senator Sessions certainly knew what he had given up. Time and history would demonstrate what a valuable staffer Stephen Miller has been to both President Trump and AG Jeff Sessions.

Post Q# 1504
Watch the vid again if you need clarity (speech that will get POTUS elected).

Stephen Miller has always been known as a far-right activist but had come into his own with his speech writing for President Trump. Miller is credited with writing both the 2016 Republican National Convention and 2017 Inauguration speeches for Candidate/President Donald J. Trump. Much of the deliberate constant repetition of positive campaign 'talking points' in speeches given at the numerous Trump Rallies is also credited to Stephen Miller.

Post Q# 4367
Trolling is fun!

Stephen Miller is well known for his dry witty intellectual humor. Miller had become President Trump's right-hand troll, key speech writer, and primary agitator of the crazed liberal left and their MSM allies. Miller has received very much negative press from the MSM and their DC Swamp over his steadfast support of President Trump. Incredibly Stephen Miller was invited by Stefan Halper (as he did also to Carter Page) to attend the July 2016 University of Cambridge event that SpyGate was born.

Post Q# 3616
THE GREAT AWAKENING.
You are the news now.
Handle w/care.

Foundational pillars of Stephen Miller's social media strategy has always been the melting of SJW snowflakes and the triggering of leftist libs. Many victims of Miller's sharp tongue can attest to this innate triggering ability along with professional caliber debating skills. Most observers would credit Miller as one of the sharpest Presidential staff to face the hostile news media.

Post Q# 877
The age of MSM is over.

During an infamous 2017 White House presser, Stephen Miller and CNN's Jim Acosta went at it in a verbal toe to toe match. This classic Miller beat down of Acosta was highlighted with the Statue of Liberty poem quoted from memory by Miller. Even Miller's harshest critics will acknowledge his high IQ and oratory skills. As the Southern border crisis intensifies under the illegal Biden administration, Stephen Miller has kept up the criticism via media appearances.

Post Q# 3613
What happens when 90% of the media is controlled/owned by (6) corporations?

Knowledge and historical facts always seem to slow down the progressive idealism rhetoric from the Progressive Left. Miller tagged Acosta with a classic saying as being a 'Cosmopolitan Bias', which is displayed by all of the MSM Mockingbird news media. 'Q' has dropped that "We are the news now" and that pending future displacement from controlling the narrative is what they fear.

Post Q# 4173
THE MEDIA [CONSPIRACY TV] IS DEAD.
SHADOW ARM [D].

Stephen Miller was a Duke graduate and vocal national defender of the false rape charges against their men's lacrosse team. Stephen Miller's unwavering defense of Duke propelled him into the MSM spotlight and ultimately into politics. Miller has honed his public speaking/debating skills to a professional level since his Duke college days. The MSM's coverup of the Hunter Biden 'Laptop from Hell' scandal is a classic example of the coordination of the DC Swamp and the news media in creating false public narratives. Miller was proven correct in 2024 when the Duke Lacrosse rape accuser admitted she made up this horrific tale.

Post Q# 2423
Trolling the FAKE NEWS media is FUN!

Stephen Miller has been a strong supporter of the southern 'Wall' and fixing our broken immigration system. Miller supported President Trump in a government shutdown and national emergency declaration if funding had not been provided for this national defensive border wall. Immigration is one of the main subjects that Miller is outspoken and in 2023 outlined President Trump's 2nd term plans for the defense against illegal aliens invading our Republic. Miller would ultimately be caught up in the phony Jan. 6th House Congressional investigation along with other Trump aides.

Post Q# 937
PATRIOTS UNITE.
We are winning BIG.
Watch the speech.

Stephen Miller had launched in his 2021 America First Legal organization to assist in combating attacks on our MAGA Patriot community as well as on President Trump. Miller's new legal group has gone on the offensive against the illegal Biden regime. Stephen Miller is one such 'quiet hero' that will assume the position of Deputy Chief of Staff in President Donald Trump's second term. Special Counsel John Durham has dropped criminal indictments related to SpyGate and submitted his final report in 2023. The reports from IG Horowitz and SC Durham will be the underlying foundation for future judicial accountability to the treasonous coup plotters.

Post Q# 4046
> Patriotism on the rise.
> WWG1WGA!!!

Links

The Atlantic-Trump's Right-Hand Troll

FOX News-Stephen Miller on the RussiaGate Scandal

Revolver News-Stephen Miller goes Scorched Earth for Trump's BBB

The Hill-Stephen Miller: From Behind the Scenes to Center Stage

FOX News-Trump names Stephen Miller and Dan Scavino to Senior WH Staff

Daily Mail-Stephen Miller unveils Harsh Migrant Tactics for Trump's 2nd Term

Real Clear Politics-Miller: Biden doesn't know 'Let's Go Brandon' Meme

DEFCON News-Miller: When, How and Why Republicans should take Down Biden

FOX Business-Stephen Miller knocks Misconception of Catch and Release

Business Insider-Susan Rice burned Sage in Her West Wing Office

Washington Examiner-Miller: Safety under Trump or Lawless Mayhem of Left

NY Magazine-Who really Writes Trump's Speeches

Bio Tree-Trump's Senior Advisor: Stephen Miller

Business Insider-32 Year Old Adviser to POTUS

The Atlantic-Trump's Oval Office Address was Classic Stephen Miller

The Guardian-Trump Adviser has Controversial College Writings

Vanity Fair-How Miller Rode Rage from Duke to W/H

Video-Stephen Miller's Trolling Tendencies

Clinton Foundation Timeline-July 7, 2016: Stephen Miller Invited to Cambridge 'SpyGate' Event

Clinton Foundation Timeline-2025 Crossfire Hurricane Docs

Justice.gov-2023 SC John Durham Report

(Answer is:) HRC's Dirty Chief of Staff
(Question:) Who is Cheryl Mills ?

Cheryl Mills [CM] was to HRC exactly what Valerie Jarrett was to BHO, an original gangster prototype 'Consigliere.' Mills goes back to the Slick Willy days where she defended him in the Monica Lewinsky impeachment trial. The recycling of proven corrupt political lawyers is the norm around the DC Swamp. The FEC would fine in 2022 the DNC and HRC's campaign over $1M over the payments to Fusion GPS for opposition research developed (Steele Dossier) during the 2016 Presidential election.

Post Q# 578
[Nothing is ever truly erased/deleted].

Mills served HRC as her Chief of Staff/State Dept and as Legal Counsel. [CM] and Huma Abedin were the central conduits between the State Department and the Clinton Foundation (CF). Mills was heavily involved with HRC's 2016 campaign and will be included in future criminal indictments rising from the SpyGate probes. President Trump would file in 2022 a federal RICO lawsuit against those that promoted the false Russian collusion narrative during the 2016 election cycle.

Post Q# 4078
Locked on target [painted].

Skippy Podesta arranged for Eric Schmidt (Google/Alphabet) to meet in 2014 with Cheryl Mills/Robby Mook. Eric Schmidt started massive fundraising efforts as well as offering his new Groundwork computer services to HRC's 2016 campaign.

Post Q# 1717
Public: FBI/DOJ/O-WH/SD
Private: Clowns Clowns Clowns.
Expand your thinking.

This new Google company called Groundwork, provided on an exclusive basis voter data and cyber assistance. Google threw their company endorsement weight behind HRC well in advance of the 2016 election (they never thought she would lose). Executives from both Google and cyber forensic firm CrowdStrike assisted in the false Alfa Bank server collusion started by HRC and Perkins Coie lawyers. The false Alfa Bank and Russia Dossier are scary examples of private outside contractors coordinating criminal schemes with government officials.

Post Q# 1266
They thought she would never lose.
Insurance w/o cover.
Nothing is deleted.

Cheryl Mills was highlighted in IG Horowitz's 1.0 report on the HRC email investigation. FBI Randy Coleman/Agent Peter Strzok/DOJ David Laufman unethically allowed Mills to attend the 7/2/16 HRC FBI interview session. Special Counsel (SC) John Durham received Horowitz's criminal referrals and has indicated Perkins Coie/Clinton campaign lawyer Michael Sussmann which connects HRC, DNC, Media and Big Tech.

Post Q# 3841
> If dirty cops ran the investigation into [HRC] private server/email scandal, could an argument be made that it was corrupt?
> The truth will be made public.

What makes the HRC interview so bizarre, is the fact [CM] herself was a target in this same ongoing FBI probe. Mills along with Heather Samuelson and overseer David Kendall, personally culled and deleted the infamous 33,000 State Department related emails from HRC's private home-based unsecured email server.

Post Q# 89
> What countries donated big money to CF?

Generously former FBI Director James Comey granted Cheryl Mills limited immunity from government prosecution. [CM] along with Samuelson/Combetta/Pagaliano/and Bentel, all received unique special limited immunity arrangements normally not afforded the targets of the high-profile FBI/DOJ investigations.

Post Q# 453
> Hillary Clinton investigation (including her 33,000 illegally deleted emails).

Mills was in the spotlight with scandals such as Benghazi, ordering Paul Combetta to BleachBit the Clinton's server, and the Clinton Foundation 'pay to play' enrichment via political favoritism. Mills and HRC have been court ordered to give depositions in the current Judicial Watch FOIA lawsuit.

Post Q# 1828
> [SPY OP]
> [[HRC] [BC] [HA] [CM].......] [FAKE NEWS]

Mill's contact call-logs at the State Department show routine interactions with the CF. What is the most pivotal email publicly released to date was to Skippy Podesta saying, "We need to clean this up."

Post Q# 2725
> Chatter - Bill and Hillary's 'public' health will begin to rapidly deteriorate.

The cryptic reference "clean this up" is about several HRC to BHO emails stored on her private server hardware. HRC specifically sent emails to BHO while she was traveling abroad, so as to entrap him in the illegal personal non-government email accounts.

Post Q# 2872
> Hillary Clinton and Foundation.
> Crime Against Children.

Everyone knew about HRC's private email system, and they all exchanged email messages routinely. All of BHO's top staffers were using their own private non-government email systems and these messages will do them in. Cheryl Mills spends her time at BlackIvy Group, which is an NGO focused on building enterprises in Africa.

Post Q# 4820
> THE CLINTON FOUNDATION.
> WHITE HOUSE FOR SALE.

Special Counsel John Durham has dropped criminal indictments and submitted his final report in 2023. President Trump would bring in 2022 a federal RICO lawsuit against those that promoted the false Russian collusion narrative during the 2016 election. The entire ObamaGate/SpyGate cast of villains is a massive spiderweb of failed conspiracy plots and bizarre evil characters. With the re-election of President Trump in 2024, many past hidden political secrets will be finally revealed.

Post Q# 4550
People are waking up in mass.
Biblical.

Links

Politico-Cheryl Mills gets Immunity

Just the News-Chuck Grassley Condemns FBI Handling of HRC's Emails

Clinton Foundation Timeline-2025 Crossfire Hurricane Docs

Law and Crime-Judge orders Investigation of Clinton Lawyers

NY Post-How the FBI Wound Up Destroying Evidence

Real Clear Investigations-The Apparent Trump-Hillary Double Standard: For Her

FOX News-DNC/HRC campaign pay FEC Fines over Fusion GPS Payments for Trump dossier

Daily Beast-3 Clinton Witnesses given Immunity by FBI

Politifact-Making Sense of Bleach and Hammer Claims

Real Clear Politics-RussiaGate: HRC/Perkins Coie/Fusion GPS/CrowdStrike

PJ Media-FBI gave Clinton Aide and Lawyer Mills Immunity Deals

Judicial Watch-JW: Strzok/Page Emails show FBI Accommodation of HRC Witnesses

Epoch Times-Lisa Page's Testimony: Mills got Special Immunity/Laptop Deal

Red State-HRC's Lawyer is in the Crosshairs

Washington Examiner-FED Judge Shocked by Mills Immunity Deal

National Review-HRC sent Emails to BHO

Red State-DOJ 'Did Not Want' FBI to Examine Laptops

Breitbart-Cheryl Mills "Better Clean This Up"

Observer-Cheryl Mills Destroys HRC's Emails

Judicial Watch-JW Releases Testimony of HRC Email Administrator

Black Ivy Group-Cheryl Mills

State Dept.gov-FOIA: HRC Recovered Emails

Crossfire Hurricane Docs-State Department Steele Binder

Justice.gov-2023 SC John Durham Report

ObamaGate Dirty Couple Murray and King: Steele's State Department Conduit

The past IG Horowitz's reports have shown that Bruce/Nellie Ohr were the conduits between Fusion GPS and the FBI. The other route traveled by the infamous Chris Steele Russia Dossier was via the U.S. State Department over to the FBI. Beyond public debate now was a sophisticated coup plot against candidate Trump by government officials coordinating plans with private contractors. President Trump would file in 2022 a federal RICO lawsuit against HRC/DNC/Fusion GPS/and others related to the promotion of the false Russian collusion narrative during the 2016 election.

Post Q# 2700
Establish 'financial checks/reviews' of those in senior (critical) positions (audits) + direct family (close proximity).

Shailagh Murray and Neil King Jr. (1959-2024) are yet one more married couple involved with the unfolding scandals of ObamaGate/SpyGate. Shailagh Murray was first VP Biden's Deputy Chief of Staff, then went onto join BHO's White House Communications team. Many feel the illegal Biden administration is the third term of BHO with many alumni back into government.

Post Q# 2129
[LIVE STREAMING] WH HUSSEIN NON-OVAL [SITUATION ROOM] COORDINATION.

Neil King Jr. was employed at Fusion GPS while his wife Anita worked at BHO's White House. Devin Nunes has sent criminal referrals to the DOJ concerning Neil and Shailagh about their connections to the Chris Steele Dossier. Law firm Perkins Coie hired research group Fusion GPS to develop an opposition white paper against the Donald Trump in 2016.

Post Q# 964
BIDEN/CHINA VERY IMPORTANT MARKER.

Shailagh Murray was snatched up later by BHO to become the first ever White House Chief Digital Officer. Her co-worker Colin Kahl (VP Biden's NSA) is also being referred by Nunes for his involvement in handling the Christopher Steele Russia Dossier. The spider web of co-conspirators involved with SpyGate and infamous operations like Crossfire Hurricane.

Post Q# 2330
[Part re: Fusion GPS, Perkins Coi now being revealed?]

Neil King has worked in the past for the Wall Street Journal (Shailagh also work at WSJ and WAPO) and was friends with Glenn Simpson. So much so Neil King was hired on in the early days of this research firm when Simpson was first forming the infamous Fusion GPS (aka Bean LLC). Corrupt politicians and government officials often use outside contractors like Fusion GPS and CrowdStrike to do operations they lawfully cannot conduct against American citizens.

Post Q# 436
[DNC BREACH / DOSSIER].

The relationship with King's wife and the obvious Fusion GPS conflict of interest, has gotten the attention of key U.S. Congressional committees. IG Horowitz/SP Huber/SC Durham have all been working on criminal investigations stemming from illegal FISA surveillance warrants and the BHO-era SpyGate coup plot.

Post Q# 1632
> With power cones corruption.

Devin Nunes had finished Phase 2 of the House Intelligence Committee's investigation into this second fake Trump-Russia Dossier. Phase 3 had focused on CIA Director John Brennan and the intelligence community's role in this failed coup plot. Senators Grassley and Johnson will finish what the probes that Rep. Nunes has begun. IG Michael Horowitz had running parallel investigations into SpyGate and the walls are closing in upon this entire cabal.

Post Q# 1164
> Public: Dossier FISA.

Devin Nunes had referred over 42 individuals for testimony to several Senate committees. Both King and Murray have appeared in front of this House Task Force for testimony and now are under review by Special Counsel (SC) John Durham. Durham's indictment of Perkins Coie/Clinton campaign lawyer Michael Sussmann connects HRC and the DNC.

Post Q# 1515
> Why did the Podesta Group close?

The Second Dossier was authored by longtime Clinton enforcers Sid Blumenthal/Cody Shearer. Their material was added to what Chris Steele had gathered to help form his final opposition research work product. Many nefarious characters contributed at least in part to the different aspects of this SpyGate coup plot.

Post Q# 2171
> Define 'Projection.'
> Define 'Censorship.'

Victoria Nuland and Jonathan Winer were officials from BHO's U.S. State Department and have admitted to their involvement in the handling of Steele's Dossier. DOJ's 'Secret Society' nicknamed this part of their coup operation Crossfire FISA. The SpyGate scandal represents a coordinated sophisticated treasonous plan that involved multiple governmental agencies and officials.

Post Q# 1708
> Creation of fake intel dossier using ex-spy.

Steele's Dossier was given to a few reporters to be funneled/passed around as part of this intelligence 'laundering.' This circular flow between Fusion GPS/State Department/and Mockingbird news media, was to lend extra creditably to this fake opposition research. The State Department officials would give parts of the Steele dossier ti both the FBI and MSM news reporters.

Post Q# 4011
> CROSSFIRE HURRICANE
> CROSSFIRE TYPHOON

Coup plot four main components of Operation Trump:

> Exonerate HRC/Aides (ObamaGate)
> False Dossier(s) creation/distribution (RussiaGate)
> FISA Title-1 Warrents/Section 702 (SpyGate)
> The 'Insurance Policy' (Crossfire Hurricane)

Post Q# 4014
    Define 'insurgency.'

Bruce/Nellie Ohr and Neil/Shailagh had direct connections between Fusion GPS as well as each other. Joining this cast of 'Dirty Couples' are McCabe/Strzok/Ohr/Pientka/Dunn-Bauer/Abedin-Weiner/Power-Sunstein and many more. One of the most incredible plots in this movie was the deliberate recruiting of married couples into this treasonous plot against President Trump and his allies. Neil King passed away in Denver in 2024.

Post Q# 1286
    Fusion GPS.
    The Brits-raw intel/dossier/5 Eyes.

The law provides an extra layer of legal court protection against testimony of a married spouse. This is a classic picturesque 'Ship of Married Fools' awaiting their criminal indictments and very long sentences via Special Counsel John Durham, who submitted his final report in 2023. With the re-election of President Trump in 2024, Judgement Day is coming and justice will be restored to our Republic.

Post Q# 4124
    Why do they always include their spouse, son, daughter, etc.?
    Follow the money.

Links

 Politico-BHO Picks Murray from Biden's Staff

The Federalist-FBI/DOJ Declined to Charge Russia Collusion Hoaxer

Clinton Foundation Timeline-2025 Crossfire Hurricane Docs

Breitbart-Nunes Refers 10 BHO Officials to DOJ

Washington Times-Steele Dossier: FBI Nurtured biggest Hoax in American History

Daily Caller-CNN's Undisclosed Ties to Fusion GPS

Techno Fog-Durham: Hundreds of e-mails between Fusion GPS and Reporters

The Federalist-The Fusion GPS Scandal Implicates Media

Washington Examiner-Fusion GPS received Small Business Loans during Pandemic

Real Clear Politics-RussiaGate: HRC Campaign/Perkins Coie/Fusion GPS/CrowdStrike

Dawson Field-Perkins Coie and HRC Campaign

The Federalist-35 Key People Involved in the Russia Hoax

Markets Work-Nunes Referral List of 42 Names

Daily Caller-House Panel Questioning Sheila Murray

Buster Hyde-The Dung Castle: Operation Crossfire Hurricane

Institute of Politics-Shailagh Murray

Crossfire Hurricane Docs-State Department Steele Binder

Justice.gov-2023 SC John Durham Report

George Nader: Planted 2016 Trump Team "Transition Spy"

Hat Tip to Dan Bongino (TV Analyst/Ex-Secret Service) for coming up with his 'Dirty Up' theory involving ObamaGate/SpyGate. Dan outlines those certain 'dirty' individuals were deliberately planted into Trump World, so as to later demonstrate the fake Russian collusion narrative. President Trump would file in 2022 a federal RICO lawsuit against those officials involved with the promotion of the false Russian collusion narrative.

Post Q# 1508
Plants need water.

As details continue to unfold with SpyGate evidence is surfacing about several inserted intelligence assets of the CIA and Confidential Human Sources (CHS) of the FBI. These paid operatives were spies or LURES deliberately planted into Trump World for entrapment.

Post Q# 3790
If FISA warrants deemed to be illegal [ALL SURV LEAPFROG HOPS] what happens to MUELLER's case(s)?

DOJ IG Michael Horowitz has produced a report on the FBI's program involving the CHS and the excessive annual cost. IG Horowitz found flaws in the initial vetting/long term retention policy that allowed for a convicted child porn (Nader) CHS to be employed in the first place.

Post Q# 2727
In the past, what was the punishment re: a TRAITOR?
Coincidence?

These paid spies/LURES went into the Trump Campaign/Transition teams to accomplish their planned mission. Crossfire Hurricane/Operation Dragon/and Crossfire FISA were part of these spy/surveillance plans.

Post Q# 461
What makes a movie GOOD?
GREAT actors.

The Deep State enemy additionally planted several intelligence assets early into the Trump campaign team. Nader has recently been indicted by the DOJ for a multi-million conduit campaign contribution case involving HRC.

Post Q# 4916
Inappropriate [sick] to you?
Normal to them?
Dark secrets.

Leftists MSM repeated the false Russian collusion narrative during both the Trump campaign and transition time periods. Russia Russia Russia has been the Coup Plotters cry since the 2016 election results.

Post Q# 224
Who knows where the bodies are buried?
Purpose for time being spent here.

'Dirty-Up' individuals were purposefully inserted like Stefan Halper / Alexander Downer / Joseph Mifsud / Carter Page / Paul Manafort / George Papadopoulos / Natalia Veselnitskaya /and now

George Nader. George Nader had been sentenced on child porn and trafficking minors but only received a slap on the preverbal wrist.

Post Q# 2129

USE OF BACKCHANNEL SURV / SPY INSERTION [BODY 1, 2, and 5]

The 'plants' all had direct contact with various Trump campaign associates in 2016 and 2017. George Nader was a cooperating witness for Special Counsel (SC) Robert Mueller and has already given sworn testimony in the Russian witch-hunt. The Deep State historically has used blackmail techniques via using compromising material (underage sexual partners) as pressure points against targeted individuals.

Post Q# 4561

Who will put an end to the endless?

George Nader has been tied directly to Bill Clinton and has been photographed together on several occasions. The picture above is from a Punta Cana/Dominican showing George Nader/Slick Willy Clinton/ Tony Podesta and pals having a blast together in early January 2017. Oddly Slick Willy Clinton traveled extensively around the globe with known pedos like Jeffrey Epstein and George Nader.

Post Q# 3131

[Will the rich and powerful influence the court to prevent the unsealing?]
Follow the ATTORNEY.
Who took the pic?
Who is located behind the camera?

George Nader has advised the Crown Prince (UAE) Mohammed bin Zayed Al-Nahyan over the past few years. Nader is always scene in public with his provider and keeper of the well-known Crown Prince. Traveling worldwide in the entourage of the Crown Prince had its benefits to Nader as well as his Deep State handlers.

Post Q# 97

Define hostage.
Define leverage.

George Nader is Lebanese born and a regular jack of all trades for the Middle East. Nader has operated as an international mediator and back-channel UN diplomat in the past. Nader had been known as a big-league fixer of scandals which was ideal to be hovering around the Clinton Crime Family. George Nader would ultimately be sentenced to 10 years in prison over child sex charges.

Post Q# 158

What is a honeypot?

George Nader has earned a reputation as a person of intrigue/speculation/high-level access/ and that of an admitted PERVERT. Perfect candidate for the international intelligence community and their famed 'honey pot' entrapment operations. The globalist needs to recruit low life individuals to actively participate in their evil corrupt schemes.

Post Q# 1164

Not Public: Five Eyes/UK/AUS POTUS targeting using pushed RUS decoy meetings/campaign insertions.

Congressional Committees had focused in on 2 specific meetings set-up and attended by Nader and Prince bin Zayed. It appears Robert Mueller had providing strategic cover for George Nader and preventing his testimony to various those Congressional committees. Nader would be officially charged with illegally funneling over $3.5 million into HRC's 2016 Presidential Campaign.

Post Q# 4388
All systems go.

This cover afforded to George Nader is very much like that the DOJ had been covering for Stefan Halper, the first inserted spy uncovered. Nader's activity happened after the election period; thus, he is the Deep State's "Transition Spy". In the development of the SpyGate detail operational plans, one plan must smoothly transition to the next until your get to the final listed option being the 'Insurance Plan.'

Post Q# 1939
'This is the case with Halper, who is now proven to be a spy, possibly (Australian Ambassador) Alexander Downer."

The FIRST meeting of interest was in December 2016 was held at the Trump Tower with Kushner/Bannon/Joel Zamel/ and Prince bin Zayed. In addition to any dirt on HRC the sales pitch for this meeting was a social media platform to help with campaign marketing strategy.

The SECOND and more critical meeting was in the Seychelles (off Africa) in January 2017. Attending this meeting was Prince bin Zayed/Russian Kirill Dmitriev/and Erik Prince.

Post Q# 4482
Difficult truths.
This is not another 4-year election.

George Nader claims a back-channel was talked about between Russia/Trump via Erik Prince. Erik Prince has said no such back-channel talk was discussed and these public interactions were strictly social in nature. The known closeness to the Trump Family by Blackwater founder Erik Prince was a given that was attempted to be exploited by the treasonous coup plotters.

Post Q# 1589
ILLEGAL SPYING.
FRAME.
INSERT ASSET.

Of side interest is Nader's personal lawyer, who is none other than the infamous Kathryn Ruemmler. Ruemmler was BHO's W/H Counsel and also now represents Susan Rice in this unfolding ObamaGate/SpyGate political corruption spectacle. Interest has developed around this January 2017 hot tub pic, 'Q' had pointed out to 'fellow the lawyer' and Anons feel it is indicated lawyer Michael Sussmann.

Post Q# 2116
YOU MUST TARGET, REMOVE, AND SILENCE ALL THOSE ILLEGALLY TARGETED FOR FISA SURV......

Always known as a shadowy figure, Nader was arrested but not convicted in 1985 on child pornography charges. Nader later plead guilty to a 1991 charge of entering the USA with illegal child pornography. Nader now has been sentenced to 10 years in federal prison due to new child sex charges. SC John Durham indicated Perkins Coie/Clinton campaign lawyer Michael Sussmann and it is believed he was present at the now infamous January 2017 Bill Clinton 'water party photo.'

Post Q# 1928
Coming SOON to a theater near you.

Inquiring minds now want to know, was Nader the second 'spy' planted into Trump World by the FBI/DOJ. We know for sure that Stefan Halper is the confirmed ObamaGate/SpyGate campaign spy and looks like Nader took over from Halper post 2016 election to be the transition spy. Judgement Day is coming to return President Trump and restore our nation. SC Durham submitted his final report in 2023. With the re-election of President Trump in 2024, many previous hidden political secrets will finally be revealed.

Post Q# 1892
BLACK OPS AGAINST USA.
TRAITORS ALL.

Links

New Tree Hints-Bill Clinton Pictured with Multiple Pedophiles

Clinton Foundation Timeline-2025 Crossfire Hurricane Docs

The Federalist-SpyGate 101: A Primer on the Russia Collusion Hoax

Washington Examiner-Mueller Witness Nader pleads Guilty in Illegal Scheme

NBC News-Russia Probe Witness Charged with Funneling Millions to HRC in 2016

Susan Whitney-George Nader

Epoch Times-Mueller probe Witness (Nader) Pleads Guilty to Child Porn

Law and Crime-George Nader Sentenced to 10 Years

Market Watch-Mueller Witness George Nader Arrested on Child-Porn

Washington Examiner-HRC should Apologize for Biggest Political Hoax

Corey's Digs-Nader/Khawaja/Clintons/Pope Francis and Elite

Washington Times-Mueller Witness Conspired to Conceal Donations

Vanity Fair-Mueller Probe got Weirder

VOX-George Nader Mysterious Figure

Epoch Times-SpyGate: The True Story of Collusion

The Atlantic-Why was Nader Allowed into the White House

Haaretz: Back-Channel Mediator between Israel/Arab Countries

Crossfire Hurricane Docs-Christopher Steele Binder

Justice.gov-2023 SC John Durham Report

Who is SpyGate's Victoria Nuland ?

Then Representative Devin Nunes had several former BHO officials in for questioning by the special Congressional House Select Joint Task Force. Among these special SpyGate related individuals chosen was multiple administration State Department official Victoria Nuland. History will show Nuland was personally involved with both the SpyGate and UkraineGate political scandals. The 2022 Russian special military operation into Ukraine would exposure both US funded bioweapons labs and an extensive Nazi presence. Nuland had a direct hand in the BHO planned overthrow in 2014 of the democratically elected Ukrainian government.

Post Q# 4301
Who was the quarterback?

Victoria Nuland was BHO's Assistant Secretary of State for Europe/Eurasia. Scary to think that Nuland was slotted to be the next Secretary of State to President HRC administration. Biden specifically wanted Nuland (like many other BHO era alumni) to return to government duty and is currently the Undersecretary State Department for Political Affairs. No shock that today Nuland is in the middle of the brewing Russia/Ukraine possible WW3 senecio. Both Nuland and Eric Ciaramella had a hand in the Massacre in Kiev and latter passed out cookies to the survivors.

Post Q# 2633
US SEN NO NAME and
NEWS SHOP and
BUZZF and
You have the keystone.

Judicial Watch has reported Victoria Nuland provided classified documents to multiple Senators about ObamaGate/SpyGate on 1/5/17. BHO held in the White House Oval Office a meeting on that exact same day, with carryovers James Comey/Sally Yates in attendance and since historically immortalized by then NSA Susan Rice's infamous CYA memo.

Post Q# 1318
State C_A next?

Nuland's partner in crime at the U.S. State Department was Jonathan Winer. Both Nuland and Winer have publicly admitted to passing along opposition research concerning Donald Trump from Christopher Steele to the FBI in July 2016. Additionally both Nuland and Weiner, as well as other State Department staffers, were involved with HRC in the Benghazi horrific debacle.

Post Q# 1669
Not 'official' product-5 Eyes.

The U.S. State Department was first given this opposition research to Nuland/Winer by longtime Clinton enforcers Sid Blumenthal and Cody Shearer. Cody and Sid developed several fake memos in what Devin Nunes refers to as the 2nd HRC Trump-Russia Dossier.

Post Q# 1617
Only the beginning.
Power to the people.

Nuland also received information from another ex-State Department official and No Name assistant David Kramer. Kramer worked at the No Name Institute and gave the Chris Steele dossier to news outlet BuzzFeed, with orders to spread it around Washington DC. Many public and private groups teamed up in a joint effort to remove President Trump.

Post Q# 2633

"McCain associate shared unverified Steele dossier with BuzzFeed, court filing says."

This false additional opposition research work product was used to reinforce the validity of Steele's main Trump-Russia Dossier. This sneaky process was done by funneling the 2nd Dossier in a circular fashion back through the State Department and then Fusion GPS, ultimately ending conveniently at the FBI.

Post Q# 3129

THIS IS NOT A GAME.

Throw in a loyal Mockingbird reporter or two into this mix, now you have extra "circular validation" to be used by the FBI. In intelligence profession circles, the term used is for this method of validation is 'intelligence laundering.' Of odd but perhaps an interesting connective note is the husband of Nuland is Robert Kagan who is a longtime Senior Fellow at the Brookings Institute.

Post Q# 1286

The Brits-raw Intel / dossier /5 eyes.

Rep. Devin Nunes had released to the U.S. Senate investigation committees both Phase Two and Three of his past probes into prior DOJ wrongdoing. The House Intel Committee's concern was primarily in the origin and authorship of the several memos referred to as the second HRC Trump-Russia Dossier.

Post Q# 2245

[House of Cards].
Military planning at its finest.

Two sections from Sid/Cody's phony memos were ultimately included in the final version of Chris Steele's finished Russia dossier. These two targeted research memos now implicate the U.S. State Department in this failed coup plot against then candidate Donald Trump.

Post Q# 1840

[Fish]ing is fun.
These people are stupid.

The direct involvement of the U.S. State Department opens up the personal involvement of then Secretary John Kerry. As this puzzle finally gets solved, all roads will inevitably to lead back to BHO. Many of BHO era alumni are back in government service with the illegal Biden administration. The Russia/Ukraine conflict of 2022 shows exactly how corrupt officials like Nuland can set-off WW3. The forced revelations under US Senate testimony, Nuland had to confirm the existence of US sponsored biological labs in Ukraine.

Post Q# 3176

THEY WILL BE HELD ACCOUNTABLE.
NOBODY WALKS AWAY FROM THIS.

Victoria Nuland was caught in 2014 of bad mouthing the European Union in several leaked audio recordings. This brought Nuland much international negative notoriety and exposed her truly nasty vindictive side. Nuland was also directing back in BHO's choice of the new leadership of Ukraine via the Color Revolution assistance offered by the CIA. Victoria Nuland would forever be nicknamed the 'Color Revolution Architect.' Later it would be revealed that much of the operational funding for 'UkraineGate' was via misdirected funds from USAID.

Post Q# 3837
BIGGER THAN YOU CAN IMAGINE.
Crimes against Humanity.

Victoria Nuland did not have a glowing reputation abroad and her leaked rude statements went viral on social media. Nuland is at a loss to explain her State Department underlying Kathleen Kavalec's October 2016 Chris Steele meeting. Kavalec wrote up a report strongly questioning the basic truthfulness of Steele's entire research and Nuland got a copy. As part of the ObamaGate 'Dirty Couples' crew, Nuland's husband Robert Kagan is a Senior Fellow at the Brookings Institute.

Post Q# 4362
Keyword: Insurgency

Victoria Nuland additionally reached out in 2016 to DNC operative Alexandra 'Ali' Chalupa to help sabotage candidate Donald Trump's campaign. Chalupa released a lot of the negative Paul Manafort material including the infamous false Ukrainian 'Black Ledger.' It would later be revealed that much of the funding for UkraineGate came through corrupt USAID via misdirected programs.

Post Q# 1892
BLACK OPS AGAINST USA.
TRAITORS ALL.

Ali Chalupa highlighted Manafort's ties to prior corrupt Ukraine leadership. Paul Manafort and his famous lobbying firm had a long history of shadowy foreign election interferences. Nuland was neck deep in 2014 with helping with the coup in Ukraine along with Eric Ciaramella/Alexandra Chalupa/Biden/Kerry and others.

Post Q# 4130
Advocating overthrow of Government?

Nuland is the current CEO of the Center for a New American Society. Victoria Nuland will ultimately be dragged in front of Congressional Committees to face tough questions and surly Special Counsel (SC) John Durham was tasked to inquire about her exact ObamaGate/SpyGate role. President Trump would file in 2022 a federal RICO lawsuit against all those who promoted the false Russian collusion narrative during the 2016 election cycle.

Post Q# 3590
Kerry's son
Biden's son
Hint: Geo location: Ukraine
Hint: Energy

These historic events will turn out to be the biggest political scandal in our history- ObamaGate/SpyGate. This coup plot is unfolding act by act and we are witnesses a true Second American Revolution. The tentacles of this elaborate scheme run from the Halls of Congress's through Big Tech with international co-conspirators as well. The 2022 Russian invasion has brought sunlight to the past corruption between the USA and Ukraine. Fortunately, in 2024 Victoria Nuland announced her retirement from government service.

Post Q# 2165
>FISA GOES BOTH WAYS.
>HOOAH!

Nuland has returned to the world stage in confirming Ukraine had biological labs and the Putin is taking them all out with his military. OIG Michael Horowitz's prior reports have led to criminal investigating of the DOJ/FBI for past FISA abuses. Scarily Victoria Nuland would boast about Trump never returning to the White House two days before the Butler/PA assassination attempt in 2024. Probes headed now by SC John Durham has dropped criminal indictments and submitted his final report in 2023. With the re-election of President Trump in 2024, hidden secrets finally will be revealed to usher in the Great Awakening.

Post Q# 3634
>[D]'s (internal) infiltration issue(s) w/protecting NAT SEC.
>[Kerry] direct relay— Iran pre/post Iran deal [future marker].
>IF KNOWN— WHY IS IT ALLOWED TO HAPPEN.

Links

MSNBC-Ambassador Nuland on Korea: US Needs to get back to Diplomacy

The Federalist-Unsealed Crossfire Hurricane Docs prove RussiaGate a Hoax

Reuters-Leaked Audio reveals Embarrassing U.S. Exchange on Ukraine

Transcend-US Gov't Perpetuated 2014 Coup in Ukraine

Revolver News-Story behind the Ouster of Deep State's Color Revolution Architect

Tore Says-Ukraine/BHO/Biden: Mafia Global Election Interference

Just the News-Viktor Shokin Firing Timeline

Breitbart-Nunes Refers 10 BHO Officials to DOJ

CBC News-QAnon Conspiracy about Ukraine Bioweapons became Mainstream Disinformation

Tablet Magazine-Ukraine's Deadly Gamble

Consortium News-The Mess that Victoria Nuland Made

Clinton Foundation Timeline-Victoria Nuland Archives

Real Clear Investigations-Unpacking the Other HRC Russia Dossier

Markets Work-Biden Officials had Roles in Surveillance on Trump

Salon-Meet the Woman at the Center of the Benghazi Scandal

Markets Work-Victor Pinchuk, Clinton's and Endless Connections

Daily Caller-Former State Department Official destroyed Records at request of Steele

Markets Work-New Details on Nuland's Role in the Steele Dossier

WSJ-Pentagon's Work with Ukrainian BioLabs becomes Flashpoint in Russia's War

Real Clear Investigations-Victoria Nuland tells All on Steele Dossier

Markets Work-Nuland/Chalupa/Ukraine/and Steele Dossier

Brookings Institute-Senior Fellow Robert Kagan

Crossfire Hurricane Docs-State Department Steele Binder

Justice.gov-2023 SC John Durham Report

ObamaGate: The 16-Year-Plan to Destroy America

To see the 40,000-foot view of this plan, we must expand our thinking to understand all of these connected treasonous failed schemes. ObamaGate/SpyGate may go down as the biggest political corruption event in our history. Essential to the Global Reset program is the '16-Year Plan' to destroy America. Domestic traitors combined with globalist pushing for the Islamic Muslim Brotherhood and the Chinese CCP to destroy the Western world. BHO claimed publicly that Biden is completing his third term and the world is witnessing the second half of the 16-Year Plan that President Trump interrupted.

Post Q# 2727
In the past, what was the punishment re: a TRAITOR?
Coincidence?

ObamaGate/SpyGate is the criminal activity of governmental officials during the 8-year reign of BHO. A Deep State International Cabal (NWO) has combined with the Progressive Marxist Communist Left to takeover and transform America utilizing this infamous '16-Year Plan.' The NWO ruling elites have been fixated on a Global Reset that will leave them total world control. BHO promised to fundamentally transform America and was groomed to be the 'Manchurian Candidate' to destroy our country from within.

Post Q# 1328
THERE WILL COME A TIME THEY WILL NOT BE SAFE WALKING DOWN THE STREET.

This societal changing plan was dreamed up by the Deep State primarily involving two consecutive back-to-back Democrat Presidencies totaling 16 years. As it turns out BHO would take the initial first 8 years, followed then by 8 years under an expected President HRC. This would be the final nail in the coffin of the last major democracy on the planet. The world would be on the brink of World War 3 in 2023 with the Ukraine conflict and the Hamas sneak attack on Israel.

Post Q# 140
What if China, Russia, and others are coordinating w/POTUS to eliminate the NWO?

By almost divine intervention President Trump stopped this evil plot after the first 8 years. President Donald Trump's unexpected victory caused the Operation Crossfire Hurricane plans to be hurriedly implemented to remove POTUS. Sadly, we are witnessing the resumption of the final half of the evil 16-Year Plan with the carnage of our country by Team Biden. One sad example demonstrated in 2022 was the dominance of both Russian and China in the realm of space when the U.S.'s own satellites were shown to be vulnerable to missile destruction.

Post Q# 4545
We are living in Biblical times.

The Progressive Left's master plan is based more on a religious movement than normal domestic politics. Cultural Marxism and the radical Islamic Muslim Brotherhood are joining forces to turn against America and all that we stand for as a nation. Since they never thought she would lose, Biden is rushing to kickstart the remaining elements that President Trump had interrupted. Using Islam as a wedge religion against both Christians and Jews, helps to spur on constant global conflict.

Post Q# 4620

> [infiltration]
> Welcome to the Revolution.

Author Diana West laid it out nicely in her series "The Red Thread." Ms. West highlights the communist's long-term plan of fundamentally changing and transforming the USA. Timeline shows Edward Snowden began his NSA theft in 2013, exactly when John Brennan took over at the CIA for BHO. In 2021 we are witnessing Biden carrying out BHO's third term and by Biden repeatedly telling the media he is 'not allowed' to answer certain questions signals a Shadow Presidency.

Post Q# 4153

> [Background] [SOROS - HUSSEIN - HRC]

Rich Higgins also threw up a similar warning flare with his 2017 NSC memo that cautioned President Trump against the growing Muslim Brotherhood. Higgins was part of General Flynn's trusted inner/circle staffers known as the "FlynnStones" and Rich Higgins authored this critical NSA warning memo. The illegal Biden administration is carrying out the second half (HRC's job) of the 16-year plan to destroy America. The Globalist and Biden needed to instigate World War 3 as a keystone to their 16-Year Plan and military conflicts in Ukraine/Middle East were teed up.

Post Q# 570

> They Never Thought She Would Lose.
> [The 16 Year Plan to Destroy America]
> decode: 8 BHO + 8 HRC = 16-Year Plan

MAIN THEMES 16-YEAR PLAN:

- Progressive/Socialist Ideology
- Install Rouge Operators (Clowns)
- Operation Northwoods/FF's
- Education Infiltration-CRT Teaching
- Military Industrial Political Complex
- One World Gov't/Open Borders
- Two-Tier Justice/USSC Puppets
- Edward Snowden's NSA Operation
- Alinsky Tactics of Resistance/Antifa
- Weaken NSA/Degrade US Military
- Sell-Off Tech/Special Access Programs
- Muslim Brotherhood/CCP Alliance
- Weaponizing Government Agencies
- End NASA and Space Dominance
- Start World War 3-Global Nuclear
- The 'Great Reset'/15-Minute Cities

Post Q# 936

> The Nazi order.
> NWO [N does not refer to "New"].
> The Sum of All Fears.

Many have been yelling about the anti-American steps taken by the Progressive Left to undermine the USA. Antifa/BLM is an outgrowth and represents a large force of trained BHO foot soldiers to act as street enforcers in this extensive infiltration campaign. This has all been planned out by evil forces and is ongoing in our country today. Special Counsel (SC) John Durham was tasked to explore the criminal referrals from IG Michael Horowitz related to past crimes of the political SpyGate scandal.

Post Q# 1010

MASS EXT EVENTS DESIGNED TO DECREASE THREAT LEVEL OF POPULATION.

The '16-Year Plan' was stopped dead with President Donald Trump's 2016 election. With the public exposure of Klaus Schwab's Great Reset plan, elements from the 16-Year Plan can be obvious to any observer. Special Counsel John Durham was tasked at exploring SpyGate and submitted his final report in 2023. Biden's open borders policy combined efforts the the planned financial collapse of the U.S. Dollar, the second half of the 16-Year Plan is obvious to all. With the re-election of President Trump in 2024, the coming 'Storm' represents the Second American Revolution and the return to America First policies featuring equal justice under the law.

Post Q# 14

Was HRC next in line?
Was the election supposed to be rigged?

Links

QAGG: 16-Year Plan meme

FOX News-Patel found Thousands of Sensitive Trump Russia Probe Docs

The Last Refuge-Original BHO and HRC 2008 Agreement

The Federalist-Unsealed Crossfire Hurricane Docs prove RussiaGate a Hoax

Lee Smith-Who Runs the Regime?

Revolver News-BHO: A Shadowy Cryptic Figure

Ron Carolina's-The 16 Year Plan Reference Materials

Tablet Magazine-Hoax of the Century

Newsweek-Donald Trump: RussiaGate Hoax

Patel Patriot-Devolution Part 14: The Invisible Enemy

Epoch Times-3 Warfare's Doctrine underpins CCP's Campaign of Infiltration

Sara Westall-Pushing Back on The Plan to Destroy America

The Millennium Report-16 Year Plan to Destroy America

American Thinker-Archbishop Vigano's startling Warning to the American Peoples

Front Page-The Party of Treason

The Blaze-BHO's Plan to Destroy America

The Atlantic-Muslim Brotherhood and The Question of Terrorism

National Review-How BHO Sided with the Muslim Brotherhood

Rense-Listed of Military Fired/Purged under BHO

Imperator Rex-Victory is Near: SpyGate is Timed to Blow

The Federalist-BHO/Biden Key Oval Office Meeting was on January 5th (2017)

YouTube: The 16-Year Plan to Destroy America

ObamaGate Counter Surveillance Measures Utilized Xbox Live Party Chat

Surveillance is all about information gathering or its prevention. Microsoft's Xbox game consoles are the most popular systems in the international gaming world. The illegal surveillance against President Trump and his circle is the keystone of the SpyGate scandal.

Post Q# 4200
> Proof game 'chat logs' discussion(s)_legitimate?

The latest enhancement is the Xbox Live Party Chat feature. Chat allows players (coup plotters) to message each other in real-time to allow instant communication between competing opponents. Anons found an example of this with the infamous 'Palpatine's Revenge' chat in which FBI/DOJ officials are discussing the appointment of Robert Mueller.

Post Q# 1891
> Texts, emails (gmail), drafts (gmail), HAM comms, PS/Xbox chat logs.

Advancements in gamer technology has enabled these Xbox units to allow communication between individual operators via Wi-Fi Bluetooth. Not so well advertised is the fact these Xbox Live Party Chat "logs" can be captured and are not secure communications.

Post Q# 365
> Shall we play a game?
> How about a nice game of chess?

Electronic counter surveillance refers to various measures deliberately undertaken to prevent surveillance. Surveillance is the secret periodical/continuous watching of persons, vehicles, places, or objects to obtain information/intelligence. The U.S. Government would build Sensitive Compartmented Information Facilities (SCIF) nicknamed 'tanks' to prevent the interception of communications and secret information.

Post Q# 1905
> Anyone have problems w/their 'Xbox Live' account shortly after the drop yesterday?

The distilled surveilled information can then be analyzed concerning the targeted individuals and their activities. It is all part of the continuing cat and mouse game played by intelligence operatives around the world. The gaming industry would rollout in 2023 online game chat live communications via new AI computer software (hello Big Brother).

Post Q# 1279
> Fake emails.
> Game forum comms.
> Gmail comms.

As the Deep State should have guessed in advance, all of the Xbox Chat logs are obtainable. It should become clear that Nellie Ohr's HAM radio transmissions, the Gmail 'Ghost Draft' messages, and all of these Xbox chat logs are in the hands of the good guys. Biden's Special Counsel obtained in 2023 President Trump's Twitter messages and 'ghost draft' posts in an effort to undermine the rule of law.

Post Q# 4004
> Why would in-game chat be disabled during [FF event(s)]?

'Q' has been advising that there will be a process of "Dark to Light" with the upcoming Great Awakening. IG Horowitz's 2.0 Report concerning FISA/FISC outlined many abuses has led directly into Special Counsel (SC) John Durham handling these criminal referrals. When all else fails in surveillance, you can always go with the direct intrusion approach as our government has done in the past to FOX TV Greg Rosen/CBS Sharyl Attikkson/and Tucker Carlson.

Post Q# 2489
[Placeholder - OIG report - OTR_C_]
decode: OTR-Off the Record 'communications' as in Nellie Ohr's HAM Radio, Gmail 'Ghost Drafts', and Xbox Live Chat logs.

SC Durham has dropped criminal indictments and this has confirmed many of the past 'Q' drops. SC Durham submitted his final report in 2023. Disclosures about ObamaGate/SpyGate operations will focus the public's attention on the past failed illegal coup attempt and lead to mass arrests. With the historic re-election of President Trump in 2024, 'Judgement Day' is coming as well as the return of the rule of law.

Post Q# 3602
Rebellion or Empire?
Private [invite only] faction(s).

Links

 Xbox-Fortnite Chapter 2 Remix

FOX News-Democrats pulled Greatest Con Job Ever

The Verge-Call of Duty/Activision to Employ AI Voice Moderation

The Guardian-Xbox Live Targeted by UK and US Spy Agencies

Just the News-Special Counsel obtained Trump's Twitter Messages/Ghost Draft Posts

Western Journal-Tucker Carlson worries NSA Broke into His Secure Messages

Gadget-NSA's Tailored Access Operations Intercepts Computer Data

CNBC-World of Spycraft: NSA Infiltrates Gamers' Data

How to Geek-Chatting with Friends on Xbox Live

The Verge-Could NSA use Xbox to Spy on You?

Dean Groom-What You Need to Know about Xbox Live Party Chat

Niche Gamer-Billionaire George Soros invests $45M into Activision

Euro Gamer-NSA and GCHQ can Listen to Xbox Communications

Regen-Demo Video on How to Use Xbox Live Party Chat

It's Tactical-How to Detect Surveillance and Counter

Windows-How to View and Delete Xbox Messages

The Last Refuge-FISA 702 Searches

Clinton Foundation Timeline-2025 Crossfire Hurricane Docs

Justice.gov-2023 SC John Durham Report

O.F.A.— Ensuring there was NO 'Peaceful Transition of Power'

Organizing For Action (OFA) is the BHO stepchild born out of Organizing for America. This Democratic core political group boasts of over 30,000 trained volunteers and several hundred field office locations. The world would see these foot soldiers in action during the Summer of 2020 with the burning of cities by BLM/Antifa armies. Many BHO alumni would return in the Biden/Harris administration in 2021 as well as named in the 2022 RICO federal lawsuit filed by President Trump against those involved with the SpyGate scandal.

Post Q# 3613
Why, after the election of 2016, did [D]'s and media corps jumpstart a [coordinated and planned] divisive blitz intended to create falsehoods re: illegitimacy of election, character assassination of POTUS.

BHO made the headquarters for his OFA Anti-Trump Cabal in DC just down the street from the White House. OFA's goal is pushing the Progressive Communist Lefts political agenda and preservation of the BHO legacy. BHO would use HRC's phony 2016 Russia Dossier to launch the next phase against Donald Trump with FisaGate and operation Crossfire Hurricane. Records in 2023 would confirm that BHO/Brennan/and Comey knew about HRC's RussiaGate' plans against candidate Trump before the FBI opened their investigation.

Post Q# 1443
Hussein [WH [call] [tarmac] BC/LL].

President Trump is the imbedded thorn in the side of the Deep State/NWO Globalist. The OFA volunteers undergo training seminars and are given detailed manuals for public protesting/civil disobedience. Many correctly claim that the 3rd term of BHO was in fact the first term of Sleepy Joe Biden and backing Kamala Harris for his potential 4th term. Through the grace of God by deflecting an assassins bullet in 2024, President Trump promises to end the era BHO in his second term.

Post Q# 4231
WHO ASKED AMB KISLYAK TO CALL FLYNN [SET UP _FBI entrap + FISA [late] justify]?

George Soros is one of the main financiers of OFA and a backer of BHO. Prior to OFA, BHO began ACORN in Chicago days as a street political organizer (Saul Alinsky formula). A group of former BHO Alumni have formed in 2017 the political action committee called National Security Action (NSA), solely as an Anti-Trump think tank coalition. Not surprisingly many of these NSA members would form the core of illegal Biden administration in 2021.

Post Q# 1887
What is Hussein's background?
Muslim by faith?
Operation Cyclone - Mujahideen/Afghanistan.

Characters like Ben Rhodes/Susan Rice/Samantha Power/Denis McDonough/and Jake Sullivan are going after Trump via NSA/OFA. This is the 'Shadow Government' at work against the interest of the Republic. The trained individuals would become BHO's Army and lead the Antifa/BLM riots of 2020.

Post Q# 4024

A deeply entrenched enemy who controls the vast majority of communications is only defeated by.......
Game theory.

We see the actionable plans now in the form of the mass protests, ICE offices overrun, Trump Officials harassment, protest marches in the streets, mass censorship, migrant caravans, bizarre viruses, etc. The current riots and organized violent Antifa protests are the end product of this organized infiltration scheme. As part of the Russia 'collusion narrative', it was revealed in 2024 that the US Intel community asked partners from FIVE EYES (FVEY) to illegally spy/bump upon targeted Team Trump campaign aides back in 2016.

Post Q# 3856

Define Renegade [Hussein USSS code name].
Standard definition.

The long-term goal is to get back on the path to total transformation of the U.S. into a Socialist Communist Utopia. Globalists and the New World Order crowd have planned for decades, this slow takeover of America from within. A Great Reset is underway per Klaus Schwab and the virus/VAX is a tool of this evil global scheme. Prior to his departure from the White House on 1/5/2017, BHO held a pivotal Oval Office meeting with Trump carryovers James Comey and Sally Yates, along with VP Biden and NSA Susan Rice, finalized the coup plot against incoming President Trump.

Post Q# 151

How do you capture a very dangerous animal?

The term 'Manchurian Candidate' seems to accurately depict a certain infamous Chicago community organizer. A Shadow Government has purposely been put into place by these failed Deep State coup plotters. Many believe that Biden is in effect carrying out BHO's third term and the second half of the 16-Year Plan to destroy America. The continuing relationship between BHO/Biden and Iran/Muslim Brotherhood would be evident with the 2023 military conflict with Israel and Hamas.

Post Q# 4098

Why did [Hussein, Barry] choose RENEGADE as USSS codename?
[Hussein, Barry] parents both fluent in Russian?
Farm work takes special skills.

The Deep State opposition needed to stop President Trump at all costs due to the past crimes he could expose. OFA/NSA coordinated the mobilization an army of street foot soldiers. BLM and Antifa activists took to the streets for civil unrest, creating racial conflicts, and the burning of many cities in the riots of 2020. It would later be revealed that BHO used funds from USAID to finance his 'Army' and all of the destructive riots they organized.

Post Q# 3694

Never forget who directed.

For the Progressive Utopia to become a reality, the Deep State must delegitimization and remove our duly elected POTUS. When will this crowd ever admit that they were wrong because "They Never Thought She Would Lose" and begin to make our country great again together? Biden claiming today to the media that his handlers will not allow him to answer certain questions is a sign of a Shadow Presidency. BHO would hold regular Sensitive

Compartmented Information Facilities (SCIF) meetings with Biden during his false Presidency and never would allow anyone to listen.

Post Q# 4645
THE SHADOW PRESIDENCY OF 44

Judicial Watch is seeking to legally depose HRC/Ben Rhodes/Cheryl Mills/Susan Rice about Benghazi. FOIA requests have unearthed the official Benghazi talking points memo and the coverup surrounding this entire tragic event. Many of these individuals are being repurposed into the Biden administration for the third term of BHO. The MSM's coverup of the Hunter Biden 'Laptop from Hell' is an example of corrupt DC Swamp politicians coordinating with fake news allies to craft false public narratives.

Post Q# 3754
FED Gov't [HUSSEIN] - Pearson Publishing
Pearson Publishing - [HUSSEIN]
Follow the money.
Corruption.

The narrative loss of Russia/Impeachments/China Virus/Shadow Presidency and now race riots, has set up the final confrontation between 'Good vs Evil'. Special Counsel John Durham has dropped criminal indictments related to the SpyGate/RussiaGate and submitted his final report in 2023. After the failed assassination attempt on President Trump in July 2024, BHO ushered out Biden for Kamala Harris continuing his behind the scenes control of the White House. Even after President Trump's historic re-election victory in November 2024, BHO would continue to thwart the peaceful transfer of power. The Great Awakening will usher in a new age of honest politics and equal justice again.

Post Q# 4957
Peaceful protests?
Riots?
"Summer of Love" redux?

Links

The Nation-Ben Rhodes: Crisis of Liberal Foreign Policy

Front Page Mag-Organizing for Anarchy

The Federalist-BHO used NPR to Launder Lies

Revolver News-BHO Lackey Ben Rhodes might Wanna Lawyer Up

The Last Refuge-Original BHO and HRC 2008 Agreement

Clinton Foundation Timeline-2025 Crossfire Hurricane Docs

AMG-Bigger than WaterGate

Britannica-BHO: Spring Scandals and Summer Challenges

Broken Anthem-BHO: Total Control

Brookings Institute-Deception and the Iran Deal

Lee Smith-BHO's January 5th Conspiracy

Tablet Magazine-The BHO Factor

The Federalist-BHO and Biden January 5th Meeting was Key to Trump Operation

Revolver News-CIA and FBI Agents Confirm BHO was behind Russia Hoax

PJ Media-Biden/BHO Officials Sought to Torpedo incoming Trump Adm

National Review-Inside BHO's ACORN

PJ Media-Ric Grenell Destroys Biden and His 'Obama Third Term Crew'

Tablet Magazine-RussiaGate began with BHO's Domestic Spying

Markets Work-Time Magazine Article details Campaign against Trump

American Report-The 'Hammer' is the Key to the Coup

American Thinker-BHO/OFA and the Death Throes of the Democratic Party

FOX News-Former BHO Officials form Anti-Trump Think Tank

Markets Work-Listing of Participants

Millennium Resort-The Trojan Horse That Rolled into America

Gatestone Institute-China Trying to Break Up the Five-Eyes Intel Network

Time-Secret History of the Shadow Campaign (2020 Election)

Senate Intelligence Committee: 2021 DECLAS

Crossfire Hurricane Docs-Christopher Steele Binder

Justice.gov-2023 SC John Durham Report

Bruce and Nellie:
A Modern Day Bonnie and Clyde OG Couple

Bruce and Nellie Ohr's criminal roles expand with every new revelation in the ObamaGate/SpyGate scandals. They sadly are part of a growing list of 'Dirty Couples' acting as a modern-day Bonnie and Clyde criminal teams. Fusion GPS (owner Glenn Simpson) and the Ohr's will be shown to have played pivotal roles in both the development and promotion of the various false Trump-Russia dossiers. In President Trump's 2022 federal RICO lawsuit, both of the Ohr's along with Fusion GPS/HRC/and DNC are named for activities related to the unfolding SpyGate political scandal.

Post Q# 2700
Establish 'financial checks/reviews' of those in senior (critical) positions (audits) + direct family (close proximity).

Trusted reporter John Solomon has said that Bruce Ohr [BO] may turn out to be the number one whistleblower in the SpyGate scandal. Ohr's leaked testimony to date has implicated high level individuals connected to the past BHO/Biden administration. Special Counsel (SC) John Durham has already gotten a guilty plea from FBI lawyer Kevin Clinesmith and indicated Perkins Coie/Clinton campaign lawyer Michael Sussmann.

Post Q# 2004
The FARM requires select skill-sets.

Ex-FBI Peter Strzok admitted publicly that Bruce Ohr gave the FBI the original Christopher Steele dossier. Jonathan Winer. Nellie Ohr and Fusion GPS were directly involved with the circular flow of fake information in an attempt to legitimize the outrageous Russian collusion claims.

Post Q# 4153
[FBI Floor 7] [UK assist] Steele - B_Ohr - N_Ohr - Fusion GPS [shell 2]

Husband/Wife pairs that are involved with high treasonous crimes normally are very rare. For some reason BHO/HRC have convinced several married couples to risk everything for their Progressive Leftists NWO Marxist global Great Reset agenda. The 16-Year Plan to destroy America was interrupted by President Trump but now re-activated under the illegal Biden administration.

Post Q# 436
BRIT INTEL.
HRC CAMP PAY.
DNC PAY.
STEELE.

Bruce Ohr was the former Associate Deputy Attorney General (# 4 spot at DOJ) prior to several internal demotions. [BO] is a cooperative witness and has been giving countering testimony to those previously called to testify. 'Q' has pointed out the phrase 'When does a bird sing" and is a reference to witnesses telling all they know to prosecutors.

Post Q# 2159
Panic in DC.
Bruce Ohr [in effort to save Nellie Ohr] testifying against Rosenstein, Yates, Lynch, and Comey?

Nellie Ohr was employed at Fusion GPS during the Spring through the Fall of 2016. Nellie Ohr coordinated the preparation and distribution of the infamous Christopher Steele Dossier for her employer Fusion GPS. Both the Ohr's would be used as conduits for the flow of disinformation surrounding the entire SpyGate portion handled by Fusion GPS.

Post Q# 1939
> BO and Alexander Downer (FVEY) (EX1).
> BO unlocks UK / F_intel [FVEY].

Bruce Ohr met several times in the Fall 2016 with Glenn Simpson (Fusion co-founder) to discuss Chris Steele. Ohr acted without prior approval or knowledge of his superiors at the DOJ for these clandestine rendezvouses. These professional indiscretions would be used in two departmental demotions before Ohr finally left the DOJ.

Post Q# 1988
> "Just learned BO was not interviewed by Huber."

[BO] was the main conduit between the Justice Department and Fusion GPS. Orbis/UK employee Christopher Steele was contracted to do opposition research for Fusion in creation of the now infamous Trump-Russia Dossier. The law firm of Perkins Coie would hire Nellie Ohr and Fusion GPS on behalf of the DNC and HRC.

Post Q# 1876
> HAM radio instructions if remote-5.

Nellie Ohr's released Congressional testimony highlights a meeting on 7/30/16 at the Mayflower Hotel/DC. Nellie along with hubby Bruce meet with Chris Steele to exchange 'Dossier' intelligence. John Durham would continue to push in 2022 for more previously held as 'privileged' documents from Fusion GPS/Perkins Coine/DNC/and HRC.

Post Q# 1316
> Bruce Ohr, Associate Deputy Director Attorney General-Demoted 2x-cooperating
> witness [power removed].

Bruce Ohr previously headed the DOJ's Organized Crime Drug Enforcement Task Force. Bruce Ohr had been involved with both Operation Cassandra and Congressional IT aides the Awan's. It is not unusual to see the same names appearing in various past political scandals as the corrupt DC Swamp loves to recycle their trusted foot soldiers.

Post Q# 3065
> NELLIE OHR = C_A?

Bruce Ohr would be demoted several times by the DOJ but was kept on at DOJ so as to continue ongoing testify. Bruce Ohr has had over a dozen sessions with IG Horowitz's team and undoubtedly been chatting with SC John Durham. [BO] resigned on 10/14/20, which was a day before he was to be fired by AG Bill Barr.

Post Q# 1435
> NELLIE OHR HAM RADIO.
> Avoid NSA data college.
> It failed.

Nellie Ohr's worked at Fusion GPS (aka Bean LLC) and did more than just help compile the Dossier. It has been said Nellie is the co-author, as she helped in developing most of the Trump-Russia collusion material used to form this false narrative. Nellie Ohr would ultimately assemble the various memos generated by Fusion GPS along with Steele's discredited researcher Igor Danchenko into the infamous Russian Dossier.

Post Q# 2004
What is the significance of Nellie Ohr being fluent in Russian?

Nellie Ohr has a unique background which includes a Ph.D. in Russian history/she is fluent in Russian/a known Stalin apologist/former CIA analyst/and expert Ham radio operator. It has been discovered that Nellie may have started working for Fusion GPS up to one year earlier than has been previously stated.

Post Q# 4124
Why do they always include their spouse, son, daughter, etc.?
Follow the money.

In Nellie Ohr's released Congressional testimony, she claims to have used additional sources besides Chris Steele to compile the final Dossier. Sid Blumenthal and Cody Shearer worked with State Department Nuland/Winer officials, to insert their own two memos to be included with Steele's compiled opposition research dossier. The Christopher Steele Dossier went via the FBI/DOJ and the Blumenthal/Shearer Dossier went via BHO's U.S. State Department.

Post Q# 2261
FISA = START.
FISA BRINGS DOWN THE HOUSE.
WHEN DO BIRDS SING?

In 2010 the three paths between Bruce/Nellie and Glenn Simpson crossed. This event was a CIA Open Source Works program and a known 'clown' gathering workshop. The intelligence community often created various official 'work shops' as both a recruitment and communions venue.

Post Q# 1928
[Movie 1]
Showtime.
BO - CS and BO - NO ands NO - BO.
decode: BO=Bruce Ohr CS = Christopher Steele NO=Nellie Ohr

By actively attending CIA sponsored seminars, the 'Clown' influence is real hard to shake off in later years. This method of 'soft' recruitment has been employed many times by various intelligence agencies. There has been an active battle between the CIA and the NSA for years.

Post Q# 4853
Wife: CIA
Husband: DOJ

Sen. Chuck Grassley previously sent out a 12-page questionnaire to several top BHO Alumni. Many of these very specific questions involve Fusion GPS, Perkins Coie, CrowdStrike and the Chris Steele Trump Dossier. Special Counsel (SC) John Durham has indicated Perkins Coie/Clinton campaign lawyer Michael Sussmann and this connects back to all of these players.

Post Q# 1286
Fusion GPS.
The Brits-raw intel/dossier/5 eyes.

The answers to Senator Grassley's tough questions may just ignite the fuse for grand show finale. Truth and sunlight will be the best disinfectant for the corrupt DC Swamp.

Post Q# 2633
"McCain associate shared unverified Steele dossier with BuzzFeed, court filing says."

It is looking like Nellie Ohr will get ultimately get credit as a co-author of Steele's Dossier. Lovely Molly has earned the title of Dossier #3 and hubby Bruce Ohr has testified to those facts. The FEC would fine in 2022 the DNC and HRC's campaign over $1M for payments to Fusion GPS in their creation of the false Steele Dossier during the 2016 election cycle.

Post Q# 4072
Treason doesn't pay well in the end.

Listed below are just some of the DIRTY COUPLES uncovered with direct connections to ObamaGate/SpyGate. 'Q' has reminded Anons to watch the families and for obvious good reasons. Judgement Day is coming and SC John Durham dropped criminal indictments as well as submitted his final report in 2023. With the historic re-election of President Trump in 2024, many past hidden political secrets will finally be revealed.

- Andy/Jill McCabe
- Bruce/Nellie Ohr
- Peter Strzok/Melissa Hodgman
- Glenn Simpson /Mary Jacoby
- Cass Sunstein/Samantha Power
- Anita Dunn/Robert Bauer
- Shailagh Murray/Neil King
- Joe/Melissa Pientka
- Huma Abedin/Anthony Weiner
- BC/HRC (ringleaders)

Post Q# 3483
Why is Bruce Ohr still @ Justice?
Nellie Ohr _C_A.
Fluent in Russian?

Links

Jeff Carlson-Bruce and Nellie Ohr

Western Journal-FBI Opened Grand Conspiracy Probe everything RussiaGate

FOX News-DOJ Bruce Ohr and Wife Nellie Ohr's Emails

Daily Mail-FBI Secret Declassified Document Reveals Origins of Trump Probe

Clinton Foundation Timeline-Perkins Coie Contracts with CrowdStrike and Fusion GPS

American Spectator-Nellie Ohr: Woman in the Middle

NY Magazine-Fusion GPS and Steele Dossier

Real Clear Investigations-Ex DOJ Official and Wife had Bigger Roles

WSJ-Fusion GPS's 'Attorney-Client Privilege' Cover

The Federalist-SpyGate 101: A Primer on the Russia Collusion Hoax

Real Clear Politics-RussiaGate: HRC Campaign/Perkins Coie/Fusion GPS/CrowdStrike

The Last Refuge-Bruce and Nellie Ohr

NY Post-Inside the HRC Dossier and Con behind RussiaGate

The War Economy-Fusion GPS

The Last Refuge-Admiral Rogers/FISA 702

Real Clear Investigations-FBI Man Undercuts Ohr's Claim in RussiaGate Role

American Thinker-Both Ohr's in Troubled Water

New Yorker-Pete/Lisa and Bruce/Nellie

The Federalist-The Bruce Ohr Archives

Epoch Times-Did FBI use Formal Interviews with Ohr to Transmit Steele Info?

The Last Refuge-Nellie Ohr/Glenn Simpson

Spectator-Nellie Ohr: Woman in the Middle

Justice.gov-Crossfire Hurricane Timeline

Crossfire Hurricane Docs-Bruce Ohr Interview

Crossfire Hurricane Docs-Nellie Ohr Interview

Justice.gov-2023 SC John Durham Report

HAM Call-Sign KM4UDZ: aka "Lovely Molly"

Department of Justice (DOJ) twice demoted and later fired employee Bruce Ohr [BO], had testified to Congress that he personally gave the Christopher Steele Dossier directly over to the FBI. Bruce Ohr conveniently first received the final work product of Chris Steele from his loving wife Nellie (aka Lovely Molly) Ohr. The use of married couples throughout the SpyGate scandal is a shocking subset of these treasonous coup plots against candidate/later President Donald Trump. Both Bruce and Nellie Ohr along with Fusion GPS/HRC/DNC/and others are included in President Trump's 2022 federal RICO lawsuit for damages surrounding those who promoted the false Russian collusion narrative during the 2016 election cycle.

Post Q# 2004
The FARM requires select skill sets.

Various Congressional committees have received testimony from Nellie Ohr about her involvement with the Christopher Steele Dossier in organizing all of the various oppostion research memos. IG Michael Horowitz had also received sworn testimony from hubby Bruce and Nellie Ohr, as he has been singing like a bird in an effort to save his 'Lovely' Nellie. Nellie Ohr is credited as the main collator of the various fabricated memos into what history will term the infamous Steele Dossier.

Post Q# 1745
FISA BRINGS DOWN THE HOUSE.

Bruce and Nellie Ohr are a modern-day versions of the original gangsters Bonnie and Clyde. Nellie Ohr has revealed that Ukrainian Serhiy Leshchenko was one source for her portion of the final opposition research work product. Nellie Ohr was hired by research firm Fusion GPS to develop anti-Trump research in 2016. Nellie Ohr also relied heavily upon the fake memos provided by Steele's primary researcher Igor Danchenko.

Post Q# 2116
Think Steele and BO [Post FBI firing] intel collection.

Leshchenko was a Ukrainian parliamentarian and gave false opposition research to Nellie/Fusion GPS from his "black ledger." From Russian Oligarch Oleg Deripaska to Clinton enforcer Sid Blumenthal, everyone had a hand in the final development of Steele's Dossier. The DNC and HRC retained law firm Perkins Coie to hire both Fusion GPS and cyber firm CrowdStrike to put a lid on developing problems.

Post Q# 3602
How do 'select' bad actors attempt comms w/o SIGINT collection?
Dark - Light.

The personal call-sign code KM4UDZ HAM Radio License is very central to ObamaGate/SpyGate. Nellie "Molly" Ohr [NO] holds that specific HAM Radio identification call-sign as well as that catchy nickname by POTUS. The use of HAM messages and other covert communications is a basic counterintelligence tool employed by trained intelligence agents. The coup plotters knew for certain that all normal communication methods were unsecure considering the vast collection power of the NSA.

Post Q# 1435

Avoid NSA data collection.

It failed.

President Trump reminded everyone in a tweet that her personal HAM radio operator personal handle was "Molly." Nellie Ohr is a key (keystone) person in today's unfolding ObamaGate/SpyGate political scandals. The complex plans involved with just one operation like Crossfire Hurricane and its infamous 'Insurance Policy' demonstrates the length the DC Swamp would go to remove President Trump.

Post Q 4153

[FBI Floor 7] [UK assist] Steele - B_Ohr - N_Oh - FusionGPS [shell 2]

The use of a HAM Radio is a classic counter surveillance method often deployed in spy tradecraft to avoid being monitored. Also bear in mind that 'Lovely' Nellie has been involved on several levels with the CIA in her past. The old 'Q' saying goes "Clowns in America-Once a Clown always a Clown."

Post Q# 1286

Fusion GPS.

The Brits-raw intel/ dossier / 5-Eyes.

Some of Nellie Ohr's foremost characteristics are a big Stalin apologist, fluent in Russian (plus others), Ph.D. in Russian history, former CIA analyst, HAM Radio operator, and Fusion GPS Russian opposition research expert. Fusion GPS's Glenn Simpson and Nellie Ohr are key figures in the entire RussiaGate/SpyGate operations against candidate Donald Trump.

TWEET # T-3726

"Bruce Ohr (and his lovely wife Molly)"

Nellie Ohr originally claimed her employment at Fusion GPS began the Spring of 2016. Records now indicate that Lovely Molly started back in late 2015 working for her old pal Glenn Simpson/Fusion GPS.

Post Q# 1939

BO unlocks UK / F_intel (FVEY).

Lovely Nellie is the theorized partial co-author of the Christopher Steele Trump-Russian Dossier. Ohr's language skills in Russian and her intelligence background, lends credence to her being a major contributing author to Steele's final dossier.

Post Q# 1164

Re-read Five Eyes.

Avoid US data collection laws.

Public: Dossier FISA.

Clinton enforcers Cody Shearer/Sid Blumenthal also claim part authorship of Dossier # 2 (HRC additions). Their work product memos were combined with Steele's research to make the final full Russian Dossier. Cody/Sid received assistance from Victoria Nuland and Jonathan Winer at BHO's State Department.

Post Q# 1891

Texts, emails (gmail), drafts (gmail), HAM comms, PS/Xbox chat logs.

Parts of Bruce Ohr's Congressional testimony confirms he passed Nellie's own research to the FBI. Lovely Molly is credited now with being the co-author of Dossier #3 as well as 'Dossiers' on Paul Manafort and the Trump children.

Post Q# 2158
> Bruce Ohr [in effort to save Nellie Ohr] testifying against Rosenstein, Yates, Lynch and Comey?

Strategically placed at Fusion GPS, Nellie is the beloved wife of DOJ top official Bruce Ohr. Bruce Ohr was the # 4 person at the Department of Justice until being demoted several times and is now actively cooperating to help save wife Nellie's life. Bruce Ohr resigned from the DOJ on 10/14/20, a day before AG Barr was to fire him.

Post Q# 4200
> Proof game 'chat logs' discussion(s)_legitimate?

The Ohr's form part of ever-growing community of Dirty Couples/Husband and Wife criminal teams. To name just a few of the married pairs that were directly connected to ObamaGate/SpyGate: McCabe/Strzok/Pientka/Power-Sunstein/Simpson-Jacoby/Dunn-Bauer/Murray-King/Abedin-Weiner/etc.

Post Q# 2004
> What is the significance of Nellie Ohr being fluent in Russian?

The Ohr's were the main spoke or conduit of the fake Russian-Trump opposition research. This Cabal used 'intelligence laundering' by passing memos between each other. The Christopher Steele Dossier went through the FBI/DOJ and the Sid Blumenthal/Cody Shearer Dossier went through the BHO U.S. State Department.

Post Q# 3126
> Is 'RUSSIAN' a common language to learn?
> [Think Nellie Ohr].

This Dossier flowed in both directions (circular manner) between the Justice and State Departments. Add in MSM reporters then spun around again to Fusion GPS prior to the FBI/DOJ. Special Counsel (SC) John Durham was appointed to investigate criminal referrals from Congress related to the unfolding SpyGate political scandal.

Post Q# 1876
> HAM radio instructions if remote-5?

Direct cash payments and sudden job promotions were given out during this time period. Benefits sprung forth to the active ObamaGate/SpyGate couples as did the economic rewards. The FEC would fine in 2022 HRC's campaign and the DNC for payments to Fusion GPS in their preparation of the false Steele Dossier during the 2016 election cycle.

Post Q# 4853
> Wife: CIA
> Husband: DOJ

All while under the 'marriage clause' concerning future testimony against each other. Convenient how they recruited married couples into this treasonous coup plot against candidate Donald Trump. SC John Durham is also working on many criminal referrals from IG Michael Horowitz related to HRC/DNC/Fusion GPS/and law firm Perkins Coie in the development of the phony Steele Dossier.

Post Q# 3064
> OHR cooperating witness.

One of Nellie's infamous quotes goes "The terror and excitement of the Stalin era is just overwhelming". Spoken like a true Communist and Progressive Leftist core believer. SC Durham's indictment of Perkins Coie/Clinton campaign lawyer Michael Sussmann connects directly back to Lovely Molly and Glenn Simpson's Fusion GPS.

Post Q# 247
> Wife connection?
> What is the pattern?
> Follow the wives.

The Steele Dossier is the central piece of evidence used to start this fake Russia scandal and launch the FBI investigation. Brennan's I.C.A. also used this unverified dossier (also nicknamed 'Crown Material') as pivotal proof of Trump-Russia collusion. SC Durham submitted his final report in 2023. With the historic re-election of President Trump in 2024, past hidden political secrets will finally be revealed.

Post Q# 3065
> NELLIE OHR = C _A?

Links

The Federalist-Did Fusion GPS's Researcher avoid Detection with HAM Radio?

Daily Mail-FBI Secret Declassified Document Reveals Origins of Trump Probe

The Federalist-FBI Revelations Show the Mueller Special Counsel was a Cover-Up

Real Clear Investigations-Ex DOJ Official and Wife had Bigger Roles

John Seaman-Durham Investigation: Answering the 5 W's

Just the News-Trump suing HRC/DNC over Russia Collusion Narrative

Epoch Times-2015 Employment of Nellie Ohr by Fusion GPS raises Questions

Real Clear Politics-RussiaGate: HRC Campaign/Perkins Coie/Fusion GPS/CrowdStrike

The Last Refuge-Nellie and Bruce Ohr

NY Mag-Fusion GPS Lights Candle for the 'Pee Tape'

The Last Refuge-Admiral Rogers/FISA 702

Newsweek-Who is Molly Ohr? Trump Butchers Name

American Spectator-Nellie Ohr: Woman in the Middle

Markets Work-FBI Docs detailing Bruce Ohr Conversations shed Light on SpyGate

Wireless FCC-HAM Radio License # KM4UDZ (Nellie Ohr)

The Last Refuge-Nellie Ohr/Glenn Simpson

The Hill-Nellie Ohr's "Hi Honey" emails to DOJ about Russia should Alarm Us

American Thinker-How Husbands/Wives Figure in Latest Scandal Revelations

Jeff Carlson-Bruce and Nellie Ohr

Epoch Times-Ukrainian Connections in Early Attacks on Trump

The Last Refuge-Origin of Russia Probe

Senate Judiciary Committee: 2021 Crossfire Hurricane DECLAS

Justice.gov-Nellie Ohr/Fusion GPS/and Steele Dossier

Crossfire Hurricane Docs-Nellie Ohr Interview

Justice.gov-2023 SC John Durham Report

U1—Going to Haunt like a "GHOST STORY"

In June 2010 Robert Mueller's FBI rolled up a network of ten Russian spies that were based in the USA. The FBI's "Operation Ghost Stories" was one of the country's biggest and most impactful counterintelligence/foreign spies busts ever. The incredibly scary but true story was made into a hit TV series that ran for 6 successful seasons. President Trump would bring several of the original characters from Ghost Stories (FBI's Bob Mueller/Peter Strzok) back into the limelight with a federal RICO lawsuit over the past SpyGate activities and promoting the false Russian collusion narrative.

Post Q# 1626
> Putin / U1 will connect post summit.
> America for sale.

Future proves past yet again as we discover FBI agent Peter Strzok was on the "Ghost Stories" DOJ's Task Force. This means in essence Peter Strzok began working with Mueller as well assisting HRC way back in 2010. We have been told in the past by 'Q' that the DC Swamp runs deep, and criminal relationships often involve several family members.

Post Q# 3
> It finally came out that Rod/Bob were key players in the Uranium scandal.

HRC wanted this bad espionage news about the '10 Russian Spies' to quickly disappear. Mueller did respond to her request with the deportation of all ten Russian spies over the 2010 Christmas Holiday time period. HRC was concerned with the negative publicity as one of the Russian spies got very close to her.

Post Q# 3858
> THIS REPRESENTS A CLEAR AND PRESENT DANGER TO THE
> CONSTITUTIONAL REPUBLIC OF THE UNITED STATES OF AMERICA.

These true events would mirror in what would be a successful TV series called 'The Americans' on FX. The Americans TV show ran from 2013-18 and garnered decent rating. This actual network of Russian sleeper operatives included two sets of biological family members and a famous model.

Post Q# 2657
> Post public release of CLAS NSA PRO and U1?
> What country was involved with U1?

These highly trained intelligence assets began to target HRC in 2008. One Russian agent poised as an accountant and she in fact got very close to HRC in 2010 by giving large personal donations. According to Cold War experts, this TV drama was fairly realistic in showing undercover KGB agents masquerading as normal American suburbanites.

Post Q# 3915
> THE TRUTH WILL SHOCK THE WORLD.

Regain power by any means necessary.

William "Doug" Campbell is the secret Uranium One (U1) undercover FBI informant that has turned state's evidence. Mr. Campbell gave his testimony to several Congressional committees and to IG Horowitz/SP Huber/SC Durham about the illegal activities surrounding the U1 deal. SC

John Durham's court filings related to his ongoing criminal investigations are slowly unveiling the total rot within the FBI/DOJ as well as other governmental institutions.

Post Q# 1345
U1 [donations to CF].

In addition to the bribery scheme involving U1, Campbell told of the parallel track Russian spy ring trying to compromise then Secretary HRC. Any good operation has vital contingency backup plans that help in overall success and the Russians are professionals at black operations. The goal of infiltrating HRC's political orbit was one of the main purposes of the entire Russian spying operation.

Post Q# 2512
Mueller will face charges re: U1.
He's working to save himself.

Please keep in mind the timeframe of the Obama/Clinton 'Russian Reset' is when these U1/Spy Ring events are occurring. Vladimir Putin had interest in both the Uranium One (cornering the world market) deal as well as the Skolkovo Silicon Valley (Hypersonic Missile) joint technology development project. Both of these Russian operations were designed to funnel off American critical strategic assets.

Post Q# 1345
The 'Exchange.'
U1.
Risk the welfare of the world.

The Clinton Foundation received nearly $145 million in kickback donations (Peter Schweizer's "Clinton Cash") stemming directly from Russian deals surrounding the entire U1 scheme. Canadian Frank Giustra would quarterback the funneling of all of these questionable U1 contributions. Russia seemed to both the boggy man when convenient for the narrative and the piggy bank when needed for funding of Deep State operations.

Post Q# 3836
Think U1 [sale of US uranium to Russia]
Sold out US to benefit Russia for personal financial gain?

Please remember the short $500k Moscow speech given by Bill Clinton. That speech was followed by an in-person meeting with Vlad Putin to solidify this Russian/U1 criminal 'pay-to-play' arrangement. Not often acknowledged is besides U1, Clinton also pushed the Skolkovo project. Special Counsel (SC) John Durham has dropped criminal indictments related to the Clinton Foundation/SpyGate and submitted his final report in 2023.

Post Q# 1306
What if U1 material ended up in Syria?
What does U1 provide?
Uranium to Iran/Syria?
SUM OF ALL FEARS.

Robert Mueller's FBI sentenced/deported the captured Russian spies over the 2010 Christmas holiday to minimize the MSM news coverage. This lot of foreign spies were exchanged for several Americans and one Britain that were being held within Russia. The exchange of captured spies has been a centuries old tradition. Russia's 2022 special military operation into Ukraine would bring back both disinformation operation as well as the Uranium One deal. Hunter Biden's

'Laptop from Hell' would show the public in 2022 the inside of international nepotism corrupt business deals and how they can a direct effect on our national security via 'foreign capture' operations.

Post Q# 4620
> [infiltration]
> Traitors everywhere.
> Welcome to the Revolution.

Incredibly as fate would have it, the one returned double agent back to the U.K. was Sergei Skripal. Skripal and his daughter were poisoned and almost killed by the toxic nerve agent Novichok last year in Salisbury. Skripal was personally connected to Christopher Steele and his infamous Russian dossier. Reports from IG Michael Horowitz and SC John Durham will ultimately bring all of the same characters together when future judicial justice is administered. With the re-election of President Trump in 2024, Vald Putin will play a key role in stabilizing both Uranium as well as Ukraine.

Post Q# 1626
> Putin / U1 will come out post summit.

Links

FX TV Series "The Americans"

Revolver News-Will Patel and Bongino Investigate this Massive FBI Scandal?

Clinton Foundation Timeline-2025 Crossfire Hurricane Docs

CBS News-Operation Ghost Stories: Russian Spies Living among Us

Breitbart-Uranium One: 7 Facts

AP News-Spy Swap: A Look at 4 Russians Freed in 2010

Just the News-The BHO/Biden/HRC Nuclear Giveaway to Russia

The Hill-U1 Informant makes Clinton Allegations

Larry Beech-Uranium One and CrowdStrike

NY Post-Durham Report proves HRC was Putin's Puppet not Trump

CBS News-How the FBI took Down Russian Spies in USA

NPR-Ghost Stories: FBI Releases Documents

Just the News-Russia/Ukraine Scandals: How they have Profited

The Hill-FBI's 37 Secret Page Memo about HRC and U1

The Guardian-The Day we Discovered our Parents were Russian Spies

American Thinker-How much did Mueller/Rosenstein know about Uranium One

LA Times-Russian Spies were Succeeding in 2011

North Jersey-Montclair Sleeper Spies

New Yorker-5 Questions about the Clintons and Uranium One

Daily Caller-HRC Russian Ghost Stories

FBI.gov-Operation Ghost Stories

The Guardian-Anna Chapman: NYC Model and Russian Spy

Web Archive.org-Uranium One Timeline

Justice.gov-President of Transportation Company (Mark Lambert) Found Guilty

Dark Docs-Operation Ghost Stories: Secret FBI Mission to Catch Spies in USA

Badlands Media-The Biggest Cover Up in American History

Crossfire Hurricane Docs-Halper Files

Justice.gov-2023 SC John Durham Report

The Keystone to BHO's PDB was Operation Latitude

The group of ladies that earned the nickname of BHO's "West Wing Power Trio" were Susan Rice/Kathryn Ruemmler/and Lisa Monaco. All gals were very close advisors to BHO and highly instrumental in forging his domestic and foreign policies. Rice and Monaco spearheaded the unmaking requests and Evelyn Farkas passed out intelligence to friendly reporters from BHO's President's Daily Brief (PDB). The PDB is a daily recap prepared by CIA analysts and dates back to the JFK administration. All 3 of these high level BHO gals would return under the illegal Biden administration to continue to wreak havoc in our Republic.

> **Post Q# 1980**
> What if a paper trail exists?
> PDB via No Such Agency.

A secondary less classy nickname given to this power trio was the 'Mod Squad.' Under all the glamour and glitz, lay the foundation for the expanded mass broadcasting of BHO's special orders via the PDB. The BHO administration needed the assistance of the MSM Mockingbird news media to spread the material gleaned from illegal surveillance monitoring. The RussiaGate/SpyGate political scandal would become center stage in 2022 as the various investigations are publicly unveiled.

> **Post Q# 2071**
> WHO ORDERED? [PDB].

Operation Latitude was the deliberate mass dissemination of select coup information via BHO's PDB. Often scandalous unconfirmed intelligence, raw FISA 702 data, and unmasked names were routinely included in BHO's PDB. Personal conversations we unmasked involving individuals in Trump World and then released to the media in hopes of damaging reputations.

> **Post Q# 4646**
> Nothing [digital] is ever really lost.

Purposely inserted into the PDB was opposition research derived from the Christopher Steele Dossier. Also included was information captured by NSA FISA 702 'about queries' searches using upstream capture filters. The abuse of the NSA data base by private outside contractors is illegal under current surveillance laws.

> **Post Q# 2128**
> PDB REGULAR UPDATE + [LIVE STREAMING] WH HUSSEIN NON-OVAL [SITUATION ROOM] COORDINATION FISA [FULL] BRINGS DOWN THE HOUSE [WH].

Admiral Mike Rogers stopped outside contractors like Fusion GPS and CrowdStrike from having full access to raw FISA 702 intel data. The direct result of this shutdown was the start of human assets being placed within Trump World and launching Crossfire Hurricane/SpyGate.

> **Post Q# 1943**
> How would updates occur?

The quarterback of spreading out the 'dirt' on candidate Trump via the PDB was Lisa Monaco. Lisa Monica was a DHS Official assigned to the White House. BHO began holding secret White House basement meetings in July 2016 concerning operation Crossfire Hurricane. History would later reveal that Lisa Monaco would be involved in Biden's AutoPen scandal.

Post Q# 1991
    Ms. Ugoretz oversaw intelligence products and briefings for the FBI Director and the
    Attorney General, as well as FBI analysts' contributions to the President's Daily Brief."

Lisa Monaco made sure all the 'Secret Society' members were included into this special
intelligence loop. Minor DOD official Evelyn Farkas would in turn leak the PDF information to
her various Mockingbird media allies. Monaco was BHO's Homeland Security and
Counterterrorism expert with emphasis on Syria. Lisa Monaco is now Biden's Deputy Attorney
General (DAG) serving under wacky Merrick Garland. DAG Monaco would come under her own
criminal investigation over her use of pseudonymous email account related to the Jan. 6th events.

Post Q# 1944
    Who has access to the PDB?

A prime example of the extended reach of this bogus information was displayed with Dr. Evelyn
Farkas. The distribution channel was over 50 individuals, where in past administrations only a
handful ever had access to the ultra-top-secret PDB.

Post Q# 559
    HUSSEIN CABINET/STAFF.
    Who used private email addresses?
    What was the purpose?

Dr. Farkas famously bragged on MSNBC as to the existence on this network within the BHO
government. Evelyn Farkas let the cat out of the bag about that BHO White House authorized
surveillance efforts against candidate Trump.

The four main components of the coup plot nicknamed Operation Trump:
* Exonerate HRC/Aides (ObamaGate)
* Fake Trump-Russia Dossier creation/distribution (RussiaGate)
* FISA Title-1 Surveillance Warrants/Section 702 (SpyGate)
* The 'Insurance Policy' (Crossfire Hurricane)

Post Q# 3246
    [No Name] [Media - [JB] [JC] Leaks - POTUS Daily Brief/FBI]

Evelyn Farkas had a key strategic purpose being included in the BHO PDB loop. Besides Farkas's
many media contacts, she had several Congressional insider friends up on the 'Hill.' History will
show the elaborate coup plot against candidate Donald Trump that was nicknamed SpyGate.
President Trump would file in 2022 a federal RICO lawsuit against those who promoted the false
Russian collusion narrative during the 2016 election cycle.

Post Q# 1912
    "Concerned dedicated resources in-place are not adequate to shelter against the PDB in
    which several agencies contribute...."

Under BHO the previously top secret and compartmentalized PDB was now spread out to over
three dozen administration officials. The 'Secret Society' could be kept up to date on the big
picture without having to assemble as one group and risk operational exposure. Plausible
deniability is the unspoken order given to protect the top ringleaders of this coup plot.

Post Q# 4153
    [NO NAME ASSIST [SENATOR STAMP _credible] _FBI Floor 7 _DNI _POTUS
    PDB]

Rounding out BHO's Mod Squad are former Ambassador Susan Rice/NSA Director and lawyer Kathryn Ruemmler, who was the White House Counsel. This group scarily was nicknamed around the White House as BHO's 'Muses.' Lisa Monaco is now Biden's DAG and Susan Rice runs Domestic Policy at the White House (Shadow President).

Post Q# 436
> [FISA 2]. PRES DAILY B

Valerie Jarrett [VJ] oversaw this Muse Mod Squad supervisory wise and along with Samantha Power (Unmasker), you have all of BHO's power-mad crazed muses! This core cabal of gals really were the gatekeepers of BHO's domestic and foreign policy.

Post Q# 3815
> They will not be able to walk down the street.
> THE GREAT AWAKENING.

With the mass distribution of the PDB and coordinated leaks to MSM, you have the backbone of the entire Operation Latitude. BHO used the White House PEOC bunker for several in-person "Trump" strategy briefings with his co-conspirators. It was revealed in 2024 that the US Intel community requested its FIVE EYES (FVEY) foreign partners to illegally spy upon targeted Team Donald Trump aides back in 2016 setting up RussiaGate.

Post Q# 1990
> Who inserts the discovery into the PDB?

Special Counsel John Durham has dropped criminal indictments related to SpyGate and submitted his final report in 2023. False opposition research combined with illegal surveillance of candidate Donald Trump was the origin of SpyGate. The overall treasonous coup plot against President Trump is now being uncovered slowly through public disclosures. With the re-election of President Trump in 2024, he will lead us all to walk through the darkness.

Post Q# 120
> Why is the NSA limited re: ability to capture and unmask US persons?
> Who cannot violate this rule?

Links

Politico-BHO's West Wing Power Trio

The Federalist-Declassified Docs Further Implicate BHO in Russia Hoax

FOX News-BHO's Cronies created Trump Russia Hoax

Tore Says-Through the Memory Hole: Lisa Monaco from FISA Files to Epstein

The Last Refuge-Original BHO and HRC 2008 Agreement

Sharyl Attkisson-BHO Era Surveillance Timeline

NY Post-No ObamaGate is Not a Conspiracy Theory

Daily Caller-Deputy AG involved Investigation Allegedly using Pseudonymous Email Address

The Hill-Lisa Monaco is BHO's Key Player on Syria

American Spectator-The Scandal Obama still won't Acknowledge

Observer-All the President's Muses

The War Economy-Lisa Monaco

Law and Crime-Lisa Monaco: What to Know

Daily Caller-Swamp Reunion: BHO's 3 Muses Reappear

The Last Refuge-The Susan Rice Memo

The War Economy-SpyFall

National Review-5 more Things about Susan Rice

Jeff Carlson-Operation Latitude/Unmasking

The Federalist-8 Times U.S. Intelligence Set People Up to Fabricate the Russia Story

The Last Refuge-FISA 702 Searches

Epoch Times-SpyGate: The True Story of Collusion

DNI.gov-BHO Executive Order 12333-Raw SIGINET Procedures

Justice.gov-Lisa Monaco Remarks at Chatham House

Crossfire Hurricane Docs-Christopher Steele Binder

Justice.gov-2023 SC John Durham Report

FISA's Russian Agent: Meet Carter (UCE) Page

Claimed publicly as an 'Agent of a Foreign Power', meet FBI's Undercover Confidential Employee (UCE) Carter Page. The DOJ/FBI secured the first of four highly unusual FISA Title-1 surveillance spy warrants on Carter Page in October 2016. Carter Page and former British spy Christopher Steele would become household names via the infamous dossier. President Trump would file in 2022 a federal RCIO lawsuit against many of the SpyGate related officials that promoted the false Russian collusion narrative.

Post Q# 2129
> USE OF BACKCHANNEL SURV / SPY INSERTION [BODY 1, 2, AND 5] BY UK/AUS [PRIMARY].

Carter Page is accused by the DOJ/FBI of being a foreign Russian intelligence spy. This was the sole basis for the FISA warrant foundational claim as part of the fake Christopher Steele Trump-Russia Dossier. Factual committed crimes need to be the basis upon any FISA inquiry should normally be based upon. HRC's created 2016 Russia Dossier was the setup BHO needed to launch the next phase against Donald Trump including FisaGate and Crossfire Hurricane.

Post Q# 1928
> [Movie 1]
> When did [RR] learn of involvement [BO] [NO]?
> What happens if [RR] knew PRIOR TO signing CP FISA?

THE FOUR COUP PLOT ELEMENTS:
- Exonerate HRC and Related Aides (ObamaGate)
- Dossier Collect/Redistribute 'Oppo Research' (RussiaGate)
- FISA Title-1 Surveillance of Carter Page (SpyGate)
- Insurance Policy (Crossfire Hurricane)

Post Q# 4096
> "Information warfare."
> Imagine that.

Entering into this picture of political espionage is UCE # 1 aka Carter Page. Carter Page is an ex-Navy and an energy Industry consultant with extensive business connections within Russia and other neighboring countries. To be a usual tool or plant for this coup operation, Page needed to have legitimate real life Russian business connections. The DOJ began in 2016 a surveillance operation called Crossfire Razor as part of the overall SpyGate coup plot.

Post Q# 1164
> Not Public: Five Eyes UK/AUS POTUS targeting using pushed RUS decoy meetings / campaign insertions.

Page would end up being an unpaid adviser on the Trump Campaign Foreign Policy board in 2016. I believe Carter Page was a targeted plant regardless of the final GOP nominee, due to his foreign credentials and prior working relations with the U.S. Government (CIA and FBI). HRC/DNC would attempt the fake Alfa Bank server in Trump Tower hoax before starting Crossfire Hurricane that would involve Carter Page.

Post Q# 1589
> FISA.
> ABUSE OF EXEC POWER.
> ILLEGAL SPYING.
> FRAME.
> INSERT ASSETS.

Funny how the FBI had first described Carter Page back in March 2016 as a past employee. Then by October 2016, the FBI told the FISA Court (FISC) that Page was now a Russian spy and required the issuance of one of the highest levels of surveillance possible. Having both the CIA and FBI in your resume history points to bring a longtime governmental informant.

Post Q# 1508
> Plants need water.

Carter Page first started to work with the FBI back in 2013. Page had been described as an Undercover Confident Informant (UCE) on the DOJ payroll. Another similar FBI term when referring to paid assistants is a Confidential Human Source (CHS). Law firm Perkins Coie was retained by HRC/DNC to foster the Russian collusion false narrative against candidate Trump. Perkins Coie hired Fusion GPS/Nellie Ohr to work with British spy Christopher Steele to 'create' a fake dossier concerning Donald Trump which featured campaign aide Carter Page.

Post Q# 1910
> Who signed the CP FISA?

Per IG Michael Horowitz's 2.0 report, Page told one FBI CHS in October 2016, that "He had an 'open checkbox' from certain Russians to fund a think tank project." With Page's past connections to Russia, these were the primary elements used by the DOJ/FBI to justify the FISA warrants.

Post Q# 3603
> FISA goes both ways.
> Information warfare.

Carter Page helped to break-up oddly enough a large network of Russian intelligence agents based in NY City. The Deep State kept an eye on Page and in 2016 decided he was useful to their efforts once again. Page's work history with the CIA has been scrubbed from the public internet. Ultimately it would be the New York FBI Field Office in conjunction with the DOJ Southern District New York that first open 'Russian' probes against newly appointed Trump campaign energy adviser Carter Page.

> Post Q# 3621
> Spy_insert(s)?
> Puppets have masters.

The first of these Russian spies Evgeny Buryakowhich confessed and plead guilty on 3/11/16. This espionage case was broken thanks to the dutifully help of the FBI's UCE-1/Carter Page. Today Special Counsel (SC) John Durham is spearing the criminal referrals from IG Michael Horowitz concerning SpyGate scandal.

Post Q# 553
> What must we LEGALLY demonstrate in order to gain such warrants?
> FISA?

It appears that Carter Page went onto yet another assignment for his bosses at the DOJ/FBI. History will tell if Page was duped while over in London or was he a paid plant. 'Q' has pointed to Carter Page as being just one of several individuals inserted into Trump World as plants.

Post Q# 3966

FISA lead-in [stage 1 act 1]

The DOJ/FBI Trump-Russia probe officially began on July 31, 2016. The specific reasons required by the DOJ to launch this investigation never existed for a credible predication. In retrospect an overhead bar conversation does not normal meet the high threshold by the FBI to being an official foreign counterintelligence operation.

Post Q# 3178

ILLEGAL MANUFACTURED EFFORT [ATTEMPTED COUP] TO TAKE DOWN THE PRESIDENT OF THE UNITED STATES.

Paid intelligence assets like spies and LURES were inserted much earlier than false FBI start date of 7/31/16. Elements of the infamous Operation Crossfire Hurricane goes back to at last the Winter of 2016. Just as in any ultra complex Deep State operation like JFK or 9/11, years of detailed planning is involved. It was revealed in 2024 that the US Intel community requested from its FIVE EYES partners to illegally spy upon selected Team Donald Trump aides like Carter Page back in 2016.

Post Q# 1008

Why is Mueller going after inside plants?

Shady meetings were originated by Stefan Halper and Joseph Mifsud for Carter Page and campaigning co-chair Sam Clovis in the Summer of 2016. These both occurred within a few months of the infamous George Papadopoulos London Pub Crawl also organized by Halper/Mifsud. Again talk in a public pub never holds sway in a court of law let alone qualify for the grounds of a DOJ criminal investigation. Evidence in 2023 would show that Ambassador Downer never told US authorities that 'HRC email Dirt' was discussed by Papadopoulos in the English pub.

Post Q# 2176

PANIC IN DC.

With the Carter Page warrants in place by the corrupt FISA Court (FISC), the Title-1 FISA could allow for the HOPS in communication chains. Title-1 allowed the total surveillance and record culling for all of Trump World lawfully via these illegally obtained warrants. The DOJ/FBI officials are required by law to present truthful and highly vetted information to the FISC. Fired FBI Andy McCabe admitted in 2024 that the FBI made many mistakes in the Trump/Carter Page FISA scandal.

Post Q# 3337

Important to remember.
Page public.
Remainder are still classified.
+Cruz.

Title-1 FISA warrants allow for a total of 2 HOPS of communications between individuals. This means the person you called plus two people they call are all covered under this umbrella-like blanket total surveillance. When using a Five Eyes (FVEY) intelligence sharing partner like the

United Kingdom, they allow for one more additional HOP making 3 total comms jumps permitted. The DOJ would later admit it lacked probable cause in the four FISA warrants issued against Carter Page.

Post Q# 1008
> Carter Page was a plant.
> Trace background.

Both of IG Michael Horowitz's two previous reports have lead to criminal investigations tasked to Special Counsel (SC) John Durham. SC Durham has gotten a guilty plea from FBI lawyer Kevin Clinesmith specifically for alterations with Page's FISA and indicated Perkins Coie/Clinton campaign lawyer Michael Sussmann. SC Durham submitted his final report in 2023. With the re-election of President Trump in 2024, the 'Storm' has arrived that will trigger Judgement Day and will usher in the Great Awakening to the entire world.

Post Q# 3595
> C_A HUMINT domestic placement - T campaign.

Links

National Review-Carter Page FISA-FBI Relied on the Unverified Steele Dossier

Grassley.Senate.gov-DOJ Admitted it Lacked Probable Cause in Carter Page FISAs

American Thinker-FBI Confirms Nellie Ohr Lied to Congress

The Federalist-Durham Report Reveals FBI Vendetta against Carter Page

Real Clear Investigations-Cater Page's FBI Timeline

Tablet Magazine-FISA's License to HOP

Sharyl Attkisson-Being Carter Page

Just the News-FBI's Arctic Haze

Sharyl Attkisson-BHO Era Surveillance Timeline

Front Page Mag-BHO used HRC's Dossier to Spy on Trump

The Last Refuge-Carter Page and Bill Priestap

Washington Examiner-Timeline: The Carter Page FISA

The Last Refuge-Carter Page FISA/Gang of 8

Markets Work-FBI Testimony on Cater Page FISA Reveal Broken System

Judicial Watch-DOJ Discloses no FISA Court Hearings on Carter Page Warrants

Epoch Times-SpyGate: The Inside Story

The Hill-London Bridges Falling Down

The Last Refuge-SpyGate: The Big Story

Markets Work-FISA Title One Surveillance Warrants

Justice.gov-Review of Four FISA Applications

Senate Judiciary.gov-Declassified Docs undercut Steele Dossier/Page FISA Warrants

Scribd-June 2020 FISA Opinion (4 x Carter Page)

OIG.Justice.gov-DOJ OIG FISA Report

Mysterious White Hat Simply Known as Kash

Post Q# 4933
> Watergate x 1000.

Kashyap (Kash) Pramod Patel was on President Trump's National Security Council (NSC) and was Chief of Staff to acting Secretary of Defense Chris Miller. Kash has dutifully served as a top aide to both Representative Devin Nunes and acting Director of National Intelligence (DNI) Richard Grenell. Born and raised in New York, the Patel family originally is of Gujarati background from India. As we suffer under the illegal Biden regime and await the return of President Trump, Kash has started a successful podcast called "Kash's Corner" in conjunction with the Epoch Times.

Post Q# 1481
> Kashyap Patel - name to remember.

Kash's SpyGate role became public on 3/21/17 with the infamous adventures of the Team Nunes Posse into the basement of the White House. In the lower levels of the White House is a very secure Sensitive Compartmentalized Information Facility (SKIF) that holds top secret classified documents. Devin Nunes and Kash were let into this SKIF by NSC Ezra Cohen-Watnick (FlynnStone member) and White House lawyer Michael Ellis. The past illegal surveillance and unmasking of Team Trump officials were just some of the information shown to Nunes/Patel in this dungeon exploring adventure.

Post Q# 3993
> Think NUNES memo v SHIFF.

With Kash at his side, Representative Nunes held a press conference on March 23, 2017, to outline some of the 'incidental spying' done against the Trump campaign by the BHO administration. Nunes then headed various Congressional committee investigations into the developing SpyGate scandal and Kash was the lead investigator into these official probes. Currently Special Counsel (SC) John Durham is revealing via criminal indictments the entire scope of the illegal surveillance and unmasking of Trump World by BHO and HRC.

Post Q# 1125
> What was just released to Nunes?

The House Permanent Select Committee on Intelligence (HPSCI) in early 2018, chaired by Nunes, released a four-page memo outlining surveillance abuses by the FBI. Nunes would follow up his infamous memo with 14 different criminal referrals over to the DOJ. Kash was lead investigator for the HPSCI and personally conducted many of the sworn depositions of the main SpyGate culprits.

Post Q# 2462
> Who briefed NUNES on classified Intel?

Kash Patel served on President Trump's NSC alongside dungeon explorers Ezra and Ellis. Towards the end of President Trump's first term, Kash was assigned to be Chief of Staff to acting Secretary of Defense Miller. Hints by 'Q' and the fine work by Patel Patriot have led many to look at the possibility of Continuation of Government plan put into motion by President Trump after the 2020 election steal. Integral to this secret plan to say our Republic, is the loyalty factor placed upon trusted individuals such as Kash Patel.

Post Q# 3539
> Attempts by D's to prevent disclosure of FVEY material (re: Nunes non_official ways) was DENIED.

President Trump asked Kash to serve as senior adviser to Ambassador Richard Grenell, who was appointed acting DNI in early 2020. The DNI heads all 17 branches of the different individual branches of our entire government. The 'White Hats' would be considered the Patriots fighting alongside Donald Trump in this global conflict against the New World Order (Deep State). Patel Patriot's excellent Devolution series highlight the critical role that Kash would continue to play post President Trump's first term. Kash Patel would join with Devin Nunes in launching President Trump's new social media platform TruthSocial in 2022. Many believe that Kash Patel will play a big role in the next Trump administration and Kash has publicly stated a top priority will be to go after judicially the corrupt 'Government Gangsters' and their compliant corporate news media co-conspirators.

Post Q# 4738
> Spying [surveillance + campaign insert(s) + W/H insert(s)].

Spying conducted against any sitting President of the United States is an issue of the utmost national security concerns. Kash Patel and friends have been singular focused upon getting out to the American public all of the treasonous details surrounding the 'Plot against the President' (SpyGate). Kash Patel has repeatedly said in various news media interviews that "John Durham has trapped the all", referring to the RICO-type filings made to the court. IG Michael Horowitz revealed in 2024 that the DOJ spied on US House staffers like Kash Patel that we're investigating the Crossfire Hurricane political scandal.

Post Q# 2938
> Think Nunes' statement "not through normal collection, gathering, and reporting/oversight (re: FVEY)."

SC Durham has dropped criminal indictments directly related to the prior criminal referrals made by Nunes/Kash and submitted his final report in 2023. The shocking public revelations confirming illegal spying committed against candidate and then President Trump, have validated the claims of a treasonous coup plot. Kash Patel would file in 2023 a $23 million lawsuit against Politico for defamintation over RussiaGate coverage. RussiaGate/SpyGate will historically rate a thousand-fold more serious than those related to WaterGate. The Great Awakening is upon the entire world and Patriots such as Kash Patel, confirmed as the new FBI Director under Trump 2.0, will long be considered to be part the 'White Hats' Patriot heroes.

Post Q# 3898
> The key that opens all doors.
> The 'Start.'

Links

AP News-Trump Loyalist Kash Patel Confirmed as FBI Director

FOX News-Patel found Thousands of Sensitive Trump Russia Probe Docs

Breitbart-DOJ obtained Email/Phone Data of Kash Patel

Wired-Kash Patel: The Hero QAnon has been Waiting For

The Federalist-NYT still Refuses to Admit Kash Patel was Right about RussiaGate

PJ Media-DOJ Spied on Incoming FBI Director Kash Patel

AFP-Kash Patel: Trump's FBI Pick is QAnon's 'Name to Remember'

Just the News-DOJ Spied on Congress that was Probing Crossfire Hurricane

Media Matters-Nunes/Patel Appealed to QAnon to Build TruthSocial

The Federalist-SpyGate 101: A Primer on the Russia Collusion Hoax

Dauntless Dialogue-DEVOLVED: A New Cold War

Independent Sentential-Kash Patel interviews DJT

The Federalist-Kash Patel: A Trump Staffer who Exposed the Russia Hoax

Washington Examiner-Durham preparing 'Well-Laid Out' Conspiracy Charges

Real Clear Politics-Kash: All Roads led to FBI McCabe/Strzok

The Atlantic-Full Text of the Nunes Memo

Daily Beast-Kash Patel gets Senior White House Security Job

Western Journal-Film reveals Key Role one Man Played

Fight with Kash-Richard Grenell on John Durham Probe

American Thought Leader-Kash Patel: Inside Story of SpyGate

Crossfire Hurricane Docs-Christopher Steele Binder

Justice.gov-2023 SC John Durham Report

Sneaky Deplorable PEPE the Frog—Ever Lurking

Voted in some polls as the most influential figure of 2016, was our hilarious pal Pepe the Frog. The Deplorables and 'Q' Army of 2020, will be calling once again for the return of our good luck campaign mascot Pepe the Frog. The creator of Pepe the Frog Matt Furie launched non-fungible token (NFT) in 2021 based upon the continued popularity of his famed meme. Pepe the Frog would remain in headline news in 2023 as Elon Musk would send out a tweet of a Pepe meme on his 'X' social media platform.

> **Post Q# 2857**
> Pepe is proud and has never been more popular.

The character of Pepe the Frog has long been the mascot of the Anons from the Chan Boards and millions of memes have flowed featuring lovable Pepe. Pepe's last confirmed public appearance was during the Hillary Clinton and Huma Abedin vacation trip to India in 2018. Pepe interrupted these girls international shopping spree, when he accidentally tripped HRC while she was descending a large Indian staircase.

> **Post Q# 3876**
> Thank you, Baker(s)!
> THE BEST IS YET TO COME!

That little green Trickster almost caused HRC to take a tumble and the funny memes of this event flowed throughout the web. Rumor has it but still yet unconfirmed, that Pepe was next spotted in Canada around the 2019 G7 gathering, causing some 'Tredeau' shenanigans.

> **Post Q# 2599**
> PEPE THE BAKER?
> Think POTUS Tweet re: PEPE.
> Trolling the FAKE NEWS media is SO MUCH FUN!

Always the cleaver little trickster, Pepe was intent on making a dramatic point during these Canadian festivities. Several memes showed Pepe lurking about as if on the prowl for good old fashion entertainment. History will show the strategic successful victory of the Anons in the intense meme warfare that transpired in both the 2016 and 2020 election cycles.

> **Post Q# 3971**
> .....and frogs to destroy them.

No pictures exist (hint to Anon meme makers), but Pepe was observed spraying some type of solvent into the air during the Canadian G7 Summit. Attention on deck to our outstanding Anons, in remembering to keep Pepe our classic mascot, out in the forefront of action in this final meme war.

> **Post Q# 4964**
> Beware of false prophets.
> We are not prophets.
> Focus on the mission.

This secret aerosol spray was known to dissolve glue and other types of adhesives in the application of fake eyebrows. Restrained laugher broke out through the crowd of dignitaries, as Trudeau's eyebrow slowly slide out of place down the side of his face. Protesters from Hong Kong to the France yellow vest crowds have all supported Pepe the Frog. The 'Meme Wars' will long be remembered by Anons as well as historians. Additionally history will show that Pepe the Frog remained a political focal point into Trump 2.0.

Post Q# 4211
> We are ready to unleash hell.
> Memes ready?

Pepe was born on 4chan out of an ancient Egyptian prophecy and became the beloved mascot of the MAGA movement. We need the return of Pepe to spearhead the counterattack informational warfare against the Deep State. Special Counsel John Durham has dropped criminal indictments related to SpyGate and submitted his final report in 2023. President Trump/Team 'Q'/and the faithful Anons are behind Pepe's until the bitter end of this epic struggle. The re-election of President Trump in 2024, Pepe/Anons will continue to support the MAGA agenda.

Post Q# 2599
> Anon to Q: I SEE a FROG.
> 'Q' answered: Confirmed.

Links

Daily Beast-Pepe the Deplorable

USA Today-Trump and Pepe the Frog: 2016 Campaign turned Meme Political

Palm Beach Post-Pepe the Frog and Trump's Truth Social

Latin Times-Trump Sneaks Alt Right Easter Egg into Truth Social Meme

Yahoo Finance-Pepe hits Record High

Deadline-Elon Musk Tweets about Pepe the Frog

NY Times-Extremist Signs/Symbols at Capitol Riot

The Conservation-Ancient Egyptian God Spurred the Rise of Trump

Deplorable Gary-Paying Tribute to Pepe (video)

Bit Coin News-Pepe the Frog Creator launches NFT

NY Times-Decoding the Far-Right Symbols

Snopes-QAnon still Thrives on Facebook

Forbes-Full Tale of Pepe's Journey from Cartoon to Racist Icon

SCMP-How Pepe the Frog Became the Face of Hong Kong Protests

The Atlantic-It's Not Easy Being "MEME"

The Federalist-35 Key People involved with Russia Hoax

The Truth about Pepe the Frog and the Cult of Kek

Daily Mail-Pepe Creator sues InfoWar

BuzzFeed-The Pepe the Frog Store Fractured

AP News-Judge Refuses to Toss Lawsuit over Pepe the Frog

Odyssey-Top 10 Memes: HRC Point of No Return

Wired-Pepe the Frog Foretold the World of Modern Memes

Perkins Coie: Providing Deep State Lawyers and Legal Cover

Perkins Coie law firm is headquartered in Seattle/WA with 14 regional offices nationwide. Three of Perkins Coie's prior partners of interest in regards to SpyGate/ObamaGate are Robert Bauer/Michael Sussmann/and Marc Elias. Robert Bauer caught everyone off guard with his retirement from Perkins Coie top leadership in 2020. Oddly Marc Elias resigned soon afterwards on 8/23/21 from Perkins Coie just in advance of Special Counsel (SC) John Durham's indictment of fellow lawyer Michael Sussmann on 9/16/21. President Donald Trump would begin to seek legal recourse by filing a federal RICO lawsuit in 2022 against Perkins Coie/HRC/DNC/and others related to the ever unfolding SpyGate political scandal revelations.

> **Post Q# 436**
> HRC CAMP PAY
> DNC PAY
> CLAS: 1-4 PAY
> STEELE.

All three noted Perkins Coie lawyers have long histories of bailing out very high-profile Democrats who get into legal trouble and various political scandals. The Clintons and BHO have had ongoing legal working relationships with infamous law firm of Perkins Coie. The DC Swamp has relied upon shady law firms like Perkins Coie time and time again for legal rescue from various political scandals. SC Durham would slowly unveil in 2002 court filing a vast 'Joint Venture Conspiracy' involving both government officials as well as outside private contractors (lawyers). Michael Sussmann would receive a not guilty verdict in his DC trial, but this case unveiled HRC's direct involvement in RussiaGate as well as the Perkins Coie maintained FBI workspace/computer portal facility at their DC office complex.

> **Post Q# 2331**
> [Part re: Fusion GPS, Perkins Coie now being revealed].
> "Former FBI general counsel James Baker met during the 2016 season with at least one attorney from Perkins Coie, the Democratic National Committee's private law firm."

Mark Elias goes back to Slick Willy and then on through representing the DNC/HRC in 2016 as the Presidential campaign's General Counsel. Bob Bauer was BHO's White House Counsel as well as one of his main personal lawyers. Bauer would go on to organize for Perkins a special political legal division of the law firm. SC John Durham is said to be filing a criminal indictment against Michael Sussmann for lying to the FBI in 2016.

> **Post Q# 3718**
> Durham discoveries can lead to early retirement[?]

Michael Sussman's good buddy is Shawn Henry, who coincidentally is the President of CrowdStrike and the DNC email leak probe. Sussman also had contacts with FBI lawyer James Baker regarding Christopher Steele's infamous Trump-Russia dossier. The assistance of several Perkins Coie lawyers was directly involved with the entire SpyGate plot.

> **Post Q# 3858**
> Control of the narrative = power.
> THIS REPRESENTS A CLEAR AND PRESENT DANGER TO THE
> CONSTITUTIONAL REPUBLIC OF THE UNITED STATES OF AMERICA.

Perkins Coie had partner Robert Bauer form a brand new Political Legal Division recruited from trusted Deep State lawyers. Bauer would become BHO's White House Counsel and the keeper of the secrets. Robert Bauer oversaw many of the BHO scandals and provided legal cover throughout this time period. Bauer would be brought into the national spotlight again in 2023 representing Biden in his classified (SCI level) documents scandal.

Post Q# 4153
[FBI Floor 7] James Baker - Perkins Coie [shell 2]

Robert Bauer would bring over in time several other BHO staffers to fill out this new political legal division. Don't forget about Bob's dear wife Anita Dunn, who is credited with getting Joe Biden the 2020 so-called victory. Anita Dunn was BHO's White House Communications Director and a pivotal inside source for the Deep State coup plotters while returning to assist the Biden administration. History will show that Bauer and Dunn would be neck deep in the Biden 'Autopen' scandal as well as assisting BHO in his 3rd term shadow Presidency.

Post Q# 1959
China hacked HRC server?
Access was granted.

This married corrupt pair joins the likes of McCabe's/Strzok's/Ohr's/Pientka's/Priestap's and other 'Dirty Couples' connected to the ObamaGate/SpyGate scandals. It is incredible the criminal element that has driven these betraying couples. We can see the generational element with these criminal families clearly with the public actions of Hunter Biden, Chelsea Clinton, and Chris Heinz.

Post Q# 1510
Why are Hussein records sealed?

Perkins Coie law firm has become involved with four main political scandals and they seem to be somewhat related. Perkins Coie indirectly paid for legal services on behalf of the HRC campaign to foreign sources for the Trump opposition research and was ultimately fined by the FEC over this action.

Post Q# 3621
Puppets have masters.

Several Russians were directly being paid for information gathered through Christopher Steele. These foreign payments are specifically not allowed under U.S. Presidential Campaign Law. FOIA requests have turned up FBI emails confirming that Perkins Coie had a copy of murdered DNC staffer Seth Rich's laptop.

Post Q# 436
[DNC BREACH / DOSSIER].
CROWDSTRIKE.

FIRST Perkins Coie goes back to the "Birth Certificate" authenticity of BHO's. In response to many serious questions about the existence of a Hawaiian original certificate, a long-form copy was finally put up on the W/H website.

Sheriff Joe Arpaio and his Cold Case Posse questioned the validity of this long-form copy. New forensic evidence produced in January 2018 calls the 'copy' into question. Mike Zullo from CCP discovered 9-points of fraud from this false long-form birth certificate.

History will reflect that longtime Clinton operative Sid Blumenthal first floated the BHO birther issue and not by citizen Donald Trump as has been attempted to falsely portray. HRC would highlight this claim during the contested 2016 Democratic Presidential primary campaign.

SECOND was the hiring on 4/12/16 of Fusion GPS with funds from both the DNC and HRC Campaign. Also, additional funds from BHO would be included. The mission this time was to find incriminating data/opposition research on then candidate Donald Trump. Perkins lawyer Marc Elias was neck deep in the Steele dossier and pushed to include the infamous Russian hotel 'Pee Pee Tape' false memo as part of the final opposition research work product.

Post Q# 4130
Advocating overthrow of Government?

Perkins Coie attorney Michael Sussman has direct contact with FBI James Baker. James Baker has testified that he gave Trump-Russia Dossier material to Sussman prior to the official start of the Trump-Russia investigation.

The phony Alfa Bank wiretap accusations of Russians at Trump Tower would characterize this clown show. Sussmann additionally pawned the false Alfa Bank tale to the CIA and brought the agency's top lawyer Caroline Krass into this hoax. The Alfa Bank nonstarter leads to the SpyGate portion of this coup plot.

THIRD is an older story but has recent value-Future Proves Past. BHO had hired Fusion GPS back in 2012 to dig up dirt on then candidate Mitt Romney. Strange how these cycles keep repeating and with the same crooked cast of criminals are always at the center.

The Deep State rewards those outside private companies that have proven to be beneficial with continued business. Perkins Coie is emblematic of a high-powered law firm knowingly provide legal assistance in RICO type criminal endeavors.

FOURTH was in late April 2016 when Perkins Coie hired CrowdStrike to inspect the DNC's computer server suspected of a breach. Perkins lawyer Michael Sussmann and Skippy Podesta thought CrowdStrike better than the FBI to handle inquiry. Per FOIA, FBI emails confirm that Perkins Coie had a copy of Seth Rich's laptop.

The DNC computer intrusion breach and subsequent fake findings by CrowdStrike of Russian origin, is the foundational event that triggered the Trump-Russia false narrative. The DNC intrusion operation follows out of the failed attempt with the Alfa Bank hoax story about Russian servers at Trump Tower.

Post Q# 3990
FBI CHAIN OF COMMAND DNC HACK? [CIA BRIDGE - UKRAINE - CROWDSTRIKE_BRENNAN]?

We all remember the Russian Fancy/Cozy Bear fantasy hackers were to blame and not an internal leak of the DNC emails. Eric Schmidt/Google invested over $100 million into the development of CrowdStrike in 2015. From one corrupt political deal to another, cleaver attorneys are required for legal cover with the exception for criminal activity involving said cleaver lawyers.

Post Q# 1008
No "direct" investigation into DNC computer/software?

Former FBI lawyer James Baker had testified that Perkins Coie/Clinton campaign lawyer Michael Sussmann gave him the FBI phony Alfa Bank collusion allegations. These false accusations involved a Russian bank located at Trump Towers/NYC and lead to the early development of the collusion narrative. Special Counsel (SC) Durham has indicated Sussmann, and this connects directly to HRC, DNC, and Google/Alphabet.

Post Q# 1866
Why did POTUS move his entire operation out of TT the DAY AFTER the ADM ROGERS [SCIF] MEETING?

Robert Bauer suddenly resigned from Perkins Coie in 2020 after many years of service. There seems to be no end to the tangled spider web of political corruption and direct connections to the failed coup attempt. With the 2021 resignation now by Marc Elais and conviction of Sussmann, a bizarre pattern seems to be developing over at Perkins Coie. The DNC would publicly part ways with Marc Elias in 2023 only to be once again rehired as head campaign lawyer, this time by the 2024 Kamala Harris for President crew.

Post Q# 2331
[Part re: Fusion GPS, Perkins Coie now being revealed?].

Exposure of long-time Deep State connections are found within this ObamaGate/SpyGate scandal. The SpyGate story continues SC John Durham has submitted his final report in 2023. Late in 2022 Elon Musk would call out Perkins Coie/Michael Sussmann for an "Attempt to corrupt a Presidential election." The FEC would fine the 2016 HRC Campaign in 2022 for improper payments to Perkins Coie concerning the infamous Steele Dossier. With the re-election of President Trump in 2024, Marc Elias vows to continue the fight in the upcoming 2026/28 election cycles. President Trump would pull the security clearances in March 2015 from Perkins Coie due to national security risks.

Post Q# 2369
Baker Testimony - House [what was learned]? [D].

Links

Law.com-Perkins Coie Cuts Pay for Lawyers and Staff

The Federalist-The FBI Set Up Trump and We Watched it Happen

FOX News-Democrats pulled Greatest Con Job Ever

Just the News-HRC Plan tying Trump and Russia

Clinton Foundation Timeline-Gatekeepers Involved in Biden Autopen Scandal

White House.gov-Addressing Risks from Perkins Coie

American Conservative-Democratic Law Firm Behind Russian Collision

Nick Moseder-Dark Money Election Summit: The Plot to Steal 2024

FOX News-Who is Bob Bauer?

Biz Pac Review-Gaetz: FBI Maintains Workspace in Office of Perkins Coie

Real Clear Politics-RussiaGate: HRC/Perkins Coie/Fusion GPS/CrowdStrike

Clinton Foundation Timeline-Durham found Evidence Sussmann Misled the CIA

Breitbart-Marc Elias: Clinton Campaign Lawyer tied to 'Pee Dossier'

Dawson Field-Perkins Coie and HRC Campaign

PJ Media-Trump 'Secret Server' Hoax was Subplot of DNC SpyGate Strategy

The Federalist-BHO's Campaign paid $972k to Law Firm that Paid Fusion GPS

Markets Work-FBI Outside Contractors, DNC Servers and CrowdStrike

Epoch Times-SpyGate: The Inside Story

Doc Cloud-Perkins Coie/Fusion GPS "Contract Letter"

Clinton Foundation Timeline-Perkins Coie

Justice.gov-SC Office: Michael Sussmann Indictment

Crossfire Hurricane Docs-FISA Notes

Justice-gov-2023 SC John Durham Report

The Petraeus Trap: Gmail 'Ghost Draft' Messages

Former CIA Director General David Petraeus had unsuccessfully tried to hide communications via 'Gmail Drafts.' Petraeus was having an extramarital affair with his biographer Paula Broadwell and setup a joint Google Gmail account to hide their secret love messages between 2011-2012. Petraeus would reappear on the media stage in 2021 for his Afghanistan two cents as well as in 2022 for his incorrect Ukraine political analysis.

Post Q# 1891
> Texts, emails (gmail), drafts (gmail), HAM comms, PS/Xbox chat logs.

By allowing several individuals access passwords to select Gmail accounts, this gives freedom to explore the saved/unsent 'draft' message folders. This tactic is employed as a counter-surveillance method to avoid the capture of information. Tampa socialite Jill Kelly reached out to FBI agent Fred Humphries, famed for his terrorism cases, to see about helping close personal friend Paula Broadwell, concerning her extramarital General Petraeus affair. Mr. Fred Humphries demonstrated true professionalism and honest FBI behavior in the entire Petraeus affair. Mr. Humphries is assisting my First Amendment legal case against Amazon for unconstitutionally stopping to print my two prior bestselling political books .

Post Q# 2476
> [There is a reason why 'directly' after the drops MS shut down their entire network to erase 'collected and stored material.'

There is no limit to the number of drafts, user access, and virtual worldwide instant message responses. Gmail 'ghost drafts' are used by both cheating spouses as well as professional Deep State intelligence actors. DNI Clapper encouraged Petraeus to resign as CIA Director on November 9, 2012, thus paving the way for BHO's appointment of John Brennan.

Post Q# 1502
> Access Kills.
> GMAIL DRAFTS?

This type of secret messaging system is employed primarily by international terrorist organizations and criminal cabals. It is a very effective surveillance countermeasure and would certainly be known by the Director of the CIA and obviously Team-'Q'. History would bring the decades long Afghanistan conflict back to center stage once again under the illegal Biden administration.

Post Q# 4774
> What did we learn this week?
> 1. Check Gmail?

Gmail drafts have become once again relevant today by Q-drops indicating that top level FBI/DOJ officials were using this clandestine method. Rumor has it that the DOJ's small group aka the 'Secret Society', used this as one of their main forms of communication. The previously used General Petraeus Trap now seems to work both ways (boomerang).

Post Q# 1283
> Lawmakers learned gmail draft comms yesterday?

Lest we forget Fusion GPS researcher Nellie Ohr who also used an old intelligence tradecraft trick of HAM Radio for secret message broadcasts. Also, the chat logs of Xbox Live game console systems were additionally used by the failed coup plotters and were all ultimately captured by the

White Hats. General Petraeus was considered a solid troop commander from his military units but got caught up in an extramarital affair.

Post Q# 1279
> We have it all.
> Many drafts.

"We have it all-Baby" will be the final nail in the coffin of these disastrous failed treasonous coup schemes. IG Horowitz's FISA abuse report leads directly into the criminal investigation phase of these several interwoven political scandals. General Petraeus has called the illegal Biden administration's handling of Afghanistan nothing short of catastrophic. Biden's assigned Special Counsel would obtain in 2023 President Trump's Twitter messages and 'ghost draft' posts in efforts to final bring him down.

Post Q# 26
> Think about it logically.
> The only way is the military.

Military commanders have testified before Congress that Biden received their strategic Afghanistan withdrawal advice contrary to his public denials. Patriots have been waiting for the final unraveling of the entire ObamaGate/SpyGate scandals. SC John Durham has dropped criminal indictments related to SpyGate and submitted his final report in 2023. With the re-election of President Trump in 2024, the 'Great Awakening' is ongoing and leading directly to the grand finale of this historic movie.

Post Q# 3602
> How do 'select' bad actors attempt comms w/o SIGINT collection?

Links

Newsweek-David Petraeus, HRC and the Perils of Email

Geller Report-AG Bondi backs Investigation after Bombshell Report Reveals FBI Botched

Clinton Foundation Timeline-2025 Crossfire Hurricane Docs

Sharyl Attkisson-BHO Era Surveillance Timeline

Just the News-Special Counsel obtains Trump's Twitter Messages/Ghost Draft Posts

NY Times-Petraeus Email Investigation

CBS News-FBI Agent in Petraeus Scandal Seen as a Hero

The Hill-Petraeus: Mariupol becoming a 'Ukrainian Alamo'

The Verge-Petraeus FBI Email Investigation

Techno Fog-U.S. Intelligence Operations against Americans

WSJ-General Petraeus on Afghanistan Withdrawal

Tampa Bay Times-Petraeus Scandal: Outed FBI Agent's Family still feels Betrayed

Tablet Magazine-How RussiaGate began with BHO's Iran Deal

REXXURECTION-Did BHO Frame/Remove Petraeus for Brennan?

CBS News-Face The Nation: David Petraeus

CNET-Petraeus uses Draft Emails to Communicate with Mistress

BBC News-David Petraeus and the Fall of a General

Wired-Obama's Drone Grandfather going to Powerful CIA

Huffington Post-Why David Petraeus' Emails should Make you Nervous

CNBC-5 Takeaways for IG Report: Comey's Gmail

Life Hacker-How CIA Director David Petraeus' Gmail were Traced

NY Times-Petraeus Resigns: FBI found Evidence of Affair

Rexxurection-BHO removes Petraeus for Brennan

Crossfire Hurricane Docs-Christopher Steele Binder

Justice.gov-2023 SC John Durham Report

Who is Joe Pientka? How is He Connected to SpyGate?

FBI Special Supervisory Agent (SSA) Joe Pientka III had by all appearances a normal government career. Pientka drew an interview assignment that however would alter his life both professionally and personally. Joe Pientka and his wife Melissa would join several other married couples deeply involved with the unfolding SpyGate political scandal. President Trump would file in 2022 a federal RICO lawsuit against HRC/DCN/Comey/Strzok/and others involved with the promotion of the false Russian collusion narrative during the 2016 election cycle.

Post Q# 2042
> FISA warrant issued/approved Flynn.

Joe Pientka was paired up with infamous FBI 'Super-Agent' Peter Strzok to interview the then incoming NSA Director General Mike Flynn. This ambush-style unscheduled entrapment interview took place on January 24, 2017, at the White House at direction of top FBI officials James Comey/Andy McCabe.

Post Q# 3626
> Targeted and silenced (gag) for a reason?
> Pain coming.

The FBI's '302 Form' is the official document that memorializes witness interview sessions. So accepted as fact are FBI 302s, they are used legally as factual evidence in courtroom proceedings. Pientka and Strzok had teamed up before when they gave then candidate Trump his first intelligence briefing in 2016.

Post Q# 4424
> Infiltration at the highest levels of government, media science, health, military COC.....
> FINAL LEVEL.

Joe Pientka is referred to as Case Agent 1 reporting under Peter Strzok in IG Horowitz's chain of command summary report for Crossfire Hurricane investigation. Pientka to this day has been shielded and transferred around the country by upper levels of the FBI.

Post Q# 2217
> In the end, all will be right.
> Patriots protect Patriots.

What has come into play was the strange interpretation of these General Flynn 302's by higher ups within the DOJ/FBI. Pientka claims he believed General Flynn was telling the truth during this interview and Pientka has been under a protective order by the DOJ.

Post Q# 2165
> SESSIONS and FLYNN [targeted] for [immediate] removal/recusal?

Agent Peter Strzok's notes seem to back up this professional gut feeling by fellow FBI agent Pientka about Flynn's truthfulness. It appears only Director Comey and Deputy Director McCabe came to a much different conclusion or interpretation of this improper ambush interview.

Post Q# 1286
> Flynn pleads guilty to no crime committed?

Rep. Devin Nunes's House Committee has already concluded with the beliefs of Pientka/Strzok, that there was no indication NSA Mike Flynn was intentionally lying during this interview.

Senators Grassley and Johnson looks like they are leaning in this same direction and will be holding hearings related to Crossfire Hurricane.

Post Q# 1282
> Who interviewed Flynn?
> Why did Flynn take the bullet?

This apparent entrapment/sting operation was to remove NSA Flynn from the new Trump Administration. DOJ's Sally Yates advised POTUS of the "blackmail" threat posed by NSA Flynn misleading VP Pence about the Russian Ambassador Kislyak phone conversation as well as bogus Logan Act violations.

Post Q# 3966
> FISA lead-in [stage 1 act 1]
> We are ready [think Barr public].

General Flynn had a phone call during the President Elect Trump transition period with the Russian Ambassador Sergey Kislyak. This phone call concerned prior BHO's sanctions (Diplomat removals) was both intercepted and quickly leaked out to the Mockingbird media.

Post Q# 1573
> Re_read drops re: 302 mod.
> DOJ forced to supply.
> Fireworks.

Team Mueller's lone charge against General Flynn was making false statements during his FBI interview. General Flynn did not have legal counsel present during this FBI interview but plead guilty to the charge to relieve pressure being applied by Team Mueller to his son.

Post Q# 2548
> Flynn has provided significant assistance.

It has come to light that DOJ's Bruce Ohr met with both Pientka and Strzok during this same time period. Joe Pientka and a few fellow FBI agents all seem willing to now testify (when does a bird sing). IG Michael Horowitz and Rep. Devin Nunes have both sent criminal referrals related to SpyGate to Special Counsel (SC) John Durham to prosecute.

Post Q# 2632
> Why would the FBI DIR take the time to visit ALL 56 FBI FIELD OFFICES around the entire United States?
> Completed this week.
> Logical thinking.

Bruce Ohr received a memory stick from his wife Nellie and her boss Glenn Simpson, containing all of Fusion GPS/Chris Steele's Trump-Russia Dossier. Bruce Ohr has testified that he gave this memory thumb drive to FBI agent Joe Pientka in December 2016. Bruce Ohr's wife Nellie was the Fusion GPS researcher who coordinated the fake Trump-Russia dossier.

Post Q# 1538
> Why still employed?
> Purpose?

These cooperative FBI agents will have a lot to talk about Comey/McCabe/Strzok/and others. They want to be called while on active government duty, so their high legal fees will be covered by the government.

Post Q# 1283
> If the FBI found NO evidence of lying why was Flynn charged?

Rod Rosenstein had been delayed releasing some of the documents related to the General Flynn case to Senator Grassley. The never shy Chuck Grassley says [RR] refusals are "disingenuous and extremely disturbing". Grassley and Senator Ron Johnson have vowed to get to the bottom of Crossfire Hurricane/SpyGate and have issues dozens of subpoenas.

Post Q# 2107
> Think Steele - BO [post FBI firing] intel collection.

In released documents it appears FBI Deputy McCabe did urge Flynn to meet with Strzok and Pientka without a lawyer present. Multiple different FBI 302's has also surfaced as well as Lisa Page's testimony she altered Strzok's own 302 report by throwing into question the entire General Flynn 'official' interview.

Post Q# 1661
> Think stages.
> What role can MIL INTEL play?
> What role can NSA play?
> BANG!

Historians will be focused in on Pientka's notation that General Flynn made an odd reference three times during this January 2017 surprise interview. Flynn said looking out a White House window, "Whet a wonderful Dark Sky" (aka The Storm). Incredibly it would come out in John Durham's 2023 final report that Joe Pientka claimed he was never shown selective intelligence surrounding HRC's plan that countered the FBI narrative about Trump-Russia.

Post Q# 4595
> THE SWAMP RUNS DEEP.

DNI Ratcliffe declassified FBI notes relating to defensive briefings given to then candidate Trump/General Flynn in August 2016. It appears now that Pientka and Strzok were paired together for these 'campaign time' intelligence briefing sessions. The same group of corrupt DOJ officials surround every aspect of this treasonous coup plot nicknamed SpyGate.

Post Q# 3880
> Prepare for the storm.

It is a classic sting entrapment ploy by the FBI that sadly has become standard operating practice. Joe Pientka appears in IG Michael Horowitz's FISA report as Supervisory Special Agent 1 and now the Senate would like to chat with this purposefully kept secret FBI agent. SC John Durham has dropped criminal indictments related to SpyGate and submitted his final report in 2023. With the re-election of President Trump in 2024, past hidden mysteries and criminal activity will finally be publicly revealed.

Post Q# 3693
> [302]_mod [1] count.
> FBI agent [1] [P] - FLYNN interview.......

Links

Washingtonian-Picture of FBI Agent Joe Pientka

FOX News-Soros' Alleged Ties to RussiaGate Exposed

Clinton Foundation Timeline-FBI Revelations Show the Mueller Special Counsel was a Cover-Up

FOX News-FBI Agent who Requested Validation of Steele Dossier left Crossfire Hurricane

Ivan Raiklin-Joseph Pientka III

Politico-FBI used Trump's Briefings to Advance Russia Probe

Clinton Foundation Timeline-2025 Crossfire Hurricane Docs

The Federalist-SpyGate 101: A Primer on the Russia Collusion Hoax

Epoch Times-FBI Special Agent Joseph Pientka is the DOJ's Invisible Man

FOX News-IG Horowitz's Report Spotlights little known FBI Agent's Role

Empty Wheel-Joe Pientka warned Trump to be Worried about His People

The Federalist-Graham kept Senators in Dark about Interview of Joe Pientka

Jeff Carlson-Joe Pientka and Bruce Ohr

Epoch Times-FBI Agent who Interviewed General Flynn

Washington Examiner-Trail of FBI Interviews

Markets Work-New FBI 302 Document Reveals Interview w/Agents not Flynn

Clinton Timeline-FBI Agent Joe Pientka

Just the News-FBI Joe Pientka Report on August 2016 Trump Briefing

Scribd-FBI Joseph Pientka/Senate Judiciary Testimony (8/27/20)

Crossfire Hurricane Docs-Steele Dossier through Simpson and McCain

Crossfire Hurricane Docs-Flynn Interview by Strzok and Pientka

Justice.gov-2023 SC John Durham Report

TRUST KANSAS— President Trump's "Fixer"

KANSAS has demonstrated his ability to help assist in the prevention of Global Nuclear War and other international incidents. Secretary Mike Pompeo (aka KANSAS) has acted as a carrier mule of secret information as well as gifts in the past, on behalf of President Trump. History will be very kind to the unselfish service Mike Pompeo has displayed for several decades. Even under the illegal Biden regime, KANSAS continues to assist President Trump as the world awaits his lawful return to office.

Post Q# 1318
Why did MP set into the C_A prior to Sec of State?

KANAS had publicly delivered for President Trump as a sign of goodwill, Elton John's classic "Rocket Man" CD to North Korea's Kim Jong-un. This secret hand-off occurred during delicate nuclear peace discussions with North Korea. Pompeo foreshadowed the risk China and it's proxies like North Korea poise against the USA. To this day, KANSAS is provided a 24/7 security detail for his safety against the ongoing death threats from Iran and others.

Post Q# 3774
Moves and countermoves.
The 'silent' was continues.

In President Trump like fashion, let's start off with a check list of big-league course corrections performed for President Trump's Mr. Fixer/KANSAS:
- CIA/Intelligence Community
- US State Dept./Foggy Bottom
- North Korea/Peace Plan
- Armenia Revolution
- Global Green Cult/Paris Climate Accord
- Cancel Iran Nuclear Deal
- Migrant Invading Caravans
- Iran/ISIS/Global Terrorism
- Trade Deals: TPP/China/USMCA
- Afghanistan/Taliban Peace Agreement
- Venezuela/Maduro Regime
- Middle East Peace Plan/Israel last
- China/Coronavirus Pandemic

Post Q# 3607
THE GREAT AWAKENING.

Mike Pompeo/KANSAS has served this country with honor for several decades. KANSAS graduated first in his West Point class and had a distinguished record of armed service to our country. It is a rare military honor to graduate top of your class and normally points to an outstanding future commanding officer.

Post Q# 2609
Yes.
(Anon question: Is there a plan in place for AFTER Trump?)

KANSAS served proudly as an Officer (Captain) in the famed 7th Calvary/General Custer. Pompeo personally patrolled the Iron Curtain sectors around the famed Berlin Wall of East

Germany. Captain Mike Pompeo's stellar military career set him on a disciplined path to government service.

Post Q# 950

Anon question to Q: Pompeo is Trump's guy?

Q reply to Anon: TRUST KANSAS.

After distinguishing active-duty KANSAS went on to earn his law degree from Harvard. Ever the student and natural leader Mike Pompeo strives constantly to be the best citizen, role model, and a civic leader even today after government service. Pompeo has spoken out as a soldier and as an official that was in the Chain of Command that Biden and Milley need to be held fully accountable for the Afghanistan disaster.

Mike seems to be tracking nicely for a major "2024 role."

Post Q# 4486

What advantages might exist to Sec of State re: former Dir of CIA?

Mike Pompeo gets his 'Q' nickname from his four-terms as a House Representative from Kansas. Mike Pompeo became one of the first Tea Party candidates ever elected to the U.S. Congress. KANSAS has demonstrated those foundational principles in his differing official duties. Many Anons feel Pompeo continues to drop crumbs post the Q-Team going silent after the 2020 election steal. Leadership is earned and we can all see in the current Biden era the efforts being displayed by Mike Pompeo.

Post Q# 4844

Wasn't referring to Kansas' statement re: Clinton emails.

Trump has tasked KANSAS first with cleaning up/out the 'Clowns' at C_A and CIA Director Gina Haspel took over the much-needed house cleaning. Pompeo then went on to skimming out the entrenched pond scum over at Foggy Bottom/US State Department. Two huge tasks in the beginning efforts to clean out the DC Swamp. Rolling Stone (Mockingbird) news has reported that KANSAS considered assassination of Julian Assange over the CIA Vault 7 release by WikiLeaks.

Post Q# 1186

"Pompeo" most senior official to visit NK since?

Future proves past.

Mike Pompeo had helped President Trump out with the two major issues involving peace both North Korea and Iran. I would say KANSAS performed admirably and exceptionally when called upon the fix a problem. Watch out for a KANSAS to have another top Cabinet position or as VP with JD Vance for the winning ticket in the post Trump era. Special Counsel John Durham has dropped criminal indictments related to SpyGate and submitted his final report in 2023.

Post Q# 3414

[Wheels up].

Special shout out to a close colleague, co-author and good friend SerialBrain2. SB2 made the connection between KANSAS and Q's "Wheels Up" reference (frequent flyer for POTUS). Former Secretary Pompeo continues to support President Trump from continued false accusations from Team Biden. Biden has attempted to blame President Trump over the tragic withdrawal from Afghanistan. President Trump would file in 2022 a federal RICO lawsuit against those that promoted the false Russian narrative during the 2016 Presidential election.

Post Q# 1122
　　TRUST KANSAS.

President Trump has said that "He and Pompeo are always on the same wavelength". President Trump trusts and has extreme confidence in his 'Mr. Fixer'-aka KANSAS. In July 2024 Nippon Steel hired Mike Pompeo primarily to advise them about the USA steel policies. Also in 2024 singer Elton John praised President Trump's brilliant nickname of Little Rocket Man' for Kim Jong Un. I have a feeling Captain Mike Pompeo will continue to advise President Trump in his 2.0 era, even though he will not have an official position.

Post Q# 1129
　　Down She Goes......

Links

Washington Times-Mike Pompeo urges Countries to do Business with U.S.

Revolver News-New Info Shows just how Deep State Mike Pompeo Really Is

Washington Examiner-Pompeo: Sending National Guard Troops to LA Riots is 'Common Sense'

Reuters News-Nippon Steel hires Mike Pompeo

Breitbart-Elton John praises Trump's Nickname for Kim Jong Un

Washington Examiner-Pompeos Mockery of Hillary Clinton Sparked IG's Retaliation

Rolling Stone-Pompeo Reportedly considered Assassination of Julian Assange

Breitbart-Pompeo's Prophetic Warning Biden about Afghanistan

NPR-Mike Pompeo: Soldier/Spy Chief/Tea Party Republican

Washington Times-Pompeo: High Confidence Wuhan Lab Linked to China's Military

PJ Media-Secretary Pompeo warms Governors of CCP Influence

Just the News-Pompeo: BHO/Biden's 'Soft Coddling' allowed China to Walk on Us

New Yorker-Mike Pompeo: Secretary of Trump

The Guardian-Rocket Man: Trump has Pompeo Elton John CD to Kim

New Yorker-Mike Pompeo: The Secretary of Trump

WSJ-Pompeo: Biden wants to Deal with Khonar Tower Killers

FOX News-Pompeo Pushes back on Biden blaming Trump for Afghanistan Withdrawal

Crossfire Hurricane Docs-Halper Files

Justice.gov-2023 SC John Durham Report

Sidney Powell Exposed:
"Creeps on a Mission" and the "Kraken"

Former top Federal Prosecutor and bestselling author Sidney Powell successfully represented General Flynn as his legal counsel. Sidney's groundbreaking book "Licensed to Lie", exposes widespread past corruption within the Department of Justice (DOJ). History will be kind to Ms. Powell as the DOJ has dropped all charges against General Mike Flynn and she has exposed the 2020 election fraud scheme and the international cyber-attack on our voting infrastructure. History will remember Patriot Powell as a heroine of the Republic for her tireless struggles against the pervasive DC Swamp corruption.

Post Q# 4140
LET FREEDOM RING!

Sidney was involved with helping to correct an injustice against Merrill Lynch executive by the DOJ. Select top executives were singled out by Special Counsel ((SC) Robert Mueller's 'Pit Bull' Andrew Weissmann [AWW] for excessive prosecution. The notorious DC Swamp relies upon corrupt government officials and a always compliant Mockingbird MSM news media.

Post Q# 2102
What happens if Mueller 'proves' 'Free Speech Systems LLC' aka 'InfoWars' is linked to a Foreign Intel Agency or other Non_Domestic entity?

[AWW] was Mueller's lead investigator on the sham Trump-Russia 'Witch-Hunt' prosecutorial team. Ms. Powell skillfully guided General Flynn out of the Mueller guilty plea trap and highlighted all of the gross prosecutorial misconduct by the DOJ. From Enron through the 2020 election steal, Ms. Powell as been the consummate Patriot. As a reminder in 2016 Sidney Powell outlined what she was told by NYPD officers about upsetting evidence that they reviewed from the Anthony Weiner/Huma Abedin's seized laptop.

Post Q# 4025
CLEARED THE ALL CHARGES.
TRUMP ADMIN v2?

Ultimately it was proven in court, that several innocent people were sent falsely to Federal prison in the Enron fiasco. This was part of the famed Enron/Arthur Andersen bankruptcy and fraud case that AWW played such a key role. Back scratching and political protection is a mainstay of the corrupt DC Swamp and the creatures that dwell within its boundaries.

Post Q# 1829
What if those 'placed' are being investigated by Mueller, former director of 'FBI' = Bob Mueller, Special Counsel.

Both Enron/Arthur Andersen were DOJ victims and lead to each of their own corporate demise. Hardball tactics and undue pressure from federal prosecutors, were the methods applied by Weissmann's corrupt DOJ team. To bring back equity and one equal rule of justice, out of control Federal prosecutors like Weissmann.

Post Q# 1285
> Congress passed Public Law 94-503, limiting the FBI Director to a single term of no longer than 10 years."
> Reconcile.

Sidney Powell reminded us all, about the history of the Enron case which ties directly into the Mueller Trump-Russia probe. Special Counsel John Durham had dropped criminal indictments related to the SpyGate scandal and submitted his final report in 2023. Enter Mueller's lead investigator [AWW] and his past courtroom legal misconduct baggage. History will not be kind to this entire cast of failed coup plotters.

Post Q# 18
> Why did Mueller meet POTUS 1-day prior to FBI announcement if Mueller COULD NOT be offered director due to prev term limits rule?

[AWW] was the DOJ Director of the Enron Task Force and concocted bogus business transactions between Enron and Arthur Andersen. This accusation led to the false convictions (like General Flynn) of 4 top Merrill Lynch executives as well as outrageous fines to all companies.

Post Q# 2643
> The 'MUELLER' insurance policy has expired.

These Merrill executives went to prison only later to have the Weissman convictions reversed on appeal by the 5th Circuit Court of Appeals. Weissman has had a long career of judicial misconduct and has been caught in these unscrupulous actions before. Sidney Powell as witnessed firsthand the tipping of the scales of justice by the very governmental agency tasked to endure equal justice under the law.

Post Q# 4762
> Not long now.

The various false Arthur Andersen charges lead directly to its bankruptcy and caused the job loss of around 25,000 staff. The Arthur Andersen company was renamed to Accenture and ultimately all charges were reversed unanimously by the U.S. Supreme Court. The final report of Special Counsel John Durham exonerates both General Mike Flynn and his crack attorney Sidney Powell as well as the Anons. Biden's DOJ and Fulton County Georgia indicted Ms. Powell and 18 co-defendants in conjunction with the 2023 criminal charges against President Trump 2020 election related offenses.

Post Q# 4224
> Subject: Flynn.
> Can you prosecute without prosecutors?

We can thank Ms. Powell for her appropriately highlighting [AWW's] past prosecutorial misdeeds as well as her election fraud Kraken. You can hear Ms. Powell regularly as a guest on network shows like FOX New w/Sean Hannity and other national news media outlets. The 2020 election will reveal a massive cyber hack by foreign countries using our stolen software signals intelligence program nicknamed Hammer and the vote changing program termed Scorecard. General Flynn would file in 2022 a $50 million claim against the DOJ/FBI for the illegal actions related to the 2016 SpyGate/Russia probe. LawFare would entangle Ms. Powell, as well as other President Trump election advisers, by numerous legal actions to the point of submission to minor charges to avoid bankruptcy as she did in 2023.

Post Q# 3330

Will newly discovered evidence (AG Barr-SDNY) FREE FLYNN?

It is only appropriate that any Witch-Hunt has a bunch of "Creeps on a Mission". Fortunately, General Flynn was assisted by a straight-shooting fellow Patriot named Sidney. Ms. Powell is unveiling the 2020 election fraud computer hacking scheme that was captured by the White Hats via the 'Kraken.' Ongoing state forensic audits will exonerate President Trump about the 'Big Lie.' The J6 Congressional committee had subpoena Ms. Powell in utter desperation to change the stolen election narrative. With the historic re-election of President Trump in 2024, Sidney Powell and all faithful Patriots will be finally vindicated.

Post Q# 3388

There is a big [direct] reason why FLYNN'S new attorney is seeking security clearance.

Links

BBC News-The Kraken: What is it and Why has Trump's Ex-Lawyer Released

Just the News-Sidney Powell secures Legal Victory in TX Appeals Case

The Federalist-Robert Mueller's Lead Prosecutor has History of Ethics Violations

Epoch Times-USSC Rejects Appeal by Sidney Powell to Review 2020 Election

Independent-Trump and 18 Others Indicted on Election RICO Charges

Washington Examiner-Sidney Powell Subpoenaed in J6 Committee Investigation

Sidney Powell-"Creeps on a Mission" website

The War Economy-The Resistance

The Last Refuge-FISA 702 Searches

The Federalist-FBI used 'Defensive Briefings' to Spy on Trump/Flynn

The War Economy-SpyFall

Breitbart-Sidney Powell: BHO Officials committed Crimes Targeting Flynn

Hillsdale College-Sidney Powell: How to Fix Justice (March 2020)

The Federalist-Your Guide: BHO Administration's Hit on Michael Flynn

Epoch Times-Flynn's Lawyer: FBI Agent wrote 'Flynn Didn't Lie'-We have Eyewitness

Hannity.com-"Creeps on a Mission"

NPR-Enron and the Fall of Arthur Andersen

SOTT-Intelligence Community Pushed RussiaGate Conspiracy Theory

WSJ-Bad Bets Enron: Potemkin Village

YouTube Video-Sydney Powell on Weiner/Abedin Laptop

Sidney Powell.com-website contains all legal motions

Clinton Foundation Time-2025 Crossfire Hurricane Docs

Justice.gov-2023 SC John Durham Report

Samantha Power:
World Class Unmasker and Fake News Media Darling

Samantha Power [SP] seems to have plenty to say to the MSM when frequently called upon by the Fake Mockingbird news establishment. She very publicly told President Trump that it was "Not a good idea to piss off John Brennan." Power has scarily returned to government service under Biden as the 16th Administrator of the U.S. Agency for International Development (USAID), with a global staff of over 10,000. Putin would include Power in his list of 13 Americans sanctioned by Russia over the 2022 Ukraine military operation. Power should additionally fear President Trump's filed 2022 federal RICO lawsuit against all those that promoted the false Russia collusion narrative during the 2016 election cycle.

Post Q# 311
> What was the USSS codename for Hussein?
> [R].
> They knew all along.
> decode: The USSS code name for BHO was Renegade [R].

Power was the UN Ambassador under BHO and was caught unmasking hundreds of American citizens. Samantha Power is known for regularly chiming in on how the Fake News media should always couch President Trump's public statements in a negative light and downplay via MSM news coverage any positive accomplishments. Samantha Power and hubby philosopher Cass Sunstein certainly have very loud months. The Mockingbird news media is trained to pick up on the narratives being spewed by the DC Swamp insiders like lovebirds Samantha and Cass.

Post Q# 2576
> Those with the most to lose are the loudest.
> Crimes against Humanity.

Power has long been a loud public voice for the Deep State and plotters of ObamaGate/SpyGate. Power is loving wife of Alinskyite Philosopher Cass Sunstein, who was considered an USSC appointee by a future President HRC. The power Washington DC couple has held sway over several administrations. Cass Sunstein also would be called upon during the illegal Biden administration to continue to add his expertise in the suppression of all voice of opposition against the given political narrative (Ministry of Truth).

Post Q# 2700
> Establish 'financial checks/reviews' of those in senior (critical) positions (audits) + direct family (close proximity).

Power was BHO's UN Ambassador and Chief 'unmasker.' Samantha combined her talents with Susan Rice and this pair were affectionately known as the "Gruesome Twosome" of unmasking. The illegal surveillance aspect of the unfolding scandal known as SpyGate will be the Achilles Heel upon which a future RICO criminal case will be constructed. As a Biden administration official, Power has called for the continued unlimited assistance of billions of dollars to Ukraine over the Russia special military operation of 2022.

Post Q# 120
> Why is the NSA limited re: ability to capture and unmask US persons?

Samantha Power's being appointed in 2021 as the new head Administrator of United States Agency for International Development (USAID) should be a red flag for continued undermining of our MAGA movement by BHO's alumni. NWO Globalists are seeing the rise of independence and are in a panic of this Great Awakening process. Power famously has long argued for humanitarian intervention as the moral responsibility of the USA. One of the more cynical quotes most often associated with both M/M Sunstein is to "Never let a good crisis go to waste."

Post Q# 3898
> The key that opens all doors.
> The 'Start.'

France, Hong Kong, Japan, Canada and the UK are now also emblematic with the global Great Awakening/'Q' Patriot movements and the struggle against the New World Order's 'Great Reset'. Demonstrated by the protesters having 'Q' on their yellow vests in Paris worn in such defiance as well as the Pepe's in Hong Kong. Vlad Putin had enacted sanctions against many Americans as well as announced the denial of entry into Russia for many more.

Post Q# 3595
> US AMB 1 and 2 NSA unmask req.

Progressive Leftists are good at blaming others for their own mistakes or wrong calculations. They all keep pushing in unison the tired worn-out false narrative of Russia-Russia-Russia collusion at every opportunity while ignoring real enemies like China and Iran. USAID would be revealed in international funding improprieties involving the Ukraine and many other countries.

Post Q# 2129
> [LIVE STREAMING] WH HUSSEIN NON-OVAL [SITUATION ROOM] COORDINATION.

Former UN Ambassador Power alone holds the Guinness Book of World Records for unmasking innocent American citizens. Samantha Power has unmasked over 260 unknowing Americans during BHO's final term in office. Samantha Power was brought back to government service as Biden's UN Administrator of the USAID program and is authorizing millions to combat global hunger while we see homeless American veterans. It was uncovered in 2024 by America First Legal that USAIR was involved in the vast 'Censorship Complex' in silencing dissent voices.

Post Q# 4124
> Why do they always include their spouse, son, daughter, etc.?
> Follow the money.

In past testimony given to Congressional committees, Samantha Power claims that the prior vast unmasking actions must have been other people as she is innocent. Samantha Power had no memory of doing these improper/illegal revealing actions time and time again. In a classic 2003 Power penned an article for the Atlantic, Power outlines 10 steps to kill a country or in essence how to exactly destroy America. Important to watch the food controls enacted under Power/USAID, as the NWO may use food and energy as tools for manipulation of the masses.

Post Q# 1182
> How do you 'legally' inject/make public/use as evidence?

Power's infamous quote in regard to BHO's Foreign Policy on why we are in Libya "It is our responsibility to protect those people that are the most helpless". There had been a recycling of BHO era political hacks back into the illegal Biden administration and a bizarre continuance of the 'dirty couples' from SpyGate into more operations for the DC Deep State Swamp. Samantha Power and Cass Sunstein once again have political influence over our Republic.

Post Q# 2180
> Define 'Traitor.'
> HUSSEIN?
> [RENEGADE].

Cass Sunstein is her 'Philosopher King' Saul Alinsky loving husband. On a scary parallel timeline Cass Sunstein was on HRC's short list to fill Justice Scalia's empty Supreme Court seat (Loretta Lynch had to wait for RBG's retirement). Sunstein was BHO's Regulations and Information Czar put in charge of breaking up the various truth movements. The infiltration and division tactics employed by Sunstein against the 9/11 truthers is the same model being employed against the 'Q' crowd today.

Post Q# 1008
> AMERICA FOR SALE.
> Cheatin' Obama.
> Trust the Plan.

Let's keep an eye on sweet Sam as she seems to be the type of person that might be willing to spill the beans. Special Counsel (SC) John Durham is now looking to apply the right kind of judicial legal pressure with his early indictment of Perkins Coie/Clinton campaign lawyer Michael Sussmann. SC Durham is systematically working his way through the entire BHO/HRC 2016 plot against candidate Donald Trump. Samantha Power has been connected to the 2022 'Color Revolution' in Hungry.

Post Q# 1621
> You have more than you know.
> Fireworks.

It is a staggering discovery how difficult it is to find any clean staffers from the Obama or Biden regimes. We can look today at modern day Patriots and Digital Soldiers such as General Flynn/Horowitz/Huber/Kash/Durham/Ezra/Admiral Rogers/Ellis/and Charles McCullough that represent a few of the White Hats from BHO's 'Renegade' era that stayed to help President Trump. SC John Durham has dropped criminal indictments and submitted his final report in 2023. With the re-election of President Trump in 2024 and departure of Samantha Power from USAID, the forthcoming Great American is going to usher in Judgement Day.

Post Q# 4020
> Control of the narrative [control of you].
> THE WAR IS REAL.

Links

New Yorker-The Moral Logic of Humanitarian Intervention

Town Hall-The Apparent Gruesome Twosome of the Unmasking

Clinton Foundation Timeline-2025 Crossfire Hurricane Docs

Biz PAC Review-Remembering Samantha Power

FOX News-USAID: Vipers Nest of Corruption

The Hill-Samantha Power: Unmasker in Chief

Washington Examiner-USAID Administrator met with Soros Foundation

FOX News-Who is Samantha Power?

PJ Media-Biden/BHO Officials Sought to Torpedo incoming Trump Adm

American Conservative-Samantha Power Color Revolution in Hungary

Washington Examiner-Power urges Congress to Approve $33 billion in Aid to Ukraine

New York Post-Russia Sanctions 13 Americans

Time Magazine-The Samantha Power Interview

Tablet Magazine-RussiaGate began with BHO's Domestic Spying

NY Times-A Monster of a Slip

Western Journal-Sam Power Claimed Not to Recall Remember Unmasking Flynn

Jonathan Turley-Did Samantha Power Commit Perjury?

The Last Refuge-FISA 702 Searches

New Yorker-In the Land of the Possible

Jeff Carlson-Power Unmasking/Operation Latitude

Markets Work-A Letter from Devin: Unmasking the Leakers

American Thinker-Ignoring the Samantha Power Bombshells

Foundation for Freedom-USAID: Documents Reveal Government Plot to Censor

Crossfire Hurricane Docs-Flynn Interview

Justice.gov-2023 SC John Durham Report

Wife of Former FBI Bill Priestap is a Famed International Spy

Picture in your mind's eye a real life 'Evelyn Salt' (Angelina Jolie's character) as you read through this article. Oddly this real marriage of these two top intelligence professionals resembles another married couple from the hit movie Mr./Mrs. Smith (Jolie with Brad Pitt). Sabina Menschel's husband is Bill Priestap, and he would be a central figure in the political scandals known as SpyGate.

Post Q# 3899
The Silent War continues....

We all know William "Bill" Priestap as being the boss of FBI Counterintelligence agent Peter Strzok. Being the head of the FBI's Counterintelligence Division means you are in fact the 'Espionage Chief' of the entire country. Bill Priestap and several of his FBI colleagues would continue to provide testimony in the different criminal probes involving the 2016 SpyGate political scandal.

Post Q# 2552
After Mr. Priestap's departure, none of the high-ranking bureau officials involved in the two investigations will remain with the bureau.

Bill Priestap is our country's top spy catcher and its primary defensive shield against his foreign worldwide counterparts. 'SPY vs SPY' is as an age-old tradition and it was said at one time that our folks were among the best in the business.

Post Q# 2058
Bill Priestap, Head of Counterintelligence and Strzok's boss-cooperating witness [power removed].

History will note Bill Priestap was the first to step forward in a line of cooperating DOJ witnesses. These are the individuals referred by 'Q' as-"When does a bird sing"? President Trump would file in 2022 a federal RICO lawsuit against Comey/Strzok/HRC/DNC/ and others who promoted the false Russian collusion narrative during the 2016 election cycle.

Post Q# 2462
SHADOW PLAYERS ARE THE DEADLIEST.

Congressional members originally went out of their way to keep Priestap's initial cooperation a top secret. On a side note, I posted another Reddit article asking the question could William Priestap be the 'Chan Boards' famed FBIAnon.

Post Q# 1892
NEVER FORGET.
BLACK OPS AGAINST USA.
TOTAL TAKEOVER OF OUR COUNTRY.
TRAITORS ALL.

Sabina Menschel Priestap appears to be a rather unique person. A Harvard BS degree plus a MBA, lead Menschel instantly upon graduation, to a high-level position as a Special Advisor to the FBI. This gig would ultimately lead to meeting and marriage with Bill Priestap.

Post Q# 2700
> Establish 'financial checks/reviews' of those in senior (critical) positions (audits) + direct
> family (close proximity).

Menschel interacted with Lawrence Summers (old Clinton ally) throughout her Harvard college days. Sabina Menschel had the early credentials as well as key connections to excel in the field of international spy tradecraft.

Post Q# 1745
> START OF HUSSEIN SPY CANPAIGN TO RIG AN ELECTION WAS BASED ON
> FALSE INFO.

Sabina Menschel was involved with the FBI Task Force that made recommendations on intelligence transformations in response to 9/11. Post government work brought Sabina Menschel first to Kroll International, then finally onto leading spy firm Nardello and Company.

Post Q# 1385
> Did the 'covert' counterintelligence branch of the FBI end?

Nardello is known as one of the world's top private contractors for espionage services. Sabina Menchel is Nardello's President/CEO, and her headquarters office received some special guests in the form of a unique emergency protection detail.

Post Q# 436
> RAMIF: US INTEL LEGAL SPY ON PRES Candidate/PRES ELECT/etc.

In early February 2018 a total of 17 operatives from the infamous Unit 269/Israeli Military Directorate rushed to Nardello's Headquarters. Interpol had picked up a credible threat to Mrs. Priestap's life and acted rather quickly. It is a very rare occurrence when foreign paramilitary forces operate within the United States on their own accord.

Post Q# 166
> Expand your thinking.
> Jason Bourne (Deep Dream).

Israel dispatched this elite team to protect Sabina's threatened life. Mind you the Israeli's beat Priestap's own FBI Hostage Rescue Team to Nardello's headquarter office. Menschel's Nardello would return to the spotlight in 2023 as they have offered free services to investigate the hidden finances of Alex Jones/Free Speech Systems.

Post Q# 1939
> "This is the case with Halper, who is now proven to be a spy, possibly with (Australian
> Ambassador) Alexander Downer."

SPY vs SPY, oh what a tangled web can be woven. President Trump and his loyal White Hat Patriots must unravel this elaborate coup plot and bring all of these traitorous SpyGate criminals to justice. IG Michael Horowitz began the official inquiries and SP John Huber/Special Counsel John Durham have followed up on the many referrals involving the SpyGate scandal.

Post Q# 451
> Who is meeting in secret right now?
> WE SEE YOU.
> WE HEAR YOU.
> YOU EVIL SICK BASTARDS ARE STUPID!!!

M/M Bill Priestap join the growing list of 'Dirty Couples' connected to the ObamaGate/SpyGate scandal. 'Q' has pointed out in prior drops the judicial meaning of 'When does a Bird Sing' and this is emblematic of several government people testifying to save their own necks. The justice phase is commencing with Special Counsel John Durham has dropped criminal indictments related to Sabrina's hubby former FBI Counterintelligence Director Bill Priestap and submitted his final report in 2023. With the re-election of President Trump in 2024, many hope past hidden political secrets will finally be revealed.

Post Q# 4362
Keyword: Insurgency

Links

Profile Magazine-Sabina Menschel

Millennium Report-Bill Priestap's Spouse tied to Deep State

The Federalist-Senate Expands Probe into FBI's Ability to Hide Documents

Clinton Foundation Timeline-2025 Crossfire Hurricane Docs

Nardello-Sabina Menschel

Impious Digest-Israeli Special Forces Rush to Protect Wife of FBI Official

Judiciary.Senate.gov-Report shows FBI Cut Corners in HRC Email Investigation

Red State-Here Are Some of the Big Name Witnesses in the Sussmann Trial

The Last Refuge-Get to Know this Name: Bill Priestap

American Thinker-How Husbands/Wives Figure in Latest Scandal Revelations

Real Clear Investigations-FBI Man's Testimony Points to Wrongdoing beyond Spying

Markets Work-FBI Official in charge of HRC/Trump Probes: Excluded from Meetings

Tablet Magazine-RussiaGate began with BHO's Domestic Spying Campaign

FOX News-Who is Bill Priestap?

Salt: Official Extended Movie Trailer (2010)

Markets Work-FBI Counterintelligence Head Bill Priestap: Cooperating Witness

Washington Examiner-Graham asks DOJ for Docs: Undercut Steele Dossier Source

Judicial Watch-Strzok/Page Involvement in Launching Crossfire Hurricane

Syracuse University-Richard/Robert Menschel awarded Carnegie Medal

The Last Refuge-Bill Priestap and Carter Page

The Intercept-Spies for Hire

Scribd-FBI Bill Priestap 2018 Joint House Testimony

OIG.Justice.gov-DOJ OIG FISA Report

Crossfire Hurricane Docs-Bill Priestap Text Messages

Justice.gov-2023 SC John Durham Report

The Long-Awaited Return of FBIAnon— aka William Priestap

A few strange but historic events took place on July 2, 2016. First HRC's FBI interview was conducted by agents Peter Strzok and Randy Coleman. The second event was that intelligence asset Stefan Halper contacted businessman Carter Page. Additionally, around this same time period the mysterious FBIAnon first appeared on 4chan with claims of corruption within the FBI.

Post Q# 89
FBI/MI currently have open investigation into the CF.

4chan and 8chan are public message boards that anyone can post anonymous information. It is now widely accepted that the information from FBIAnon was indeed legitimate. FBIAnon held a famous Q and A session where many answers/predictions have held true to date.

Post Q# 2581
How do you protect a valuable witness (whistleblower)?

After too long of a silence, it appears FBIAnon has returned again to the Chans. Posted on 1/26/19 was a claim that a federal grand jury has indicated both FBI Director James Comey and CIA Director John Brennan. Anons are constantly watching for real whistleblowers to drop 'crumbs' at the various public message boards like 4chan.

Post Q# 2541
Future will prove past.
History books.
JUSTICE.
Enjoy the show.

Public disclosure of the entire SpyGate treasonous coup plot will be rolling out in the form of future criminal indictments and will be part of the upcoming DECLAS. FBIAnon has also said in a follow up drop, that FBI Deputy Director Andy McCabe will be indicted as part of the intentional coverup for BHO and HRC.

Post Q# 4545
We are living in Biblical Times.

If this in fact the real FBIAnon, we are in the 'quickening' of full disclosure fellow Patriots. The beginning of criminal indictments is part of the Storm that will usher in the Great Awakening. The return to an equal system of justice is essential in the rebirth of a new Republic. Special Counsel (SC) John Durham would slowly unveil in 2022 court filings a coordinated vast criminal conspiracy against candidate Donald Trump by both government officials as well as private outside contractors.

Post Q# 2552
After Mr. Priestap's departure, none of the high-ranking bureau officials involved in the two investigations will remain with the bureau.

Rumors have been circulating that Pete Strzok's boss at FBI Counterintelligence (CI) could be FBIAnon. Bill Priestap was head of FBI CI and was the first person to cooperate in the IG Horowitz/SP Huber's criminal investigations. Priestap was intentionally kept out of many meetings involving the SpyGate operation and underling Strzok routinely went directly to FBI Assistant Director Andy McCabe.

Post Q# 1288

Bill Priestap, Head of Counterintelligence and Strzok's boss- Cooperating witness [power removed].

Priestap was the first of the DOJ/FBI 'Small Group' to turn states evidence.

Cooperating Witnesses (Bird Cage):

- William Priestap (FBI Dir C/I)
- Peter Strzok (FBI Asst. C/I)
- Lisa Page (FBI Lawyer)
- Bruce Ohr (DOJ # 4 before demoted)
- Joe Pientka (FBI Special Agent)
- George Tosas (Deputy Assistant AG)
- James Baker (FBI General Counsel)

Post Q# 753

When does a bird sing?

Everything has meaning.

Time will tell if Bill Priestap was in reality the infamous FBIAnon. Priestap lead the way with the early "singing" and will be noted for that role by historians. Many of these Department of Justice employees are in damage control and looking out for self-preservation. In 2022, Bill Priestap and other government officials continue to cooperate with the different investigative committees in providing testimony related to the SpyGate political scandal.

Post Q# 1552

+FBI protection of HRC.

+FBI criminal acts.

Ref to Huber?

Priestap's released Congressional testimony states he was deliberately excluded from key Trump probe meeting by the coup plotters. Looking like Bill Priestap was not in the 'Small Group' and will be rewarded accordingly for his early cooperation. Priestap and DAG Sally Yates took the false Flynn/Kislayak story to the White House to originate his firing as President Trump's first NSA. An odd occurrence happened in 2018 when a group of Israeli Special Forces rushed to protect Mrs. Bill Priestap (Sabina Menschel) in her New York office from a viable death threat received via Interpol.

Post Q# 1939

Red-Handed comms revealed to 'encourage truthful testimony.'

OIG Horowitz's 2.0 and Nunes' phase 2/3 Congressional reports highlighted prior misconduct by the DOJ. Charges first from SP John Huber and later by SC John Durham will be in front of several grand juries as the ObamaGate/SpyGate criminal probes are all finalized. President Trump would file in 2022 a federal RICO lawsuit against all those who promoted the false Russian collusion narrative in 2016.

Post Q# 3702

This is not another 4-year election.

Game theory.

IG Michael Horowitz finished with Bill Priestap's cooperative testimony and turned criminal referrals to SC John Durham to prosecute. Bill Priestap has announced his resignation from the FBI and has returned to civilian life. In would be revealed in 2023 that the DOJ sought the personal phone/data records of Preistap and other possible whistleblowers.

Post Q# 1929
MOVIE 3 - TBA.
Enjoy the show.

These actions all point to the final act beginning [Movie 3] and is about to play out. SC Durham's indictment of Perkins Coie/Clinton campaign lawyer Michael Sussmann connects many SpyGate coup plotters. SC Durham submitted his final report in 2023. With the re-election of President Trump in 2024, stay tuned as our Republic returns to the rule of equal justice under the law.

Post Q# 4836
Combat tactics, Mr. Ryan.

Links

Just the News-FBI Agent started Enhanced Validation on Christopher Steele

Washington Examiner-Bongino finds Comey's FBI Hidden Evidence Room

Clinton Foundation Timeline-FBI Revelations Show the Mueller Special Counsel was a Cover-Up

The Federalist-Unsealed Crossfire Hurricane Docs prove RussiaGate a Hoax

Washington Times-FBI Unmasks Trump Russia Hoax

Impious Digest-Israeli Special Forces Rush to Protect Wife of FBI Official

The Federalist-DOJ Subpoenaed Phone/Email Logs of those Probing Crossfire Hurricane

Epoch Times- Email Reveals Answer to Establishment's Efforts to Oust Trump

Markets Work-SpyGate: The Inside Story

The Federalist-SpyGate 101: A Primer on the Russia Collusion Hoax

The Last Refuge-Key Brennan Email to Comey and Strzok

FOX News-Who is Bill Priestap?

The Last Refuge-Get to Know this Name: Bill Priestap

Rolling Stone-Anatomy of a Fake News Scandal

The Last Refuge-Origins of Russia Probe

Daily Caller-Former FBI Intel Chief faces Scrutiny over Steele Dossier Briefing

Markets Work-FBI C/I Head Bill Priestap Cooperating Witness

Daily Dot-What are Anons?

Clinton Timeline-Bill Priestap

The Last Refuge-Bill Priestap's 2016 London Trip

Scribd-FBIAnon (2016)

Senate Judiciary Committee: 2021 Crossfire Hurricane DECLAS

Scribd-FBI Bill Priestap 2018 Joint House Testimony

OIG.Justice.gov-DOJ OIG FISA Report

Crossfire Hurricane Docs-Bill Priestap Text Messages

Justice.gov-2023 SC John Durham Report

Blackwater Founder Mentioned by 'Q': Meet Erik Prince

Erik Prince is commonly known as Blackwater's founder and is a former Navy SEAL. Prince was an informal adviser to President-Elect Trump and is the brother of Education Secretary Betsy DeVos. Prince is now acting as a travel agent by offering air tickets out of Kabul (Afghanistan) for $6,500 per person mercifully assisting those left abandoned by Biden. Erik Prince would stay the news through 2023 with a $10 billion plan to create a private army for Ukraine in light of the Russian special military operation.

Post Q# 1948
Who provided security?
Why did [1] plane particular land outside of Iran?

Erik Prince has repeatedly been brought back into the news and has been doing some 'White Hat' type of actions in recent years. Erik Prince has long been promoting private contractor armies in Venezuela and other global hot spots versus the U.S. military. This mercenaries for hire approach very well be the future of small nations to supplement their own standing army.

Post Q# 223
Who is Betsy D?
Why is she relevant?
Expand your thinking.

As you go through this article keep in mind Erik Prince/Crew (Mitch Rapp/Jason Bourne/Scot Harvath type hombres) has been protecting in some fashion President Trump and FAMILY for a longtime. The USSS took sole protection of the POTUS (President of the US) but Erik's operators are always omnipresent around the Trump Family. Beginning in the 2018 election cycle and for all of the 2020 President Trump rallies, Erik Prince's company provided extra security to augment the Secret Service/US Military assigned protective details.

Post Q# 1442
Thank you for guarding POTUS, Erik.
QAnon answer to Anon: Not POTUS

During Bush/Obama eras, Prince became the scapegoat for civilian deaths at the hands of his sub-contractors in the Middle East. Erik Prince sold Blackwater and started Frontier Services Group and Xe Services which now operate under the name Academi. I believe history will show Prince as being a loyal Patriot to our nation.

Post Q# 765
Watch the water.

In August 2016, a special meeting was setup by George Nader to be held at Trump Tower. Besides George and his patron UAE Crown Prince bin Zayed, attending were Donald Trump Jr. and Erik Prince. Intelligence circles would describe this type of operation as a 'dirty-up' job.

Post Q# 69
God speed to those that will be put in harms way. You are the bravest men and women on earth.
We will never forget.

Offers of future campaign help were extended but no Gulf States arrangements were consolidated. A future meeting was discussed and arranged for after the 2016 Presidential election. Just be shear physical associations can the enemy paint a negative narrative against their assigned target.

Post Q# 2572
Drops 'layered' to provide 'advance knowledge.'
PANIC BUTTON PUSHED.

On Nov. 4, 2016, Erik Prince did an interview with Alex Marlow about the Anthony Weiner's sized laptop. Prince was the first to publicly unveil the illegal classified emails and salacious material recovered by the NYPD (Rudy Giuliani is in the background as holding a copy of this data).

Post Q# 2365
[Pg 294]
[Meeting between Comey and Coleman on October 4]

Laptop data supposedly contained Huma Abedin's 'Insurance File' and other documented crimes against children. The DOJ/FBI headquarters would step in to silence all leaks and smoother this critical evidence. The infamous Weiner/Abedin laptop might possibly be the keystone of enlightenment once revealed to the general public.

Post Q# 3845
Backchannels are important.
Enjoy the show!

Erik Prince explains how the NYPD threatened Lynch/Comey that they would go public, if DC didn't act in the explosive Weiner/Abedin laptop emails. FBI Director Comey then reopens the HRC email probe and AG Lynch puts the clamps on both the NY FBI and NYPD. In short order Comey would hold a presser to exonerate HRC of all charges.

Post Q# 1229
Blackwater USA.
The world is connected.

On Jan. 11, 2017, Erik Price went to a meeting in the Seychelles (off Africa) at request of the UAE Crown Prince and George Nader. A back-channel with Russia was one topic they discussed as well as a future relationship with the new Trump Administration.

Post Q# 224
Who knows where the bodies are buried?

Putin ally Krill Dmitriev accidentally bumped into Erik Prince and they had a few beers while vacationing in the Seychelles. The Deep State has another 'plant' with George Nader arranging 'dirty-up' meetings with Trump world individuals.

Post Q# 4235
Infiltration of the US GOV?
That fact alone should scare every American.

George Nader setup both of these highly suspicious meetings. I contend that Nader was a spy/LURE deliberately inserted into the Trump Transition Team by the criminal coup plotters. George Nader would later be arrested and convicted of underage criminal sex charges and is in jail.

Post Q# 2872

Hillary Clinton and Foundation.
Crime Against Children.

In March 2018, Robert Mueller expanded his investigative scope to other 'stormy' subjects. Team Mueller had looked into Erik Prince's mysterious Seychelles rendezvous and possible back-channel talk with Russian secret agents. Judgement Day is coming, and all truths will be finally revealed.

Post Q# 1091

What forces shadow No Name ?
Contractors.
Special contractors.
decode: Hired (Prince's FSG) Mercenaries are following No Name around in real-time.

Post Q# 1141

Blackwater on GUARD.
decode: Erik Prince's "Blackwater Mercs" are protecting POTUS/FAMILY.

It has been announced that Erik Prince is helping with a friendly "Occupation Force" in Syria. Erik Prince has long promoted the ideal of a civilian contractor army in place of sending our military and a privatized global intelligence network. Erik Prince would testify in the Benghazi Congressional hearings that HRC friend Sid Blumenthal had no business advising her on foreign policy affairs such as Libya.

Post Q# 4310

HOW DO YOU CIRCUMVENT THE SHADOW INTEL COMM?

President Trump had once seriously considered the option of an outside independent intelligence system to replace the corrupt "17 U.S. Intel" agencies. Erik Prince has the expertise as well as international connection to build a new spy network. Additionally Erik Prince would make a 26-page mass deportation proposal to the U.S. Government to sweep up and deport millions of illegal migrants.

Post Q# 374

Operators active.
Operators in harms way.

On a rumor basis only, Erik/Blackwater was connected to assisting the Saudi Arabia cleanup and torture of disloyal Saudi Royals. Additionally, Erik/Blackwater is credited with helping NK Kim's security during his peace talks with President Trump. Special Counsel (SC) John Durham has dropped criminal indictments related to past illegal surveillance operations and submitted his final report in 2023. Ever the economic opportunist, Erik Prince had drawn up plans for a 'Flying Tigers' air force for Ukraine in a later rejected lend-lease military arrangement.

Post Q# 4021

Think Double agents.
Public truths of some events force wars.
WWIII prevent.

FOX's hit TV series "24" has famed actor Jon Voigt playing a veiled version of the real Erik Prince. We are watching a real-life historic play unfold in front of us fellow Patriots. Prince has been helping recruit former spies to assist with Project Veritas. Erik Prince has explored in

2022/23 of the possibility of setting up a private army for Ukraine for only $10B. Haiti would enlist the expertise of Erik Prince in 2025 to help fight off the increasing use of 'assassin drones.'

Post Q# 1091
> Think Double.
> Why are we confirming this publicly?
> Why now?

IG Horowitz's two past reports highlighted Abedin/Weiner's laptop seizure and the subsequent disgusting material discovered. Erik Prince would rollout in 2024 a secure personal phone called 'Unplugged' which defeats most monitoring surveillance efforts. The reports from IG Horowitz and SC John Durham will be the foundation for future judicial accountability. With the historic re-election of President Trump in 2024, many past hidden political secrets will be revealed.

Post Q# 224
> (Anon): Betsy DeVos - Erik Prince-POTUS.

Links

Time-Erik Prince's $10B Plan for Private Ukraine Army

Revolver News-This Guy is Still Secretly Running Key Parts of the CIA

Washington Examiner-Haiti Enlists Blackwater Founder Erik Prince

The Hill-Erik Prince/Blackwater's Mass Deportation Proposal

Real Clear Politics-Erik Prince: The Theme of No Accountability Across All Government Rings True

The Hill-Erik Prince helped Raise Money to Spy on Progressives and Anti-Trump

Medium-Erik Prince: From the Seychelles to the White House

Vanity Fair-Tycoon, Contractor, Soldier, Spy

The Intercept-FBI Investigating Erik Prince: Weaponizing Crop Dusters

Washington Examiner-Schiff Sends Criminal Referral to DOJ on Erik Prince

Newsweek-Blackwater Founder wants His Mercenaries in Venezuela

The Intercept-Trump White House Weighs plans for Spies to Counter Deep State

ABC News-Putin Ally Dmitriev says Erik Prince Meeting more than Chance

NY Daily News-Blackwater's Erik Prince part of Trump-Russia Comms Effort

The Hill-Erik Prince helps Rohrabacher amid Mueller Seychelles Probe

Daily Mail-Trump comes under Fire for "Private Security Detail"

Forbes-Prince's Return to Power: Trump, Bolton and the Privatization of War

Breitbart-Erik Prince: NYPD ready to make Arrests in Weiner's Laptop Case

FOX News-Prince fights Accusations of a Russia "Back-Channel"

Oak and Institute-Return of Erik Prince: Trump's Knight

The Hill-Erik Prince Recruited Ex-Spies to Help Project Veritas

Breitbart-Erik Prince: HRC should be Unemployable

Radio Patriot-Erik Prince Transcript: Weiner Laptop

Unplugged-The Unplugged Phone

Operation Cassandra / Bruce Ohr / Hezbollah / and Imran Awan

Former AG Stealth Jeff Sessions was well known for being a very anti-drug federal officer. The ongoing FBI international anti-drug project operation known as Operation or Project Cassandra, was purposely put on hold by BHO so as to clear the pathway for his signature Iranian Nuclear Deal. Established in 1982 was the Organized Crime Drug Enforcement Task Forces (OCDETF) to combat major trafficking operations. DOJ official Bruce Ohr is a central figure with Cassandra that would continue to play a key role in 2022 with the unfolding SpyGate political scandal.

Post Q# 3532
[AWAN]
You didn't think the plea deal was the end did you?

When the halted Project Cassandra was brought to AG Jeff Sessions' attention, he formed a new special DOJ Task Force to continue this important program in the war on drugs. This task force's goal was to seriously combat the Hezbollah international criminal cartel and to cripple their drug running/money laundering programs into the United States.

Post Q# 151
How do you capture a very dangerous animal?

Project Cassandra was a decades old DEA program implemented to stop the Iran backed terror group Hezbollah. Narcoterrorism is always present from illegal drug running and weapons trafficking operations. The Muslim Brotherhood has attempted a longstanding campaign of infiltration against the USA.

Post Q# 1981
AWAN - Pakistani Intelligence?

Central to this $1 Billion annual criminal enterprise is ability to have huge cash money laundering. This untraceable cash brings directly into play the international banking industry. The late best selling author Phillip Haney had testified before Congress on this threat and written a best selling book warning about the infiltration into the U.S. of the Muslim Brotherhood (MB). The world would witness in 2024 the explosion of the MB in their wild worldwide support for Hamas over Israel.

Post Q# 85
Why is AG Sessions /POTUS prioritizing building the wall?
Immigration?
Drugs?

Drugs and the related money laundering operations will also bring in shady used car dealerships, just like the ones our favorite Pakistani spy Imran Awan (handled first by Xavier Becerra and later by Debbie Wassermann Schultz) owned in the USA. Money laundering operations need to operate with a believable valid front company and untraceable cash has always been the 'life bloodline' of the international MB.

Post Q# 3634
Awan IT scandal
IF KNOWN - WHY IS IT ALLOWED TO HAPPEN?

Also let's not forget about President Trump's first military action and subsequent tragedy in Yemen (Yalka). This is where our U.S. mission plans were somehow internally compromised and given to the 'waiting in ambush' enemy forces. The White Hats have been very interested into this vital leak of military intel which had such tragic results.

Post Q# 77
Who is Awan?
What is Awan Group?
Define cash laundering.

This operation's unplanned security compromise tragically led to Navy Seal Ryan Owen's death. The Awan Family Cabal are the prime suspects in this leak of secret military operational information and will ultimately be held accountable. Bear in mind Bruce Ohr's wife is the infamous Fusion GPS researcher Nellie Ohr who is a central character in the SpyGate scandal. It later would be revealed that a lot of the funding for both domestic and foreign illegal operations came via the corrupt USAID.

Post Q# 674
Awan/DWS/Paki Intel/MB.
decode: MB=Muslim Brotherhood

DOJ's Task Force is expected to have some preliminary findings to Congress later in 2020. Focus will be on uncovering past Project Cassandra abuses as well as prior business relationships with the Pakistani Awan's and other laundering fronts. The Islamic religion has been at war with Christians and Jews for centuries. Special Counsel (SC) John Durham was tasked to explore criminal referrals from IG Horowitz and vowed to get to the bottom of past criminality under BHO. President Trump would specifically name Bruce and his wife Nellie Ohr in his 2022 federal RICO lawsuit against those promoting the false Russian collusion narrative during the 2016 Presidential election cycle.

Post Q# 2450
We take this journey together.
One step at a time.
WWG1WGA!

Former Deputy AG Rod Rosenstein and disgraced DOJ top official Bruce Ohr had originally led this current task force. Bruce Ohr previously had run this very same program under BHO but was ordered to ignored the international terrorism, money laundering, and drug trafficking. Bruce Ohr and his 'lovely' wife Nellie will become central figures in the unfolding criminal indictments of the infamous SpyGate scandal. President Trump would specially name both Bruce and Nellie Ohr as the first married pair (more 'dirty couples' to follow) in his lawsuit related to the activities surround the unfolding SpyGate scandal.

Post Q# 2663
Something out of a movie?
The hole is deep.

President Trump had been systemically cutting off both the Deep State's access to America and attacking their funding sources. Global terror groups rely upon the untraceable cash from these drug-running worldwide operations. SC John Durham pressed Fusion GPS for documents related to both Bruce and Nellie Ohr's activities around the phony Christopher Steele Russian Dossier but got no cooperation. SC Durham dropped criminal indictments related to SpyGate and submitted his final report in 2023. With the re-election of President Trump in 2024, many hope that past hidden political secrets will finally be publicly revealed.

Post Q# 3903

[infiltration instead of invasion]

Links

The Hill-Get Tough on Hezbollah: Fix BHO's Mistake

The Federalist-FBI/DOJ Declined to Charge Russia Collusion Hoaxer

American Thinker-Is BHO Guilty of Mass Murder?

Voice of America-DOJ's Hezbollah Campaign Called Project Cassandra

New Yorker-Pete/Lisa and Bruce Ohr

The Federalist-Ohr Memo Confirms Clinton Team had Knowledge of Black Ledger

Markets Work-Indictments by DOJ Point to Multiple Global Operations

Markets Work-Hezbollah's Bomb Making, Iran Nuke Deal, and Bruce Ohr

Tablet Magazine-How RussiaGate began with BHO's Iran Deal

NY Post-BHO protected Hezbollah Drug Ring to save Iran Nuke Deal

Daily Caller-Former DEA Agent: Bruce Ohr had 'Other Priorities'

Front Page-The Party of Treason

Politico-Secret Backstory: How BHO let Hezbollah Off the Hook

Town Hall-Hezbollah hoarded Fertilizer for planned Nuclear Style Attack

PJ Media-BHO Officials Colluded with Iran to Undermine Trump

Jeff Carlson-Bruce and Nellie Ohr

Daily Caller-Awan's Car Dealerships Nefarious for Money Laundering

Epoch Times-String of Indictments by DOJ to Multiple Global Operations

Sharyl Attkisson-Cybersecurity and The Awan Brothers

NY Post-Deafening Media Silence on the BHO Hezbollah Scandal

DEA.gov-Uncover Massive Hezbollah Drug and Money Laundering Scheme

Crossfire Hurricane Docs-Bruce Ohr Interview

Justice.gov-2023 SC John Durham Report

MOAB:
When President Trump Confirms the Operation: 'Q' Day

Post Q# 55

> Look to Twitter:
> Exactly this: "My fellow Americans, the Storm is upon us......"

There is little dispute that the day will come when the Mockingbird media asks President Trump the question concerning 'Q' (QAnon). When President Trump announces or drops the validity of 'Q' on a 100% undisputed basis, that will be forever known as Q-DAY. Remember President Trump signed on 12/21/17 his Executive Order blocking the property of persons involved with corruption. Cyber Command announced a new unit designated Cyber Military Intelligence Group (CMIG) that will capitalize on open-source public data to support cyber operations.

Post Q# 4502

> The doubters will soon be believers.
> Years in the making.

Patriots from around the globe are waiting for the day we can all come out of out the 'Q' closet. 'Q' is an informational program which began in late 2017 on the public posting board known as 4Chan. The many past drops seem to forecast and indicate the future will be the glorious indeed fellow Patriots. President Trump has answered the 'Q' questions by news reporters in the past, always giving general answers to the frustration of the Mockingbird media. 'Crumbs' continue to appear since the last 'Q' drops in 2020 and the Truth Social new media site has a Q-like account. Magically the drops began again the day Roe (11.3 as a marker) was overturned on 6/24/22 after a two-year break in the posts.

Post Q# 1232

> Ready to play?
> MOAB incoming.

Q-DAY will be the beginning of the end of fighting from the shadows. Patriots await President Trump's announcement and unleashing of what General Flynn terms as the Army of Digital Soldiers. Special Counsel (SC) John Durham has dropped criminal indictments and submitted his final report in 2023. President Trump went on the offensive in 2002 with the filing of a federal RICO lawsuit against HRC/DNC/and others related to the promotion of the false Russian collusion narrative during the 2016 election cycle.

Post Q# 4050

> You are trending WW 24/7/365 w/censorship.
> Never in our history has this been attempted.

The first time the U.S. deployed a GBU-43 or M.O.A.B. (nicknamed Mother of all Bombs) in combat was in 2017. The Air Force was targeting an ISIS underground command/control complex in Afghanistan. President Trump has echoed what the entire nation feels about the treasonous withdrawal from Afghanistan by the illegal Biden regime, that it is a permanent stain on our country. One of the earliest 'Q-Proofs' was when President Trump made the specific (asked by the Anons to make) was during a 2018 White House Easter event when the term "Tippy Top" was made.

Post Q# 144

> What is No Such Agency—Q group?

MOAB was first tested at the Eglin Air Force Material Command Base on 3/11/2003. Eglin AFB is located along Florida's Panhandle not far from Pensacola and is considered one of the largest air bases in the world. Eglin boasts of several unique facilities including the world famous hot/cold aircraft testing hanger. Many feel the 'Q Operation' began in 2004 and was first made public in 2014 (NSA Q Group) then fully to the general public (Anons) in late 2017.

Post Q# 47

> You can paint the picture based solely on the questions asked.
> Alice and Wonderland.

Elgin AFB had a hand in the famed Colonel Doolittle mainland Tokyo Japan Raid during WW2. Pilots practiced take-offs at Elgin AFB prior to their historic launching from USS Lexington aircraft carrier on their Tokyo bombing runs. The Hollywood hit movie 'Midway' accurately re-enacts the Eglin AFB training portion of that important surprise air raid. Please note that the U.S. House of Representatives voted in 2020 under HR 1154 to condemn QAnon, thus adding more credibility to our worldwide movement. President Trump's lawyers argued in 2023 as part of his legal defense against false charges, that he must retain his top secret 'Q' level security clearance.

Post Q# 4496

> Digital warriors ready.
> Surender to None ['Digital Battleground'].
> WWG1WGA!!!

Massive Ordnance Air Blast (MOAB) has the common nickname of the 'Mother of all Bombs.' Dropped at Eglin's Range 70 in the early afternoon, this earth-shaking explosion created a 'Mushroom Cloud' that was visible for miles along the Florida panhandle. Local folks still will discuss the events surrounding that Florida day. Of note is that President Trump continues to make the unique reference to "Tippy Top" in public appearances leading up to the 2024 election. Steve Bannon would publicly announce in 2023 that "QAnon had been right all along". Ironically both the height of popularity of 'Q' as well as the extreme censorship of 'Q' occurred before the 2020 Presidential election.

Post Q# 991

> Anon: Tip Top Tippy Top Shape
> Q: It was requested. Did you listen today?

The MOAB is the largest non-nuclear bomb in the U.S. arsenal (20 in stock). It detonates around 6 feet above the intended target and is non-penetrating but extremely lethal due to the massive concussion wave and forced blast ratio. It is rumored UBL died in the al-Qaeda cave complex battle of Tora Bora and not in the BHO 2011 narrative killing. Under the proposed Continuance of Government concept, the coming Judgment Day will be the final great awakening for the public.

Post Q# 153

> Ask yourself an honest question, why would a billionaire who has it all, fame, fortune, a warm and loving family, friends, etc. want to endanger himself and his family by becoming POTUS?
> Perhaps he could not in good conscience see the world burn.

The Q-DAY will be like the impact of the impressive real MOAB. President Trump and Team 'Q' have mentioned carpet bombs as well as other Stealth Bombers were forthcoming, but Patriots want the MOAB. With disastrous events unfolding daily under the illegal Biden administration, the time for the truth about many scandals and absolutely right now. Special Counsel John Durham has dropped a MOAB-type BOOM by submitting his final report in 2023. Besides General Flynn, we can thank many other military Patriots like Valley/McRaven/and McInerny to name a few associated with the famed Army of Northern Virginia.

Post Q# 3716
First indictment [unseal] will trigger mass pop awakening.
First arrest will verify action and confirm future direction.
They will fight but you are ready.

NOTE FROM AUTHOR: Due to fate, I was at Eglin AFB that day of the first MOAB test in 2003. All I can say is that the blast noise, ground vibration, and image of that massive mushroom cloud remains firmly imprinted in my mind today-BOOM!!!

Post Q+ 2629
[D] Day, Patriots.
We will have our Country back!

At some point the 'question' will be ask and answered by President Trump. Our dear President Trump has already given cleaver answers to prior media questions over 'Q.' Patriots see in 2024 the unveiling of what our JoeM outlined as 'The Plan' as well as what Patel Patriot has outlined in the Continuity of Government (COG) programs that seem to be at play. In 2023-24 thankfully meaningful U.S. Congressional investigations as well as Elon Musk's Twitter Files and Jeff Bezos' Amazon Files releases over past censorship. President Trump as well as Elon Musk would troll their mutual enemies with continuous reposts on his TruthSocial of 'QAnon' related memes. With the re-election of President Trump in 2024, many feel there is a possibility of the return of 'Q'/Team.

Post Q# 2563
At some point, the Q will be asked.

Links

YouTube-President Trump Tippy Top

Salon-Trump Shares QAnon Conspiracy Theory

Clinton Foundation Timeline-2025 Crossfire Hurricane Docs

Awaken Greatly-Ask the 'Q'

MSNBC-Durbin questions Pam Bondi about QAnon

The Independent-Trump Jr.: QAnon has "Probably been Right about a Lot of Things"

Axios-Trump TruthSocial: Posts QAnon

MSMBC News-Elon Musk's QAnon Signals New Low

Vice News-Trump Supports QAnon

New Yorker-Why is Trump Openly Embracing QAnon Now?

Scientific American-What is the Mother of All Bombs?

PBS-Trump Openly Embracing and Amplifying False Fringe QAnon

WAPO-Trump 'Q' Clearance Classified Nuclear Secrets

Rolling Stone-QAnon Conspiracy: Trump Timeline

People Magazine-Trump Reportedly praised QAnon

AMG-Q: Greatest Military Intelligence Operation

Raw Story-Steve Bannon: QAnon has been Right

Martin Geddes-Information Architecture of the Q

Salon-Narrative Sociology: Conspiracy Theory QAnon

Axios-QAnon Grows before 2020 Election

Patriots Soapbox-Ret. General Paul Vallely Confirms Existence of "Q"

FED Scoop-New Army Unit will Combine Military Intelligence with Open-Source Data

Burning Bright-We Are Q

CNN-Q Group: Manhunt Under Way for NSA Leaker

My Pan-MOAB used in One Other Place -Eglin AFB

CNBC-Trump says He Appreciates Support from Followers of QAnon

Pew Research-QAnon Conspiracy Seeped into Politics (24% of USA)

New Yorker-Trump Drops the M.O.A.B. on Afghanistan

PRRI Organization-The Rise and Impact of Q in 2024

WJHG-MOAB Developed and Tested at Eglin AFB

State of the Nation-The 16-Year Plan to Destroy America

Wired-MOAB was just waiting for Right Target

Daily Beast (pre-Q)-Inside the "Q Group" Hunting Snowden

NBC News-QAnon Book Climbs Best Seller List

Intelligence Support Activity-Joint Special Ops Command (Send Me)

Science Daily-The 10% Rule (Public Acceptance)

NSA.gov-Central Security Services (CSS)

General Mike Flynn- "Army of Digital Soldiers"

VICE TV-QAnon Influencers

Congress.gov-HR 1154: Condemning QAnon

White House.gov-EO blocking Property of Persons Involved with Corruption

Crossfire Hurricane Docs-Christopher Steele Binder

Justice.gov-2023 SC John Durham Report

Ringmaster IG Horowitz's Reports have 'Set the Stage'

The Ringmaster is the master of ceremonies that introduces the "circus acts" to the audience. Inspector General (IG) Michael Horowitz is such a talented skilled Ringmaster. DOJ's IG Horowitz has produced reports on HRC's email server, FBI James Comey, FBI Andy McCabe, Confidential Informants (CI) human resource validation, and past abuses in FISA/FISC. The public would start to see in 2022 the culmination of Michael Horowitz's referrals as the SpyGate/RussiaGate criminal indictments begin to drop.

Post Q# 2462
> Who is HOROWITZ?
> Mandate charged to HOROWITZ?
> Resources provided to HOROWITZ?

IG Horowitz's report on FISC/FISA abuses during the 2016 campaign led to criminal investigations. SpyGate elements and insertion of paid intelligence assets or Confidential Informants (CI) into President Trump's election campaign staffer is under review by Special Counsel (SC) John Durham. President Trump would file in 2022 a federal RICO lawsuit against those promoting the false Russian collusion narrative back in 2016.

Post Q# 2555
> WHITAKER, HOROWITZ, HUBER, and WRAY.
> Long meeting held within a SCIF [unusual].

Carter Page's four FISA application have been deemed to be fraudulent by the OIG's report. AG Bill Barr had authority for full DECLAS as ordered by POTUS as well as announcing the outcome of current criminal probes but chose not to all at the end of 2020. Special Counsel John Durham would begin to layout a vast 'Joint Venture Conspiracy' involving many officials surrounding the 2016 false Russian collusion narratives.

Post Q# 2681
> Barr meeting Huber and OIG.
> OIG report.

IG Horowitz and his hundreds of lawyers had been working since January 12, 2017, on several investigations. Reports on the FBI Andy McCabe, the CI issue, FBI James Comey, Clinton Foundation, and HRC email probes all tie into the many FISA abuses by the DOJ/FBI.

Post Q# 4374
> Be strong in the Lord.

The OIG had been doing its primary assigned job, which is oversight of the DOJ/FBI. Per crack news reporter Sara Carter, SC Durham will deliver indictments and he did. SC Durham submitted his final report in 2023. IG Horowitz was first appointment to this position by BHO in 2012.

Post Q# 2489
> [Placeholder - OIG Report and Findings].
> [Placeholder - OIG Report-Umbrella SPY and Targeting].

The multiple fraudulent Carter Page's Title-1 Surveillance warrants and sinister interactions by intelligent assets Stefan Halper and Joseph Mifsud in 2016, will be another main focus of the ongoing criminal investigations.

Post Q# 1318

"Horowitz oversees a nationwide workforce of more than 450 special agents."

IG Horowitz had been working in secret conjunction with U.S. Attorneys Special Prosecutor (SP) John Huber and Special Counsel (SC) John Durham. This combination according to historian Jonathan Turley, is far better than appointing a second Special Counsel to review these scandals.

Post Q# 1563

Text B missing and takes (4) attempts to recover due to 'glitch.'
Text B supplied in IG report.

SP Huber and SC Durham were assigned secretly by Stealth Jeff Sessions way back in November 2017. Secrecy and no comment were the way things used to always be handled by the DOJ. President Trump has vowed to return our country to the successful ways things used to be done.

Post Q# 4957

What happens when you corner an animal?
SP John Huber/SC John Durham have full prosecuting authority over all of these following open investigations started by IG Horowitz:

- • HRC Server/Email (ObamaGate)
- • FISA Court/Fusion GSP Dossier(s)/Alfa Bank (RussiaGate)
- • Crossfire Hurricane-Crossfire Razor-Crossfire Typhoon (SpyGate)
- • Clinton Foundation/Uranium One

Post Q# 4162

$1 + 1 = 2$
Think [leak investigation].
Think Horowitz [Midyear] re: FBI_media assets.

Huber and Durham were secretly appointed by AG Sessions as a Special Prosecutors to help out the OIG. SP John Huber added prosecutorial teeth to IG Horowitz and assistance in routing out corruption at the top echelons of the DOJ/FBI/State/Intelligence agencies.

Post Q# 1517

IG started long before Huber setting stage.
IG = FBI.
Huber = DOJ (no DC).

Horowitz was appointed under BHO and was a carry-over into the Trump Administration. Deputy AG Sally Yates never allowed Horowitz to review the National Security departments of both the DOJ and FBI. Horowitz has again stayed on with the new Biden administration.

Post Q# 2501

WHITAKER (in conjunction w/OIG) approved the release of CLAS docs 1-4.

National Security Departments were the central locations of the 'Secret Society' or small group of traitors. This small group of upper-level 7th Floor officials planned and carried out the SpyGate coup plot.

Post Q# 1553

Noting that Huber would be "conducting his work from outside Washington D.C. area" and in "cooperation with Horowitz."

A total of 7 major reports have been tasked to Horowitz with only 4 of those to be made public. President Trump had organized a true legal dream team with Barr/Horowitz/Durham/Huber/and Storch to start the probes into the Deep State.

Post Q# 2676
> DECLAS?
> OIG release of findings?
> "This is not another 4-year election."

Horowitz's had been tasked with the initial inquiries and handed off via his subsequent report recommendations. Big future BOOMS are forthcoming and the emergence of the 'Great Awakening.'

Post Q# 3587
> Indictments coming

Hopefully with AG Barr's final act of elevating SP John Durham to Special Counsel (SC), the prosecutions can finally begin. Let's all remember Durham has had access to fair grand jury's and treason charges carry the death penalty. In 2022 John Durham has made filings that appear to rebuke Horowitz's prior claims on material that has been previously turned over to the Special Counsel's office.

Post Q# 2397
> OIG works w/HUBER [important to remember].

We all recall the many riveting personal text messages between the so-called FBI lovers Strzok and Page. Yet to be publicly released is a text with a 'physical threat' to President Trump and his wonderful family. IG continues under the illegal Biden administration but has given Congressional testimony outlining the past abuses of the FBI in FISA warrant applications.

Post Q# 2548
> What case(s) is HUBER + OIG + team of 470 currently working on?

FBI staff like Peter Strzok and Lisa Page went from exonerating HRC, over to the persecution of candidate Trump. Several Trump-Russia staffers were then placed onto Robert Mueller's investigative team to continue the witch-hunt. IG Horowitz's reports, along with that of SC Durham, will be the foundational documents that future judicial accountability will be based. With the re-election of President Trump in late 2024, Chris Wray would resign a day before IG Horowitz's report on the FBI's confidential human sources planted into the January 6th Capitol event.

Post Q# 1122
> TRUST HOROWITZ.
> TRUST HUBER.

Recently per Joe diGenova, 'Ringmaster' Horowitz concluded that all four Carter Page FISA's were in fact illegal. IG Horowitz has continued on in his same Inspector General duty under illegal Joe Biden. SC John Durham has dropped criminal indictments related to SpyGate and submitted his final report in 2023. It would be revealed in early 2024 by a whistleblower that James Comey assigned FBI 'Honeypot' agents into Trump's 2016 campaign and to intentionally hide this evidence from then IG Michael Horowitz. With the re-election of President Trump in 2024, he fired all Inspector Generals except Michael Horowitz and we still hope to find the real architects of the illegal SpyGate/RussiaGate coup operations.

Post Q# 3839
> It's time to wake up.

Links

National Review-IG Horowitz found 'Apparent Errors' in every FISA Reviewed

Real Clear Investigations-RussiaGate's Architects Suppressed Doubts to Peddle False Claims

Washington Examiner-DOJ IG Michael Horowitz Picked as New Watchdog for FED/CFPB

OIG.Justice.Gov-DOJ OIG FISA Report

The Federalist-Unsealed Crossfire Hurricane Docs prove RussiaGate a Hoax

The Last Refuge-OIG Michael Horowitz Testimony

Washington Examiner-James Comey used FBI 'Honeypots' to Infiltrate Trump's Campaign

Daily Mail-DOJ Spying on Crossfire Hurricane Watchdogs

The Last Refuge-IG Horowitz and Sally Yates

National Review-No IG Horowitz didn't Endorse the FBI Predication

Rolling Stone-Horowitz Report: 5 Unanswered Questions

The Federalist-SpyGate 101: A Primer on the Russia Collusion Hoax to Down Trump

Washington Examiner-Durham adds to SpyGate's Chapter on Trump Transition

The Last Refuge-IG Michael Horowitz Report

Epoch Times-IG Horowitz and FISA Abuses

Markets Work-Findings of IG Report: Significant FISA Abuse

Epoch Times-IG Michael Horowitz

The Last Refuge-SpyGate: The Big Picture

NY Post-FBI Routinely Failed to Document FISA Warrant Claims

The Federalist-DOJ/FBI knew Trump Surveillance based on Russian Disinformation

Video-IG Michael Horowitz Speaking at National Whistleblower Event

OIG.Justice.gov-FBI's Handling of it's Confidential Human Sources

OIG.Justice.gov-IG Horowitz's Review of 4 FISA Applications

OIG.Justice.gov-Report regarding Unauthorized Contacts by FBI and Media

Crossfire Hurricane Docs-Christopher Steele Binder

Justice.gov-2023 SC John Durham Report

Susan Rice—
Stand Down Artist Extraordinaire to Shadow President

Susan Elizabeth Rice [SR] had long departed from BHO's cabinet as his National Security Director/UN Ambassador, when she was asked to return to government service. Sleepy Joe announced Susan Rice as head of White House Domestic Policy Council aka acting as the Shadow President. Dementia Joe has ordered Rice to divest her $2.3M stake in an oil pipeline. Most observers agree Rice was tasked to carry on BHO's third term policies under Biden, but both have miscalculated horribly the ability to control Sleepy Joe. With horror in early 2023 Biden picked Susan Rice to implement Critical Race Theory (CRT) across the entire USA federal government. Fortunately for our country, Susan Rice decided it was time to split from Sleepy Joe and declared in mid 2023 she was once again leaving government service.

Post Q# 1623
Who just joined the Board of Netflix?

Past Congressional testimony had revealed that NSA [SR] gave the official stand-down order to the U.S. Cyber Security Chief in 2016. Rice's order forced Cyber Security to 'stand-down' against attempted 2016 Russian cyber attacks and Presidential campaign election meddling. In historical hindsight, we can now see the tactics first tried out in 2016 and later perfected with the Presidential election steal of 2020.

Post Q# 1356
The Shadow Government.

Judicial Watch has been seeking to question both Susan Rice and Ben Rhodes over the 2012 attack at Benghazi. Recent uncovered FOIA BHO-era documents outline false Benghazi talking points to be given out by Rice to MSM news reporters. Rice would come to document the January 5, 2017, Oval Office meeting with team BHO concerning Trump/Russia in her infamous January 20, 2017, CYA personal memo to self. BHO would order the continued unmasking/surveillance of those associates close to then President Elect Trump.

Post Q# 3595
US AMB 1 and 2 NSA unmask req.

Bear in mind that Susan Rice currently holds the 'Mockingbird' world record of 6 Sunday morning talk show appearances concerning the deadly Benghazi attack. Rice broke the record of 5 Sunday appearances by attorney Ginsburg in the Monica Lewinsky case against Bill Clinton. Collectively Rice/Rhodes/and Powers also jointly hold the current world record for the most 'unmasking' of U.S. Citizens, estimated at well over 300 innocent civilians.

Post Q# 2770
ABC NEWS exec producer Ian Cameron married to Susan Rice (Nat Sec Advisor-HUSSEIN)?

Rice's infamous response when questioned on this subject of media leaks "I leaked nothing to nobody." [SR] was also the quarterback when it came to the special circulation of BHO's Presidential Daily Brief (PDB) and the Evelyn Farkas spilling the surveillance beans on MSNBC.

Post Q# 1764

Think FISA.
NAME/BRENNAN/CLAPPER/RICE/HUSSEIN.

The PDB distribution was compartmentalized within the 'Secret Society' members via the Operation Latitude. Rice joined with BHO Alumni Jake Sullivan, Ben Rhodes, Jen Pasaki, Denis McDonough and Samantha Powers in forming the PAC think tank called National Security Action (oddly NSA). Many of NSA's alumni now hold high level positions in the illegal Biden administration.

Post Q# 4310

Critical thinking_what did [Susan Rice] DECLAS [Jan 5] WH meeting reveal?
RUSSIA INTEL HOLD.

NSA is the primary corporate Anti-Trump resistance headquarters group. NSA along with BHO's OFA foot soldiers like BLM/Antifa, together they form the front-line fighters against President Trump/'Q'/and the MAGA movements. The Deep State/DC Swamp will never give up their ill gained power and 'Q' highlighting that the military is the only way.

Post Q# 3954

Missing [29] connections - National.
Missing [98] connections - Local.

Susan Rice has once again in 2023 upon leaving the Biden administration, scarily rejoined the board of entertainment firm Netflix. Rice's husband is Ian Cameron, who is a longtime top executive at ABC News and strategically placed to help the Deep State Cabal. Most feel that BHO is controlling the dementia ridden Biden through Susan Rice's new West Wing office.

Post Q# 120

Why is the NSA limited re: ability to capture and unmask US persons?
Who sets the narrative?

Incredibly there are numerous 'Dirty Couples' connected to the ObamaGate/SpyGate scandals. The illegal email accounts will become more of a central issue with Special Counsel (SC) John Durham has dropped criminal indictments and submitted his final report in 2023. The Shadow President (Susan Rice) would be put in charge of the 'gun effort' in 2022 after the return of the weekly school shooting that were a common occurrence under BHO and instantly vanished under President Trump.

Post Q# 559

HUSSEIN CABINET / STAFF
Who used private email addresses?
What was the purpose?
SR
decode: SR=Susan Rice

Senators Chuck Grassley and Ron Johnson have been interested in Susan Rice's bizarre email on 1/20/17. Susan Rice had oddly emailed a classified email note to herself after leaving government service and on the day of President Trump's Inauguration (1/20/17). Sadly a group of entrenched leftists/Marxist top government officials have captured our country and the fight to restore freedom continues.

Post Q# 1708

> Co-sponsor insurance policy re: POTUS election.
> RICE.

This strange Rice "Cover Your Ass" (CYA) email memo occurred on President Trump's Inauguration Day 2017, in a very hastily prepared fashion. Meaning Susan Rice was no longer employed by the government when doing this irregular email memo that she sent to herself on NSA computer servers. The essence of the ObamaGate/SpyGate operations against Donald Trump would coalesce on the critical January 5th Oval Office meeting.

Post Q# 354

> Ian Cameron.
> Clowns In America.
> Dr. Emmett J. Rice.
> Federal Reserve.

Susan Rice's was immortalizing a White House Oval Office meeting she attended held on 1/5/17 with BHO/JB/Yates/Biden/and Comey. It appears Rice did a classic CYA email, but impartial Congressional Committees are not buying her lies after seeing the newly declassified version. Susan Rice's pal current NSA Jake Sullivan may ultimately be implicated in the various political scandals known as RussiaGate/SpyGate.

Post Q# 802

> Traitor.
> 2. a person who commits treason by betraying his or her own country.

Inquiring minds want to know exactly what BHO /Biden ordered Comey and Yates to do about incoming President Trump. Comey/Yates were the top two carry-overs into the new administration and leaders of Crossfire Hurricane failed coup plot. In late 2024 foreshadowing the forthcoming historic Trump re-election victory, Susan Rice and other BHO/Biden officials claim they will be imprisoned in the future. Former DNI Rick Grenell says Rice is currently the Shadow President of the country. Susan Rice additionally would help sabotage, in direct violation of the Logan Act, President Trump's peace proposal for the Ukraine/Russia conflict.

Post Q# 3118

> Susan Rice picture—Placeholder

Links

Brass Balls-Susan Rice is the President

FOX News-BHO Officials Mum on Allegations Manufactured Intel Launching Trump Probe

Geller Report-BHO's Ukraine Traitors

Clinton Foundation Timeline-Susan Rice is Fired from Defense Policy Board

The Federalist-Susan Rice Email Confirms Michael Flynn was Personally Targeted

Netflix-Netflix Reappoints Ambassador Susan Rice to BOD

Lee Smith-BHO's January 5th Conspiracy

Sharyl Attkisson-BHO Era Surveillance Timeline

The Federalist-BHO and Biden January 5th Meeting was Key to Trump Operation

National Review-The Susan Rice CYA Memo

Markets Work-Biden Officials had Roles in Surveillance of Trump

Judicial Watch-Susan Rice/HRC/and Benghazi

National Review-5 more Things You did not Know about Susan Rice

Judicial Watch-Susan Rice admits under Oath She emailed HRC on Personal Account

Real Clear Investigations-Susan Rice's Testimony doesn't Add Up

FOX News-Grenell: Susan Rice is the Shadow President

The Last Refuge-Susan Rice Memo

Front Page Magazine-Susan Rice's Role in Rwanda Genocide predicted ObamaGate

Daily Caller-Rice gave "Stand Down" Order

The Federalist-Rice's Role in SpyGate

Sen. Grassley-Unusual Email Sent by Susan Rice

Power Line Blog-The Silence of Susan Rice

Town Hall-Gruesome Twosome of Unmasking

Grassley.Senate.gov-Crossfire Hurricane Timeline

Clinton Foundation Timeline-2025 Crossfire Hurricane Docs

Justice.gov-2023 SC John Durham Report

The Seth Rich Murder Mystery: Morphing Iterations [187]

The tragic death of Patriot Seth Conrad "Panda" Rich (1989-2016) on July 10, 2016 can be viewed as a critical pivotal point. This in the historical perspective of the 'Q' Great Awakening movement that is unfolding worldwide today. The murder of a DNC IT staffer helped to kick off an elaborate scheme by the most powerful globalist to prevent a New York builder from winning the Presidency in 2016. Seth Rich [SR] would remain in the news as in 2023 FBI Director Wray was forced to disclose that the FBI in fact does have more information on Seth Rich.

Post Q# 2607
> No. (Anon question: Is SR Alive?)

Since the sad [SR] murder there has been many different twists and turns in an attempt to solve this high-profile assassination. Many theories have surfaced but 'Q' has stated that [SR] is truly dead and will long be remembered for his brave downloads of DNC emails. With the numerous major political scandals of today, there is an apparent lack of governmental whistleblowers for obvious reasons of personal safety.

Post Q# 3841
> RUSSIA DID NOT'HACK' [penetrate] THE DNC SERVER.
> internal DL / release.

Seth Rich's brutal murder has been described by the DC Metropolitan Police (MPDC) as a "botched robbery". The DC Metro Police homicide case review included the confiscation of Seth's personal laptop and cellphone data which has never been made public despite numerous FOIA requests. MPDC had initially offered a reward of $25,000 for any information concerning this brutal homicide. To date no one has claimed any rewards and in fact the Seth Rich murder case has had a 'cone of silence' purposely enshrouded from the jump.

Post Q# 1708
> SR
> Why do the UK gov desperately want JA?
> Think source files

The next public notice is with Julian Assange's (7/22/16) offer of an additional $20,000 reward for any solid information on the murder of DNC staffer Rich. Julian Assange would appear with Sean Hannity on FON News to repeat the [SR] reward offer to the entire world. Assange's famed WikiLeaks had never revealed the source of their whistleblower information and has been a selling point for future informants.

Post Q# 1591
> Server unlocks SR.

This widely broadcasted Assange statement led to revisiting the events surrounding Seth Rich's computer related role at the DNC. Most folks could accurately tell Assange was helping to find Seth's killer(s) as well as confirming the original source for the DNC email transfers (in Washington/DC with WL operatives Craig Murray and MacFadyen).

Post Q# 3990
> FBI CHAIN OF COMMAND DNC HACK? [CIA BRIDGE - UKRAINE CROWDSTRIKE_BRENNAN]?

Lobbyist Jack Burkman (Nov 2016) followed with assisting to the Rich Family by an additional $125,000 reward offer. Rod Wheeler was later retained by Burkman to look for the true killer(s) and produced a report that was later immortalized on Sean Hannity/FOX News. DNC communications consultant Brad Bauman would appear at this time to 'help' Seth Rich's family come to the odd decision to not wanting to pursue all options in the this bizarre murder.

Post Q# 4710
Seth Rich

Wheeler's investigative findings leaned towards a WikiLeaks connection and DNC email leak by Seth Rich. This direct connection was the primary reason for the public execution of Patriot Seth Rich in the minds of many. The DNC hired via Perkins Coie legal advice, the cyber tech firm CrowdStrike to forensically review the DNC 2016 computer intrusion.

Post Q# 3764
How does one provide content to WL?
The (Source(s)):
Interning for the DNC can be deadly.
The hole is DEEP.

Rod Wheeler's final [SR] report was re-told on the Sean Hannity TV Show, which came in the Spring of 2016. The Seth Rich Family promptly rejected the final Wheeler findings and continued in the belief of a typical robbery attempt that had gone terribly bad. Many feel that the family was approached by nefarious elements of the DNC to continue to promote the given botched robbery public narrative.

Post Q# 436
((SR 187) (MS 13 (2) 187)
DWS_DIR

decode: Seth Rich was murdered by two of the MS13 Gang, who were themselves later killed. All directed by Debbie Wasserman-Schultz as "Quarterback" of this "wet works" operation.

Post Q# 834
Why is SR back in the news?
decode meaning——Never Forget
His Name Was Seth Rich!!!

Donna Brazile's hit book stirred things up again in November 2017 by dedicating her bestselling book to the memory of [SR]. This timeframe also saw the rise of the legend of Seth Rich throughout the alternative media world and subsequent online internet commentary. After 4 years of absolute denial of possession, the FBI has finally admitted to having files from Seth Rich's personal laptop.

Post Q# 1195
Why did the D's push legal rep on family?

The Rich Family sued FOX News/Channel 5 Affiliate unsuccessful over their broadcast stories surrounding Seth's death. Then we had the attempted murder of Jack Burkman by once employee/investigator Kevin Doherty, which has caused a fuss that is still being legally resolved.

Post Q# 1493
SR 187 DISCOVERY.

Mixed reports now are circulating about an anonymous Washington Hospital Center surgeon saying (SR) was alive and recovering after his bullet wounds surgery. Special Counsel (SC) John Durham has indicated DWS's pal Perkins Coie/Clinton campaign lawyer Michael Sussmann and this will help lead to the full disclosure of this tragic murder. SC Durham would reveal in 2022 court filings of a relationship between CrowdStrike and the Rodney Joffe lead SpyGate researchers that may have relied on 'spoofed' data. SC Durham submitted his final report in 2023.

Post Q# 4153
WL publish v SR 187?

Seth Rich had a sudden reversal of health while left unattended in the ICU recovery room. The EMT's ambulance crew had reported 'stable' condition in route but he later expired in ICU. Former Ambassador Craig Murray claims he personally received the leaked DNC emails at American University, and he gave them directly to Julian Assange/WL. The British court has chided with the USA in the extradition of Assange to stand trial for espionage.

Post Q# 4016
Seth Rich internal DL hand-to-hand pass USA?

Tom Fitton/Judicial Watch has uncovered via FOIA several FBI emails incredibly involving [SR], in yet another strange occurrence in the evolving chapter of this tragic 'Murder Mystery.' The FBI in 2022 is requesting a delay of 66 years to release the FOIA requested data from Seth Rich's seized laptop. Top reporter Diana West has connected Perkins Coie as having a copy of Seth Rich's laptop. With the historic re-election of President Trump in 2024, we all hope to learn the truth about the 2016 DNC emails leak.

Post Q# 3532
DNC server(s) hold many answers.
[DWS]
House of Cards.

Links

Revolver-Seth Rich's Story just got Darker

American Thinker-Was the Death of Seth Rich a Hit?

Ada Nestor-They All Knew it was a Lie

Clinton Foundation Timeline-Trump Posts Video of Mysterious Deaths and Suicides

Just Human-Huddleston v FBI (Seth Rich FOIA)

Revolver News-Mike Benz: The CIA Assassination Manual

Newsweek-Seth Rich Laptop Turned Over by FBI Judge Rules

American Thinker-Who is Seth Rich?

Last Refuge-Trump Russia Narrative

Epoch Times-FBI Reveals more Information on Slain DNC Staffer Seth Rich

The Federalist-Special Counsel's Office is Investigating DNC Server Hack

Common Sense Show-Seth Rich leaked Emails: CF/Ukraine/Iran/and Russia

Craig Murray-FBI has been Lying about Seth Rich

WJLA News-Independent Group Releases New Report on Seth Rich Murder

Sic Sempre Tyrannis-Binney/Johnson: Why the DNC was not Hacked by Russians

Zeckelin-Seymour Hersh discusses Seth Rich and WikiLeaks

Nieuwsuur-Julian Assange on Seth Rich

MPDC.gov-Seth Conrad Rich: Reward Flyer

Vault.FBI.gov-Seth Rich Files

Crossfire Hurricane Docs-Christopher Steele Binder

Justice-gov-2023 SC John Durham Report

Ex-FBI Chief of Staff James Rybicki: Not so 'Squeaky Clean'

James Rybicki [JR] was Chief of Staff to both former Director James Comey and current Director Chris Wray at the FBI. Rybicki acted as the central clearinghouse and initial focal point of all information going to the FBI Director. History will show a small group of government officials conspired in a treasonous coup plot against then candidate and later President Trump. President Trump would file in 2022 a federal RICO lawsuit against Comey/McCabe/HRC/DNC/and others related to the SpyGate false Russian collusion narratives.

Post Q# 3673
It was over before it began.

Rybicki's names is indicated as the primary sender of key emails to the infamous FBI lovers Strzok/Page combo. [JR] was a key member of the small group or 'Secret Society' within the upper ranks of the DOJ/FBI. A core group of justice insiders hatched a plan to set up then candidate Trump by false Russian collusion accusations. Judicial Watch won in 2022 a FOIA request for the FBI to release all of the government officials listed in the 2016 Peter Strzok memo that began the FBI's operation codenamed 'Crossfire Hurricane,' the spy campaign against candidate Donald Trump.

Post Q# 2476
Dig deeper!
Re_read drops re: Gmail + PS/Xbox comms

Rybicki was the person at the hub of collecting and dispatching critical communications that were used as official FBI media talking points. The role of gatekeeper suited [JR] well, as he kept the criminal coup plans against President Trump very compartmentalized.

Post Q# 3990
FEDERAL BUREAU OF "INVESTIGATION"
Areas that Rybicki had an influence and are very alarming:
• April 2016: Rybicki/Baker meet DOJ John Carlin at White House-FISA talk.
• May 2016: Assists Comey w/HRC draft statement on "exoneration".
• June 2016: Point FBI person handling Clinton/Lynch Tarmac meeting.
• July 2016: Along with Strzok, interviews HRC not under oath.
• October 2016: Drafts McCabe's email saying HRC got "HQ Special" status.
• November 2016: Strzok/Page texts reveal Rybicki's of MSM leaking.
• January 2018: Nunes Committee asks Rybicki about a Comey/POTUS private White House meeting (General Flynn).
• September 2021: SC John Durham indictment of Perkins Coie/Clinton campaign lawyer Michael Sussmann for lying to FBI.

Post Q# 1288
Jim Rybicki, chief of staff and senior counselor-FIRED.

Senator Chuck Grassley put it well: "To have your conclusion first, fact-gathering second, the FBI should be held to a higher standard". Chuck Grassley and Senator Ron Johnson will continue to hold probative committee hearings concerning the entire ObamaGate/SpyGate scandal. History will show that a small group of DOJ officials willfully engaged in a treasonous coup plot against President Trump nicknamed SpyGate.

Post Q# 4933

Watergate x 1000.

President Trump's Justice Dream Team was organized with Barr/Horowitz/Huber/Storch/and Durham, with plans to drop the hammer on the Deep State. Special Counsel (SC) John Durham has dropped criminal indictments and filed his final report in 2023 surrounding this multi-year probe. The treasonous web of coup plotters involved with SpyGate/Crossfire Hurricane illegal surveillance operations involved both corrupt government officials and private entities like the MSM as well as Big Tech.

Post Q# 1828

[FBI [JC] [AM] [JR] [MS] [BP] [PS] [LP] [JB] [MK] [JC] [SM] [TG] [KC]].

Rybicki's fingerprints are over many of the ObamaGate/SpyGate political scandals. Watch for the reports from IG Horowitz and SC Durham to be the foundation for future judicial accountability. With the re-election of President Trump in 2024, the Great Awakening that is happening worldwide will usher in the approaching Judgement Day.

Post Q# 2692

Jim Rybicki -Chief of Staff (JC) -FIRED.

Links

NY Post-Comey's Former Chief of Staff Finally Quits FBI

Just the News-FBI Timeline Chronicles Political Interference

Washington Examiner-Bongino finds James Comey's FBI Hidden Evidence Room

The Federalist-Senate Expands Probe into FBI's Ability to Hide Docs

Clinton Foundation Timeline-FBI Revelations Show the Mueller Special Counsel was a Cover-Up

Daily Beast-Comey's Former Chief of Staff finally Quits FBI

Washington Times-Retribution for Crossfire Hurricane

Real Clear Investigations-Deception by Redaction

FOX News-FBI Director Wray replaces James Rybicki

Markets Work-FISA Title-One Surveillance Warrants

Judicial Watch-DOJ Clinton/Lynch Tarmac meeting Docs

White House.gov-Declassification of Material Related to FBI's Crossfire Hurricane

Crossfire Hurricane Docs-Christopher Steele Binder

Justice.gov-2023 SC John Durham Report

Pandora's Box: Scalia Death Mystery [AS 187]
Tarmac = LL/BC

U.S. Supreme Court (USSC) Chief Justice Antonin Scalia's (1936-2016) mysterious 2016 death in Texas has been the topic of much speculation. Team 'Q' has made references to the odd circumstances surrounding this national tragedy. The exact political leanings of the Justices that make up of the highest court in our land is of concern to all sides of the isle. The 2022 leak of the USSC's review of Roe vs Wade demonstrates the critical importance that our High Court provides to our Republic.

> **Post Q# 2261**
> PANIC IN DC.
> [LL] talking = TRUTH reveal TARMAC [BC]?

A connection has been made to the famed Tarmac meeting with BC/LL and a future open Supreme Court seat. 'Q' has hinted that [LL] would have to wait until RBG retired and not the Scalia open slot. The questionable death in 2021 of the ABC reporter Chris Sign, who broke the Tarmac story, demonstrates the extreme determination of these Deep State NWO Globalists. Justice Thomas has been championing the First Amendment of all Americans, while he tries to reign-in Big Tech's immunity under Section 230.

> **Post Q# 1147**
> SC/LL deal drop.
> Tarmac.

Justice Antonov Scalia (AS) was found dead on 2/13/2016 at a private hunting lodge in Shaffer/TX. Known as an ultra-elite sportsman property, famed Cibolo Creek Ranch was owned by John Poindexter and is strictly off limits to the fly-over deplorable folk. Unproven rumors have surrounded the nature of this particular Texas ranch in terms of 'extra services' provided to the sporting elite guests. All evidence suggests Justice Scalia's group was only into the hunting preserve and not nefarious other activities.

> **Post Q# 1190**
> Guided by LL/+ 3 CLAS.
> Think SC.

Bizarre events have plagued this sudden death including that no autopsy was ever done on AS. Additionally no medical examiner was ever on-site along with a very quick cremation and the Scalia's dead body was found in bed fully clothed with a pillow over his face, obviously calling into question the true manor of death. Many different theories have sprung out of this more than strange death of a Supreme Court Justice and hopefully in time the exact details will be revealed.

> **Post Q# 1162**
> SC-Supreme Court.
> RBG.
> AS 187 / Clown Black (Brennan).

A string of semi-coded emails was traced through WikiLeaks disclosures back to John "Skippy" Podesta. Justice Scalia's untimely death was just days after Podesta's bizarre email references to 'Wet Works.' We must recall the setting at the time where many firmly believed that HRC would replace BHO. The skipping of an official autopsy on Scalia's body naturally spawned suspicions as well as growing 'conspiracy theories.' The Deep State/DC Swamp had many reason to eliminate a hard right Republican Chief Justice of the Supreme Court.

Post Q# 4888
Pandora's 'political elite' box?

In the shady world of Spy vs Spy, intelligence experts use 'Wet Works' as lingo for an ordered assassination. The police and security services refer to homicides/murders as a [187] in their own lingo code. Intelligence operatives are known to use hard to trace exotic poisons that trigger specific human organs to quickly fail. Another narrative is that BHO wanted to become a Supreme Court justice and the elimination of Justice Scalia would fit into a future President HRC.

Post Q# 674
[SC / LL deal and AS 187].

decode: SC = Supreme Court AS = Antonin Scalia LL=Loretta Lynch RBG=Ruth Bader Ginseng

Justice Ginsburg (RBG) had prolonged ill health and was rumored to be on the verge of retirement prior to her death. 'Q' has floated that Lynch would have to wait until RBG retires to help a future President HRC with the optics. Biden now is floating expanding the USSC bench from 9 to 13 total in an obvious effort to entrench power.

Post Q# 2860
The Deal of a Lifetime?

A President HRC would pick the [AS] replacement open seat and LL would stay on as AG until the retirement announcement of RBG. Just like with the 16-Year Plan and Insurance Policy, the Deep State coup plotters are failing. The illegal Biden administration is now having to complete HRC's 8 years that President Trump interrupted from their evil plan to destroy America.

Post Q# 675
AS 187

Justice Scalia will be sorely missed, and we may never know the exact details of his coincidental passing (Dark to Light). The Great Awakening of a public enlightenment is underway, and we all must walk through the darkness to be in the light. Special Counsel John Durham has dropped criminal indictments and submitted his final report in 2023. With the re-election of President Trump in late 2024, Judgement Day is coming soon.

Post Q# 2729
Bigger than the 25th amendment attempt to remove.
Depth of this is very serious.

Links

True Pundit-HRC Promises Supreme Court Seat to LL

CNN-Skipping Scalia Autopsy Spawns Conspiracy Theory

Law and Crine-USSC Thomas calls to Limit Big Tech's Immunity under Section 230

People-Antonio Scalia was with Members of Secretive Society of Elite Hunters

Daily Caller-Confusion Reigned the Day Scalia Died

CNN-Justice Scalia's Unexamined Death Points to a Problem

Newsweek-Why some Believe Scalia was Murdered

Breitbart-Conspiracy Theories surround Scalia Death

CBS News-Donald Trump considers Theory Scalia Murdered

Washington Times-Michael Savage: Was Scalia Murdered?

FOX News-Judge Napolitano says Scalia was Wiretapped

Christian Science Monitor-Could BHO become a Supreme Court Justice?

Rense-Hacked Emails show HRC's Rage

Texas Tribune -Supreme Court Justice Antonin Scalia found Dead in West Texas

PBS-Judge Alito pushes Back against SCOTUS Criticism

WikiLeaks-The Justice Scalia Emails

Law.com-Inside Antonin Scalia's FBI File

AP News-Scalia's Last Days

Revolver News-There's a Legit Coup Underway in the US Led by Federal Judges

Crossfire Hurricane Docs-Christopher Steele Binder

Justice.gov-2023 SC John Durham Report

(Answer Is:) Morning Joe's Worst Nightmare
(Question:) Who was Lori Klausutis?

Now is the time Patriots to strike back against the MSM Mockingbird media. One perfect candidate is the early day voice of the opposition resistance, Morning "Psycho" Joe. President Trump has been steadfast in exposing the fake news and a primary mission of 'Q' was to replace the Mockingbird media. The revelation in 2022 of a coordinated deliberate media lie about the validity of Hunter Biden's 'Laptop from Hell' in the fall of 2020 just prior to the Presidential election, proves the full complicity of the corporate news media.

Post Q# 2700
Nobody should be above the law (no matter how massive the spider-web is (entangled). This will never happen again.

Psycho Joe has continued long after the end of the first term label President Trump and his supporters as openly racist white domestic terrorists. In 2017 Joe told his TV show host (future wife) Mika Brezinski that "it's our job to control what people think". The deranged Progressive Leftists and their corporate Mockingbird media allies continue to this very day to doubled down against former President Trump/MAGA/as well as 'Q'.

Post Q# 678
The ART of illusion.

Morning Joe would continue in 2023 to carry water for his NWO bosses by perpetuating the lie by falsely stating AR-15's of today are more powerful than the weapons used during the Vietnam War. President Trump is a world class brander and has come up with appropriate nicknames for many in the Fake News media. Joe now goes by 'Psycho Joe' and his romantic sidekick/current wife is 'Dumb as a Rock Mika' or just plain old 'Crazy Mika.' President Trump has repeated called out the corporate FAKE News media danger to our Republic.

Post Q# 742
The Inner Circle.
Mika Brzezinski.
End is near.

November 29, 2017, President Trump sent out a cryptic Tweet message referring to Morning Joe. This tweet highlighted the mysterious death of a young pretty Scarborough campaign staff intern from 2001. Morning Joe as well as the entire Mockingbird news media would go into Trump Derangement Syndrome (TDS) overdrive as the 2024 Presidential election looms.

Post Q# 4127
[note: they all read from a teleprompter - who controls the message?]

This sad event happened at one of Joe Scarborough's (R-FL) panhandle campaign offices more than 2 decades ago. That unfortunate young very fit campaign aide found dead was Ms. Lori Klausutis (1973-2001). The beyond mysterious death of this young political intern would be a skeleton in the closet of Morning Joe that justifiably will haunt his remaining days.

Post Q# 4896
HOW IS THE GAME PLAYED?

On July 20, 2001, the dead body of 28-year-old Lori Klausutis was found at her place of work. Lori worked for U.S. House Joe Scarborough (R-FL) at his Ft. Walton Beach/FL regional campaign office. A suspicious death would be an understatement and the subsequent coverup confirms abnormal circumstances. Always remember that once elected politicians rarely give up their reins of power unless forced into an early resignation.

Post Q# 1785
Do you think they got the [4am] memo?

Lori Klausutis was a daily runner of 5 miles and by all accounts was the picture of perfect health. No drugs or alcohol were found to be in her system from the official autopsy lab results. Her excellent athletic condition lead to many speculations about foul play as opposed to a 'medical event' as the cause of death, beginning the start of the conspiracy theories surrounding this sad event.

Post Q# 4588
Public awareness important [bypass of controlled [approved] topics].
[General public steered by MSDNC like a dog steering sheep]

Strange as it seems, Joe Scarborough had just announced that he would not seek another U.S. House representatives' term. This unexpected statement came two months after the Lori Klaisutis death and on the heels of very comfortably win during his last campaign for re-election. Even though the actual events may never be known, I maintain Mrs. Klausutis overheard or saw something she should not have as opposed to any sexual reason associated with her mysterious death.

Tweet POTUS T#-265
And will they terminate low ratings Joe Scarborough based on the "unsolved mystery" that took place in Florida years ago?

Psycho Joe then claimed he needed to spend more quality time with his beloved family. This coincidently appears to be the number one cop-out excuse for retiring public service liars and criminal politicians.

Post Q# 2902
When the real TRUTH re: Russian collusion is right in front of you, but the FAKE NEWS media prevents public awareness.

Rumors had swirled around the Florida panhandle about several affairs involving Psycho Joe. Local tales connected past promiscuous activity as the reason Joe would never run for elected office again.

Post Q# 113
What is Operation Mockingbird?

This was contrary to his recent cookie-cutter public narrative announcement about of his loving family. I'm not sure we can find many honest politicians or reporters residing in the Washington DC 'swamp.' All Patriots look forward to the second term of President Trump and the start of the New America.

Post Q# 1515
> These reporters and networks have been named in the Wikileaks to have colluded with
> the DNC or Hillary's campaign during the 2016 election cycle.
> MSNBC-Joe Scarborough.
> MSNBC-Mika Brzezinski.

Coroner's report had Lori passing out due to a rare and previously undetected fatal heart condition.
Cardiac arrhythmia caused Lori to suddenly fall over hitting her head on an office desk and
causing her instant death.

Post Q# 4468
> The Daily "Beast."

Autopsy tests could never confirm this undetectable rare arrhythmia irregular heart rhythm.
Primarily because it can only be detected while the heart is beating (victim must still be alive) and
has been used to muddy the waters in prior sketchy murder cases.

Post Q# 1270
> Happened.
> Dangerous.
> Threats.

decode: Assassination threats [187 = murder].

Surprisingly this coroner was able confirmed, without credible evidence, that the head trauma did
kill her. This case had things going sideways right off the bat, giving good indications of
shenanigans at play from higher powers.

Post Q# 2489
> [Placeholder - OIG Report-FBI, DOJ, and Media Coll].

What confounded a local WGTX reporter was right after being notified of the Lori's death, they
unexpectedly got an official statement given out by Joe and several key staffers. This statement
told a false narrative that Lori was very sticky and not been a healthy person recently.

Post Q# 4024
> A deeply entrenched enemy who controls the vast majority of communications is only
> defeated by.......
> Game theory.

Psycho Joe and his team were scrambling to build a false narrative about Lori's ill health and
connecting this to her death. This incorrect 'ill-health' theme was shot down instantly by the
Klausutis family members and by many of her close friends.

Post Q# 1500
> Access kills.
> Morning strolls are refreshing.

Joe Scarborough and his aides were pressured by her family to retract their original false public
statement concerning Lori's health. Incredibly this low-life Scarborough was more concerned with
optics than the death of this young lady. The CIA began in the 1950's Operation Mockingbird
which was the placement of trained assets into the U.S. news media. Many say that current MSN
news figures like Anderson Cooper, Rachel Maddow, and even Joe Scarborough could really be
modern day Mockingbird examples.

Post Q# 1826
Echo chamber conspiracy?
U.S. Air Force B-52 [Precision Bombs].

Dr. Michael Berkland was assigned to perform Lori's autopsy. Michael had a history of unethical conduct. Berkland was fired within a year due to faulty and incomplete official reports given on a regular basis. In a cleanup operation, often key individuals leave their previous industry and fade away out of the public spotlight.

Post Q# 572
NOBODY PLAYING THE GAME GETS A FREE PASS.

In 2008 authorities found a real life 'House of Horrors' in a rental unit leased by Dr. Berkland. Discovered were various body parts of over 100 different cadavers in this suburban U-Haul storage facility. It has been long known that criminals need the assistance of professional like corrupt coroners to assist with their ongoing crimes and coverups.

Post Q# 4141
What happens when corp media 'knowingly' pushes false [propaganda] Information?

Insanely these body parts/organs were stored in various Tupperware containers, Styrofoam cups, and garbage trash bags. Recently an old video surfaced showing Joe Scarborough joking about Lori's death surfaced, further demonstrating how truly evil and sick this entire Mockingbird media crowd truly is. The MSM's coverup of the Hunter Biden 'Laptop from Hell' is another classic example of the coordination of fake news with corrupt DC Swamp politicians to craft false public narratives.

Post Q# 2
Mockingbird 10.30.17

Special Counsel (SC) John Durham has dropped criminal indictments related to HRC/BHO/Big Tech/and the MSM. SC Durham submitted his final report in 2023. Mika's brother Mark Brzezinski is Biden's Ambassador to Poland. SC Durham would reveal in 2022 court filings that Fusion GPS regularly emailed reporters unverified claims against Donald Trump. he era of corporate legacy media is quickly coming to an end in front of our eyes today. Morning Joe and current wife Crazy Mika will have to answer for their previous collusion with their failed coup plot against President MSNBC News pulled Morning Joe off the air after the failed July 2024 assassination attempt on President Trump stating that Morning Joe is "damaging" to the country. With the historic re-election of President Trump in 2024, past hidden political secrets will finally be publicly revealed.

Post Q# 4319
Nobody is 'buying' what you are peddling [selling] any longer.
THE MSDNC IS DEAD.

Links

The Sun-Trump calls Death of Scarborough Staffer "Suspicious"

The Federalist-RussiaGate Wouldn't have been Possible without a Complicit Press

Daily Mail—Trump Never Believed Joe Scarborough's Aide Death an Accident

Mediaite-Greg Gutfeld about Joe Scarborough: "You have to Lie about your Lies"

Daily Mail-Morning Joe Scarborough responds to Claim

The Federalist-MSNBC admits Morning Joe is Damaging to the Country

Western Journal-Joe Scarborough told needs Medication after Unhindged Trump Rant

Starfire Codes-Legacy of Operation Mockingbird

Revolver News-N. Korea Wishes they had Propaganda like Morning Joe

Independent Sentinel-Mika: "It's Our Job" to Control what People Think

National Review-Scarborough calls RussiaGate Skeptics useful Idiots

NY Post-MSNBC's Morning joe Delivers Lowest Ratings since 2021

Just the News-White House faces Questions about Trump Tweets (Dead Intern)

NY Post-Trump asks if Joe Scarborough "Got Away with Murder"

Trump Twitter: T-265 on 11/29/17 @ 9:14 am

Daily Caller-Scarborough: "Everyone should get 20 Years in Prison"

Newsweek-Trump Suggests Joe Scarborough killed Intern

Miami Herald-What is Trump Ranting About Scarborough

Political Cartoons for Trump-Joe's Dead Intern

Brookings.edu-Church Committee investigated Americans Spying on Americans

Democrats Archive-Joe Scarborough/Lori Klausutis

Intel.Senate.gov-Operation Mockingbird

Clinton Foundation Timeline-2025 Crossfire Hurricane Docs

Justice.gov-2023 SC John Durham Report

Golf Caddie to Air Force One:
Meet Dan Scavino

Dan Scavino holds the record amongst all White House staffers for the longest service to President Trump. Dan Scavino has been an intricate Team Trump member from the 2015 ride down the escalator, through to the first White House term and regularly flying onboard Air Force One. 'Q' has specifically called out 'Dan' in past drops and many feel Scavino continues to post crumbs since the posts have stopped. The new media platform called Truth Social, features President Trump/Dan Scavino/Kash Patel and others interacting with the new "@q" account. President Trump has said that he admires loyalty and few non-family members have exhibited more loyalty that Dan Scavino.

Post Q# 4759
Never forget those in the background.

As part of my President Trump's 'Quiet Heroes" series, I am happy to highlight this good Patriot Dan Scavino. Many that have worked around Donald/President Trump, have developed a strong bond of loyalty and Scavino exemplifies this common trait. In the era of the illegal Biden administration and the apparent suspension of the Q drops, Scavino's personal social media accounts have become critical. Scavino would be subpoenaed and faces criminal contempt of Congress charges related to the January 6th committee fishing exhibitions.

Post Q# 88
POTUS' Twitter attack.
IMPORTANT.

The setting is 1990 and young Dan Scavino is a talented 16-year-old golf course caddy at famed Briar Hill Country Club/NY. Of historic note is today this is the famed Trump National Golf Club. Within the travel/hospitality industry the Trump moniker is well noted for top excellence. Odd that the Trump golf facility in Bedminster/NJ would be the safe location after Admiral Rogers warned of Trump Tower surveillance by BHO.

Post Q# 1711
Mueller is investigating POTUS' Tweets for obstruction?

Dan Scavino had a lucky beam from above shine on him, as Donald Trump selected young Dan from the caddy shack to be his personal golf caddy. Dan Scavino would later work himself up to become the General Manager of this fine country club. Dan Scavino has demonstrated the ability to learn new tasks quickly and perform admiralty under pressure.

Post Q# 4572
Trust Dan.

Fast forward to the Summer of 2015 and Dan Scavino is asked to assist candidate Mr. Donald Trump with his upcoming Presidential campaign. Hope Hicks and Corey Lewandowski also joined Scavino to form the core of the leanest successful team ever. This trio of early Trump loyalists deservingly get credit for a winning 2016 campaign strategy.

Post Q# 108
Analyze time stamp of my go message to BO's Tweet.

Dan Scavino was in charge of the social media and digital communications for Candidate Trump. History will show the effective use of Twitter, Facebook and other social media platforms in the run up to President Trump's historic victory. The initial 2016 campaign manager Brad Parscale worked closed with Scavino in coordinating a historic online voter positive informational program. Steve Bannon would later replace Parscale and also worked closely with Scavino in helping to elect candidate Donald Trump in 2016. The election steal of 2020 and the illegal Biden administration destroying our country, our hope is in God to help restore equal justice to our Republic.

Post Q# 536

Have you not discovered the CONFIRMED correlation between posts here and Tweets yet?

Everyone may recall the one big dust up during the campaign over the use once of the "Star of David." Dan Scavino had always set the standard for professionalism and explained this was in fact a typical U.S. Sheriff's badge. Scavino helped to oversee President Trump's total social media presence to this day as the team explores developing their own networks. Many sophisticated compartmentalized intelligence operations involve 'read-in' helpers that assist certain operational phases while not understanding the full big picture.

Post Q# 4527

3 seconds.
Dan is to blame.

Scavino's first official White House title was Director of Social Media and in 2022 Dan is helping with the launch of President Trump's new platform called Truth Social. After the departure of Hope Hicks (later she returned) from the White House staff, Scavino was named White House Communications Director but then later become the Deputy Chief of Staff. With the tens of millions of online followers, President Trump and Scavino still carry tremendous clout onto their new site Truth Social.

Post Q# 335

Timestamp [Q] post [:03] against POTUS' Tweet [:13].

Dan Scavino has been referred to by President Trump as a "Facebook and Twitter junkie". Insiders acknowledge that any strange late night or misspelled tweets, can be attributed normally to President Trump and not to Scavino. 'Q' has directly pointed to Scavino and this extra special relationship was apparent to all of the Anons. Special Counsel John Durham has dropped criminal indictments related SpyGate and submitted his final report in 2023. With the re-election of President Trump in 2024, Dan Scavino has been appointed Deputy Chief of Staff and Assistant to President Trump in his new administration (v 2.0). Speculation had originally swirled around Dan Scavino about replacing the NY Congressional seat vacated by Elise Stefanik, President Trump's new UN Ambassador.

Post Q# 4367

Trolling is fun!

Links

Business Insider-Dan Scavino: Trump Golf Caddie

FOX News-Dan Scavino: Journey of a Lifetime

Medium-Who is Behind Bonkers QAnon Conspiracy Theory?

CNN-Donald Trump and Dan Scavino

Washington Examiner-Senior Trump Adviser fuels Congressional Speculation

FOX News-Trump names Stephen Miller and Dan Scavino to Senior WH Staff

Golf Wire-Dan Scavino

VICE News-J6 Committee wants to Speak with Dan Scavino about QAnon

Breitbart-Dan Scavino: Trump was Made for this Moment

Just the News-Jan. 6 Committee recommends Dan Scavino face Criminal Contempt

Talking Points Memo-Trump Social Media partners with Anti-Vax/QAnon Video Hub

FOX News-Scavino tells Trump Officials to be Proud of Accomplishments

Media Matters-Trump has Repeatedly Amplified QAnon Twitter Accounts

Washington Examiner-Scavino to Facebook: 'Why are you Silencing Me?'

Huff Post-The Man Behind Trump's Bizarre Social Media Strategy

Golf Week-Once Trump's 16-Year Old Golf Caddie

NPR-Mystery Man behind Trump's Tweets

Video-Dan Scavino Trump's Director of Social Media

Nimrod Kamer-Trump Watching a Kamala Harris Speech

Crossfire Hurricane Docs-Christopher Steele Binder

Justice.gov-2023 SC John Durham Report

HRC's Second Trump-Russia Dossier

Then Representative Devin Nunes announced that the House Intelligence Committee had completed with Phase Two of its investigations into Trump-Russia and turned over findings to both the U.S. Senate and Special Counsel (SC) John Durham's criminal probes. Uncovered were several attempts to discredit candidate Trump with false Russian collusion narratives. A false Alfa Bank secret server in Trump Tower along with several phony dossiers would be part of HRC's treasonous 'Russia Russia Russia' plots. The FEC would fine in 2022 HRC/DNC over$1M for payments made to Fusion GPS in their 2016 preparing of the infamous Steele Dossier.

Post Q# 2876
>CLINTON PANIC.
>CLINTON FEAR.
>JUDGEMENT DAY COMING.

Rep. Devin Nunes focused initially on the dossier information provided by Cody Shearer and Sid Blumenthal, who both have been longtime enforcers for the Clinton Crime Family. Devin Nunes was tracking Christopher Steele's Dossier route via BHO's State Department and then over to the FBI with the help of outside contractors like Fusion GPS and law firm Perkins Coie. SC John Durham's indictment of Perkins Coie/Clinton campaign lawyer Michael Sussmann opened many eyes about RussiaGate.

Post Q# 4310
>[Hussein] order preventing sharing of intel re: Russia?
>Would such an order shield [Clinton] camp from discovery re: Clinton-DNC Russian collusion?

Fixers Cody/Sid have a long track record of smearing the reputations of female accusers of Slick Willy and anyone against coming out against HRC. Additionally, Cody Shearer is known for silencing many potential witnesses against the Clintons in ruthless fashion. The era of the Clintons will be long remembered for the multiple bizarre suicidal deaths forcing a new term into our vocabulary called 'Arkancide.'

Post Q# 4793
>"Trump Swift Boat Project." —Clinton OP

Cody/Sid have decades long devotional service to both Clintons and the DC Swamp. Cody Shearer has a journalistic background and contributed several memos into Chris Steele's final Trump-Russia Dossier. Sid Blumenthal is basically a political operative and has some basic journalistic training. Both characters would be hard pressed to operate in the normal 9 to 5 world as they are political tricksters.

Post Q# 1286
>The Brits-raw intel / dossier / 5-Eyes.

Rep. Nunes' committee had been tracing the origins and distribution of all of the Clinton sponsored Trump-Russia dossiers. Christopher Steele received some opposition research through the U.S. State Department via Jonathan Winer and Victoria Nuland. Both Nuland and Winer were high level State officials that were directly involved with Steele as well as hired outside contractors Fusion GPS.

Post Q# 4162
Think WL HRC_Podesta media asset(s) list.

Cody Shearer along with his sidekick Sid Blumenthal both publicly claim to be the co-authors of this fictional hit piece concerning candidate Donald Trump. This duet contributed 2 memos used to help buttress Chris Steele's own final opposition research work product the infamous dossier. Fusion GPS's researcher Nellie Ohr also contributed to Steele's final dossier. A buffet of false information and outright lies like the Pee Pee memo all came together to form the final Steele dossier.

Post Q# 1515
HRC deal request.

Cody Shearer's Brother In-Law is the famed Strobe Talbott from the Bill Clinton Presidential era. Talbott was the entrance token into the BHO's State Department for Cody and Sid due to his professional connections to Nuland/Winer. Talbott had been the Deputy Secretary of State and later headed for many years the Brookings Institute.

Post Q# 4333
HRC direct attacks re: Q?
2,200+ [attack] MSDNC articles written/pushed in past 2 years?

There was a 2-way conduit flow of opposition research information between Cody/Sid and Jonathan Winer/Victoria Nuland at BHO's State Department. Under Nuland was staffer Kathleen Kavlalec, who personally met with Chris Steele in October 2016, gave a negative evaluation of the Trump-Russia dossier. Kavlalec's instant dismissal of the Steele dossier should have halted all inquiry right then.

Post Q# 2698
[Controlled by those that worked for the Clinton's].
They have ZERO control now.

Christopher Steele also was directly involved with this special circular flow of "Anti-Trump Oppo" material. Steele passed along this extra State Department 'intel' directly to the FBI himself and had his prior outside media news sources confirm this circular flow of material.

Post Q# 1345
U1 [donations to CF].

Chris Steele primarily researcher Igor Danchenko fabricated material given to him from Sergei Millian (Source D) and the pee pee memo from Russian Oligarch Oleg Deripiska. Steele also used the two memos he got from Cody Shearer and Sid Blumenthal along with material from Nellie Ohr/Fusion GPS. HRC also promoted the false Alfa Bank story supposedly involving Russian computer servers at Trump Tower. President Trump would file in 2022 a federal RICO lawsuit against those involved with the promotion of the false Russian collusion narrative in 2016.

Post Q# 2872
Hillary Clinton and Foundation.
Crime Against Children.

Nellie Ohr worked at Fusion GPS and combined her own opposition research into the final Steele Trump-Russia Dossier. Nellie had DOJ husband Bruce Ohr give her work product over directly to the FBI. Durham indicted Perkins Coie/Clinton campaign lawyer Michael Sussmann assisted in getting false Alfa Bank information to the FBI. Nellie Ohr will be shown as the primary collator of the various fabricated memos into the final infamous Steele Dossier.

Post Q# 3856

Define Evergreen [HRC USSS code name]
Non-standard definition.
Think depopulation.

Victoria Nuland and Jonathan Winer both have admitted publicly to their direct involvement with Steele Dossier. Former AG Bill Barr has tasked both SP John Huber and SC John Durham to look into this secret 2nd Clinton Dossier and how it ultimately got into the FBI/DOJ's FISA surveillance warrants. NSA Jake Sullivan and operative Daniel Jones have been implicated in pushing the false Alfa Bank server collusion claim.

Post Q# 4402

Demons continue to serve the devil in his attempt to lead the world to from a God and into sin.

Watch for both Cody Shearer/Sid Vicious Blumenthal to become household names (like Chris Steele) in the near future. SC John Durham submitted his final report in 2023. With the re-election of President Trump in late 2024, outgoing Joe Biden unconscionably granted the Presidential Medal of Freedom to HRC. The Great Awakening is underway and justice will return to the USA.

Post Q# 1515

These reporters and networks have been named in the WikiLeaks to have colluded with the DNC or HRC campaign during the 2016 election cycle:

Links

NY Post-Anatomy of a Political Dirty Trick

FOX News-DEMs pulled Greatest Con Job Ever

Just the News-Grassley Condemns FBI Handling of HRC's Emails

Techno Fog-Durham: Hundreds of Emails between Fusion GPS and Reporters

Breitbart-Nunes Refers 10 BHO Officials to DOJ

NY Post-Inside the HRC Dossier and Con behind RussiaGate

WSJ-Hillary Clinton's other Dossier

Real Clear Politics-RussiaGate: HRC/Perkins Coie/ Fusion GPS/CrowdStrike

Daily Caller-Ron Johnson Subpoenas for Blumenthal/Shearer: HRC's Second Dossier

The Guardian-FBI Reviewing HRC's Second Dossier

Washington Examiner-The Other Secret Dossier

The Atlantic-Devin Nunes's next Target

National Review-Meet Cody Shearer

American Spectator-Cody Shearer's Dirty Dossier Role

Just the News-FBI's Arctic Haze

Breitbart-Jonathan Winer was Steele's Inside Guy

Real Clear Investigations-Unpacking the Other Clinton-Linked Russia Dossier

Judicial Watch-Weiner Timeline: How FBI gave HRC Cover during Election

"Thank You for Your Service to Our Country" TRUST SESSIONS

Patriot Jeff Sessions served with distinction in the Army Reserve from 1973-86. Known affectionately as The Silent Executioner or Stealth Jeff Sessions, earned the rank of Captain and has the judicial background qualifications to serve on any future Military Tribunals. Sessions would later serve as a U.S. Senator and become President Trump's first Attorney General. History will show that Jeff Sessions helped to stop the insidious Washington DC leak problem, the violent MS13 illegal immigration and he helped to setup up the stage for judicial accountability we call 'Judgement Day.'

Post Q# 461
What makes a movie GOOD?
GREAT actors?

Captain Sessions threw his hat back into politics in an attempt to regain his old Alabama Senate seat (Boomerang). POTUS has constantly thrown 'shade' at Sessions, which offers much needed protection for himself as well as his entire family. Remember Patriots we are watching a movie (multiple movies) and optics are important.

Post Q# 538
TRUST SESSIONS.

Stealth Jeff and his replacement Matt Whitaker were scripted as examples of President Trump's secret "Stealth Bombers." Many believe that the 'Silent Assassin' (aka Stealth Jeff Sessions), may still have another major role to play in this unfolding historic drama (BOOMERANG). Captain Jeff's previous life opens a possible part if in fact future Military Tribunals are enacted.

Post Q# 2604
SESSIONS forced release of name [HUBER] to House created another variable.
Use logic.

Annually Senator Sessions was rated the most honest member of the U.S. Senate by an independent watchdog group. History and future Patriots will be treating Mr. Jeff Sessions and the critical role he played very kindly indeed fellow Patriots. One of AG Sessions' first actions was to organize a new DOJ task force to stop the flow of classified leaks to the media and big tech.

Post Q# 3371
Sometimes you need to 'take one for the team publicly' before you are vindicated as a hero.

Like in a good movie or book, sometimes your favorite characters are written out of the script prior to the ending. Logically thinking for optics alone, it never could be Jeff Sessions to drop the 'hammer of justice' on the Deep State coup plotting criminals in terms of the DOJ.

Post Q# 3004
SESSIONS' Senate vote?
Why was SESSIONS targeted?
Who FIRED/REMOVED the traitors within the FBI/DOJ?

I feel POTUS has a future role for Sessions to play in this unfolding real-life dramatic play. Possible legal position for Stealth Jeff would be overseeing upcoming Military Tribunals. One of Stealth Jeff's early tasks was to plug the unprecedented number of classified leaks surrounding the

White House and other governmental institutions. AG Sessions would form in 2017 a special counterintelligence division of the DOJ designed specifically to entrap governmental leakers to the news media and began 27 active criminal leaking cases.

Post Q# 2462
> Role of Sessions?
> Who did Sessions appoint in NOV 2017?

Senator Jeff Sessions was the first sitting U.S. Senator to endorse then Candidate Trump in late 2015. Many folks don't recall that Sessions gave up Stephen Miller, his number one Senate staffer early on, to the 2016 Trump campaign.

Post Q# 2506
> To all those that doubted SESSIONS and HUBER you WILL ALL PAY THE PRICE VERY SOON.

Stephen Miller has been Trump's main speech writer and has been key member of his inner circle ever since. Miller is fondly remembered for his classic beat-down of Jim Acosta/CNN in a 2017 White House press briefing.

Post Q# 4153
> [FBI Floor 7] [DOJ] push Sessions recuse.

Sessions served as Alabama's Southern District Assistant U.S. Attorney (USA) from 1975-77 and Reagan made Jeff Sessions the USA from 1981-93. Jeff Sessions has long held firm positions on Pro Life, legal immigration, superior military strength, and balanced federal budgets.

Post Q# 2371
> Why did McCabe try to take out Sessions?

Jeff Sessions has also been known as a proponent of balanced fair U.S. trade deals and legal immigration. Sessions was strongly against TPP/NAFTA/Carbon Tax and other unfair slanted old global trade arrangements. A letter dated 11/22/17 sent by then Chief of Staff Matthew Whitaker, that the DOJ previously said didn't exist was unearthed exonerating AG Sessions as it advises John Huber to revisit both the Clinton Foundation and Uranium One. AG Sessions would secretly meet with those involved with the U.S. Cyber Task Force in behind the scenes 'White Hat' actions.

Post Q# 2637
> Sessions departure.
> Law.

Everyone knows Jeff Sessions' position on illegal drugs, and he has pushed hard for the 'Wall' along the Southern U.S. border. Sessions saw the direct illicit connection between illegal drugs, illegal immigration and wide-open borders. The country would witness in horror millions of illegal migrants pouring across our open southern border through 2024 under the Biden administration.

Post Q# 2197
> Activate]SESSIONS[.

AG Stealth Jeff began an all-out war on the international crime gang known as MS-13 and on the open borders policy of prior administrations. This evil transnational terror group is made up of criminal refugees from San Salvador/Honduras/Guatemala/and Mexico. President Trump designated MS13 and their South American cousins an international terror organization.

Post Q# 801
>AG Sessions.
>US Cyber Task Force.
>Important.

Stealth Jeff was amnesty's worst nightmare, and he has pushed hard for enforcement of all existing immigration laws. The southern border wall and the flow of migrant caravans invading our country always has been a big priority. Jeff Sessions may yet turn out to be the 'Executioner' that the Deep State has so long dreaded. Sessions hired both SP John Huber and now upgraded to full Special Counsel (SC) John Durham as well as unleashing IG Horowitz/IG Storch.

Post Q# 2204
>PANIC IN DC.
>SESSIONS and HUBER.
>WEEKEND MEETING(S).

AG Sessions early into his duty, had to recuse himself from the various "Russia" investigations being conducted by the DOJ because of his role during the 2016 campaign. It would come as no surprise to learn James Comey opened a FISA on Sessions due to few social Ambassador Kislyak interactions and this was the primary reason for recusal from official involvement.

Post Q# 4407
>ONLY AT THE PRECIPICE [moment of destruction] WILL PEOPLE FIND THE WILL TO CHANGE.

Since we are witnessing the greatest 'movie' of all time, Jeff Sessions will go down as one of the best actors. Thanks to shade thrown by POTUS during the Georgia Senate runoff election, Coach Tommy Tuberville beat out Jeff Sessions for the Republican slot, that was ultimately won for Alabama to take that seat back.

Post Q# 1929
>Coming SOON to a theater near you.
>Enjoy the show.

Captain Sessions would be proud of SC Durham's beginning indictment of Perkins Coie/Clinton campaign lawyer Michael Sussmann. SC Durham submitted his final report in 2023. With the re-election of President Trump in 2024, many past hiding political secrets with finally be revealed. History will be very kind to Patriot Jeff Sessions and his past service to our country will never be forgotten. 'Q' said "Thank you for your service to our country Mr. Jeff Sessions".

Post Q# 3385
>It was all under the direction and oversight of AG Jeff Sessions.

Links

NY Times-The Fall of Jeff Sessions

Badlands Media-The Biggest Cover Up in American History

NY Post-Thank You Jeff Sessions for Crushing MS-13

Epoch Times-BHO Admin Enabled Nonstop Security Leaks against Trump

Daily Beast-DOJ finds Letter Ordering Scrutiny of Clinton Foundation and Uranium One

National Review-John Sullivan interviews Jeff Sessions

Washington Examiner-"Didn't Take me 30 Seconds": Sessions advised Trump to Fire Comey

The American Spectator-John Durham's Salad Shooter

Epoch Times-DC Leak Culture was Powerless to Thwart SpyGate Investigations

WSJ-Thank You, Jeff Sessions

The Federalist-8 Times U.S. Intelligence Set People Up to Fabricate the Russia Story

War Economy-Four FISA/Crossfire Hurricane

FOX News-Sessions: DOJ has 27 Investigations into 'Epidemic' of Leaks

Washington Examiner-Sessions to Receive His Cabinet Chair from Barr/Rosenstein

Epoch Times-The Great Leak Hunt

Crossfire Hurricane Docs-Halper Files

Justice.gov-DOJ Announces Strike Force to Assess ODNI Evidence

Justice.gov-2023 SC John Durham Report

Who is Cody Shearer? How is He Connected to ObamaGate?

When we take a closer look at many of these unfolding ObamaGate/SpyGate scandals, it is apparent this group enjoyed layered levels of plans. Look no further than the SpyGate's elaborated fake dossier, illegal FISA(s), and inserted campaign spies to appreciate the total coup plot scope. HRC and the DNC were intent in 2016 of falsely framing opposition candidate Donald Trump in any means possible. President Trump would file in 2022 a federal RICO lawsuit against many of the officials involved with the promotion of the false Russian collusion narrative.

Post Q# 3837
BIGGER THAN YOU CAN IMAGINE.
Crimes against Humanity.
The Silent War Continues......

The 'Insurance Policy' was the Deep State's listed option # 4 as part of operation Crossfire Hurricane. It makes things dicey when your takeover coup plot is riding on your last contingency proposal, termed hauntingly as your insurance policy. The SpyGate scandal will go down in American history as an elaborate treasonous scheme that had gone bad.

Post Q# 4227
[Russia] narrative ALL FAKE?

HRC/BHO launched a 2-prong attack against President Trump using a fake Russia collusion narrative plan. Hiring Christopher Steele through Perkins Coie/Fusion GPS was one part of their plan. The fake dossier was launched via the DOJ/FBI and would be used to apply for various FISA surveillance warrants on Trump campaign staffers. HRC also has surrogates like Perkins Coie lawyer Michael Sussmann to proffer to FBI James Baker false Alfa Bank claims.

Post Q# 2633
"McCain associate shared unverified Steele dossier with BuzzFeed, court filing says."

Contemporaneously HRC had hacks Cody Shearer and Sid Blumenthal developed a second independent fake Trump-Russia dossier. This second opposition research dossier would be run through the U.S. State Department with the help of top officials Victoria Nuland and Jonathan Winer.

Post Q# 3605
PAY-FOR-PLAY only works when you hold a position of POWER.

Cody Shearer is nicknamed 'Mr. Fixer' and is a longtime controversial political activist as well as a former journalist. Cody Shearer along with his constant sidekick Sid "Vicious" Blumenthal, are known Clinton enforcers and cleanup artists that briefly doubled as opposition researchers.

Post Q# 1929
Coming SOON to a theater near you.
Enjoy the show.

Cody/Sid collected "oppo research" materials from foreign sub-sources, to form a two-part memo report given over to Chris Steele. This false material involved Trump's 2013 Moscow Miss Universe contest and ultimately was included in Steele's final Trump-Russia Dossier.

Post Q# 2872

Hillary Clinton and Foundation.
Crime Against Children.

Cody's famous Brother In-Law is none other than Washington insider Strobe Talbott (BC's State Department). Talbott was the initial wedge in connecting Cody/Sid with U.S. State Department officials Jonathan Winer/Victoria Nuland. The State Department conveniently gave credibility to these fictional memos by re-circulation back over to the FBI.

Post Q# 3963

Symbolism.
An informed [awake] public holds all the keys.

The Christopher Steele Dossier was pivotal in the application for FISA Title-1 surveillance warrant(s) against Carter Page. Special Counsel (SC) John Durham was tasked to look into past FISA abuses by the DOJ/FBI within the framework of a criminal probe.

Post Q# 3181

BLIND JUSTICE UNDER THE LAW WILL RETURN TO OUR REPUBLIC
There is a reason why a sword is held.

Winer/Nuland were members of BHO's State Department and have admitted publicly to being the conduit for Christopher Steele. This questionable relationship is what Devin Nunes had reviewed in his House Intelligence Phase Two report, which had been turned over to the U.S. Senate.

Post Q# 4125

WN BY ANY MEANS NECESSARY.
Everything is at stake.

Winer/Nuland passed the Sid/Cody research material along directly to Chris Steele. This was to help lend additional credibility to the Russian dossier by using circular-flow validation among media as well as each other (termed intelligence laundering).

Post Q# 520

7TH FLOOR IS NO MORE - FBI/SD.

Under just bare minimal scrutiny, Christopher Steele's research work product has proven to be fake scandalous propaganda. The Sid/Cody phony memos were eventually turned over to the FBI in October 2016 and are included in the ongoing criminal investigation.

Post Q# 3689

FISA = START

Rep. Devin Nunes had referred over to the special House Congressional Task Force for witness testimony Shearer/Blumenthal/Winer/and Nuland. Special Counsel John Durham has dropped criminal indictments and submitted his final report in 2023. With the re-election of President Trump in 2024, many hope hidden political secrets will finally be revealed.

Post Q# 2876

CLINTON PANIC.
CLINTON FEAR.
JUDGEMENT DAY COMING.

Links

Washington Examiner-A Doozy of a Dossier

Just the News-HRC Plan tying Trump and Russia

Clinton Foundation Timeline-2025 Crossfire Hurricane Docs

The Federalist-SpyGate 101: A Primer on the Russia Collusion Hoax to Down Trump

Washington Examiner-Meet the Men behind HRC's Private Spy Network

Real Clear Politics-Hillary Clinton's Greatest Masterpiece

VOX-There's a Second Trump Russia Dossier

Real Clear Investigations-Unpacking the other Clinton-Linked Russia Dossier

Daily Caller-Sen. Johnson Subpoenas Blumenthal/Shearer: HRC's 2nd Dossier

Breitbart-Fusion GPS Confirms Steele passed Material to FBI from Cody Shearer

Washington Examiner-Nunes refers Clinton Thugs Shearer and Blumenthal

Guardian-Second Dossier Being Assessed by FBI

American Spectator-Cody Shearer's Dossier Role

Daily Caller-Gowdy: FBI Info from HRC Ally to Collaborate Steele Dossier

National Review-Meet Strange Character Cody Shearer

The Federalist-35 Key People Involved in Russia Hoax need Investigated

Scribd-The Steele Dossier Documents

Crossfire Hurricane Docs-State Department Steele Binder

Justice.gov-2023 SC John Durham Report

Leftist Sin of Pride:
"They Never Thought She Would Lose"

PRIDE is said to be the foremost of all human sins. Hubris is the pathway to all of the other 7 Deadly Sins. According to the Bible, the sin of pride helped in the evil transformation of Lucifer himself. Pride leads us to take full credit for our achievements without gratitude to God and others. Patriots were correct with rejecting the Trump-Russia false narrative and history vindicated the 2016 'Trump Won' movement. Incredibly a poll in 2022 showed a majority of Democrats still believe that HRC won the 2016 Presidential election. Since President Trump was elected (shocking the DC Swamp), BHO and HRC have led complex intelligence operations to escape justice for past crimes.

Post Q# 1345
THEY NEVER THOUGHT SHE WOULD LOSE.

From the moment President Trump won, various groups had been diabolically plotting to overthrow his surprising election. Funding for the opposition resistance is compliments of George Soros and other Leftist piggy banks. The unrelenting attacks continued against President Trump even after the election steal of 2020. President Trump would file in 2022 a federal RICO lawsuit against HRC/DNC/and many others who promoted the false Russian collusion narrative in 2016/17.

Post Q# 4318
Only when information [truth] becomes free [uncontrolled] will people awaken to the levers of control placed upon them.
ANTI-TRUMP ALIGNED FACTIONS:
• Democrats-Progressive Socialists
• Mockingbird Corporate News Media
• Global Climate Crisis and Medical Elites
• Never-Trump/Fake-MAGA
• Muslim Brotherhood/Arab Spring
• Intelligence Communities/FVEY
• NWO Crowd/Family Bloodlines
• Alternative Media Attacks on 'Q+'
• Communist/Marxist/Antifa/Anarchist
• Judicial Corruption-Courts/Judges
• Global Pandemics WHO/UN Health Control
• Open Borders/Migrant Caravans
• International Trade/Tariffs Balance

Post Q# 3124
Increase in attacks (de-platforming, shill infiltration, MSM/Fake MAGA direct, link(s) to terrorism/acts of violence).

It was the very first sin of "PRIDE," that eventually changed Angels into Devils. Excess belief in one's own abilities is vanity, and this dire path leads directly to the 'Original Sin.' The political ruling elite have an unquenchable desire to stay in power using wherever means available. The world is waiting for HRC/BHO to apologize for manufacturing Trump-Russia collusion earning the dubious title of the biggest political hoax in USA history.

Post Q# 2673

FAKE NEWS control over those who do not think for themselves limits exposure of TRUTH.
[D] Party Con..

Vanity is dangerous because it blinds our understanding of the truth and the obvious facts. The followers of BHO/HRC will never fully accept the reality of her lose in 2016 or the loss of power/control of the narrative. The MSM news empire guards their control of the narrative and unleashes destruction on anyone that challenges that tight grip on information.

Post Q# 2461

YOU ARE WATCHING THE SYSTEMATIC DESTRUCTION OF THE OLD GUARD.

So many individuals and special interest groups staked everything on a 2016 HRC victory. Experts, pundits, government employees, lobbyists, industry specialists and even bettors, all were proven to be incorrect over the 2016 Presidential election outcome. The Deep State vowed this would no repeat in the 2020 election and efforts began for the crime of the century.

Post Q# 4586

Largest coordinated mis[dis]information campaign ever to be pushed by controlled entities?

Will they ever just simply admit that they were wrong about HRC and apologize sincerely for their big-league mistake? Healing as a nation will soon be required by all and part of the forthcoming Great Awakening. Bringing the guilty to full legal accountability is the first order at restoring faith in our government. The 'Orange Man Bad' narratives were spun to distract the public from their own criminal activities and done per the Alinsky form of 'projection.'

Post Q# 3310

Threat to Controlled Narrative.
THINK FOR YOURSELF.
DIVIDERS will FAIL.

'Q' stresses the unification of our country and coming to grips with an error in your judgment, is the beginning of the healing process. We are all Americans first and MAGA is our new battle cry to restore our republic. The Afghanistan debacle and subsequent confession of General Milley to treasonous conduct concerning then President Trump demonstrates mass derangement syndrome.

Post Q# 171

Good will always defeat evil.

The Anti-Trump crowd appears to be getting more unhinged daily even in his post Presidency status. Approval polls are at an all-time high for President Trump while Sleepy Joe is at his lowest point. Big Tech's censorship of President Trump and 'Q' parallels the vicious daily ongoing Mockingbird news media attacks. False criminal charges would be brought by various Federal and State prosecutors as well as the corrupt J6 Committee, in attempts to try to finally get President Trump.

Post Q# 2142

Shills only shill.
Patriots WIN.

Stigmas like self-centered, self-pity, over sensitivity, and superiority are outward symptoms being displayed. Also appearing in mass, is the common affliction is now known as Trump Derangement Syndrome (TDS). Related 'sister' illnesses include QAnon/QDS, Virus/VDS and Statue Removal/SDS to name just a couple. HRS's insane scheme to fabricate the entire Trump-Russia scandal will have implications in the unfold 2022 Russian special military operation in Ukraine. As the second term of President Trump approaches in 2024, MSM news figures like Rachel Maddow falsely claim that President Trump will have "death squads" to go after his enemies.

Post Q# 3597

> Do you think we are targeted and attacked by the largest media co's in the world because we're a LARP?

Many of BHO's Organizing For Action (OFA) staffers and his alumni were running National Security Action are now back in the incoming Biden administration. OFA has thousands of protesters trained and on the ready for coordination for the massive Antifa/BLM riots. This is done under the watchful eye of gatekeepers Valerie Jarrett and Susan Rice with final approved by BHO (Shadow President). After the disastrous debate performance by Joe Biden in June 2024, serious discussions about a HRC Presidential ticket occurred before VP Harris was anointed without receiving any Democrat primary votes.

Post Q# 4050

> You are trending WW 24/7/365 w/censorship.
> Never in our history has this been attempted.

Our country needs all citizens united again behind our POTUS/MAGA. Time for the other side to give up on their PRIDE stance and accept the upcoming justice phase for their past sins and crimes. Judgement Day is coming to the corrupt DC Swamp. In the 'Q' informational drops it was pointed out that "your President needs your help". in late 2023 a federal whistleblower revealed the existence of a public/private partnership designed to censor American citizens called the Cyber Threat Intelligence League (CTIL) as part of the vast Censorship Complex in the USA.

Post Q# 3692

> Operators are standing by.

The deranged leftist have tried impeachment, LawFare, fake dossiers, and false hoaxes in a failed effort to 'Get Trump.' HRC would say in 2024 that "Americans should be jailed for misinformation". For the traitorous failed coup plot leaders and their MSM partners, there will be no mercy/forgiveness. We welcome all Americans under the huge tent of 'Q', to becoming Digital Soldiers in this epic struggle to save our Republic. Special Counsel John Durham has dropped criminal indictments related to SpyGate and submitted his final report in 2023. With the re-election of President Trump in 2024, expect the Great Awakening to pick up more public momentum.

Post Q# 4407

> ONLY AT THE PRECIPICE [moment of destruction] WILL PEOPLE FIND THE WILL TO CHANGE.

Links

Brass Balls-How to Stop another Stolen Election

Just the News-HRC Plan tying Trump and Russia

Catholic.org-Seven Deadly Sins

Victor Davis Hanson- The Anti-Democratic Democratic Left

Washington Times-TDS Plagues the Mainstream Media

Revolver News-Flashback Trump was Right about J6 Committee Destroying Evidence

Shellenburger-CTIL Files: US/UK Military Subcontractors

Tablet Mag-A Guide to Understanding the Hoax of the Century

The Federalist-How Trump Derangement gave Birth to the Censorship Industrial Complex

New York Post-Inside the Clinton Dossier and the Con behind RussiaGate

New Yorker-Early Cover Story as President HRC

Seven Deadly Sins-The Sin of Pride

WND-Biden's Actions explained by Cloward Piven Strategy

Breitbart-Gohmert: Trump Derangement Syndrome is reason for Big Tech Censorship

American Spectator-Orange Man Bad Disease

American Thinker-Progressivism and the 7 Deadly Sins

Just the News-Clinton Foundation Meeting Timeline

Crossfire Hurricane Docs-Christopher Steele Binder

Justice.gov-2023 SC John Durham Report

Skolkovo Project: HRC's Hyper Sonic Missile Giveaway

The Putin or Skolkovo Project is much better known to the general public as the Russian Silicon Valley. Several U.S. firms partnered up in 2009 with their Russian counterparts following BHO/HRC's 'Russia Reset' policy. The Clinton foreign treachery began when Slick Willy gave the Chinese miniature Nuke ICBM technology. The world would witness the first use under active wartime conditions of Russia's new hypersonic missiles during the 2022 Ukraine special military operation and deployed into civilian cities.

Post Q# 4924
> BOOMS EN_ROUTE TOMORROW.
> This is not a drill.

Secretary HRC spearheaded, with the blessing of BHO, several U.S. technologies firms in opening joint operations within this new Russian complex. Of course, kickbacks and huge contributions to the Clinton Foundation (CF) were made mandatory. History will show that HRC followed in her husband's treasonous ways by giving Russia our brand-new hypersonic missive technology.

Post Q# 3836
> Think HRC Russia reset statement [Russia].

The Russian Skolkovo Project was an enterprise to promote the transfer (going around CFIUS) of U.S. secret technology. This devious method uses investment/acquisition into this new ultra-advanced technology complex instead of outright bribery. On March 6, 2009 in Geneva HRC gave to Russian Minister Lavrov a plastic red button marked 'Reset' as part of this elaborate scheme to transfer U.S. technology and profit personally in the process.

Post Q# 438
> HRC SAPs (private server).
> EVIL.

The stage was set for the transfer of America's top-secret technologies and Special Access Programs (SAP). History will not be kind on this betrayal of our national defensive military secrets. Safeguarding sensitive new military technologies is paramount in any successful world superpower.

Post Q# 1145
> Trust POTUS.
> Sparrow Red.
> Missiles only.
> Intel good.

Victor Vekselberg was the Russian Skolkovo Director and a major CF donor. Vekselberg paid Bill Clinton $500k for that very short Moscow speech. The corrupt Russian connections were in fact with the Clintons and not as falsely projected against candidate/President Donald Trump.

Post Q# 1241
> No missile tech prevention.
> ICBM

Clinton met with Putin right after that pricey speech. Vladimir told Bill his oligarch pal Vekselberg and Prime Minister Dmitri Medvedev would be the main overseers. Russian oligarchs like Vekselberg and SpyGate's Oleg Deripaska hold incredible sway over American politicians and government officials. Vekselberg and Deripaska would come back into the media spotlight during the 2022 Russian special military operation in Ukraine and the worldwide sanctions placed upon Oligarchs.

Post Q# 1960
Pro Tip: Look Crowdstrike
CrowdStrike managed the infiltration program based on payments to CF.
The More You Know.

Victor Vekselberg steered additional millions directly into the CF coffers per watchdogs Charles Ortel and Peter Schweizer. Thanks to some enterprising forensic bounty hunting accountant whistleblowers evidence is now being presented publicly. As is being discovered in the Arizona forensic audit of the stolen 2020 election, a comprehensive review will often turn up the underlying truth. Veksleberg would have $75 million in assets seized by the DOJ in 2023 under current Russian sanctioning laws.

Post Q# 4813
How close did we come to losing it?
What if she got in?

The 17 of the top 28 U.S. tech firms involved with the Skolkovo project became major CF donors. The U.S. Army raised concerns in 2012 over the loss of some secret military technology. It was obvious to any that looked that there was advanced American technology being used in personal profiteering.

Post Q# 1730
Specialized weapons package.
CLAS-5.

Further the Skolkovo Project concerns in 2016 forced the U.S. Air Force to hit the panic button in several Pentagon reports. The cat was out of the bag and Skolkovo was shut down from the U.S. side and quiet probes began. HRC helping to transfer top secret technology to our sworn enemies is identical to when hubby Bill gave China/CCP miniature ICBM Nuke data.

Post Q# 834
Russian ICBM tech.
Highest level of US-G.
HRC open source.
SAP.

Please check out the below Diana West article on "HRC's Hypersonic Missile Gap". Ms. West highlights the massive tech transfer of top-secret weapons information over to Russian companies. Special Counsel (SC) John Durham has dropped criminal indictments related to HRC/BHO/and other treasonous coup plotters as well as submitting his final report in 2023.

Post Q# 1011
RUSSIA TESTING NEW MISSILES.

Russian President Vladimir Putin threatened the West with his new unstoppable Intercontinental Hypersonic Nuclear Missiles (IHNM). These weapons were compliments of HRC/BHO and Skolkovo partnership venture. The wildcard nation that is the biggest threat is China/CCP and they are quickly playing catch-up in the hypersonic arms race.

Post Q# 4820
>THE CLINTON FOUNDATION.
>WHITE HOUSE FOR SALE.

President Trump gets full credit for creating both the new U.S. Space Force and our own "even faster" hypersonic nuclear missiles. In 2024 Putin sent Russian warships carrying hypersonic missiles to conduct drills en route to Cuba. Even with President Trump's successful reelection in 2024, we continue to watch the illegal Biden/Harris administration destroying our great Republic with continued warmongering and disastrous economic policies.

Post Q# 1728
>Unauthorized missile fired.
>POTUS AF1.
>POTUS re-routes.

BHO/HRC's Skolkovo project under the Russian Reset policy may indeed end up destabilizing the world. The recent successful test and deployment of the new hypersonic Russian Avangard glide vehicle and Tsirkon cruise missile may just have ignited a new superpowers arms race with USA as well as China. The planet is on the brink of World War 3 with the ongoing military conflict in Ukraine using hypersonic missiles and Putin updates Russian nuclear doctrine due to use of U.S. made long range missiles. With the historic re-election of President Trump in 2024, many feel world peace and global unity may finally be at hand.

Post Q# 570
>HRC [8] WWIII (death and weapons real).

Links

RT-Dream to Reality: Russia's 'Silicon Valley' marks 10 Year Anniversary

Reuters News-Kremlin: Hypersonic Missile Strike in Ukraine was a Warning

Just the News-Russian Warships with Hypersonic Missiles to Cuba

Free Beacon-Skolkovo: Russia gave Millions to Clinton Foundation

Newsweek-Russia's Kinzhal Missile Fundamentally changes War

Victor Davis Hanson-Russia Russia Forever

Just the News-Putin Updates Russian Nuclear Doctrine

Business Insider-DOJ Seizes 6 Luxury Properties from Russian Oligarch

Just the News-Uranium: How Russia got stronger as Bidens/Clintons got Richer

Open Secrets-Russian Oligarchs made Political Contributions to U.S.

National Review-Remembering BHO's Russia Reset and HRC's Skolkovo

WSJ-The Clinton Foundation, State and Kremlin Connections

Moscow Times-Russia's latest Tsirkon Hypersonic Missile Test

Aaron Mate-RussiaGate has No Bottom

The Guardian-Inside Skolkovo: Moscow's Silicon Valley

The Drive-China tests Fractional Orbital System and Hypersonic Glide Vehicle

FOX News-HRC Pushes for Russian Silicon Valley

NY Times-Clinton approved Technology Transfer to China

Wikipedia-Skolkovo Innovation Center/Project

BBC-Russia deploys Avangard Hypersonic Missile System

Daily Caller-HRC's Hypersonic Missile Gap

Investor's Business Daily-Revelations about HRC's "Russian Reset"

FOX News-HRC's Push for a Russian Silicon Valley

The Guardian-Russia's Skolkovo Silicon Valley

The Hill-Case for Russian Collusion against Democrats

Crossfire Hurricane Docs-DJT and Flynn Defensive Briefing

Clinton Foundation Timeline-2025 Crossfire Hurricane Docs

Justice.gov-2023 SC John Durham Report

Chris Steele/Orbis/and Skripal: Poisoning Connections

The observant young daughter (Abigail) of Colonel Alison McCourt spotted two individuals collapsed to the ground on 3/5/18. This setting was Salisbury/England, and this bizarre incident would have lasting worldwide repercussions. This poisoning would be brought up during the 2022 Russian special military operation into Ukraine in several regards. Also brought up in 2022 by Special counsel (SC) John Durham was our FBI offered to pay Christopher Steele $1 million in the Fall of 2016 to collaborate his own fake dossier.

Post Q# 1974
If the FAKE Steele Dossier constituted the 'bulk' of the facts submitted to FISC to obtain FISA warrant(s) against POTUS.......

Sergei Skripal and his daughter Yulia were victims of a poisoning that almost killed them both. A rare and very toxic military-grade nerve agent called Novichok was used as part of this assassination attempt and this pair. It has long been assumed that Sergei Skripal was yet another one of Christopher Steele and Orbis Business Intelligence (spies for hire) unreliable sources for his now discredited Russian Dossier. It was revealed that Fusion GPS had a paid working relationship with Steele/Orbis going back to 2015 and through the creation of the fake 'dossier.'

Post Q# 1164
NOT PUBLIC: Five Eyes UK/AUS/POTUS targeting.

The exotic nature of nerve agent Novichok in being used in this military grade fashion, definitely screams of a 'state sponsored' assassination attempt. Novichok is not available to the general public and almost impossible to acquire in this lab refined grade except by countries or international criminal cartels.

Post Q# 2633
"McCain associate shared unverified Steele dossier with BuzzFeed court filing says."

After two additional victims fell ill in the nearby region, the entire Salisbury area underwent a massive decontamination clean-up. Two Russian nationals were captured on closed circuit video as being at the scene and later were positively identified by authorities. Russia has long been falsely portrayed as the global bogeyman who is always up to no good.

Post Q# 2107
'KNOWINGLY' used FALSE intelligence?
Think HRC [paid for] FAKE DOSSIER [bulk].

Colonel Anatoliy Chepiga is a GRU intelligence officer and his partner Alexander Petrov, are now wanted for this murder attempt. Black Hats attempted to link Christopher Steele and his employer Orbis Business Intelligence, to the attempted murder of the well-known double agent Sergei Skripal.

Post Q# 4153
[FBI Floor 7] [UK assist] Steele - B_Ohr - N_Ohr - FusionGPS [shell 2]

International warrants and EU/Interpol alerts have been issued for this Russian pair. England has already tried them in absentia, and they are globally wanted fugitive criminals. BBC has produced a miniseries titled "The Salisbury Poisonings" that has brought additional light to the tragedy. Christopher Steele would still be in 2022 trying to legitimize his phony Russian Dossier by continuing to go to the international news media pleading his innocence.

Post Q# 2129
USE OF BACKCHANNEL SURV/SPY INSERTION [BODY 1, 2, and5] BY UK/AUS [PRIMARY] ACTIVATED UNDER DIR BRENNAN DIR CLAPPER W/PDB REGULAR UPDATES.

This was an assassination mission and obviously had several operational layers. A near death message/warning was sent out by the Kremlin to future traitors and a false trail planted to play into Steele-Russian narrative. The deadly bio-agent Novichok has been used since in the death of Dawn Sturgess and the attempted assignation of Russian politician Alexei Navalny.

Post Q# 1828
[SPY OP]
[UK PM/MI6/SIS [SPY ACTIV] - [CS]

Skripal was convicted by Russia in 2004 of espionage and sentenced to 15 years in prison. Sergei was exchanged in 2010 as part of an infamous 'spy swap' between Russia and England but involving the United States as well. Sergei and Yulia have since left England and are happily resettled in New Zealand. President Trump would include both Chris Steele and Orbis Business Intelligence in his 2022 federal RICO lawsuit in damages stemming from the unfolding SpyGate political scandal.

Post Q# 972
Intelligence A's across the globe in partnership to spy on citizens?

History will remember the other half of this spy exchange was for Anna Chapman and her sleeper agent families. FX's "The Americans" portrays the real-life spies of the FBI's 'Operation Ghost Stories.' Central characters in SpyGate include Christopher Steele, Orbis, and dossier asset Igor Danchenko. Danchenko would prove to be Steele's primary sub-source and remember that Fusion GPS/Nellie Ohr would be the main compiler of the infamous Trump-Russia Dossier.

Post Q# 895
Don't drop the soap.

Incredibly this old international spy episode involved U1/HRC/Mueller/and Peter Strzok. SC John Durham has begun to drop criminal indictments and will sort out the treasonous role played by these same characters. SC Durham would begin to demonstrate in 2022 the outline of a vast 'Joint Venture Conspiracy' in the creation and the dissemination of the false Russian collusion narrative of 2016 involving many key government officials. Some of the very same actors in the unfolding ObamaGate/SpyGate political scandals have played parts in past operations. Several Russian Oligarchs in 2022 would also mysteriously come down with unknow poisoning symptoms.

Post Q# 1944
Given magnitude of spy campaign (U.S. Presidential Election Republican Party Nominee Candidate and President Elect and President of the United States) would HUSSEIN be required to DIRECT ORDER?

President Trump filed a lawsuit in 2023 against both Christopher Steele and his company Orbis Business Intelligence for the creation of the false Russia dossier. Spy vs Spy has been a theme we have notice being played out in this historic drama. We are entering [Movie 3/The Storm] and the end to this perfectly choreographic production masterpiece. SC Durham submitted his final report in 2023. Steele would start another false story in early 2024 by suggesting that Moscow is behind the UK immigration protests. With the historic re-election of President Trump in 2024, our Republic is yearning for the return of the rule of law and equal justice once again in our land.

Post Q# 1974
BO was the 'BACKCHANNEL' between FBI/DOJ and STEELE.

Links

The Sun-Poison Probe: Who is Sergei Skripal?

FOX News-Patel found Thousands of Sensitive Trump Russia Probe Docs

Just the News-Steele Dossier Cited in 2016 ICA about Putin

Clinton Foundation Timeline-2025 Crossfire Hurricane Docs

Newsweek-Poisoned Russian Spy liked to Dossier Author

Racket News-The Spies who Hijacked America

Clinton Foundation Timeline-Orbis Business Intelligence

The Guardian-Trump sues Steele/Orbis over Dossier

Judicial Watch-Fusion GPS/Chris Steele Timeline from 2015

BBC News-Russian Spy: Poisoning Poses major Challenge to MI6

FOX News-FBI offered Christopher Steele $1M to Corroborate Trump Dossier

Daily Express-Sergei and Yulia Skripal: New Zealand after Novichok Poisonings

The Guardian-'A Chain of Stupidity': The Skripal Case

The Telegraph-Poisoned Spy Skripal close to Consultant linked to Trump Dossier

The Last Refuge-Chuck Grassley and Christopher Steele

BBC-Russian Spy: What Happened to Sergei Skripal

Time-How Skripal went from Russian Spy to Poisoning Victim

NBC News-Two Russians charged with Novichok Poisoning of Skripal

FOX News-Former Russian Spy Skripal: What to Know

The Guardian-Woman in Russian Spy Mystery is Skripal's Daughter

Video-Two Russians Charged in Skripal Novichok Poisoning

Just the News-FBI's Arctic Haze

Red Piller-Craig Murray: Sky News/Skripal Interview

Senate Intelligence Committee: 2021 DECLAS

Crossfire Hurricane Docs-Christopher Steele Binder

Justice.gov-2023 SC John Durham Report

'Q' Approved "Read-In" Helpers:
Reporters John Solomon and Sara Carter

"LISTEN AND WATCH SEAN HANNITY TODAY"

The term 'read-in' can mean the process of being 'read-in' to a compartmented operational program or a portion of the entire plan. Officially named Sensitive Compartmented Information (SCI), this is where individuals have access to only a segmented part and not read-into the entire whole operational program. John Solomon (JS) and Sara Cater (SC) are longtime top news media reporters and would be central figures at the beginning of the public awareness of the SpyGate scandal as well as later tie in the 2022 as events around the many political investigations come to fruition.

Post Q# 2121
Q also links us to Sara Carter, who is literally on Hannity every single night.
NOTE: Anon post and 'Q' confirmed

The entire 'Q' back-channel information operation began late in 2017 as a systemically arranged public informational dissemination program primarily directed at the inquisitive Anons. Non-classified intel 'crumbs' often in the form of a question, had been approved at the highest levels on public Chan message boards for distribution to worldwide Anons. Selective information would be quietly disseminated to special news media helpers like Solomon/Carter as well as figures like Congressional leaders and private non-governmental entities.

Post Q# 2626
"I have pretty good sources..."-SH.
There is a reason why SH, SC, and JS are on stage.

We all firmly believe that the core of Team 'Q' is composed of U.S. Military Intelligence active-duty personnel under the direction of President Trump. Due to the scope and complexity of this operation, a few 'read-in' helpers have got to be included to assist the overall objectives. By John Solomon's public account of this incident explained on FOX News with Mark Levin, Solomon was approached by two intelligence individuals that would continue to provide unreleased intel for him and Sara Carter to disseminate via their news reports. Sara Carter would confirm a similar approach by mysterious government agents later in that same TV interview.

Post Q# 283
Why are Sara and John getting all the 'real' scoops?

I throw out Erik Prince/Blackwater as another prime example of being 'read-in' but that's for another story. 'Q' obliviously has selected media personalities like Sara/John to appear periodically with hosts like Tucker Calrson and Sean Hannity, to receive periodic special 'insider' information to disseminate publicly. Later select media activations appear to be Catherine Herridge/Tom Fitton/Steve Bannon/Jesse Watters/Vicki Toensing and hubby JoeD as well as via Patriots like General Flynn, Rudy Giuliani and Sidney Powell to name a few Patriots.

Post Q# 900
Why are we providing this much sensitive detail in a public [known] forum?

Tucker Carlson/Sean Hannity jointly held at one time the most watched evening cable network news programs on FOX TV and Hannity also enjoys one of the largest radio audiences. Both

Sara/John have been awarded winning journalists with stellar reporting records and appear regularly with Sean Hannity. Others joining at FOX News crew that have been leading the way of truthful information are Judge Jeanine/Ingraham/Lou Dodds/and Jesse Watters. Tucker Carlson would be fired by FOX News in 2023 and would emerge stronger on Elon Musk's X/Twitter platform. Tucker Carlson would set viewing records for his new programs on Elon Musk's social media site.

Post Q# 3588

"SURV of SC/JS terminated."-Q
Relevant to upcoming 'DECLAS' events.

This extra special relationship between these three key media figures began in the Winter of 2017. Sean Hannity had Sara Carter and John Solomon on to break the secret Uranium One (U1) FBI confidential informant story of William 'Doug' Campbell. Note that also in March 2017 was then Rep. Devin Nunes presser concerning classified information about past illegal surveillance of Team Trump and the beginning of public awareness of SpyGate.

Post Q# 1934

BIG PUZZLE PIECE
Who is systemically arranging the leaks to select individuals?

decode: Sara Carter (SC) has a news articled linked to this Q drop

Of odd coincidence was the start of the public 'Q' informational drops during this same Fall 2017 time period. I maintain that SC/JS started to get the 'Q' drops first (test run) and then later the Anons were included in this dissemination flow via 4Chan/8Chan/and now 8KUN. President Trump would file in 2022 a federal RICO lawsuit against HRC/DNC/and others related to the promotion of the false Russian collusion narrative during the 2106 election cycle as demonstrated in the unfolding SpyGate political scandal.

Post Q# 2121

New shill attack to smear Sean Hannity.
Hannity is a Patriot.
Note: Anon post-confirmed by 'Q'

'Q' has repeatedly posted links on various drops to articles by both from Sara Carter and John Solomon. 'Q' has also directed folks to watch Hannity's prime time show for important news. In the era of the big 2020 election steal and illegal Biden regime, many other helpers are continuing in dropping the crumbs. The MSM's coverup of the Hunter Biden "Laptop from Hell" is a classic example of the coordination of fake news and the corrupt DC Swamp and the bonus letter from 51 former intel officials swayed over 17% of the 2020 vote towards Joe Biden.

Post Q# 4620

Intel community [NAT SEC_WH] essential to control [infiltration] to prevent DECLAS_public exposure of true events [illegal surv [R] candidates 1+2, House members 1-x, Senate members 1-x, Journalists 1-x, Amb 1-x] + CLAS 1-99 events.

There has been a direct retaliation threat made by 'Q' to the Deep State in terms of the health of all three of these specific news media personalities. The exact phrase was "Self-suicide if activated" retribution if any harm may befall SH/SC/or JS. The entire Mockingbird news has continued their attacks on 'Q' and our read-in helpers since the jump back in 2017. John Solomon would sue the DOJ/National Archives in 2023 over access to declassified Trump-Russia probe memos. PSYOPS or psychological operations have been around in one form or another forever and the news media has been an essential element of forming mass opinions/narratives. FOX/CBS reporter Catherine Herridge ('Follow the Pen') has consistently been connected to the 'Q' drops was fired and her confidential files were questionable seized by her news network prompting an appearance testifying in front of the U.S. Congress.

Post Q# 144
> Why was Sarah A. C. attacked (hack-attempt)?

Many may have suspected a few members of Congress (Nunes/Grassley/Jordan/Johnson/and now MTG and Gaetz) as bring "read-in" helpers as well. The same 'Q' helper theory would also apply to a few trusted media folks as well as other key private individuals. Dan Scavino and KANSAS continue to lead but trusted folks like Kash Patel and Ezra Cohen-Watnick also drop 'Q' related crumbs via social media. 2022 would see both John Solomon and Sara Carter continue to drop truth bombs in regard to Ukraine/SpyGate/Hunter Biden's 'Laptop from Hell.'

> Post Q# 3373
> SURV of SC/JS terminated.
> Sleep well.

President Trump had set up the table with his Justice Dream Team (Barr/Huber/Durham/and Horowitz) and we are ready for the final performances. Today heroes like Mike Lindell/Sydney Powell/Kari Lake/and our own General Mike Flynn are posting 'Q' related information like others have done. Special Counsel John Durham has dropped criminal indictments related to illegal surveillance operations and submitted his final report in 2023. The reports from IG Horowitz and SC Durham will be the foundation for judicial accountability. With the re-election of President Trump in 2024, the long expected 'Judgement Day' is forthcoming.

Post Q# 4196
> Why did [Schiff] illegally surveil [phone] members of WH legal team, media, and Congress?

Links

FOX News-John Solomon and Sara Carter Following the Facts on the Collusion Narrative

Just the News-John Solomon Sues DOJ over Trump Russia

Ada Nestor-They All Knew it was a Lie

FOX News-Clinton Campaign Paid for Anti Trump Dossier

Mark Levin-John Solomon and Sara Carter: Facts on the Collusion Narrative

Newsweek-Everything Tucker Carlson has said about QAnon

Lew Rockwell-Fox News, Ukraine, and the Onset of the New World Order

Code Monkey-Framing Techniques for Mass Persuasion

The War Economy-John Solomon meets Q-Team

Chron-Government Tracking of Journalists

FOX News-Nunes: 'Strange and Irregular' requests to Monitor Journalists

Real Clear Investigations-Theft near White House: John Solomon's Laptop

Breitbart-Judicial Watch: BHO Ambassadors Ordered Monitoring of Journalists

Real Clear Politics-Hannity/Sara/John: Uranium One FBI Informant

American Thinker-Hannity: I Think I am a Deep State's Target

The American Spectator-WAPO's Attacks John Solomon

Mediaite-Who is Sara Carter?

Judicial Watch-State Dept Records show US Embassy Monitored Reporters

Real Clear Investigations-Media Attack on John Solomon is Attack on Free Press

Sara Carter-Sidney Powell Interview (6/30/20)

Crossfire Hurricane Docs-Christopher Steele Binder

Justice.gov-2023 SC John Durham Report

Pending Return of Shadowy Contractor Edward Snowden

The profit motive surrounded Edward Snowden's [ES] choice of employers on several occasions. Snowden has been an employee of the CIA, NSA and a top government contractor in past years. History will not be kind on the mountains of classified data 'willfully' handed over to hostile nations (China/Russia) by Snowden. Assigned Special Counsel (SC) John Durham would begin to expose in 2022 with SpyGate related court proceeding, the horrors of illegal governmental surveillance operations against Americans.

Post Q# 1984
What agency did Snowden work for orig?
Did he train on THE FARM?

Snowden's background has always been with computers, and he started early with Dell Computers. Snowden found out at a young age, that top connected civilian outside contractors pays way more than does similar work for the U.S. government. A 2023 survey showed that Snowden's leak of classified data still ranks as the worst in U.S. history.

Post Q# 846
Snowden.
Welcome to China.

History will show that Snowden's 2013 disclosure of classified NSA data severely damaged the overall national security of our country. A special policing directorate within NSA called the 'Q Group' instantly began hunting Snowden. The estimated costs in damages and repairs alone exceeded $1 Billion, crippling the NSA for years afterward.

Post Q# 3920
Define 'Traitor.'
Data exchange(s) can be very dangerous.

'Q' had been hinting that we may soon find out the true allegiance of Snowden and it is not the carefully constructed 'whistleblower' continuously character portrayed by both the MSM and Alternative news media. Returning Snowden from Russia/China for a full debriefing, would help to answer many pivotal questions of his past loyalties and real employer.

Post Q# 3691
Snowden
#HOMECOMING2020

Snowden was employed by the CIA as a computer technician back in 2006. By 2009 [ES] had become a contract employee from top technology firm Booz Allen Hamilton, subbing out with the NSA. Many would look back upon Snowden working via outside governmental contractors as a CIA trained ploy to penetrate safeguards.

Post Q# 2767
Snowden.
What will happen when Russia gives you up?
Will the C_A protect you?
Sleep is important.

[ES] then went to a full-time employment status with the NSA in 2011. 'Q' has hinted that Snowden had an educational stop at 'THE FARM' during this same time period. Note the NSA began actively hunting down Edward Snowden (Q Group Directorate) with a dedicated team way back in 2013.

Post Q# 790
> SNOWDEN.
> WHERE ARE YOU?
> NOT RUSSIA.
> [EYES ON].

Booz Allen Hamilton is one of the largest subcontractors of various products to the U.S. government. They employed Snowden through late 2012 and is the company of record during his incredible betrayal escapade. As a historical lesson in governmental security, the use of outside contractors should be limited when dealing with the most classified top-secret information.

Post Q# 900
> Why are we giving him this much attention?
> Why are we providing this much sensitive detail in a public [known] forum?

Edward Snowden first reached out to reporters Glenn Greenwald and Laura Poitras in December 2012/January 2013. Snowden had identified himself under the pseudonym of 'Citizen Four' (later a hit Hollywood movie). Edward Snowden was offering the disclosure of NSA secret operations and classified data. Both Greenwald/Poitras as well as Snowden were members of John Parry Barlow's Freedom of the Press (SecureDrop).

Post Q# 770
> Snowden
> You are now a liability.

Snowden departed the U.S. for Hong Kong on May 19, 2013, to meet up with Glenn and Laura. Assisted by Julian Assange/WikiLeaks in his escape route, experts still marvel on how Snowden cleared any point of entry while his passport had a worldwide hold alert issued. Canada has granted asylum to four Sri Lankan refugees who hide Snowden in their Hong Kong apartment.

Post Q# 151
> What was Snowden's real primary mission?
> Was Snowden truly acting on his own?
> Nothing is as it appears.

It is estimated that over 1.5 million files were downloaded in total from two NSA sites. Printed out these stolen files would stack over 3 miles high. To date he has given to these two reporters over 200,000 of the copied NSA files. Dennis Montgomery would steal more files from the NSA than Snowden a few years later but not as top secret sensitive.

Post Q# 570
> Launch 'good guy' takedown (internal remove).
> Snowden open source Prism/Keyscore (catastrophic to the US Mil v. bad actors (WW) + Clowns/-No Such Agency).

Snowden would shortly travel from Hong Kong to his final destination of Russia via Jason Bourne type tactics. His wife later joined him in Moscow, where asylum has been extended by the Russians through 2020 (Welcome Back Home Snowden). Anons point out that Snowden's treason was an integral component to the 16-Year Plan.

Post Q# 732
> What if Snowden was still a Clown?

Odd that Snowden did not use the regular official whistleblower route to raise his objections about the practices of the NSA. SecureDrop was a whistleblower drop box and a big part of the Freedom of the Press (FOTP) group that many believe had been taken over the C_A. Snowden would reveal NSA's PRISM (Planning Tool for Resource Integration, Synchronization, and Management) computer data tool for the collection of foreign intelligence.

Post Q# 2657
Where did Snowden work prior to NSA contractor ACCEPT.

FOTP leading members included Greenwald and Poitras along with John Perry Barlow/James Dolan/Daniel Ellsberg/ and Julian Assange. Snowden may have known something that other whistleblowers [SR] didn't know about who really controlled (Clowns/C_A) SecureDrop.

Post Q# 2612
Negotiating for return.
Traitor.
Mission to harm NSA.

'Q' has dropped the C_A/Clowns have taken control of SecureDrop. Snowden's stolen NSA source codes allow the 4am MSM 'talking points' to be transmitted to the Mockingbird media via SecureDrop daily statements. The late John Perry Barlow and the Electronic Freedom Foundation played a key role in the development of SecureDrop.

Post Q# 875
Who performs in a circus?

In addition to the economic and obvious optics, various intelligence streams and even field operatives' lives have been lost due to this treasonous data disclosure. Snowden's 'Leak' has been the largest loss of classified top-secret information in our country's history up to 2013. Many intelligence agents believe Snowden has been parsing out the stolen data to China and Russia in exchange for his residency.

Post Q# 166
Expand your thinking.
Jason Bourne (Deep Dream).

Analysts now believe that Snowden's primary role was on behalf of the CIA, was to damage rival NSA's intelligence gathering abilities. By exposing NSA's most secret technical tools and methods, it did in fact severely cripple NSA. Anons are exploring Snowden's helping Brennan/Clapper with surveillance tools like the 'Hammer', PRISIM, and the 'Bridge' programs. History will judge Edward Snowden in terms of his actions being treasonous, but most agree his predictions about the United States turning into a 'surveillance state' has proven accurate decades later.

Post Q# 836
Who leaked Vault7 to WL?
OP Name: Fiddler.
Snowden.

Thankfully Admiral Rogers came to the later rescue of both the NSA and on November 17, 2016, of our POTUS. NSA has vowed to bring Snowden back to stand justice for the damage he has done to our national security. Snowden has agreed to forfeit over $5M in sales from his book 'Permanent Record.' Russia has given Snowden permanent residency and path to citizenship. In

2023 the DOJ was awarded by the VA District Court a final judgment and permanent injunction against Edward Snowden's book.

Post Q# 874
How did Snowden clear customs/immigration in HK AFTER the public release?

In 2014 the movie "Citizen Four" was released featuring the real Edward/Glenn/and Laura. Oliver Stone would follow by producing the big screen Hollywood hit "Snowden" in 2016. The NSA's internal police termed the 'Q Group' has been hunting Snowden since 2013. Snowden stays active on social media as evident in his 2022 comments on Joe Rogan/COVID-19. Edward Snowden would say in 2023 marking 10 years in exile that he has "No Regrets ".

Post Q# 3024
WELCOME HOME, SNOWDEN.

In this unfolding complex drama, we all may have to wait until the very end to sort of the real White vs Black Hats. President Trump/NSA/Team 'Q' have all helped to expose the "enigma" of Edward Snowden and I feel they will hold [ES] fully accountable for his treacherous actions. SC John Durham has dropped criminal indictments related to illegal surveillance operations and submitted his final report in 2023. With the re-election of President Trump in 2024, some incoming Cabinet members are inclined to revisit a pardon of Edward Snowden.

Post Q# 3053
Whistle while you work.....
Have you screen the movie 'Snowden'?

Links

Discord Image-Snowden the Fiddler

NY Post-Edward Snowden has Allies in Trump White House

The Guardian-Edward Snowden: No Regrets after 10 Years in Exile

The Defender-Edward Snowden: Citizen Four

Sharyl Attkisson-BHO Era Surveillance Timeline

Techno Fog-U.S. Intelligence Operations against Americans

Daily Mail-Canada grants Asylum: Sri Lankan Refugees who Hide Snowden

The Guardian-Speculation grows over Pardon for Edward Snowden

The Federalist-5 Myths about Snowden Reinforced by Movie

Daily Beast (pre Q)-Inside the "Q Group" Hunting Snowden

John Stossel-Edward Snowden Interview

Vice News-Snowden: Assange Arrest/Mueller Report Show 'Two-Tiered' Justice

Forbes-Helped by Assange/WikiLeaks: Snowden needs Perry Mason

Washington Free Beacon-CIA and NSA Missed Signs of Snowden's Betrayal

Business Insider-Timeline of Snowden's Leaks

ARS Technica-US Gov't Entitled to all Snowden Book Proceeds

CNET-What is the NSA's PRISM Program?

The Guardian-NSA Whistleblower Edward Snowden Video

ENDEVR-Meeting Edward Snowden Documentary

Movie Trailer-2014 Citizen Four

Justice.gov-Final Judgement and Permanent Injunction against Edward Snowden

Crossfire Hurricane Docs-Halper Files

Justice.gov-2023 SC John Durham Report

Soros' Open Society Foundation—
The Gift that Keeps on Giving

George Soros (aka Gyorgy Schwartz) was born in Hungary and has become one of the richest most powerful people in the world. Soros admitted to offering assistance to the Nazi regime in the confiscation of Jewish property during WW2. Many today feel that George Soros [GS] is one of the primary globalists pushing The Great Reset. The Russian 2022 special military operation in the Ukraine exposed one hub of the New World Order and major financial funders like puppet master Soros. President Trump would file in 2022 a major lawsuit against George Soros as well as HRC/DNC/and others related to the creation of the SpyGate/RussiaGate false narrative.

Post Q# 4393
What happens if Soros funded operations get violent and engage in domestic terrorism?

[GS] began in 1992 his global charity called the Open Society Foundation (OSF). Considered one of the three pillars of international global power, when George Soros calls, progressive leftist run to answer. Globalist Klaus Schwab under the World Economic Forum has initiated a Global Reset with assistance from OSF. The passing of the family baton would occur in 2023 as Godfather George turned over control to son Alex Soros.

Post Q# 4635
Soros history.
Assault on America.

OSF is the second largest worldwide charity behind only the Bill/Melinda Gates Foundation. Money buys influence as well as posh awards, bizarrely demonstrated by George Soros being named the 2019 Philanthropist of the Year. Non-Governmental Organizations (NGO) are being used to help fund these various global schemes from climate change to vaccine passports.

Post Q# 490
Think GS pays for Antifa out of his own pocket?
The hole is deep.

Soros uses his philanthropy charities to promote NWO agendas and an universal one-world global philosophy. Massive donations are deliberately directed toward Progressive Communist Leftist causes and ultra-liberal socialists' programs to influence political policy. Money talks and Soros is known as the Progressive's supplier of this vital ammunition.

Post Q# 99
Foundations?
Institutes?
Soros.

Soros has turned over his accumulated wealth of $18 billion directly into his OSF charity as a protective shield against confiscation. Over the last 3 decades, Soros has donated over $10 billion towards various Progressive Liberal causes. Socialist employs tactics of 'Color Revolution' to help overwhelm their target country with race wars and public rioting. One of the evilest campaigns by the Soros Family has been to bankroll crocked State Attorney Generals as well as supporting 'defund the police' local state-wide political candidates.

Post Q# 2
Why did Soros donate all his money recently?

George Soros is often referred to as "The Godfather of the Left" and is one of the NWO's main fundraisers. Soros belongs to an exclusive shadowy club of billionaires referred to loosely as the Democracy Alliance. A primary goal of the globalist is to destabilize the USA via infiltration of every aspect of society. Special Counsel (SC) John Durham has connected Soros to the Alfa Bank/Trump Tower fake server hoax through operative Daniel Jones. Soros along with his NWO Globalist pals would cheer in 2022 Biden's creation of a 'Ministry of Truth' section under DHS to combat domestic misinformation ala George Orwell's infamous '1984' book.

Post Q# 3749

> Threat: If a major police party can be [controlled] does that represent a clear and present danger to the United States of America?
> [GS]

In 2002 Soros gave one of his charities over to Robert Redford along with $5 million to influence the Sundance Films. The Deep State is pushing out progressive narratives via Hollywood hit film movies to achieve global social change. Soros appointed Mark Mallock-Brown, who is the head of Smartmatic Voting Software as new president of OSF at the end of 2020. Son Alex Soros has pledged over $125M to help the Democrats in the 2022 midterms. It would later revealed that Soros/OSF received millions In misdirected funds from the corrupt USAID, which funded their various political activities.

Post Q# 619

> Do you expect HRC, GS, Hussein, etc to stand in a PUBLIC courtroom w/ potential crooked judges and tainted 'liberal' juries?

[GS] combined with HRC/Harold Ickes in 2006 forming the Shadow Party. Yet more threads of the spider web that all seem to connect to Soros' pocketbook. Sadly, it is understood that the U.S. Congress and corporate heads are in alliance under the puppet master strings of [GS]. Records show Soros has put in over $1M in support Governor Newsom in the California recall election. A Soros-backed group would help in 2022 a Latino media group purchase 18 Spanish radio stations in an attempt to control the narrative of this critical voting group.

Post Q# 4153

> [Background] [SOROS - HUSSEIN - HRC]
> SOROS/OSF is involved with the following:
> • Refuge Caravan/Immigration Waves
> • Major donor to BHO's O.F.A.
> • Funding for the Reparations Movement
> • Int'l Activism: Ukraine/Albania/Romania/Vatican
> • 2016 $8M toward HRC Campaign
> • 18 Spanish and 200 English Radio Stations
> • 2020 $40M into Voter Super PAC
> • Paymaster to Daniel Jones/Alfa Bank
> • Sponsorship of Hamas/ISIS/Hizballah
> • Smartmatic Voting/Election Fraud
> • Paymaster of Antifa, BLM and Defund the Police
> • Behind NFL 'Take a Knee' and Black National Anthem
> • Funded World Health/UN Climate Groups
> • $50M toward Chris Steele Dossier 2.0
> • The Great Reset/Vaccine Passports
> • USAID misdirection funding fraud
> - • Alex Soros $125M for 2022 Midterms and 2024 Elections

Post Q# 330

We have a special place picked out for GS

OSF pushes for open borders and unlimited illegal immigration. Globalists want a borderless world to help achieve their primary NWO domination goals and overall population reduction. Vaccine passports will lead into a digital tracking ID cards for even more control of the world populace. Soros has also been caught funding several state Attorney General and District Attorney candidates who endorse radical judicial policies. George Soros would turn over control over in 2023 total control of OSF to his oldest son Alex, who begun closing OSF offices worldwide.

Post Q# 142

How did Soros replace family 'Y'?
What happened during WWII?

The flooding of Europe and now the USA by waves of illegal Muslim immigrants incredibly funded in part by our own USAID funding, is the future planned by globalists for the entire Western world. Glenn Beck forewarned that George Soros had "Messianic Fantasies" toward total global world domination (like an evil movie villain). This current global battle of Good vs Evil is on a winner take all trajectory. SC Durham submitted his final report in 2023 and will be the foundation for future judicial accountability. Americans would witness in the endless legal cases filed against President Trump, the efforts by Soros/OSF to fund election campaigns of crazed Marxist state Attorney Generals. Soros/OSF would bid in 2024 for control of debt ridden Audacy and their over 200 USA radio stations in yet another attempt to control the media/narrative.

Post Q# 15

PS, Soros is targeted.

Soros insists on his own blend of Progressive Socialism/Liberalism/and Communism and continues to fund Afghanistan refugees and Southern border migrant invasion caravans. The Patriots say no to the Great Reset and the NWO. Special Counsel John Durham submitted his final report concerning SpyGate in 2023. Judgement Day is coming for George Soros and his paid revolutionary globalist communist minions. With the re-election of President Trump in 2024, outgoing Biden unconscionably awarded the Presidential Medal of Freedom to George Soros and HRC.

Post Q# 2502

Thank you, Mr. Soros.

Links

The Atlantic-Soros and the Demonization of Philosophy

FOX News-Soros' Alleged Ties to RussiaGate Exposed

Town Hall-The USAID/Soros Nightmare Continues

Just the News-Tom Fitton unmasks George Soros Alliance with USAID

Washington Times-Soros Grip on Democratic Party Loosened

FOX News-FCC Launches Probe into Soros Backed Radio Stations

Real Clear Policy-How Trump's USAID move Impacts Soros Empire?

Marissa Hansen-USAID Funding to Soros/Open Society Foundation

Bloomberg News-Soros Shutters OSF Offices Worldwide

Badlands Media-George Soros: Shadow Network

NY Post-How George Soros Co-opts the Media

Victor Pinchuk Foundation- Davos Ukrainian Breakfast

Independent Sentinel-George Soros: Plan to Destroy America

Front Page-Three Foreign Billionaires financed Dark Money in 2020 Election

PJ Media-Soros Connected to Alfa Bank Fake Russia Hoax

Millennium Report-The Fake Great Reset and End of Civilization

Revolver-Transition Integrity Project: Soros Group Plotting a "Color Revolution"

Breitbart-George Soros Pouring $220M into Radical Justice Movement

Sunshine State News-Billionaire Leftist George Soros bought America's Media

Millennium Report-The Trojan Horse that Rolled into America

The Guardian-The George Soros Philosophy and Flaws

City Journal-Connoisseur of Chaos

Washington Times-Soros Still on Quest to Destroy America

Clinton Foundation Timeline-2025 Crossfire Hurricane Docs

Justice.gov-2023 SC John Durham Report

The Sundance Kid 'Partners-Up' with George Soros

Already political and ideological bedfellows, George Soros and actor Robert Redford (The Sundance Kid) keep expanding their business relationship. Various political fund raisers and connected charities had matched up these two unique characters in the past. The 2022 Russian special military operation in the Ukraine will expose a big center of operations for the New World Order and their major sponsors like George Soros. In 2023 George Soros would remain one of the global leaders in the struggle of the Great Reset versus the Great Awakening.

Post Q# 4635
> Soros history.
> Assault on America.

President Trump would file a major lawsuit in 2022 against George Soros/HRC/DNC/and others for the manufacturing of the false Russia collusion narrative in 2016. Preliminary discussions were started in 2011 to form a merger with Sundance Institute. The globalist George Soros could see the Hollywood appeal and having access to famous actor Robert Redford, worked into his long-term political agenda.

Post Q# 2658
> Remember when D's and the FAKE NEWS media [+ FAKEWOOD] pushed mass fear that POTUS would start WW111 re: North Korea?

The Soros Open Society Foundation (OSF) had a film division called the Documentary Fund (DF). The DF changed its name to The Sundance International Documentary Fund upon this dual charity merger. A cozy working relationship that perfectly blends Hollywood films with the plans of the New World Order globalists. After the complete capture of Hollywood, the next target was the independent filmmakers and studios for infiltration/takeover.

Post Q# 140
> Families combined (TRI) = NWO.
> What is the keystone?

Included with this slick new name change was a large $5 million donation to Sundance. George Soros committed to yet another $5 million to be given again in 2009 as a built-in future booster shot. History will show that Soros and his many well-funded organizations will never stop at their goal of a global Great Reset.

Post Q# 275
> SOROS controls organizations of people.

Soros has quickly become the 'Ministry of Truth' for the entire Progressive Left. George Soros remains in solid control of his cherish title of 'The Godfather of the Left.' Sundance co-founder Sterling van Wagenen would be charged with sex abuse in 2019. General Flynn would state that in 2021 we are witnessing communism coming to America with Biden.

Post Q# 330
> We have a special place picked out for GS.
> Really special.

Sponsored films have pre-packaged propaganda slanted narrative themes scripted right into upcoming documentaries and Hollywood films. This is a hideous form of subliminal messaging that creeps unnoticed into our daily culture and is propaganda on public display. A Soros-backed group would purchase in 2022 a total of 18 Spanish radio stations in the USA in an overt attempt to control the Latino narrative and thus this critical voting group.

Post Q# 3911

Have you ever witnessed the media, Hwood, [D] party [full], [F] leaders, [F] media, etc. push so much hatred towards a sitting President?
Define propaganda.

A communist and malcontent seemingly from birth, Robert Redford has portrayed a much different character on the big screen. His Sundance Film Festival is internationally known as the premier launching platform for new independent films and avant-garde producers. The NWO Globalist would cheer in 2022 Biden's creation of a 'Ministry of Truth' department under DHS ala Orwell's 1984 scenario. It would later be revealed that Soros/OSF received millions in misdirected funds from the corrupt USAID and this help fund their various causes.

Post Q# 3931

This is not about politics.
It has been projected [normalized] by stars.
[Symbolism will be their downfall]

Sundance showcased a documentary movie called "Gasland" at the annual 2010 film gathering. Afterward "Gasland" was highlighted, it turned into a hit documentary on cable HBO. The gain notoriety by the film ultimately was the kiss of death as the Deep State reacted to a threat to their narrative. Control and shaping of the public narrative are some of the most critical elements involved with the planned 'Great Reset' by the NWO Globalists. The NWO hierarchy baton passing came in 2023 from Godfather George to son Alex as the heir to the Soros Empire/OSF. Soros/OSF bid in 2024 to take control of debt ridden Audacy and their over 200 radio stations (second largest in the USA), in yet another attempt to control the media/narrative. The FCC later would launch an investigation into the particulars behind the Soros attempt to control the radio airwaves.

Post Q# 923

Brainwashed.
They thought the SHEEP would follow the STARS.

The American Shale Gas industry is still trying to recover from the negativity highlighted against the fracking practice. Award winning journalist John Solomon wrote a 14-year follow up article proving the predictions/anti-fracking statements failed to come true. Hollywood can make or break an industry just by these types of selected narrative targeting. It is the identical game plan that the MSM news uses in a coordinated gaslighting attack from all angles. Soros/OSF would continue to financially support far-left causes such as election rigging, USSC protests over Roe vs Wade, and to lead boycotts against Elon Musk's Twitter. George Soros stated publicly in 2023 that he would "meddle" in the 2024 Presidential Election if Trump is the Republican nominee.

Post Q 666

Marriage for POWER, not LOVE.
Soros/Clinton.

What if you have been misled and conditioned to believe lies and illusions your entire life? Soros has been connected by Special Counsel (SC) John Durham to the Alfa Bank hoax through his operative Daniel Jones. SC Durham submitted his final report in 2023 and will be the foundation for future judicial accountability. The unexpected 2023 box office hit 'Sound of Freedom' just might demonstrate that the Hollywood worm has turned. The re-election of President Trump in 2024, outgoing Biden unconscionably awarded the Presidential Medal of Freedom to George Soros and HRC. Thing bigger and expand your knowledge fellow Patriots as the Great Awakening is quickly arriving.

Post Q# 4153

[MSM + SOCIALM] [HOLLYWOOD] propaganda push_coord establish 1-7 movement(s) ANTIFA silence-stop endorse_POTUS (pro).

Links

Biography-Butch Cassidy Sundance Kid: The Real Story

FOX News-Soros' Alleged Ties to RussiaGate Exposed

Washington Times-Soros Grip on Democratic Party Loosened

Just the News-Gasland: Predictions/Anti-Fracking Fail to come True

Inside Radio-George Soros $415 Million Stake in Audacy

FOX News-FCC Launches Probe into Soros Backed Radio Stations

Just the News-Shuttered USAID routed Funds to Soros Causes

David Yeagley-The Soros Sundance

Deadline-Sundance gets $5M Grant from George Soros Foundation

Badlands Media-George Soros: Shadow Network

NPQ-OSF Grants $5 Million to Sundance

Burning Bright-Hegelian Hydra

Independent Sentinel-George Soros: Plan to Destroy America

Front Page-Three Foreign Billionaires financed Dark Money in 2020 Election

Breitbart-Soroswood: Intersection of Politics and Hollywood Propaganda

Front Page-Sundance, Soros and Robert Redford

PJ Media-Soros Connected to Alfa Bank fake Russia Hoax

News Busters-Some Inconvenient Facts for Redford's Climate Change Cry

American Thinker-Soros Propaganda Machine vs Shale Gas

Breitbart-Citizen Soros Funding Anti-American Film

GNBS-Redford and Soros Agenda Connection

LVB-George Soros and The Sundance Kid

Breitbart-Soros Funded Documentary Embraces Left-Wing Terrorists

Sundance: Institute Receives $5 million from OSF

Deadline-Sundance Panel with Robert Redford Plagued by Video Failure

NY Post-HRC's Plan to Smear Trump with Russia Collusion

Clinton Foundation Timeline-2025 Crossfire Hurricane Docs

Justice.gov-2023 SC John Durham Report

Top Echelon of Justice:
Tangled "Spider Web" of Corruption

'Operation Trump' was an elaborate scheme engineered at the top levels of the Department of Justice (DOJ). The DOJ National Security Division combined with its counterpart the FBI Counterintelligence Unit, to form this 'Secret Society' against candidate Donald Trump. President Trump would file in 2022 a federal RICO lawsuit against HRC/DNC/and many government officials involved with the promotion of the false Russian collusion narrative during the 2016 election cycle.

Post Q# 2700
Nobody should be above the law (no matter how massive the spider-web is (entangled).
DOJ National Security Division:
• Loretta Lynch / Sally Yates / John Carlin / Bruce Ohr /David Laufman
FBI Counterintelligence Unit:
• James Comey / Andy McCabe / Bill Priestap / Peter Strzok / Lisa Page / James Baker
OPERATION TRUMP:
• Exonerate HRC/Aides (ObamaGate)
• Trump-Russia Dossier creation/distribution (RussiaGate)
• FISA Title-1 Warrants/Section 702 (SpyGate)
• The Insurance Policy (Crossfire Hurricane)

Post Q# 100
Secret Society.

What made this group seemingly untouchable was the special exemption from any oversight by OIG Horowitz. On July 20, 2015, Sally Yates issued a statement allowing top officials from the National Security sections (DOJ and FBI) to ignore IG Horowitz or any other official inquiry.

Post Q# 4944
Are you ready to finish what we started?

Additionally, the required notification to Congress about Trump-Russia Probe (Rep. Stefanik questioning Comey) by the FBI to the Gang of Eight, was not done at all timely. In fact, it was almost one year later Comey did advise the Congressional committee but not within the normally required 3 months' time period.

Post Q# 2489
[Placeholder - OIG Report-FBI, DOJ, and Media Coll].

FBI Asst. CI Director Bill Priestap clearly noticed that FBI Director James Comey had just threw him under the preverbal bus by his Congressional testimony. Priestap was one of the first cooperating witnesses (songbirds) with IG Horowitz/SP Huber/SC Durham and IG Storch conducting differing investigations.

Post Q# 520
THINK BIG.
THINK BIGGER.
THINK BIGGEST.

Strzok/Page refer in their personal text messages to this group being the 'Secret Society' McCabe's own catchy nickname for this DOJ ultra-insiders club was the 'Small Group.' FBI

General Counsel James Baker and Perkins Coie/Clinton campaign lawyer Michael Sussmann colluded to present false Alfa Bank information to bolster Russian collusion.

Post Q# 586

What would happen if texts originating from a FBI agent to several [internals] discussed the assassination (possibility) of the POTUS or member of his family?

The very strict compartmentalized nature of this band of criminals from the upper ranks of the Justice Department, helped to keep tight operational secrecy. History will be harsh on this high government level cabal of traitors and failed coup plotters. SC John Durham's criminal investigations have led a few indictments and his final report submitted in 2023, along with those from IG Michael Horowitz will be the foundation for future judicial accountability.

Post Q# 3967

These people are pure evil.
This is not about politics.

Always big on nicknames, this 'small group' internally referred the HRC probe the 'Mid-Year Exam' (MYE). Whereas they came up with tougher names like "Crossfire Hurricane" when referring to investigations into Donald Trump. Additional cleaver nicknames like Crossfire Razor, Dragon FISA, Cross Wind, and Crossfire Typhoon were part of this treasonous coup plot. It would later be revealed that James Comey deployed in late 2015/into 2016 two female FBI 'Honeypot' Agents to infiltrate the Donald Trump Campaign.

Post Q# 2729

Bigger than the 25th amendment attempt to remove.
Depth of this is very serious.

The 'Insurance Policy' was the last element in their Operation Trump plan. First, they exonerated HRC, next was the Dossier collection/dissemination, and then the FISA Title-1 Surveillance of Trump World via the warrant HOP rule (P to X/X to Y/Y to Z). It was revealed in 2023 that the FBI/DOJ subpoenaed phone/email records of FBI agents Bill Priestap, Joe Pientka, as well as Congressional staff involved with probing Crossfire Hurricane.

Post Q# 953

How bad is the corruption ?
FBI (past/present). DOJ (past/present).

There had been an effort to remove the top echelon of both the DOJ and FBI and many were gone one way or another by the end of Trump's first term. The 7th Floor of Justice hopefully one day will be dutifully wiped clean and the Intelligence Community has been purged of disloyal holdovers. The DOJ/FBI would be caught in 2023 of protecting Biden from UkraineGate scandals in the same fashion as they protected BHO from SpyGate indictments.

Post Q# 4832

SHADOW PRESIDENT.
COLOR REVOLUTION.
INSURGENCY.

Many now feel the FBI's raid upon President Trump's Mar-A-Lago home to to obtain the RussiaGate/Crossfire Hurricane classified documents folder. Let's all hope for the return of President Trump to complete long overdue justice. President Trump's dream team of Durham/Horowitz/Storch/and Huber tried to untangle this spider web of political corruption, deception, manipulation and treason. President Trump's 2024 re-election victory left the officials at DOJ/FBI 'stunned,' as they know real justice will be forthcoming. The Great Awakening is on the horizon and the 'Storm' has begun leading to the return of equal justice.

Post Q# 2723

A Traitor's Justice.
RATS EVERYWHERE.

Links

New Republic-Anti Intelligence: What Happens when the President goes to War

FOX News-DOJ Receives Gabbard's Criminal Referral

Just the News-FBI Opens Grand Conspiracy Probe

Sara Carter-FBI to Investigate Comey's Covert Operation to Deploy Female 'Honeypots'

The Federalist-FBI Revelations Show the Mueller Special Counsel was a Cover-Up

The Last Refuge-FBI Corruption and Deliberate Misconduct

Markets Work-DC Establishment Concerned Trump has Classified Binder

Lee Smith-BHO's January 5th Conspiracy

Tablet Magazine-How the FBI Hacked Twitter

NY Post-FBI Knew all about Joe and Hunter's Business Dealings

The Last Refuge-Sally Yates/DOJ/and FBI

Markets Work-Sally Yates: Bypassing the Inspector General

Washington Times-Steele Dossier: FBI Nurtured biggest Hoax in American History

Washington Examiner-RussiaGate claim exposes FBI and DOJ's Misinformation Campaign

Just the News-FBI 'For Sure' committed Crimes Investigating Trump

American Report-HAMMERING Out their Cover Story 2 Days before Inauguration

Epoch Times-SpyGate: The Inside Story

The War Economy-James Comey and the FBI

NY Post-Team BHO Invented whole RussiaGate Scandal

Epoch Times-SpyGate: The True Story of Collusion

Lew Rockwell-Onward into Darkness

Red State-Remembering Strzok/Page 'Insurance Policy' Exchange

Real Clear Investigations-The Brennan Dossier: Prime Mover of RussiaGate

C Reason-The Clinton Cabal

Markets Work-FBI Contractors and FISA Abuse

Ann Phelm Scoop-ObamaGate Movie

Senate Judiciary Committee-2021 Crossfire Hurricane DECLAS

Intelligence.House.gov-The Intelligence Community 51 CIA Contractors

Crossfire Hurricane Docs-Christopher Steele Binder

Justice-gov-2023 SC John Durham Report

Provocateur Found Guilty:
Robert Mueller Does "Get Roger Stone"

Roger Stone, Jr. has been the 'Wizard' that was behind the curtain of Presidential politics for decades. First a campaign aide to President Nixon (large Nixon tattoo on his back), a consultant to Reagan, and finally an early Trump Presidential Campaign informal adviser. Stone is still making the headline news now with his direct involvement with the January 6th Capitol events. Additionally, the lude subject of Republican sponsored 'drug-filled orgies' was brought up by Madison Cawthorn and quickly disavowed by professed sex expert Roger Stone.

> **Post Q# 2500**
> CORSI [attempt infiltrate] Q.
> THERE ARE BAD PEOPLE THAT PRETEND TO BE GOOD.

Roger (aka Snuggles) Stone is a self-described political trickster, Libertine and has often overstated his roles with government officials. The endearing 'snuggles' nickname comes from Stone's New York City live-in sexual partner and had a longstanding relationship with Kristin Davis, aka the infamous 'Manhattan Madam.' Kristin Davis was imprisoned over the 2008 Gov. Elliot Spitzer prostitution ring affair and would pop up in 2024 assisting RFK Jr.'s campaign. Bob Dole gave him his first paid government job but fired him due to Roger Stone posting public ads asking for 3-way sex partners (swing fever). Stone revealed late in 2021 that his wife Nydia had cancer via a new fundraising campaign and thankfully she seems to be doing fine in 2023.

> **Post Q# 2556**
> Controlled Narrative?
> People awake are what they FEAR THE MOST.
> LOSS OF CONTROL.
> THE GREAT AWAKENING.

Stone was infamously found guilty on a 7-count federal indictment over his claimed' Julian Assange/WikiLeaks (WL) connections and his prior (now proven to have been false) U.S. Congressional testimony. Roger Stone has publicly stated he had direct communications with Assange/WL over HRC's emails but this self-promoting claim was a lie. Ensnared under Robert Mueller's Trump/Russia review, charges only related to Stone's past interviews given under sworn oath to the U.S. Congressional House PSCI that all were proven to be just grandiose false statements made by Stone.

> **Post Q# 3622**
> Spy_insert(s)?
> Puppets have masters.

Roger Stone was part of the Black, Manafort, Stone and Kelly (BMSK), one of the first and most powerful DC lobbying firms. For decades BMSK was the place to get agendas and laws tailored per their paying clients exacting stated requirements. Many feel the undue influence exerted by various lobby firms has been a leading factor in institutionalize corruption in the DC Swamp.

> **Post Q# 3683**
> Put on the full armor of God, so that you can take your stand against the devil's schemes."

This obvious Roger Stone connection helped to enable Paul Manafort to become Candidate Trump's campaign manager. Paul Manafort was recruited just prior to the 2016 Republican Convention to help in securing Trump's previously won critical voting convention delegates.

Post Q# 2102
>There is a lot more to this than you realize.
>Think 'collective' attacks v 'Q.'

Stone has been convicted on false statements, obstruction of justice, and witness tampering. Roger Stone had claimed prior knowledge from Julian Assange about the 2016 WL drops involving the Podesta/DNC leaked emails. Assange publicly stated that WikiLeaks did NOT have any discussions with Stone pointing out all of Roger Stone's predictions did not materialize.

Post Q 1164
>POTUS targeting using pushed RUS decoy meetings / campaign insertions.

Federal charges stem from Stone's several false statements to the House Permanent Select Committee on Intelligence (HPSCI). Roger Stone and Michael Caputo exchanges texts about a $2M fee needed to obtain 'dirt' on HRC from some connected Russians. After lying to Congress about his exact relationship with WikiLeaks/Julian Assange, Stone ending up begging for a Presidential pardon or commuting of his prison sentence.

Post Q# 2128
>NXIVM?
>When does a BIRD sing?
>EYES WIDE OPEN.

Both Stone and Caputo conveniently did not remember these 2016 discussions when put under testimony. Roger Stone attempted to get witnesses to alter testimony to match his own narrative as per his federal conviction.

Post Q# 2089
>Why are the majority of 'Q' attacks by 'PRO_MAGA' supporters coming from AJ [MOS backed] and/or AJ known associates?

Additionally, Stone has acknowledged contact with Romanian hacker Guccifer 2.0 over claimed HRC hacked emails. These interactions were part of Mueller's probe and include conduits Jerry Corsi/Alex Jones/and Randy Credico. Similar to the MSM news, the Alternative Media has an old establishment guard that protects its various economic grifting schemes.

Post Q# 1343
>Destroy through [misinformation].
>Absorb the 'confused.'
>Re-route traffic to other platforms.

Guccifer 2.0 first posted hacked emails on 6/16/16 which conveniently was the day after the announcement of the DNC computer intrusion. Evidence pointed directly to Guccifer 2.0 intentionally by planting Russian 'markers' (CIA Vault 7) to assist with the false collusion narrative and possibly a Ukrainian operation. Assange's WikiLeaks released some of the stolen CIA vault 7 hacking tools and everyone uses this intrusion masking trick today.

Post Q# 4712
>Guccifer 2.0

Stone has been written books disputing the official narrative of both the JFK and JFK Jr. deaths. It can be argued that Stone has kept up the fight for the final complete disclosure of the decades long sealed JFK assassination archives. President Trump had released most of the final JFK files and Ezra Cohen-Watnick is overseeing the scheduled last public release.

Post Q# 2123

Last and final comment(s) re: AJ and Associates [attempts].
Attempts to deceive AUTISTS/ANONS will FAIL.
We are a threat to their livelihood [+CLAS].

Roger Stone has been described by many as a political 'Dirty Trickster.' Stone cherishes the media exposure regardless of its negative or positive press coverage. Both sides agree that the ugly side of political campaigns as exemplified by the infamous dirty trickster should be long over. History may show that Roger Stone's personal involvement in the January 5/6th U.S. Capitol events in 2020 relating to 'Stop the Steal' rallies. Stone had a Danish film crew filming a documentary titled 'A Storm Foretold' at the time of January 5/6th and shocking statements were made by Stone regarding President Trump issuing last minute pardons.

Post Q# 3740

NOBODY is above the law [not anymore].

Stone's top quote "Politics is not about uniting people; it's about dividing people." Always with a lot to say other than anything about 'Q' ('known associates'). Roger Stone has plead the 5th Amendment to a Senate panel inquiry in 2018 after giving extensive House testimony. As fate would have it Stone has again plead the 5th this time to every question the Congressional select committee asked.

Post Q# 1794

"Never Interfere with an Enemy While He's in the Process of Destroying Himself."

Alex Jones has described his prior employee Roger Stone as an "Albatross around his neck." The 'Q' outed traitorous Jerry Coris has additionally filed a large defamation lawsuit against Roger Stone. Both Stone and Alex Jones are neck deep in the 1/6/21 Capitol events and the lies are already piling up. Many feel that some leaders of the 2020 'Stop the Steal' campaign like Roger Stone were promoting violence like was displayed by certain associated groups on January 5 and 6th at the U.S. Capitol Building.

Post Q# 1862

FAKE NEWS = ENEMY OF THE PEOPLE.
['They' prey on emotionally unstable (helpless) individuals and use them as PAWNS]

I have to believe that Roger Stone's past NXIVM cult connections are also at play. Stone was on Keith Raniere's payroll and the entire NXIVM sex-trafficking ring is under federal criminal investigation. The IRS would compel Stone to pay millions in back taxes and several defamation lawsuits would continue to haunt provocative Stone. Troubles would follow Stone in 2023 as connections to the 2020 election related to slates of alternative electors and 'Stop the Steal' associations.

Post Q# 1368

Allison Mack [NXIVM] arrested [date]?
When does a bird sing?

Robert Mueller has demanded "Get Me Roger Stone." Stone is the second top InfoWars/Alex Jones personality that was ensnared in the Muller probe (Corsi). Odd that Roger refused to take the stand in his own trial nor did his counsel offer any witnesses for the defense. Karma has a way of catching up to bullshit artists and ultimately grifters have to owe to their own past lies.

Post Q# 3990
> FBI CHAIN OF COMMAND FISA-RUSSIA-POTUS-FLYNN-STONE-PAPADOP-MANAF?

President Trump had criticized the Stone jury verdict, saying "HRC and Mueller should be Indicted." President Trump made comment as to the appearance of anti-Trump bias among the jury, the COVID situation in the jails and Stone's old age as factors that lead to the last-minute commutation of federal sentencing to jail. President Trump before departing from his first term would pardon Roger Stone, Paul Manafort, and others in late 2020.

Post Q# 365
> Shall we play a game?
> How about a nice game of chess?

Stone received 3 years and 4 months in prison due to 'process crimes. Four of the prosecution team have withdrawn from this case and have been reassigned within the DOJ or resigned. LawFare is now beginning against Stone by the government for unpaid taxes as well as civil defamation cases brought by individuals like Larry Klayman and Jerome Corsi. Additionally, the Congressional January 6th Commission is pursuing both Roger Stone and Alex Jones for their active participation.

Post Q# 4196
> IRREGULAR WARFARE.
> THE GREATEST POLITICAL SCANDAL IN HISTORY.

Stone had filed notice of appeal based on jury and DOJ misconduct and been ordered to begin prison sentence. Of odd note has been the sudden health change from a lifelong gym rat/body builder to claimed illnesses to prevent self-surrender. Classic Stone legal tactics on public display as miraculous full health was restored upon receiving his Presidential clemency and continued his many donations appeals upon the Patriot community.

Post Q# 1828
> What assets (people) were placed (spy) in POTUS' campaign?
> What if those 'placed' are being investigated by Bob Mueller, Special Counsel?

President Trump granted Stone a last-minute commutation of his guilty verdict. Biden's DOJ is investigating claims Stone offered BitCoin for a Presidential pardon. Roger Stone has been served a subpoena by the DOJ for his role in the January 6th Capitol events and is going to plead the Fifth Amendment. Special Counsel John Durham has dropped criminal indictments related to SpyGate and submitted his final report in 2023. With the historic re-election of President Trump in 2024, many past hidden political secrets will finally be revealed.

Post Q# 3596
> What advantages might exist when you know the other sides playbook?
> Enjoy the show!

Links

The Atlantic-Roger Stone's Secret Messages with Wikileaks

The Federalist-FBI Revelations Show the Mueller Special Counsel was a Cover-Up

Rolling Stone-Roger Stone and 2020 Fake Electors Plot

Variety-Roger Stone: 'A Storm Foretold' Review

Daily Mail-Inside Roger Stone's Swinging Marriage

Business Insider-Manhattan Madam: Kristen Davis

Rolling Stone-Roger Stone on Trump: 'Greatest Single Mistake in US History'

PJ Media-The Vow: Shocking HBO Doc Reveals NXIVM Sex Cults Links

Abramson-Roger Stone Buries Himself in New Interview

Yahoo News-FBI Docs Reveal Communications between Stone and Assange

New Yorker-Roger Stone's Crimes

Washington Examiner-Smears, Swingers and Dirty Tricks: Roger Stone

Empty Wheel-Stone/Gates/and Caputo Met Around the DNC/Podesta Hack

BBC-Democrat Hack: Who is Guccifer 2.0?

Pittsburgh Post Gazette-Roger Stone/Michael Caputo/and A Russian

New Yorker-The Dirty Trickster (classic old article)

Newsweek-How is Roger Stone Connected to NXIVM

Now This News-Roger Stone comes Unhinged in Court Deposition

Netflix: "Get Me Roger Stone" documentary

Newsweek-Trump Pardons Kushner's Father, Paul Manafort, Roger Stone, and 23 Others

PBS/Frontline-United States of Conspiracy

Crossfire Hurricane Docs-Halper Files

Justice.gov-2023 SC John Durham Report

Disgraced FBI Lovers Legacy
Immortalized in Hateful Text Messages

Many people had been captivated by tens of thousands of text messages between FBI 'Love Birds' Peter Strzok and Lisa Page. Many messages have not been released due to current ongoing criminal investigations by Special Counsel (SC) John Durham. Lisa Page has once again returned to the media spotlight as she is married to the judge handling a recent Durham indictment. President Trump would pick out both of the 'Love Birds' as part of his 2022 filed $24M federal RICO lawsuit related to the events surround the SpyGate political scandal.

Post Q# 2643
RE: MUELLER deleted 'critical' text messages between PS+LP?

SC Durham's indictment of Perkins Coie/Clinton campaign lawyer Michael Sussmann connects HRC and the DNC to these political scandals. Perkins Coie law firm hired both research company Fusion GPS and cyber firm CrowdStrike in 2016 in conjunction with the SpyGate/Crossfire Hurricane coup plot. The planting of paid spies and the use of international 'LURES' against your political opposition is tantamount to treasonous and seditious conduct.

Post Q# 1589
PS/LP texts are only scratching the surface.

Threats of a Presidential assassination and harm to the First Family will be uncovered and confirmed publicly in forthcoming Strzok/Page texts. One tidbit discovered in the OIG Michael Horowitz's previous reports showed how much this coup group enjoyed calling their operations by special pet nicknames for their elaborate plans.

Four main components of the elaborate coup plot nicknamed Operation Trump:
- Exonerate HRC/Aides (ObamaGate)
- Fake Trump-Russia Dossier creation/distribution (RussiaGate)
- FISA Title-1 Surveillance Warrants/Section 702 (SpyGate)
- The 'Insurance Policy' (Crossfire Hurricane)

Post Q# 586
What would happen if texts originating from an FBI agent to several [internals] discussed the assassination (possibility) of the POTUS or members of his family?

This small group or 'Secret Society' called the HRC email probe the Midyear Exam (MYE). Colorful code names for SpyGate operations included Crossfire Hurricane/Crossfire FISA/Crossfire Razor/Crossfire Typhoon and Operation Dragon. FBI counterintelligence agent Peter Strzok was having an office affair with FBI lawyer Lisa Page. Over the course of 2016-17 this pair of FBI love birds exchanged over 60,000 social media messages while on their federal jobs.

Post Q# 3848
The bottom half was instructed (99% good).
The first will send a shock wave.

The central plan that the SpyGate coup was operation Crossfire Hurricane involving domestic and international surveillance. Lisa Page's Congressional testimony refers to a second known surveillance warrant nicknamed Dragon FISA. The target of this FISA Title-1 surveillance warrant is not known but could have been 2016 Presidential Republican candidate Ted Cruz as we know Crossfire Razor was against Lt. General Michael Flynn.

Post Q# 2794
> The Corinthia Hotel.

Texts messages repeatedly called the final Trump option as the 'Insurance Policy.' Top FBI officials Peter Strzok/Lisa Page were allegedly having an extramarital affair and exchanged a voluminous amounts of text/email messages. Many feel that former FBI counterintelligence director Randy deliberately match Strzok/Page to assist in this coup plot and only to pretend to be office lovers as operational cover. In an ironic judicial twist, Strzok/Page would both settle in 2024 with the DOJ, their individual lawsuits over wrongful termination due to their SpyGate activities and privacy claims. Additionally Peter Strzok/Lisa Page would settle for $2 million (Pete $1.2m and Lisa $800k) in a lawsuit against the DOJ for publicly releasing their personal text messages.

Post Q# 1605
> PS "Texts were taken out of context."

Peter Strzok was considered our country's top Counterintelligence FBI agent. In essence meaning Strzok is one of our best spies and enemy counterintelligence expert (ala James Bond or a modern-day Jason Bourne). Strzok along with fellow FBI agents Joe Pientka and Kevin Clinesmith gave then candidate Trump his first official Intel briefing. Clinesmith has plead guilty to SC John Durham for altering the Carter Page FISA warrant applications. Lisa Page would admit under oath to DNI Ratcliffe in 2019 that BHO ordered the DOJ to 'stand down' in regards to HRC's email/documents scandal.

Post Q# 247
> Who is Peter Strzok?
> How was he paid?
> Who is Melissa Hodgman?
> Strzok/Page FBI Highlights:
> • APRIL (2016): Interviews Mills and Abedin
> • MAY: Strzok goes to London/UK
> • JUNE: Changes Comey HRC Memo
> • JULY: Interviews HRC w/Laufman
> • AUG: Trump-Russia FBI Counterintelligence Probe and Intel Brief to candidate Trump
> •. SEPT: Another London trip w/Page
> • OCT: Wife Hodgman SEC promotion
> • TEXTS: "We'll Stop Trump" / "Insurance Policy" / "Secret Society" / "Obama wants to know everything" / "HRC could be POTUS".
> • MAY (2017): Strzok/Page joins Mueller
> • JULY: Strzok removed by Mueller
> • SEPT: Strzok demoted to HR Dept.
> • MAY (2018) Lisa Page resigns
> • AUG (2018) Bowdich fires Strzok
> • MARCH (2019) Lisa Page admits BHO ordered stand down on HRC
> • AUG (2020) Clinesmith pleads guilty
> • SEPT (2021) Sussmann indictment

Post Q# 250
> Date Peter/Comey cleared Weiner emails?

Please bear in mind both Lisa Page was fired, Strzok as well, shortly after giving their sworn OIG testimony. Remember they both stayed working (cooperating) while many others have voluntarily quit or been outright fired. It was Mrs. Strzok that first discovered this alleged marital affair and not the overseers at the FBI. Thanks to SC Durham's court filings with the Michael Sussmann case, notes have surfaced from Peter Strzok demonstrating that he purposefully pushed false narratives related to the SpyGate/Crossfire Hurricane operations. Publicly exposed key figures exposed in SpyGate like Pete and Lisa would ultimately receive cushy TV gigs and lucrative book deals.

Post Q# 4153
[FBI Floor 7] deep-cover operatives crosswalk CIA-FBI [PS]

Inquiring minds now want to know if Strzok/Page were even having an extramarital affair. Strzok is a trained spy and the 'lovers' element may have been cleaver tradecraft work as cover for their Crossfire Hurricane plot. Strzok post FBI would snag MSM gigs that would allow him to spew falsehoods and is especially rich in attacking Elon Musk in 2022. Karma would strike Lisa Page in 2023 as she divorced her husband of 15 years DC lobbyist Joe Burrow. SC John Durham has submitted his final report in 2023. With the re-election of President Trump in 2024, many hope past hidden political secrets will finally be revealed.

Post Q# 3715
Propaganda.
GoFundMe next?

Links

FOX News-DOJ Settles with Strzok/Page over Release of Texts

Judiciary.Senate.gov-Report shows FBI Cut Corners in HRC Email Investigation

Clinton Foundation Timeline-FBI Revelations Show the Mueller Special Counsel was a Cover-Up

Just the News-FBI's Arctic Haze

National Review-Peter Strzok Text: "We'll Stop Trump from Becoming President"

Epoch Times-Lisa Page admitted BHO Ordered DOJ to Stand Down

Politico-FEDs Settle Page/Strzok Privacy Claims

FOX News-Figures Exposed in Durham Report Rewarded with Cushy TV Gigs/Lucrative Book Deals

Daily Mail-Cheating FBI Lawyer Lisa Page Files for Divorce

Clinton Foundation Timeline-Mid Year Exam (MYE)

The Federalist-Notes Show FBI Agents Mislead DOJ on Trump-Russia Investigation

Ann Phelm Scoop-ObamaGate Movie

Just the News-Peter Strzok led the FBI's Investigation into Trump

The Last Refuge-Crossfire Hurricane

NY Post-FBI Lovebird Strzok/Page Conspired in Michael Flynn Case

Daily Caller-FBI used 'News Hooks' in Crossfire Hurricane

Red State-Lee Smith: Insurance Policy more Than the Coup Itself

The Last Refuge-Mid Year Review/Exam

Epoch Times-SpyGate: The Inside Story

Brass Balls-Peter Strzok Worked for CIA and FBI at the Same Time

New Yorker-Pete and Lisa

Grassley.Senate.gov-Crossfire Hurricane Timeline

Crossfire Hurricane Docs-Strzok and Page Text Messages

Justice.gov-2023 SC John Durham Report

Jake Sullivan: Dude The "Deep State" Just Loves

Jacob "Jake" Sullivan is a very popular person when it comes to building a solid Deep State team. Sullivan's colorful prior employers include HRC, Biden, BHO, Yale College, and National Security Action (NSA/PAC). Sullivan has returned to the DC Swamp stage now as Biden's National Security Advisor (NSA). Sullivan has publicly threatened China with 'consequences' over possible future aid to Russia during the Ukraine invasion. President Trump would include Jake Sullivan along with HRC/DNC/and others in his 2022 federal RICO lawsuit related to the damaging activities surrounding the false Russian collusion narrative promoted during the2016 election cycle.

Post Q# 1356
The Shadow Government.

Sullivan was Secretary HRC's Chief of Staff at the State Department. Sullivan served VP Biden as his National Security Advisor (a role he sought under a President HRC). The illegal Biden administration has announced Sullivan to be his NSA and the country prays he will do limited damage. Sullivan has demonstrated his skills in the handling of our Southern border security, Afghanistan military crisis and the events in Ukraine during the Russian special military operation. Jake Sullivan played a crucial role in the early stages of the 2016 false Russian collusion narrative against candidate Donald Trump with his official HRC campaign letters about the fake Alfa Bank servers.

Post Q# 4443
People are waking up [[D] party con].

Under BHO's rule, Jake Sullivan served as the White House Deputy Assistant. Sullivan has served faithfully and proven his loyalty to DC's Deep State Swamp time and time again. The NWO globalist encourage the recycling of Sullivan type individuals into new administrations. Sullivan would be one of 13 Americans sanctioned by Putin over the 2022 Ukraine military operation.

Post Q# 4241

Think Chess.
Do you attack the KING in the beginning or middle-to-end?
QUEEN protects KING?

Jake Sullivan was a senior adviser to HRC's failed 2016 presidential campaign. Sullivan was Chief Foreign Policy advisor to Secretary HRC. After leaving government service, Sullivan accepted a periodic lecturer job at Yale Law School between his government gigs.

Post Q# 236
Revelations coming very very soon.

Sullivan was co-chair of National Security Action (NSA), which is a national political action committee (PAC) think tank. NSA is the tip of the resistance for Anti-Trump activities and packed with progressive BHO-era alumni. It was discovered in 2023 that Jake Sullivan sent then Secretary of State HRC email marked 'Top Secret' bringing into question the security of classified government documents.

Post Q# 4352
Thank you for playing.
Have a Nice Day.

In recent times Jake Sullivan has been sought out for employment by Google/Alphabet/and the Schmidt Group. Making political headlines was the new NSA think tank with Ben Rhodes/Susan Rice/Denis McDonough/Cheryl Mills and Samantha Power. Biden would tap Sullivan to become his National Security Advisor and Jake would become point person for disputes in Ukraine and Brazil in 2022.

Post Q# 43
Resistance will be dealt with swiftly.

Cleverly named as National Security Action (NSA), it is a political advocacy hit squad. The other shadowy co-chair is Ben Rhodes and what a pair of wannabes and vocal anti-Trump advocates these two clowns make together. In what would be scene as the third term of BHO, in 2020 many NSA members would become part of the incoming Biden administration.

Post Q# 1354
LOOP.

decode: Loop Capital Corporation

The NSA attack group consists of around 40 alumni from the dark BHO days. NSA receives generous donations from George Soros and other rich leftist's puppet masters. These NWO globalist are always looking to recruit talent such as Mr. Popular aka Jake Sullivan to the team. Sullivan tends to side with China/CCP at every opportunity and his true alliances have long been in question.

Post Q# 2499
EXTREME PANIC IN [DC].
WWG1WGA!

NSA has been coordinating plans with the shadow government of BHO's Organizing For Action (OFA). OFA headquartered base is scary close to the President Trump's White House. OFA acts as the quarterback in greenling mass protests, lawsuits, demonstrations, etc.

Post Q# 1868
Do not link to [CF].
[CF] docs kept in NYC and UT.

Sullivan first came to public notoriety when he was helping out HRC during the Benghazi 2013 Congressional hearings. Jake Sullivan assisted HRC with legal advice throughout her long memory-challenged testimony (remember her prescription glasses).

Post Q# 1345
U1.
Risk the welfare on the world.
U1 [donation to CF].

In the past, Jake Sullivan has been questioned by various Congressional Committees over his prior official email exchanges with HRC. The emails in question were discovered through the Wikileaks exposure as well as FOIA requests by Tom Fitton's Judicial Watch and revolve around Benghazi. Sullivan additional would be tied directly into the UkraineGate scandal with his past involvement with Victoria Nuland/Ali Chalupa/and Eirc Ciaramella with the BHO planned coup to overthrow the elected Ukraine government in 2014.

Post Q# 1559

DECLAS.

LP "Viva Le Resistance."

Classified information was sent and received by HRC over unsecured non-governmental email accounts. Documented foreign intrusion hacks by China and others has been discovered on HRC's private home-brewed email server. Special Counsel (SC) John Durham indicated Perkins Coie/Clinton campaign lawyer Michael Sussmann over lying to the FBI about Alfa Bank. As Biden's NSA, Jake Sullivan would boldly announce in 2023 of the very peaceful atmosphere in Israel/Middle East just days before the surprise attacks by Hamas. Senator Blackburn and others have since called for the removal of NSA Jake Sullivan for his continued incompetence.

Post Q# 484

Coincidence all donations to the CF terminated post defeat?

Let's see how 'Mr. Popular' comes out as he like Sussmann was a promoter of the false Alfa Bank server collusion scheme. The Clinton Foundation is under official DOJ criminal investigation as is the entire cabal via SC John Durham. Sullivan is back as NSA to Biden and his latest verbiage connects Election integrity to national security. Sullivan is getting the proper share of blame over the disastrous Afghanistan debacle. Jake Sullivan damaged our relationship with Saudi Arabia when the Crown Prince Mohammed bin Salman yelled at Jake over the Jamel Khashoggi questionable death.

Post Q# 953

How bad is the corruption?

Projection.

Russia and D/HRC.

IG Horowitz's 2.0 report highlighted the Blumenthal/Shearer/Talbott involvement with the Chris Steele Russian Dossier. [MOVIE 3] is the start of the Storm. SC Durham has dropped criminal indictments and submitted his final report in 2023. Sullivan has been identified as Clinton 'Foreign Policy Advisor' in the Michael Sussmann indictment. Popcorn time Patriots, as the final acts are played out as the entire world watches. The House GOP would demand answers in 2024 under official testimony from NSA Jake Sullivan over the deadly and shameful exit from Afghanistan in August 2021. With the historic re-election of President Trump in 2024, many past hidden political secrets will be revealed.

Post Q# 1849

Welcome to THE SWAMP.

Ex 1 GOOG

State Dept [HRC] - Eric Schmidt - Lisa Shields.

Links

Foreign Policy-Sullivan's own Mea Culpa

Just the News-HRC's 2016 Post Mortem Confirms Plan to Smear Trump with Russia

Clinton Foundation Timeline-2025 Crossfire Hurricane Docs

Daily Mail-Durham Probe: Biden's NSA Jake Sullivan in Hot Seat

Washington Times-Jake Sullivan: The Master of Media Misinformation

Real Clear Investigations-What did Clinton Know about the RussiaGate Smear?

Foreign Policy-Jake Sullivan's Closing Arguments at Brookings Institute

Breitbart-Jake Sullivan claimed Biden Admin De-escalated Gaza Crisis

The Last Refuge-Jake Sullivan

Business Insider-MBS Yelled at Jake Sullivan when He brought up Jamal Khashoggi

New York Post-Russia Sanctions 13 Americans

Tablet Magazine-Ukraine's Deadly Gamble

Washington Examiner-Jake Sullivan repeatedly Promoted Alfa Bank Story

Real Clear Investigations-HRC Aides that Allied w/Fusion GPS push Trump Dossier

Daily Caller-Benghazi led Directly to Crossfire Hurricane

FOX News-Former BHO Aides form Anti-Trump PAC

Wikileaks-Sullivan and HRC Emails

The Hill-Sullivan/Rice/Rhodes launch Anti-Trump Group

Grassley.Senate.gov-Crossfire Hurricane Timeline

State Dept.gov-FOIA: HRC Recovered Emails

Crossfire Hurricane Docs-State Department Steele Binder

Justice.gov-2023 SC John Durham Report

Cass Sunstein: The 'Alinskyite' Philosopher King

It is mind boggling how many married couples are connected in some way to the developing ObamaGate/SpyGate scandals. History will show a Bonnie and Clyde criminal coupling that transpired within the SpyGate scandal crew. I swear you can't make this up but here below are a few of the 'Dirty Couples' that have a part in this treasonous coup plot termed SpyGate. The use of married couples in a criminal venture is helpful both in the secrecy element of the operation as well as legal rules governing court ordered testimony against a legal spouse.

Post Q# 3628
> Enemy of the People.
> Facts matter.

McCabe's / Ohr's / Strzok's / Pientka's/Jacoby and Simpson / Dunn and Bauer / Murray and King / Abedin and Weiner / etc. are just some of the married couples connected to SpyGate. History will record a bizarre common thread with this political scandal as the recruitment of husband/wife pairings. President Trump would file in 2022 a massive Federal RICO lawsuit against all those that promoted the false Russian narrative surrounding candidate and later President Donald Trump.

Post Q# 1832
> Who are we taught to trust the most?

Samantha Power and Cass Sunstein met while both were advisors to BHO's 2008 Presidential Campaign. Cass Sunstein went on to become BHO's Administrator of White House Office of Information and Regulatory Affairs (2009-2012)-nicknamed the Regulations/Information Czar.

Post Q# 4362
> Keyword: Insurgency

Samantha Power became the UN Ambassador for the U.S. appointed by BHO. Power currently holds the world record for the most unlawful unmasking of U.S. citizens as her exact role crystallizes in the unfolding ObamaGate/SpyGate scandal. Special Counsel John Durham was tasked to prosecute criminal referrals from IG Michael Horowitz revolving around the treasonous SpyGate operations.

Post Q# 1953
> Stay LOCAL (U.S.).
> GLOBAL = reflection of LOCAL.

It is estimated that Sam Power alone ordered the unmasking of 300 innocent American victims. Power now incredibly claims these were done in her name without her permission or advanced knowledge of these unmasking orders. Illegal surveillance was the cornerstone of the entrapment scheme against candidate Donald Trump in the 2016 campaign cycle.

Post Q# 1241
> Who funds WW leftists' events?

Following in Saul Alinsky's footsteps, is the omnipotent voice of Power's husband Cass Sunstein. Hailed as the new Philosopher King of the Technocrats, Cass Sunstein is the educated voice of the hard Progressive Communist Left. The subtle infiltrate of the West has been a decades long plan by the Muslim Brotherhood and their globalist masters.

Post Q# 1489
PEOPLE SLEEPING ATTACH TO OPINION/PERSONALITY/GROUP THINK.

Sunstein co-wrote the book "Nudge" with the theory of being able to push or nudge the general public in certain directions due to their laziness. He has since refined his mass sales pitch toward the "Cognitive Infiltration". The complete infiltration and destruction of the 9/11 Architects and Engineers truth movement was tasked by BHO for Sunstein to control early in his first term.

Post Q# 2576
Those with the most to lose are the loudest.
Crimes against Humanity.

The "Cognitive Infiltration" program has governmental agents infiltrating extremists web sites/social media/and public platforms for disruption and division. Our 'Q' movement has witnessed paid fake MAGA infiltration employing in the classic Alinsky divide and conquer strategy. The tactics employed today against 'Q' and the Anons are exactly the same used to attack prior movements that counter the given approved narrative.

Post Q# 1585
Censorship applied to scale down impact/reach.

During the BHO reign Cass Sunstein was viewed and considered the country's Regulation Czar demonstrated by his spewing endless rules to govern over the mass populace. Sunstein headed the infiltration of alternative media with the goal of derailing the general truth movement and 9/11 crowd in particular. The NWO globalist insist on total power and control of the media narrative is paramount.

Post Q# 529
4-6% LOST FOREVER.

Cass Sunstein was always thought highly by two-time Presidential loser HRC. It has been rumored Sunstein was a President HRC's pick (making LL wait for RBG) for the then open SCOTUS seat-R.I.P. (AS). I believe the 16-Year Plan to destroy America would have played out under a President HRC assisted by the likes of Cass Sunstein.

Post Q# 3903
[infiltration instead of invasion]

America is too democratic for Socialism or Marxism to ever fully succeed. Leftist teachers gear curriculum toward a slow cultural transformation and try to sway the young impressionable minds of our nation. Today's Critical Race Theory is the poster child of this mindset. Cass Sunstein's infiltration of the 9/11 truther movement set the example for the draconian cancel culture/censorship demonstrated in the 2020's surrounding 'Q.'

Post Q# 192
Why are Russia and China communist?

These are the favored themes pushed out by Cass Sunstein and his Saul Alinsky followers. Socialists/Marxist crave the day their warped idealism becomes the law of the land in a global New World Order (NWO). The World Health Organization (WHO) appointed Sunstein to head new COVID psychological unit.

Post Q# 3595
US AMB 1 and 2 NSA unmask req.

Sunstein Initiated the efforts to censor the Internet via enlisting big tech Silicon Valley. Cass Sunstein recommended limits on Blogs and penalties for providers of extremism, aka free speech that the left disagree about. The origins of what is called 'Cancel Culture' today. The FBI launched COINTELPRO in the 1960/70's to monitor communists and PATCON post 9/11 to track terrorists (foreign and domestic) but Cass Sunstein took targeting enemies of the state to new levels.

Post Q# 3891
> Nothing can stop what is coming.
> Nothing!

Sunstein also championing the Progressive Leftists efforts to change English words and define free speech. Cass Sunstein demonstrated that by emphasizing plain language alternatives, it would reinforce their idealistic goals and hamper any criticism. Mrs. Sunstein (Samantha Power) would be one of 13 Americans sanctioned by Putin over the 2022 Ukraine military operation.

Post Q# 1941
> Did ANTIFA organically form?

One of Sunstein/Alinsky's core objectives is the complete transformation of America into their false NWO utopia. 'Q' reminds us of that God; confidentiality does win in the end. A global Great Reset is the goal of the illegal Biden administration and President Trump is still trying to stop. Sunstein's developed methods of silencing all voices of opposition to the given political narrative would be continued to be deployed in Biden's new DHS 'Ministry of Truth' Czar.

Post Q# 520
> THE PUPPET MASTERS HAVE BEEN REMOVED.
> STRINGS CUT.

The assault on American's freedom and values has been unrelenting for way too long. These Marxist Communist have been attempting to infiltrate America for decades and hopefully we are awake now to recognize this Insurgency. Special Counsel John Durham has dropped criminal indictments related to SpyGate/Samantha's colleagues and submitted his final report in 2023 (stay tuned).

> Post Q# 4832
> SHADOW PRESIDENT.
> SHADOW GOVERNMENT.

Some bizarrely view Samantha/Cass as a prime example of the modern left 21st Century Power Couple. 'Liars' is a new book penned by Sunstein published in 2020 and emphasizes producing excessive mass fear. Sunstein joined illegal Biden's DHS in shaping immigration policy-God really help us all. With the historic re-election of President Trump in 2024, many hope past hidden political secrets will be revealed.

Post Q# 3608
> PREV EXPOSURE OF TRUTH.
> INFORMATION WARFARE.

Links

Glenn Beck-Casa Sunstein Proves to be the Most Dangerous Man

FOX News-Democrats pulled Greatest Con Job Ever

Clinton Foundation Timeline-2025 Crossfire Hurricane Docs

Human Events-BHO and the Fear of Modern Philosopher Kings

New York Post-Russia sanctions 13 Americans

Human Events-W.H.O. appoints Cass Sunstein to Head COVID Psych Unit

The Atlantic-Our Nudge in Chief

The Guardian- 'Liars' by Cass Sunstein Review: In Search of Chill

Washington Examiner-Nunes: BHO Ambassadors went Wild with Unmasking

The Intercept-How Covert Agents Manipulate the Internet

Jonathan Turley-Did Samantha Power commit Perjury?

New Yorker-How a Liberal Scholar became Subject of Right-Wing Conspiracies

Empty Wheel-Advocate of Secret Infiltration: Cass Sunstein

Above The Law-Reason Sunstein Going to Harvard

Salon- Sunstein's Spine-Chilling Proposal

Washington Examiner-Unmasking the Unmaskers

Esquire-Cass and Sam: 21st Century Power Couple

Front Page-Cass Sunstein: Poster Boy for Liberalism

American Thinker-Sunstein's Despicable Ideas

Foreign Policy-Sam says Cass is 'Sleeping on the Couch Tonight'

Epoch Times-FBI's Operation to Infiltrate Right Wing Extremist Groups

Revolver News-FBI Sinister PATCON Program

Crossfire Hurricane Docs-Halper Files

Justice.gov-2023 SC John Durham Report

Clinton's Roommate and HRC's Second Russia Dossier: Meet Strobe Talbott

Strobe Talbott is a longtime Clinton 'crony' and who started the whole 'Friends of Bill' (BC) club. Talbott was first a college roommate at Oxford and later President Clinton's Deputy Secretary of State. Talbott's Brookings Institute is a central point involving several different scandals against former President Trump and his associates. The Brookings Institute would publish an extensive report in 2021 titled 'How to Respond to the QAnon Threat', in a coordinated campaign with other media outlets to craft a false narrative surrounding 'Q.'

Post Q# 717
> Public: FBI/DOJ/O-WH/SD.
> Private: Clowns Clowns Clowns.
> Expand your thinking.

Strobe Talbott certainly had the top inner circle Washington/DC political connections via Slick Willy in the 1990's. The old DC adage of 'who you know' is political capital to be cashed in. Talbott's rule over the famed Brookings Institute established his dominate role in DC politics. Brookings Institute's Igor Danchenko would be Christopher Steele's top researchers in developing his infamous Russian dossier. In 1994, then President Bill Clinton and Strobe Talbott helped to craft an agreement that Ukraine would renounce nuclear weapons and helped to lead to the 2022 Russian special military operation.

Post Q# 1220
> Clinton Foundation conflicts of interest.

Strobe Talbott's past Clinton State Department duties kept him looped into the international political scene. Talbott has been a top adviser to George Soros, a successful journalist at Time Magazine, and was the head of the Brookings Institute for many years. Brookings Institute staffers Fiona Hill and Igor Denchenko will join Talbott in answering for their roles in the development and circulation of the infamous Christopher Steele Dossier.

Post Q# 861
> Note from Anon to Q: "I had breakfast with Pinchuk. He will see you at the Brookings lunch." (State Department email sent to HRC June 2012)

Rumors swirled around Talbott's improper communications with Russian SCR operative Sergei Tretyakov. Talbott claimed he was duped and tricked into exchanging classified information with this crafty Russian. Brookings Institute Senior Fellow Fiona Hill and staffer Igor Denchenko would play important roles in several Trump created scandals. The so-called brain trust at Brookings would lend feedback of support in 2022 for illegal Joe Biden's new 'Ministry of Truth' department under DHS.

Post Q# 3925
> Do people really believe the biggest scandal in modern US history will go unpunished [Scot-Free]?

Strobe Talbott has an infamous Brother In-Law who is none other than Cody Shearer, a decades long Clinton enforcer. These two family members are both tied into the Trump-Russia collision extravaganza with direct connections to dossier author Chris Steele. President Trump would file in

2022 a federal RICO lawsuit against those who promoted the false Russian collusion narrative during the 2016 Presidential election.

Post Q# 1334
Rank and File.
DOJ, FBI, C_A, State.
Not Forgotten.

Strobe Talbott got involved with the Steele's opposition research assembly (aka fake Russian Dossier) and distribution through Victoria Nuland and Jonathan Winer. Nuland/Winer were BHO State Department officials working with Christopher Steele at the urging of higher ups. Important to the SpyGate operation was to add false credibility to the Christopher Steele Dossier.

Post Q# 1840
[Fish]ing is fun.
These people are stupid.

Cody Shearer and his constant sidekick Sid "Vicious" Blumenthal are credited with creating the second Trump-Russia Dossier. Several fakes memos were given to Chris Steele and were included in his final opposition research work product that was turned over to the FBI.

Post Q# 4245
HOW DO YOU CREATE A DIVERSION?
HOW DO YOU SHIFT THE NARRATIVE?

Shearer/Blumenthal's memos went through BHO's State Department not through Fusion GPS. This combined final Steele Trump-Russia Dossier headed ultimately over to the FBI/DOJ. Critical to giving the false dossier credibility is the circular distribution of the information to/from the State Department to the FBI.

Post Q# 4003
Logical thinking.
All assets deployed.
Win by any means necessary.

Talbott is included in the Wikileaks drops from the HRC/Podesta email release. Strobe Talbott has been connected to the dissemination of the research about candidate Trump by Jonathan Winer's own admission. SpyGate coup plot relied on past political associations to assist in this planned coup plot. The Brookings Institute crowd would attempt in 2024 a resurrection of the false RussiaGate narrative in an effort to once again try to derail President Trump.

Post Q# 3168
Nobody walks away from this.

Talbott's son Devin also was caught up in questionable fund raiser events for HRC in 2016. AG Barr appointed Special Counsel (SC) John Durham was tasked to look into all events surrounding the failed coup plot referred to as ObamaGate/SpyGate and criminal referrals from IG Michael Horowitz. Additionally Senior Fellow at Brookings Robert Kagan is husband to Victoria Nuland, thus adding another connecting tentacle to RussiaGate/SpyGate as well as the numerous married 'Dirty Couples' of ObamaGate.

Post Q# 1935
Define 'Projection.'
Define DARK MONEY.

SC John Durham's criminal probe findings will be problematic for both Strobe Talbott and his State Department co-conspirators Jonathan Winer and Victoria Nuland. Other Brooking's coup plotters will ultimately include Fiona Hill and Igor Danchenko. Fireworks will be flying soon as per 'Q'- "we have it all." Also of note was that in 2018 former FBI General Counsel James Baker took a stop at Brookings on his way over to Twitter, only later to be publicly fired by Elon Musk in December 2022.

Post Q# 4864
'Q' inserted meme -Ministry of Truth (see George Orwell's 1984).

Talbott took the helm of famed think tank the Brookings Institute in 2002 and many coup plotters connect during his reign. Strobe Talbott suddenly quit recently after 15 years of service, as so many others recently have done. SC John Durham had dropped criminal indictments and the walls are rapidly closing upon the failed coup plotters. SC Durham submitted his final report in 2023. With the re-election of President Trump in 2024, many expect past hidden political secrets to finally be revealed.

Post Q# 4832
SHADOW GOVERNMENT.
COLOR REVOLUTION.
INSURGENCY.

Links

The Federalist-Why Durham Subpoenaed the Brookings Institute?

FOX News-Democrats pulled Greatest Con Job Ever

Just the News-Evidence Suggests FBI Conspired with HRC to Legitimize RussiaGate

Clinton Foundation Timeline-2025 Crossfire Hurricane Docs

The Federalist-5 Years Ago the Russia Collusion Hoax Fell Apart

Brookings Institute-How to Respond to the QAnon Threat

Breitbart-Nunes Refers 10 BHO Officials to DOJ

Politico-Strobe Talbott: The Full Interview

American Spectator-The Friends of Igor Denchenko

Epoch Times-SpyGate the Inside Story

Daily Caller-Gowdy: FBI Info from HRC Ally to Collaborate Steele Dossier

The Guardian-HRC's Second Russia Dossier from Cody Shearer

Just the News-Steele's Primary Sub Source Triggers Focus on Think Tank

National Review-Steele updated Clinton Ally on Dossier

Real Clear Investigations-Unpacking the Other Clinton-Linked Russia Dossier

Daily Caller-Christopher Steele Provided Info to Longtime Clinton Crony (Talbott)

Politico-Talbott Stepping Down from Brookings

Washington Exam-Power Profile: Strobe Talbott

Brookings Institute-Fiona Hill

Brookings Institute-Former FBI Official James Baker joins Brookings

Crossfire Hurricane Docs-State Department Steele Binder

Tarmac Meeting / Loretta Lynch / and Chris Sign

We can all thank Christopher Sign from ABC15 (morning TV award winning anchor) News for breaking the Bill Clinton-Loretta Lynch Tarmac meeting. This plane-to-plane event happened at the Phoenix Sky Harbor International Airport on June 27, 2016. Mr. Sign would later reveal in his bestselling book that he had received a credible tip (Q Team) to go out to the airport that day. Loretta would be hired in 2022 by the NFL to handle a racial discrimination suit brought by Miami Dolphins coach Brian Flores.

Post Q# 2860

> The Deal of a Lifetime?
> SC/[LL] deal presented by BC?

Bill Clinton's (BC) plane was only 30 yards from Loretta Lynch's [LL] private government jet, so why not stroll on over to talk about golf and grandkids. When BC boarded Lynch's jet, it was just [LL] and her husband Stephan Hargrove onboard as all staff members had disembarked.

Post Q# 1556

> Bridge LL and BC.
> +1 BC and LL (TARMAC) Witness.

Bear in mind the obvious fact that high ranking government officials never leave themselves without one staffer (witness) present. Additionally, it is hard to ditch any Secret Service or FBI protection detail, without having violated strict security protocols previously agreed upon.

Post Q# 3868

> Date of tarmac meeting?
> Date of [HRC] investigation END announcement?
> 1 + 1 = 2
> It's going to be a very hot [spring/summer].

The FBI security detail for [LL] knew that the former President and accompanying Secret Service would waiting be at the Phoenix airport. A similar mad scramble happened over at the main DOJ headquarters, once this strange rendezvous became general public knowledge.

Post Q# 3364

> What happens when Loretta Lynch can no longer provide legal cover for the Clinton's?
> Tarmac meetings_END.

The FBI was concerned about who had leaked this meeting and how best to spin the 'talking points' to the media. [LL] had to evidentially recuse herself officially from the HRC 'matter' due to the horrible optics being generated from this face-to-face meeting with Slick Willy.

Post Q# 2861

> Just another coincidence we dropped [LL] was offered a SC seat on Feb 6th and backed up by POTUS on April 5th.
> Enjoy the show!

This paved the way for FBI Director James Comey's full exoneration of the infamous HRC presser media event on July 5, 2016. Time will reveal all of the criminal plans and conspiracies connected to ObamaGate/SpyGate and the plot to remove our dully elected President Trump. Special Counsel (SC) John Durham has been tasked to investigate the many criminal referrals from IG Horowitz surrounding the HRC's emails/Clinton Foundation/and SpyGate.

Post Q# 674

Tarmac meeting [SC/LL deal AS 187].
decode: Supreme Court seat/ Lynch deal/Murder of Antonin Scalia. Also LL would stay on as AG until RBG's seat became available, not open AS seat.
Bonus Question: Who was one of HRC's picks for the open AS SC seat (since LL had to wait)?
Answer: Sam Power's husband Cass Sunstein

Post Q# 1149

RBG steps down.
LL steps up.
New AG.
'The Plan.'

There ensured a frantic scramble over at main Justice trying to get ahead of this damaging breaking tarmac story. Top level FBI/DOJ officials exchanged a flurry of emails to better coordinate the exact company narrative. Special Counsel (SC) John Durham was tasked to work on criminal referrals from IG Horowitz and has dropped indictments related to SpyGate. It was revealed in 2023 that the FBI questioned BHO's DOJ in the HRC email probe and the 2016 related 'Tarmac Meeting.'

Post Q# 36

What if the wizards and warlocks tipped off a local as to the supposed unscheduled stop?

Thanks to a FOIA request by ACLJ, we know that [LL] used the alias of Elizabeth Carlisle in many of these DOJ communications. Rumors abound of a NSA taping system that captured all of the tarmac plane conservations. SC John Durham submitted his final report in 2023 concerning SpyGate related crimes. Loretta Lynch was with JP Morgan and they have assisted the Jan. 6th committee in obtaining private citizen banking records. Lynch now is a partner at Paul Weiss Law is actively lobbying the Pentagon on behalf of Chinese firms.

Post Q# 1443

Hussein [WH [call] [tarmac] BC/LL]

Besides the obvious suspicious nature of this meeting, inquiring minds want to know what was promised to [LL]. IG Horowitz's report (page 203) put Loretta/Elizabeth back on the public center stage. In the summer of 2021, Chris Sign mysteriously dies at only 45 years of age, only adding to this entire sorted affair. With the historic re-election of President Trump in 2024, many pray that hidden political secrets will finally be publicly revealed.

Post Q# 2860

Security reports indicate USSS (sec detail [BC] and FBI (sec detail [LL]) planned for meeting?

Links

Newsweek-After Clinton/Lynch Meeting: FBI Scrambled to Find and Punish Source

The Federalist-FBI never Investigated Evidence for Loretta Lynch's Role in Cover Up

Real Clear Politics-When Loretta met Bill on the Tarmac

Clinton Foundation Timeline-2025 Crossfire Hurricane Docs

Just the News-Clinton Foundation Meeting Timeline

Sharyl Attkisson-Collusion against Trump Timeline

Blunt Force Truth-What Happened During the Tarmac Meeting

FOX News-New Details from Clinton/Lynch Clandestine Tarmac Meeting

The Blaze-IG Report Blows Holes in LL/BC Tarmac Meeting

The Last Refuge-SpyGate: The Big Picture

NY Post-Lynch Tapped to Assist AG's NYPD Probe

Observer-Inside Security Source detail Tarmac Meeting

Markets Work-Listing of Participants

Rick and Bubba-Chris Sign: What Clinton/Lynch Discussed on Tarmac

WHNT-New Anchor Chris Sign Dead at 45

FBI Press Office-Director Comey's Statement on July 5, 2016

Just the News-FBI's Arctic Haze

Justice.gov (page 203)-Review of Actions by FBI/DOJ in Advance of 2016 Election

Grassley.Senate.gov-Crossfire Hurricane Timeline

Senate Judiciary Committee: 2021 Crossfire Hurricane DECLAS

Crossfire Hurricane Docs-FISA Notes

Justice.gov-2023 SC John Durham Report

Locations of 3 Critical Laptops:
MPDC / USCP / and NYPD

The public had witnessed in late 2020 just prior to the Presidential election, with the coordinated suppression of the now infamous Hunter Biden 'Laptop from Hell,' an effort to keep key information from the voting public. Since the unexpected election of President Trump in 2016, the Deep State DC Swamp has been on a mission to prevent legal accountability for past criminal conduct. The massive Big Tech censorship along with a willing compliant news media has led to the truth deliberately being hidden from the general American public. Many key laptops would be seized by various authorities in the course of different political scandal investigations.

Post Q# 4891
Why would H. Biden have such material on his laptop?

United States Capitol Police (USCP) are currently in the possession of a mysterious backpack. This backpack contained a laptop and was found in an old phone booth in the Rayburn Office Building/U.S. Congress. This would be one of several key laptops secured by officials for criminal investigations. Of odd note is that in 2022 confiscated laptops like Hunter Biden's 'Laptop from Hell' would continue to play important roles in the unfolding SpyGate political scandal.

Post Q# 4484
Importance of SDNY control.
Weiner evidence collection.
Clinton Foundation.

What makes this laptop found by Capitol Police so unusual was the ID card of IT worker Imran Awan. Additionally discovered was a package marked 'Attorney Client Privilege' and several letters to authorities/prosecutors. To even the casual observer, this type of deliberately left information only points to a witness desperate to exchange information for future legal leniency.

Post Q# 1195
SR connects to DNC.

Lordy it just so happens that once this laptop is turned on it displays [DWS]. This laptop could be the "keystone" to uncovering Pakistani espionage and extortion ring run by the Awan's. Without question the initials of DWS represent Awan's handler and top Congressional Democrat Debbie Wasserman-Schultz.

Post Q# 1364
Who knows where the bodies are buried?
Rudy.
Now comes the pain.

The Imran Awan family cabal used remote servers illegally connected to the U.S. House of Representatives mainframe computers. This convenient 'tap' allowed downloaded of unlimited data including top House committees.

Post Q# 1512
IT scandal Awan.

The New York Police Department (NYPD) was working on an underage child pornography case in September 2016. Incredibly this sex case involved former Congressman Anthony Weiner and subsequently his then current wife Huma Abedin.

Post Q# 3168

Nobody walks away from this.

The laptop and other devices the NYPD seized in that arrest were discovered to contain over 600k emails from his semi-estranged wife Huma. Huma Abedin had been officially connected to HRC and many of these emails were government related.

Post Q# 3163

The RULE OF LAW is being returned to our GREAT LAND.
WWG1WGA!!!

Huma Abedin has been a decades long advisor and constant body companion of HRC. Once this laptop was reviewed by NYPD, they properly notified the FBI NYC field office. Many would speculate about the specific extent of their very personal relationship.

Post Q# 2365

[Page 294].
[Meeting between Comey and Coleman on October 4].

The FBI was notified because of the possible classified top-secret nature of some emails between Huma Abedin and HRC. The FBI was given Weiner's hard drive, but the NYPD retained a full backup copy as a safeguard.

Post Q# 247

Think HRC emails, Weiner laptop, etc.

When James Comey and Andy McCabe sat on this explosive Anthony Weiner email information for over 1 month, the NYPD threatened to go public. Comey was forced to reopen the Mid-Year Exam aka HRC's email probe and Loretta Lynch handled New York.

Post Q# 4016

Seth Rich internal DL hand-to-hand pass USA?

This round two of threats by the FBI came just days before the 2016 Presidential election. IG Horowitz noted on page # 294 of his initial report, the scary remarks by Randy Coleman, Crime against children" and "HRC and Foundation."

Post Q# 1512

Note CF children drop in IG report.

Metropolitan Police District of Columbia (MPDC) is currently in the possession of a laptop from murder victim Seth Rich (SR). On July 10, 2016, Seth Rich (1989-2016) was murdered and apparently 'robbed', as he walked home from a local bar in his DC neighborhood.

Post Q# 4616

NOTHING CAN STOP WHAT IS COMING.
NOTHING.

The police have described the brutal public murder as a "botched robbery". Of very odd notation is this killing occurred coincidentally just prior to the infamous WikiLeaks (WL)/DNC and John Podesta email dump. The FBI admitted they did in fact have files from Seth Rich's laptop after 4 years of absolute denials of possession.

Post Q# 1591

Server unlocks SR.

Since that tragic murder several theories have arose due to Julian Assange/WL's reward offer for information on (SR). Donna Brazile dedicates her book to the memory of fallen Seth Rich and ignites the many discrepancies involved with this famous botched robbery.

Post Q# 4089
> Sometimes you can't TELL the public the truth.
> YOU MUST SHOW THEM.

The MSM/Mockingbird Media has ignored the (SR) to the point of a total blackout. The Rich Family's failed lawsuit against FOX News was only minor headlines, as have the other entities they have legally gone after. Author Diana West believes Rich's laptop data is being held under National Security laws.

Post Q# 1180
> "Insurance File."
> Quiet until now.

Strange events have also been occurring between Jack Burkman and his past investigator Kevin Doherty. Burkman was almost killed by Doherty over the handling of this case and Kevin is currently in jail awaiting trial on this attempted murder. Special Counsel (SC) John Durham had been tasked to explore criminal referrals from IG Horowitz related to illegal surveillance operations as well as the DNC computer intrusion involving Seth Rich.

Post Q# 4845
> Roger that, Madam Secretary.
> [C] = classified [State]
> Nothing is ever truly deleted.

The bizarre story surrounding the untimely death of this DNC IT staffer has had many strange twists and turns. Everyone wants to know what happened to: His Name Was Seth Rich. All three of these captured critical laptops will be key components of the Great Awakening. SC Durham has dropped criminal indictments and submitted his final report in 2023. The reports from Horowitz and Durham will be the foundation for future judicial accountability. With the historic re-election of President Trump in 2024, past hidden political secrets will finally be publicly revealed.

Post Q# 3532
> [AWAN]
> [DWS]
> You didn't think the plea deal was the end did you?

Links

NY Post-Classified Documents among Huma's Emails on Weiner's Laptop

The Last Refuge-The Weiner/Abedin Laptop

Town Hall-Comey's FBI Deliberately Sandbagged Clinton Server Investigation

Clinton Foundation Timeline-2025 Crossfire Hurricane Docs

Just Human-Huddleston v FBI (Seth Rich FOIA)

Just the News-Clinton Foundation Meeting Timeline

The Last Refuge-Key Brennan Email to Comey and Strzok

The Hill-Huma Abedin: Anger over Weiner almost Killed Me

FBI.gov/Vault-Seth Rich (part 1 of 2)

FOX News-Wassermann Schultz to Allow Laptop Scan after Stonewalling

Judicial Watch-Federal Court Hearing on Awan Brothers

Just the News-Documents confirm FBI Stalled 1 Month on Weiner Laptop Search

The Hill-Huma Abedin's Ties to the Muslim Brotherhood

The Last Refuge-Mid Year: Abedin/Weiner Laptop

Real Clear Politics-Why is This not A Story

Judicial Watch-Luke Rosiak/Daily Caller Interview: Imran Awan

Real Clear Investigations-Bulk of Weiner Laptop never Examined

FOX News-Luke Rosiak with Lou Dobbs on Awan's

Buster Hyde-Weiner Laptop

Vault FBI.gov-Discovery of HRC's Emails on Weiner Laptop

Zeckelin-Seymour Hersh Discusses Seth Rich and WikiLeaks

Radio Patriot-Erik Prince Transcript: Weiner/Abedin Laptop

Crossfire Hurricane Docs-State Department Steele Binder

Justice.gov-2023 SC John Durham Report

Infamous Trump Tower Meeting: Classic 'Sting Op'

A complex entrapment/sting operation unfolded at the New York Trump Tower (TT) on 1/9/2017 during the Trump transition period. This planned meeting was part of the Deep State's (DS) coup plot against President Trump nicknamed Operation 'Crossfire Hurricane.' Trump Tower would play a role in the Alfa Bank hoax, Don Jr. setup meeting, and Admiral Mike Rogers advising of planted surveillance bugs. President Trump would file in 2022 a federal RICO lawsuit involving HRC/DNC/Fusion GPS/and others related to the SpyGate operations and those that spread the false Russian collusion narrative during the 2016 election cycle.

Post Q# 1794
"Never interfere with an Enemy while he's in the Process of Destroying Himself."

There is much more to be gleaned by the long-standing relationships between Natalia Veselnitskaya, Glenn Simpson, Bruce Ohr, and Chris Steele. Natalia Veselnitskaya had hired Simpson/Fusion GPS back in the Spring of 2014 to help with the repeal of the global 2012 Magnitsky Act and the campaigns by Sergei's lawyer Bill Browder.

Post Q# 2043
[SETUP EX 1]
[Natalia Veselnitskaya] - Manafort.
FISA warrant issued/approved - Manafort.

It appears now that Russian lawyer Natalia Veselnitskaya used talking points in the infamous TT meeting that were created by Fusion GPS's Glenn Simpson. Glenn Simpson meets just prior to and right after the TT meeting with Natalia Veselnitskaya and her Russian assistant/interpreter.

Post Q# 3214
Anon Question: TT was bugged most likely=confirmed by Q.

In the shadowy international intelligence world, the tradecraft terms used are 'Dispatch and Recovery.' Handlers send off their assets and perform debriefings after the mission as demonstrated by Glenn Simpson and Natalia Veselnitskaya. Fusion GPS would because embroiled in several coup plots against both candidate and President Trump. The infamous Trump Tower Meeting was just one of many setup attempts to 'dirty up' President Trump as well as his inner circle of aides.

Post Q# 3389
Why did POTUS move his transition command center (base of ops) from TT the VERY NEXT DAY?

The FBI had contacted Oleg Deripaska back in 2009 to help with the release of captured Robert Levinson from the Iranians. Deripaska spent $25 million of his own money and had contact with DOJ official Bruce Ohr and Chris Steele during this effort. Bruce Ohr's wife Nellie was the lead researcher from Fusion GPS tasked to produce false information against both Donald Trump and his family.

Post Q# 3595
C_A HUMINT domestic placement - T campaign.

As a note of history Oleg Deripaska had Levinson's release all setup and deal were killed by HRC. Oleg Deripaska had been promised restoration of his US travel privileges and that promise/his money both vanished. In another twist of SpyGate fate, Deripaska would brag to FBI Andy McCabe that he made up the 'Pee Pee' memo from the infamous Steele Dossier.

Post Q# 3858

> THIS REPRESENTS A CLEAR AND PRESENT DANGER TO THE CONSTITUTIONAL REPUBLIC OF THE UNITED STATES OF AMERICA.

British music publicist Rob Goldstone emailed Don Trump Jr. on 6/3/2016 outlining some dirt on HRC. A meeting was setup for June 9th at TT. A total of 8 people with Rob/Veselnitskaya/lobbyist Rinat Akhmetshin along with Don Jr./Paul Manafort/and Jared Kushner and interrupters.

Post Q# 2740

> Why was [NV] barred from entering prior to?
> decode: [NV] = Natalia Veselnitskaya

Shortly after the meeting finally began, it was apparent that Natalia Veselnitskaya was pushing only for the repeal of the Magnitsky Act. It seemed painfully obvious that sweet Natalia did not have any material/dirt on HRC to offer but was exclusively pushing the Magnitsky Act mantra.

Post Q# 3212

> Think Rogers T-Tower meeting (right after SCIF set up in Tower).
> Think POTUS campaign leaving T-Tower (base of operations) THE VERY NEXT DAY.
> 1 + 1 = 2.

This little get together was over as soon as it had begun due to the obvious bait and switch tactics. British promoter Goldstone had met Don Jr. previously in England, but it looks like intelligence operative Joseph Mifsud ordered Rob to organize this meeting.

Post Q# 1506

> Plants need water!

There was an underlying agenda in regard to Bill Browder and the Magnitsky Act. Veselnitskaya had hired Fusion GPS via Baker Hostetler a few years earlier to investigate Browder. Mrs. Melissa Pientka also worked for Fusion GPS and coordinated activities with her hubby FBI Special Agent Joe Pientka.

Post Q# 1866

> Why did POTUS move his entire operation out of TT the DAY AFTER the ADM ROGERS [SCIF] MEETING?

In related breaking news the Russian Deputy AG (their [RR]) has died in a helicopter crash. Saak Karapetyan was the handler of Veselnitskaya and the power behind the ongoing global efforts in lifting the U.S. 2012 Magnitsky Act. Trump Tower would initially be the first attempt to tie candidate Donald Trump to nefarious anonymous Russians.

Post Q# 2043

> [LL] and paper trail and special entry [Natalia Veselnitskaya] and Manafort.

FBI General Counsel James Baker has testified that Perkins Coie/Clinton campaign lawyer Michael Sussmann gave knowingly false information to the FBI about Alfa Bank. This phony intel concerns a Russian bank operating a computer server out of Trump Tower and was part of the initial surveillance operations against President Trump. Special Counsel (SC) John Durham has indicated Sussmann and many more are expected to flow from these illegal activities.

Post Q# 2331

> [Part re: Fusion GPS, Perkins Coie now being revealed?]

This HRC setup meeting assisted the Russian narrative development within the upper ranks of the DOJ. It all is part of the final element of the 'Insurance Policy' under the elaborate Operation Crossfire Hurricane. 'Q' has said FISA surveillance warrants were also issued against Jarred Kushner/Ted Cruz/General Flynn/and many others. SC Durham would outline in 2022 court filing of a vast conspiracy against then candidate Donald Trump by HRC/Fusion GPS/Perkins Coie/and many others.

Post Q# 2740

Why did [LL] [ATTORNEY GENERAL OF THE UNITED STATES] grant 'special entry' to Natalia Veselnitskaya (Don Jr. 'set up' meeting)?

The false narrative that POTUS and Donald Trump Jr. had detailed discussions after this meeting has been debunked. Any questionable interactions were strictly between Team HRC and the Russians in attendance. The creation of false flag events as well as false narratives is the trademark of the corrupt Deep State that we battle for control of our Republic.

Post Q# 1828

[SPY OP]
[FUSION GPS] (Shell2) (CS) [NO NAME] [PERKINS COIE] (Shell2).

The failed coup plotters planted these ObamaGate/SpyGate intel assets deliberately into Trump World. Part of a classic entrapment sting operation involving 'dirty-up meetings' against Team Trump. SC Durham has dropped criminal indictments related to all of the illegal surveillance activities and submitted his final report in 2023. With the historic re-election of President Trump in 2024, many past hidden political secrets will finally be revealed.

Post Q# 4011

CROSSFIRE TYPHOON
CROSS WIND

Links

The Federalist-Facts behind Trump Tower meeting: Incriminating but Not for Trump

The Blaze-The Case against Clinton/Brennan/and Comey is Stronger than Ever

NY Post-Durham Closer to obtaining Fusion GPS Records: Judge agrees to Review Docs

NPR-Senate releases Report on 2016 Trump Tower Meeting

FOX News-Clinton Campaign paid to 'Infiltrate' Trump Tower/White House Servers

New Yorker-Contested Afterlife of Alfa Bank

FOX News-Magnitsky Act Explained: Meeting with Russian Lawyer

Just the News-Mueller's hidden Evidence: Translator Exonerated Don Jr.

The Federalist-8 Times U.S. Intelligence Set People Up to Fabricate the Russia Story

Clinton Foundation Timeline-Trump Tower Archives

Real Clear Investigations-Trump Tower Meeting: Translator telling FBI 'No Collusion'

The Hill-DOJ let Russian Lawyer into US before Meeting with Trump Team

Real Clear Investigations-Trump Tower Setup by Russian Operatives

Undercover Huber-Trump Tower

FOX News-Fusion GPS's Ties to Clinton Campaign

Markets Work-Ongoing Fusion GPS Revelations

Inside Edition-Secret Service President-Elect to Move out of Trump Tower

Judiciary.Senate.Gov-Crossfire Hurricane Interviews

Clinton Foundation Timeline-2025 Crossfire Hurricane Docs

Justice.gov-2023 SC John Durham Report

Predictably Unpredictable: Trump's 'Sixth Sense' Gene

"It's been a long time since we've had a non-corrupt President who works on behalf of the American people and not himself."-Q

In one of the first drops from 'Q' we are asked a question about President Trump being ahead of most things in an almost clairvoyant fashion "Why Trump ran for President". Anyone would question why a successful billionaire would give up a cushy lifestyle to run for President. Candidate Trump would explain that our country has given him so much, he felt the need to give back to the country that he loves. President Trump instituted the back-channel information program known as 'Q' in 2017 and potentially triggered the 'Devolution' process with the Continuity of Government (COG) operations after the 2020 election steal.

Post Q# 14
Was TRUMP asked to run for President?
How is POTUS always 5-steps ahead?

It is hard to deny that President Donald Trump has that rare ability or gift to foreshadow certain future events. Candidate Trump had called well in advance (against the international bookies odds) the upcoming highly controversial British Brexit vote, as well as his own 2016 Presidential victory as well as the 2020 election steal. The ability to accurately judge future events is a unique gift not afforded to many others. Famously President Trump correctly predicted and publicly stated that his campaigns was being spied upon as well as the entire corporate media complex bring nothing but 'Fake News.' Podcaster Joe Rogan would claim that the media has been engaged in a 'Psy-Op' against President Trump for many years.

Post Q# 2504
Has POTUS ever made a statement that hasn't been proven to be correct (future)?

President Trump has additionally predicted dramatic world events in Sweden, North Korea, Iran and Saudi Arabia. Domestically he called out the rigging of both the 2016 Democrat Primaries against Bernie Sanders and both the 2016/2020 Presidential general elections. The 'Q' drops outlined in late 2017 that 11.3 (the 2020 election) would be the first marker. President Trump would file in 2022 extensive RICO federal lawsuit against many of the government officials involved with the SpyGate false Russian collusion narrative political scandal.

Post Q# 2565
Scott Free = WWG1WGA
Q0 = Q+

After publicly broaching the subject of the illegal wiretapping of candidate Trump's phones, the Mockingbird media went crazy with the false narrative of Russia Russia Russia. Future proves past as the FISA Title-1 surveillance warrants on Carter Page back up what President Trump has said about 'tapping' his phones and the illegal surveillance of his close advisers. In 2023 President Trump correctly predicted the golfing world merger of the PGA Tour with the LIV League.

Post Q# 4
Why is POTUS surrounded by generals?

Most of the prior top leadership of the DOJ FISA's are under legal scrutiny by Special Counsel (SC) John Durham. IG Michael Horowitz's 1.0/2.0 FISA reports had outlined many past abuses and his referrals are were tasked to be explored by SC John Durham. SC Durham completed his report in 2023 and will lead into future judicial accountability. We are finding that SpyGate lead into the virus, which directly leads to the 2020 election steal.

Post Q# 2962
> Protect MGL

I don't buy into every wild theory that is out there regarding Trump's special forecasting talents. Claims of President Trump being a 'time traveler' from the distant future or using secret ancient advanced technologies, are highly speculative at best but since Project Looking Glass was mentioned by 'Q', like Anons normally do, all possibilities need to be logically considered. Proven correct yet again, was President Trump's prediction of higher gasoline prices if Biden gets elected.

Post Q# 2936
> At what stage in the game do you play the TRUMP card?

'Q' reminds us however to always think bigger, just like Patriot William Cooper (R.I.P.) who like President Trump has clairvoyant abilities. With the launching of a our U.S. Space Force, it seems our future will be truly universally infinite. President Trump knows the military importance of space and properly set our country back on the proper trajectory. Bill Cooper successful predicted many events such as 9/11, rise of the NWO, population control via biological weapon, secret space programs and much more.

Post Q# 167
> POTUS opened the door of all doors.
> What is the keystone?

We have to give credit where credit is due as it seems President Trump definitely does have a 6th 'sense' gene. He has been correct way more times than he has wrong and certainly on the really big issues. It is often said that President Trump has never made a substantial claim that has not been proven correct. Patel Patriot has written about the Devolution theory involving the continuity of government being enacted by then President Trump. Many would say following the failed assassination attempt on President Trump in July 2024 during a rally in Butler/PA, that God's 'Divine Providence' deflecting the bullet just one inch saved his life. Within two months time, another sniper attempted to kill President Trump while putting on the fifth green at his Florida Trump International Golf Club focusing everyone on the USSS protective details lapses in coverage.

Post Q# 4963
> You have seen the truth.
> Time to show the world.

President Trump is known to be a skilled chess player, and most would believe we are way past your average checkers game. The stakes could not be any higher and the future freedom of the entire free world is at play as the scripted 'Storm' is played out to the public. SC John Durham has dropped criminal indictments related to the treasonous conduct surrounding the ObamaGate/SpyGate scandals. The 2022 Russian special military operation into Ukraine will expose to the world the extent of the corruption and biological warfare experiments that have been occurring.

Post Q# 2807
> Kennedy was an outsider [assassinated].
> POTUS is an outsider [CLAS HIGH].

It is a plus for our country to have such an omnipotent leader currently at the helm in these turbulent world times. President Trump's predictive ability seems to be going strong these days and leading us all toward the Great Awakening. President Trump's record of accurate predictions utterly drives his opponents mad leading inevitably to derangement. Most recent predictions to come true was the removal of historical statues like Thomas Jefferson and the news media will completely tank in rankings post Trump would ultimately occur. President Trump had no wars in his first term demonstrating a 'Peace through Strength' international foreign policy.

Post Q# 4812

> He gave up everything.
> A man who had everything.
> Why do it?

A White House insider has let out a very 'Q' type of an entrapment strategy. Trump's 'Shutdown Trap' is designed to permanently thin out our overpopulated federal DC Swamp. Of historical importance is uncle Dr. John Trump, a famous MIT scientist who examined Nikola Tesla's papers in 1943 on behalf of the FBI. President Trump's uncle John had been given the nickname of the 'Nuclear Uncle.' Please read Patel Patriot's 'Devolution' series as he comes to similar conclusions about President Trump's plan independent of our 'Q' drops. The Continuity of Government operations is central to the devolution implementation. President Trump additionally would be proven prophetic in his 2015 call about the dire situation in Syria regarding the extermination of targeted civilians.

Post Q# 661

> POTUS is safe.
> Protected By PATRIOTS.

Yet again in 2023 President Trump is proven correct with his prediction concerning the corrupt J6 Committee in regards to the deliberate destruction of documents and video testimony. God seems to have sent us a savior that has successfully eliminated the deadly 16-year plan to destroy America. It is not often highlighted but ever Anon knows who is Q+ (POTUS). Please keep President Trump/Family in your prayers constantly fellow Patriots. Thankfully 2025 marks the historic return of President Trump and the long expected judicial Judgement Day.

Post Q# 3585

> Project Looking Glass?
> Going Forward in Order to Look Back.

Links

Open Democracy-Can Donald Trump Predict the Future

FOX News-CIA Report makes Clear Trump was Framed

Clinton Foundation Timeline-2025 Crossfire Hurricane Docs

Victor Davis Hanson-Conspiracies Too Awful to Imagine

The Federalist-Miracle: Divine Providence Protected Trump from Deadly Bullet

Revolver News-Flashback: Trump was Right about J6 Committee Destroying Evidence

Real Clear Politics-Washington/Lincoln/and Donald Trump

Newsweek-Donald Trump: RussiaGate Hoax

Sharyl Attikisson-Media Mistakes in the Trump Era

America Media Group-Military Intelligence: Trump's Ace Card

Golf Digest-Donald Trump Predicted LIV Golf/PGA Tour Merger

American Greatness-Trump: 'I Was Proven Right About the Spying'

Revolver News-Trump was Right Again with Prophetic Call on Syria

American Thinker-"Replacing a Failed and Corrupt Political Establishment"

Empire of the Wheel-Just when you Thought it Couldn't get Weirder

US News-Trump Predictably Unpredictable

The Guardian-Trumpadamus: Trump's Tweets Predict his own Future

The Week-10 Times Trump Bragged Ability to Predict Future

David Wilcock-Ancient Alien Technology Predicts Future

Quod Verum-Shadow Warriors: Trump's Praetorian Guard

American Thinker-So God sent Us a Salesman

Video-Jim Breuer: Trump Derangement Syndrome

New Yorker-Donald Trump's Nuclear Uncle

YouTube-This Video will get Donald Trump Elected

Crossfire Hurricane Docs-DJT and Flynn Briefing

Justice.gov-2023 SC John Durham Report

The US 470th Military Intelligence Brigade and 'Q'

Post # 2007
>   HUBER + IG + 470?

Below is an authorized official comment from Ms. Monica Yoas, the Public Affairs Officer of the US 470th Military Intelligence Brigade. 'Q' has repeatedly dropped references to 470 and I thought best to go to the source and ask. I had first posed this question to Ms. Yoas back in 2018:

My Question:

Does the 470th MI Brigade have anything official to say about 'Q"/QAnon (Patriot)?

Her Answer:

"There is no connection between the 470th Military Intelligence Brigade and QAnon (Patriot). The 470th MI Brigade -Theater sets the theater for intelligence for Army South (ARSOUTH) and U.S. Southern Command's (USSOUTHCOM) area of responsibility by providing multi-disciplinary intelligence in support of multinational operations and security cooperation, in order to obstruct and deter trans-regional threat networks while strengthening regional security through an enterprise methodology. We provide trained and tailored teams as well as other enterprise capabilities to support global contingency operations. Our headquarters are located at Fort Sam Houston, Texas."

Post Q# 1660
>   Think 470.
>   The more you know.

'Q' has directly pointed out the 470th in several prior board drops. It is only natural that we reached out to this fine military unit for an official comment. I would like to personally thank Ms. Yoas for her time and prompt reply. Anons know of the service and dedication of all of our loyal armed services and understand we are partnered in this epic struggle together.

Post Q# 2007
>   Who prosecutes?
>   Team of 470?

The 470th was originally activated in 1944 at the end of World War 2 (WW2) hostilities. Primary responsibility of this prestigious unit was the protection of the Panama Canal Zone. Military intelligence operations are the key informational reports that commanders need to make accurate decisions both in war and peacetime.

Post Q# 1659
>   Who has that kind of manpower?
>   470.

The Panama Canal was a critical military passage point for our Navy between the Atlantic and Pacific oceans. As the European WW2 theatre conflict wound down, all troops were transferred over to the Pacific region. By all records this unit performed exceptionally in defeating the Japanese empire.

Post Q# 1318
>   Horowitz oversees a nationwide workforce of more than 450 special agents, auditors, inspectors, attorneys, and support staff.

The 470th mission statement highlights that they provide tailored multi-disciplined intelligence and counterintelligence services. Primary support is now provided to the US Army (ARSOUTH) and U.S. Southern Command (USSOUTHCOM).

Post Q# 1553

General Michael Horowitz who is working with Huber has a staff of 470 investigators.

A speech quote from General Mike Flynn that confirms our 'Q' mission, outlines his belief in a very large "Digital Army of Citizen Journalists." General Mike Flynn says, "This was irregular warfare at its finest in politics." This is our basis for General Flynn's Army of Digital Soldiers and our belief in WWG1WGA.

Post Q# 755

MILITARY INTELLIGENCE BRIGADE (STRATEGIC SIGNALS INTELLIGENCE)

Per our good friend Praying Medic, 'Q' is a psych operation designed to change the way we think, to change our collective minds in a good way. A classic example of psych operation is when Morpheus gives Neo the Red Pill and he awakenings from the sleepy grip of the Matrix. A parallel can also be drawn from an accidental revelation by Sydney Powell as to the mysterious identity of a White Hat Hacker (305th MI Battalion) helping the Arizona forensic audits.

Post Q# 2072

Huber.....assigned team of 470 investigators (attorney) + IG + legal jurisdiction across all 50 states, is not a 'special counsel' so therefore nothing is being done.

We have noticed the extra special working relationships with Sean Hannity/Sara Carter/and John Solomon in regard to drops from Team-Q. In a prior post I mentioned the fact of 'read-in' assistants often being an integral component of any intel operations and are given limited compartmentalized information. Patel Patriot has written in his Devolution articles about the Continuance of Government (COG) plan that is believed to have been initiated by then President Trump. As yet another example of President Trump's love of our military, on many occasions the credit is given to General Dunford's encouragement to run for President in 2016.

Post Q# 270

Adm R
No Such Agency (WW) + POTUS/USMIL =
Apply the Keystone.
Paint the picture.

I agree with those that have pointed out super computers and AI programs are at work here in this 'Q' back-channel information operation. The 'Black Widow' supercomputer at Ft. Mead in particular, has been credited with helping Team-Q as well as various assisting military intelligence units. Under the illegal Biden regime, the debacle in Afghanistan was a blow to our entire military as well as the populace. Special Counsel (SC) John Durham had been tasked to investigative many of the criminal aspects related to prior illegal spying on then candidate Donald Trump and later President Trump.

Post Q# 11

Military Intelligence vs FBI CIA NSA.
State Secrets upheld under SC.
Very important?
Who surrounds POTUS?

Of Anon interest, is that one of our own has mentioned her (FeistyCat) past military association with the 470th MI. Even though the Public Relation Officer (Ms. Yoas) semi-disavowed the 'Q' association, as 'Q' often says "The military is the only way." Units like the 470th very well come into play with the implementation of the oncoming Storm. Besides assisting SC John Durham with his criminal investigations into SpyGate, it's possible many units like the 470th and similar units like the 305th are involved with the COG operations. President Trump has vowed to go after Transnational Criminal Organizations (TCO) and has filed in 2022 a federal RICO lawsuit against those that promoted the false Russian collusion narrative during the 2016 election cycle.

Post Q# 2169
Military planning at its finest.

In a sad related news story, a soldier from the 470th MI was found dead along with his entire family at their home near the base. Ms. Yoas and San Antonio police chief issued a statement the incident "was no accident" and preliminary being ruled murder/suicide. SC John Durham has dropped criminal indictments related to SpyGate and submitted his final report in 2023 signaling the oncoming Judgement Day. 'Future proves Past' comes true with President Trump's 2022 RICO federal lawsuit against HRC/DNC/and others over the false Russian collusion narrative, as the term '470 entities' is mentioned within the filing paperwork. With the re-election of President Trump in 2024, many past hidden political secrets will be revealed.

Post Q# 4050
You are trending WW 24/7/365 w/censorship.
Never in our history has this been attempted.

The US Army SOF would produce in 2022 an excellent video titled 'Ghosts in the Machine' (link below) that is a must watch into actual military psychological military operations of today. Please read Patel Patriot's 'Devolution' series as he came to similar conclusion independent of the 'Q' posts. Thank you to all of the fine men and women serving our country in uniform. A special shout out to all of the Patriots from the 470th MI Brigade and many White Hat helpers like the ISA/Army of Northern VA/Gray Fox/Send Me/and the Q-Team!

Post Q# 1659
Who has that kind of manpower?
470

Links

US 470th MI Brigade-Unit Patch

US Army SOF-GHOSTS IN THE MACHINE

Military News-Trump says Dunford Played Role in Decision to Run for President

Raleigh News and Observer-Secretive Army Group's Recruitment Video

Patel Patriot-Devolution - Part 22

Newsweek-The Continuation of Government Operations

INSCOM-470th MI Brigade

Wikipedia-US 470th MI Brigade

17 SOG-The President's Army

Military.com-470th MI Soldier found Dead apparent Murder/Suicide

KSAT News-Family of 6 found Dead in SUV at Home

Fort Sam Houston-Stationed Units

Current Ops-470th Military Intelligence Brigade

Joint Base San Antonio-New Leadership 470th Military Intelligence

Wiki Talk-The US 470th MI Brigade

Military.com-Special Ops Profile: Intelligence Support Activity (Gray Fox)

Army University Press-This Month in NCO History: Intel NCO saves Lives in Panama

SOCOM-2025 Army Special Forces Recruitment Video

DHS.gov-A Study of the Military Intelligence Support of Law Enforcement

Intelligence Support Activity-Joint Special Ops Command (Send Me)

Video-USAF Band: "Send Me"

General Michael Flynn-Their Plans for Us

The Federalist-Over 200 Retired Admirals and Generals Endorse Trump

Video-General Mike Flynn: "Army of Digital Soldiers"

Crossfire Hurricane Docs-Christopher Steele Binder

Justice.gov-2023 SC John Durham Report

Attempted 2016 and Now 2020 Election Fraud: Not a 'Big Lie'

One of the first actions taken by President Trump was forming the 2016 voter fraud commission. President Trump knew the national counts were wrong and he wants the real totals from 2016. Future proves past as the 2020 election fraud will go down in the history books. The individual state forensic ballot/machine audits will pave the way for both Voter ID as well as the return of our rightful POTUS. Patriots were correct about the false Trump-Russia narrative and will again be vindicated with the 'Trump Won' movement. History will show that a $400M infusion of 'Zucker Bucks' by Mark Zuckerberg's Facebook into the 2020 election cycle played a significant factor in the overt fraud committed.

Post Q# 2463
> VOTER LAW = DEATH OF D PARTY.
> Boomerang Suicide?

Maine's Secretary of State Matthew Dunlap was part of the original 11-member team to investigate 2016 election voter fraud claims. Incredibly this group was thwarted by many individual States at every point in this important investigation into the voter fraud issue. In 2021, similar obstruction tactics have been employed against any attempted State ballot audit. 'Stop the Steal' and the 'Big Lie' have been the Patriot's rallying cries since November 3, 2020. Polls taken in 2022 incredibly still show a majority of Democrats believe HRC won in 2016 and Trump lost in 2020.

Post Q# 2610
> 2019 push Voter ID based on verifiable intel (fraud).
> 2020+ safeguarded.

Secretary Dunlap continued with his mission and won court battles to get vital voting history records from many States from the 2016 election cycle. An estimated 3-5 million illegal votes were casted via mass ballot harvesting, voting machine manipulation and straight up fraudulent count tallies for 2016. The 2020 election will show a massive foreign cyber hack attack into machinery software and altering the national vote totals as well as syncing with the ground level cheating figures.

Post Q# 26
> The only way is the military. Fully controlled. Save and spread (once 11.3 verifies as 1st marker).

In classic master trolling, President Trump has continued to bring up the critical subject of the 2020 election fraud in all of his rallies and social media posts. Quoting our great leader on this subject, "They like to say, Oh that's a Conspiracy Theory, not a conspiracy theory folks". On election night 2016, the hours long delay for the final Pennsylvania results, would be a window into the 2020 fraud tactics they would trigger. Many later would connect the dots between the Wuhan Lab/COVID outbreak and their direct funding from the corrupt USAID, as instrumental foundational elements in the 2020 Presidential election steal.

Post Q# 4521
> Everything you are witnessing [past and present [future]] centrally revolves around the Presidential Election of 2020.

Historically there are many occurrences where the same person voted in an election many different times. Voter rolls need to be updated in terms of reported deaths and valid legal U.S. citizenship must be mandatory via mandatory voter ID. Sidney Powell educated the public as to the international cyber hacking of the 2020 election results and that the White Hats captured in real time these critical data packets via the 'Kraken.' The coordinated coverup from 51 Intelligence Committee members of Hunter Biden's 'Laptop from Hell' just prior to the 2020 election was a deliberate attempt to rig this Presidential election.

Post Q# 3913
What is the primary benefit to keeping public in mass-hysteria re: COVID-19?
Think voting.

On May 11, 2017, President Trump issued an Executive Order forming the Presidential Advisory Commission on Election Integrity. This panel was headed by VP Mike Pence and Chaired by Kris Kobach. Even though this group was disbanded, they helped to lay the foundational framework that would assist in the trap of 2020 election steal. The international cyber intrusion into selects state election equipment flipped votes away from President Trump. Additionally President Trump asked the Cybersecurity and Infrastructure Security Agency (CISA) to help protect our voting systems from cyber hackers both foreign and domestic.

Post Q# 25
Proof to begin 11.3.
We all sincerely appreciate the work you do.

Many Democratic States had refused to share election data of current voter roll information, let alone inspect any voting equipment. DEMs got the GAO to apply additional pressure to force the closing of this Presidential investigation panel in January 2018. The 2020 election fraud revealed the past tactics with voter machine manipulation combined with ground level ballot fraud shenanigans. Proving what we already knew, famed Rasmussen Polls revealed in 2023 that 20% of the voters in the 2020 Presidential Election admitted to filling out multiple mail-in fraudulent ballots.

Post Q# 2926
Intel awareness pre_2016.

Then DHS Secretary Nielsen thought voter fraud best handled ultimately by the DOJ. NSA/Cyber Command General Paul Nakasone took over control of safeguarding the 2020 Presidential election in terms of tracking and the implementation of the Kraken software to capture this theft. President Trump has called the 2020 election the 'Crime of our Century' and all past voter fraud needs to uncover prior to any future elections. Big Tech played their role by censoring MAGA (as well as 'Q') and allowing algorithms to favor their leftist comrades. The January 6th US Capitol protest is directly related to the stolen 2020 election and Rep. Barry Loudermilk's Congressional committee has uncovered evidence of being a staged event.

Post Q# 4951
How do you 'safeguard' US elections Post POTUS?

The Department of Defense additionally will play a crucial role in election integrity as well as any future corrective measures. The manipulation of active-duty military election ballots brings in another level of justice to this ongoing 'Big Lie' about the 2020 election steal. National full forensic audits for all 50 states are required for 2020 and photo voter ID going forward. It was revealed in 2024 about a coordinated mass 'Censorship Industrial Complex' that altered the 2020 election cycle. Special Counsel (SC) John Durham has dropped criminal indictments and submitted his final report in 2023 related to HRC/DNC/BHO/and many others.

Post Q# 153

Who owns the voting machines?
What about voter ID laws?
Photo ID?

Screams continue from the Progressive Left of discrimination by the mere suggestion of checking the voter rolls and standard citizen voter ID laws. There is a need to implement a National Photo ID Card to all citizens and insuring election integrity for the future. Innovations like blockchain accountability and QR codes must be incorporated into future elections. The use of 'ballot mules' that stuffed voter boxes during the 2020 Presidential election will be a turning point in the public awakening of the historic election fraud. Exhibited in both 2016/2020 were long used tools of election cheaters like voter role manipulation as well as fraudulent signatures on mail-in ballots. On the State level driver licenses were issued to illegal migrants and on a Federal level non-citizens were Social Security benefits assisting illegal voting to ultimately occur.

Post Q# 4960

Who controls the elections?

History will show a massive cyber-attack occurred on 11/3/20 by foreign countries using our own stolen software called the Hammer and Scorecard. Influence campaigns were done by China, Iran, and other foreign countries to prevent the re-election of Donald Trump. Then DNI James Clapper had used Hammer program to illegally spy on Americans and added a program termed Scorecard to alter voting totals. President Trump has described the actions on 11/3/20 correctly as being the crime of the century. Evidence of the 2020 fraud continues to drip out in 2022 and all Patriots hope the cheating methods have been stopped. Clapper and former CIA Director John Brennan would gather 51 intelligence officials to sign a letter claiming Hunter Biden's 'Laptop from Hell' was not real and only a product of Russian disinformation prior to the 2020 Presidential election.

Post Q# 4620

10. Promote mail-in voting as only 'safe' method _bypass NSA election security [installed midterms +1].

Full disclosure will let the public know what has transpired in regard to past voter fraud and our election integrity. Arizona hired the Cyber Ninjas to perform a complete forensic audit of Maricopa (AZ) County's election ballots/machines on the 2020 vote. Censorship played a big role in 2020 and the banning of Patriot media accounts were directly related to the coverup of Hunter Biden's 'Laptop from Hell' explosive story. The Wisconsin assembly has been the first state to vote to decertify their 2020 electors for Biden and the Pennsylvania high court ruled mail in ballots are unconstitutional.

Post Q# 570

[pop vote and easily manipulation illegal votes Soros machines].

Safeguards and voter ID laws will better prevent future voter fraud occurring against the American electorate. President Trump/ 'Q' have assured us that the 'Kraken' program captured the election hack, and the data is irrefutable. Documentaries like '2000 Mules' and 'Rigged 2020' further reveal to the public the full scope of the 2020 Presidential election steal. The need for guaranteed election

467

integrity and permanent Voter ID is the reason it 'had to be this way' through the darkness. Late in 2022 Elon Musk would reveal the exact nature of the coordinated Big Tech censorship leveled against President Trump/MAGA to alter the 2020 Presidential election. With President Trump's re-election in 2024, many feel CISA is credited with 'fortifying' of our critical Presidential election.

Post Q# 4219

People used as pawns in their attempt to [provide cover] for vote-by-mail?
Is this about the virus OR THE ELECTION?

Links

The Guardian-How Republicans Came to Embrace the Big Lie

Just the News-Trump Calls for Special Prosecutor to Investigate 2020 Election

Western Journal-USAID helped DEMs Steal the 2020 Election

CISA.gov-CISA DIrector Easterly: Security of 2024 Elections

Breitbart-CIA Interfered in 2020 Election with Discredited Hunter Laptop Story

Vigilant Fox-This Looks very Bad for the 2020 Campaign

Washington Examiner-1 in 5 Admit to 2020 Election Fraud

WND-Who Undermined Election Integrity in 2016 and 2020?

Western Journal-'Ballot Mules' Delivered Tens of Thousands of Votes for Biden

Revolver News-DOGE Investigation into Social Security proves Illegals have been Voting

The Federalist-Testimony explains how Leftist Money Infiltrated Elections in 2020

New York Post- New York Times finally Admit Hunter's Laptop is Real

Epoch Times-How Google Stopped the Red Wave

Real Clear Politics-The Plot to Fix the 2024 Election

Front Page-Three Foreign Billionaires financed Dark Money in 2020 Election

Daily Dot-Facebook Shut down QAnon Groups before 2020 Election

American Thinker-Darryl Cooper: Martyr Made's Mega Thread

Marshall Report-Sidney Powell's 'Kraken' is a DOD Cyber Warfare Program

The Federalist-10 Lies Democrats Tell about our Elections

Time Magazine-Secret History of Shadow Campaign that Saved 2020 Election

Epoch Times-Infographic: China's 2020 Election Interference

Just the News-Iran Tried to Stop Trump's Election

Patel Patriot-Devaluation: Part 3 Addendum

Rep. Barry Loudermilk-January 6th Initial Findings Report

OIG.DOJ.gov-Report on 2020 Election Fraud

Just the News-DHS/OIG: 2025 Cybersecurity System Review

CISA.gov-Vulnerabilities Affecting Dominion Voting Systems

White House.gov-Risks from Government Censorship

Clinton Foundation Timeline-2025 Crossfire Hurricane Docs

[MOVIE 1] Nomination for Best Supporting Actress [DWS]

IMRAN AWAN - [DWS] - SETH RICH

Nothing to see here, please move along! U.S. Representative Debbie Wasserman-Schultz [DWS] finds herself as the pivotal connecting point between two major political scandals. DWS is central to IT work surrounding Congressional staffer Imran Awan and DNC staffer Seth Rich. President Trump in 2022 would specially list DWS as well as HRC/DNC and others in his federal RICO lawsuit over the events surrounding the false Russian collusion narrative as well as unfolding criminal SpyGate political scandal.

Post Q# 4153
> [FBI Floor 7] [DNI] [CIA] [DNC] [WH] primary [bulk]

His name was Seth Rich (1989-2016), and his unsolved murder is still in the news years later. Pakistani 'Mystery Man' Imran Awan like Seth Rich have both been involve in the past with 'Noodles' aka DWS. Historians will find it odd that the law firm of Perkins Coie is also connected to DWS as well as both IT staffers. 'Q' has stressed we are watching a movie(s) and in 2022 playing simultaneously FisaGate/Guardians of the Pedophiles/and Panic in DC featuring DES.

Post Q# 674
> AWAN/DWS/Paki intel/MB.

decode: MB = Muslim Brotherhood

Seth (Panda) Rich was employed at the DNC under DWS as the Voter Expansion Data Director. A loyal Bernie Sanders follower, Seth became a whistleblower for election fraud/voter suppression in the 2016 Democratic Primaries. The so-called 'hack' of the DNC server in 2016 would remain a key intersection in the entire planned coup against Donald Trump.

Post Q# 1226
> Q: SR.
> DNC to initiate lawsuit (pre-planned).

Records now show that the DNC leak event was the starting point of the entire Trump-Russia collusion hoax. We can thank the false DNC intrusion reporting by CrowdStrike who ultimately blamed Russian hackers Fuzzy/Cozy Bear. Special Counsel (SC) John Durham's criminal indictment of Perkins Coie/Clinton campaign lawyer Michael Sussmann started to bring the truth to the public.

Post Q# 4904
> All [3] movies playing simultaneously?

Imran Awan was the leader of a family group of Pakistani nationals that all worked as IT aides for the US Congress. Starting in 2004 the family combined receive over $6 million in inflated pay. The Muslim Brotherhood has planned for decades to infiltrate our governmental agencies, and many feel the Awan cabal are prime examples.

Post Q# 3532
> [AWAN]
> [DWS]
> House of Cards.
> You didn't think the plea deal was the end did you?

Spanning over a dozen years and millions in inflated salaries, this Cabal had access to 44 Democratic House members. The Awan's mysteriously got waived the normal required of all Congressional staff full background security checks. A red light should have gone off to any counterintelligence folks normally tasked to spot such penetration.

Post Q# 1250

When did AWANs mission op go green?
2004
Follow the timeline.
Here is a timeline and brief outline of some major activities in these scandals:
• 2005: DWS assumes 'handler' role for Imran Awan from Xavier Becerra.
• 4/30/16: DNC aide reports computer intrusion in main computer servers.
• 5/5/16: CrowdStrike blames Russians.
• 7/10/16: Murder of Seth Rich.
• 7/22/16: Wikileaks drop DNC Emails.
• 7/24/16: DWS resigns Chair DNC and instantly joins HRC campaign.
• 2/2/17: U.S. House cuts off Awan's access.
• 4/16/17: DWS laptop found with Imran's ID/documents by Capitol Police.
7/24/17: Imran attested
• 7/24/17: VIPS Report by Thomas Drake and Bill Binney-'Leak not a Hack.'
• 9/16/21: Perkins Coie/Clinton campaign lawyer Michael Sussmann indicated by Durham

Post Q# 4592

The Great [D]eceivers.

Per President Trump orders, NSA whistleblower Bill Binney was told to brief KANSAS (Pompeo) on forensic testing results by his cyber team on the DNC server. The documented very fast download transmission rate speed proved it was a 'Leak not Hack.' This unique physical fact eliminates the Russian hacking theory by CrowdStrike and lends credence to the thumb drive download by Seth Rich.

Post Q# 436

DNC.
(SR 187) (MS13 (2) 187).
DWS/DIR.

'Q' has mentioned not only [DWS] but also Seth and Awan's. The answers and details surrounding both of these historical scandals will prove vital. Special Counsel (SC) John Durham was tasked to explore the criminal referrals from OIG Michael Horowitz surrounding all of these political scandals. The DNC as well as DWS would be key players in the Perkins Coie/HRC coordinated spying operation against then candidate Donald Trump.

Post Q# 4016

Was the DNC (was) hacked by Russia?
Seth Rich internal DL hand-to-hand pass USA?

Setting aside the MS-13 [2] element, [DWS] is neck deep in several major investigations. Let's pray that Seth Rich's murder will be avenged and the Pakistani spy ring fully exposed and prosecuted. SC John Durham has dropped criminal indictments and submitted his final report in 2023. SC Durham additionally had looked into the 2016 DNC alleged computer 'hack' of the email system and release by WikiLeaks prior to the election.

Post Q# 551
DWS FAILED TO FLEE.

Incredibly Judge Tanya Chutkan who oversaw the Awan case, would be assigned in 2023 President Trump's criminal case related to January 6th. It appears Imran Awan has skated with time served but let's hope he 'sang' big league to earn such a generous deal. 'Q' has led us to believe this is part of the 'show' and justice will result from these espionage activities. The reports from IG Horowitz and SC Durham will be the foundation for future judicial accountability. With the re-election of President Trump in 2024, many Deep State villains will now finally face justice.

Post Q# 3634
[D]'s (internal) infiltration issue(s) w/protecting NAT SEC?
Deliberate?
Awan IT scandal

Links

Daily Wire-Scandals Reopen

The Federalist-FBI never Investigated Evidence for Loretta Lynch's Role in Cover Up

NY Post-FBI never Probed Confidential Talks

Clinton Foundation Timeline-2025 Crossfire Hurricane Docs

Observer-DWS: Corruption Scandals are Pilling Up

FOX News-DWS to Allow Laptop Scan after Stonewalling

Real Clear Politics-RussiaGate: HRC/Perkins Coie/Fusion GPS/CrowdStrike

Judicial Watch-Luke Rosiak/Daily Caller Interview: Imran Awan

Markets Work-IT Intrigue: Imran Awan and Debbie Wassermann Schultz

Breitbart-7 Fast Facts Imran Awan: Debbie Wassermann Schultz's Jailed Vendor

Daily Caller-44 House DEMs Exempted Awan's from Background Checks

Clinton Foundation Timeline-DWS Admits to helping HRC Win DEM Nomination

Sharyl Attkisson-Cybersecurity and The Awan Brothers

Sun Sentential-Wasserman Schultz calls Conspiracy Theory about Seth Rich Vile

Daily Caller-Police believe Awan Planted Laptop

FOX News-Luke Rosiak with Lou Dobbs on Awan's

Rense-Valentine's Massacre says DWS from Awan Probe

Zeckelin-Seymour Hersh Discusses Seth Rich and WikiLeaks

Char74Trump-DWS and Awan's

FBI.gov/Vault-Seth Rich (part 1 of 2)

Crossfire Hurricane Docs-Christopher Steele Binder

Diana West Forecasted 'Red Coup' and '16-Year Plan to Destroy America'

When focusing in on the scandal known as ObamaGate/SpyGate, the question of motivation must be paramount when dissecting this treasonous plan. You must set aside the narrative that everything was done for HRC and the 3rd term of BHO under the illegal Biden administration to view the larger picture that is at play behind these treasonous actions. The clever Saudi Crown Prince Mohammed bin Salman (MBS) would take full advantage of the 2022 Ukraine conflict to reach beneficial arrangements with both Russia and China.

Post Q# 1953
Know your enemy.
"Every battle is won before it's ever fought."

A much larger force is going on, one of an idealistic progressive leftist cultural Marxist movement. Criminal coup plots seem to have trumped normal Washington DC swamp politics. Massive criminal conduct has occurred with this failed coup against President Trump. Domestic traitors combined with globalist like the Chinese CCP and the Muslim Brotherhood is promoting this plan to destroy America.

Post Q# 14
Was HRC next in line?
Was the election supposed to be rigged?

Very few people are connecting the dots on what are the underlying factors driving top ranking government officials to commit treason. Shockingly several married couples have literally committed high crimes together in this unfolding ObamaGate/SpyGate scandal. The public would witness in 2002 via Hunter Bidne's "Laptop from Hell' how foreign governments 'capture' US officials through planned compromise operations.

Post Q# 2640
What was the 16-year plan to destroy America?
EYES ON TARGET.

Bestselling author/MSM journalist/TV guest host and stage star is Diana West. Diana West in 2010 was one of the co-authors along with Andy McCarthy of the hit bestselling book "Shariah: The Threat to America". Ms. West has long been on the trail of the Muslim Brotherhood and exposing their infiltration efforts within the United States.

Post Q# 4961
Endless lies.
Who will put an end to the endless?

Ms. West again gained national attention in 2012 when she and Sheriff Joe lead the 'Birtherism' push. Diana West has published several bestselling books in recent years and is on TV network news programs regularly as a featured expert contributor. Remember in 2012 Rep. Michele Bachmann attempted to start investigations into Huma Abedin/Muslim Brotherhood.

Post Q# 4076

This is about regaining POWER.
Every asset deployed.
WIN OR DIE.

Since December 2017, Diana West has been publishing several short stories called the "Red Thread Series". Ms. West has eight fascinating articles that center around the theme of a Communist plot involving a "16-Year Plan" to transform (destroy) America. Beginning with the coordination of 9/11 with the Islamic caliphate and today with the detailed infiltration of the USA by the Chinese CCP.

Post Q# 166

Expand your thinking.
Jason Bourne (Deep Dream).

The basic principle is a total Progressive Leftist Communist/Red Progressive revolution in the USA. Tactics rely on using the powers of the Deep State against an unsuspecting general population, that is purposely being brainwashed continually by the partnering Mockingbird media. The global Great Reset is to bring in a one world government controlled by the ruling elites.

Post Q# 2313

Darkest days.
This evil must be destroyed.

Futuristic authors like Huxley and Orwell have warned us not so long ago, with their dire advanced predictions of a global surveillance state. Future does prove past in many chilling scary examples from recorded human history. The ultimate goal of the ruling elite is a planned global Great Reset with a large majority of the population being killed off.

Post Q# 570

[The 16 year plan to destroy America]
HUSSEIN [8].
HRC [8] WWIII.
They Thought She Would Never Lose.

This "Red Coup" is more than just politics, it is about a fundamental ideology and societal transformation. West's 8-part series starts with "Does a Red Thread run through the Anti-Trump Coup" and continues with this dangerous narrative through her thrilling published series. Early Patriots like Bill Cooper also warned of this coming 16-year plan to infiltrate then destroy our once great Republic.

Post Q# 4361

God save America.

Ms. West's articles begin to bring this 16-year plan into current focus with subject titles like: When American collusion looks like Russian deception / Red Thread through Foggy Bottom /and From Magnitsky to Steele. Diana West has stated she believes the government is holding the data from Seth Rich's laptop under National Security laws. Peter Schweizer's 2024 bestselling book 'Blood Money' vindicates Ms. West in her predictions concerning the Chinese conducting unrestricted warfare against the USA.

Post Q# 3586

Define 'black op' [clandestine].

The entire series is a must read as well as some of Diana's many other syndicated stories. Ms. West is a regular contributor to many news publications and deemed an authority. Scarily illegal Biden administration is completing the second 8-years that were to have been completed by HRC after BHO. Special Counsel John Durham has dropped criminal indictments related to SpyGate and submitted his final report in 2023. Reports from IG Horowitz and SC Duration will be the foundation for future judicial accountable.

Post Q# 154
Who financed 9-11?

Perhaps someday people will understand 'they' had a plan to conduct 'another' mass extinction event.

The hard Progressive Left of today is very similar to the Communist/Marxist of yesterday. The NWO Globalists and the Leftists have similar overall objectives and pair up constantly to achieve those ends. Today Biden is repeatedly telling reporters he is 'not allowed' to answer certain questions implying handlers in a Shadow Presidency. Globally we can witness the unholy alliance between Red and Green, the odd bedfellows of the Communist CCP and the Muslim Brotherhood.

Post Q# 192
Why are Russia and China communist?

We can no longer afford to ignore this dangerous threat as it has been spreading in our country for many decades. Saul Alinsky's playbook has been the model on which BHO/HRC have built their transformational strategy. Ms. West is currently exploring the relationship of Perkins Coie law firm and Seth Rich's laptop.

Post Q# 3903
[infiltration instead of invasion]
West's Red Thread Series and 16-Year Plan:
- Progressive Communist Utopia
- 2-TierJustice System and Courts
- Total Surveillance and Censorship
- The Great Reset (Virus/VAX)
- Permanent Shadow Gov't/Deep State
- Adherence to the UN/NWO Cabal
- Open Boarders/Sanctuary Country
- Middle East/Regional Conflicts
- Takeover of Education and Media
- Global Policies-Climate/Laws/etc
- Red/Green/Brown Alliances

Post Q# 3607
Define 'Projection.'
THE GREAT AWAKENING.
SHEEP NO MORE.

The world would focus upon the global Islamic vs West struggle with the 2024 war between Israel and Hamas. Diana West joins fellow heroines Sidney Powell/Sara Carter/Cheryl Attkisson and others in helping to exposure political corruption. Diana West was also one of the first to point of 2020 election fraud as it occurred. Please support Ms. West's outstanding books, blog posts, and impactful educational lectures. With the historic re-election of President Trump in 2024, many hope past hidden political secrets will finally be revealed.

Post Q# 4382

Police ordered to stand down by [D] mayor(s) [D] gov(s)?
ANTIFA [coordinated] SAFE ZONES?

Links

American Thought Leaders-Diana West (2020)

The Federalist-China's Spying Expanded Rapidly under Biden/Harris

Ron Carolina's-The 16-Year Plan Reference Materials

Breitbart-'Blood Money': The Secret Chinese Military Warfare Manifesto

CCP Bio Threats-Project One

WSJ-The Red Green Alliance: Pro Hamas Protests

Lori Anderson-2015 Admiral James Lyons on Muslim Brotherhood Threat

The Federalist-Hunter Biden's Laptops Scandal exposes how Communists Work

Newsweek-Understanding the Red/Green Alliance

Patel Patriot-Devolution Part 14: The Invisible Enemy

Arab News-Muslim Brotherhood using Woke Europeans

American Thinker-Archbishop Vigano's startling Warnings to the American People

Daily Caller-Soviets subverted US in 1930's

970 The Answer-Diana West (interview 4/20/20)

State of the Nation-The 16-Year Plan to Destroy America

Markets Work-Time Magazine details 'Shadow Campaign' against Trump

Politics and Prose-Diana West: "American Betrayal"

Front Page-The Party of Treason

American Thinker-CAIR: An Islamic Trojan Horse

C-SPAN-2011 Interview with Diana West

Diana West Blog-Supersonic Missile Gap

Epoch Times-57,000 Communist Takeover of DNC

Town Hall-Diana West Biography

US House Oversight-The Muslim Brotherhood's Global Threat

Clinton Foundation Timeline-2025 Crossfire Hurricane Docs

Justice.gov-2023 SC John Durham Report

'Q' asks "When Does a Bird Sing"?
When Put Into a [BOX] by SC Durham

We are all about to see the fruits of cooperating government witnesses when the unsealing of indictments begins. Horowitz/Huber/Storch/Bash and now Special Counsel (SC) John Durham have been working first with Bill Priestap and a later few other co-conspirators in testimony about SpyGate. Finally, indictments are beginning to flow as first FBI lawyer Kevin Clinesmith plead guilty and Perkins Coie/Clinton campaign lawyer Michael Sussmann was indicted by SC Durham.

Post Q# 2476
> Dig deeper!
> Sometimes people need to see the future in order to save the past.

Bill Priestap/Lisa Page/James Baker/Peter Strzok/Joe Pientka/Mike Kortan/and Bruce Ohr have all been early cooperating witnesses in the various probes. Their testimony is developing criminal cases against higher ups the chain of command of DOJ/FBI/Intelligence/and former White House officials. President Trump would file in 2022 a federal RICO lawsuit against many of the main characters connected to the SpyGate false Russian collusion narrative. James Baker would be the first 'singer' to be made public and indications are Bill Priestap will be the next on center stage.

Post Q# 2554
> WHITAKER, HOROWITZ, HUBER, and WRAY.
> Long meeting held within a SCIF [unusual].

FBI Counterintelligence Director William Priestap may be remembered by historians as the very first 'singer' from the ObamaGate/SpyGate coup plotters. Rumor has it Priestap was also the infamous FBIAnon doing drops at 4chan in July 2016. 'Q' later began posting drops in late October 2017 at the public message board called 4chan followed by 8chan/8KUN. Bill Priestap and others would remain key figures in the ongoing criminal probes into the SpyGate political scandal.

Post Q# 3870
> THEY WILL BE HELD ACCOUNTABLE.
> NOBODY WALKS AWAY FROM THIS.

Bill Priestap was the head of the FBI's Office of Counterintelligence and was FBI agent Peter Strzok's direct boss. Bill Priestap and Joe Pientka have not been mentioned much in the public arena by design and over possible safety concerns as witnesses. Priestap and Pientka were involved with candidate Trump's first intelligence briefings in 2016 and with the setup interview of General Flynn in early 2017.

Post Q# 1278
> Cooperating

Media silence is a customary practice extended to most major cooperating government and whistleblower witnesses. Continued government employment is also standard practice until their usefulness as productive witnesses is deemed over. Many of these early witnesses were retained by the DOJ as evidence as they were the last to leave government employment.

Post Q# 100
> Secret Society.

By all reports Bill Priestap was the first to turn over testimony and begin the rush into the 'Bird Cage.' FBI Director James Comey tried to setup Bill Priestap and throw him under the bus in his past Congressional testimony on investigation compliance. History has shown that coup plotters will eventually turn in themselves in a rush of self-preservation when the jig is up.

Post Q# 2558

It's all just a CONSPIRACY.
Nothing To See Here.

Rep. Stefanik questioned James Comey for not advising Congress in the required timely fashion about the official FBI's official start of the Russia probe into Donald Trump. Comey blamed delay directly on Priestap s asks took no responsibility. It had been customary to alert Congress within 3 months' time of the opening of these types of sensitive probes and had always previously been done by the FBI in the past.

Post Q# 564

When does a bird sing?

An old theory in cases like this goes "If they are still working, then they are still cooperating". Still collecting government paychecks up to the end of President Trump's first term were the traitorous figures likes of Bruce Ohr and Joe Pientka. The entire SpyGate scandal involves not only many American officials but plenty of international co-conspirators.

Post Q# 3125

The PUBLIC must be prepared for what is about to come.
"THE CLINTON FOUNDATION"

DOJ/FBI employees that have been linked to this political scandal termed loosely as RussiaGate/ObamaGate/SpyGate, have mostly retired or have been fired. All have given official statements that will be used in upcoming Congressional and criminal investigations.

Post Q# 1288

Bill Priestap, Head of Counterintelligence and Strzok's boss-cooperating witness [power removed].
Lisa Page, attorney with the FBI Office of the General Counsel-cooperating witness [power removed].
Conspiracy?

Please note that Lisa Page, Peter Strzok, and James Baker have been fired by the FBI. Bruce Ohr has been demoted (power removed) several times. The mysterious Joe Pientka has been treated like he is in the witness protection program and totally kept off all radar screens and his FBI assignments scrubbed from all public records.

Post Q# 1385

Did the 'covert' counterintelligence branch of the FBI end?

It appears that the DOJ 'Bird Cage' is being emptied out as criminal investigations proceed. 'Q' asks "When does a Bird Sing" and the answer is when it's cornered in a [BOX] by AG Barr/IG Horowitz/IG Storch/SP Huber/SP Bash/SC Durham/and the 470th MI Brigade.

Post Q# 2552

"After Mr. Priestap's departure, none of the high-ranking bureau officials involved with the two investigations will remain with the bureau."

The past retirement of Bill Priestap signaled a new phase was ready to begin. SC John Durham will bring Judgement Day as he has submitted his final report in 2023. With the re-election of President Trump in 2024, let the pain and justice phase of the 'Storm' commence upon all of these failed traitorous coup plotters.

Post Q# 3824

Open your eyes to see the TRUTH.

Links

Clinton Foundation Timeline/2025 Crossfire Hurricane Docs

The Federalist-FBI/DOJ Declined to Charge Russia Collusion Hoaxer

Judiciary.Senate.gov-Report shows FBI Cut Corners in HRC Email Investigation

Epoch Times-Testimony reveals FBI Official Excluded from Key Meetings

FOX News Who is Bill Priestap?

Rolling Stone-How did RussiaGate Start?

Seaman Substack-FBI: Coverup of the Crime of the Century

The Federalist-SpyGate 101: A Primer on the Russia Collusion Hoax to Down Trump

Clinton Foundation Timeline-Mid Year Exam (MYE)

The Last Refuge-Get to Know this Name: Bill Priestap

FOX News-FBI Agent who Requested Validation of Steele Dossier left Crossfire Hurricane

Markets Work-Brennan and Clapper: Complicity, Lies, and Bill Priestap

Daily Caller-Former FBI Intel Chief Bill Priestap faces Scrutiny over Steele Dossier Briefing

Washington Examiner-DOJ Unearths more Notes from Peter Strzok and Others

American Thinker-Is Lisa Page Singing to Durham Prosecutors?

FOX News-FBI Leadership Fired Up about Trump Russia Bank

Epoch Times-SpyGate: The Inside Story

Markets Work-Bill Priestap Cooperating Witness

Capital Research Center-Cast of the Trump Russia Collusion Hoax

Markets Work-SpyGate: The Inside Story

OIG.Justice.gov-DOJ OIG FISA Report

Crossfire Hurricane Docs-Christopher Steele Binder

Justice.gov-2023 SC John Durham Report

A Trump 'Stealth Bomber': Meet Big Matt Whitaker

With the resignation of Stealth Jeff Sessions, President Trump appointed Matthew Whitaker as Acting AG. 'Q' previously outlined some upcoming "Stealth Bomber" attacks and now we know the 'temp' role of one of those selected players. History will show that Whitaker enabled a smooth transition from AG Jeff Sessions to AG Bill Barr for President Trump and the plans of the Patriots.

Post Q# 2381
How do you navigate around installed corrupt [FBI] [DOJ].
USE A STEALTH BOMBER.

"Trust the Plan" and understand that every move can't be telegraphed to the watchful enemy. Many had hoped Stealth Jeff would be activated to go on the attack but apparently, he has played his role perfectly as per the 'plan.'

Post Q# 2495
Attacks on WHITAKER will only intensify.
SENATE WAS THE TARGET.
53 - 47

President Trump has always stressed to "Trust Sessions" and 'Q' posted thanks for all Jeff has done. Whitaker was Stealth Jeff's Chief of Staff since returning to the DOJ in October 2017.

Post Q# 2525
When your 'enemy' feels in control...
PANIC re: WHITAKER?

Steering the ship of 'Justice' on the proper legal course, Matt has assumed oversight of Team Mueller. Whitaker also insists that a federal prosecutor is still looking into FBI/DOJ misconduct and the Clinton Foundation probe(s) is ongoing.

Post Q# 2766
WHITAKER remain DOJ senior staff?
Senior counselor in the associate attorney general's office?
Planned?

Matt Whitaker was appointed U.S. Attorney for the Southern District of Iowa in 2004 by Bush. Whitaker won the Republican primary for Iowa Treasurer in 2002 but lost to the Democratic incumbent in the general election.

Post Q# 2165
Drop [daily] carpet bombs [RATS RUNNING] and drop/release MOAB?

Matt Whitaker appears to have political ambitions in addition to his outstanding justice background. Whitaker is exactly the type of 'temp hire' that can shake things up properly within the rotten DC swamp.

Post Q# 2459
Imagine if the new Acting AG now releases all previously 'blocked' doc requests by the House (including the [RR] secondary CLAS Scope doc.

Whitaker is an imposing figure at 6.4 feet tall and played tight end for the Iowa Hawkeyes in the 1991 Rose Bowl. Big Matt is a big Christian Nationalist and President Trump has said "He is a great guy, I mean, I know Matt Whitaker."

Post Q# 2462
> Who was SESSIONS' CHIEF OF STAFF?

Matt Whitaker assumes the mantel of oversight with the Mueller probe from [RR]. Big Matt Whitaker also has announced the full support of the DOJ over Trump's right to limit illegal entry/asylum into the U.S. An email was unearthed that sent by Whitaker at the behest of then AG Sessions on 11/22/17 advising John Huber to revisit the Clinton Foundation and Uranium One probes.

Post Q# 2676
> Re_read drops re: 'Scaramucci' model.
> Purpose?

Another critical role for Whitaker was in the upcoming declassification of the FISA documents. President Trump recommend John Laush to be the liaison at DOJ to help speed up production of requested documents to the requesting Congressional committees.

Post Q# 4595
> THE SWAMP RUNS DEEP.
> v2_change you can believe in.

IG Michael Horowitz was additionally tasked by President Trump to determine 'sensitive information within the Carter Page FISA(s). President Trump had signed off on the full declassification of all the related FISA/DOJ documents and given AG Barr final release authority.

Post Q# 3410
> Stealth Bomber.
> B(2).

Personal friends of Whitaker include China Ambassador Terry Barnstad, Sam Clovis, and Senator Chuck Grassley. Matt embodies the Biblical view of justice and is demonstrated in his work demeanor.

Post Q# 2554
> WHITAKER, HOROWITZ, HUBER, and WRAY.
> Long meeting held with a SCIF [unusual].

Matt Whitaker had suggested publicly for a full investigation into HRC, the Clinton Foundation, and cutting off funding to the Mueller investigation. This is the type of aggressive judicial offense that is required by President Trump in helping to remove all 'blockades'.

Post Q# 2937
> [zero leaks - none]
> Transfer from AG1 to AG2?

After having the DOJ ethics officers look at any conflicts of interest, Matt Whitaker oversaw the Robert Mueller probe. This is very bad news to the Deep State Cabal and 'BLOCKADE' removal tactics were well underway across the board.

Post Q# 2501
> WHITAKER (in conjunction w/OIG) approved the release of CLAS docs 1-4 as requested by the House Committee and as ORDERED BY THE PRESIDENT OF THE UNITED STATES.

With the subsequent confirmation of AG William Barr, Whitaker was more than qualified to become Deputy AG. [RR] announced his resignation and Whitaker would have been an ideal selection.

Post Q# 2468

> Temp hire to remove embeds 'untrustworthy' staffers?
> Temps can be very dangerous to those who are targeted.

The House DEMs had been pressuring Whitaker into disclosing all contacts with the Trump legal team. This concern centered around possible Special Counsel (SC) Bob Mueller's findings being shared with Team Trump. The entire Mueller witch-hunt against President Trump will be a stain on our judicial system forever.

Post Q# 2676

> Stealth bombers silent?
> What is the purpose of WHITAKER?

'Q' has posted in prior drops that FISA will "Bring down the House." Whitaker had moved the ball forward, doing his role in the ongoing SpyGate/ObamaGate scandals and related indictments. SC John Durham has dropped criminal indictments and submitted his final report in 2023. After President Trump's 2024 re-election, Matt Whitaker would be nominated to become the new U.S. NATO Ambassador.

Post Q# 2504

> Locked and (who is) Loaded?

PS: As for possible other stealth bombers used by POTUS: Bill Barr, Jeff Sessions, John Huber, John Durham, and Richard Grenell are a few other prime examples.

Links

BBC News-Matthew Whitaker: Trump defends Acting AG

Real Clear Investigations-RussiaGate's Architects Suppressed Doubts to Peddle False Claims

Seatle Times-What to Know about Matthew Whitaker

Just the News-Trump Taps Matthew Whitaker for NATO Ambassador

Epoch Times-Matthew Whitaker is Owed an Apology

Time-Whitaker suggests Cutting off Mueller's Funding

Republican Herald-Spying, indeed, took Place

Real Clear Politics-Why the RussiaGate Scandal Outranks the Rest

Breitbart-Matthew Whitaker: "Above the Law"

Washington Examiner-Eric Holder Orchestrated ObamaGate says Whitaker

FOX News-3 Things to Know about Matthew Witaker

Daily Beast-DOJ finds Letter Ordering Scrutiny of Clinton Foundation and Uranium One

NBC News-Matthew Whitaker has Left the Justice Department

The Hill-5 Things about Matthew Whitaker

Epoch Times-A New AG for New Phase of SpyGate

Clinton Foundation Timeline-Matt Whitaker

Justice.gov-Conspiracy to Defraud the United States

Who is Jonathan Winer?
How is He Connected to ObamaGate?

Jonathan Winer was a U.S. State Department Official under BHO. Winer's first stint at State was under Bill Clinton as Deputy Assistant Secretary for International Law Enforcement. Winer along with other government officials would become neck deep in the SpyGate political scandal and become involved with the fake Steele Dossier. President Trump would file in 2022 a federal RICO lawsuit against those officials involved with the promotion of the false Russian collusion narrative back in 2016.

Post Q# 1431
TRUST the plan.
Conspiracy NO MORE.

Please note that Winer was hired in 2013 by BHO at the insistence of then Secretary of State John Kerry. I suspect Jonathan Winer's old Clinton ties posed an initial hurdle that obviously John Kerry had to clear with BHO. There has always been a level of distrust and outright hate between team Clinton and BHO.

Post Q# 1345
U1 [donations to CF].

Between Winer's State Department gigs, he was with APCO Worldwide. APCO has done extensive pro bono work for the Clinton Global Initiative (CGI) and has had prior business relations with Tenex/Uranium One. The corporate world has embraced the direction being promoted by the NWO globalist in wanting a Great Reset.

Post Q# 3815
They will not be able to walk down the street.
THE GREAT AWAKENING.

Jonathan Winer has admitted to meeting regularly with Christopher Steele in 2016. Winer and his State Department sidekick Victoria Nuland facilitated Steele's Dossier getting into the hands of the FBI. Recent records reveal Winer destroyed State Department records at request by Steele. Incredibly indicated Perkins Coie lawyer Michael Sussmann doesn't want his past meetings and prior personal contacts with Jonathan Winer brought up during his trial.

Post Q# 3083
These people are sick and evil.
It is not a coincidence.
It never is.

In discovered emails former Deputy Assistant Secretary Kathleen Kavalec had direct communicates with both Steele and DOJ's Bruce Ohr. Kavalec worked under State's Victoria Nuland and subsequently President Trump just pulled her pending Ambassador nomination. Normally if Kavalec had said that the Steele dossier information was bogus, that would have ended this charade right then.

Post Q# 2129
[LIVE STREAMING] WH HUSSEIN NON-OVAL [SITUATION ROOM]
COORDINATION.

In addition to assisting Steele with the compilation of his Trump-Russia Dossier, two old Clinton enforcers were involved. Winer/Nuland meet regularly with Clinton hacks Sid Blumenthal and Cody Shearer for additional opposition research into candidate Donald Trump. Then representative Devin Nunes referred Winer/Nuland and several others in 2018 to the DOJ in criminal referrals surrounding their suspicious U.S. State Department activities.

Post Q# 1935
Define 'Projection.'
Define DARK MONEY.

Sid/Cody added their two opposition research memos into the final main 35-page discredited Chris Steele Dossier. It is also thought Fusion's Nellie Ohr contributed her own research work into what is now the 'Third Russia Dossier.' SpyGate will be shown as detailed coordination between governmental agencies and independent contractors.

Post Q# 4245
HOW DO YOU CREATE A DIVERSION?
HOW DO YOU SHIFT THE NARRATIVE?
Time to end the horror show?

Christopher Steele was able to help authenticate his Dossier just by the circular rotation between the State Department and Fusion GPS. Throw in a few Mockingbird news reporters and now you have instant verification of false 'laundered' intelligence information.

Post Q# 2601
NOBODY IS ABOVE THE LAW.
THE WORLD IS WATCHING.

Of interesting note is that Winer has worked in the past for the lobbying industry with several foreign clientele. Inquiring minds want to know if the FARA laws were broken by the very shady Jonathan Winer. The exact relationship between the State Department and private outside contractors like Fusion GPS are being explored by Federal grand juries.

Post Q# 2043
[LL] and paper trail and special entry and [Natalia Veselnitskaya] and Manafort.

Continuing with Winer's questionable connections, who pops up but the notorious William Browder. Browder was the force behind the U.S. Magnitsky Act and much of the overall friction with Vladimir Putin/Russia.

Post Q# 4915
A dark world is being exposed.
The truth won't be for everyone.

Browder had hired Fusion GPS a few years ago to help campaign with the implementation of the Magnitsky Act. The June 2016 entrapment operation at Trump Tower involving Russian lawyer Natalia Veselnitskaya, revolved not around 'HRC Dirt' but the Magnitsky Act. Jonathan Winer now has his own legal firm specializing in 'DC Consulting.'

Post Q# 3168
Nobody walks away from this.

IG Michael Horowitz's 2.0 report highlighted the past FISA/FISC abuses at DOJ/FBI. Departing AG Barr upgraded to Special Counsel status John Durham to look into these criminal referrals by IG Horowitz. SC Durham has dropped criminal indictments and submitted his final report in 2023.

With the re-election of President Trump in 2024, Judgement Day is coming and will usher in the Great Awakening.

Post Q# 1318
Think LOGICALLY.
Mass exodus in DC?

Links

Washington Examiner-The Weird Tales of Jonathan Winer

Just the News-HRC Plan tying Trump and Russia

Clinton Foundation Timeline-2025 Crossfire Hurricane Docs

Real Clear Investigations-Top Kerry Aide Key Conduit for Steele Dossier

Real Clear Politics-RussiaGate: HRC Campaign/Perkins Coie/Fusion GPS/CrowdStrike

FOX News-Report Spotlights FBI Agent Role in Russia Probe

The Federalist-Why Durham Subpoenaed the Brookings Institute?

Breitbart-Nunes Refers 10 BHO Officials

Daily Caller-Former State Department Official destroyed Records at request of Steele

Markets Work-Steele's Meeting with US Officials Casts Doubt on FBI Story

Epoch Times-Jonathan Winer and Chris Steele

Real Clear Investigations: Trump-Russia and Clinton-Libya: 2 Probes and FBI

Breitbart-Jonathan Winer: I feed Oppo Research from Sid Blumenthal to Chris Steele

Clinton Foundation Timeline-Jonathan Winer Archives

The Federalist-HRC's Fingerprints are All over Dossiers

Markets Work-Details of Victoria Nuland's Role in SpyGate

The Hill-State Department's Kathleen Kavalec met Christopher Steele Prior to FISA

Real Clear Investigations-Unpacking the Other HRC Russia Dossier

Winer Legal-Jonathan Winer Lawyer

Crossfire Hurricane Docs-State Department Steele Binder

Justice.gov-2023 SC John Durham Report

The Insubordinate FISA Signer: Meet Sally Yates

Legendary illegal FISA signer and who willingly disobeyed a direct Presidential order, meet Sally Yates [SY]. As Carter Page's FISA applications became declassified and be proven illegally obtained, Sally Yates will have played an important role in this past coup plot against President Trump. BHO used HRC's 2016 false Russia Dossier as grounds to spy on then candidate Donald Trump. Assigned Special Counsel (SC) John Durham has dropped criminal indictments in 2022 related to the past surveillance of Team Trump and submitted his final report in 2023. Combined with the prior reports submitted by IG Michael Horowitz, the exact scope of the coup plot against Donald Trump will become crystal clear.

Post Q# 2118
>FISA SIGNATURES.
>FISA 10/?/16.
>SSA?-Comey-Yates-DOJ?

Sally Yates was the former Deputy and then acting U.S. Attorney General under President Trump. Sally Yates was a carryover from the BHO administration into Team Trump and her non-loyalty was on full public displayed. President Trump would file in 2022 a federal RICO lawsuit against those officials that created and promoted the phony Russian narrative during the 2016 election cycle.

Post Q# 2727
>In the past, what was the punishment the: a TRAITOR?
>Coincidence?

Yates was painted into a legal corner by both Senators Grassley and Johnson by their Senate Committees. Through prior testimony by Bruce Ohr and James Baker, Sally Yates's prior Senate under-oath testimony is looking to be very questionable as many FBI agents are now apparently cooperating with SC Durham's' probes.

Post Q# 1928
>Page [ ]-Sally Yates.

IG Michael Horowitz was seeking redemption from being prohibited by Yates from his oversight into the National Security Divisions of DOJ/FBI. This was the home of the infamous 'Secret Society', where the treasonous coup plot was hatched and managed by this small internal group.

Post Q# 953
>Who makes arrests?
>FBI and DOJ?
>Can you make arrests w/ a crooked FBI team?

Senate Judiciary Committee had sent out a 10-page questionnaire to Yates back in 2018. These forms were sent to several other high ranking former BHO alumni including CIA Brennan and DNI Clapper in attempts to get a few of these individuals under oath.

Post Q# 4310
>What was really discussed during [Jan 5] meeting?

Completion of these Senate forms was made mandatory by Congressional Committee subpoenas, of which only a few were ever complied. President Trump's AG Bill Barr's appointed team of special prosecutors and counsels (Huber/Bash/and Durham) have been cross referencing prior statements to those now being made to grand juries.

Post Q# 2017
Sally Yates, Deputy Attorney General and Acting Attorney General-FIRED.

Yates's name is brought up in a few of these questions and the answers and will ultimately prove damaging. The early cooperative songbirds are sure to undercut SY's prior testimonies.

Post Q# 3595
F2F 1-4 US person(s) initiate scope memo.

SC John Durham's criminal investigation is slowly rolling out to the public and a vast 'Joint Venture Conspiracy' (RICO) case seems to be developing. Popcorn time fellow Patriots, as this historic play unfolds in the year of Justice.

Post Q# 1351
What happens if FED [criminal] indictments are brought forth to a corrupt FBI/DOJ/FED Judge?

Sally's biggest past public notice was of course early on in President Trump's administration over during the Travel Ban. Historically Acting AG's follow all orders from the President except if your first name happens to be Sally Yates.

Post Q# 3717
First indictment [unseal] will trigger mass pop awakening.
First arrest will verify action and confirm future direction.

Yates chose on her own to ignore a lawfully given order direct from President Trump. President Trump was directing DOJ to enforce these new travel related regulations and entry rules enacted.

Post Q# 2376
[Sally Yates].

This unbelievable insubordination led to Yates quickly being 'You're Fired' on 1/31/16. SCOTUS later upheld the major elements of President Trump's travel ban executive order and it is recorded today to have helped prevent bizarre Chinese viruses.

Post Q# 953
How bad is the corruption?
DOJ (past/present).
1
2

decode: 1=AG Loretta Lynch and 2=Dept. AG Sally Yates.

An Oval Office meeting occurred on 01/05/17 in which Susan Rice has immortalized with her 'Memo to Self.' This memo was on Trump's Inauguration Day and when Rice was no longer working/employed by the government.

Post Q# 1891
Texts, emails (gmail), drafts (gmail), HAM comma, PS/Xbox chat logs.
JC-BO-CS-LL-# 2-NO-SY.

FBI Director James Comey and Yates were the only top tier 'Secret Society' holdovers going into the Trump Administration. This was the final time to coordinate Operation Crossfire Hurricane and the 'Insurance Policy.' BHO pushed to apply the Logan Act to General Flynn and to continue the Trump-Russia narrative.

Post Q# 1316

Sally Yates, Deputy Attorney General and Acting Attorney General-FIRED.

The question is now was it BHO's "By the Book" as per Rice's memo. Inquiring minds what to know what BHO/JB/SR/JC and Yates said during that January 2017 White House Oval Office meeting-"Panic in DC." SC John Durham has dropped criminal indictments related to illegal SpyGate surveillance operations and submitted his final report in 2023. With the re-election of President Trump in 2024, many past SpyGate secrets will finally be made public.

Post Q# 3117

Sally Yates picture=Placeholder

Links

Breitbart-Former Acting AG Yates Surprises herself over Support for Liz Cheney

Just the News-FBI Timeline Chronicles Political Interference

Clinton Foundation Timeline-2025 Crossfire Hurricane Docs

The Last Refuge-Sally Yates

Lee Smith-BHO's January 5th Conspiracy

Real Clear Politics-Ratcliffe: Brennan Briefed Obama and Biden about HRC's Plan

The War Economy-Sally Yates/The Resistance

The Last Refuge-Why Flynn Lied

Jeff Carlson-Strzok's Notes

American Thinker-Flynn Prosecution turned on the Logan Act Hoax

The Federalist-BHO/Biden White House Meeting on January 5th was KEY

The Last Refuge-Crossfire Hurricane

Markets Work-FISA Abuse/4 Coincidences/and DNC Server

Front Page Mag-BHO used HRC's Dossier to Spy on Trump

Markets Work-Bypassing the IG: Sally Yates/DOJ's National Security Carve-Out

Washington Examiner-Did Sally Yates enable Bruce Ohr to Assist with Dossier

NY Post-Sally Yates was the Real Blackmailer

War Economy-Four FISA/Crossfire Hurricane

The Federalist-BHO Holdover Sally Yates helped Sink Michael Flynn

Washington Examiner-Page FISA Approved in 'Unusual Way' by Yates/McCabe/Baker

Markets Work-The Injustices BHO's Justice Department

DNI.gov-FISA Memo 2017

FBI.Vault.gov-FISA Surveillance Court Applications

Crossfire Hurricane Docs-FISA Notes

Justice.gov-2023 SC John Durham Report

WikiLeaks Ambassador was a 'Mule' for the DNC Leaked Emails

Craig Murray was the UK Ambassador to Uzbekistan from 2002-2004. Murray is an author, historian, broadcaster, human rights activist, and a known WikiLeaks (WL) data mule. Julian Assange and his WikiLeaks organization has become pivotal in the unfolding SpyGate surveillance scandal. Assigned Special Counsel (SC) John Durham had revealed in 2022 court filings of a direct relationship between Julian Assange's WikiLeaks and the unfolding events of the 2016 SpyGate/RussiaGate scandal.

Post Q# 1870
Not seen since WL Podesta dump?

Murray claims to be the middleman between Julian Assange's WL and the DNC email leaker. Craig said he meet the 'disgusted' DNC insider in a wooded area by the American University in DC and received the data to give to WL. The DNC, Debbie Wassermann-Schultz, and HRC are at the initial starting point of the false Trump-Russia collusion narrative.

Post Q# 1515
These reporters and networks have been named in the WikiLeaks to have colluded with the DNC or HRC campaign.

Ambassador Murray had flown from London to Washington in September 2016 to meet this DNC whistleblower (aka Seth Rich). Additional helpers involved with this go-between handoff operation were Kim Dot Com and Gavin MacFadyen. Murray has had long ongoing relations with Julian Assange, Kim Dotcom, MacFadyen and Randy Credico to be an official WikiLeaks operative.

Post Q# 3764
How does one provide content to WL?
The hole is DEEP.

Included in this clandestine meeting/data transfer handoff were the DNC emails, John Podesta's emails and HRC emails relating to 'Pay to Play' schemes operating at the Clinton Foundation. The subsequent public revelation of these emails would alter to course of the 2016 Presidential election cycle. The 2022 documentary titled '2,000 Mules' brings us to the understanding of the importance of secure votes and the consequences of deliberate interference in democratically held elections.

Post Q# 1195
SR connects to DNC.

Thanks to Bill Binney/Thomas Drake/VIPS partners for proving the DNC emails were a 'Leak not Hack.' Proven forensically the download data transmission rate was too fast by a factor of 4 to be anything but an insider leak made direct to a storage device/thumb drive unit.

Post Q# 1591
JA in the news.
Think JC.
Server unlocks SR.

Murray was not without controversy during his brief tenure as a British Foreign Service Ambassador. In 2003 Murray left his wife/children for a very young exotic Uzbekistan lap dancer, that Murray had fallen madly in love with.

Post Q# 1286
   Why no contact w/WL/JA?

Nadira Alieva ran off with Murray and it caused a major international stir. Nadira later publicly claimed "Love had nothing to do with it. It was the quickest way out and onto the UK/US".

Post Q# 3764
   The (Source(s)):
   Feeder [1]
   Recipient [1]

Of odd note was that the US has denied entry to Murray back in 2006. Craig Murray was invited to receive the prestigious Sam Adams Award for whistleblowing but couldn't attend due to VISA issues. Note Murray would ultimately be granted travel privilege and received this earned award.

Post Q# 436
   [DNC BREACH/DOSSIER]
   [WL]

Murray ultimately would be let go by the Foreign Office due his criticism of his host country Uzbekistan. Craig Murray said that Uzbekistan was 'torturing' individuals and was not a "functional democracy".

Post Q# 4016
   Seth Rich internal DL hand-to-hand pass USA?

Rep. Dana Rohrabacher traveled to London to meet personally with Julian Assange. Dana and Rand Paul later conveyed the given Julian Assange DNC email information directly to President Trump. A recent report has then CIA Director Pompeo considering kidnapping or outright assassination of Julian Assange over the release of the classified Vault 7 files.

Post Q# 3774
   If Russia didn't [hack] the DNC (insider breach)...... and US INTEL supported Russia
   [breach] claim.......
   What does that tell you?

Ambassador Murray has been extremely vocal about the deplorable conditions within the Ecuadorian Embassy and now prison. WikiLeaks founder Julian Assange had been hiding out at this embassy for 7 years and in 2023 Assange lost his final deportation hearings and extradition from England to the USA appears imminent. Organizations worldwide have plead with the British government to release Assange over compassionate humanitarian reasons. In mid-2024 the British courts are still mulling over Assange's final appeal pending extradition to the USA. In a surprise plea deal by the U.S. DOJ in June 2024, Assange has agreed to violating the Espionage Act and is now free from prison for time served.

Post Q# 2499
   [House Of Cards] re: Maggie NYT re: WL.

Murray is the key central player in the entire DNC email 'transfer' scandal. Inquiring minds want to know when will Murray/Assange both publicly testify. SC John Durham has dropped criminal indictments related to the 2016 Russian collusion false narrative and submitted his final report in 2023. All of these political charged scandals connect directly back to HRC/DNC/Big Tech/BHO/Julian Assange and the Seth Rich murder mystery. With the re-election of President Trump in 2024, we pray to finally get the truth behind many of these past political scandals.

Post Q# 1009

JA?

Seth Rich?

No investigation into WL receipt of information?

Links

Craig Murray-The CIA's Absence of Conviction

AMG News-Assange calls Trump for Private Meeting

Ada Nestor-They All knew it was a Lie

Just the News-Julian Assange makes Public Appearance following Prison

Revolver News-Seth Rich's Story just got Darker

CBS News-Julian Assange to Plead Guilty to Violating the Espionage Act

The Guardian-Julian Assange Granted Permission to Appeal Extradition to USA

Newsweek-Seth Rich Laptop Turned Over by FBI a Judge Rules

Last Refuge-Russia Russia Russia Narrative

Medium-Scientific Journalism, Julian Assange, and a World without Leaks

FOX News-DOJ Pressuring Journalists to Aid Persecution of Assange

The Federalist-Researchers said DNC Hack Relied on 'Spoofed' Data

Washington Examiner-Emails Prompt DARPA to deny Involvement in 2016 DNC Hack

The American Spectator-John Durham and Disappearing DNC Hack

Yahoo News-Pompeo Considered the Assassination of Assange

Craig Murray-FBI has been Lying about Seth Rich

Daily Mail-Former Ambassador names One of Assange's Alleged Sex Victims

Craig Murray-In the Word of Truth or Fact: RussiaGate is Dead

Washington Times-Wikileaks Figure says 'Disgusted' Democrat Leaked Emails

Daily Mail: Ex-British Ambassador: DNC Emails were Handed to Him

Craig Murray-The Stink without a Secret

Gadgets-NSA's Tailored Access Operations intercepts Computer Data

FBI.gov/Vault-Seth Rich (part 1 of 2)

Crossfire Hurricane Docs-Christopher Steele Binder

Justice.gov-2023 SC John Durham Report

About the Author

Roy D. Davis (CaptainRoyD) is one of the original posters on Reddit about QAnon and the many subjects related to the 2016 elections and SpyGate. Like many Q-Scribes—that courageous cadre of Patriots who were early citizen journalist addressing these topics—censorship and de-platforming has been a brutal reality numerous times. As disheartening as it has been for some to see countless hours of research and writing vanish, these attempts to suppress them have failed.

Roy is a U.S. Merchant Marine Officer/Master Captain and retired from the travel industry. He is currently living on a boat in Florida, where he continues to pursue telling the truths that the mainstream media seeks to hide or minimize. He is the proud father of two sons and a granddaughter and is motivated to share what he has learn by a sense of patriotic duty.

About the Artist

Alexander "Lex" Caldwell is a visual storyteller whose work blends symbolism, design, and narrative. His cover art for The SpyGate Conspiracy captures the intrigue and urgency at the heart of the story.

About the Publisher

Relentlessly Creative Books offers an exciting new publishing option for authors. Our "middle path publishing" approach includes many of the advantages of both traditional publishing and self-publishing without the drawbacks.

For more information and a complete online catalog of our books, please visit us at http://relentlesslycreative.com or write us at books@relentlesslycreative.com

Glossary of Acronyms

#2: Andrew McCabe Former FBI Director

+: Soros Family

+++: House of Saud

187: to murder, assassinate: Q's reference likely comes from California Penal Code 187

8chan: Refers to the discussion boards formerly at http://8ch.net where Q used to post drops and Anons use to post research information related to Q posts.

ACLU: American Civil Liberties Union

AF1: Air Force One

AFB: acid: fast bacillus

AG: Attorney General

AJ: Alex Jones

Alt media: alt = alternative. News sources outside of the mainstream media that have sprung up on both sides of the controversy. Often they are citizen journalists trying to get the truth out. But, be careful who you follow. Not all are telling the truth

Anon: Anonymous

ANTIFA: Anti: Fascists, Soros backed domestic terrorists

APCO: Initialism of Association of Public: Safety Communications Officials

ARSOUTH: Army South

AS: Adam Schiff

ASAP: as soon as possible

AUS: Australia

AUSA: Assistant United States Attorney

Bakers: The people on the Chans who do the Baking

BANG: Bay Area News Group

Barr: Attorney General William Barr

BC: Bill Clinton

BDT: Bulk Data Transfer (as in NSA info from Hawaii to USA)

BHO: Barack (Hussein) Obama

Boards: Before the World Wide Web, we had bulletin boards. They are a place you can go (now on the Web) to have discussions with others on a common topic

BOB: Robert Mueller former Director of FBI

BROWN: Central /SA Migrant Caravans

BS: Bernie Sanders

BUZZF: BuzzFeed

BW: Black Water

CA: California

CA: Canada

CBS: Columbia Broadcasting System

CBTS: Calm Before the Storm (gaming clan)

CP: Command Post

CP: Copilot

CP: Candle Power

CCP: Cold Case Passe

CEO: Chief Executive Officer

CF: Clinton Foundation

CFIUS: Committee on Foreign Investment in the United States

CFO: Chief Financial Officer

CFPB: Consumer Financial Protection Bureau

CFR: Council on Foreign Relations

CGI: Clinton Global Initiative

CI: Counter Intelligence

CIA: Clowns In America

CIA: Central Intelligence Agency

Clowns: Negative CIA Agents

CNN: Cable News Network

COMMS: Communications

Controlled opposition: People who appear to be supporting the white hats but are actually controlled by the black hats

COO: chief operations officer

D5: A reference Q gave us in Post 2494 that referred to Dec. 5.

DC: Dick Cheney

DC: District of Columbia

De-Platforming: Censorship by banning

DEA: Drug Enforcement Administration

DECLAS: declassification, specifically of the FISA applications

Deep State: The corrupt people who have infiltrated and work within and around governments around the world. This includes people working in businesses, charities, pharmaceutical companies and others that often control government outcomes through payoffs and bribes

DNC: Democratic National Committee

DNI: Director of Nat'l Intelligence (over the NSA)

DNI: Director of National Intelligence

DOD: Department of Defense

DOJ: Department of Justice

DOUG: Dumb Old Utility Guy

Drain The Swamp: Indicting and arresting corrupt deep state workers and leaders.

DS: The Deep State

DWS: Debbie Wasserman Schultz

EEE: The Electronic Frontier Foundation

EH: Eric Holder

EMT: Emergency medical technician

EO: Executive Order

EU: European Union

Fake MAGA: someone who is using the MAGA or QAnon movements to build an audience for a hidden agenda, disloyalty. This is an example of "controlled opposition" (above).

Fake News: The mainstream media outlets that control the primary broadcast stations on Cable TV endlessly release lies and propaganda that President Trump refers to as Fake News. Fox is the only one that is not considered Fake News, however, beware as even Fox is owned by a liberal globalist. Rupert Murdoch is a member of the Council on Foreign Relations, a known globalist think tank

False Flag: An event, usually a terror event, that is planned in advance and carried out for nefarious reasons. Example: For many years the black hats have carried out false flag mass gun shootings around the world. This was an effort toward gun control and eventually banning guns in worldwide

FARA: Foreign Agents Registration Act

FBI: Federal Bureau of Investigation

FIFA: International Federation of Association Football

FISA: Foreign Intelligence Surveillance Act

FISC: Foreign Intelligence Surveillance Court

FLOTUS: First Lady of the United States

FLYNN: Michael Flynn, former National Security Advisor to President Trump

FOB: Friends Of Bill

FOIA: Freedom of Information Act

FOTP: Freedom Of the Press

FOTP: Freedom Of The Press Foundation

FVEY: Five Eyes, an intelligence alliance comprising Australia, Canada, New Zealand, the United Kingdom and the United States

G7: group consisting of the finance ministers of seven industrialized nation

GITMO: Guantanamo Bay Naval Base military prison and detention camp

GJ: Grand Jury

GOOG: GOOGLE, NASDAQ Designation

GOP: Grand Old Party

GPS: global positioning system

GREEN: Radical Muslim Brotherhood

GRU: Russian General Staff's Main Directorate

HAMR: Health and Medical Response

HEC: House Ethics Committee

HHS: Health and Human Services

HM: Hidden Mickey

HPSCI: House Permanent Select Committee on Intelligence

HRC: Hillary Rodham Clinton

HSGAC: Homeland Security and Government Affairs Committee

HUMA: Harvard University Muslim Alumni

Huma: Huma Abedin

Human trafficking: Trading in human beings, including babies and children, for the purpose of sexual abuse, prostitution, slavery, ritual sacrifice, cannibalism or organ harvesting

HUMIT: Human Intelligence Assets

Hussein: Obama

ICA: Intelligence Community Assessment

ICU: intensive care unit

ID: Identification

IDEN: Identification

IG: Inspector General

IMI: International Military Tribunal

INTEL: Integrated Electronics

INTEL: Intelligence

IRS: Internal Revenue Service

ISIS: Israeli Secret Intelligence Service

JA: Julian Assange

JC: James Clapper, Former DNI Director or James Comey, Former FBI Director

JFK: John Kennedy, former President of the USA before being assassinated in 1962

JP: John Podesta

KANSAS: Mike Pompeo

Larp: Live action role play(er).

LL: Loretta Lynch

LLP: limited liability partnerships

LP: Lisa Page (disgraced FBI attorney/ assoc with Peter Strzok)

Lurking: reading online posts without revealing your presence

MAGA: Make America Great Again, Trump Slogan

MB: Muslim Brotherhood

McCain: One who shall not be named

JK: John Kerry

JK: Jared Kushner

MI: Military Intelligence

MOAB: Massive Ordnance Air Blast

Mockingbird media: The mainstream media outlets that control the primary broadcast stations on Cable TV and receive their 4:00 AM Talking Points

MS13: Latino Drug Cartel

MSM: Mainstream Media

MYE: Mid-Year Exam

NAFTA: North American Free Trade Agreement

NASA: National Aeronautics and Space Administration

NAT G: National Guard

NK: North Korea

NM: New Mexico

NP: Nancy Pelosi or Non-Profit

NSA: National Security Agency

NSD: National Security Division

NWO: New World Order

NXIVM: The sex/slave cult that Keith Raniere created. He, Clare Bronfman and Alison Mack have been arrested in this case.

NY: New York

NYC: New York City

NYPD: The New York Police Department

OFA: Organising For Action

OIG: Office of Inspector General

OP: Original poster also Operation(s)

Op: Original Poster of Operation

Operation Mockingbird: CIA infiltration of mass media

OSF: Open Society Foundation

OSI: Open Society Institute

PAC: premature atrial contraction

Patriot: Someone that supports freedom and truth

PDB: Presidential Daily Briefs

PDS: Presidentall Daily Briefings

PEOC: Presidential Emergency Operations Center

Pizzagate: A sex cult involving Comet Ping Pong pizzeria in Washington DC. Despite the fact that Wikipedia (controlled opposition) claims it has been debunked. Stay tuned. More to come

POTUS: President of the United States

PQG: Penn Quarter Group

PRN: Platte River Networks

Psyop: Psychological operation. Any operation (possibly false flag) intended to affect people psychologically

Q: Alice in Wonderland

Q-Drop: Posts created by Q are often called Q-drops

Q: Person (Q-Person) with extremely high level of security clearance

RBG: Ruth Bader Ginsburg

red pill: A reference to the movie "The Matrix" used to indicate someone has opened their eyes and seen the truth

RED: Progressive Communist Left/SJW

Reddit: A website used by many Q followers in the early days. Reddit has many boards that people can converse on many subjects anonymously. http://reddit.com.

RFTP: Resilient File Transfer Protocol

RICO: Racketeer Influenced and Corrupt Organizations

RINO: Republicans: Republican in name only

RIP: Rest in Peace

RNC: Republican National Committee

RR: Rod Rosenstein

RYAN: Paul Ryan, Speaker of the House

SA: Saudi Arabia

SAP: Special Access Program

SC: Supreme Court

SC: Special Counsel

SCI: Sensitive Compartment Information

SCIF: Sensitive Compartment Information Facility

SCOTUS: Supreme Court of the United States

SDNY: Southern District of New York

SEC: Security or Secure

SESSIONS: Jeff Sessions (Attorney General)

SF: Schmidt Futures

Soros: George Soros

SP: Samantha Power

SP: Special Prosecutor

SR: Seth Rich

SR: Susan Rice, Obama National Security Advisor

Subreddit: Each primary created discussion topic on Reddit is referred to as a Subreddit.

SVR: systemic vascular resistance

SY: Sally Yates

TAC: The Analysis Corporation

TBA: to be announced

TDIP: The Democracy Integrity Project

The Great Awakening: Refers to the event currently taking place that involves waking up the public to see the truth of the world they live in. The world that has been previously and deliberately hidden from them

The Chans: Reference to 4ch.org (4chan) and 8ch.net (8chan). Q began by posting on 4chan but moved to 8chan when 4chan became compromised

TPP: Trans Pacific Partnership

Trip code: A code that Q uses when logging in to 8chan that is also displayed in each of the Q posts

Truther: One who believes in telling the truth

TSA: Transportation Security Administration

TT: Trump Tower

U1: Uranium One

UAE: The United Arab Emirates

UBL: Osama Bin Laden

UCCI: Under Cover Confidential Informant

UCE: Undercover Confident Informant

UFO: Unidentified flying object

UN: United Nations

US: United States

USB: Universal Serial Bus

USCP: United States Capital Police

USD: United States dollar

USMIL: United States Munitions Import List

USSOUTHCOM: United States Southern Command

USSS: United States Secret Service

VIP: very important person

VISA: Visa International Service Association (credit card company)

VISA: Virtual Instrument Software Architecture

VISA: Voluntary Intermodal Sealift Agreement

VISA: Vancomycin Intermediate/Resistant Staphylococcus Aureus

VJ: Valerie Jarret

WH: White House

WL: WikiLeaks

WSJ: Wall Street Journal

WWG1WGA: Where we go one we go all

WWII: World Wide Allotment Area II

YC: Yellow Cake

www.ingramcontent.com/pod-product-compliance
Lightning Source LLC
Chambersburg PA
CBHW080223270326
41926CB00020B/4127